GW01606544

UPDATED EDITION

The Daily Telegraph

Football Chronicle

A season-by-season account of the soccer stories that made the headlines from 1863 to the present day

Norman Barrett

TED SMART

Specially produced for The Book People
in association with Carlton Books Limited
20 St Anne's Court, Wardour Street, London W1V 3AW

Updated Edition 1994

ISBN 1-85613-848-8

Project editor – Martin Corteel
Design – Steve Wilson
Production – Sarah Schuman

Printed and bound in Great Britain by
Butler & Tanner Limited, Frome and London

ACKNOWLEDGEMENTS

The author would like to acknowledge the use of extracts from reports and articles that have appeared in *The Daily Telegraph* and *The Sunday Telegraph* by the following correspondents: Michael Calvin, Robert Dick, Charles Freeland, Colin Gibson, Edward Giles, William Johnson, Denis Lowe, Colin Malam, Roger Malone, Bill Meredith, John Moynihan, Robert Oxby, Ian Peebles, and Donald Saunders.

Thanks are also due to David Ballheimer, Neil Tunnicliffe, David Prole, John Boteler and Mary Morton (editorial help), Juliet Duff (picture research), Fred Gill (indexing), and to Hugh Godwin of Colorsport for his unstinting help with the pictures.

***Previous page: (left)* Johan Cruyff, Holland; *(right)* George Best, Manchester United.**

CONTENTS

England v Scotland, 1905.

Ted Drake, Arsenal.

Stanley Matthews, Stoke City.

Stan Cullis, Wolves.

John Charles, Leeds United.

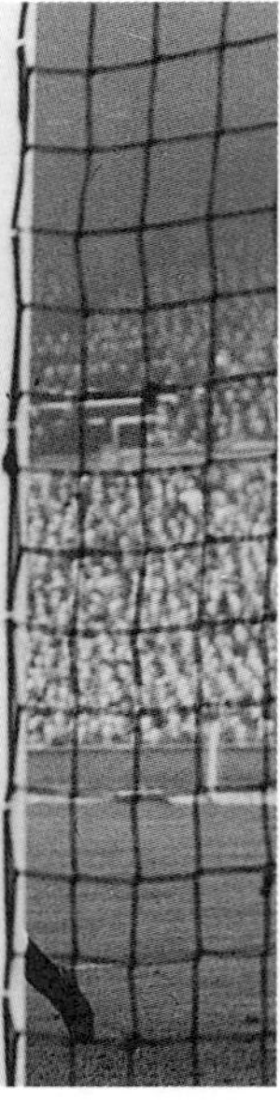

England v Hungary, 1953.

Danny Blanchflower, Tottenham Hotspur.

INTRODUCTION

In compiling and writing this Chronicle, choices have had to be made all down the line. While a large proportion of the entries have been automatic choices – the major milestones, important finals, great achievements, tragedies and triumphs – other factors have been taken into consideration. In order to provide a greater breadth of coverage, not every Cup final between Celtic and Rangers, or League triumph by Liverpool, has been featured. Rarer, if not worthier, achievements by lesser clubs have been given priority. And while it is not possible to be comprehensive in covering some 130 years of football history, the Football Focus feature of every year has proved useful in tying up loose ends.

The match reports and other stories are not taken verbatim from the newspaper. In fact, for earlier years, when The Daily Telegraph did not give the unrivalled coverage to football that it now boasts, the pieces have been compiled from the author's vast library of histories, reference books and biographies. Admittedly, they are written with hindsight, but hopefully topicality has been retained and anachronisms avoided. It is only from the 1970s, when more space was available per year, that any substantial extracts from Telegraph reports have been used, and the writers of these have been duly acknowledged elsewhere in this book.

There is an intentional bias in the Chronicle towards British football, particularly in the early years. As international competition has grown, so has its coverage here, and this is reflected both in the stories and in the statistics. Each World Cup has been featured from the start, even though one would be hard put to find much about the prewar tournaments in any British newspaper.

Special features on the personalities of the game cover each generation of football stars, from Goodall to Giggs. 'Years' have been based on British seasons, and there have been no strict rules as to where events in the 'close season' are included. In the Final Score statistical boxes, the European Footballer of the Year – chosen always at the end of a calendar year – has been placed in the season covering the end of that year. Results of that benighted competition, the World Club Championship, are given in the season when the European clubs concerned won the European Cup, even though the match is regularly played well into the next season. This seemed tidier, if perhaps not entirely logical.

The journey through the seasons has been a fascinating one. Every period threw up its headlines, its triumphs and its tragedies, its heroes and its occasional villains. The changes over the years appear to be astonishing, yet David Jack's transfer for £10,000 in 1928 made no less a stir than Paul Gascoigne's for 600 times that amount some six decades later.

Working through the years, reliving the highlights of this great game in words and pictures, has been sheer joy, and it is hoped that the spirit and flavour of each era have been conveyed to the reader. Much has happened in football in the twelve months since the first edition – England's humiliation at the hands of Norway, the United States and Holland, a new England supremo, Manchester United's classic double, Arsenal's European triumph and the woes of their north London neighbours, and, of course, the 1994 World Cup, in which Brazil stirred the memories and FIFA took the first steps towards making the game of football "beautiful" again.

Norman Barrett
July 1994

The Busby Babes, 1958.

Kevin Keegan, England.

Birth of Association Football

ON MONDAY, 26 October 1863, a meeting was convened of representatives from a dozen of the leading London and suburban football clubs to form an association and to establish an agreed set of rules for the game. The meeting, which took place at the Freemasons' Tavern in Great Queen Street, formed the Football Association, with 11 of the 12 clubs present enrolling as founder members. But it has taken another six meetings to formulate the rules of football.

The problem has been coordinating the disparate codes of football played around the country. There was a strong body of opinion in favour of banning some of the practices allowed by the Rugby (School) code, already outlawed by the Sheffield Rules of 1857 and the Cambridge Rules of 1862 and 1863. But representatives of the Blackheath club, strong advocates of the Rugby game, were unyielding. They insisted on the inclusion of two clauses in the rules: first, that "A player may be entitled to run with the ball towards his adversaries' goal if he makes a fair catch" and, second, "If any player shall run with the ball towards his adversaries' goal, any player on the opposite side shall be at liberty to charge, hold, trip or hack him, or wrest the ball from him..."

Finally, at a meeting held on 8 December, the dispute came to a head. The proposal by the Blackheath group to adjourn the meeting was defeated by 13 votes to 4, and as a consequence they withdrew from the Association. The Laws of the Game, evolved from the Cambridge Rules and now agreed by the Association, were formally accepted, heralding the birth of Association Football.

Wanderers win the Cup

THE WANDERERS FC beat the Royal Engineers by a goal to nil at Kennington Oval on 16 March 1872 to win the newly inaugurated Football Association Challenge Cup competition. A crowd of some 2,000 spectators saw C.W.Alcock, captain of the victorious team, presented with the trophy, a silver cup scarcely 18 inches high.

It was highly appropriate that Mr Alcock should be the recipient of the trophy for, as secretary of the Football Association, he was the moving spirit in the inception of the competition, which was born on 16 October 1871. There were 15 entrants, eight of them from London, but no northern clubs, their fixture cards for the season having already been completed. Donington School from Lincolnshire entered and so did Queen's Park of Glasgow, the first Scottish football club.

Both of these clubs were given byes in the first round, and then Queen's Park had a walkover in the second when Donington scratched. With five clubs left in the third round, Queen's Park received another bye, so were in the semi-finals without having played a match. They were drawn against the Wanderers, and travelled to London from Glasgow with the help of public subscription. After a hard-fought goalless draw, Queen's Park, whose accurate passing style was a complete revelation in the South, could not afford to stay in London for a replay and had to scratch. So Wanderers were in the final.

The Royal Engineers were favourites to win the final at odds of 7–4 on, but the Wanderers were a strong side composed of the best players to have graduated from the public schools and universities. Their star player, the Rev. R.W.S.Vidal, was famed as the "Prince of Dribblers", and it was he who broke away and passed to M.P.Betts who proceeded to score the only goal of the game.

There was a bad-luck story for the gallant losers, for Lieutenant Cresswell broke a collar-bone 10 minutes after the start, but bravely played on to the end of the game. For the victors, there was not only the glory of winning the Challenge Cup, but also the privilege of exemption next year until the final, when they would also have choice of venue.

The Royal Engineers, who appeared in three of the first four FA Cup finals, losing two and winning the third.

No goals in history-making Scotland-England encounter

THE GAME WAS a long time in coming, Scotland versus England on 30 November 1872 at the West of Scotland Cricket Ground, Partick. For some time, the idea of a Scotland-England match had been brewing in men's minds. On 5 March 1870, England took on a Scottish representative side in the first of five matches played over two years at the Oval, in London. The result was a 1–1 draw, and in all England won three and drew two of these unofficial internationals with what was a "London Scottish" side.

It was the Scots who first suggested the match, seeking help in spreading the game north of the border, where no more than 10 football clubs had been established. The FA accepted the invitation, and on 24 October wrote to all the member clubs requesting assistance in paying the railway expenses of England's 11 chosen representatives and officials. The prime mover for the FA was C.W.Alcock, their first secretary. He was due to captain the team, but had to withdraw because of injury, and travelled as England's umpire.

More than 2,000 spectators turned out to watch the match in Partick, paying £109 at the gate, and they were not disappointed with the action despite the absence of goals. The Scots, six of them from Queen's Park, were smaller and lighter than their adversaries, giving away an estimated two stone per man, and it called for an outstanding performance from their two backs, J.J.Thomson and R.W.Ker, to save the day. For England, the magnificent dribbling of the captain, C.J.Ottaway, A.S.Kirke-Smith and J.Brockbank was greatly admired by the crowd, who kept the utmost order.

Scotland 0 England 0 — a selection of sketches from the match.

Playing the game by electric light

TWO TEAMS drawn from the Sheffield area and captained respectively by the brothers W.E. and J.C.Clegg, both England internationals, played an historic match at Bramall Lane, Sheffield, on 14 October 1878 under electric lights. There were four lamps standing on 30-foot wooden towers erected in each corner of the ground, and powered by portable generators. Nearly 20,000 people saw this novelty on a crisp moonlit night.

Other clubs have repeated this experiment, including Birmingham and Accrington, although the first night match to be played in London, at the Oval on 4 November, was not such a success, owing to uneven illumination and high winds.

Football by floodlight — an impression of the Sheffield scene.

FOOTBALL FOCUS

- A return England-Scotland match was played at the Oval on 8 March 1873 and England won 4–2. Alexander Bonsor (Old Etonians and The Wanderers) went into the record books as the scorer of England's first-ever international goal. Thereafter the match became an annual fixture, alternating between the two countries. The Scots pulled off a hat-trick of victories towards the end of the decade, culminating in their remarkable 7–2 triumph at Queen's Park in 1878.
- In March 1873, the Scots instituted their own Cup competition and founded the Scottish Football Association. With a credit balance of only £1.11s.4d in its first year, the Scottish FA had to seek donations from its member clubs to pay for the trophy and badges, which cost £56.12s.11d.
- The Royal Engineers, from Chatham, appeared in three of the first four FA Cup finals, losing twice before beating Old Etonians 2–0 in 1875. During that period, they lost only three out of 86 matches, mostly played against leading clubs, and boasted an extraordinary goalscoring record of 244 scored and a mere 21 conceded.
- Wales entered the international scene for the first time, losing 4–0 to Scotland in Glasgow in 1876 and 2–1 to England at London's Kennington Oval in 1879.

FINAL SCORE

FA Cup Finals

1872	Wanderers	1	Royal Engineers	0
1873	Wanderers	2	Oxford University	0
1874	Oxford Uty.	2	Royal Engineers	0
1875	Royal Eng.	1	Old Etonians	1
Replay:	Royal Eng.	2	Old Etonians	0
1876	Wanderers	1	Old Etonians	1
Replay:	Wanderers	3	Old Etonians	0
1877	Wanderers	2	Oxford University	1
	(after extra time)			
1878	Wanderers	3	Royal Engineers	1
1879	Old Ets.	1	Clapham Rovers	0

Scottish FA Cup Finals

1874	Queen's Pk.	2	Clydesdale	0
1875	Queen's Pk.	3	Renton	0
1876	Queen's Pk.	1	Third Lanark	1
Replay:	Queen's Pk.	2	Third Lanark	0
1877	Vale of Leven	0	Rangers	0
Replay:	Vale of Leven	1	Rangers	1
Replay:	Vale of Leven	3	Rangers	2
1878	Vale of Leven	1	Third Lanark	0
1879	Vale of Leven	1	Rangers	1
	(Vale of Leven won replay by default)			

Artisans beat the aristocrats

THE PLUMBERS and weavers of Blackburn Olympic beat the gentlemen of the Old Etonians to take "t'Coop" up North for the first time in its 11-year history.

Blackburn, in existence for only five years, needed extra time to win the 1883 final 2–1 after reaching it with 6–3, 9–1, 8–0, 2–0, 4–0 and 4–0 victories in the earlier rounds. They had been moulded into an imposing force by half-back and trainer Jack Hunter, who before the final took his team away to Blackpool to prepare them for the great day, the first time such systematic training had been implemented.

Old Etonians, the Cup-holders, fielded six internationals, including the Hon. A.F.Kinnaird, a veteran of the competition who was playing in his ninth final. There was little to choose between the two sides in the first half, although the Etonians took the lead through Goodhart.

Blackburn began to press in the second half, but Kinnaird, who was playing magnificently, hit a place-kick through the posts only to have it disallowed because the ball did not touch an opponent. This was the turning point of the game. Matthew dribbled down the right and hit an angled shot to equalize, and then Dunn went off injured, a severe handicap for the Etonians, who were tiring fast.

The 10 men managed to contain the Olympians for the remainder of the 90 minutes. But they were no match for their fitter opponents in extra time, and Crossley converted a pass from Dewhurst soon after the change-over for the winner.

Sketches from the 1883 Cup final between Blackburn Olympic and Old Etonians.

England's new formation Scotched

ENGLAND, having lost seven of their last eight annual internationals to the Scots, and conceded 36 goals in the process, appeared for the 1884 game at Cathkin Park, Glasgow, with a revolutionary defensive formation. Instead of the customary two half-backs and six forwards, they turned out with three half-backs and only five forwards. This might have had the effect of restricting the Scots to a single goal, but Scotland still triumphed 1–0 for their fifth win in a row.

As always, despite the individual brilliance of the Englishmen, it was the smaller Scots' greater cohesion and understanding that won the day. And an historic day it is, for with this victory Scotland have won the first International Championship, having already roundly beaten Wales (4–1 in Glasgow) and Ireland (5–0 in Belfast).

'Offside' storm as Villa beat the favourites

IN THE FIRST all-Midlands Cup final in 1887, Aston Villa beat West Bromwich Albion 2–0 after a hotly disputed goal gave them the lead on the hour. West Bromwich, confident after their unexpected but comprehensive 3–1 semi-final win over Preston, dominated the game in the first 20 minutes. Only the brave goalkeeping of Warner kept their hungry forwards at bay. On more than one occasion, he scooped the ball up and over his own cross-bar to avoid being bundled into the goal.

It was a different story in the second half. Villa, 3–1 conquerors of Glasgow Rangers in the semi-finals, began to take charge. With the wind now at their backs, they proceeded to demoralize their opponents. But when they did score, it caused a furore. West Bromwich keeper Roberts, assuming Hodgetts was offside, made no attempt to stop the Villa winger's shot. The umpires on both sides, however, ruled in favour of Villa, much to the distress of the Albion side and the wrath of their supporters.

Two minutes from the end, the game was appropriately wrapped up by Villa's captain and inspiration, Archie Hunter. Intercepting a back-pass, the centre-forward defied Roberts's effort to block him, and slid the ball into the net for a 2–0 victory.

West Bromwich centre-forward Bayliss heads towards Villa's goal.

Blackburn Rovers, a 'hat-trick' of Cup wins with victories over Queen's Park (twice) and West Brom.

Joy for the Rovers

BLACKBURN ROVERS celebrated their third successive Cup triumph, equalling the Wanderers' feat of the 1870s, when they beat West Bromwich Albion 2–0 at the Racecourse Ground, Derby, in the replayed 1886 final after the goalless draw at the Oval. They received a silver shield for their achievement.

The Rovers' record in the eighties has been one of remarkable accomplishment. When they reached their first Cup final in 1882, they had gone 35 games without defeat against some of the best sides in the land, including a 16–0 trouncing of Preston in North End's first professional fixture. Old Etonians beat them in the final, but Rovers came back in 1884 to take over the Cup mantle of their neighbours Blackburn Olympic, beating Queen's Park to take the trophy. They repeated their victory over the Scottish challengers the following year, and now they have "scored a hat-trick", with seven of their players appearing in all three of the finals.

FOOTBALL FOCUS

- The Scotland-Ireland fixture in 1884 completed the six-match cycle amongst the four home countries, and the International Championship was born. Scotland won four of the eighties Championships outright and shared the title with England in 1886.
- Professionalism was recognized in England in 1885. Blackburn Rovers left-half James Forrest, at 19, became the first professional to play for England against Scotland, despite Scottish protestations that both teams should be strictly amateur.
- England won the International Championship for the first time in 1888 with a thumping 5–0 victory in Scotland, after beating both Wales and Ireland 5–1.
- In 1887–88, Preston scored 51 goals in six FA Cup ties, including a Cup record 26–0 defeat of Hyde, before losing 2–1 to West Bromwich in the final.
- Scottish Cup-winners Renton beat FA Cup-winners West Bromwich in 1888 in a match for the "Championship of the World".
- The Football League was inaugurated on 17 April 1888 at the Royal Hotel, Manchester. It was the brainchild of a Scot, William McGregor, a director of the Aston Villa club. The 12 clubs forming the League, all from the Midlands or the North, were Accrington, Aston Villa, Blackburn Rovers, Bolton Wanderers, Burnley, Derby County, Everton, Notts County, Preston North End, Stoke, West Bromwich Albion and Wolverhampton Wanderers.

Bon Accord lambs to the slaughter

ON 5 SEPTEMBER 1885, in the first round of the Scottish FA Cup, Arbroath beat Bon Accord 36–0, a record for any British first-class match. The visitors, playing in their working clothes and without a proper pair of football boots between them, had replaced their unfit keeper with a half-back who had never played in goal before.

The Arbroath goalkeeper was not called upon to touch the ball once, and winger John Petrie scored 13 goals — a record for an individual player. On the same day, Dundee Harp beat Aberdeen Rovers 35–0.

Invincible Preston's twin triumphs

PRESTON NORTH END have gone through the first League season, 1888–89, without losing a match and have become the first League champions. In addition, they have won the FA Cup without conceding a goal. They are indeed "double" champions.

With the emphasis on attack, Preston scored 74 goals in their 22 matches, and only at Accrington were they denied scoring. They finished 11 points ahead of runners-up Aston Villa, with 40 points out of the maximum 44. And they conceded only 15 goals.

Centre-forward John Goodall was the brains of the side, with inside-right Jimmy Ross a prolific goalscorer. They were well supported by the Scottish half-back trio of Sandy Robertson, David Russell and John Graham. The keeper, Jimmy Trainer, known as the "Prince of Goalkeepers", is a Welshman. He joined Preston from Bolton only a few months after Preston had knocked 12 goals past him in one match!

Preston eased their way through to the semi-finals of the FA Cup, where they met West Bromwich, who had beaten them in last year's final. This time Preston won 1–0. In the final they easily beat Wolves 3–0 in front of a record 22,000 crowd. They truly earned their nickname "The Invincibles".

FINAL SCORE

Football League Champions

1888-89 Preston North End

FA Cup Finals

Year	Winner		Runner-up	
1880	Clapham R.	1	Oxford University	0
1881	Old Carthusians	3	Old Etonians	0
1882	Old Etonians	1	Blackburn Rovers	0
1883	Blackburn Olyp (after extra time)	2	Old Etonians	1
1884	Blackburn R.	2	Queen's Park	1
1885	Blackburn R.	2	Queen's Park	0
1886	Blackburn R.	0	WBA	0
Replay:	Blackburn R.	2	WBA	0
1887	Aston Villa	2	WBA	0
1888	WBA	2	Preston N. E.	1
1889	Preston N. E.	3	Wolves	0

Scottish FA Cup Finals

Year	Winner		Runner-up	
1880	Queen's Park	3	Thornlibank	0
1881	Queen's Park (after 2–1 cancelled)	3	Dumbarton	1
1882	Queen's Park	2	Dumbarton	2
Replay:	Queen's Park	4	Dumbarton	1
1883	Dumbarton	2	Vale of Leven	2
Replay:	Dumbarton	2	Vale of Leven	1
1884	Queen's Park beat Vale of Leven on default			
1885	Renton	0	Vale of Leven	0
Replay:	Renton	3	Vale of Leven	1
1886	Queen's Park	3	Renton	1
1887	Hibernian	2	Dumbarton	1
1888	Renton	6	Cambuslang	1
1889	Third Lanark (after 3–0 cancelled)	2	Celtic	1

International Firsts

1882 Wales v Ireland (at Wrexham, 7–1)
1882 Ireland v England (at Belfast, 0–13)
1884 Ireland v Scotland (at Belfast, 0–5)
1884 International Champ. (Scotland, 6 pts)

Townley goes to town

WILLIAM TOWNLEY, playing on the left wing for Blackburn Rovers, hit three goals in the 1890 FA Cup final as Rovers beat Sheffield Wednesday 6–1. He is the first player to score a hat-trick in the final.

Rovers, who themselves scored a hat-trick of Cup wins in the mid-eighties, were favourites to beat their Yorkshire rivals in this first ever "War of the Roses" final, at Kennington Oval. They included only Forrest, Lofthouse and Walton from those earlier triumphs, but boasted nine internationals among their ranks.

Wednesday fielded all local products, but were not dismayed at the prospect of playing the mighty Rovers. They had, indeed, accounted for three Football League sides on their progress to the final — Accrington, Notts County and, in the semi-finals, Bolton Wanderers, conquerors of "Proud" Preston in the previous round. Bolton were certainly a prize scalp, having humiliated Belfast Distillery 10–1 and Sheffield United 13–0 before overcoming Preston.

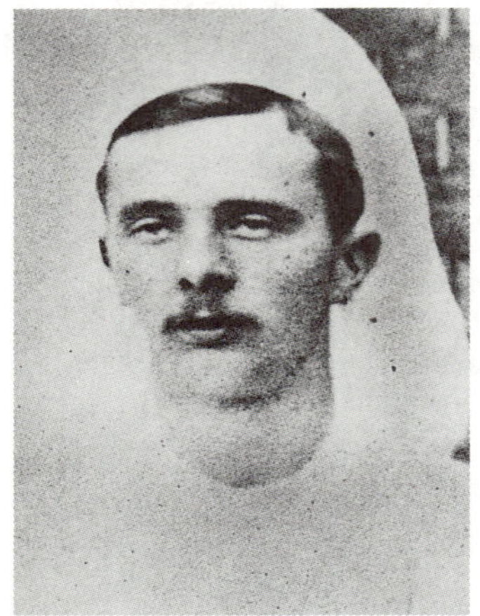

William Townley, Rovers' hat-trick hero in the 1890 final.

In the final, however, Wednesday were outplayed, but to their credit they never gave up. They were disadvantaged by some "primitive" keeping by their custodian Smith, while his counterpart in the Rovers goal, Horne, had little work to do. At the end, the crowd sportingly carried off the little Wednesday right-back Hadyn Morley for a gallant display against the odds.

Descent of Darwen

DARWEN FINISHED BOTTOM of the Second Division in 1899 and were not re-elected to the League. This is not surprising in view of their record, only nine points from 34 games. Their away record was extraordinary, one point from 17 games, with six goals for and an unprecedented 109 against. They were beaten 10–0 on three occasions: by Manchester City, the Second Division champions, by Walsall and, incredibly, by Loughborough, who finished second from bottom but were re-elected. Other crushing defeats for Darwen included 9–0 by Newton Heath, 9–2 by Grimsby, 8–0 by Small Heath, 8–1 by Luton and 7–0 by New Brighton.

No game for ladies!

THE BRITISH LADIES' Football Club was formed in 1895, and played their first match at Crouch End. Some 10,000 spectators turned out to watch this novelty, regarded by the football authorities as a "farce". The ladies turned out in nightcaps and heavy, cumbersome skirts, and wore shinguards.

The British Ladies play their first match at Crouch End, North London.

Bassett hounds Villa

WILLIAM BASSETT, who as an 18-year-old inspired West Bromwich Albion to their shock Cup final victory over Preston in 1888, has done it again. Albion once more started as underdogs, this time to their neighbours Aston Villa. But Albion had knocked out Blackburn Rovers, depriving them of a chance to notch another hat-trick of Cups.

Only four minutes had passed when the diminutive right-winger raced down the line and crossed for Geddes to shoot home. Bassett repeated the performance, this time for 20-year-old centre-forward Nicholls to send Albion in with a 2–0 interval lead. Right-half Reynolds completed the scoring in the second half, with a long shot into the net — the first time nets and crossbars have been used in the final.

Scots get their own League

A SCOTTISH LEAGUE, first mooted 10 years earlier, was formed in 1890. Eleven clubs joined the League: Abercorn, Celtic, Cowlair, Cambuslang, Dumbarton, Hearts, Rangers, St Mirren, Renton, Third Lanark and Vale of Leven. Renton, however, were kicked out after five games, having been found guilty of professionalism. There were plenty of goals in this first season, 409 in 90 matches, without a single goalless draw. Dumbarton and Rangers shared the inaugural Championship, each finishing with 29 points from their 18 games and drawing a play-off decider 2–2.

Jimmy Logan, who scored three goals in the Cup final.

Cup-winners stay in Division Two

NOTTS COUNTY of the Second Division beat Bolton Wanderers 4–1 in the 1894 Cup final, but failed to win promotion to Division One when, after finishing third in their division, they were beaten 4–0 by Preston in a "test match".

James Logan was County's hero in the final, played at Everton's Goodison Park, scoring a hat-trick to equal Townley's record for Blackburn of four years ago. But the Second Division side outplayed the beleaguered Bolton side, who unwisely fielded four or five men in various states of injury or unfitness. Indeed, were it not for an heroic performance in their goal by John Sutcliffe, who knows what the score might have been!

FOOTBALL FOCUS

● On 15 March 1890, England fielded two international sides on the same day, beating Wales 3–1 at Wrexham and Ireland 9–1 at Belfast.

● There was some heavy scoring in the first round of the 1890–91 FA Cup. Darwen, whose 3–1 win over Kidderminster was cancelled after a protest, won the replay 13–0. Aston Villa beat Casuals 13–1, and Sheffield Wednesday beat Halliwell 12–0. The other Sheffield side, United, lost 9–1 at home to eventual finalists Notts County. But pride of place must go to their neighbours Nottingham Forest, who chalked up a record away win, 14–0 at Clapton.

● James Forrest equalled the record of five Cup winners' medals when he helped Blackburn Rovers win their fifth Cup final in 1891, 3–1 over Notts County. Remarkably, only a week earlier, County had won 7–1 at Blackburn.

● The Scottish FA recognized professionalism in 1893, and a 10-club Second Division was introduced.

● The English Second Division came into being in 1892 with 12 clubs. At the end of the season, "test matches" took place in which the bottom three of Division One played the top three in Division Two (in reverse order), to determine promotion or relegation.

● There was a new venue for the FA Cup final in 1895, Crystal Palace, in London, and over 42,000 saw Aston Villa beat West Bromwich 1–0 with a goal scored in just 40 seconds by John Devey.

Sheffield on the razor's edge

SHEFFIELD UNITED, last season's League champions, eventually won their first FA Cup, beating Derby County in the 1899 final, but what a time they had to get there! In the semi-finals, it took them a record four games to account for Liverpool. The first was a 2–2 draw. In the second, at Bolton, they were 4–2 down with eight minutes to play before Fred Priest scored twice to earn a second replay. This was played at Fallowfield, and abandoned when the crowd encroached on to the field with Liverpool leading 1–0. Sheffield finally settled the tie with a 1–0 win at Wolverhampton.

A record 73,833 crowd for the final saw Sheffield's right-back Harry Thickett turn out with two broken ribs, protected by some 50 yards of bandages. The match turned on the duel between United's captain and left-half, Ernest "Nudger" Needham, and Derby's prolific goalscoring inside-right, Steve Bloomer. Needham won the encounter, although Bloomer uncharacteristically missed several chances. Sheffield were a goal down at half-time, after Boag shot past goalkeeper Foulke, but with four goals in the second half, scored by Bennett, Beers, Almond and Priest, they ran out easy winners. At the end of the match, the brave Thickett passed out with the pain.

FINAL SCORE

Football League Champions

1889–90	Preston North End
1890–91	Everton
1891–92	Sunderland
1892–93	Sunderland
1893–94	Aston Villa
1894–95	Sunderland
1895–96	Aston Villa
1896–97	Aston Villa
1897–98	Sheffield United
1898–99	Aston Villa

FA Cup Finals

1890	Blackburn R.	6	Sheffield Wed.	1
1891	Blackburn R.	3	Notts County	1
1892	WBA	3	Aston Villa	0
1893	Wolves	1	Everton	0
1894	Notts Co.	4	Bolton W.	1
1895	Aston Villa	1	WBA	0
1896	Sheff Wed.	2	Wolves	1
1897	Aston Villa	3	Everton	2
1898	Nottm For.	3	Derby County	1
1899	Sheffield Utd	4	Derby County	1

Scottish League Champions

1890–91	Dumbarton and Rangers (joint)
1891–92	Dumbarton
1892–93	Celtic
1893–94	Celtic
1894–95	Heart
1895–96	Celtic
1896–97	Hearts
1897–98	Celtic
1898–99	Rangers

Scottish FA Cup Finals

1890	Queen's Pk.	1	Vale of Leven	1
Replay:	Queen's Pk.	2	Vale of Leven	1
1891	Hearts	1	Dumbarton	0
1892	Celtic	5	Queen's Park	1
	(after 1–0 cancelled)			
1893	Queen's Pk.	2	Celtic	1
1894	Rangers	3	Celtic	1
1895	St Bernard's	2	Renton	1
1896	Hearts	3	Hibernian	1
1897	Rangers	5	Dumbarton	1
1898	Rangers	2	Kilmarnock	0
1899	Celtic	2	Rangers	0

International Champions

England 1890 (joint), 1891, 1892, 1893, 1895, 1898, 1899
Scotland 1890 (joint), 1894, 1896, 1897

The rise of professionalism

ORGANIZED FOOTBALL began as an amateur sport, played purely for fun and for exercise, with no commercial reward. The Football Association was founded by amateurs in 1863, and the FA Cup, inaugurated in 1872, was contested by all amateur clubs. The "amateur era" was dominated by sides such as the Wanderers, Old Etonians and Oxford University.

Opposing the Cup

In the early days, there was no thought of players being paid. It was against all the ideals of sport and sportsmanship. Things began to change with the advent of competition in the shape of the FA Cup. For the Cup had its opponents when it was first mooted, whose chief objection was that the rivalry generated would lead to the destruction of the true spirit of the game. In some respects they were right. A direct outcome of the enthusiasm to win the "little tin idol" was the subversive growth of professionalism.

England's Vivian Woodward beats the Scottish defence to the ball at Bramall Lane in 1903. A dedicated amateur, he scored 29 goals in 23 full internationals, over 50 in amateur internationals, and won two gold medals with the UK Olympic football team.

Bob McColl, the Scotland and Queen's Park centre-forward, who turned professional to play for Newcastle in 1901, returned to Glasgow in 1904 with Rangers, and went back to Queen's Park in 1907 as a reinstated amateur.

The first obvious signs of a chink in the amateur code came in the FA Cup of 1879. Lancashire club Darwen reached the last six, but were not expected to trouble Old Etonians. Nor did they look likely to when they trailed 5–1 at the Oval with 15 minutes to go. But they shocked the old boys with four goals in that time. Old Etonians declined to play extra time, as was their right, so Darwen had to return for a replay. They drew this, too, causing quite a stir. How could a virtually unknown provincial club hold one of the best teams in the land twice? They lost the second replay 6–2, but they had made their mark. Among their side were two Scots, Fergus Suter and James Love, arguably their star players. Now what were two Scotsmen doing playing for an English club?

The answer was that they had played against Darwen when their Scottish club Partick Thistle were on tour, and had been persuaded to stay on. Rumours soon became rife that they would find money in their boots on returning from their after-match baths.

Darwen, of course, were not the only northern club in this situation. Football had become extremely popular in the North, especially in Lancashire, where it was soon appreciated that a successful football club could help bring prosperity to its town. There was a desire to challenge the superiority of the southern masters. Under-the-counter payments to players became rife; "shamateurism" began to rot the very soul of football.

Scottish clubs, for their part, were producing fine players, well versed in the passing game and other tactical skills found only north of the border. They were attracted by the greater opportunities to be found in the industrial North of England. And so, gradually, the flow of Scots across the border developed from a trickle to a torrent.

FA members split

The surreptitious infiltration of professionalism caused a rift in the FA. There were those who felt it was degrading for "respectable men to play with professionals" — this view mainly from the North and Midlands. On the other side, paradoxically, were the greatest advocates of amateurism, from the South. These more enlightened members of the old guard included FA secretary C.W.Alcock, who pioneered both the FA Cup and the first internationals. While no supporter of professionalism himself, he defended the right of players to embrace it and regarded it as a necessity for the growth of the game.

He objected to the idea that professionals were the "utter outcasts some people represent them to be". He realized, too, that the deadlock would continue until professionalism was legalized and could be controlled.

The struggle continued, however. The so-called "importation" of players by amateur clubs, who paid them, was banned, and protests began to be lodged by one club against the other for playing these "importations" in Cup ties. The FA brought in a rule in 1882 prohibiting any payments to players other than strict expenses or compensation for wages lost through taking part. Any player breaking this rule would be barred from Cup games and internationals, and guilty clubs would lose their FA membership.

But the rising tide of professionalism could not be stemmed. People were getting fed up with all the bickering and endless meetings and commissions. Preston were disqualified from the Cup when their opponents alleged they had used professionals, and the club openly admitted it. Everyone was doing it, they said, so why pick on them? Bolton managed to fool an investigative commission, but later owned up to having paid their players. Such confessions brought the situation to a head and suddenly opposition to professionalism began to melt away. On 20 July 1885, a Special General Meeting of the FA in a Fleet

Prolific amateur goalscoring centre-forward G.O.Smith of the Corinthians.

Street hotel, with the necessary two-thirds majority (35-15), voted to legalize professionalism.

Bringing professionalism into the open did not end all the arguments immediately. Strict regulations were laid down, and indiscriminate "importation" banned. But the game could now grow, unfettered by subversion and by regulations constantly broken. The most dramatic effect of the change was to pave the way for the formation of the Football League in 1888.

Scottish resistance

In Scotland, the persecution of professionalism was even greater than in England. Thus when it arrived south of the border, the difference in status led to the breaking-up of relationships between clubs that had been on good terms and enjoyed regular fixtures. When Rangers — who as FA members regularly entered the FA Cup — found in 1885 that they were drawn against professionals, they withdrew (the FA fined them 10 shillings). Two years later the Scottish FA banned their clubs from entering the English competition.

Open professionalism in England was attracting even more Scottish players south. The top northern clubs began to send their scouts in disguise, to save them from being beaten up. But English clubs did not always find it possible to lure a player with the promise of "gold", as Accrington once found to their embarrassment when they offered international Frank Shaw £120 per annum to join them. Football in Scotland had always been promoted as a middle-class sport, and Shaw's reply began: "Dear Sir, On return from a fortnight's cruise among the Western Islands on my yacht, I found your letter... "

Attempts to prevent the poaching of Scotland's best players by legalizing payment in Scotland were repeatedly destroyed by the more powerful upholders of pure amateurism. Thus the only way to counter the temptations of England was to make illegal payments. This went on openly, and the Scottish FA turned a blind eye. The champions of amateurism were powerless.

But to be able to make these payments, regular fixtures between the top teams became essential. The success of the Football League in England persuaded the Scottish clubs that this was the solution. Several clubs met in semi-secrecy to found the Scottish League in 1890. When the rules were made public, there was an outcry in the Press, *Scottish Sport* going so far as to declare: "The entire rules stink of... moneymaking and money grabbing." Nevertheless, the League was an immediate success, and sure enough the expected gate money came rolling in.

The League grew in membership, with all the leading clubs clamouring for admission — except for Queen's Park, that last bastion of amateurism, who resented the idea of linking themselves with a body of clubs who were swaying towards professionalism. But the prime mover of the Scottish League, J.H.McLaughlin, had no doubts: "You might as well try to stop the flow of Niagara with a kitchen chair as endeavour to stem the tide of professionalism." In 1893, the Scottish FA finally succumbed to popular demand and opened its doors to the paid player.

A slow transition

The professional clubs of the North and Midlands soon began to dominate the Football League and FA Cup. But this is not to say that the amateur clubs disappeared. The South remained amateur for some years (Royal Arsenal were the first to embrace professionalism, in 1891), and one amateur club the professionals continued to fear was Corinthians. In 1884, the year before professionalism came in, they beat Cup-winners Blackburn Rovers 8–1. In 1886 they supplied nine players to the England side (the other two came from Blackburn Rovers), and in 1904 they beat the Cup-winners Bury (6–0 conquerors of Derby in the final) by 10 goals to three! The Corinthians, who had been founded in 1882 from old boy and university players, did not enter the Cup — it was against their rules to play in competitions. Had they done so, they most certainly would have won it, but they carried the torch of amateurism well into the 20th century.

FA secretary C.W.Alcock, who defended the right of players to embrace professionalism.

The Preston side of 1889, with chairman Major William Sudell (standing, third from right) who openly admitted to paying players.

Villa supreme

John Devey, highly-successful captain of Aston Villa.

SHEFFIELD UNITED, not surprisingly, failed to beat Burnley by eight goals at Turf Moor, so Aston Villa pip them by two points for the Championship. This is Villa's fifth title in seven seasons, during which they have also won the Cup twice. At the beginning of a new century they reign supreme.

Three players shared in all seven of these successes. Captain and inside- or centre-forward John Devey played in 143 out of a possible 158 matches in the five Championship seasons, centre-half Jimmy Cowan one fewer, and outside-right Charlie Athersmith in 137.

The 1900 League triumph was hard fought. With two-thirds of the season gone, Sheffield United were unbeaten, two points ahead of Villa and with two games in hand. But Villa were the stronger finishers, suffering only one defeat in their last 13 matches and dropping only one point in their last six games. They finished their programme on 16 April, leaving Sheffield needing to win their remaining two matches — both away — by at least eight goals in aggregate. They beat Wolves 2–1, but they failed at the last to do the impossible at Burnley.

Loughborough lurch out of League

LOUGHBOROUGH TOWN, who have been clinging to League membership ever since they were elected to the Second Division in 1895, finally had to let go. Their position has steadily deteriorated — 12th in 1896, 13th, 16th (bottom), 17th, and finally 18th and bottom in 1900.

With only eight points from 34 matches, one fewer than Darwen's dismal record last season, it is hardly surprising that they failed to gain re-election this time. They achieved but a single victory, 2–1 over Burton United in January, but lost all 17 of their away games. They gave away 100 goals, 74 of them in away matches, in which they scored only six — not as bad as Darwen's record, though. They also suffered some heavy defeats, the greatest being a 12–0 massacre by Woolwich Arsenal.

Non-Leaguers 'Buryed'

SOUTHAMPTON came to Crystal Palace with high hopes of becoming the first "outsiders" to win the FA Cup since the inception of the Football League. But Bury proved too much for them and ran out easy 4–0 winners.

Perhaps it was the occasion that got to the non-Leaguers, although they had played on the ground in the semi-finals. They had also disposed of three First Division sides on their way to the final — Everton 3–0, Newcastle 4–1 and West Bromwich 2–1 — all at the Dell. Only fellow Southern Leaguers Millwall gave them any trouble, drawing their semi-final 0–0 before going down 3–0 in the replay at Reading.

Nearly 69,000 turned out on a blazing hot April day to watch the final. Southampton kicked off with the sun in their eyes, and found themselves three goals down within 23 minutes, two of them from centre-forward McLuckie. They came back into the game for spells in the second half, but never seriously challenged Bury's lead, and a fourth goal for the northerners 10 minutes from time was the final nail in their coffin.

A rare Southampton attack in the final against Bury.

FOOTBALL FOCUS

- With 77 goals, Aston Villa are the leading scorers in Division One for the sixth season running.
- Racehorse owner Lord Rosebery attended the Scotland-England match at Parkhead and somehow persuaded the Scottish FA to allow the team to play in his racing colours of primrose and pink. Whether this Derby-winning combination had any galvanizing effect on the players is a moot point, but the Scots won 4–1, aided by a hat-trick from centre-forward R.S.McColl, the last remaining amateur in the side and the only representative from Queen's Park.
- Celtic retained the Scottish Cup, beating Queen's Park 4–3 in the final after losing a 3–1 half-time lead. They scored 25 goals in their six Cup matches, including a 4–0 win over Rangers in a semi-final replay.
- Rangers ran away with the Scottish League Championship again, although this season they lost four points — three of them to Celtic.

FINAL SCORE

Football League
Division 1: Aston Villa
Top scorer: Bill Garratt (Aston Villa) 27
Division 2: Sheffield Wednesday

FA Cup Final
Bury 4 Southampton 0

Scottish League
Division 1: Rangers
Division 2: Partick Thistle

Scottish FA Cup Final
Celtic 4 Queen's Park 3

International Championship
Scotland, 6 pts

Spurs win their first Cup

THE 1901 CUP FINAL drew a record crowd of 110,820 to the Crystal Palace and produced the first draw for 15 years. In the replay Tottenham Hotspur beat Sheffield United 3–1 to become the first club from outside the League to win the Cup since the League started. Their hero was centre-forward Alex "Sandy" Brown, the first player to score in every round of the Cup. He got both of their goals in the first final, and scored again in the replay for a record 15 goals in one tournament.

Tottenham, who won the Southern League last season, are the first team to break the dominance in the Cup of the great northern and Midlands clubs. They were unlucky not to win the final at the first attempt, for the Sheffield equalizer was a dubious affair. The linesman gave a corner, but the referee, who was hardly in a position to see, decided the ball had crossed the line before being cleared, and awarded a goal.

Sheffield, with the 20-stone Willie Foulke in goal, took the lead after 40 minutes in the replay at Burnden Park, Bolton, when Needham put Priest through. But the Spurs, in front of a much smaller crowd of 20,470, came back strongly in the second half for a thoroughly deserved victory with goals by Cameron, Smith and — inevitably — the remarkable Brown.

United repel a Spurs attack in the replay.

Brown scores for Spurs in the first match.

FOOTBALL FOCUS

- The scorer of England's first goal against Scotland in the drawn international at Crystal Palace was Blackburn (Blackburn) — Fred Blackburn of Blackburn Rovers, that is.

- Celtic beat Rangers in the Scottish Cup for the third successive season, this time in the first round. But they failed to bring off a hat-trick of Cups, losing 4–3 in the final to Hearts. Like their opponents Queen's Park last year, they fought back to equalize after being 3–1 down, but Hearts scored a late winner. Rangers won their third League title running.

- The bottom of Division One at the end of the 1900-01 season had a curious look to it — four of the last five clubs had formerly won either the Championship or the Cup or both. Sheffield United and the lately supreme Aston Villa stayed up. But both "Proud" Preston and West Bromwich were relegated to Division Two.

- On 23 February, Scotland beat Ireland 11–0, their highest international score, but they drew their other two games and England won the Championship.

- The Sheffield United keeper Billy "Fatty" Foulke, who lined up against Tottenham Hotspur in the 1901 Cup final, stood 6ft 2½in and weighed an amazing 20 stone.

Liverpool at last

AFTER NEARLY A DECADE of ups and downs between the divisions, Liverpool have finally won the League title. Their 1–0 victory over relegation-doomed West Bromwich at the Hawthorns was enough to put them two points clear of Sunderland and clinch the Championship.

Liverpool made a bright start to the season, winning their first three games. But in-and-out form left them well adrift of Sunderland, and when they suffered their third defeat in four games, at Bolton in mid-February, there was no thought of the Championship. Then came the turning point. They went to Roker Park and beat Sunderland 1–0, the start of a 12-match unbeaten run that took them through the field to the title.

Even so, it was a close-run thing. Sunderland finished their programme with a 2–0 victory at Newcastle, to take them two points clear. Liverpool beat Nottingham Forest 2–0 to draw level, but with a far inferior goal average. They needed just a draw in their last game, and West Bromwich bravely held them scoreless until Liverpool got a late goal to settle the issue.

With only 59 goals, Liverpool have nevertheless broken the First Division scoring dominance of Aston Villa, who finished well down the table with only 45. But their real strength has been in defence, with Scottish international centre-half Alec Raisbeck outstanding in the middle.

Alec Raisbeck, outstanding for Liverpool and Scotland.

FINAL SCORE

Football League
Division 1: Liverpool
Top scorer: Steve Bloomer (Derby County) 24
Division 2: Grimsby Town

FA Cup Final

Tottenham Hotspur	2	Sheffield United	2
Replay: Tottenham H.	3	Sheffield United	1

Scottish League
Division 1: Rangers
Division 2: St Bernard's

Scottish FA Cup Final

Hearts	4	Celtic	3

International Championship
England, 5 pts

Terrible disaster at Ibrox Park

A COLLAPSE in the new stand at Ibrox Park, Glasgow, during an international match has caused 25 deaths, with hundreds more injured, many of them seriously. Most of the crowd were oblivious to the horrific scenes under the stand. The match was stopped, but first reports were of just a few injuries, and the authorities decided to continue the game to prevent panic. Only after the match was the full scale of this catastrophe revealed.

Three Scottish clubs vied to stage the lucrative Scotland-England international: Celtic, Rangers and Queen's Park. Most recent internationals have been played at Celtic Park or Hampden Park, but Rangers "won" this time, largely because of the new West Stand constructed at a cost of £20,000. It was a fatal decision.

The Ibrox Park stadium is said to hold 80,000, but there were more likely nearly 100,000 crammed in, such is the fanaticism of the Scots for the game. As the eastern terrace became full, latecomers made a dash for the new stand, constructed of wooden planking set on steel pylons. The game was only six minutes old when there was a sudden rending of timber as a vast hole appeared in one section of the terracing. The unfortunate spectators there just fell through the gap, 40 feet to the ground below and on top of each other. Seven rows of wooden planking had collapsed, leaving a gap 30 yards wide.

The result of the match, which was played without passion and more as an exhibition, was a 1–1 draw, but this will not count in the records. It has been determined to replay the fixture next month in England, when the proceeds will go to a fund set up for the bereaved and injured.

The dead and dying are brought out from the collapsed Ibrox stand.

The gaping hole through which the unfortunate people fell.

Sunderland's Scots do it again

WHILE NOT AS commanding as their "Team of All the Talents" of the mid-nineties, Sunderland have won their first League title for six years. And again they have done it by packing their side with Scots, regularly fielding a team with at least nine men from across the border.

Two players remained from their last title-winning team, Scottish internationals Ted Doig, their goalkeeper, and centre-forward Jimmy Millar. For both it was their fourth Championship medal. But Millar, who spent four seasons with Glasgow Rangers before returning to Sunderland in 1900, also has two League and two Cup medals from Scotland.

Only Everton have provided any kind of challenge to the new champions. But, with games in hand, Sunderland have kept their noses comfortably in front, and their 3–0 victory over Bury has clinched the title with 10 days of the season remaining.

Sunderland finished with 44 points to Everton's 41, with Newcastle United in third place on 37. West Bromwich topped Division Two with 55 points, a record.

FINAL SCORE

Football League
Division 1: Sunderland
Top scorers: James Settle (Everton), Fred Priest (Sheffield United) 18
Division 2: West Bromwich Albion

FA Cup Final

Sheffield United	1	Southampton	1
Replay: Sheffield Utd	2	Southampton	1

Scottish League
Division 1: Rangers
Division 2: Port Glasgow

Scottish FA Cup Final

Hibernian	1	Celtic	0

International Championship
Scotland, 5 pts

FOOTBALL FOCUS

- A maximum wage of £4 per week was introduced in England.

- The result of the Scotland-England game, scene of the Ibrox disaster, did not count towards the International Championship. The replay a month later at Villa Park ended in a 2–2 draw. These were the first matches in which both sides fielded all-professional teams.

- The Cup final was contested by the previous two years' beaten finalists, Southampton and Sheffield United, but the Southern League club lost again. It was a second consecutive replayed Cup final running for Sheffield. This time they won 2–1, after a 1–1 draw. The celebrated amateur, C.B.Fry, played right-back for Southampton. The Crystal Palace provided seated accommodation for 12,000, with "crowds of almost any size" watching from the slopes. The gate for the 1902 final was 76,914, although only 33,068 turned up for the replay, also at Crystal Palace, a week later.

- Scoring in Division One of the Football League reached a new low, averaging 2.75 goals per game.

Sunderland fail to sabotage Scots

ENGLAND were favourites to beat Scotland in 1903 and clinch the International Championship. They had beaten the other two countries, whereas Scotland had suffered their first defeat at the hands of Ireland, and that at home, in Glasgow, too.

Scotland had six Anglo-Scots in the side, and three of these — the keeper and the two backs — were from Sunderland. It was learnt from official quarters that Sunderland tried to prevent their players, Doig, McCombie and Watson, from taking part, threatening them with the loss of their wages. The three men played, and Scotland won 2–1. It was much easier than the score suggests, for the English keeper Baddeley made save after save from the marauding Scots, who were brilliant on the day.

The win gave Scotland a share in the Championship with England and Ireland, who were the first country other than the "big two" to win such an honour. The three Sunderland players did not suffer, as after the game the Scottish treasurer received instructions to "commemorate the game in a generous manner"! And Sunderland won their League match without them.

'Threatened' Doig repels a rare English attack in the internationl match played at Sheffield.

FOOTBALL FOCUS

- A change in pitch markings for the 1902-03 season — the goal area is now a rectangle measuring 6 x 20 yards, and there is a penalty spot (at 12 yards) and a penalty area (at 18 yards).
- A crowd of 22,000 paid to see a junior Scotland-England match at Celtic Park, a tribute to the Scottish enthusiasm for international football. The full international, played at Bramall Lane, Sheffield, drew 33,000, and some 6,000 of those were Scots.
- When Sunderland lost a crucial Championship match 1–0 at home to Sheffield Wednesday, displeased fans stoned the referee's carriage as he left the ground, as a result of which Roker Park was ordered to be closed for a week.
- A storming Championship finish by Aston Villa, who won their last five games (four of them at home) in 15 days, with a goal record of 15-3, was just too late, as they finished a point behind winners Wednesday.

Newcastle sabotage Sunderland's Championship hopes

CHAMPIONS Sunderland went to St James's Park on 25 April for their last game of the season knowing that a win would ensure that they retained their Championship title. Their League record at Newcastle was four wins in four seasons, although they had lost there in the Cup last year. Sadly for them, they lost again, 1–0, and Sheffield Wednesday, having finished their programme a week ago with a 3–1 win over West Bromwich, are the new League champions.

Sunderland did not even finish second, being beaten to that position, on goal average, by Aston Villa.

It has been the tightest title race so far, with Sunderland favourites to win again. But they lost a vital match at home to Wednesday on 21 March, and their form has been in and out since then. It is ironic, considering Sunderland's strong Scottish connections, that it should be a Scot — Newcastle's goalscorer Bob McColl — who finally ended their chances.

This is Wednesday's first League title. They won it despite 11 defeats, more than any other previous champions. They owe their success largely to their home record, where they lost only twice and conceded just seven goals, equalling Preston's record in the first League season, when there were 11 home matches as opposed to 17 now. Their outstanding players this season have been Scottish centre-forward Andy Wilson, who scored 12 goals and made many more with his accurate passing, and stalwart centre-half Tom Crawshaw, a local lad and a great favourite with the fans.

Bury break Cup records

BURY'S 6–0 DEFEAT of Derby County at Crystal Palace is a record margin of victory in an FA Cup final. That's 10 goals without reply for the "Shakers" in two finals over four years. And this time, they did not concede a goal in the Cup at all, only the second side to accomplish this feat (Preston did it in 1889).

The match as a contest was over soon after the interval, when Bury scored four goals in 12 minutes to add to their half-time lead of 1–0. Derby disappointed. They just did not put up any kind of showing. True, they were without the injured Steve Bloomer, their ace goalscorer, but there can be no excuses. Their keeper was hurt trying to save a goal and left the field when they were 5–0 down, but by then they were well beaten.

So Derby's record of "failure" in the FA Cup continues. In eight seasons from 1896, they have lost three times in the semi-finals and now three times in the final.

FINAL SCORE

Football League
Division 1: Sheffield Wednesday
Top scorer: Alec Raybould (Liverpool) 31
Division 2: Manchester City

FA Cup Final

Bury	6	Derby County	0

Scottish League
Division 1: Hibernian
Division 2: Airdrieonians

Scottish FA Cup Final

Rangers	1	Hearts	1
Replay: Rangers	0	Hearts	0
Replay: Rangers	2	Hearts	0

International Championship
England, Ireland, Scotland, 4pts

The mighty Quinn

CELTIC'S young centre-forward Jimmy Quinn plundered a hat-trick in the Scottish Cup final against deadly rivals Rangers to give his side a dramatic 3–2 victory after the Cup-holders had built up a 2–0 lead. The new Hampden Park, opened on 31 October and staging its first Cup final, could not have had a better introduction. With solid earth terracing for the spectators, rather than the wooden steps and scaffolding that caused the Ibrox disaster, and much reduced admission prices, 65,000 turned up to see the "show".

Quinn's success was a triumph for manager Willie Maley, who has patiently built up this exciting Celtic side despite the doubters and the criticism. His courageous policy of removing the old guard and, instead of buying established players, finding and rearing junior talent, has paid off. Even the directors, however, were beginning to doubt his wisdom in persevering with Quinn, a shy, unassuming lad whom he had nurtured from the juniors, mainly on the left wing. The breakthrough came in 1902, when Celtic beat Rangers 3–2 for the Glasgow Exhibition Trophy, Quinn scoring all three from the centre-forward position. Since then, he has gone from strength to strength, but the directors were still dubious when Maley put him in for the regular centre-forward Alec Bennett for the Cup final.

Celtic were in for an early shock at Hampden, when Speedie twice penetrated their defence to put Rangers two up. But they fought back furiously, and Quinn burst through to pull one back and then hit an unstoppable shot for the equalizer before half-time.

The younger Celts continued to press in the second half without being able to find the net. Then, with 10 minutes to go, the mighty Quinn — all 5ft 8in of him — broke away again. He scythed his way through the Rangers defence, brushing aside tackles from those redoubtable backs Smith and Drummond, to fire the ball past Watson for the clincher. It had been a wonderful match, and this was a goal worthy of winning any Cup final.

The 1904 Scottish Cup final at the new Hampden Park.

'Welsh Wizard' clinches it for City

OUTSIDE-RIGHT and captain of Manchester City, Billy Meredith, scored the only goal of the game against Bolton Wanderers in the first all-Lancashire Cup final. There was just a suspicion of offside as Meredith received the ball from his right-wing partner Livingstone, but the referee had no doubts. Meredith went on to round Bolton left-back Struthers before netting in the 23rd minute.

Manchester City, challenging leaders Wednesday for the League Championship, were only slight favourites against Second Division Bolton, who are renowned Cup fighters. They deserved their half-time lead, but Bolton pressed strongly for most of the second half, and would have improved their chances of victory had they shot more frequently and more effectively. On the other hand, Meredith, apart from scoring, did not live up to his glowing reputation as the finest winger in the land. Had he played to his usual brilliant form, City's win would surely have been more convincing.

Billy Meredith scores the winning goal in the FA Cup final at Crystal Palace.

FOOTBALL FOCUS

- Relegated Liverpool scored 49 goals in Division One, one more than Wednesday, champions for the second year in succession. Wednesday scored only 14 away goals to Liverpool's 25.
- Woolwich Arsenal won promotion from Division Two and will be the first southern side to play in the top division.
- Sheffield FC, founded in 1857 and the oldest club in existence, won their first major honour, the FA Amateur Cup, which itself was founded in 1893.
- The Scottish First Division was extended to 14 clubs, and Third Lanark won the title for the first time.
- The managers of the winners of the FA Cup and Scottish Cup are brothers, Tom Maley of Manchester City and Willie Maley of Celtic.
- A "world governing body" for football was formed on 21 May in Paris by representatives of Belgium, Denmark, France, Holland, Spain, Sweden and Switzerland. It is to be called the Fédération Internationale de Football Association.

FINAL SCORE

Football League
Division 1: Sheffield Wednesday
Top scorer: Steve Bloomer (Derby County) 20
Division 2: Preston North End

FA Cup Final
Manchester City 1 Bolton Wanderers 0

Scottish League
Division 1: Third Lanark
Division 2: Hamilton Academical

Scottish FA Cup Final
Celtic 3 Rangers 2

International Championship
England, 5 pts

Villa spoil Newcastle's 'double' dreams

NEWCASTLE'S visions of bringing off the Cup and League "double" were shattered by Aston Villa in the FA Cup final. The Villa, without a trophy to their name for five years, are nevertheless still a powerful side, as they soon demonstrated to Newcastle's discomfort at Crystal Palace. Spencer, Leake and Bache all played for England a fortnight ago, and in centre-forward Harry Hampton, six days from his 20th birthday, they have a brave, no-nonsense spearhead who has already built up a reputation for himself back in Birmingham, where he is more popular than local politician Joseph Chamberlain.

The Villa's brand new style of attacking football, in which the dynamic Hampton swings long balls out to the wings and then does the damage when they are returned, was soon in evidence. After only three minutes he gave them the lead, latching on to a loose ball after Newcastle failed to clear a cross from left-winger Hall, and rifling it inside the right-hand post. Villa dominated for most of the match, and Hampton clinched it when he pounced after Lawrence had dropped another cross from Hall. It was their fourth FA Cup win, only one short of the record held jointly by Backburn and Wanderers.

Harry Hampton (white shorts, centre) fires in Villa's first goal in the Cup final.

Newcastle make up for Cup defeat

NEWCASTLE'S victory at Middlesbrough on the last day of the season has earned them the Championship, their first major trophy. Overcoming the disappointment of losing to Aston Villa in the Cup final, they produced a powerful finish and have beaten Everton by a point.

Packed with Scottish talent, the "Geordies" have succeeded with the type of close-passing game favoured north of the border, built on triangular movements involving inside-forward, winger and wing-half. Their all-Scottish half-back line of Alex Gardner, Andy Aitken and Peter McWilliam has been the backbone of the side, while up front their centre-forward, bustling Bill Appleyard, and right-wing Jack Rutherford, already capped against Scotland at 20, have provided the punch.

A series of seven wins in eight games — their only defeat coming at Blackburn on 1 April, when they sportingly released five of their players for the England-Scotland international (four of them played, all Scots) — set them up for their exciting finish. But as they were losing to Villa in the Cup, Everton were winning their League match and going three points ahead of them and Manchester City. Newcastle had a game in hand, however; although they lost at home 3–1 to Sunderland, they ended up needing to win their last two matches, both away, to take the title.

The first match was at the Wednesday, the outgoing champions whom they had thrashed 6–2 earlier in the season. And despite finding themselves a goal down with only 10 minutes left, they bravely fought back, and goals from Orr, Howie and McWilliam gave them a precious 3–1 victory. Then came the 3–0 defeat of Middlesbrough at Ayresome Park — the match that earned Newcastle the title in style.

FOOTBALL FOCUS

- On 5 December, Woolwich Arsenal beat a visiting side of French "Internationals" 26–1.
- Wales's 3–1 victory at Wrexham was their first ever over the Scots. It was the 30th match between the two countries and Wales had conceded 120 goals.
- The first £1,000 transfer fee was paid by Middlesbrough to Sunderland for England international inside-right Alf Common in February.
- Everton were unlucky to finish as runners-up in the League. They lost at Arsenal 2–1 in their penultimate match, a replay of a game abandoned earlier in the season through fog, with just a few minutes to go. At the time they were leading 3–1.
- Rangers made a gallant effort to bring off the first ever Scottish Cup and League "double". They lost the Cup final after a replay, and then lost the League title in a play-off, after finishing level with Celtic on points. On the English system of goal average, Rangers would have been champions, with a goal record of 83-28 to Celtic's 68-31.

Alf Common — the subject of a record transfer.

FINAL SCORE

Football League
Division 1: Newcastle United
Top scorer: Arthur Brown (Sheffield United) 23
Division 2: Liverpool

FA Cup Final

Aston Villa	2	Newcastle United	0

Scottish League
Division 1: Celtic
Division 2: Clyde

Scottish FA Cup Final

Third Lanark	0	Rangers	0
Replay: Third Lanark	3	Rangers	1

International Championship
England, 5 pts

Promoted Liverpool win title

LIVERPOOL have won the League Championship for the second time, although it needed a season in Division Two to sharpen up their goalscoring. After their relegation in 1904, they set the Second Division alight last season with 93 goals, 60 of them at home, where they were unbeaten.

It is the first time that a promoted side have won the League title in the following year. Yet they made a poor start to their campaign, losing the first three games. Indeed, in their very first match, away to Arsenal, they not only went down 3–1, but they lost their speedy centre-forward Jack Parkinson with a broken wrist that kept him out of the game for several weeks. Although he did come back to score six goals in nine games, his injury enabled Liverpool to bring in Joe Hewitt, whose 22 League goals were an invaluable contribution.

Another success was goalkeeper Sam Hardy, bought from Chesterfield for £500, who replaced veteran Ted Doig early in the season. Still there from Liverpool's 1901 Championship team were left-back Billy Dunlop, centre-half Alec Raisbeck, outside-right Jack Cox and prolific centre-forward Alec Raybould.

It was not until late October that Liverpool asserted their authority, putting together nine wins and a draw in 10 matches. The only dropped point was at home to Preston, who in the end ran them closest for the title. But they won 2–1 at Deepdale at the end of March to give them some breathing space, and finished four points clear.

Liverpool's Parkinson breaks a wrist and sees his effort go wide of the Arsenal goal.

FINAL SCORE

Football League
Division 1: Liverpool
Top scorers: Bullet Jones (Birmingham City), Albert Shepherd (Bolton Wanderers) 26
Division 2: Bristol City

FA Cup Final

Everton	1	Newcastle United	0

Scottish League
Division 1: Celtic
Division 2: Leith Athletic

Scottish FA Cup Final

Hearts	1	Third Lanark	0

International Championship
England, Scotland, 4 pts

Raisbeck is the rock on which England's forwards founder

THE ENGLISH forwards found the commanding figure of centre-half Alec Raisbeck of Division One leaders Liverpool too much for them at Hampden Park, where they lost the international 2–1. Raisbeck, arguably the best centre-half in Britain, and his fellow "Anglo-Scots" Andy Aitken and Peter McWilliam, both of Newcastle, were dominant in the air. Scotland surely have never had such a fine half-back line.

Crowds began converging on Hampden Park for hours before the start, on foot, in cabs and trolleys and from scores of special trains from all around the country. It was the first official 100,000 gate for an international, and although the match was not a classic, the Scots were delighted to see their team dominate the "Saxon invaders" until a late England goal produced a misleading scoreline.

Scotland failed to press home their superiority until five minutes before the interval, when Jim Howie, another Newcastle exile, crashed a fierce shot at James Ashcroft. The Arsenal keeper held the ball, but the force of it spun him round, and the referee judged it to have crossed the line. Howie added another, in the second half, after a fine run by outside-left Alec Smith. England's consolation was scored with a low free-kick by centre-forward Albert Shepherd, the only time he escaped Raisbeck's attentions all afternoon.

The win produced only a share in the International Championship for Scotland, who had lost to Wales, but it deprived England of the outright title.

FOOTBALL FOCUS

- Last season Liverpool put six goals past Chesterfield keeper Sam Hardy in one match. Yet they bought him, and he won a Championship medal with them.
- Bristol City set two records when they won the Second Division title. Their 66 points is the highest total yet in either Division and they ran up 14 consecutive League wins.
- England joined the Fédération Internationale de Football Association (FIFA) in 1905, and the FIFA Congress of 1906 in Berne elected Daniel Burley Woolfall of the Football Association as their new president.
- The first international in South America took place, for the Lipton Cup, between Argentina and Uruguay, and was drawn.

Everton make it a Merseyside double

EVERTON BEAT Newcastle United in the FA Cup final to make sure that both of this season's major trophies go back to Liverpool. This is Everton's first Cup triumph, and they inflicted a second consecutive defeat in the final on poor Newcastle, this one by a single goal after 75 minutes scored by Sandy Young from a right-wing centre by Jack Sharp.

The Cup has been a harder grind this year, with the competition proper increased from five rounds to six (including the final). Everton won all their ties at the first attempt, including an exciting 4–3 win over Sheffield Wednesday in the quarter-finals and — the one that pleased their fans most — a 2–0 victory over neighbours and champions-elect Liverpool in the semi-finals.

The final itself was disappointing as a spectacle. Newcastle never played up to their known standards, with their much-vaunted half-back line of Gardner, Aitken and McWilliam having an off day. Everton deserved their win, but it was the case of the poorer side losing.

Arsenal go top

WOOLWICH Arsenal beat champions Liverpool 2–1 at Plumstead on 6 October to become the first southern club ever to top the First Division table. They were a goal down at half-time, but after the interval outside-left David Neave, who established his first-team place last season with seven goals in 18 games, opened his account for this term, scoring both of Arsenal's goals. Beaten only once so far this season, Arsenal now have 11 points out of a possible 14.

Twenty-two thousand fans and a dog see Arsenal beat Liverpool and go top of Division One.

Wales win the Championship

THE ENGLAND-SCOTLAND dominance of the International Championship has been ended at last. When Scotland held England to a 1–1 draw at St James's Park, Newcastle, on 6 April, it meant that Wales had won the Championship outright, for the first time, with five points to England's four.

The international season began on 16 February, when England beat Ireland 1–0 at Goodison Park. A week later Wales also beat Ireland, 3–2 in Belfast. Then, for the third season running, Wales beat Scotland, 1–0 at Wrexham on 4 March.

Two weeks later they held England to a 1–1 draw at Craven Cottage, Fulham, thanks to a goal by inside-forward William "Lot" Jones of Manchester City, who also had scored against the Irish, and were assured of at least a share in the Championship. But they had to wait until the England-Scotland match on 4 April before they knew that they were outright winners.

The inspiration of Wales has, as usual, been right-winger Billy Meredith, now with Manchester United after moving across town from City last May. In the England match, he was making his 25th appearance in the red shirt of Wales.

The International Championship has now been contested 24 times, with England winning it outright on 10 occasions to Scotland's nine and now one by the Welsh. There have been three titles shared by England and Scotland, and in 1902–03 there was a triple tie between the "Big Two" and Ireland.

FOOTBALL FOCUS

- The Football League season opened, on 1 September, in searing heat, over 90°F in most of the country. This did not appear to bother Chelsea, who beat Glossop 9–2, with George Hilsdon scoring five goals on his debut. Chelsea went on to win 18 of their 19 home games, losing only to Nottingham Forest and earning promotion to Division One for the first time.

- It hardly seemed worth the fare when Crystal Palace, languishing near the bottom of the Southern League, were drawn to play mighty Newcastle at St James's Park in the first round of the Cup. But they went up there and beat them 1–0.

- In winning the League title for the second time in three years, Newcastle dropped only one point at home. This was in their last home match, but the point they earned from their goalless draw with Sheffield United was enough to clinch the title.

- Celtic became the first club to do the Scottish League and Cup "double". They ran away with the Championship, their third consecutive title, finishing up seven points ahead of Dundee. They lost only twice and scored 80 goals in their 34 matches. They beat Rangers 3–0 at Ibrox in the quarter-finals of the Cup, but needed two replays in the semi-finals to get past Hibs, before beating Hearts in the final.

- Arsenal faded after their brief spell at the top of the League, finishing seventh, but only one point behind third-placed Everton. They toured Europe in May, playing eight games in 16 days and winning seven of them — including 9–1 in Berlin and 9–0 in Budapest.

FINAL SCORE

Football League
Division 1: Newcastle United
Top scorer: Alec Young (Everton) 30
Division 2: Nottingham Forest

FA Cup Final

Sheffield Wed	2	Everton	1

Scottish League
Division 1: Celtic
Division 2: St Bernard's

Scottish FA Cup Final

Celtic	3	Hearts	0

International Championship
Wales, 5 pts

Bristol's small wonder

ARSENAL MIGHT have topped the League briefly early on, but newly promoted Bristol City came with a late run in Division One, winning their last four games to finish up in second place, three points behind Newcastle and three in front of Everton. This is the highest position yet achieved by a southern club.

Bristol's remarkable progress in their first season in the top echelon has in no small part been due to their centre-half Billy "Fatty" Wedlock. Standing only 5ft 4$^{1}/_{2}$in, he nevertheless dominates the middle of the field with his skills, and his lack of inches does not seem to affect his heading prowess. He has boundless energy, roaming the pitch in support of his forwards, yet his powers of recovery enable him to get back to his defensive duties whenever necessary. The Bristol-born pivot fully deserved to win his first cap this season, and played in all three of England's internationals.

Bristol City were founded as recently as 1894, and joined the Football League only six years ago. Progress indeed!

Billy Wedlock, Bristol City.

Newcastle's Cup 'jinx' strikes again

THERE MUST BE a jinx on Newcastle in the FA Cup, beaten in the 1908 final for the third time in four years. It was almost gift-wrapped for them — four home draws and then a semi-final against Second Division Fulham, which they won 6–0. But they lost to Wolverhampton Wanderers, who finished only ninth in Division Two, in the final.

The Newcastle side was packed with internationals, from England, Scotland and Ireland. Wolves, on the other hand, were a team made up largely of unknowns. But somehow Wolves were able to impose their style of play — based on speed and strength — on their more illustrious opponents. Yet there was never any suggestion of "strong-arm" tactics. It might have been a different story had Newcastle taken their early chances. But Wolves delivered a double blow just before the interval, and never looked like losing after that. The first goal came from amateur international the Rev. Kenneth Hunt on 40 minutes, followed three minutes later by one from centre-forward George Hedley, twice a Cup-winner with Sheffield United and who played once for England in 1901.

Newcastle could not get their famous short-passing game going, although Scottish cap Jim Howie gave them a glimmer of hope when he scored with 17 minutes left. But Billy Harrison settled it for Wolves 12 minutes later, and six of the Newcastle side sadly went to collect their third runners-up medal. It must seem as though they will never win the Cup.

Wolves, shock Cup-winners when beating Newcastle at Crystal Palace.

FOOTBALL FOCUS

● The British attendance record, 110,000 for the 1901 Cup final, was beaten when between 120,000 and 130,000 crammed into Hampden Park on 4 April to see the Scotland-England international. The result was a 1–1 draw.

● Manchester United continued to dominate Division One, running up 10 consecutive wins, making it 13 in the first 14 games, in which they scored 48 goals. They faltered in the second half of the season, but such was their lead that they won the title by nine points.

● All-conquering Celtic were outdone in just one department — goalscoring. Their 86 League goals were bettered by one club, Falkirk, whose 103 is the highest ever total in the Scottish League, and the first ever hundred.

● England played their first full international on foreign soil on 6 June 1908, beating Austria 6–1 in Vienna. Within a week, they repeated the dose — 11–1 this time — and beat Hungary 7–0 and Bohemia 4–0.

FINAL SCORE

Football League
Division 1: Manchester United
Top scorer: Enoch West (Nottm Forest) 27
Division 2: Bradford City

FA Cup Final
Wolves 3 Newcastle United 1

Scottish League
Division 1: Celtic
Division 2: Raith Rovers

Scottish FA Cup Final
Celtic 5 St Mirren 1

International Championship
England, Scotland, 5 pts

Who can stop United now?

United captain Charlie Roberts.

MANCHESTER UNITED, in only their second season back in the top flight, have taken Division One by storm. Their extraordinary 6–1 win over champions Newcastle at St James's Park is their seventh in the eight games they have played, and they have already built up a commanding lead.

Credit for the 27 goals they have scored so far must go not only to the forwards, fired by wingmen Billy Meredith and George Wall, but also to the masterly half-back line of Dick Duckworth, Charlie Roberts and Alec Bell. Roberts, the captain, has been the inspiration of the side. Will he lead them to the title? It's early days yet, but it's difficult to see who will stop them.

Another double Scotch!

CELTIC, who brought off the first ever Scottish League and Cup "double" last year, have done it again. They clinched it at Ibrox Park, too, beating Rangers 1–0 to confirm the mastery they have exerted over their Glasgow rivals and, indeed, over the rest of Scotland. They still have two games to play, but no other club can catch them now.

Pity poor Rangers, beaten twice in the League by Celtic as well as in the second round of the Cup and in the final of the Glasgow Cup. Celtic, who also beat Queen's Park 3–0 in the final of the Charity Cup, won every tournament they entered. Their only defeats were at Aberdeen and Dundee in the League. In last week's Cup final, they romped to a 5–1 victory over an overawed St Mirren, who offered little resistance. Such is Celtic's form and consistency that it is difficult to see anyone mounting a challenge to their supremacy.

In the past five seasons they have won the Championship four times and the Scottish Cup three times.

Newcastle 1 Sunderland 9

YES, THE SCORELINE is correct. Believe it or not, England's top team — twice League champions and three times Cup-finalists in the last four years, and now challenging for the League title once more — have been beaten 9–1 at home by their neighbours.

There was no inkling that such a shock was in store at half-time, with the score at 1–1. But in the space of 28 second-half minutes, Sunderland hammered eight goals past the hapless Magpies, the last five coming in eight minutes. Newcastle were just stunned by the onslaught.

Sunderland have an excellent recent record at St James's Park, having won seven of their last 10 League games there. But nothing could have prepared even their wildest fans for the goal glut to come after the interval. Newcastle-born Billy Hogg added another three to his first-half goal, and George Holley also helped himself to three.

With Everton beating champions Manchester United to go further ahead in the table, it remains to be seen whether Newcastle can recover from this extraordinary setback and keep up their challenge for the League title.

George Holley, who scored a hat-trick for Sunderland.

The United Kingdom team, with Hunt top left and Woodward seated centre.

England win Olympic soccer tournament

BEATING DENMARK 2–0 in the final at the White City Stadium, the United Kingdom, represented by an England side chosen by the Football Association, won the gold medals in the London Olympic Games. All the competitors in the tournament were, of course, amateurs, England's best-known players being their captain, the Tottenham and England inside-forward Vivian Woodward, and the Rev. Kenneth Hunt, who won an FA Cup medal with Wolves last season.

The six entrants to the competition included two teams from France. In the semi-finals, however, the French "A" side let in 17 goals, 10 of them scored by Sophus Nielsen. England, meanwhile, had accounted for Sweden 12–1, C.H.Purnell of Clapton scoring four, and Holland 4–0, all scored by Harry Stapley of Glossop. The final was a hard-fought match, with the Danes a little unlucky to lose to goals from centre-half F.W.Chapman (South Notts) and Woodward.

FINAL SCORE

Football League
Division 1: Newcastle United
Top scorer: Bert Freeman (Everton) 38
Division 2: Bolton Wanderers

FA Cup Final

Manchester United	1	Bristol City	0

Scottish League
Division 1: Celtic
Division 2: Abercorn

Scottish FA Cup Final

Rangers	2	Celtic	2
Replay: Rangers	1	Celtic	1

(Cup withheld)

International Championship
England, 6 pts

FOOTBALL FOCUS

- The 1908 League champions Manchester United played Southern League winners Queen's Park Rangers for a new trophy in September, the Charity Shield, winning 4–0 after a 1–1 draw.
- Leicester Fosse, already doomed to relegation, lost 12–0 at Nottingham Forest on 21 April, a record score for Division One.
- Newcastle won the League despite their 9-1 home defeat by Sunderland. They won 10 out of their next 11 matches, and won at Roker Park, 3–0 in the fourth round of the Cup, after a 2–2 draw at St James's Park.
- After the trauma of the Cup final riots, Celtic found themselves needing six points from four games in five days to win the League. Thanks to a couple of hat-tricks from Jimmy Quinn, they achieved their fifth Championship on the trot, a Scottish record.

Whisky fuels fire of Hampden riot and rules out Celtic 'double'

THE 1909 SCOTTISH CUP has been withdrawn following the riot at Hampden Park after the replayed final between Celtic and Rangers. The action by the Scottish FA, readily agreed to by the clubs concerned, confirms the seriousness in which they regard the events, and puts paid to Celtic's chances of completing the Cup and League "double" for the third season running.

The trouble started when the replay was drawn after 90 minutes. Many of the players and most of the crowd expected extra time. But the rules had been laid down beforehand and could not be changed, extra time being possible only for a second replay.

Some of the crowd became unsettled and spilled on to the pitch. The police moved in, and the violence escalated into a full-blown riot, with fires started and an attempt to burn down the pay boxes using whisky as fuel. When the fire brigade arrived, they were attacked and their hoses cut. Hundreds of people were injured. Both clubs have shamefacedly agreed to help compensate Queen's Park for the extensive damage done to the ground.

The First Heroes

FOOTBALL is a team game, but right from the start it has produced its heroes, the men the crowd love to watch. There has always been more glamour attached to certain positions. The wingers and the goalscorers, as well as the tricky providers, are purveyors of the more spectacular skills. But the crowds appreciate the great defenders, too, the brave and the skilful, the men who get their side out of trouble when the going gets tough.

Amateur days

In the early days, there were the great amateurs. There was the Hon. A.F.Kinnaird, later an earl and president of the FA, unmistakable with his red beard and long white trousers. He played in nine FA Cup finals, for the Wanderers and the Old Etonians, and earned five winners' medals. In those days when hacking was legal, he was a fearsome opponent. It is said that when Captain Marindin of Royal Engineers fame called on Kinnaird's mother, she expressed her fear that her son would come back one day from that horrid rough game with a broken leg. The reply was: "Don't worry, ma'am, it won't be his own."

Lord Kinnaird, the "W.G.Grace" of football.

Centre-forwards

John Goodall, perhaps the most brilliant of the Preston "Invincibles", played inside-right or centre-forward for England, and was one of the pioneers of scientific football in the country. Another outstanding centre-forward in the 1890s was G.O.Smith of Oxford University, Old Carthusians and the Corinthians. With a frail physique and gentle disposition, he did not look a footballer. But he had courage, a fine tactical brain, and was a lethal finisher. He gained 20 caps for England. Emulating Smith in the early 1900s was Vivian Woodward, also an amateur, with Spurs and Chelsea, who played for England in 23 full and 43 amateur internationals, winning two Olympic gold medals. Renowned for his sportsmanship, he was fast off the mark and scored 29 goals for England, 53 in amateur internationals.

The most prolific scorer of all was Steve Bloomer, an inside-forward famed for his quick thinking and first-time shooting. His career with Derby, Middlesbrough and Derby again lasted from 1892 to 1914, when he was 40. He scored 353 goals in 598 League appearances, and 28 in 23 matches for England. In many of those nineties internationals, he had G.O.Smith on one side of him and either William Bassett or Charlie Athersmith on the other.

John Goodall of Preston's "double"-winning side.

Wingmen

Bassett was the outside-right supreme, a little man (5ft 5½in) for the big occasion, whether playing for England or West Bromwich Albion. He sprang to fame as a young lad when West Brom beat Preston in the 1888 Cup final, and won an England cap on his showing. For a decade he was in a class of his own. He inspired West Brom to another Cup success in 1892, against Villa, after his legendary display in the third semi-final with Forest. That day, in a blinding snowstorm, Bassett was magnificent. All Albion's goals in their 6–2 victory came as a result of his crosses.

Yet there was another outside-right who would challenge Bassett in those days, another Billy, Meredith of Wales, whose career with the two Manchester clubs ran from 1894 to 1923. He played a record 48 times for Wales, his international career spanning 25 years. Patrolling the touchline and chewing the inevitable toothpick, he could score goals as well as make them, and helped both his clubs to major honours.

Billy Bassett, a little man for the big occasion.

Scottish idol

Contemporary with Meredith, but a left-winger, was Scottish idol Alec Smith of Rangers, who won 20 international caps between 1898 and 1911. Taking the ball straight up to an opponent and then slipping round him at the last moment, he electrified the crowds with his dashes up the wing, and was a model of consistency. With Rangers, he won six Championship and four Cup-winners' medals, and was one of five Rangers men in Scotland's side that beat England 4–1 at Celtic Park in 1900.

Half-backs

Two half-backs also stand out from that match. Scotland's centre-half Alec Raisbeck was so often a thorn in England's side, a tower of strength for Liverpool as well as his country. He played the pivotal role to perfection, always thinking, moving around the field in defence and attack, perpetual motion personified.

Ernest "Nudger" Needham, England's left-half, was a polished performer, the "Prince of Half-backs". Never known to shirk a tackle, he was a key figure in Sheffield United's side from 1891 for 22 years, inspiring them to two Cup wins and a League title.

Villa men

The most successful English side of the 1890s and early 1900s were Aston Villa, with six League titles and five Cup wins before the Great War. Archie Hunter, captain and centre-forward who led them to the first of their Cup victories in 1887, was idolized by the Villa crowd. John Devey, another inside- or centre-forward, took over as skipper from Hunter and was a key figure in Villa's success. So was Scottish international Jimmy Cowan, their attacking centre-half who was fast enough to win the Powderhall Handicap. Even faster, though, was outside-right Charlie Athersmith, whose combination with inside partner Devey was devastating. The versatile Jimmy Crabtree played in every defensive position, but Villa rated him their best ever wing-half. Later, before the Great War, Joe Bache and Harry Hampton shot them to further honours. Centre-forward Hampton, lethal in front of goal, scored a club record 213 in the League, while Bache, a scheming inside-forward, was always among the goals.

Sunderland talents

When Villa weren't winning the League in the 1890s, it was usually Sunderland, the "Team of All the Talents", packed with Scottish footballers. They were much feared, and famed for their goals — from that powerhouse of a centre-forward John Campbell and tricky inside-right James Miller. But the dominant personality of their side was right-half Hugh Wilson. His anticipation in defence was legendary, his throw from the touchline unsurpassed, and his shot as deadly as any forward's.

Custodians

Prominent between the posts were those literally "great" keepers Billy "Fatty" Foulke and Albert Iremonger. Foulke, an enormous man, was 15 stone when he joined Sheffield United in 1894, and five more when he played for Chelsea and Bradford City over 10 years later. Yet despite his bulk, he was remarkably agile and one of the finest keepers of his era, winning major honours with Sheffield and playing once for England. Iremonger, capped for England in the early 1900s and a stalwart of Notts County, stood 6ft 6in, but had difficulty getting down to low balls. The safest of all was Sam Hardy, of Liverpool and Villa, capped 21 times for England over 14 years.

Hugh Wilson led Sunderland's "Team of All the Talents".

Combinations

With full-backs Bob Crompton and Jesse Pennington, Hardy formed a matchless defensive combination for England in the pre-war years. Crompton, of Blackburn Rovers, amassed 41 caps and was an influential skipper, a man of great presence and the accepted leader of English football from 1902 to the outbreak of war. Pennington, of West Bromwich, was the perfect complement, always covering, relying on skill rather than brawn.

Many players, like these, are remembered for their partnerships or combinations. Perhaps the most famous pre-war half-back combination was Duckworth-Roberts-Bell of the Manchester United League- and Cup-winning sides. The power of Dick Duckworth, thighs like tree-trunks, allied to the more delicate skills of Alec Bell on the left, flanked the commanding figure of the constructive Charlie Roberts in the middle. A dominating six-footer, Roberts was the most complete centre-half of his day, mixing power with perfect touch. His pioneering work with the Players' Union and his rebellious nature — his penchant for short shorts prompted the FA to rule in 1904 that "footballers' knickers must cover the knee" — did not perhaps endear him to the England selectors and he won only three caps.

Celtic stars

One of the outstanding attacking combinations was the Celtic inside-forward trio of Jimmy McMenemy, Jimmy Quinn and Peter Somers. Quinn, a charismatic character, the archetypal centre-forward, robust, courageous and a goalscorer supreme, was the idol of the Celtic crowd for years as he terrorized opposing defences, always, it seems, saving his best performances for the clashes with Rangers. McMenemy and Somers were perfect foils, subtle schemers, the former the "Napoleon" of the side, the latter a nimble conjurer. That whole Celtic side were stars, with six pre-war League wins on the trot and averaging a Cup win every other year.

"Fatty" Foulke towards the end of his career, flanked by Chelsea team-mates.

'Dirty' jibes as Newcastle break their Cup jinx

NEWCASTLE FINALLY buried their Cup jinx, beating Second Division Barnsley 2–0 in the replayed final at Goodison Park. But the manner of their victory left much to be desired, and there were unprecedented cries of "Dirty Newcastle" heard around the ground before the end of the match.

It seemed that certain Newcastle players came out on to the pitch determined to win at all costs. Early on, Alex Higgins floored the Barnsley keeper Mearns, who, when he recovered, had to be restrained by the referee and a team-mate as he chased after the culprit. Barnsley right-back Downs, limping from a foul in the first half, was laid out after the interval by a kick in the stomach and had to be carried off for treatment. The punishment was a mere free-kick, but even his Newcastle team-mates showed their disapproval with the offender.

Albert Shepherd, scorer of both Newcastle goals

There is no denying that Newcastle had the better of the play, with their captain and right-half Colin Veitch outstanding in a goalless first half. They adapted better to the muddy, churned-up pitch than their lighter opponents, and went one up through centre-forward Albert Shepherd, who ploughed through the middle to finish off a move started by Veitch seven minutes after the interval. Barnsley missed a glorious chance to equalize and then gave away a penalty for a trip on Higgins. It was Shepherd's privilege to score from the first penalty ever conceded in an FA Cup final.

So Newcastle — albeit having sullied their hitherto fine reputation for fair play — have finally added the Cup to their three League titles.

FOOTBALL FOCUS

● Vivian Woodward became the first player to score double hat-tricks in two games, when he hit six goals for England in the amateur international against Holland at Stamford Bridge on 11 December. The famous Tottenham Hotspur centre-forward and Olympic gold-medallist had scored a phenomonal eight times against France three years earlier, also in an amateur international.

● Aston Villa won their sixth League title, their first for 10 years, finishing with a record-equalling 53 points, five points ahead of runners-up Liverpool.

● Ireland drew with England and then beat Scotland, but, with the Championship at their mercy for the first time, they went down 4–1 to Wales, giving Scotland their first outright win for eight years.

Vivian Woodward – goalscorer supreme.

Promotion scramble goes Oldham's way

THE LAST DAY of the season began with Manchester City on top of Division Two with 54 points and assured of promotion barring a couple of adverse 9–0 results. Below them, however, there were three clubs in contention to join them, and anything could happen.

Hull City, with 53 points, needed a draw to go up, but they were due to meet Oldham Athletic, two points behind them and with a superior goal average. Derby, with the worst goal average, were on 52 points, and needed to win at West Bromwich if Hull opened the door for them by slipping up at Oldham. Well, Hull did slip up at Oldham. They lost 3–0. But Derby failed to take advantage, being held to a goalless draw.

So all three finish up on 53 points, a point behind the new Division Two champions Manchester City, who lost 3–2 at Wolves. And it is Oldham, with their superior goal average, who deservedly win promotion, too. They deserve it because, having accounted for Derby 4–0 in mid-week, they have beaten the two other contenders comprehensively inside five days and so proved their superiority.

A new name on the Scottish Cup

DUNDEE HAVE WON the Scottish Cup for the first time, beating Clyde 2–1 at Ibrox Park in the second replay of the final.

What a remarkable Cup campaign Dundee have fought. After two goalless draws in their semi-final against Hibs, they won the second replay 1–0 to reach their first final. And they looked dead and buried 11 days ago against Clyde, when they were 2–0 down with only seven minutes to go. But goals by John Hunter and Johnny Langland earned them a replay, which ended in another goalless draw.

FINAL SCORE

Football League
Division 1: Aston Villa
Top scorer: John Parkinson (Liverpool) 29
Division 2: Manchester City

FA Cup Final

Newcastle United	1	Barnsley	1
Replay: Newcastle United	2	Barnsley	0

Scottish League
Division 1: Celtic
Division 2: Leith Athletic

Scottish FA Cup Final

Dundee	2	Clyde	2
Replay: Dundee	0	Clyde	0
Replay: Dundee	2	Clyde	1

International Championship
Scotland, 4 pts

New Cup stays in Bradford

THE NEW TROPHY for the FA Cup was made in Bradford, and after the replayed Cup final at Old Trafford it is staying there. Bradford City beat Newcastle 1–0 to win their first major honour.

For Newcastle United it is the same old story. They reached the Cup final for the fifth time in seven years, a truly remarkable feat in itself. They were again unable to win at Crystal Palace, and after a poor match there, in which they sorely missed last year's scoring hero Albert Shepherd, it was expected that their scientific play and individual skills would prevail against the rugged Bradford defence in the replay.

In the event, however, it was the resolute Bradford rearguard that prevailed. Bolstered at centre-half by the outstanding Torrance, who had missed the first match, Bradford enjoyed another fine performance from full-backs Campbell and Taylor. A bad goalkeeping error by Lawrence, who had played in all his club's five finals, allowed Scottish international inside-forward Jimmy Speirs the chance to score a simple goal after 15 minutes, and Newcastle could find no answer.

Speirs scores the winning goal for Bradford City.

Dramatic finish to title race

THREE DAYS after Bradford City won the Cup at Manchester United's new home, Old Trafford, the ground was the scene of a great United victory, 5–1 over Sunderland, which gave them their second League title in four years. Again they won with 52 points, and again it was Aston Villa who were runners-up, but this time by only one point instead of nine.

Manchester made a wonderful start to the season, with seven wins in their first eight matches. But it looked all over for them when Villa edged in front on goal average last Saturday by beating the Reds 4–2 at Villa Park in a bad-tempered match in which a player from each side was sent off in the closing minutes. Villa had a game in hand, but could only draw at Blackburn on Monday, setting up the last day for a dramatic finish. They crashed 3–1 to Liverpool at Anfield, and Manchester's resounding defeat of third-placed Sunderland won the day.

United have triumphed with largely the same team that won the League in 1908 and the Cup a year later. New signing Enoch West led the scorers with 19 goals, although Alec Turnbull still made a valuable contribution with 18. Charlie Roberts was again an inspiring captain, and the incomparable Billy Meredith was still chewing his toothpick and teasing full-backs on the right wing.

Manchester United with the League Championship trophy, won for the second time in four years.

FOOTBALL FOCUS

- Newcastle did not hold on to the FA Cup for long last year. The FA presented the trophy to Lord Kinnaird to mark his 21st year as president, and commissioned a new design for this season because the old one had been pirated for a minor competition in Manchester.

- Twelve Scots played in this year's FA Cup final, eight of them for the winners, Bradford City. The attendance for the replay at Old Trafford was a midweek record 66,646.

FINAL SCORE

Football League
Division 1: Manchester United
Top scorer: Albert Shepherd (Newcastle United) 25
Division 2: West Bromwich Albion

FA Cup Final

Bradford City	0	Newcastle United	0
Replay: Bradford City	1	Newcastle United	0

Scottish League
Division 1: Rangers
Division 2: Dumbarton

Scottish FA Cup Final

Celtic	0	Hamilton Acad	0
Replay: Celtic	2	Hamilton Acad	0

International Championship
England, 5 pts

New order over the border

CELTIC'S SUPREME reign in Scotland has finally come to a close. Admittedly they won the Cup — after a stuttering campaign — but fifth place in the League after winning it six times on the trot is evidence of a dramatic decline. Their defence has not been the problem — 18 goals conceded is better than in any of those six Championship years. But their goalscoring has fallen from a peak of 86 in 1907–08 to a dismal 48 this season.

Despite home draws in every round, Celtic struggled to reach the semi-finals of the Cup, particularly in the second round, when they scraped past non-League Galston 1–0. They beat Aberdeen by the same score in the semi-finals, and they needed a replay before they beat lowly Hamilton 2–1 in the final.

Rangers have taken full advantage of their rivals' fall from grace in the League, emerging four points clear of Aberdeen in the title race.

Battling Barnsley show Yorkshire grit

BARNSLEY played six goalless games in an extraordinary Cup campaign that saw them reach the final for the second time in three years, a record for a Second Division club. This time they emerged victorious, beating West Bromwich 1–0 after extra time in the Cup final replay.

Their saga is a story of attrition rather than glamour, their triumph down to stamina and heroic defending. They played 12 matches, of which three went to extra time, and conceded only four goals. The first final was a dull affair for the spectators, with brilliant defence dominating. The speed and tackling of Barnsley's, with right-back Dicky Downs in his element, smothered Albion's attacks before they got too near goal. And despite Barnsley's poor attack, it was the Albion's goal that had the luckier escapes.

Both sides performed better in the replay, with Barnsley's wing-halves Glendinning and Utley to the fore. But the match seemed to be heading the same way, when Barnsley suddenly broke away with two minutes of extra time to go. Utley broke up an Albion attack on the left before hitting a cross-field pass to inside-right Harry Tufnell, standing on the half-way line. Showing remarkable stamina after two hours of solid effort, the Barnsley forward made for the Albion goal, swerving past the formidable challenge of England left-back Jesse Pennington and taking the ball on another 30 yards before shooting past the advancing keeper. It was a glorious goal to win the match and, for Barnsley, a fitting climax to an epic Cup journey.

Harry Tufnell — scored a solo winner for Barnsley.

FOOTBALL FOCUS

- In the first round of the FA Cup, Wolves were held to a 0–0 draw at Watford and won the replay 10–0.
- After a third drawn Cup final in a row, the FA determined that extra time would in future be played in the first match if level after 90 minutes.
- Rangers retained the Scottish League title, finishing six points clear of Celtic, who retained the Cup.
- Blackburn Rovers, five times Cup-winners, won their first League title, beating runners-up Everton by three points. Their total of 49 points is the lowest since Division One was increased to 20 teams in 1905.
- In a consolation tournament staged for teams eliminated in the first two rounds of the Olympic football tournament, Germany beat Russia 16–0.

FINAL SCORE

Football League
Division 1: Blackburn Rovers
Top scorers: Harry Hampton (Aston Villa), George Holley (Sunderland), Dave McLean (Sheffield Wednesday) 25
Division 2: Derby County

FA Cup Final

Barnsley	0	WBA	0
Replay: Barnsley	1	WBA	0

(after extra time)

Scottish League
Division 1: Rangers
Division 2: Ayr United

Scottish FA Cup Final

Celtic	2	Clyde	0

International Championship
England, Scotland 5 pts

Danish keeper Hansen in action against England in Stockholm.

Another Olympic triumph for England

ENGLAND represented the United Kingdom again and retained their Olympic title in Stockholm. And again it was Denmark who provided the strongest opposition, but England beat them more convincingly in the final this time, by four goals to two. The tournament took place between 29 June and 5 July, and it was so hot that buckets of water were placed by the touchlines so that players could refresh themselves during the game.

Out of 14 original entrants, all from Europe, France and Belgium were late withdrawals and Bohemia could not be accepted because they were not members of FIFA. Six of the 11 teams had to play a preliminary round, and then in the first round proper both England and Denmark enjoyed 7–0 victories, Harold Walden scoring five of England's goals against the Hungarians.

England coasted through their semi-final against Finland, winning 4–0 and ostentatiously hitting a penalty over the cross-bar when they considered the award too harsh. Denmark also scored four in their semi-final, while conceding a single goal to Holland, who gave them a good match.

England gained a well-deserved win in the final, although Denmark were unlucky to lose Buchwald owing to a sprained wrist with the score 2–1. England went in at half-time with a 4–1 lead. The Danes, with Nils Middleboe moving from defence to centre-forward, pressed hard in the second half, scoring again, but never managed a serious threat to England's supremacy.

Battle of the giants ends level

THE BATTLE of the giants has ended with honours even. Sunderland, a week after losing to Aston Villa in the Cup final, have beaten Bolton 3–1 to clinch the League Championship. Three days ago they went to Villa Park and earned a brave draw that put paid to Villa's title hopes. The Wednesday were still in with a chance, but now they have lost 3–1 at Everton the title is Sunderland's, whatever happens in the last games next week.

What a battle it has been, with two teams both going for the League and Cup "double". Sunderland's League campaign has been quite extraordinary. They failed to win any of their first seven matches, managing only two draws and conceding 18 goals. A dip into the transfer market in October to bolster their defence transformed their season. Joe Butler, a reliable keeper from Glossop, and Charlie Gladwin, an inspirational right-back from Blackpool, shored up the holes at the back and enabled the right-wing "triangle" of Frank Cuggy (right-half), Charlie Buchan (inside-right) and Jackie Mordue (outside-right) to weave their intricate attacking patterns.

Sunderland stormed up the table with five straight wins. They lost a couple of away games, but they beat Villa 3–1 and Liverpool 7–0, with Buchan scoring five times. In 17 matches from 28 December, they have lost on only one occasion.

In the Cup, meanwhile, Villa charged through to the semi-finals with three 5–0 victories. Sunderland's progress was hardly less impressive, although they needed two replays to dispose of Newcastle in the quarter-finals. They also needed a replay in the semi-finals before beating Burnley 3–2, while Villa reached the final with a 1-0 victory over Oldham.

The final drew a record crowd of 120,081 to see a battle royal between the two Championship challengers. It was a thrilling, if bruising, match. A series of clashes between Villa centre-forward Harry Hampton and Sunderland centre-half Charlie Thomson could have had them both sent off. (Indeed, they and referee A. Adams were all suspended for a month by the FA, the players for their behaviour and the official for his leniency.)

Early on Villa were awarded a penalty — only the second in the history of the Cup final — but Charlie Wallace shot wide. Defences got on top, but when Villa keeper Sam Hardy had to go off for 20 minutes in the second half with an injury, Sunderland failed to capitalize on their chances. With Villa centre-half Jim Harrop wearing the keeper's jersey, Sunderland peppered away at goal and twice hit the upright. Hardy returned, and with 15 minutes to go, Wallace sent a corner-kick to the edge of the penalty box. Right-half Tom Barber met it with his head, and the Sunderland defence watched spellbound as the ball rolled into the corner of the net.

That was the only score, so Villa won the Cup for the fifth time, equalling the record of the Wanderers and Blackburn Rovers. But they could not emulate their own feat of League and Cup "double", achieved back in 1896-97, as the other "giants" Sunderland have gone on to win the battle for the League.

Butler (Sunderland) foils Villa's Hampton in the Cup final.

FOOTBALL FOCUS

- Despite England's disastrous start, losing to Ireland, they beat Wales and Scotland to win the International Championship.
- Sunderland won the League Championship with a record number of points, 54, after gleaning only two from their first seven games.
- Rangers completed a hat-trick of League titles in Scotland, but there was a new name on the Scottish Cup, Falkirk. Neither they nor runners-up Raith Rovers had reached the final before.
- Morton of the Scottish Division One created a curious record — every player who appeared for them in the League scored, even the keeper, who converted a penalty kick.

Ten Irish heroes

ENGLAND LOST to Ireland for the first time in an international, going down 2–1 in Belfast. The England side, described as "the greatest ever sent across the Irish Sea", was full of stars. Sunderland's Charlie Buchan, making his England debut, headed them in front after 10 minutes. And when, shortly afterwards, Ireland lost inside-left James McAuley of Huddersfield with a knee injury, only one result seemed possible.

But the 10 Irish heroes fought like tigers, and Sheffield United centre-forward Billy Gillespie scored twice with shots deflected by English defenders.

About three minutes from time, the referee blew for a free-kick to Ireland. The crowd, thinking it was the final whistle, surged on to the field and carried their heroes off shoulder-high. There was no way that the referee was going to get the game restarted in those circumstances, and the amazing result stood.

FINAL SCORE

Football League
Division 1: Sunderland
Top scorer: David McLean (Sheffield Wednesday) 30
Division 2: Preston North End

FA Cup Final

Aston Villa	1	Sunderland	0

Scottish League
Division 1: Rangers
Division 2: Ayr United

Scottish FA Cup Final

Falkirk	2	Raith Rovers	0

International Championship
England, 4 pts

A great day for the Irish

IRELAND have won the International Championship outright for the first time in their history. A draw with Scotland in Belfast was enough to secure them the title with five points. When before has the Championship been decided by mid-March?

But you have to go back a couple of months, to Wrexham in January, for the start of this epic story. Before a goal was scored, Ireland lost Everton's Harris with a torn ligament, but they took charge of the game and beat Wales 2–1.

In February, Ireland confounded the critics again and won for the first time on English soil, 3–0 at Middlesbrough. They outplayed England, and a magnificent goal from Gillespie, sandwiched between two from Lacey, did not exaggerate their superiority.

The stage was set for the showdown with Scotland on 14 March. A record Irish crowd of 26,000 turned out in appalling weather to watch their heroes. Yet again the Irish side, without the forceful Gillespie, were soon affected by injury, and once more they showed the greatest fighting spirit in the face of desperate odds. First, centre-half O'Connell had to leave the field with an arm injury. Then right-back McConnell was carried off. Worse was to follow. Goalkeeper McKee, hurt in a collision, carried on until just after the interval, when he could no longer continue. So into goal went the injured McConnell!

With O'Connell back in the fray, the nine-and-a-half Irish warriors held out against the rampaging Scots until 20 minutes from time, when makeshift keeper McConnell inadvisedly left his charge and Donnachie found the unguarded net. That should have been the end, but you cannot write off these remarkable Irishmen. Centre-forward Young grabbed an equalizer eight minutes from time and, with the crowd swarming on the touchlines, they held out for the draw that gave them a richly-deserved Championship.

Celtic back with a 'double'

THEY LAUGHED at the little waif when he first took the field at Parkhead. But the jeers changed to cheers as soon as small, fragile-looking Patsy Gallagher touched the ball. The control, intelligence, skills and toughness of this seven-stone "mighty atom" made him an instant hero. And now, in his third season with Celtic, he has revitalized the forward line and finished as top scorer, with 21 goals in the League.

It needed a replay before Hibs were convincingly conquered in the Cup final. Celtic then finished their League programme six points ahead of Rangers, with 81 goals scored and only 14 conceded in their 38 matches. It is their third League and Cup "double", and they are still the only Scottish side to have achieved the feat.

FOOTBALL FOCUS

- Preston have changed divisions again — relegated from Division One in 1912, promoted in 1913, they have now gone straight down again to Division Two.
- Playing for Stockport against Fulham on 4 October, Norman Wood headed an own goal, gave away a penalty for hands from which the visitors scored, and then missed a penalty. Stockport lost 3–1.

King at Palace for Cup final

KING GEORGE V became the first reigning monarch to see the Cup final, when he presented the trophy at the Crystal Palace to the winning captain, Burnley's centre-half Tommy Boyle. It was a great occasion for football, if not a great match. For the fourth consecutive season, the result was 1–0, although the last two finals have not needed a replay.

Neither Burnley nor Liverpool had enjoyed a particularly distinguished season in the League, and the first half bore witness to their lowly positions in the table. The goal, a fierce shot by England international centre-forward Freeman after 58 minutes, changed the mood of the game, however, and the King, along with the 72,000 spectators at this last final at the Crystal Palace, was treated to a lively last half-hour in which Liverpool strove vainly for an equalizer.

Burnley goalkeeper Sewell, deputizing for injured regular Dawson, made some vital saves — one, when the ball hit him in the face, completely by accident.

The captains are presented to the King.

FINAL SCORE

Football League
Division 1: Blackburn Rovers
Top scorer: George Elliott (Middlesbrough) 31
Division 2: Notts County

FA Cup Final

Burnley	1	Liverpool	0

Scottish League
Division 1: Celtic
Division 2: Cowdenbeath

Scottish FA Cup Final

Celtic	0	Hibernian	0
Replay: Celtic	4	Hibernian	1

International Championship
Ireland, 5 pts

Freeman's shot beats Liverpool keeper Campbell for the only goal of the game.

A change of uniform

Buchan in Sunderland strip and (right) Grenadier Guards uniform.

THE DECISION to continue with the League and Cup programme while the country was engaged in war had been a controversial one. Both the English and Scottish authorities were motivated by the desire to provide "an antidote to the war", and in August, when Britain declared war on Germany, few people expected hostilities to last more than a few months, anyway.

But as the war dragged on, and news came back of terrible casualties at the front, the football authorities began to view the situation with growing concern. The season was allowed to finish, although the fixtures played out with little enthusiasm. It was understandably difficult for the players to concentrate on football when their fellow men were fighting — and dying — in the trenches. As soon as the season was over, there was a rush to change their football strip for uniforms of the armed forces.

FOOTBALL FOCUS

- The result of Oldham's game at Middlesbrough, abandoned by the referee with the score 4–1 against them, was allowed to stand. Billy Cook, the player who refused to leave the field when sent off, was suspended for a year. Oldham, severely reprimanded and fined £350, finished runners-up to champions Everton, just a point behind. The title had been theirs for the taking, but they lost their last two matches, both at home.

- A debate in Parliament about shells failing to explode in battle — the implication being that munitions workers had possibly not been concentrating on their work — led to an FA decree that no games were to be played near munitions factories during working hours. As a result, the second-round Cup replay at Lincoln between Bradford City and Norwich was played behind closed doors.

- There was a three-way tie in Scotland's Division Two, necessitating three play-off matches. Cowdenbeath won both theirs to finish top, with Leith second and St Bernard's third. But none of them won promotion, as only the top division played during the war.

- League champions Everton owed their success largely to their results away from home, where they won 11 times and conceded just 18 goals in 19 games. Only bottom club Spurs won fewer than Everton's eight at home. Everton's winning total, 46 points, was the lowest since the First Division was increased to 20 clubs, and only six points separated them from West Bromwich Albion in 11th place.

The man who wouldn't go

IN AN UNPRECEDENTED incident at Middlesbrough on Easter Monday, Oldham's left-back Billy Cook refused to go when ordered off by the referee. So the referee himself left the field, and the match ended half an hour early.

Oldham had arrived at Ayresome Park full of confidence. They were challenging for the First Division title, in fourth position but only two points behind leaders Manchester City. But as the game progressed, their frustration built up. Not only did they find themselves three down in 20 minutes, but they felt aggrieved at some of the decisions that were going against them, including a penalty appeal that had been turned down.

Then, 10 minutes after the interval, the referee gave Middlesbrough a penalty for a Cook foul on Carr. Tinsley scored from the spot to complete his hat-trick. Shortly afterwards, Cook again fouled Carr and the referee stopped the game and sent him off — or at least he tried to. The Oldham left-back seemed reluctant to go, and his team-mates crowded round the referee. The harassed official, Mr H.Smith of Nottingham, then gave Cook a minute to leave the field. When he still stood his ground, Mr Smith, after looking at his watch, walked off, with the players of both sides following. The spectators could hardly believe their eyes.

The Khaki Cup final

WITH THE WAR in progress since August, the Cup final was a very low-key affair. It was held at Old Trafford in wet, gloomy conditions, with thousands of servicemen in uniform among the near 50,000 crowd, many of them bearing signs of injuries sustained at the front.

The outcome was an easy 3–0 win for Sheffield United over a Chelsea side whose forwards never managed to reproduce the form that got them to the final. Chelsea's defence, on the other hand, had nothing to reproach themselves for, and held their opponents to a single goal until seven minutes from the end. For Sheffield, their captain and left-half George Utley was outstanding, just as he was for Barnsley three years ago.

In a poignant speech to the crowd after presenting the trophy and medals to the players, Lord Derby said that the clubs and their supporters had "seen the Cup played for, and it was now the duty of everyone to join with each other and play a sterner game for England".

FINAL SCORE

Football League
Division 1: Everton
Top scorer: Bobby Parker (Everton) 35
Division 2: Derby County

FA Cup Final

Sheffield United	3	Chelsea	0

Scottish League
Division 1: Celtic
Division 2: Cowdenbeath

Scottish FA Cup
No competition

International Championship
No competition

The Great War (1914–18)

BRITAIN entered what has become known as the Great War on 4 August 1914, when Germany invaded Belgium. Britain sent forces to help stop the German advance across France, and few thought that they would not return before Christmas. But by 1915 the opposing sides had dug themselves into a system of trenches that zigzagged along the Western Front, a battlefield extending some 450 miles across Belgium and North-eastern France to the border of Switzerland. They remained deadlocked in this trench warfare until 1918.

Aiding the war effort

At the beginning of the war, there was no conscription. But the continuation of the football programme caused a great deal of controversy. Criticism was vociferous and widespread. Clubs were accused of helping the enemy, and the Dean of Lincoln wrote to the FA of "onlookers who, while so many of their fellow men are giving themselves in their country's peril, still go gazing at football".

But the FA had consulted the War Office before taking its decision to stage the 1914–15 Cup. And while many players quit their clubs to volunteer for the armed forces, the League, too, decided to carry on with their programme. The football authorities contributed to war charities, and more importantly assisted in the recruitment of volunteers — some half a million, it was claimed, by early 1915.

As the war took a grip in 1915, more players began to enlist, and gates dwindled. In July, it was decided to cancel the regular League and Cup programmes, and replace them with regional leagues. The players would not be paid, and nor would there be any medals or trophies. No internationals would be played, either. Matches were to be scheduled only for Saturdays and holidays, so there would be no midweek games to interfere with work in the munitions factories. In Scotland, although the Cup was cancelled, the First Division of the League continued. But players were not allowed to make a full-time living from the game, being paid a maximum of £2 a week. And players not in the forces were required to work in a war-related industry.

Sam Hardy kept for Forest during the war.

'Match-fixing'

Allegations of "match-fixing" that first surfaced in the Manchester area near the end of the 1914–15 season, and had been published in the *Sporting Chronicle* on 24 April, developed into a full-blown scandal during the year. The accusations, first printed on a handbill issued by a firm of bookmakers, were that a Manchester match at Easter had been squared for the home club to win by a particular score. There were only two matches this could apply to, and the *Sporting Chronicle* demanded a Football League inquiry.

The Football League did indeed set up a committee to look into these serious allegations, but it was Christmas before they delivered their final report. The verdict caused a sensation. Manchester United's match against Liverpool at Easter turned out to be the fixture under investigation, and it transpired that considerable wagers had been struck in the area at odds of 7–1 that United would win 2–0. Eight players, four from each side, were found guilty of conspiring to fix the match and were suspended from football for life. But, perhaps because there were more important things going on in the world, the result was allowed to stand.

The Liverpool players involved were Tom Fairfoul, Tommy Miller, Bob Purcell and Jackie Sheldon, a former Manchester United player who acted as the go-between. Of the four United players, three — Laurence Cook, Sandy Turnbull and Arthur Whalley — did not play in the match in question. The fourth was Enoch "Knocker" West, who was the only player not to have the ban lifted after the war.

FOOTBALL FOCUS

- Steve Bloomer, England's most prolific pre-war goalscorer, retired in 1914 and took up a job coaching in Germany, where he was interned for the whole of the war. With other British footballers at the Ruhleben camp, he set up an "association" and they played league matches every day on a nearby racecourse for the duration of the war.

- With midweek matches banned, clubs in Scotland were occasionally called upon to play two matches in one day. On 15 April 1915, Celtic beat Raith 6–0 at home in the afternoon, while Motherwell lost 3–0 to Ayr, also at home. Then, in the evening, Celtic went to Motherwell and beat them 3–1.

- In unofficial "Victory" internationals at the end of the 1918–19 season, England and Scotland drew 2–2 at Goodison Park and England won 4–3 at Hampden Park.

Celtic supreme

Glasgow Celtic's remarkable unbeaten run that stretched over 17 months and 62 matches finally came to an end on 21 April 1917 when they lost 2–0 at home to Kilmarnock in the last game of the 1916–17 season. For their last defeat — also 2–0 — you have to go back to 13 November 1915, when they lost at Hearts.

Celtic's almost complete domination of Scottish football during the war led to rumours and suggestions that the club's war effort was not all it should be. But the club and players made their contributions in many and various ways, just like other clubs. Players served in the forces, worked in the factories and shipyards, and down the mines. The club made half-time appeals for more volunteers to the forces, made their ground available for recruiting rallies and fund-raising events, sent footballs to recruits in training and to the soldiers at the front, and did whatever they could to help wounded soldiers back in hospital and prisoners-of-war in Germany.

In the 1917–18 season, Rangers controversially broke Celtic's supremacy, winning the League title by a single point in a struggle that went to the last day

Steve Bloomer was interned in Germany throughout the war.

of the season. But they were heavily criticized for the manner in which they went about doing it. During the war, "temporary transfers" were permitted in which players were allowed to turn out for other clubs at short notice as they found themselves in different locations on account of their war service. Rangers, it seemed, took undue advantage of this to gather in star players stationed in Scotland to replace their own missing men. The *Glasgow Observer* in particular was scathing in its reference to the "conglomeration of Queen's Park, Oldham Athletic, Hearts, Hibernian, Clyde, Dumbarton, Raith Rovers, Dundee, Morton and Sheffield Wednesday" players that masqueraded in Rangers' colours during this title-winning season.

The great rivalry between the two Glasgow clubs was becoming even more intense, and in the 1918–19 season, which began before the end of the war, Celtic sprang back to the top in what was another two-horse race. Five points behind at the turn of the year, they gradually eroded Rangers' lead and finished with a run of 20 matches unbeaten to pip them by a point.

The 'Championship'

In both 1918 and 1919 there were two-legged play-offs between the Lancashire and Midland Regional winners for the "League Championship", with gate receipts going to the National Footballers' War Fund. Leeds City (Midlands winners) won the 1917–18 Championship cup, beating "Lancashire" winners Stoke 2–0 at home and holding them to a single goal in the return.

In the following year's play-offs, Nottingham Forest were held at home by Everton to a goalless draw, but went to Goodison and beat the Lancashire champions 1–0 in the return. In goal for Forest was England and Aston Villa keeper Sam Hardy, who guested for them during the war.

FINAL SCORE

Scottish League Champions

1915–16	Celtic
1916–17	Celtic
1917–18	Rangers
1918–19	Celtic

Wartime League Championship

1917–18	Leeds City
1918–19	Nottingham Forest

Lancashire Regional Tournament

1915–16	Manchester City
1916–17	Liverpool
1917–18	Stoke City
1918–19	Everton

Midland Regional Tournament

1915–16	Nottingham Forest
1916–17	Leeds City
1917–18	Leeds City
1918–19	Nottingham Forest

London Combination

1915–16	Chelsea
1916–17	West Ham United
1917–18	Chelsea
1918–19	Brentford

Aftermaths

Football took a time to find its feet again when hostilities were finally over in November 1918. Many clubs needed reorganization, and grounds needed repair.

There was a move by the clubs of the Football League to renew the FA Challenge Cup for the 1918–19 season on a modified scale. Their suggestion was to dispense with the qualifying competition, in which hundreds of clubs usually took part, and restrict entry to just 64 clubs — the 40 in Divisions One and Two together with 20 members of the Southern League and another four selected clubs. But the FA decided against it, on the grounds that it would be unfair to the vast body of their membership.

"Knocker" West, banned for match-fixing.

'We wuz robbed'

SPURS felt they had cause for grievance when they found themselves in the Second Division at the restart of the Football League after the war. Admittedly, they had finished bottom of the First Division in 1914–15, the last season before hostilities stopped play. But the League has been augmented by two extra teams in each division. The last time that happened, in 1905, no teams were relegated. But this time there was a certain amount of activity behind the scenes.

The result was that Derby and Preston, first and second in Division Two, were promoted as expected, and Chelsea, second from bottom in Division One, were re-elected (the match-fixing scandal in which Manchester United players were involved saw to that). But Spurs were replaced by their new North London neighbours Arsenal, who had finished only fifth in Division Two. Arsenal chairman Sir Henry Norris might have used his influence to ensure an election for the remaining Division One place, for which seven clubs put their names forward, but the voting went Arsenal 18, Spurs eight, with the other five clubs sharing the remaining 15 votes.

England hand it to Wales

ENGLAND came back from 4–2 down at half-time to beat Scotland 5–4 at Hillsborough, but in doing so they handed the International Championship to Wales, who beat them 2–1 at Highbury last month. Nevertheless, this remarkable victory over Scotland was reward in itself, gained as it was in one of the finest and most thrilling matches in this long series of internationals.

The match was played at hectic pace in driving rain. The England heroes were two new caps who scored the second-half goals, Bob Kelly (Burnley) two and Fred Morris (West Brom) one, all in the space of seven minutes midway through the half.

FOOTBALL FOCUS

- With 42 matches instead of 38, it was not surprising that the points records for both divisions were broken this season, West Bromwich winning the League title with 60 and Spurs the Second Division with a massive 70. Both scored over 100 goals, and West Brom's 104 is a record for the top division.
- In the newly expanded Scottish League, Rangers accumulated a record 71 points from their 42 games, and scored 106 goals. Celtic had to take a back seat this time with "only" 68 points. There was no Division Two.
- There was a new name on the Scottish Cup, Kilmarnock. The runners-up were even more surprising — Albion Rovers, who finished bottom of the League but had the audacity to beat Rangers in the semi-finals after two replays.
- Semi-final winners Shelbourne won the Irish Cup by default. In the other semi-final, both teams were disqualified, Belfast Celtic being blamed for the disruption when shots were fired in the crowd, and Glentoran for fielding an ineligible player.

FINAL SCORE

Football League
Division 1: West Bromwich Albion
Top scorer: Fred Morris (WBA) 37
Division 2: Tottenham Hotspur

FA Cup Final
Aston Villa 1 Huddersfield Town 0
(after extra time)

Scottish League
Division 1: Rangers
Top scorer: Hugh Ferguson (Motherwell) 33

Scottish FA Cup Final
Kilmarnock 3 Albion Rovers 2

International Championship
Wales, 4 pts

Bargain buy hits Cup-winner in extra time

THE ROMANCE of the Cup is back with us. At its new venue, Stamford Bridge, the final went to extra time before Aston Villa beat Huddersfield 1–0 with a goal scored by inside-right Bill Kirton, a converted full-back whom Villa had picked up for £250 when the Leeds City players were auctioned earlier in the season.

So Villa win the Cup for a record sixth time. In the final they had much the better of the play. But when the goal came after 10 minutes of the first period of extra time, there was a touch of luck about it. As the heads went up for a corner from outside-left Dorrell, the ball flew into the net. The referee later said it had come off a defender, but the goal has been credited to Kirton, who as Villa's best forward deserves the honour.

Villa captain Andy Ducat clears in the new setting of Stamford Bridge.

Sale of the century

PLAYERS OF DISGRACED Leeds City were auctioned at the Hotel Metropole in a most bizarre sale in October, a week after the club were expelled from the League for irregularities in payments to players during the war. Meanwhile Port Vale have taken over their fixtures in the Second Division, as well as the 10 points already won from the eight games Leeds had played.

After allegations made by a player earlier in the year, the FA and Football League set up a joint commission to investigate Leeds's affairs. During the war years, no fewer than 35 "guest" players had turned out for Leeds, including seven internationals. When the club refused to produce their accounts for the last two seasons, the League had no choice but to expel them.

Although the League regretted the decision, recognizing that Leeds were a new club with bright prospects, they regarded the charges of breaking wartime regulations by paying players more than the permitted rates as extremely serious. So much so that they also banned four Leeds directors and two previous managers, Herbert Chapman and George Cripps, from taking any further part in football management or even attending football matches.

The players fetched a total of little more than £10,000, going at bargain prices, ranging from £250 to £1,250, to managers who flocked to Leeds from clubs in various parts of the country. Some of those managers must have had mixed feelings, for it was no secret that Leeds were not the only club to have stretched the wartime regulations by paying "generous" expenses.

Spurs beat Wolves on quagmire of pitch

NEWLY PROMOTED Tottenham beat Second Division Wolves 1–0 in the FA Cup final at Stamford Bridge in the most terrible conditions. Despite continuous rain and an increase in admission prices to keep the numbers down, a crowd of nearly 73,000 began streaming into the ground over four hours before the kick-off and spilled on to the pitch surrounds.

They paid record gate money of £13,400, but because of the conditions the match turned out to be a poor spectacle.The pitch was a quagmire, enveloping the football skills of the Spurs stars — their captain and left-half Arthur Grimsdell, inside-right Jimmy Seed, and the left-wing pair of Bert Bliss and Jimmy Dimmock. It was the dogged persistence of Dimmock that won them the game eight minutes into the second half, rather than the artistry they have become known for.

Stopped in his tracks by Woodward, the opposing full-back, Dimmock regained the ball, dragged it through the mud into the penalty area, and hit a shot that skidded across the keeper into the far corner. It was not the most elegant of goals, but Spurs were worthy winners and have brought the Cup back south for the first time since they first won it 20 years ago.

Peter McWilliam, their manager, is the first man to play in and then manage a cup-winning team. He was in the Newcastle side in 1910.

Dimmock of Tottenham defies mud and defenders to score the winning goal.

Third division for League

THE NEW LEAGUE season starts with 66 clubs, made up of three divisions of 22. An *en bloc* application from the Southern League's First Division to join the League was accepted, and the new Third Division is composed of those clubs with the exception of Cardiff. The Welsh club go straight into Division Two at the expense of Grimsby Town, who were demoted to the new Third Division. There will be automatic promotion and relegation of one club between Divisions Two and Three.

Lincoln City, who finished second from bottom of Division Two last season, were not reelected. Their place in Division Two has been taken by Leeds United, the club that sprang up like a phoenix from the ashes of the disgraced Leeds City and who will operate from the same Elland Road ground.

FINAL SCORE

Football League
Division 1: Burnley
Top scorer: Joe Smith (Bolton Wanderers) 38
Division 2: Birmingham City
Division 3: Crystal Palace

FA Cup Final
Tottenham Hotspur 1 Wolveerhampton W 0

Scottish League
Division 1: Rangers
Top scorer: Hugh Ferguson (Motherwell) 43

Scottish FA Cup Final
Partick Thistle 1 Rangers 0

International Championship
Scotland, 6 pts

Burnley defeated at last

BURNLEY'S RECORD League run without defeat has finally been broken. Last beaten way back on 4 September, 2–0 by Bradford City, they went 30 matches in the League without losing, 21 wins and nine draws. Now, on 26 March, they have lost 3–0 at Maine Road to their challengers for the Championship, Manchester City.

What an extraordinary season this has been so far for Burnley, who started off with three straight defeats. Then on 6 September they beat Huddersfield 3–0, the start of the run that has given them 51 points and put them in a commanding position at the head of the First Division table. The only blemish in their season so far has been their 3–0 defeat at Second Division Hull in the third round of the Cup, a big shock in view of their 7–3 win at Leicester in the first round.

They have been particularly strong at home, where they have lost only their first match of the season, 4–1 to Bradford City. Their home triumphs have included 7–1 victories over Oldham and Aston Villa and 6–0 over Sheffield United. Centre-forward Joe Anderson and inside-right Bob Kelly have scored most of the goals, while Jerry Dawson has been as safe as always in goal, and centre-half Tom Boyle an inspirational skipper.

FOOTBALL FOCUS

- The Third Division got off to a good start with gates of 25,000 at Millwall and 20,000 at Portsmouth and Queen's Park Rangers on the first Saturday, while Swindon beat Luton 9–1. Crystal Palace, who lost 2–1 at Merthyr Town, eventually finished top.
- After their record run was broken, Burnley won their next two games, including revenge over Manchester City by 2–1, and although they failed to win any of their last six matches, they ran out easy League winners by five points from Manchester City.
- Cardiff, promoted at the first attempt, will play in the First Division next year — the first Welsh club to do so.
- The biggest non-event of the season was Stockport's home game with Leicester on 7 May, the last day. Already relegated, and with their own ground under suspension, they had to play at Old Trafford, where a record low "crowd" of 13 on the vast terraces were entertained to a goalless draw.
- The pendulum continues to swing Rangers' way in Scotland, where they amassed a record 76 points, with only one defeat (at home to Celtic), and won the title by 10 points from Celtic. Their Cup "hoodoo" continues, however. They lost 1–0 to Partick in the final, despite being odds-on favourites.

Liverpool wrap title up at Easter

Keeper Elisha Scott, solid at the back.

LIVERPOOL are the new kings of English football. They beat last year's champions Burnley 2–1 on 17 April to complete their Easter programme. With three games to go, Burnley can no longer catch them, and nor can Spurs, in second place, who lost their last chance when they went down 1–0 at Oldham.

Liverpool's third Championship has not been a spectacular one, but has been earned by good defence — they have kept a clean sheet in 17 of the 39 matches played so far — and a consistency that saw them, after losing their first match, go through 30 more with but one further defeat. Irish international Elisha Scott has established himself in goal in the best tradition of Liverpool keepers, and with four international full-backs to call on, it is not surprising that they have had no problems in defence.

FOOTBALL FOCUS

- Dumbarton goalkeeper James Williamson died after the game with Rangers on 12 November.
- Stockport, relegated from Division Two last season, have gone straight back up again as the first winners of the new Division Three (North).
- The reorganized Scottish League, with a new 20-club Division Two, saw Alloa promoted by right as champions, but three Division One clubs relegated, including Queen's Park for the first time.
- Southend, who finished bottom of the Third Division (S), scored only 34 goals. Their top scorer was a full-back, Jimmy Evans, whose 10 goals were all penalties.
- Celtic are back in business as the "Auld Firm" struggle continues in Scotland, beating Rangers by a point for the title, while Rangers are again beaten in the Cup final.

Preston's Cup of woe

WHILE HUDDERSFIELD were popular winners of the Cup, the final itself was a depressing affair and it is perhaps appropriate that the result should have turned on a disputed penalty. There can be no doubt that a deliberate foul brought England outside-left Billy Smith down. But there can be little doubt either that the offence was committed outside the penalty area. However, the referee saw fit to award the spot-kick, Smith picked himself up to score, and few neutrals at the match felt it was an unjust result.

Preston right-back Hamilton, who fouled Smith from behind when the winger was making for goal, should have been sent off for such a disgraceful offence, and shame on once "Proud" Preston for protesting, even if the referee failed to follow the letter of the law. Perhaps the best entertainment of the match came when their bespectacled amateur keeper J.F.Mitchell tried to put Smith off by dancing around on his line.

Ignoring the match, but looking back on Huddersfield's progress to the final, they are to be congratulated for their spirited play in earlier rounds and overall for their revival since the dark days of their financial crisis just after the war. Then, but for the generosity of their fans, the club would have been transplanted to the ground at Elland Road vacated by the disbanded Leeds City.

Their new manager, Mr Herbert Chapman, is to be congratulated, too. The first thing he did on his appointment last year was to pay Aston Villa £4,000 for the veteran inside-forward Clem Stephenson. And it is Stephenson's leadership on the field that has knitted the young players of Huddersfield into such a formidable side

Clem Stephenson, inspired Chapman buy.

Another Third Division

WITH THE ADVENT of the new Third Division North, the League has virtually doubled in just two years. Clubs from the North were invited to apply for membership, and 20 clubs were accepted into what is now officially called the Northern Section of the Third Division. Last year's Third Division, still 22 clubs, is the Southern Section. The top club from each section will be promoted in place of the bottom two clubs of the Second Division. The last two clubs of each section will have to apply for re-election.

FINAL SCORE

Football League
Division 1: Liverpool
Top scorer: Andy Wilson (Middlesbrough) 31
Division 2: Nottingham Forest
Division 3S: Southampton
Division 3N: Stockport County

FA Cup Final
Huddersfield Town 1 Preston North End 0

Scottish League
Division 1: Celtic
Top scorer: Duncan Walker (St Mirren) 45
Division 2: Alloa

Scottish FA Cup Final
Morton 1 Rangers 0

International Championship
Scotland, 4 pts

Crowd chaos at Cup final: 'mounties to the rescue!'

IT IS A MIRACLE the game was played at all, incredible that no one was killed in the crush. The first Cup final to be staged at Wembley Stadium took place in spite of the greatest crowd chaos ever witnessed. The official attendance has been given as 126,047, but there must have been close to a quarter of a million packed inside the ground, overflowing right up to the boundaries of the pitch itself.

At one stage, before the start, the crowd almost completely covered the pitch, and there seemed little hope that the match could possibly take place. Thousands upon thousands of fans had scaled Wembley's outer walls and broken down the flimsy barriers. A few mounted police on the pitch managed to clear portions of it at a time, one officer in particular, Constable Scorey, on a white horse, earning the cheers of the "gallery" as again and again he resourcefully coaxed the crowd back.

At last the reinforcements arrived, hundreds more police on foot and on horseback, and gradually they herded the crowd back over the lines and behind the goals. The match started 40 minutes late and, within two minutes, Bolton were in front with a goal from David Jack, scored while a West Ham player was still struggling to get back on to the pitch after retrieving the ball for a throw-in. Eight minutes into the second half, Bolton scored a second, a thunderbolt shot from Jack Smith that rebounded from the wall of spectators pressed against the net and almost hit him on the way back. That was the end of the scoring. Bolton deserved their win, although West Ham, a Second Division side pressing for promotion, never showed their true ability.

Immediate reactions to the crowd fiasco have been for an official inquiry to be set up. The size of the crowd was drastically — almost fatally — underestimated by the British Empire Exhibition authorities, who handled the match arrangements, and by the police.

The great stadium, completed only four days earlier, will have its barriers strengthened, and there have been calls for future Cup finals to have ticket-only admission.

The crowd overflows on to Wembley's pitch. PC Scorey is circled.

David Jack (white shirt) scores the first goal.

FOOTBALL FOCUS

- During the 1922 close season, the players' maximum wage was cut from £9 to £8 a week. A strike was threatened, but, as usual, nothing came of it.
- A player in a preliminary round FA Cup tie scored seven goals and finished up on the losing side! He was Billy Minter, whose team, St Alban's City, lost 8–7 to Dulwich Hamlet on 22 November.
- Liverpool smoothed their way to a second consecutive League title, leading virtually from start to finish. Again, though, they scored only 20 goals away from home.

FINAL SCORE

Football League
Division 1: Liverpool
Top scorer: Charlie Buchan (Sunderland) 30
Division 2: Notts County
Division 3S: Bristol City
Division 3N: Nelson

FA Cup Final

Bolton Wanderers	2	West Ham United	0

Scottish League
Division 1: Rangers
Top scorer: John White (Hearts) 30
Division 2: Queen's Park

Scottish FA Cup Final

Celtic	1	Hibernian	0

International Championship
Scotland, 5 pts

West Ham go up

WEST HAM, beaten at home by Notts County, still win promotion on what has been the most dramatic last day of the season in Division Two. And what a week it's been for the East London club, striving to get into the top division for the first time. After their depressing, and exhausting, experience at Wembley last Saturday, they had to pick themselves up for an away game at Sheffield Wednesday on Monday. They did, and won 2–0, to go back on top of the table on goal average from both Leicester and Notts County.

The scene was set for a last day of many possibilities, with West Ham entertaining Notts County and Leicester away to disinterested Bury. A shock for West Ham — County beat them 1–0. But all was not lost, because Bury beat Leicester, and West Ham are promoted in second place on goal average behind Notts County.

West Ham earned their success by dint of their excellent away record — 42 goals scored (twice as many as at home!) and 11 games won, including, in hindsight, the crucial 6–0 victory at Leicester back in February. Their promotion gives London four teams in Division One for the first time.

West Ham's Vic Watson was a fine centre-forward, well worth his first England cap, which he celebrated with a goal against Wales. Ted Hufton (goal) and winger Jimmy Ruffell also shone.

Long division settles First Division

AFTER THE CLOSEST battle for the League title yet, Huddersfield have beaten Cardiff on goal average by 0.024. It does not seem much after a long, hard season, but the mathematicians had their slide-rules out on the last day, working out the possibilities. Basically, all Cardiff had to do was win. Huddersfield, who seemed to have it all sewn up, dropped some vital points in the later stages, leaving themselves a point behind Cardiff with one match to play.

Huddersfield were playing at home to Nottingham Forest, but the drama was all at Birmingham for Cardiff's last game. Cardiff were awarded a penalty when an opponent handled the ball on the goal-line. None of the senior players would accept the responsibility of taking it, so Len Davies stepped up for his first ever spot-kick. The keeper saved it, and the match finished 0–0. Meanwhile, Huddersfield won 3–0. It was just enough. Huddersfield's 60–33 beats Cardiff's 61–34. Those are the rules.

The Championship is another triumph for manager Herbert Chapman, who not only transformed the side by signing the inside-forward Clem Stephenson, but has made further inspired signings and initiated improvements at the club for the benefit of both the playing staff and the fans.

Huddersfield: Football League champions — just.

FINAL SCORE

Football League
Division 1: Huddersfield Town
Top scorer: Bill Chadwick (Everton) 28
Division 2: Leeds United
Division 3S: Portsmouth
Division 3N: Wolverhampton Wanderers

FA Cup Final

Newcastle United	2	Aston Villa	0

Scottish League
Division 1: Rangers
Top scorer: Dave Halliday (Dundee) 38
Division 2: St Johnstone
Division 3: Arthurlie

Scottish FA Cup Final

Airdrieonians	2	Hibernian	0

International Championship
Wales, 6 pts

Wales win Triple Crown

THE "TRIPLE CROWN", victory over each of the other nations in the International Championship, has gone to Wales for the first time. England have accomplished the feat seven times and Scotland four.

Wales clinched it in Belfast, the first time they have won there since 1913. All they needed was a draw to make sure of the Championship, but they won 1–0 thanks to a penalty goal scored by veteran Plymouth right-back Moses Russell.

Wales started the season with a 2–0 victory over Scotland at Cardiff on 16 February. This was a particularly proud day for Cardiff, as their club provided both captains — centre-half Fred Keenor of Wales and left-back Jimmy Blair of Scotland. This left the Championship table in a decidedly unusual state — Wales and Ireland top with two points, Scotland and England bottom without a point, as Ireland had beaten England 2–1 at Everton in October. Then came the Welsh victory over England, 2–1 at Blackburn earlier this month.

The only other time Wales have won the Championship, 13 years ago, they needed England to draw with Scotland. They won't need any help this time when the two clash at Wembley in April.

FOOTBALL FOCUS

- The Scottish League increased its membership again by the introduction of a 16-club Third Division with promotion for two clubs.
- England played their first match at Wembley, drawing 1–1 with Scotland for their only point in the Championship.
- In a Division Two match against Manchester United on 6 October, Oldham full-back Sam Wynne scored twice for each side, a free-kick and a penalty for his own team and two own goals for the visitors. Oldham won 3–2.
- Newcastle right-back Walter Hampson was 41 years 8 months when he played in the Cup final, and is believed to be the oldest player to do so, at least since the 1870s.

The Welsh team, Triple Crown winners for the first time.

Airdrie a third force in Scotland

AIRDRIEONIANS have established themselves in just two seasons as real rivals to Rangers and Celtic in Scotland. Not only have they now won the Cup, beating Hibernian 2–0 in the final, but they have again finished second in the League to Rangers, relegating Celtic to third place.

A young team with tremendous forward power, they have matched Rangers goal for goal this season, with their small but highly effective centre-forward Hughie Gallacher to the fore.

Drastic change in offside law

ONE WORD has been changed in football's offside law — one word that could have untold effects on how the game is played. Football, since it restarted after the Great War, has lost much of its entertainment value, bogged down as it is in defensive tactics, particularly the "offside-trap" as perpetrated so successfully by Newcastle United.

After 15 years of argument, the FA arranged a trial at Highbury between sides of Amateurs and Professionals. One 45-minute period was played under an offside law that stipulated a player needed only two rather than three (the one-word change) opponents behind him to remain onside. The other period was played under the present offside law but with the onside area extended. On the flimsy evidence of this highly inadequate experiment, the FA decided on the former solution at their meeting in London on 15 June. It was the Scottish FA who put the proposal to the International Football Association Board, by whom it has now been ratified. The change becomes effective next season.

The following Proposals by the Scottish Football Association were adopted :—

PRESENT LAW.	PROPOSED ALTERATION.
6.—When a player plays the ball, any player of the same side who at such moment of playing is nearer to his opponents' goal-line is out of play and may not touch the ball himself nor in any way whatever interfere with an opponent, or with the play, until the ball has been again played, unless there are at such moment of playing at least three of his opponents nearer their own goal-line. A player is not out of play when the ball is kicked off from goal, when a corner-kick or a throw in is taken, when the ball has been last played by an opponent, or when he himself is within his own half of the field of play at the moment the ball is played by any player of the same side.	From the first sentence of Law 6 delete the word "three" and substitute the word "two."
7.—When the ball is played behind the goal-line by a player of the opposite side, it shall be kicked off by any one of the players behind whose goal-line it went, within that half of the goal area nearest the point where the ball left the field of play; but, if played behind by any one of the side whose goal-line it is, a player of the opposite side shall kick it from within 1 yard of the nearest corner flagstaff (*a*). In either case an opponent shall not be allowed within 10 yards of the ball until it is kicked off.	Add— "and the kicker shall not again play the ball until it has been played by another player."

Changes in the offside and corner-kick laws.

The 'mighty atom' strikes

LITTLE Patsy Gallagher scored a goal of extraordinary audacity in the Scottish Cup final, never to be forgotten by the fans who saw it, because they are not likely to see its equal again. And what a time to score it, with Dundee leading 1–0 and holding everything that Celtic could throw at them in the closing stages.

With 15 minutes remaining, Gallagher, the "mighty atom", picked up a flighted free-kick from Paddy Connolly and, surrounded by blue shirts, began to wriggle his way towards goal, squeezing past and through defenders until he was held up a few feet short of the posts. Tackled heavily, he stumbled to the ground, but, with amazing presence of mind, kept the ball lodged between his feet and somersaulted into the net with it.

Hampden Park, chock-full of Celtic fans, went wild, and Dundee wilted visibly. Minutes from the end, Jimmy McGrory, Celtic's leading scorer, snatched the winner with a diving header. So Celtic chalk up their 11th Scottish Cup win to overtake Queen's Park's record. It is consolation for another season's trailing in the wake of Rangers and Airdrieonians in the League.

Patsy Gallagher, acrobatic scorer for Celtic.

FOOTBALL FOCUS

- The law allowing players to score directly from corner-kicks came into operation this season, and Huddersfield's Billy Smith scored the first such goal in the League, against Arsenal on 11 October. The law was so vaguely worded, however, that many people in the footballing community were under the impression that players could dribble the ball from the flag. The law has now been clarified, and a player may not touch the ball more than once when taking a corner.

- Huddersfield, winning their second successive League title, were undefeated in their first 10 and last 17 matches, and collected more points away than at home. The club's reserves won the Central Lague, too.

- After Cardiff's near misses, Welsh success came in the Third Division (S), when Swansea, unbeaten at home, won promotion this season.

Wake goes to sleep

After last season's heart-stopping anti-climax to the League season, Cardiff fans were put through the mangle again, this time in the Cup. In the first round, they were twice held to goalless draws by Third Division Darlington before beating them 2–0 at Anfield. In the fourth round they needed a history-making goal from Willie Davies, who scored with the last kick of the game against Leicester direct from a corner, the first Cup goal under the new law.

But now, at Wembley, after a good 3–1 semi-final win over Blackburn, their luck ran out. In front of hordes of Welshmen who flooded into London for what was an "international" Cup final, Cardiff right-half Harry Wake belied his name and went to sleep, allowing Sheffield United's Fred Tunstall to rob him of the ball and run in to score the only goal of the game after half an hour. It was one of the few scoring chances allowed to either side's attack by two strong defences.

FINAL SCORE

Football League
Division 1: Huddersfield Town
Top scorer: Fred Roberts (Manchester City) 31
Division 2: Leicester City
Division 3S: Swansea Town
Division 3N: Darlington

FA Cup Final
Sheffield United 1 Cardiff City 0

Scottish League
Division 1: Rangers
Top scorer: Willie Devlin (Cowdenbeath) 33
Division 2: Dundee United
Division 3: Nithsdale Wanderers

Scottish FA Cup Final
Celtic 2 Dundee 1

International Championship
Scotland, 6 pts

£100-a-goal Buchan fails to score

Buchan gets in a header against Spurs on his debut for his new club.

ARSENAL CHAIRMAN Sir Henry Norris watched with mixed feelings as controversial new signing Charlie Buchan made his debut in the opening match at Highbury on Saturday. Under the terms of his transfer, Arsenal will pay Sunderland an extra £100 this season for every goal the veteran inside-forward scores. He didn't add to his price against Spurs, but none of his colleagues could find the net either, and Arsenal lost 1–0.

When new manager Herbert Chapman said he wanted the 34-year-old former England star to bolster his flagging forward line, Sir Henry had to swallow his aversion to high transfer fees and make the money available. He was certainly taken aback by Sunderland's asking price, £4,000, but when their manager Bob Kyle justified it for the 20 goals Buchan was "bound to score" in his first season with the Gunners, Sir Henry turned this to his own advantage by offering £2,000 plus £100 a goal.

The flood-gates opened

WITH THE CHANGE in the off-side law, the expected goal glut arrived. The total number of goals scored in the Football League rose from last season's 4,700 to 6,373 this season. The rise was most spectacular in the First Division, where Manchester City conceded 100 goals and were relegated, and Burnley conceded 108 and stayed up. Four Third Division clubs scored 100 goals or more, and none of them was promoted.

The initial reaction of the clubs had been to play full-backs squarer and closer to their goal. But this enabled forwards to move unchallenged into shooting range. The free-scoring abated noticeably in the second half of the season, as defences realized they were allowing attackers too much space and tightened up.

Hat-trick for Huddersfield

LEAGUE CHAMPIONS again, Huddersfield have become the first club to win the title three seasons running. Their achievement is a monument to Herbert Chapman, who left them to manage Arsenal before the start of the season. He built up the side and he made the club famous. And before he left he made one of his typical swoops in the transfer market, snatching Alex Jackson from under the noses of Liverpool.

The 19-year-old Scottish international Jackson proved a valuable buy, at £2,500, from Aberdeen. A roaming, goalscoring outside-right, he contributed 16 goals to Huddersfield's 92 in his first season with them, and made many more for others, particularly centre-forward George Brown, who set a club goalscoring record in the First Division with 35.

Alex Jackson, a coup for Chapman.

FOOTBALL FOCUS

- With a number of clubs in the Scottish Division Three getting into financial difficulties, the whole League was suspended before the programme was completed.
- Charlie Buchan cost Arsenal an extra £2,000, with 19 League goals and one in the Cup, so Sunderland's manager was spot-on with his forecast.
- Bobby Skinner of Dunfermline set a British record with 53 goals in the Scottish Division Two.

Goals but no glory

MANCHESTER CITY have become the first Football League club to reach the Cup final and be relegated in the same season. They went down in most unfortunate circumstances only eight days after losing 1–0 to Bolton at Wembley.

What an extraordinary season it has been for City. They scored 89 goals, more than any relegated club in the history of the League. And they stormed into the Cup final after an orgy of goalscoring in earlier rounds. Then they couldn't score a single goal at Wembley. But it was a thrilling final.

On the last day of the season, with Notts County already condemned to the drop, Leeds United and Burnley were a point behind Manchester. So City, with a superior goal average, needed only to draw their game at Newcastle even if the other two won. City lost 3–2 after missing a penalty, the other two both won 4–1... and City were down.

FINAL SCORE

Football League
Division 1: Huddersfield Town
Top scorer: Ted Harper (Blackburn Rovers) 43
Division 2: Sheffield Wednesday
Division 3S: Reading
Division 3N: Grimsby Town

FA Cup Final

Bolton Wanderers	1	Manchester City	0

Scottish League
Division 1: Celtic
Top scorer: Willie Devlin (Cowdenbeath) 40
Division 2: Dunfermline Athletic

Scottish FA Cup Final

St Mirren	2	Celtic	0

International Championship
Scotland, 6 pts

English Cup goes to Wales

CARDIFF CITY beat Arsenal 1–0 at Wembley to take the FA Cup out of England for the first time, with a remarkable goal scored by centre-forward Hughie Ferguson in the 75th minute. It was a personal tragedy for Arsenal's Welsh international keeper Dan Lewis, who seemed to have the shot under control, but allowed the ball to squirt out of his hands and over the line.

The key to Cardiff's victory was the play of veteran left-half Billy Hardy, the only Englishman in the side, who managed to keep Charlie Buchan quiet for most of the time. When Buchan did manage to break free, the chances he laid on for his colleagues were not taken. The powerful tackling of Cardiff captain Fred Keenor was another major factor. But Arsenal's half-back line of Baker, Butler and John were also splendid, and the two sides were restricted to a handful of shots on target over the 90 minutes.

When the goal did come, it was totally unexpected. Ferguson shot hard, and Lewis caught and held the ball while on one knee. But in turning to avoid a challenge from Len Davies, he swung round and spilled the ball, which spun away from him and over the line. It was the difference between winning and losing.

The ball slips away from the unfortunate Lewis.

Scot is new Tyneside idol

HUGHIE GALLACHER has sparked a revival on Tyneside in his first full season with Newcastle, leading them to the League Championship for the first time since 1909. The little Scottish international centre-forward, bought from Airdrie last season for £5,500, has set a club record with 36 League goals in his 38 games.

Newcastle virtually acquired the title in front of their own fans, winning a record 19 home matches and dropping only three points at St James's Park. Their derby with Sunderland in March drew a record 67,211 attendance, and they have rewarded their supporters with goals galore, averaging over three per home game. It did not matter that they lost 10 away matches. They still won the title with ease, five points ahead of Huddersfield.

Hughie Gallacher, Tyneside hero in his first season.

FOOTBALL FOCUS

- The first football match broadcast on radio was the Arsenal-Sheffield United League game on 22 January. An "announcer" gave a running commentary while a colleague called out numbers referring to sections of the pitch, to help listeners follow the play on a simple chart.
- Jimmy McGrory set a Scottish First Division record with 49 goals for Celtic despite missing the last five matches through injury. Celtic scored 101 goals but could still finish only third to Rangers. They won the Cup, but McGrory missed the final.
- England beat Scotland 2–1 at Hampden Park for the first time since 1904, thanks to two goals from Everton's Bill Dean, their new centre-forward, who has scored 12 goals in five games for his country, including hat-tricks against Belgium and Luxembourg.

More goal records tumble

MIDDLESBROUGH have won promotion to Division One largely through centre-forward George Camsell. His League record of 59 goals makes up nearly half their total, 122, also a League record. Camsell hit nine hat-tricks, and that's never been done before either. Middlesbrough's first four games produced only one goal and one point.

While Middlesbrough were coasting into the First Division, there was an almighty struggle going on behind them for the other promotion place. Portsmouth and Manchester City were level on points on the last day, but Portsmouth had the better goal average. Manchester had already scored 92 goals, and proceeded to thrash bottom club Bradford City 8–0. Portsmouth, whose match against Preston had kicked off 15 minutes later, were 4–1 up when the news filtered through that, unless they scored another, City would beat them. They did, in the last few minutes, and were promoted with a goal average of 1.77551 to City's 1.77049.

George Camsell — 59 goals in Division Two.

FINAL SCORE

Football League
Division 1: Newcastle United
Top scorer: Jimmy Trotter (Sheffield Wednesday) 37
Division 2: Middlesbrough
Division 3S: Bristol City
Division 3N: Stoke City

FA Cup Final

Cardiff City	1	Arsenal	0

Scottish League
Division 1: Rangers
Top scorer: Jimmy McGrory (Celtic) 49
Division 2: Bo'ness

Scottish FA Cup Final

Celtic	3	East Fife	1

International Championship
England, Scotland, 4 pts

Scottish masters give England a lesson: wizard show at Wembley

SCOTLAND came to Wembley at the end of March and, in the pouring rain and in front of 80,000 people, proceeded to give England a lesson in how football should be played. The "Wee Blue Devils" — hat-trick hero Alex Jackson was the tallest of the forwards at 5ft 7in — turned on an exhibition of ball skill and artistry that left their opponents breathless, bewildered and thoroughly beaten.

Scotland took the lead in three minutes. Left-half Jimmy McMullan set up a string of passes with Jimmy Gibson and the mercurial Alex James, who put Alan Morton away on the left. Over came the cross, and there was Alex Jackson on the other wing steaming in to head the ball home. James put them two up, shrugging off a challenge as only he can do and volleying the ball past the hapless Hufton from 25 yards.

In the second half the Scots really turned it on. Morton came into his own on the left and made two more for Jackson. In between, James scored the fourth, smashing in a loose ball after Gallacher had been tackled. The rout was complete. A late goal by Kelly made it 5–1, but the skill and science of the Scots had triumphed over the more direct English style.

McMullan leads the Scots out at Wembley, followed by Jackson and Gallacher.

FINAL SCORE

Football League
Division 1: Everton
Top scorer: Billy Dean (Everton) 60
Division 2: Manchester City
Division 3S: Millwall
Division 3N: Bradford Park Avenue

FA Cup Final

Blackburn Rovers	3	Huddersfield Town	1

Scottish League
Division 1: Rangers
Top scorer: Jimmy McGrory (Celtic) 47
Division 2: Ayr United

Scottish FA Cup Final

Rangers	4	Celtic	0

International Championship
Wales, 5 pts

Dixie Dean does it! Hat-trick to reach 60

THE SCENE is Goodison Park, the date 5 May 1928. Everton already have the League title sewn up, but a crowd of over 48,000 turn up for the last game of the season, against Arsenal, to see what they hope will be the climax of the greatest feat of individual goalscoring in the history of the League. Billy "Dixie" Dean has 57 League goals to his credit and needs another three to beat the record set last season by Middlesbrough's George Camsell in the Second Division.

Arsenal scored within two minutes of the kick-off. But less than a minute later Dean converted a Critchley corner, and when, after only a few more minutes, Dean was brought down in the box and netted the resultant penalty, the crowd went wild. They had to wait with bated breath, however, until the 82nd minute before Alec Troup, provider of so many of Dean's goals, placed a perfect corner for Dean to rise above the Arsenal defence at the far post and power a typical header into the net. The resulting roar from the crowd could be heard all over Merseyside.

FOOTBALL FOCUS

- Jimmy McGrory scored eight goals, a Scottish Division One record, when Celtic beat Dunfermline 9–0 on 14 January.
- A week after their Cup triumph, Rangers made sure of the League, too, for their first ever "double".
- Jim Smith of Ayr United scored a British record 66 goals in the Scottish Division Two.
- Millwall scored a League record 127 goals in Division Three (S) and were promoted.

Dean (left) heads his 60th goal of the season.

Rangers beat Cup hoodoo

THE HOODOO — a very real hoodoo to their fans — was finally laid to rest at Hampden Park when Rangers beat Celtic 4–0 to win the Scottish Cup for the first time since 1903. A crowd of 118,000, divided into blue and green, turned out to see this fifth "Old Firm" final.

It was mostly Celtic in the first half, when only the brilliance of Tom Hamilton in the Rangers goal kept them from taking advantage of a strong wind. The match turned on a penalty in the second half, given away when Celtic captain Willie McStay handled the ball on the goal-line with his keeper beaten. Rangers captain David Meiklejohn courageously took the responsibility for the kick himself, and converted it to an explosion of relief and joy among the fans in blue. Bob McPhail then scored a second and right-winger Sandy Archibald made certain with two spectacular goals hit from near the touchline.

Jack's the lad for £10,000

LIKE THE Canadian Mounties, Arsenal manager Herbert Chapman always gets his man – even if the asking price is twice the transfer record. When Charlie Buchan decided to retire last season, Mr Chapman knew he had to find a replacement quickly. As always he set his sights on the best, and there is none better than David Jack of the celebrated body-swerve, whose goals have helped Bolton to two Cup triumphs at Wembley,

The first problem was getting Bolton to agree to sell. Whatever Mr Chapman did to persuade the Bolton board, they finally gave him a price — £13,000. It took another week and two more meetings between the clubs before the final figure was agreed — £10,890, which knocks the previous record out of sight.

The FA president, Sir Charles Clegg, has stated that no player in the world is worth £10,000. Arsenal feel they have got themselves a bargain in the England inside-right, at 29 one of the most cultured footballers in the country. And Mr Chapman's record in getting his money's worth from players speaks for itself.

David Jack, subject of a transfer record.

First defeat — England slip in Spain

ENGLAND LOST for the first time to a foreign side when they went down 4–3 to Spain in Madrid on 15 May. Coming as it did at the end of an arduous tour in which this was their third match in a week, it is perhaps not so surprising that they were found wanting. But it is still a shock to discover that the Continentals are catching up.

Even without Dean, England won easily in France (4–1) and Belgium (5–1), with Camsell scoring two and four goals respectively. They should have been warned, however, that Spain had just accounted for Portugal 5–0 and France 8–1, and were not the Continental pushovers England were accustomed to facing. And Spain's crafty coach Fred Pentland, the 46-year-old former Middlesbrough and England winger, had made sure that the match would be played when the sun was at its height.

Unfortunately Camsell had to miss the game through injury, but without him England still gained a half-time lead. The torrid heat, however, was beginning to take its toll. After the interval, with 30,000 excited fans urging them on and the ball bouncing shoulder-high on the bone-hard pitch, the Spaniards' fine dribbling and passing skills began to bear fruit. England led 2–0 and 3–2, but finally wilted and Spain gained a famous 4–3 victory, truly a milestone in the history of the game.

The combination of the conditions, the strange atmosphere and skilful opponents had proved too much for an inexperienced England side who relied too much on full-backs Cooper and Blenkinsop.

FOOTBALL FOCUS

- Numbered shirts were worn in the League for the first time on 25 August, by Arsenal at Hillsborough and Chelsea against Swansea at Stamford Bridge.
- Hughie Gallacher scored a record five goals for Scotland in their 7-3 win over Ireland in Belfast on 23 February.
- Scotland beat England 1–0 at Hampden Park when Alex Cheyne scored in the dying minutes direct from a corner, the first such goal in an international.
- Bradford City won Division 3N with a League record 128 goals, 82 of them at home. They opened the season with an 11–1 win over Rotherham and hit eight goals three times, including once away.
- Bolton won their third Wembley final, and keeper Dick Pym kept his third clean sheet.
- After last year's triumphant "double", Rangers' Cup hoodoo paid them a return visit, when Jock Buchanan became the first player to be sent off in a final. Rangers, who lost only once in the League and won the title by a record 16 points from Celtic, lost 2–0 at Hampden to unfancied Kilmarnock.
- Despite Sheffield Wednesday's fine home record, they were outscored at home by six other clubs, including Leicester and Sheffield United, who both enjoyed 10–0 victories, over Portsmouth and Burnley respectively, neither of whom were relegated. Cardiff, the only side in Division One to concede fewer than 60 goals and who conceded fewest goals away, were relegated.

Seed sprouts League title

WHEN WEDNESDAY manager Bob Brown made veteran Jimmy Seed captain last season, he inspired the Sheffield club to rise from the bottom of the table to 14th, with 17 points in their last 10 games. The transformation has continued this season, and although the 33-year-old former Spurs inside-right is not as sprightly as he was, his influence on the team has been paramount in their annexation of the League Championship. Wednesday's success has been achieved despite an away record that would not look out of place at the bottom of the table. They were, however, unbeaten at Hillsborough. In early October they started a run of 16 matches with only one defeat that took them into the lead at the start of December, and they remained there until the finish, to claim their third League title.

Jimmy Seed, influence behind Wednesday's success.

FINAL SCORE

Football League
Division 1: Sheffield Wednesday
Top scorer: Dave Halliday (Sunderland) 43
Division 2: Middlesbrough
Division 3S: Charlton Athletic
Division 3N: Bradford City

FA Cup Final
Bolton Wanderers 2 Portsmouth 0

Scottish League
Division 1: Rangers
Top scorer: Evelyn Morrison (Falkirk) 43
Division 2: Dundee United

Scottish FA Cup Final
Kilmarnock 2 Rangers 0

International Championship
Scotland, 6 pts

Heroes of the Twenties

THE GAME in the 1920s was blessed with two of the most prolific goalscorers in the history of British football, Dixie Dean and Jimmy McGrory. Admittedly, with the change of the offside law in the mid-twenties, there was a sudden explosion of goals. But these two stars, Dean of Everton and McGrory of Celtic, continued to find the net regularly long after defences had got to grips with the new law.

Heading for success

Dean began to hit the headlines in the first season after the change, 1925–26, when as an 18-year-old he scored 32 goals in 38 matches. Two seasons later, he was never out of the headlines, as the whole country followed his successful pursuit of the League record. Tremendously strong and with two good feet, he was famed for his heading ability, and he scored 17 goals in 13 games for England in the twenties.

At Celtic, McGrory had a hard act to follow — Jimmy Quinn. But he became the greatest goalscorer in British football, and was perhaps Celtic's best-loved player. He was not particularly tall, but he was fast and powerful, with a deadly knack for converting the half-chance. He scored perhaps a third of his goals with his head, many by diving full length to meet low crosses.

Scottish masters

McGrory's international career was limited because he happened to be the contemporary of Hughie Gallacher, rated by many as the best centre-forward of them all. The little Scot stood barely 5ft 6in, but he was a giant among footballers, and idolized in Scotland, where he played for Airdrie, and on Tyneside, where he starred for Newcastle. He had all the gifts — powerful shooting, the ability to poke the ball in with little backlift, a flair for the unexpected, speed off the mark, a deceptive body-swerve, ball control and, despite his lack of inches, remarkable heading ability. He scored 22 goals in 17 internationals before he went to Chelsea in 1930.

Alan Morton, the "Wee Blue Devil".

For Scotland, Gallacher played between two of the finest wingers they have ever had, Alan Morton and Alex Jackson. Left-winger Morton helped Rangers to seven League titles in the twenties (and two more afterwards), and won 31 Scottish caps, tormenting every right-back England tried. Only 5ft 4in, he possessed fabulous dribbling skills, speed and close control. The goalscoring Jackson, on the right, had gazelle-like speed and style, and for Scotland was adept at getting on the end of Morton's floated crosses. He played for Scotland in his first League season, with Aberdeen, and became the idol of the fans at Huddersfield and known as the "Laughing Cavalier" to crowds everywhere, but retired surprisingly early.

Forward for England

In addition to Dean, the English stars who were playing up front in this period included Middlesbrough's equally prolific George Camsell, a man who never let England down, and a quartet of inside-forwards — Charlie Buchan, Joe Smith, Billy Walker and David Jack. Smith and Buchan, who both came to prominence before the Great War, were inspiring captains, Smith leading Bolton to two Cup wins, while Buchan became the brains of Arsenal after an outstanding career with Sunderland. The elegant, thoughtful Jack also starred for Bolton before, like Buchan, signing for Arsenal in a record transfer. Billy Walker was a long-time inspiration for Aston Villa and scored nine goals in 17 games for England during the twenties.

Dean climbs above the Arsenal defence at Highbury.

Hughie Gallacher (left) and Alex Jackson.

The 'Old Firm'

Even in their lean years, when Rangers reigned supreme, Celtic had their heroes. Patsy Gallagher was still with them till the mid-twenties, rivalling McGrory in their affections before joining Falkirk. Rangers' stronger all-round squad of players, apart from Morton, included their impressive and authoritative skipper David Meiklejohn at centre-half, forceful winger Sandy Archibald, and Andy Cunningham, a powerhouse of an inside-forward with an explosive shot.

Wales and Ireland

Wales won three International Championships in the twenties, and both their success and Cardiff's rise to fame was in no small measure due to Fred Keenor, an outstanding captain and centre-half. Ireland, for their part, were unable to repeat their triumph of 1914. But Sheffield United captain Billy Gillespie, a star of that era, guided them throughout the twenties, and with Celtic's Patsy Gallagher often in the other inside-forward berth Ireland managed to achieve a degree of respectability in the international arena.

Charlie Buchan leads Arsenal out.

Quick-thinking James schemes Arsenal victory

A SLICK PIECE of thinking by Alex James from a free-kick after 16 minutes set Arsenal on their way to victory over Huddersfield in the Cup final at Wembley. James, fouled by Goodall, placed the ball on the ground and knocked it out to Cliff Bastin without even straightening up, having paused just long enough to get the nod from the referee. The young winger beat his man on the left before slipping the ball inside again to James, who took it in his stride and slammed it past Turner. And it was from James's pass out of defence that Lambert scored late on to clinch the game 2–0 for Arsenal.

When the two teams came out in pairs — a new idea — it must have been a very proud moment for Arsenal manager Herbert Chapman, who built the Huddersfield club into such a footballing force in the 1920s. James and Bastin, both signed by Mr Chapman last summer, were the Arsenal stars. But the scoreline does not do justice to Huddersfield's second-half rally. Preedy in Arsenal's goal brought off some fine saves, but he also made some appalling blunders which remarkably went unpunished. For Huddersfield, left-winger Billy Smith was most dangerous, but the chances he made went begging.

This is Arsenal's first major honour. Mr Chapman has tried various forward permutations, but finally seems to have got it right at the expense of his old club. Huddersfield's half-back line were outstanding, and they contributed to one of the best finals seen for some years.

An uninvited visitor to the Cup final, the German airship Graf Zeppelin over Wembley.

FOOTBALL FOCUS

- Jim Dyet scored eight goals on his first-class debut, in King's Park's 12–2 win over Forfar in the Scottish Division Two on 2 January.
- Five days before the Cup final, Arsenal drew 6–6at Leicester, the highest-scoring draw in British first-class football.
- Plymouth finally made it into the Second Division, winning Division Three (S) by seven points, after finishing second for six of the last eight years. They were unbeaten at home again, and in the last nine years have lost only nine League games at the well-named Home Park.
- The first World Cup took place in Uruguay in July, and the hosts beat deadly rivals Argentina 4–2 in the final. Thirteen countries took part. There were no British entries, the home countries having left FIFA.

Tactical talk key to England success

FOR THE first time, the England players met on Friday evening to discuss their match the next day against Scotland at Wembley. If the result is anything to go by, the tactical talk worked wonders, as England won 5–2. It won them the International Championship outright for the first time since before the war, and it was their best victory over Scotland since the 1890s, going some way towards wiping out memories of the 5–1 defeat by the "Wembley Wizards" two years ago.

England were one up in 11 minutes, and scored another three in a five-minute spell midway through the first half. All four goals were made by Derby outside-right Sammy Crooks, who had a brilliant match on his international debut. The other winger, Ellis Rimmer of Sheffield Wednesday, also playing his first game for his country, scored twice.

Skipper David Jack, doubtful up to the day of the match, limped through most of the last hour, otherwise the score might have been greater.

Scotland never stopped trying, however, and made a fine match of it in the second half.

Slip it to Joe

"SLIP IT TO JOE" was the cry at Celtic Park, as Northern Ireland ran up their biggest ever win, 7–0 over Wales in the International Championship. And nearly every time the big centre-forward Joe Bambrick got the ball, he seemed to put it in the net — six goals, the highest individual tally for any British player in an international. The last time the lads in green scored seven — the only time — was back in February 1891, when Ireland beat Wales 7–2, also at Belfast.

Bambrick, from Linfield, was up against doughty centre-half Fred Keenor, the Welsh captain, who could not have had a more embarrassing match. In the Welsh defence, however, apart from Keenor, only left-back T. Jones, with three caps, had experienced international football before.

Joe Bambrick, six goals for Northern Ireland.

FINAL SCORE

Football League
Division 1: Sheffield Wednesday
Top scorer: Vic Watson (West Ham United) 41
Division 2: Blackpool
Division 3S: Plymouth Argyle
Division 3N: Port Vale

FA Cup Final

Arsenal	2	Huddersfield Town	0

Scottish League
Division 1: Rangers
Top scorer: Benny Yorston (Aberdeen) 38
Division 2: Leith Athletic

Scottish FA Cup Final

Rangers	0	Partick Thistle	0
Replay: Rangers	2	Partick Thistle	1

International Championship
England, 6 pts

The World Cup kicks off

When FIFA were founded in 1904, they included in their statutes a clause giving them the sole right to organize a World Championship. It was another 26 years before such a competition came about, and by that time the four British associations, who had been in and out of FIFA twice, were no longer members.

THE MAN who pioneered the World Cup was Jules Rimet, a French lawyer who became president of FIFA in 1921. Uruguay won the Olympic football competition in 1924, but in 1926 FIFA decided that, because of the difference in standards between amateur and professional football, the Olympics were no longer representative of the top level of the game. At the FIFA meeting during the 1928 Olympics at Amsterdam, it was decided to stage a World Championship every four years from 1930.

There were six contenders to stage the first World Cup — Holland, Hungary, Italy, Spain, Sweden, who had originally opposed the idea, and Uruguay. The South Americans were the obvious choice. Not only had they won the last two Olympic football tournaments, but they were due to celebrate their independence centenary in 1930, they undertook to build a special 100,000-capacity stadium for the World Cup and, an important consideration, they promised to pay the full expenses of every participating country.

Even so, the response from Europe was disappointing. The problem was the time that players would have to be away — with travel to and from Uruguay by boat, at least two months. The major Continental soccer powers, including Germany, Italy and Spain, all declined. With eight weeks to go, there was not a single entry from Europe. It required the intervention of M.Rimet to persuade France to go, and likewise the Belgian FIFA representative Rudolphe Seeldrayers secured his country's entry. King Carol of Romania selected a side himself and arranged their release from work. Yugoslavia were a late entry, making Europe's contingent up to four. They joined seven South American countries, Mexico and the United States.

WORLD CUP FOCUS

● Hector Castro, the centre-forward who played in one group match and the final for Uruguay and scored in both, had the lower part of one arm missing.

● Argentina's captain and centre-forward Manuel Ferreyra missed the game against Mexico to take his university exams. His replacement Guillermo Stabile scored a hat-trick, stayed in the team with Ferreyra at inside-left, and finished as the tournament's top scorer.

● When the referee gave a foul against the United States in the semi-final, their medical attendant rushed on to the pitch to protest, threw down his bag, smashing a bottle of chloroform, was overcome by fumes and had to be helped off.

● The two halves of the final were played with different balls after an argument between the two sides.

Nasazzi (Uruguay), left, and Ferreyra (Argentina) toss up before the final.

Qualifying groups

The original idea to stage a knock-out tournament was dropped because of the low number of entrants, and the 13 countries were divided into four groups, the winners of each to qualify for the semi-finals. The Uruguayan hosts provided armed guards — soldiers with fixed bayonets — for all the teams. Although the four European teams were given a huge welcome when they arrived in Montevideo, they were by no means the cream of European football, and none of them was seeded. The four seeds were Argentina, Brazil, Uruguay and, surprisingly, the United States.

There were no drawn matches in the qualifying groups, each semi-finalist coming through with a 100 per cent record. The first ever World Cup match took

Soldiers with fixed bayonets guarded all the teams . . . boatloads of Argentinians crossed the River Plate and were searched for arms

place on 13 July, France beating Mexico 4–1 despite losing their keeper after 10 minutes with a kick on the jaw. This was the group of four countries, and the organization was such that France had to appear again two days later to play Argentina.

In the meantime, Belgium had gone down 3–0 to the United States, a team, nicknamed the "shot-putters" by the French, that included five former Scottish professionals, and also an Englishman. But the other European entries, Yugoslavia and Romania, had victories over South American teams.

Stabile, arm in air, puts Argentina 2-1 up in the final.

Argentinian anger

The first signs of trouble came in Group One, when the Brazilian referee blew for time some six minutes too soon, with Argentina one up on France. The Argentine fans in the crowd invaded the pitch, while the French players harangued the referee. After consulting his linesmen, he managed to restart the match, which finished with no further score. The Argentine players, angry that the Uruguayan crowd had supported France throughout, were further incensed when they carried two Frenchmen off shoulder-high at the finish. There were complaints to the organizing committee, and Argentina threatened to go home.

They completed their matches, however, though not without incident. In their game with Mexico, the Bolivian referee awarded five penalties, each side scoring from two, and against Chile, "hatchet-man" centre-half Luisito Monti started a brawl that needed the police to quell. Nevertheless, Argentina qualified for the semi-finals, where they joined Yugoslavia and the United States, who both went through comfortably.

Uruguay, the hosts, who had to wait for the late completion of the Centenary Stadium before they could start their matches, struggled to beat Peru, but found their form in the group decider against Romania.

Semi-final slaughter

The two great rivals, Uruguay and Argentina, Olympic finalists two years earlier, emerged from their semi-finals with comprehensive victories, both 6–1. Uruguay, with the nucleus of their Olympic side, went a goal down, but proved far too strong in the end for the Yugoslavs. Argentina, too, proved too strong — literally — even for the fit and fast American "shot-putters", who found themselves only one down at half-time but with one player missing (broken leg after 10 minutes), another suffering from a kick on the jaw, and their keeper also badly injured. It was not surprising that Argentina put five goals past them in the second half.

Trouble-free final

The final took place in the Centenary Stadium, Montevideo, on 30 July. Boatloads of Argentinians crossed the River Plate for this "local derby" and were searched for arms. The rivalry between the opposing sets of fans was intense, bitter even. The referee, the Belgian John Langenus, in his customary plus-fours, agreed to officiate only hours before the start, having secured a guarantee of his and his fellow officials' safety. Yet the game itself, expected to be a cauldron of emotion, went off without any trouble.

Uruguay scored first through Dorado after 12 minutes. But Peucelle equalized for Argentina, and centre-forward Guillermo Stabile, who had been brought in for their second match and already scored seven goals, put them ahead 10 minutes before the interval with a disputed goal. Thankfully, the Uruguayan fans accepted the referee's courageous decision.

In the second half, Uruguay's renowned half-back line — the "Iron Curtain", as it was known — of Andrade, Fernandez and Gestido began to take charge, and Uruguay exerted their technical superiority. The goals came though Cea, Iriate and Castro, and they ran out deserved 4–2 winners.

The trophy was presented by Jules Rimet to the winning captain, José Nasazzi. Montevideo went wild, and the authorities proclaimed the next day a national holiday. Sadly, in Buenos Aires, the Uruguayan consulate was stoned, such is the uncontrollable nationalism that so often surfaces in the name of sport.

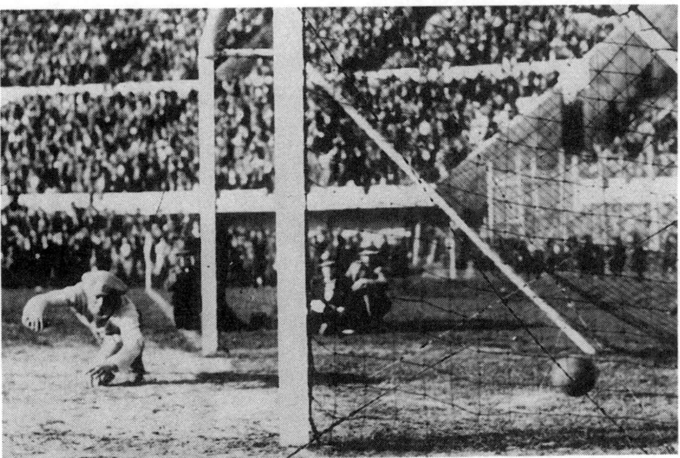

Argentine keeper Botasso is helpless to stop Uruguay's third goal.

FINAL SCORE

Group 1

France	4	Mexico	1
Argentina	1	France	0
Chile	3	Mexico	0
Chile	1	France	0
Argentina	6	Mexico	3
Argentina	3	Chile	1

	P	W	D	L	F	A	P
Argentina	3	3	0	0	10	4	6
Chile	3	2	0	1	5	3	4
France	3	1	0	2	4	3	2
Mexico	3	0	0	3	4	13	0

Group 2

Yugoslavia	2	Brazil	1
Yugoslavia	4	Bolivia	0
Brazil	4	Bolivia	0

	P	W	D	L	F	A	P
Yugoslavia	2	2	0	0	6	1	4
Brazil	2	1	0	1	5	2	2
Bolivia	2	0	0	2	0	8	0

Group 3

Romania	3	Peru	1
Uruguay	1	Peru	0
Uruguay	4	Romania	0

	P	W	D	L	F	A	P
Uruguay	2	2	0	0	5	0	4
Romania	2	1	0	1	3	5	2
Peru	2	0	0	2	1	4	0

Group 4

United States	3	Belgium	0
United States	3	Paraguay	0
Paraguay	1	Belgium	0

	P	W	D	L	F	A	P
USA	2	2	0	0	6	0	4
Paraguay	2	1	0	1	1	3	2
Belgium	2	0	0	2	0	4	0

SEMI-FINALS

Argentina	6	United States	1
Uruguay	6	Yugoslavia	1

FINAL

Uruguay	4	Argentina	2

Montevideo, 30 July 1930. Attendance 90,000

Uruguay: Ballesteros, Nasazzi, Mascheroni, Andrade, Fernandez, Gestido, Dorado, Scarone, Castro, Cea, Iriarte (Scorers: Dorado, Cea, Iriate, Castro)

Argentina: Botasso, Della Torre, Paternoster, Evaristo J, Monti, Suarez, Peucelle, Varallo, Stabile, Ferreyra, Evaristo M (Scorers: Peucelle, Stabile)

Leading scorers: 8 Stabile (Argentina) 5 Cea (Uruguay) 4 Subiabre (Chile)

Division One record for Arsenal

ARSENAL, the first southern club to win the League Championship, have done so with a record 66 points. Their goal tally was only one fewer than the new record of 128, set by runners-up Villa, seven points behind Arsenal. Arsenal's remarkable away record — won 14, drawn five, lost two, identical to their performance at home — sets new First Division figures for matches won and points scored away from home. And their 60 away goals is a new League record — no club in the four divisions has reached 50 before.

The shining star of this Arsenal triumph has been little Alex James, revelling in his new role of making goals rather than scoring them. Those to benefit have been his left-wing partner Cliff "Boy" Bastin (28 goals), bustling centre-forward Jack Lambert (38, a new club record), peerless inside-right David Jack (31) and right-winger Joe Hulme, the "Highbury Express", who provided a splendid service for the central attackers as well as scoring 14 goals.

Arsenal started the season with five straight wins and never looked back. They suffered their first loss on 11 October, 4–2 at Derby, their only defeat in the first 18 games. They failed to score in only one match, a goalless draw at home to Huddersfield on 7 March, which, oddly enough, was the first time they kept a clean sheet themselves. Their only lapse was a 5–1 reverse at Villa Park in mid-March, revenge for Villa who had lost 5–2 at Highbury and were knocked out of the Cup by Arsenal in the third round. But that was Arsenal's last defeat.

Bastin – goals from Arsenal's left wing.

FOOTBALL FOCUS

- Celtic were 2–0 down in the Scottish Cup final against Motherwell with eight minutes left, but a goal from McGrory and an own goal in the last seconds earned them a replay, which they won 4–2. Over 200,000 saw the two games at Hampden Park.
- West Bromwich became the first club to win the Cup and promotion in the same season, finishing seven points behind Everton, whom they beat in the semi-finals.
- On a disastrous tour in May, Scotland suffered their first foreign defeats, losing 5–0 to Austria and 3–0 to Italy, before beating Switzerland 3–2.

FINAL SCORE

Football League
Division 1: Arsenal
Top scorer: Pongo Waring (Aston Villa) 49
Division 2: Everton
Division 3S: Notts County
Division 3N: Chesterfield

FA Cup Final
West Bromwich Albion 2 Birmingham City 1

Scottish League
Division 1: Rangers
Top scorer: Barney Battles (Hearts) 44
Division 2: Third Lanark

Scottish FA Cup Final

Celtic	2	Motherwell	2
Replay: Celtic	4	Motherwell	2

International Championship
England, Scotland, 4 pts

Pongo Waring, leading League scorer.

Giant-killers slain

GALLANT SOUTHPORT from the Third Division North, Cup conquerors of three sides from higher divisions, were finally put in their place by Second Division leaders Everton. There were no half-measures at Goodison Park, where Dixie Dean and company, still smarting from last season's relegation, thrashed the upstarts 9–1, a record win for the sixth round.

After wins over Millwall, Blackpool and Bradford PA, Southport's hopes of reaching the semi-finals were shattered. Dean, who scored four goals when Everton won 6–0 at Crystal Palace in the fourth round, collected four more.

Dean heads one of his four against Southport.

Throstles singing in the rain

THE MIDLANDS came into their own at Wembley in the wettest Cup final seen for years, when Second Division West Bromwich Albion beat their First Division neighbours Birmingham 2–1. With centre-forward W.G.Richardson, scorer of their two goals, in splendid form, the Throstles really were on song. Such was their team spirit and their superior teamwork that, were it not for the brilliance of England's Harry Hibbs in the Birmingham goal, they would have won by a cricket score.

Despite the dreadful conditions, the football was of a high standard. The 21-year-old Billy Richardson — the phantom "G" is for "Ginger" to distinguish him from the Albion centre-half of the same name — opened the scoring after 26 minutes. England leader Joe Bradford equalized for Birmingham 12 minutes into the second half, but Richardson restored Albion's lead straight from the kick-off, and after that there was only one team in it.

Tragedy of Celtic keeper

WHEN 23-YEAR-OLD Celtic keeper John Thomson died, there were 30,000 mourners at Glasgow's Queen Street Station to see his coffin off, and 3,000 attended his funeral. He was a much-loved hero at Parkhead, and had already established himself in the Scotland side.

Thomson was renowned for his dashes off the line and his daring saves at the feet of onrushing forwards. So it was no surprise when he left his goal to thwart a Rangers attack when the two great Glasgow clubs met at Ibrox Park on 5 September. As Rangers' Sam English collected a long through-ball and ran it into the penalty area, Thomson threw himself at the attacker's feet to deflect the ball wide of goal. But this time he didn't get up. His skull was fractured in the collision, and he died five hours later in the nearby Victoria Infirmary.

Thomson joined Celtic as a 17-year-old, having been spotted in a junior game in his native Fife. He was at first reluctant to sign for the big club and make soccer his career, because his mother had dreamt that he would be seriously injured keeping goal. He won two Cup-winners' medals with Celtic, and was set to keep goal for Scotland for the next decade before his tragic death.

John Thomson goes down to make his fatal save.

'New' England outclass Scots

ENGLAND wrapped up the International Championship with a 3–0 victory over Scotland at Wembley, finishing with maximum points and a 12–3 goal record.

With an experimental eleven that included five new caps, England outclassed a poor Scottish side, although they needed two goals in the last 10 minutes to confirm their superiority. The outstanding player of the match was a newcomer, left-half Sam Weaver of Newcastle, whose 30-yard throw-ins have brought a new dimension to wing-half play.

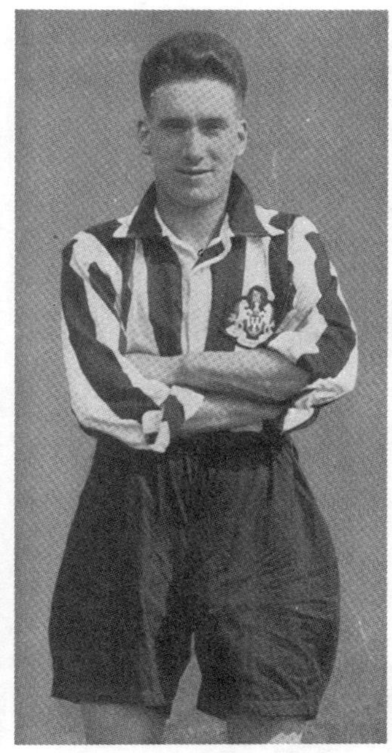

Sam Weaver, throw-in expert.

FOOTBALL FOCUS

- Wigan Borough of Division Three (N) became the first League club to resign during a season. They had played only six games, and their record was expunged.
- Motherwell won their first ever Scottish title, beating Rangers by five points and scoring a record 119 goals. Centre-forward Bill McFadyen, who played in 34 of their 38 games, scored 52 goals, a Scottish Division One record. Motherwell were the first club outside the Glasgow "Old Firm" to triumph since Third Lanark 28 years earlier.
- Everton won the League title in their first season back, with a Division One home record of 84 goals, including nine against Leicester and third-placed Wednesday, eight against Cup-winners Newcastle, and seven against Chelsea, with Dean twice notching five.
- England gained revenge over Spain for their 1929 defeat, winning 7–1 at Highbury in December.

FINAL SCORE

Football League
Division 1: Everton
Top scorer: Dixie Dean (Everton) 44
Division 2: Wolverhampton Wanderers
Division 3S: Fulham
Division 3N: Lincoln City

FA Cup Final

Newcastle United	2	Arsenal	1

Scottish League
Division 1: Motherwell
Top scorer: Bill McFadyen (Motherwell) 52
Division 2: East Stirlingshire

Scottish FA Cup Final

Rangers	1	Kilmarnock	1
Replay: Rangers	3	Kilmarnock	0

International Championship
England, 6 pts

Cup final controversy ends Arsenal's 'double' dream

A frame from the news film shows the ball clearly over the line.

ARSENAL, striving to become the first club this century to achieve the elusive League and Cup "double", had their hopes dashed when Newcastle beat them 2–1 at Wembley after the Gunners had taken an early lead through Bob John.

It was not a great Cup final, but the game will go down in history as one of the most controversial because of Newcastle's hotly disputed equalizer. When Jimmy Richardson chased the ball to the byline, it seemed to have gone out of play before he crossed it for Jack Allen to shoot in from close range. The Arsenal defence certainly thought so; they made no attempt to stop Allen. But the referee was unrepentant: "It was a goal... As God is my judge, the man was in play. I was eight yards away." But if British Movietone News were judge, the ball was clearly over the line and the referee was 20 yards away!

Arsenal had come to the final as favourites, despite missing their injured midfield genius Alex James. But they just weren't the same without the little Scot to weave his magic. Allen scored a second after 71 minutes, and Newcastle held on to run out worthy winners.

England beat Austria's 'Wunderteam'

ENGLAND WON the long-awaited showdown at Stamford Bridge on 7 December with the much-vaunted "Wunderteam", but were given a fright by the skilful Austrians before they emerged 4–3 victors.

Austria, coached by former Bolton player Jimmy Hogan, arrived with an imposing reputation, earned by such victories as their 5–0 shaming of Scotland (admittedly without any Rangers or Celtic players) in Vienna in May 1931. They had compiled an 18-match unbeaten run, including 15 wins, before they met England.

England, however, expected to win. Their own reputation on the Continent was formidable, the only real blemishes being their 1929 defeat in Madrid and a 5–2 reverse in Paris last year. At home, where Austria were only the third team to be invited, they could look back on a 6–1 defeat of Belgium in 1923 and their 7–1 humiliation of the overawed Spaniards a year ago.

Austria, too, seemed overawed, despite their standing as the "unofficial champions of the Continent". Before they could settle down, England scored through Blackpool centre-forward Jimmy Hampson, who added another after 27 minutes.

It is a great tribute to the Austrians that they did not fall apart at this stage. Calmed down during the interval by their manager Hugo Meisl, the architect of Austrian football, they began to play with their accustomed confidence, and some of their moves brought the sporting English crowd to their feet in admiration. They soon put England under greater pressure, with their elusive centre-forward Matthias Sindelar, the "Man of Paper", continually pulling the English defence out of position. Nevertheless, England always managed to keep in front.

England score through Hampson before Austria settle down.

FOOTBALL FOCUS

● Wales, who won the International Championship, scored their best ever win against Scotland and their first on Scottish soil since 1906, when they won 5–2 at Tynecastle despite playing with 10 men for 80 minutes.

● Numbered shirts were worn for the first time in the FA Cup final, winners Everton being numbered from 1 (the keeper) to 11 and Manchester City from 12 to 22 (keeper).

● Motherwell (114 goals) outscored Rangers by one goal again, but Rangers regained their League title from them by three points, and they were also pipped for the Cup by Celtic.

Numbered shirts were used in the Cup final.

Mighty Arsenal are humbled by Walsall

LOWLY Third Division Walsall pulled off perhaps the biggest shock in the history of the FA Cup when they beat League-leaders Arsenal 2–0 in the third round. True, Arsenal had just hit a bad patch with three defeats in five games, and a flu epidemic going round the country had robbed them of Eddie Hapgood, Jack Lambert and Bob John. But this should not have mattered. Nor should the fact that Walsall were unbeaten at home in the League. Perhaps manager Herbert Chapman made a rare mistake by replacing his stars with three players who had never appeared in the first team before and by dropping the off-form Joe Hulme.

The tiny ground was unfamiliar, and if Walsall's over-vigorous game took undue advantage of a lenient referee, they cannot be blamed for playing in the only way that would upset the First Division giants.

Arsenal were, indeed, thrown out of their stride. Alex James took a severe battering. And the new players proved a disaster. Charlie Walsh, who thought he was the best centre-forward on Arsenal's books, was a bag of nerves. He missed chance after chance and completely disrupted their attack. Outside-right Billy Warnes was too fragile for such a baptism of fire, and left-back Tommy Black allowed himself to get rattled.

When centre-forward Gilbert Alsop headed in a corner on the hour to put Walsall in front, the roar of the crowd could be heard two miles away. Five minutes later, Bill Sheppard completed the job, converting a penalty after Black had badly and gratuitously fouled Alsop — something so alien to Arsenal tradition that Black was immediately put on the transfer list.

FINAL SCORE

Football League
Division 1: Arsenal
Top scorer: Jack Bowers (Derby County) 35
Division 2: Stoke City
Division 3S: Brentford
Division 3N: Hull City

FA Cup Final

Everton	3	Manchester City	0

Scottish League
Division 1: Rangers
Top scorer: Bill McFadyen (Motherwell) 45
Division 2: Hibernian

Scottish FA Cup Final

Celtic	1	Motherwell	0

International Championship
Wales, 5 pts

Death of a sporting colossus

ARSENAL manager Herbert Chapman is dead. The shock news came out on the morning of Arsenal's home match with Sheffield Wednesday, and players and fans learned of it from the newspaper billboards on their way to the ground. He died at three o'clock on Saturday morning, 6 January, having bestrode the football world like a colossus, not only as a club manager, but as a tactician and an innovator. He brought success to every club he managed, and he was adored by both spectators and players, whose welfare was always uppermost in his mind.

Mr Chapman died in the course of his duty. He caught a chill watching a game at Bury on New Year's Day, but still decided to go to Sheffield the following day to watch Wednesday, Arsenal's next opponents. Despite a high temperature, he ignored doctor's advice and went to Guildford to see Arsenal's reserves. When he finally took to his bed, it was too late, for pneumonia had set in.

Born in Sheffield, Herbert Chapman was an enthusiastic wing-half or inside-forward with a number of clubs — he was Spurs' leading scorer in 1905–06 with 11 goals in the Southern League — before joining Northampton as player-manager in 1907. He transformed them from nonentities to Southern League champions in 1909. He joined struggling Second Division club Leeds City as secretary-manager in 1912, building them up to wartime champions before transferring his efforts to managing an arms factory.

He was lost to football after the war, when Leeds were expelled from the League and club officials banned for irregular payments to players during the hostilities. But he cleared his name of any involvement in the scandal before taking over at Huddersfield in 1921. His successes since then are legion: the Cup and the first two of Huddersfield's record three successive Championships, followed at Arsenal by the Cup and two League titles in the last four years as he transformed them into the most famous club side in the world. He leaves Arsenal on top of the League again as they begin the New Year without him.

Herbert Chapman (bottom right) with one of his early Arsenal teams.

FOOTBALL FOCUS

- Scottish League and Cup champions Rangers beat Blairgowrie 14–2 in the first round of the Cup, and Jim Fleming scored nine.
- Broadcaster and Arsenal managing director George Allison took over as secretary-manager at Highbury on the death of Herbert Chapman. His first buy, centre-forward Ted Drake from Southampton, scored seven goals in 10 games to help Arsenal retain the Championship.
- A crowd of 84,569, a record for any English club game other than the Cup final, saw eventual Cup-winners Manchester City beat Stoke 1–0 at Maine Road in the sixth round on 3 March.
- Stanley Rous, a Hertfordshire schoolteacher, refereed the Cup final and was then appointedsecretary of the Football Association.

Teenage keeper faints after Cup victory

FRANK SWIFT, Manchester City's 19-year-old goalkeeper, was so overcome at the end of the Cup final that he collapsed under his cross-bar and had to be helped to the Royal Box to collect his winners' medal. It was a close game, and Swift blamed himself for the goal that gave Portsmouth a half-time lead. In the dressing-room during the interval, centre-forward Freddy Tilson, trying to console the youngster, told him not to worry because he would score a couple in the second half. He was true to his words!

Swift, who joined City as a 17-year-old, has played only half a season in the first team. So it is not surprising that the nervous tension got to him in the end, especially with photographers behind his goal counting away the last minutes.

The tall keeper with the huge hands felt he should have done more than just touch Rutherford's cross-shot on its way to the net after 27 minutes of the first half. But City became only the second team to recover from a goal deficit at Wembley when Tilson took advantage of Portsmouth centre-half Allen's temporary absence to equalize, and then scored the winner four minutes from time.

Frank Swift, Manchester City's young keeper.

FINAL SCORE

Football League
Division 1: Arsenal
Top scorer: Jack Bowers (Derby County) 35
Division 2: Grimsby Town
Division 3S: Norwich City
Division 3N: Barnsley

FA Cup Final

Manchester City	2	Portsmouth	1

Scottish League
Division 1: Rangers
Top scorer: Jimmy Smith (Rangers) 41
Division 2: Albion Rovers

Scottish FA Cup Final

Rangers	5	St Mirren	0

International Championship
Wales, 5 pts

Italy win — by a fluke!

WORLD CUP QUOTES

"It was a brawl, not an exhibition of football."

HUGO MEISL,
Austria's supremo, after his team's 2–1 victory over Hungary in the quarter-finals.

"I was off balance and late to react when Orsi scored from eight yards."

FRANTISEK PLANICKA,
Czechoslovakia's perfectionist goalkeeper, blaming himself for Italy's late equalizer in the final from Orsi's freak shot. Next day, Orsi — watched by photographers — tried 20 times to reproduce the shot, but without success.

"Every one of our guests felt the pulsating of the masculine energies of a bursting vitality, in this our Mussolini's Italy."

GIOVANNI MAURO,
Italian delegate to FIFA and one of the tournament's organizers.

"In the majority of countries, the World Championship was called a sporting fiasco, because, beside the desire to win, all other sporting considerations were non-existent."

JOHN LANGENUS,
Belgian referee who had taken the 1930 final and one of the first-round matches in 1934.

In this second World Cup, Europe showed that South America had not cornered the market in violent play and fanatical nationalism, while the standard of refereeing still left much to be desired. There were again no British teams, and the South American contingent was weak, so Austria and Italy were the favourites.

THE 1934 WORLD CUP was the first international football competition exploited for propaganda purposes. Italy, with a Fascist government, won the right to stage Europe's first World Cup only after eight meetings of FIFA. They had the resources, the stadiums and sufficient big cities to handle what had now become a prestigious event, with political capital an extra prize for the victors. There were originally 32 entrants, but the holders, Uruguay, were missing, piqued at the poor response from Europe when they staged the first World Cup and beset with domestic troubles. The countries were divided into 12 geographical groups to produce 16 finalists. Even Italy had to qualify by playing Greece. Brazil and Argentina qualified without playing when their scheduled opponents withdrew, and the United States beat Mexico 4–2 in an extra qualifier in Rome before the start of the tournament proper.

The finals were organized as a straight knock-out event, with eight of the 16 teams seeded in the first round. Both Brazil and 1930 runners-up Argentina, who, having already lost some of their players to Italian football, had left more of their stars at home, were beaten and found themselves making the long return trip after only one game.

Italy, who had selected three Argentinians of Italian extraction, including the ruthless centre-half Monti of Montevideo notoriety, beat the other long-distance travellers, the United States, by 7–1. Egypt, the African representatives, put up a spirited fight against Hungary in Naples before succumbing 4–2. Every team scored in the first round, which, apart from the football, was relatively free from incident. Hat-tricks were scored by Schiavio for Italy and Conen for Germany, 5–2 winners over Belgium.

Austrian keeper Platzer thwarts Italy's Schiavio in the semi-final.

European mayhem

The last eight now represented what was virtually a European Championship. And that's when the trouble started. Spain took the lead against Italy in Florence, but what had been a rough game went into an even more brutal extra time. The Italian ruthlessness went unpunished by the referee, and only a brilliant display by captain and keeper Ricardo Zamora enabled the crippled Spaniards to hold on for a replay. This took place the next day, and seven Spaniards, including the influential Zamora, as well as four Italians, were unfit to play.

If the Belgian referee for the first game had failed to control the mayhem, the Swiss official

Home advantage tells again in a 'sporting fiasco' where 'beside the desire to win, all other sporting considerations were non-existent' — JOHN LANGENUS, one of the 'intimidated' referees.

Combi dives too late to stop Puc's goal in the final, but Italy recovered to win in extra time.

for the replay was so poor that he was later suspended by his national association, adding fuel to the accusations of intimidation that abounded during the finals. It was a tough game for both sides, but the fitter Italians — manager Vittorio Pozzo had instilled discipline and prepared his squad physically and mentally in a secluded resort for six weeks before the finals — outlasted the Spaniards despite a fine display from the young replacement keeper Noguet.

The clash between neighbours and rivals Austria and Hungary promised to be a classic but developed instead into a brawl, with players arguing and Markos, the Hungarian right-winger, sent off. Austria played some good football, however, and deserved their win.

The Austrians should have been fresher for their semi-final than the Italians, who were playing their third match in four days. But they weren't, and the heavy rain in Milan before the kick-off produced a muddy pitch and the sort of conditions detested by the skilful passers and dribblers of the Viennese school. The Italians were also skilful, and they had been better prepared. A goal after 18 minutes by one of their Argentinian wingers, Guaita, settled the match.

In the other semi-final, played in Rome, Germany, conquerors of Sweden in the quarter-finals, met Czechoslovakia, who, in Frantisek Planicka, had perhaps the best goalkeeper of the tournament. The Czechs had improved as the finals progressed, and they outplayed the unimaginative Germans. They served up inventive, entertaining football, and their finishing proved better than that of their otherwise methodical opponents. The manner of their 3–1 victory, with Oldrich Nejedly scoring twice, promised a combative final with Italy.

A freak equalizer

The final provided a curiosity – both captains were goalkeepers. In a goalless first half, the Czechs looked the more dangerous side, with Antonin Puc proving a handful on the left for the Italian defence. At the other end, Planicka safely thwarted the Italian forwards. It was Puc, returning after going off with cramp, who stunned the crowd 20 minutes from time with a goal from a long shot for which Giampiero Combi dived too late. The Czechs could then have clinched the match. Centre-forward Sobotka should have done, but missed an open goal. Then inside-right Svoboda hit a post.

The Italians, watched by dictator Benito Mussolini, desperately piled on the pressure, but it took a freak goal by their Argentinian left-winger Raimondo Orsi to beat Planicka eight minutes from the end of normal time. Orsi, lured out of South America by Juventus in 1929, was noted for his speed, skill and powerful shot. He used the first two of these attributes as he took a ball from Guaita and hared through the Czech defence. He feinted with his left foot and then, eschewing the third of his qualities, somehow struck a right-foot shot-cum-lob that swerved and dipped crazily over Planicka and into the net.

In extra time, the Italians lasted the pace better, despite having inside-right Guiseppe Meazza limping on the wing. The Czechs had tended to ignore him, but he was no passenger, as he proved seven minutes into the first period. Receiving the ball on the right, he crossed it to Guaita, who in turn found Schiavio. The centre-forward neatly sidestepped a defender and shot past Planicka for what proved to be the winning goal. Tired as they were, the two sides continued to battle it out, with both keepers kept busy right to the end.

At the final whistle, the Italian players still had enough strength to hoist Pozzo on to their shoulders in triumph, and Combi was presented with the trophy by a jubilant Mussolini, gratified that the team's success had enhanced the prestige of his Fascist regime.

FINAL SCORE

FIRST ROUND

Italy	7	United States	1
Czechoslovakia	2	Romania	1
Germany	5	Belgium	2
Austria	3	France	2
Spain	3	Brazil	1
Switzerland	3	Holland	2
Sweden	3	Argentina	2
Hungary	4	Egypt	2

QUARTER-FINALS

Germany	2	Sweden	1
Austria	2	Hungary	1
Italy	1	Spain	1
Czechoslovakia	3	Switzerland	2

Replay

Italy	1	Spain	0

SEMI-FINALS

Czechoslovakia	3	Germany	1
Italy	1	Austria	0

THIRD-PLACE MATCH

Germany	3	Austria	2

FINAL

Italy (after extra time)	2	Czechoslovakia	1

Rome, 10 June 1934. Attendance 55,000

Italy: Combi, Monzeglio, Allemandi, Ferraris IV, Monti, Bertolini, Guaita, Meazza, Schiavio, Ferrari, Orsi
(Scorers: Orsi, Schiavio)
Czechoslovakia: Planicka, Zenizek, Ctyroky, Kostalek, Cambal, Krcil, Junek, Svoboda, Sobotka, Nejedly, Puc
(Scorer: Puc)

Leading scorers
4 Conen (Germany) Nejedly (Czechoslovakia) Schiavio (Italy)

Vittorio Pozzo (left) encourages his team before extra time.

Battle of Highbury

IT WASN'T SO much a football match, more a pitched battle, when England beat world champions Italy 3–2 at Highbury. Battered but unbowed, the eleven English heroes were queuing up for treatment after the match in the dressing-room, which looked more like a casualty clearing station.

When, after two minutes, Luisito Monti, Italy's ruthless Argentinian centre-half, broke a foot in a clash with Ted Drake and had to go off, the rest of the side went berserk. Pushing, elbowing, kicking, even jumping on players in their efforts to "retaliate" for what the crippled Monti had claimed was a deliberate foul, the Italians forgot about the football.

Italy's Ceresoli saves, with England's Drake (right) in close attendance.

England, with seven Arsenal players, a record for one club, were three up in 15 minutes despite missing a penalty. The culprit, outside-left Eric Brook, soon made amends, heading in a cross from 19-year-old right-winger Stanley Matthews and then whacking in a free-kick. England's new captain Eddie Hapgood received an elbow in his face and was off the field having the resultant broken nose treated when Drake hooked in a Matthews cross.

To the fore for England was rugged left-half Wilf Copping, whose famous shoulder-charge and tackle were never put to better use. It is a mystery, however, why the Swedish referee did not take a firmer hand. His reluctance to send anyone off might have been due to fear of causing a riot, as the Italian contingent in the 50,000 crowd was considerable.

After the interval — and spurred on by a pep-talk from Vittorio Pozzo — the Italians began to play football at last, and their skilful and stylish centre-forward Guiseppe Meazza scored twice in a four-minute spell and later hit the cross-bar. England, bruised and limping, managed to hold out, with keeper Frank Moss outstanding. Their unbeaten home record against foreign teams was still intact, even if the same could not be said of their players.

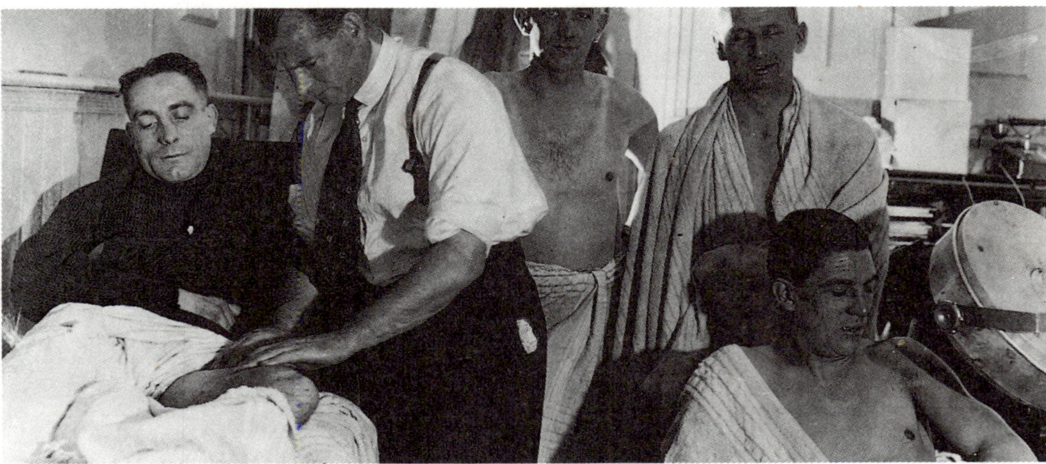

Tom Whittaker treats Copping, while Moss, Bastin and Drake wait their turn.

Arsenal complete a hat-trick

ARSENAL built another monument to the late Herbert Chapman when they tied up their third consecutive League title, emulating Huddersfield's feat in the twenties — which was also inspired by the great man. Carrying on the Chapman policies and the style that has become the hallmark of Arsenal, manager George Allison has steered the Gunners to another comfortable win, by four points from Sunderland. His two early-season signings, half-backs Crayston and Copping — both players Chapman had sought — have fitted in perfectly to the Arsenal machine. And Ted Drake, signed near the end of last season, has electrified the attack with his lion-hearted play. He topped the League scorers with 42 goals, and so did Arsenal with 115.

FINAL SCORE

Football League
Division 1: Arsenal
Top scorer: Ted Drake (Arsenal) 42
Division 2: Brentford
Division 3S: Charlton Athletic
Division 3N: Doncaster Rovers

FA Cup Final

Sheffield Wed	4	WBA	2

Scottish League
Division 1: Rangers
Top scorer: Dave McCulloch (Hearts) 38
Division 2: Third Lanark

Scottish FA Cup Final

Rangers	2	Hamilton A	1

International Championship
England, Scotland, 4 pts

FOOTBALL FOCUS

- Carlisle, who finished bottom of Division Three (N), were earlier humiliated 6–1 at home in the Cup by non-League Wigan Athletic.
- Rangers brought off their second successive League and Cup "double", their fourth in all, to beat Celtic's record of three. It was their third Championship on the trot, their eighth in nine seasons.

Rimmer the winner in Wembley thriller

IN ONE OF the most exciting finals seen for years, Ellis Rimmer scored twice in the last three minutes to give Sheffield Wednesday their first Cup victory since 1907. West Bromwich, with nine of their winning side of four years ago, were looking for a repeat performance, but were never in front.

Wednesday opened the scoring through Palethorpe after only two minutes, but Albion left-winger Boyes equalized with a spectacular drive after racing half the length of the field. When Sandford equalized again for Albion soon after Hooper's 67th-minute goal, it began to look like extra time would be needed. But outside-left Rimmer kept up his record of scoring in every round when he beat the Albion keeper to a bouncing through-ball and headed in, and he clinched the match with another goal a minute from time.

Wounded-knee Drake scores seven

RAMPAGING centre-forward Ted Drake equalled the League goalscoring record at Villa Park on 14 December when he scored all Arsenal's goals in their 7–1 win. With the triple champions struggling to remain in the title race, this burst of scoring came out of the blue. The schemer-in-chief of Arsenal's goal machine, Alex James, was missing, and Drake himself played despite the handicap of an injured knee, which had troubled him for some time and was strapped up.

Villa, struggling to stave off relegation, begin brightly enough, and there is no hint of the devastation to come. Early on, Drake skids off the pitch and falls flat on his face, to the great amusement of the Villa fans. This is the last time they laugh all afternoon.

It starts for Arsenal, and Drake, after 15 minutes. Moving out to the left to collect a pass from Pat Beasley, he pushes the ball through the legs of Tommy Griffiths, Villa's recently acquired Welsh international centre-half, and runs on to shoot past keeper Harry Morton. The next goal, after 28 minutes, rounds off a typical solo run after Bastin puts him clear 10 yards inside the Villa half. Shouldering off challenges from Griffiths and left-back George Cummings, he slams the ball past the helpless Morton. He notches his hat-trick after 34 minutes, presented with an open goal after a Beasley shot rebounds from a defender.

When Drake puts another two in the net within five minutes of the interval, the Villa crowd begin to sense a record is on. First, he chases a ball that Griffiths thinks is going out, catches it just in time and flicks it past the bemused keeper. Then good work by Bowden and Bastin sets him up for a first-time shot for his fifth goal.

Another first-time shot from just outside the box, after a poor Villa clearance — 58 minutes, six shots, six goals! The whole Villa half-back line is now making a concerted effort to shackle the Arsenal centre-forward, and Drake's next shot crashes down from the underside of the bar and is cleared by a defender. Then Villa score their only goal, a header by centre-forward Jack Palethorpe. Drake has to wait until the 89th minute for his seventh. He finds space for himself to take another Bastin pass and joyfully blasts the ball home.

The Villa players sportingly applaud Drake's history-making performance, and all sign the match ball before it is presented to the seven-goal hero, who has matched James Ross's seven for Preston against Stoke in 1888.

Ted Drake, Arsenal's seven-goal hero.

FOOTBALL FOCUS

- Chelsea's game against Arsenal at Stamford Bridge on 12 October drew 82,905, a League record. Result: 1–1.
- Ted Drake's knee lasted another six matches after his seven-goal spree before it needed an operation. In his comeback match, a try-out at Highbury for the Cup final, he scored the only goal of the game — against Aston Villa — and proceeded to do the same to win the final against Sheffield United..
- Aston Villa and Blackburn Rovers, original members of the League, were both relegated from the First Division for the first time.

FINAL SCORE

Football League
Division 1: Sunderland
Top scorer: W. "Ginger" Richardson (West Bromwich Albion) 39
Division 2: Manchester United
Division 3S: Coventry City
Division 3N: Chesterfield

FA Cup Final

Arsenal	1	Sheffield United	0

Scottish League
Division 1: Celtic
Top scorer: Jimmy McGrory (Celtic) 50
Division 2: Falkirk

Scottish FA Cup Final

Rangers	1	Third Lanark	0

International Championship
Scotland, 4 pts

Third-choice centre-forward Payne hits 10

JOE PAYNE, a reserve wing-half with Luton Town in the Third Division South, was given the job as makeshift centre-forward on 13 April when Luton's regular No. 9 and his deputy were injured, and he proceeded to rewrite the record books with 10 goals in the 12–0 thrashing of poor Bristol Rovers.

It took the 22-year-old Payne 20 minutes or so to settle into his new role, but once he got the hang of it he couldn't stop scoring. Four goals up at half-time, with three of the goals having been scored by the newcomer, Luton took Rovers apart in the second half. Every time Payne got the ball, the cry went up, "Come on, Joe, let's have another one". And nearly every time, Joe obliged.

Ten-goal Joe Payne, Luton's makeshift record-breaker.

Everything went right for him. For his last goal, after 86 minutes, he was lying on the ground outside the penalty box with his back to goal. As the ball came to him, he swivelled and swung his boot to send it unerringly into the net.

Derbyshire-born Payne originally joined the club as a centre-forward, but failed to make the grade in their reserves. It is safe to say he has now returned to his rightful position.

Payne's record surpasses the nine goals scored by Robert "Bunny" Bell for Tranmere only four months earlier, in the 13–4 win over Oldham on Boxing Day. Tranmere, beaten 4–1 at Oldham on the previous day, responded by equalling the League record score by a club in a single match and — with Oldham's help — set an aggregate record as well.

Sunderland's Cup at last

SUNDERLAND HAVE WON the FA Cup for the first time in their long and illustrious history. At long last, after a difficult campaign, they reached the final, and now, coming back typically from a half-time deficit, they have beaten Preston 3–1 at Wembley.

They needed a replay to beat Luton in the fourth round and two before they slammed Wolves 4–0 in the sixth. And they were a goal down against Third Division Millwall in the semi-finals before emerging 2–1 winners.

In what was by no means a great final, Preston's Scottish international centre-forward Frank O'Donnell put them ahead after 38 minutes. Sunderland, under the astute generalship of their captain and inside-right Raich Carter, took charge in the second half, and Bobby Gurney equalized after seven minutes with a header following a corner. Carter put them ahead 20 minutes later from a Gurney pass, and shortly afterwards, Eddie Burbanks shot home from a narrow angle to clinch the match and the Cup for this talented, and delighted, Roker side.

Carter (striped shirt, behind goalkeeper Burns) puts Sunderland in front.

World record crowd at Hampden Park

IT DIDN'T SEEM to matter that Scotland were playing England for second place in the International Championship, Wales having already sewn up the title and the Triple Crown, as 149,547 fans passed through the Hampden Park turnstiles, a world record attendance. It is estimated that at least another 10,000 broke in and saw the game without paying. This huge mass of spectators were not disappointed. They saw what they came for — defeat of the "auld enemy" by 3–1. But they had a fright in the first half, when England went into a goal lead that should have been three.

Playing in numbered shirts for the first time, they gave a superb exhibition of football, with right-winger Stanley Matthews outstanding, but all they had to show for it was a goal by Matthews's Stoke team-mate Freddie Steele.

It was a different story in the second half, when Scotland, inspired by Hearts inside-right Tommy Walker, equalized after just two minutes through Frank O'Donnell of Preston. In a classic match, England were then floored by two goals from Bob McPhail of Rangers in the last 10 minutes.

Tommy Walker, inspired Scotland.

Freddie Steele, goal for England.

FINAL SCORE

Football League
Division 1: Manchester City
Top scorer: Freddie Steele (Stoke City) 33
Division 2: Leicester City
Division 3S: Luton Town
Division 3N: Stockport County

FA Cup Final

Sunderland	3	Preston North End	1

Scottish League
Division 1: Rangers
Top scorer: David Wilson (Hamilton Academical) 34
Division 2: Ayr United

Scottish FA Cup Final

Celtic	2	Aberdeen	1

International Championship
Wales, 6 pts

FOOTBALL FOCUS

- A Scottish Cup record attendance of 144,433 watched the final at Hampden Park.
- Everton's Dixie Dean passed Steve Bloomer's record of 352 League goals, and finished the season with 375.
- Both Division Three (N) and Three (S) goalscoring records were broken with 55 goals, by Ted Harston (Mansfield) and Joe "10-goal" Payne (Luton) respectively.
- England, who beat Hungary 6–2 at Highbury in December, with Ted Drake scoring three, hit 18 goals without reply on their three-match Scandinavian tour in May. Joe Payne scored two in his only appearance, an 8-0 defeat of Finland.

Millwall make history

LITTLE MILLWALL made football history when they beat First Division giants Manchester City 2–0 at the Den to become the first Division Three side to reach the semi-finals of the FA Cup. The giant-killer had to be a David, of course — player-manager Dave Mangnall, who scored both Millwall's goals. But all eleven Millwall players were heroes to the 42,000 crowd as they swept the Championship challengers aside — Peter Doherty, Eric Brook and all.

Millwall's only excursion away from the Den was in the first round, when they thrashed lowly Aldershot 6–1. This was followed by a 7–0 trouncing of Third Division North strugglers Gateshead, and then further home victories over Second Division Fulham (2–0), First Division Chelsea (3–0) and Derby County (2–1) in front of a ground record 48,672 crowd.

The London club have reached the semi-finals twice before, in 1900 and 1903, when they were a Southern League side. Their next hurdle is another formidable First Division outfit, Sunderland, at Leeds Road.

In addition to Millwall's historic effort, the cup produced one remarkable result — when Second Division Tottenham Hotspur beat First Division Everton 4–3 in a fifth-round replay, after being two down with only four minutes left.

Penalty drama at Wembley

AFTER 119 minutes of dull, featureless football, the Cup final between Huddersfield and Preston suddenly came to life when the referee blew for a penalty. It was the first to be awarded in a Wembley Cup final, and the first time extra time had been necessary.

The fans had already begun to depart, referee Jimmy Jewell was consulting his watch, and BBC radio commentator Commander Tom Woodroofe had promised his listeners: "If they score now, I'll eat my hat." Suddenly George Mutch, Preston's Scottish international inside-right, was making a determined run on goal. There seemed little danger, however, as England centre-half Alf Young, a rock for Huddersfield all afternoon, was about to challenge. But his tackle was mistimed, and over went Mutch. Was it a foul? Was it in the penalty area? The referee had no doubt and pointed to the spot.

A still dazed Mutch picked himself up and slammed the ball into the net off the cross-bar. It was the last kick of the match.

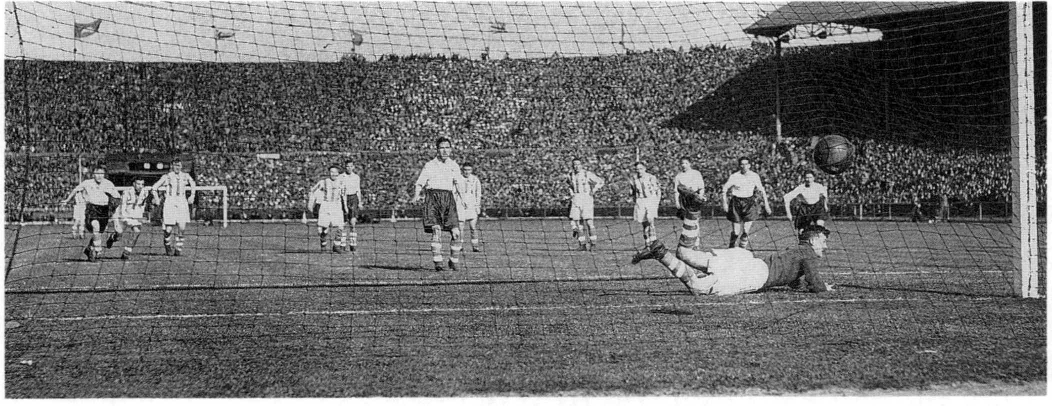

Goalkeeper Hesford dives, but Mutch's penalty is straight.

England give Nazi salute, then humble Germany 6–3

THE ENGLAND players did not want to do it, but the British ambassador felt it would be a serious snub not to give the Nazi salute, so the team reluctantly complied. The scene was the impressive Olympic Stadium in Berlin, where two years ago Herr Hitler had used the Olympics in an attempt to whitewash his evil regime.

Fortunately for the German team, including some Austrian players who had been absorbed into the side with the recent annexation of their country, Hitler was not among the 110,000 present to see them turned over, although his henchmen were — Goering, Goebbels and company. The swastikas came out briefly when Germany equalized an early Bastin goal, but the crowd were stunned into silence as England built up a 4–2 half-time lead. The Germans, carefully selected after months of trials and fresh from 10 days' special training in the Black Forest, were no match for the determined English. The game was capped with a dream goal, as Stanley Matthews, who had run the German defence ragged all afternoon, mesmerized them once again before sending over one of his flighted crosses to West Ham's Len Goulden, who struck a 25-yard left-foot volley screaming into the net. The final score was thus a triumph for sport over politics: Germany 3 England 6.

A reluctant England team, in the traditional white shirts, give the Nazi salute.

FOOTBALL FOCUS

- East Fife became the first Division Two side to win the Scottish Cup.
- Raith Rovers won the Scottish Division Two with a British record 142 goals in only 34 games. They scored 74 away goals, including eight three times.

Champions relegated — top scorers City go down

IN AN UNUSUALLY close First Division campaign, only 16 points separated winners Arsenal (52) from the relegated pair Manchester City and West Bromwich. Wolves, top by a point as the season went into its last day, lost 1–0 at Sunderland, while Arsenal beat Bolton 5–0 to take their fifth title in eight years.

But the biggest drama was unfolding at the other end of the table. On Cup final day, a week before the end of the season, any of the bottom 11 teams could have been relegated, including Cup-finalists Huddersfield.

The last day saw six teams joint bottom with 36 points. Birmingham got out of trouble with a 4–1 win at Leicester, while Grimsby, Portsmouth and Stoke all had home wins. The crucial match was Huddersfield v Manchester City. Huddersfield won it 1–0 to stay up and doom City, First Division top scorers (80 goals) and champions a year ago.

FINAL SCORE

Football League
Division 1: Arsenal
Top scorer: Tommy Lawton (Everton) 28
Division 2: Aston Villa
Division 3S: Millwall
Division 3N: Tranmere Rovers

FA Cup Final

Preston North End	1	Huddersfield Town	0

(after extra time)

Scottish League
Division 1: Celtic
Top scorer: Andy Black (Hearts) 40
Division 2: Raith Rovers

Scottish FA Cup Final

East Fife	1	Kilmarnock	1
Replay: East Fife	4	Kilmarnock	2

International Championship
England, Scotland, 4 pts

Goals galore as Italy retain World Cup

WITH FIFA membership up to 57 countries, there were a record 36 entries for the 1938 World Cup. Of these, for the first time, the holders, Italy, and the host country, France, did not have to qualify. The rest had to be whittled down to 16 for the finals.

Uruguay, the first World Cup-winners, were still suffering a professionalism crisis and did not enter. Argentina, upset at being overlooked as hosts, prevaricated before finally withdrawing. This left Brazil as the only South American representatives. They qualified automatically along with Cuba from their group, as Mexico, the United States and others also withdrew.

In Europe, war-torn Spain also pulled out before being allocated qualifying fixtures. But the Austrians, who had qualified in October 1937 when they eliminated Latvia, found their nation swallowed up by Germany in the 1938 Anschluss, and their best players were greedily incorporated within the German team. This left the way open for England, but the FA spurned FIFA's overtures.

In other qualifying groups, Norway eliminated the Republic of Ireland and Hungary beat Greece by a record 11–1. In the Far East, Japan's withdrawal let the Dutch East Indies through to the finals.

Again, England stayed aloof from the World Cup, even though they were offered a late entry to take part in France. A competition without the home countries, and with Argentina and Uruguay also missing, would again be a World Championship in name only. But the Axis powers Germany and Italy were out to milk it for all the propaganda they could get. Italy indeed retained the trophy after a severe fright in the first round, but the Germans came an early cropper.

Swiss repel Germans

Of the seven first-round matches (Sweden had a bye), five went to extra time, and two of these required a replay. And the replays provided the two shock results of the round, Germany and Romania going out to Switzerland and Cuba respectively.

The Germans, although demoralized by their 6–3 defeat at the hands of England a few weeks earlier, were among the tournament's favourites. They had a new manager, Sepp Herberger, and an injection of Austrian talent. But Switzerland had beaten the touring England side 2–1, and had little respect for the Germans — to the extent of refusing to give the Nazi salute during the playing of the national anthem. Germany had to hang on for a draw after having Pesser, one of their four Austrians, sent off. In the replay, the Swiss won a remarkable 4–2 victory, recovering from a two-goal deficit despite playing most of the game with 10 men or with the injured Aebi a passenger.

The biggest surprise of the first round, however, was Cuba. They held the experienced and tactically superior Romanians to a 3–3 draw, and then dropped their widely praised keeper Carvajeles for the replay. His replacement, Ayra, performed even better, and limited Romania to a solitary first-half goal before his team-mates scored two in the second.

Goal feast

The tie of the round turned out to be Brazil's clash with Poland, a goal feast that stood at 4–4 after 90 minutes before Brazil edged it 6–5. Their acrobatic little centre-forward Leonidas da Silva became the first player to score four goals in a World Cup match — followed a few minutes later by his opposite number Ernst Willimowski for Poland.

The only first-round matches that did not go to extra time were Hungary's predictable rout of the Dutch East Indies and France's smooth victory over Belgium. Italy, however, were stopped in their tracks by the Norwegian team of amateurs, who had beaten Germany in the 1936 Olympics and run eventual gold-medallists Italy close. They did so again, after Italy had taken the lead in the second minute. Norway hit the woodwork three times before equalizing, and a goal in extra time by Piola saw a relieved Italian side through.

The goals continued to flow in the quarter-finals, at least for Sweden, playing their first game. The tired Cubans were no match for the fresh Swedes, who swamped them 8–0, with outside-right Gustav Wetterstroem hitting four to the dismay of recalled keeper Carvajeles. Switzerland, also suffering replay fatigue and without skipper Minelli, were no match for Hungary. And Italy, producing a much better display against the hosts, went through 3–1, their brilliant

Piola scores Italy's fourth to clinch the World Cup final victory over Hungary.

A Jekyll and Hyde performance from Brazil hints at South American magic, while a spate of goals sees attacks come out on top

Vittorio Pozzo, four years older, with the trophy again and another jubilant team.

FINAL SCORE

FIRST ROUND			
Switzerland	1	Germany	1
Hungary	6	Dutch East Indies	0
France	3	Belgium	1
Brazil	6	Poland	5
Czechoslovakia	3	Holland	0
Italy	2	Norway	1
Cuba	3	Romania	3
Replays			
Switzerland	4	Germany	2
Cuba	2	Romania	1
QUARTER-FINALS			
Sweden	8	Cuba	0
Hungary	2	Switzerland	0
Italy	3	France	1
Brazil	1	Czechoslovakia	1
Replay			
Brazil	2	Czechoslovakia	1
SEMI-FINALS			
Italy	2	Brazil	1
Hungary	5	Sweden	1
THIRD-PLACE MATCH			
Brazil	4	Sweden	2
FINAL			
Italy	4	Hungary	2

Paris, 19 June 1938. Attendance 55,000

Italy: Olivieri, Foni, Rava, Serantoni, Andreolo, Locatelli, Biavati, Meazza, Piola, Ferrari, Colaussi
(Scorers: Colaussi 2, Piola 2)
Hungary: Szabo, Polgar, Biro, Szalay, Lazar, Saș, Vincze, Sarosi, Zsengeller, Titkos
(Scorers: Titkos, Sarosi)

Leading scorers
8 Leonidas (Brazil)
7 Zsengeller (Hungary)
5 Piola (Italy)

centre-forward Silvio Piola ominously scoring twice.

After Brazil's first-round goal-fest and Czechoslovakia's cool extra-time execution of the Dutch, this seemed an appropriate pairing for the opening of Bordeaux's new stadium. But the match set record lows in World Cup thuggery. Brazil's Zeze started the carnage with a gratuitous kick at Nejedly, one of the leading scorers from the last World Cup. The Brazilian was sent off, but Leonidas put the South Americans ahead. The game then degenerated into a brawl, and just before half-time Machado and Riha became involved in their own private scrap and both received their marching orders. Brazil conceded a penalty for handball, and Nejedly equalized before he too went off, with a broken leg. The game finished at one each — and nine men each — with the Czech keeper Planicka having bravely played on with a broken arm.

The replay, with 15 new players, turned out to be a mild affair, and the crowd were treated to some good football. The Czechs badly missed the influential Planicka and Nejedly, and their left-winger Puc, but they took a first-half lead through Kopecky, who soon went off with an injury. Brazil, with a far stronger squad, had retained only their keeper Walter and the prolific Leonidas, the latter equalizing and the former recovering a ball thought by many to be well over his goal-line. Right-winger Roberto finally broke the magnificent Czech defence once more with a rasping hook shot, and Brazil marched confidently into the semi-finals.

Brazilian blunder

Perhaps the Brazilians were overconfident. Their coach Ademar Pimenta made wholesale changes again for their clash with Italy. Only three players kept their places and — to the utter disbelief of everyone following the World Cup — Leonidas, the "Black Diamond", the jewel in Brazil's crown, was omitted. According to Pimenta, Leonidas and his inside partner, the ball-juggling expert Tim, were being saved for the final.

It was a gamble that did not come off. Colaussi put Italy ahead after 55 minutes, and shortly afterwards Domingos, Brazil's hitherto immaculate right-back, conceded a penalty. Admittedly, Piola made a meal of the foul, and this antagonized the Brazilians. After Meazza converted the spot-kick, they allowed their tempers to interfere with their acknowledged artistry. They pulled a late goal back, but the Italians in the end earned an impressive victory.

Sweden made a sensational start in the other semi-final, left-winger Arne Nyberg scoring with only 35 seconds gone. But the Hungarians appeared not in the least perturbed by this setback and soon took complete control. Inside-right Gyula Zsengeller contributed a hat-trick to a classy 5–1 victory.

In the third-place match three days later, Sweden were 2–1 up at half-time. But Brazil, with Leonidas restored as captain, put on a brilliant exhibition and ran out 4–2 winners, with another two from the "Black Diamond" to take him to the top of the scoring list.

Win or die!

It was rumoured, after the final, that the Italian players had received a telegram warning them "Win or die!" Whether or not there was any truth in this, the Italians won, and won well, without any hint of undue pressure. It was an exciting final with plenty of fine play and movement. Outside-left Colaussi put Italy in front, finishing off a quick break in which right-winger Biavati raced almost the length of the field. The neat Hungarians replied two minutes later, when Titkos rifled the ball in from a narrow angle.

Italy soon exerted their control over midfield, however, and began to take advantage of the weak right flank of the Hungarian defence. Piola put them ahead again, and Colaussi gave them a 3–1 half-time lead. An opportunist goal from Sarosi unexpectedly put Hungary back into the game after 65 minutes. But the Italians re-exerted their superiority, and with 10 minutes left finished off their opponents with a flourish — a back-heel from Biavati arrowed home by the triumphant Piola.

No one could deny that Italy were worthy winners. They were better than the 1934 champions, of whom only Meazza and Ferrari remained. More organized and more direct, they were a credit to Vittorio Pozzo, who had rebuilt the side in the intervening years. Of the others, the Brazilians had shown some quite remarkable ball skills, but poor organization and a brittle temperament let them down. It was a great shame there were no British representatives in this increasingly exciting tournament. And with war clouds threatening over Europe, it would be a long time before the fathers of soccer would test themselves against the new rising powers of the game.

Lambs devour Wolves

IT WAS LIKE lambs to the slaughter, Pompey taking on the Wolves at Wembley in the FA Cup final — or so the pundits would have it. Wolves, second in the League, had stormed through to the final with a 19–3 goal record. They had beaten the new League champions Everton 2–0 in the quarter-finals and thrashed them 7–0 in a League match. At 5–1 on, they were the biggest favourites in years.

But Portsmouth, having just fought clear of the First Division relegation zone, had other ideas, and they had their secret weapon — manager Jack Tinn's lucky spats. Whether or not the ritual that veteran outside-right Freddie Worrall went through of buckling the famous white spats on his manager's feet (left one first!) before the game had anything to do with boosting their confidence, Portsmouth came out at Wembley and caned the Wolves 4–1. Once inside-left Bert Barlow — a Wolves player only two months ago — had given them the lead on the half-hour, there was only one team in it.

FOOTBALL FOCUS

- Aided and abetted by an unplayable Stanley Matthews and an unselfish Tommy Lawton, inside-right Willie Hall of Spurs equalled England's scoring record with five goals against Northern Ireland on 16 November at Maine Road.
- The Rangers-Celtic match at Ibrox on 2 January drew a record League crowd of 118,567.

FINAL SCORE

Football League
Division 1: Everton
Top scorer: Tommy Lawton (Everton) 35
Division 2: Blackburn Rovers
Division 3S: Newport County
Division 3N: Barnsley

FA Cup Final

Portsmouth	4	Wolves	1

Scottish League
Division 1: Rangers
Top scorer: Alec Venters (Rangers) 34
Division 2: Cowdenbeath

Scottish FA Cup Final

Clyde	4	Motherwell	0

International Championship
England, Scotland, Wales, 4 pts

England hold world champs despite fisted goal

THE MATCH was billed as "The Masters of Association Football versus the World Cup-holders", and it lived up to its advance publicity. England took on Italy in Milan on 14 May, and although any misgivings that England might have had that this would be another Battle of Highbury were soon dispelled, the fists of the Italians featured prominently in the drama.

The incident that will be remembered above all else was Italy's second goal. Young Lawton had headed England into a first-half lead, which the speedy winger Biavati cancelled out soon after the interval. Centre-forward Piola then took centre-stage, fisting the ball into England's goal from five yards out as he fell. Everyone in the 70,000 crowd saw it, and most of them were laughing. The players saw it. The Italian Crown Prince and FA secretary Stanley Rous saw it from the Royal Box. But German referee Dr Bauwens apparently did not see it. After consulting his linesman when England protested, he still awarded a goal. Even the "scorer" looked suitably embarrassed, and Mr Rous diplomatically refused the Crown Prince's request that they go down and jointly explain to the referee that the goal was illegal!

The England players got on with the game. Joe Mercer was magnificent in midfield. The forwards threw everything at Italy's goal, and the Italians brought everyone back to protect it. England rained in shot after shot. One goalbound effort was certainly fisted out by the left-back, others were handled, too, and the ball crossed the line more than once. Dr Bauwens finally had to give a goal when Willie Hall crashed the ball into the net.

The England players had arrived prepared for the worst, but came away at the end proud to have taken part in what had been a sporting and hard-fought draw — despite the curious decisions of an idiosyncratic referee.

Willie Hall, five-goal hero against Ireland, equalized in Milan.

Bryn Jones, Arsenal's record-breaking buy.

'Moneybags' splashes out again to sign Bryn Jones

ARSENAL MANAGER George Allison unscrewed his fountain pen on 4 August and signed a cheque for £14,000 to secure Welsh international inside-forward Bryn Jones from Wolves. When Arsenal want something, they usually get it. But "Moneybags" Allison had to smash the transfer record to obtain what he hopes will be a replacement for schemer-in-chief Alex James.

It is 10 years since Allison witnessed his predecessor as Highbury manager, Herbert Chapman, break the old record by paying Bolton nearly £11,000 for David Jack, and he later acquired James from Preston for £9,000. If Jones achieves half the success of either of those two marvellous inside-forwards, it will again be money well spent.

Jones, who is 25, is not much taller than James, but a clever player and a strong character, something of a late developer. He had trials with Southend and Swansea, and played in Ireland, for Glenavon, before joining Aberaman, where Wolves discovered him.

Heroes of the Thirties

THE THIRTIES were a glamorous decade for football — high attendances, high-scoring teams and, outside the United Kingdom, three World Cups.

On either side of the border, Dixie Dean of Everton and Jimmy McGrory of Celtic were still operating at the highest level. Dean's international career was almost over at the start of the thirties (18 goals in 16 games), McGrory's short one (six in seven) just beginning. But they both accumulated huge aggregates in domestic football. Dean broke Bloomer's all-time Football League record (352) in 1936 and went on to total 379 in 437 matches. McGrory amassed 410 goals in 408 matches, the only British goalscorer to average more than a goal a game.

Spoilt for choice

It might appear strange that the international careers of these thirties idols were comparatively short. But there were so many wonderful centre-forwards around, especially in England. Middlesbrough's George Camsell played only nine internationals, scoring in every one — 18 goals in all. Other fine leaders enjoyed even fewer appearances: long-striding opportunist Pongo Waring of Aston Villa (five caps/four goals); Freddy Tilson (four/six) of Manchester City, quick thinker with an elusive body-swerve; fearless, swashbuckling Ted Drake (five/six) of Arsenal; Fred Steele (six/eight), who set several scoring records for Stoke. "Ten goal" Joe Payne of Luton scored twice in his sole international, against Finland. Joe Bambrick of Linfield and Chelsea scored 12 goals in 11 games for Northern Ireland, six of them in one match.

The careers of those fine inside-forwards of the twenties, David Jack and Billy Walker, spilled well into the thirties. Later, Spurs' Willie Hall, considered to be one of the most complete inside-forwards in the game, scored nine in 10 games for England, including five in a memorable match against Ireland. Tommy Walker (Hearts) was a fixture at inside-right for Scotland from the mid-thirties, and scored some important goals.

Arsenal's Alex James is away, leaving three of Manchester City's defenders gasping at his wizardry.

The supreme artist

But perhaps the most famous player of the thirties was another Scottish inside-forward, who made but a handful of appearances for his country — Alex James of the baggy pants and shuffling gait. Herbert Chapman transformed him from the goalscorer of Preston and "Wembley Wizards" fame into arguably the greatest scheming inside-forward of all time, the maestro who made Arsenal tick. Not only was he the supreme artist, but he had the gift to spark the genius in others. Whenever he got the ball, a thrill of expectation surged through the crowd, waiting in awe to see how this Chaplinesque figure would accomplish his next piece of magic.

On England's right wing for much of the thirties was another goalscorer, the fast and direct Sammy Crooks of Derby, until he could no longer keep out Stoke City's young Stanley Matthews, an entirely different kind of winger, with unsurpassed ball control and crossing ability that centre-forwards dream about. Derby had another fast-raiding man on the left, Dally Duncan, who took over for Scotland when Alan Morton's record international career finally ended.

Young England and Stoke right-winger Stanley Matthews.

Rangers were to Scotland in the thirties what Arsenal were to England, only more so. They had many heroes as well as Morton, notably Bob McPhail, a prolific goalscoring inside-left, Jimmy Simpson, Scotland's first stopper centre-half, and the cultured George Brown at left-half. On the other side for Scotland was Alex Massie of Hearts and Aston Villa, converted from a moderate forward into a scintillating right-half.

Alf Strange of Sheffield Wednesday took a similar route, blossoming from centre-forward to a fine wing-half for England in the early thirties. Behind him was a solid England defence, with Harry Hibbs (Birmingham) in goal, Tom Cooper (Derby) or Roy Goodall (Huddersfield) at right-back paired with Wednesday's Ernie Blenkinsop on the left, before Arsenal's Male and Hapgood took over.

Long live the King

In the latter thirties were players whose careers were to be curtailed or at best interrupted by the war, notably two wonderful ball-playing inside-forwards who could also score goals, Peter Doherty of Blackpool, Manchester City and Northern Ireland, and Raich Carter of Sunderland and England. Still in his teens, but already twice the League's leading scorer, Tommy Lawton looked like doing the impossible — filling the shoes of the legendary Dixie Dean for Everton and England. The King is dead; long live the King.

World War II (1939–45)

IT WAS 2 SEPTEMBER 1939. With German armies marching all over Europe and now the sudden Nazi invasion of Poland, Britain was teetering on the edge of war. Nevertheless, the football season had started, and in England the teams had just completed the third round of League matches. The Sunday papers next day printed the first set of League tables.

Blackpool were sitting on top of Division One, the only side with maximum points. Just below them were Arsenal, 5–2 victors over Sunderland at Highbury, with Ted Drake scoring four. Tommy Lawton scored two for champions Everton in their draw at Blackburn. It looked like being another exciting season. But there would be no more League football for seven years. Hardly had the Sunday papers hit the door-mat than Britain declared war on Germany. All sport came to a temporary halt. But it was not long before regional football leagues and cups were organized in both England and Scotland and, as in the First World War, clubs were permitted to field "guest" players who were stationed locally. This ruling kept the game going during the hostilities, although it was often abused.

One club who gained particular benefit from guest players was Third Division Aldershot. As the traditional home of the British Army, they enjoyed the services at various times of most of the leading internationals.

The England half-back line — Britton, Cullis, Mercer — often turned out for Aldershot.

Maine Road massacre

ENGLAND thrashed Scotland 8–0 at Maine Road, Manchester, on 16 October 1943, emphasizing their wartime superiority over the Scots. This was their sixth win against Scotland's two in the 10 unofficial internationals played so far.

England were irresistible. With a forward line that read Matthews, Carter, Lawton, Hagan, Denis Compton, backed up by a half-back line of Britton, Cullis and Mercer, they tore the unfortunate Scottish defence to shreds. Tommy Lawton scored four, including a first-half hat-trick in 10 minutes. One of his goals was hooked in while sitting on the ground with his back to the net.

Stanley Matthews tormented Scotland's left flank throughout the match, laying on goal after goal. He capped a wonderful display and brought the house down — a capacity 60,000 — when near the end he dribbled in and out of the bemused Scottish defence on a run from the halfway line and rounded the keeper to score the last goal. Even the Scottish fans generously joined in the applause.

England's Tommy Lawton climbs above the Scottish defence.

Barriers collapse at Burnden Park — 33 crushed to death, hundreds more hurt

A TERRIBLE TRAGEDY occurred at Burnden Park on 9 March 1946, as the sixth-round FA Cup tie between Bolton and Stoke got under way. It was the second leg, the ties of this first post-war Cup being played on a home-and-away basis, and Bolton had won the first leg 2–0.

A huge crowd passed through the turnstiles to see, among others, Stoke's Stanley Matthews. The gates were closed, with some 65,000 having paid, but another 20,000 were milling around outside and many managed to force their way in. Suddenly, two crash-barriers collapsed under sheer weight of numbers. The result was horrific. Spectators piled on top of each other, and many were trodden underfoot.

The match kicked off as casualties were being attended to, but as soon as it was known that there were fatalities, the referee called the players off the pitch. The police recommended the resumption of play to avoid panic, as most of the crowd were unaware of the disaster. The match continued, without an interval or any score. The death list totalled 33, and more than 500 spectators were injured.

FOOTBALL FOCUS

- On Christmas morning 1940, Brighton travelled to Norwich with only five players, hoping to recruit more on the way — not so unusual in wartime. They made up their team with some Norwich reserves and soldiers from the crowd of 1,419, but were beaten 18–0.
- Arsenal's pre-war reserve back Leslie Compton played two seasons at centre-forward during the war, scoring 76 goals in 70 regional league and cup games, including 10 against Clapton Orient on 8 February 1941, when his brother Denis also scored two in Arsenal's 15–2 win.
- England agreed to let Stan Mortensen, their 12th man, go on as substitute for Wales in the second half of their match at Wembley on 25 September 1943 for the injured Ivor Powell, as Wales had no spare players. It made little difference — England won 8–3.
- The 1946 FA Cup was played on a two-legged home-and-away basis before the semi-final stage. Bradford PA lost their fourth-round home leg 3–1 to Manchester City and then proceeded to win 8–2 at Maine Road.
- Aberdeen beat Rangers 3–2 on 11 April 1946 in the final of the Scottish Southern League Cup, the forerunner of the League Cup.

The Moscow mysteries leave British soccer agog

IN AND OUT in just over two weeks, those marvellous men from Moscow took Britain by storm. With names like Stankevitch, Blinkov, Archangelski and Bobrov, Moscow Dynamo arrived in Britain in mid-November 1945 for a four-match tour. Nobody knew anything about them before they came, and we know little more now that they've gone — except that they certainly can play football.

Before they agreed to the tour, Moscow presented the FA with a dozen or more conditions, including the use of substitutes and that their own referee would be allowed to take at least one match. They also expressed the desire to play Arsenal. While the Dynamo and embassy officials of our recent wartime allies seemed intent on making propaganda out of the tour, the players proceeded to give spectacular demonstrations of teamwork.

Their first match, against Chelsea, was a lock-out. Nearly 85,000 people crammed into Stamford Bridge, overflowing on to the dog track. The Dynamo team, all in blue, came out 15 minutes before the start to practise, and when they later emerged with Chelsea, each man carried a bouquet of flowers for his opposite number. Despite this embarrassment, Chelsea, playing in red, took a 2–0 half-time lead. But the Dynamos, fast and physically fit, showed what they were capable of after the interval and held their hosts to a 3–3 draw.

The Dynamo players come out at Stamford Bridge with flowers for their opponents.

The next match was at Ninian Park, against a Cardiff City team composed mainly of working men who came straight from their jobs — some in the pits — to play. They were no match for the rampant Russians, who trounced them 10–1.

Next came a controversial match with Arsenal, who were still playing at White Hart Lane because Highbury had been converted into an Air Raid Patrol Centre during the war. A reluctant Arsenal, with most of their leading players still abroad, needed to draft in six guests, including Matthews and Mortensen, and the Russians objected strongly. However, they had their own referee, the match was played in dense fog, and they somehow managed to convert a 3–1 deficit into a 4–3 victory. The game ended in complete farce — the referee disallowed a goal by Ronnie Rooke (a guest from Fulham), tried to send Arsenal's George Drury off, and allowed Dynamo to play for a time with 12 men!

Even so, the Arsenal team, among the few who could see what was going on, were impressed with Dynamo's first-time passing and the way they all ran into position. The goalkeeper, "Tiger" Khomich, made some remarkable saves to inspire his team's recovery. And the Russians gave a last exhibition of their skills at Ibrox Park, where 90,000 saw them hold Rangers to a 2–2 draw. Then they went home — to be made "Heroes of the Soviet Union".

A close thing at Ibrox in Dynamo's last match.

FINAL SCORE

League Cup

1939–40	West Ham United
1940–41	Preston North End
1941–42	Wolverhampton Wanderers
1942–43	Blackpool (North)
	Arsenal (South)
1943–44	Aston Villa (North)
	Charlton Athletic (South)
1944–45	Bolton Wanderers (North)
	Chelsea (South)

Regional Leagues

1941–42	Blackpool (North)
	Arsenal (London)
1942–43	Blackpool (North)
	Arsenal (South)
1943–44	Blackpool (North)
	Tottenham Hotspur (South)
1944–45	Huddersfield Town (North)
	Tottenham Hotspur (South)
1945–46	Sheffield United (North)
	Birmingham City (South)

FA Cup Final 1946

Derby County 4 Charlton Athletic 1
(after extra time)

Scottish Regional Leagues

1939–40 Rangers (S/W) 2 Falkirk (N/E) 1
Southern: 1940–45 Rangers
Southern League "A": 1945–46 Rangers

Scottish Southern League Cup

1940–43,1945	Rangers
1944	Hibernian
1946	Aberdeen

Two for Stamps' collection after ball bursts

WITH THEIR RECENTLY purchased inside-forwards, Peter Doherty and Raich Carter, two of the finest in the United Kingdom, it is perhaps surprising that Derby needed extra time to beat Charlton in the first FA Cup final since the war. In a thrilling match of end-to-end football, the talking points will be Bert Turner's own goal to put Derby ahead near the end, and then his equalizer in the next minute from a free-kick that was deflected into the net. Jack Stamps might have won it for Derby, but the ball burst as he shot, and Bartram held it easily.

In a whirlwind extra-time finish, however, Derby's class told, and they hammered three goals without reply. It was a triumph for Stamps, who had been injured in the war at Dunkirk and told that he would never play again. He broke away from the restart, and sent over a perfect cross for Doherty to restore Derby's lead. The centre-forward then scored two more to make sure of Derby's first major honour after 58 years of effort.

Debut boy hits six in record Newcastle win

OCTOBER the 3rd was a special day for inside-forward Len Shackleton. He was making his debut for Newcastle United, having just been transferred from Bradford PA for £13,000, a record sum for a Second Division club. If he was nervous, he didn't show it, and by the end of the game he had put six goals past the unfortunate Charlie Turner in Newport's goal. And what a day it was for Newcastle, too. They amassed 13 goals, a Second Division record and equalling the League best.

It did not start out like being Newcastle's day. There were 52,000 fans at St James's Park, and they groaned when Charlie Wayman missed a penalty after just two minutes. But the centre-forward soon made amends and opened the scoring three minutes later. Shackleton opened his account in the seventh minute, and the pair of them proceeded to run Newport ragged. Wayman scored four, Jackie Milburn chipped in with a couple from the right wing, and inside-right Roy Bentley got into the act with one. But for a fine performance by Turner and several near misses, the score could have been in the region of 20.

Len Shackleton (right), a scorer six times on his record debut for Newcastle.

Duffy breaks deadlock and Charlton win the Cup

THE 1947 FA Cup final at Wembley will be remembered for the winning goal, six minutes from the end of extra time, if for nothing else. The dreadful prospect of a replay was beginning to look a certainty when Chris Duffy's spectacular volley hit the back of Burnley's net to break a boring deadlock such as Wembley had probably never witnessed before.

The final was representative of this first post-war League campaign — long, dominated by defence, and short on goalmouth action. But what a contrast this sweltering day was to the big freeze-up responsible for extending the League season until June, and playing such havoc with the earlier rounds of the Cup.

The only incident of note in the first half was when the ball burst — for the second final running, a million to one chance. Midway through the second half, Harry Potts hit the Charlton bar in a rare Burnley attack. But the game went into extra time in a strange atmosphere, the players wilting in the heat and the crowd subdued.

With the first Cup final replay since 1912 now very much on the cards, Charlton suddenly struck. Centre-forward Bill Robinson picked up a pass on the right and pulled the ball back into the centre. Don Welsh went up for the ball, but it merely grazed off the top of his balding head, dropping on to Duffy's boot. The scorer's reaction was an equally spectacular gallop down the field, pursued by his colleagues, before they caught him in a mass embrace.

Duffy, arms upraised, sees his volley win the cup for the first time in Charlton's history.

FOOTBALL FOCUS

- Newport conceded 133 goals in Division Two and were relegated, but they had their revenge on Newcastle, who finished fifth, beating them 4–2 in the return game in June.
- In winning Division Three (N), Doncaster Rovers set four League records: most points 72, wins 33, away points 37, away wins 18. They equalled the fewest defeats (three) for the division, and had the League top scorer, Clarrie Jordan (42).
- At the end of a long, protracted season, Stoke went to Bramall Lane on 14 June and lost 2–1 to Sheffield United, handing the League title to Liverpool and finishing fourth themselves to equal their best ever position.

SOCCER SOUNDBITES

"What if I was off form? What if my colleagues did not fit in with me or I with them? What if I muffed chances and things went wrong?"

LEN SHACKLETON'S
thoughts before he scored six of Newcastle's 13 on his debut.

"It seemed as though we could see into each other's minds."

TOM FINNEY,
on England's 10–0 defeat of Portugal.

England run wild in Portugal

ENGLAND finished their two-match end-of-season tour on a high note in Lisbon, thrashing Portugal 10–0. The Portuguese, encouraged by England's 1–0 defeat in Switzerland, felt they had a chance. They did everything they could to put England out of their stride. They changed the ball, they changed their captain and they changed their goalkeeper. But nothing short of changing the England forward line would have made any difference.

Last-minute injuries had forced England to reshuffle their side, and Blackpool's Stan Mortensen won his first full cap, partnering his new club-mate, Stanley Matthews, recently transferred for £11,500, on the right. With left-winger Bobby Langton out, the selectors decided to try Tom Finney there, to partner Mannion, thus, at a stroke, solving the long Matthews-Finney debate of which one to play.

The start was held up because of a dispute about the ball, Portugal wanting to use their smaller one. England team manager Walter Winterbottom won the argument, but England's ball lasted only 20 seconds, the time taken for Lawton to head it into the Portuguese net. After that, the smaller one mysteriously appeared.

It made not the slightest bit of difference. England ran riot. Finney was fantastic; there is no other word for it. He turned Portugal's captain and right-back Cardoza inside-out, to the extent that Cardoza's manager persuaded him to feign injury so that he could be substituted. And after the hapless Azevedo, jeered by his own crowd, had fished the ball out of the net for the fifth time — including an oblique shot from Finney after an electrifying run from half-way that brought the house down — he, too, was replaced, without even bothering to simulate damage.

Again it failed to stem the tide of England's attack. Lawton and Mortensen scored four each, and Matthews, not wishing to be left out, allowed himself the luxury of a solo goal to round off the bloodless massacre.

Tom Finney, torturer-in-chief of the Portuguese.

Britain trounce Rest of Europe 6–1

Mannion (second left) scores Britain's first goal as keeper Da Rui dives in vain.

A COMBINED Great Britain side celebrated the post-war return of the four home countries to FIFA by giving a Rest of Europe XI a lesson in football at Hampden Park. Despite a long, hard season, which is set to continue for another month in England because of the winter freeze-up, the British side outplayed the cream of Europe to the tune of six goals to one.

Wilf Mannion, aided and abetted by his England wing partner Stanley Matthews, was outstanding for Britain, and scored three goals. Tommy Lawton scored two, and Billy Steel — who had played only 10 Scottish League games at the time of his selection — cracked in a raking drive from 35 yards. The 135,000 crowd were treated to an exhibition match, hard-fought but without a single intentional foul. It lived up to its billing as the "Match of the Century", although allowances had to be made for the European team, drawn from nine countries and comprising players with little knowledge of their colleagues. Captain Johnny Carey of Manchester United was the only one with English as his native language. Teams:

Great Britain: Swift, Hardwick (E), Hughes (W), Macaulay (S), Vernon (NI), Burgess (W), Matthews, Mannion, Lawton (E), Steel, Liddell (S)

Rest of Europe: Da Rui (Fr), Peterson (Den), Steffen (Switz), Carey (Eire), Parola (It), Ludl (Cz), Lambrechts (Bel), Gren, Nordahl (Swed), Wilkes (Neth), Praest (Den)

FINAL SCORE

Football League
Division 1: Liverpool
Top scorer: Dennis Westcott (Wolves) 37
Division 2: Manchester City
Division 3S: Cardiff City
Division 3N: Doncaster Rovers

FA Cup Final

Charlton Athletic	1	Burnley	0

(after extra time)

Scottish League
Division A: Rangers
Top scorer: Bobby Mitchell (Third Lanark) 22
Division B: Dundee

Scottish FA Cup Final

Aberdeen	2	Hibernian	1

Scottish League Cup Final

Rangers	4	Aberdeen	0

International Championship
England, 5 pts

Victory at Wolves — now Liverpool must wait

IN A STORMING finish to their League programme, Liverpool have beaten Division One leaders Wolves 2–1 at sunbaked Molineux to take over at the top, and now they must wait to see how Stoke fare in their last match. Because of the fixture pile-up due to the winter freeze-up, Liverpool found themselves playing their last four games away. They dropped only one point. Indeed, they have won seven and drawn one of their last eight matches to make a marvellous bid for the Championship.

Jack Balmer, who has been with Liverpool since 1935, opened the scoring in the match at Molineux, and Albert Stubbins, their £13,000 early season buy from Newcastle who scored 244 goals in wartime football, put them two up before half-time, joining Balmer as the Anfielf outfit's joint leading scorer on 24 League goals for the season.

Wolves managed to pull one back after the interval, but Liverpool held out to take the two points that put them on top with 57. Stoke City are currently situated two points behind Liverpool in the table with a better goal average. They must beat Sheffield United at Bramall Lane on 14 June if they are to win their first League Championship. It is a long, nerve-wracking time for Liverpool to wait.

Lawton in shock record transfer to Third Division Notts County

AFTER ONLY ONE full season at Chelsea, Tommy Lawton has been the subject of a sensational transfer to Notts County. The Third Division side paid £20,000 for the unsettled England leader, £5,000 more than the previous record, and they had to throw in wing-half Bill Dickson for good measure. Lawton, with 20 goals in 19 games for England (as well as 25 in 23 wartime internationals), leaves after a protracted dispute with Chelsea. A part-time job goes with his new contract, but at 28 years old, it is a tragedy that Lawton's supreme talents are now lost to first-class League football, and his international career must surely be in some considerable jeopardy.

Tommy Lawton makes his debut for Notts County.

Classic Cup final goes United's way

IF EVER A team deserved to win the Cup it was Manchester United. Their epic 6–4 victory at Villa Park in the third round set the ball rolling. All five of their opponents on the way to Wembley were First Division sides, United scoring 18 goals to six. But Blackpool were no slouches, 18 goals and only one conceded, and that in their heart-stopping semi-final at Villa Park with Spurs, when Mortensen equalized with four minutes to go and completed his hat-trick in extra time.

When two great attacking sides play to their form to a man, and some above it, you have a classic. The Manchester forward line — Delaney, Morris, Rowley, Pearson, Mitten — were brilliant. For Blackpool, Matthews, the first Footballer of the Year, was his scintillating self until United cut off his supply of passes in the second half. Mortensen was ever-dangerous with his electric speed, while right-half and captain Johnston worked furiously in defence.

The first drama occurred with 12 minutes gone, when Mortensen went racing through on goal and was brought down from behind by Chilton. Was it a penalty? It looked outside the box. But if the referee's decision was not right, it was certainly just, and Shimwell scored from the spot. It took United 16 minutes to equalize, when Rowley made the most of a mix-up in the Blackpool defence. But Mortensen restored their lead just before half-time with a typically opportunist goal.

Manchester began to take charge after the interval, but there were only 21 minutes left when Rowley equalized again with a spectacular diving header. The turning point came 10 minutes later. Mortensen broke through again and smashed a shot at goal which Crompton brilliantly held. He cleared the ball to right-half Anderson, who transferred it to Pearson, and the inside-left ran on to crack a low 25-yarder in off a post. Three minutes later, Anderson hit a speculative shot from way out, which curled into the net off a Blackpool defender. That was the end of a great Cup final.

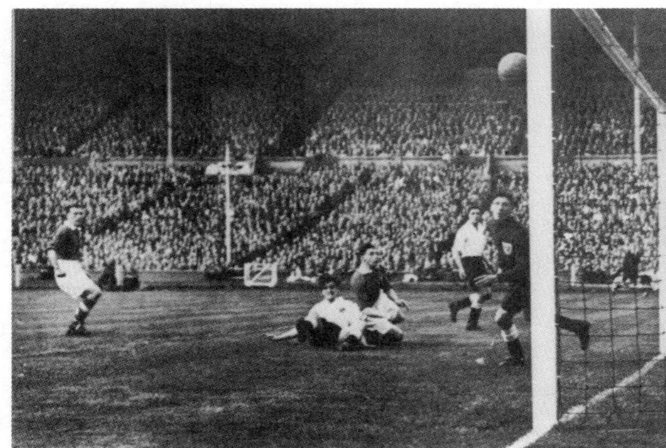

Rowley (dark shirt, on ground) heads Manchester United's second equalizer.

FOOTBALL FOCUS

- A Football League record crowd on 17 January of 83,260 saw Manchester United draw 1–1 with Arsenal at Maine Road (United's temporary post-war home).
- On 27 March, a British record gate for a non-final club game of 143,570 saw Rangers beat Hibs 1–0 in a Cup semi-final at Hampden Park. A record midweek gate of 133,570 saw the replayed final on 21 April, when Ragers defeated Morton 1–0.
- Stan Mortensen scored in every round of the Cup for Blackpool, 10 goals in all.
- Arsenal led the First Division from start to finish, winning their sixth title in 11 seasons to equal the total of Aston Villa and Sunderland. They conceded only 32 goals, a record for Division One, and over two million people saw their games.
- Newcastle sold Len Shackleton to Sunderland for a record £20,050 in February, but still won promotion without him.

Aston Villa just fail in a thriller

HERE WAS a match worthy of a final, this third-round tie in front of 65,000 half-drenched spectators at a muddy Villa Park. In 14 seconds, the crowd were on their feet as keeper Crompton became the first United player to touch the ball when he picked it out of the net. It had been put there by right-winger Edwards — what a start for Villa. Who'd have thought they would be 5–1 down by half-time!

Inspired by their captain Johnny Carey, United's forwards proceeded to play some of the most breathtaking football ever seen at Villa Park. Within six minutes they were level, through Rowley, and Morris (two), Pearson and Delaney also scored before the interval.

Unbowed, Villa came back out better equipped than United in the strength-sapping mud. Gradually they clawed their way back to 4–5 with nine minutes to go. The menacing Ford hit the bar for Villa. Could United hold out? They did so in the only way they know — by attacking. They won a corner. Mitten took it and Pearson shot the ball home — 6–4. What a game!

Magnificent Matthews

STANLEY MATTHEWS played possibly his greatest game as England continued where they left off last season with an impressive win on the Continent. This time it was in Brussels, and their 5–2 victory over Belgium was down to the Blackpool wing wizard.

Matthews made every goal. England were ahead in 15 seconds as he put a cross right on Tommy Lawton's head. Another pinpoint centre, a Lawton deflection, and Mortensen was through. Then Matthews was fouled, took the kick himself, and this time Finney headed in to put England 3–0 up in 20 minutes.

Belgium came back strongly with two goals, and with the 70,000 crowd behind them, they looked like completing their revival — until Matthews took charge again. Picking the ball up at half-way, he beat tackle after tackle as he made his way to the byline, and then chipped the ball over the keeper for Finney to walk it into the empty net.

He wasn't quite finished. The only way to stop him was to foul him. But then he put another free-kick on Lawton's head for the last goal. It was sheer, unadulterated magic.

England draw shroud over Turin

MANY HAVE been England's famous victories down the years, over the Scots and against increasingly stronger Continental opposition. But they reached new heights on 15 May 1948, when they beat the rampant, arrogant Italians 4–0 in Turin.

It needed one of the most memorable goals in England's history to set them on their way and silence the frenzy of the 85,000 Latin crowd in the sweltering heat of the Comunale Stadium. The Italians, fresh from special training in a mountain retreat and wins against Czechoslovakia and France, made a confident start. Then, after four minutes, Matthews, dropping back, collected the ball from Wright. A feint and a jink wrong-footed two defenders, but instead of taking his usual route up the touchline he hit a left-footed pass inside the back for his Blackpool team-mate Mortensen to run on to. Taking the ball in his stride, Mortensen accelerated through the Italian defence towards the byline. Just outside the penalty box and only a few feet from the line, with an opponent moving in to tackle, he swivelled at speed and lanced in a shot that flashed past the startled keeper at the near post.

It was like a shot in the arm for the England side. But they needed all the brilliance of Frank Swift, the first keeper to captain England this century — as well as the fearless honesty of the Spanish referee Escartin, who disallowed two Italian efforts for offside — to stay ahead as Mazzola and company brought all their dazzling skills to bear. Then came another breakaway, the same as before, Matthews sending Mortensen away on the right. This time he pulled the ball back for Lawton to drive home. Half-time, and England were 2–0 ahead.

Both teams were wilting in the humidity, but the Italians came back strongly. Then Swift threw the ball out to Scott, who switched it to Wright, then on to Mannion and Lawton, for Finney to waltz it round the keeper. What a beautiful move, and it knocked the stuffing out of the Italians. Finally, Mortensen streaked away again and made another for Finney. That left them with a scoreline of Italy 0 England 4 — Turin was like a morgue that night.

FINAL SCORE

Football League
Division 1: Arsenal
Top scorer: Ronnie Rooke (Arsenal) 33
Division 2: Birmingham City
Division 3S: Queen's Park Rangers
Division 3N: Lincoln City
Footballer of the Year: Stanley Matthews (Blackpool)

FA Cup Final

Manchester United	4	Blackpool	2

Scottish League
Division A: Hibernian
Top scorer: Archie Aikman (Falkirk) 20
Division B: East Fife

Scottish FA Cup Final

Rangers	1	Morton	1
Replay: Rangers	1	Morton	0

Scottish League Cup Final

East Fife	0	Falkirk	0
Replay: East Fife	4	Falkirk	1

International Championship
England, 5 pts

Ronnie Rooke (Arsenal), League leading scorer.

Mortensen (on ground, left) scores from a seemingly impossible impossible angle.

Sunderland slope off after Yeovil defeat

GIANT-KILLERS Yeovil from the Southern League have done it again. Mighty Sunderland came down from the North-East to play on their infamous slope in Somerset, and went back home again with their tails between their legs. It was Second Division Bury in the third round, and now they have a First Division scalp.

Nobody really gave the non-Leaguers a chance. When Yeovil's keeper was hurt in training, and had to be replaced by 23-year-old solicitor's clerk Dickie Dyke, with only one senior outing under his belt, it became a question of how many Shackleton and company would score. The odds lengthened further against Yeovil when winger Hargreaves pulled a muscle after 10 minutes and became a passenger.

The only Yeovil player with any League experience was their captain and player-manager Alec Stock, 30, who had played for Charlton and QPR before the war. And it was he who put the skids under Sunderland after 26 minutes, cracking in a flick-on from the edge of the box — his first goal of the season.

Robinson equalized for Sunderland after an hour, after Dyke, who had an heroic game, made his only mistake of the match and dropped the ball at the forward's feet.

As fog began to swirl around, the game went to extra time, with the fighters of Yeovil still on top. The 17,000 spectators packed into the ground, hundreds of them on beer crates set up as extra seating, and hundreds more outside listening on police car radios, could feel in the atmosphere that something momentous was about to happen. Sure enough, Yeovil took the lead again just before the turnround. Eric Bryant finished off a slick four-man move and sent a low shot past the Sunderland keeper from 15 yards.

Now Sunderland were stung into attack. The Yeovil defenders hacked the ball away, anywhere they could. The referee blew for a free-kick just outside their box, and the crowd invaded the pitch, thinking it was over. They had to be cleared before Sunderland could take the kick. They made a mess of it. Now it was all over, and the party could begin.

SOCCER SOUNDBITES

"Player–managership is violent exercise on top of a pile of worries."

ALEC STOCK,
player-manager of giant-killers Yeovil.

Stand-in keeper Dyke clears once again on the greatest day in Yeovil's history.

'No-star' Portsmouth's championship at last

UNFASHIONABLE Portsmouth, never before better than fourth in Division One and without a single international in their side, won the League title in their jubilee year. It has been a fine team performance, and they proved unbeatable at Fratton Park, where they won 18 games and drew the other three.

They led the table for most of the season, and a remarkable 5-0 victory at St James's Park over nearest rivals Newcastle in early April put them well clear. They looked on course for the "double" before suffering a shock defeat in the Cup semi-finals by lowly Second Division side Leicester, who won 3–1 at Highbury. But they clinched the title with three games to spare, and finished on 58 points, five ahead of Manchester United, second for the third season in a row, and Derby.

Reg Flewin, Portsmouth captain.

Treble chance comes off for Rangers

THERE WASN'T much left for Glasgow Rangers to do, and now they've done it. They have completed the Scottish "treble" — League, Cup and League Cup. Their 4–1 defeat of Clyde last Saturday in the Cup final was merely the end of a veritable stroll through the tournament. Their League Cup success did not come so readily, especially in the group stage, when they recovered from a bad start to qualify for the last eight at the expense of Celtic. And Division B champions Raith gave them a run for their money in the final in March, before going down 2–0.

The League proved their toughest hurdle, and in the end it was out of their hands. Two days after the Cup final they won 1–0 at Morton to lead Dundee by a point. But on Wednesday Dundee leapfrogged back to the top with their game in hand, and it was all down to the last Saturday. Rangers went to Coatbridge and beat Albion Rovers 4–1, Willie Thornton scoring a hat-trick. They could do no more. Poor Dundee, however, lost 4–1 at Falkirk, and the Championship — and the "treble" — went to Rangers.

FOOTBALL FOCUS

- Giant-killers Yeovil, without home advantage, crashed to Manchester United 8–0 (Jack Rowley 5) at Maine Road in the fifth round of the Cup, and were cheered to the echo by the 81,565 crowd.
- Derby paid a record £25,000 for Manchester United inside-forward Johnny Morris in March.
- Cup-finalists Leicester needed three points from their last three games to stay in Division Two, and then one point from their last match, at Cardiff: they drew 1–1, condemning Nottingham Forest to the drop.

England fall to Scottish Steel at Wembley

ENGLAND, with only one defeat in 18 post-war internationals, were shocked at Wembley by a Scottish side given little hope after the 3–0 defeat the Scottish League suffered at Ibrox last month at the hands of the Football League. England, on paper, looked stronger, while the Scots chose only two players from the Inter-League game.

Two of the Scottish heroes were keeper Jimmy Cowan and forward Billy Steel. Cowan, of Morton, recently recovered from a broken arm that threatened to end his career, kept England at bay with some marvellous saves in the first 20 minutes, when England were on top. Then Jim Mason (Third Lanark) broke away to score with a shot that went in off the foot of a post.

Steel (Derby), Scotland's fireball of an inside-left and the only "Anglo" in the side, put Scotland two up on 50 minutes after a fine move, and the cultured Hibernian Lawrie Reilly clinched it before Newcastle's new cap, Jackie Milburn, scored a consolation goal for England.

Steel (left) scores the second goal for Scotland with goalkeeper Swift helpless.

FINAL SCORE

Football League
Division 1: Portsmouth
Top scorer: Willie Moir (Bolton Wanderers) 25
Division 2: Fulham
Division 3S: Swansea Town
Division 3N: Hull
Footballer of the Year: Johnny Carey (Manchester United)

FA Cup Final

Wolves	3	Leicester City	1

Scottish League
Division A: Rangers
Top scorer: Alec Stott (Dundee) 30
Division B: Raith Rovers

Scottish FA Cup Final

Rangers	4	Clyde	1

Scottish League Cup Final

Rangers	2	Raith Rovers	0

International Championship
Scotland, 6 pts

Easy as Pye for Wolves in the end

LEICESTER CITY put up a brave show at Wembley, but in the end were no match for Wolves. The lowly Second Division side sorely missed the inspiration of the sick Don Revie, their 21-year-old inside-right. But they gave Wolves a fright in the second half, halving their 2–0 lead and being desperately unlucky to have an equalizer disallowed for offside.

Wolves had appeared to be coasting to victory after Jesse Pye's two first-half goals, the first a header from a fine Johnny Hancocks cross, the second an opportunist prod-in. But two minutes after the interval, Leicester struck. Bert Williams parried a scorcher from Ken Chisholm, only for Mal Griffiths to hook the ball into the net.

Now Leicester were giving as good as they got, and it needed all of England captain Billy Wright's experience to keep them at bay. With 67 minutes gone, Chisholm put the ball in the net, but the referee gave him offside, a close call. A minute later, Sammy Smyth picked up the ball in midfield and carried it forward for 30 yards or more against the retreating Leicester defenders, evading their tackles before planting the ball past the advancing keeper. That knocked the stuffing out of Leicester, and Wright was soon collecting the Cup from Princess Elizabeth.

Pye heads the ball past Bradley, Leicester's keeper, for the first goal.

Champions killed in air crash

THE CREAM of Italian football died in an air crash on 4 May, when the plane carrying the Torino team back from a game in Portugal hit a hillside at Superga, just outside Turin. The tragedy claimed the lives of 18 players, including the bulk of the Italian national side. Among the stars who died was Italy's captain Valentino Mazzola. In all, 31 people perished, including journalists, club officials and their English manager Leslie Lievesley.

The finest club team in the history of Italian football, Torino had won four consecutive League titles and were four points clear on the day of the crash. Their youth team completed their last four fixtures against the youth teams of their opponents, winning them all to earn a sad consolation for the grief-stricken club.

England Rio-bound, but Scotland won't go to World Cup as losers

THE SCOTLAND-ENGLAND match in April had more than national pride and the Home International Championship riding on it. An extra prize this time was qualification for the World Cup finals in the summer. In fact, with the British countries now eligible for their first World Cup, FIFA had generously offered them two places for the tournament, to be held in Brazil. But the stubborn, insular Scottish FA had announced that they would go only as champions.

With Wales and Northern Ireland already well beaten by both sides, the Hampden match was the decider. And Scotland, as holders, needed only a draw. The England experiment of playing Chelsea leader Roy Bentley as inside-left to Mortensen's centre-forward, creating a twin spearhead, paid off when an interchange between the two allowed Bentley to score midway through the second half. It turned out to be the winner, although a shot from Willie Bauld hit the underside of the bar and bounced down on England's line.

After the match, England captain Billy Wright begged his opposite number George Young to appeal to the Scottish FA, as the whole England side wanted Scotland to join them in Rio. But Young's pleas fell on deaf ears.

Bentley's goal puts England on the road to Rio.

Championship thriller as Pompey pip Wolves

THE FIRST Division Championship went down to the last day, with three teams still in the race. Last season's champions Portsmouth led with 51 points, on goal average from Wolves, who had started the season with six straight wins, and Sunderland were just a point behind.

In reality, Portsmouth needed only to win, so superior was their goal average. In the event, they beat Aston Villa 5–1. Wolves hammered bottom club Birmingham 6–1 to become only the second side to miss the title on goal average, and Sunderland beat Chelsea 4–1, but had to be content with third place. In the end, only six points separated the first nine clubs.

Big 'ead to the rescue

WITH ARSENAL a goal down in their pulsating Cup semi-final with Chelsea at White Hart Lane, and only five minutes to go, centre-half Leslie Compton ignored his captain's instructions and went up for a corner. Compton, known affectionately by the Highbury fans as "Big 'ead" for his dominance in the air as a stopper, arrived in the Chelsea goalmouth at the same time as his brother Denis's inswinger, and he headed it powerfully into the net.

That completed a dramatic comeback for Arsenal from two down, and earned them a replay.

Chelsea had surprised Arsenal in the first half with two beautifully taken goals from centre-forward Roy Bentley. Arsenal clawed one back somewhat luckily with the last kick of the half, when a corner from right-winger Freddie Cox, no stranger to White Hart Lane, swerved into goal at the near post. Time had then looked like running out for Arsenal until Compton took a hand. Captain Joe Mercer will have forgiven him for disobeying orders.

Leslie Compton is mobbed after his semi-final equalizer.

England in Carey Street

THE REPUBLIC of Ireland scored a shock win over England at Goodison Park on 21 September. Inspired and orchestrated by their captain Johnny Carey in their first ever international on English soil, they grew in confidence as the match progressed. Tommy Godwin played the game of his life in goal, Con Martin gave them a shock lead when he converted a penalty after 36 minutes, and as England began to fade they scored a second five minutes from time. It was England's first home defeat by a team outside the four home countries, although with nine of the Irish playing for English club sides, Carey and company could hardly be described as foreigners.

England, as usual, had started as strong favourites. Taking the opposition too lightly, perhaps, the selectors brought in three new caps: Derby's Bert Mozley at right-back and, in place of Matthews and Mortensen, Portsmouth's pacy winger Peter Harris and Jesse Pye of Wolves.

England attacked from the start, but Pye missed two easy chances before Mozley, making his debut on his 26th birthday, gave away the penalty. Bert Williams got a hand to Martin's fierce shot but could not prevent it from crossing his line.

With Carey containing Finney, Eire began to see more of the ball. As much as Billy Wright pushed England forward in the second half, Godwin, a carpenter and a part-timer with Shamrock Rovers, continued to foil England's forwards, and when England were caught square, Peter Farrell of Everton, playing for the away team on his home ground, lobbed the second goal.

Arsenal's 'capital' victory in Cup

ARSENAL have won the FA Cup without having to leave London. Drawn at home in the first four rounds, they progressed each time at the first attempt. The only replay they needed was in the semi-final against Chelsea, and both ties were played at White Hart Lane. Now they've beaten Liverpool 2–0 at Wembley.

Liverpool also had a local derby in their semi-final, beating Everton 2–0. Both Cup-finalists were high in the League, and indeed both had tilts at the title. Liverpool went unbeaten at the start for a record 19 games, but fell off the pace later. Arsenal, after a poor start, came within three points of leaders Liverpool before Christmas, but a 2–0 defeat at Anfield on New Year's Eve left them with just too much to do.

Nevertheless, at Wembley, Arsenal always had the edge. Their half-back line of the fiery dynamo Alex Forbes, the rock-like Leslie Compton and the inspirational Joe Mercer, Footballer of the Year, was outstanding. In inside-right Jimmy Logie they had the man of the match, and young centre-forward Peter Goring proved a handful for the Liverpool defence. It was Logie who produced the perfect through-pass for Reg Lewis to score after 18 minutes. Lewis, an ice-cool finisher, got a second on 63 minutes after a Denis Compton cross had been touched on by Cox.

With the rain pouring down, Liverpool made gallant efforts to come back, none more so than their star outside-left Billy Liddell. But they were denied even the goal they deserved by an excellent Arsenal defence, none of whom would see the right side of 30 again!

Joe Mercer (6) shows his delight as Reg Lewis (10) glides through for his first goal.

FINAL SCORE

Football League
Division 1: Portsmouth
Top scorer: Dickie Davis (Sunderland) 25
Division 2: Tottenham Hotspur
Division 3S: Notts County
Division 3N: Doncaster Rovers
Footballer of the Year: Joe Mercer (Arsenal)

FA Cup Final

Arsenal	2	Liverpool	0

Scottish League
Division A: Rangers
Top scorer: Willie Bauld (Hearts) 30
Division B: Morton

Scottish FA Cup Final

Rangers	3	East Fife	0

Scottish League Cup Final

East Fife	3	Dunfermline Ath	0

International Championship
England, 6 pts

Arsenal's captain Joe Mercer, Footballer of the Year.

FOOTBALL FOCUS

- Centre-half John Charles (Leeds United) became Wales's youngest international, at 18 years 71 days, when he played in the 0–0 draw against Northern Ireland at Wrexham on 8 March.
- Northern Ireland suffered two massive defeats in the Home International Championship, 8–2 by Scotland at Belfast in October, and 9–2 by England at Maine Road in November.
- Rangers completed their second hat-trick of Cup wins and won the championship, but did not manage another "treble", losing to East Fife in the semi-finals of the League Cup.

Fabulous Finney, but this England team won't do for Rio

MEMORIES OF their 10-goal triumph must have come flooding back to Wright, Finney, Mannion and Mortensen when the England team returned to Lisbon after three years. They won again, but this time their victory was not so convincing and does not bode well for the coming World Cup. Finney, with the help of two penalties, scored four of their five goals, but a leaky defence let in three. But for the impressive Williams in goal, it would have been more.

Finney put England ahead from the penalty spot after he had been brought down when right through, and Mortensen and Finney again put England 3–0 up at half-time. Any thoughts of another double-figure massacre were soon dispelled after the interval, when centre-forward Ben David pulled one back with a fine header. Finney restored England's three-goal margin with a gem of a goal, beating man after man before slamming the ball into the net for his hat-trick.

Portugal would not lie down, however, and pulled the score back to 3–4 as they dominated the game for 20 minutes. Thankfully, right-back Alf Ramsey kept calm and saw England out of further trouble. Finally, Finney cut through the Portuguese defence once more, was brought down, and scored from the spot again to clinch the game for England.

England humiliated

Brazil, the hosts, and England, who were newcomers to the World Cup, were joint favourites to win the 1950 tournament. Brazil fell at the last hurdle, and the whole nation mourned. England, the traditional home of football and feared for so long by the rest of the world, did not make the final pool. They met with an accident on the way, and the headlines read: England 0 United States 1.

WORLD CUP FOCUS

- Brazil might not have got through their first-round group but for an accident to Yugoslavia's inside-right, Rajko Mitic, who cut his head on a girder outside their dressing-room. By the time he made it on to the pitch, Ademir had scored Brazil's first goal.
- After their elimination by Spain, the England squad, instead of staying to be educated, left for home — together with all the English journalists.

THERE WERE only 31 original entries for this first post-war World Cup, and a number of withdrawals left an unwieldy 13 finalists. Italy qualified automatically as holders, but West Germany were not yet members of FIFA. The home countries were allotted two places in the finas, with the International Championship as their qualifying group, but Scotland incomprehensibly refused to go as mere runners-up, and withdrew. Portugal, who had been eliminated by Spain, declined to replace them. Yugoslavia qualified at the expense of France, who were given a reprieve when Turkey withdrew, but backed out when they heard their travel programme. Sweden eliminated the Republic of Ireland.

The four South American places were decided without a match being played, because of withdrawals, including Argentina, from the qualifying groups. Mexico beat the United States 6–0 and 6–2, but they both qualified above Cuba. Late withdrawals by Turkey and India, after both had qualified, left a lop-sided tournament.

Gaetjens glances the ball past Williams to the horror of all England.

No World Cup final

A new system was used in the finals. The countries were divided into four groups of four, with the winners of each group to go into a final pool, where they would play each other. The winners of this pool would be the world champions. Brazil, England, Italy and Uruguay were seeded, but because of the lateness of the withdrawals, the groups could not be rearranged, so there was one group of three countries and one of two. In the latter, Uruguay beat Bolivia 8–0, so they were in the final pool without having to play any qualifying games and having had only one match in the finals.

A freak result

The group that made the headlines was England's. With Chile and the United States as virtual "makeweights", England did not anticipate any problems until their last match, against Spain. England's World Cup debut, against Chile in the massive, unfinished Maracana Stadium in Rio, was ponderous, but they came through with goals from Mortensen and Mannion.

Meanwhile, the United States were giving Spain the fright of their lives, holding on to a 1–0 half-time lead until Spain hit three face-saving goals in the last 10 minutes.

Forewarned, England should still have thrashed this team of part-timers, captained by one Eddie McIlvenny, a Glasgow-born right-half who had played seven games for Wrexham in 1947 and had then been given a free transfer. But even with an unchanged line-up that included Billy Wright, Alf Ramsey and Tom Finney, and a post-war record of 23 wins and only four defeats in 30 internationals, the expected flood of goals did not materialize.

On a bumpy pitch at Belo Horizonte, in front of barely 10,000 spectators, England struck the woodwork four times, a Mullen header was cleared from a position seemingly a yard behind the line, and two plausible penalty appeals were turned down.

Instead, the Americans defen-ded valiantly, grew in confidence, and scored in the 37th minute when Haitian-born Larry Gaetjens beat Bert Williams to a cross, deflecting it with his head past the astonished keeper. The impossible, the unthinkable had happened.

The four finalists

England still had a chance to qualify for the final pool — if they beat Spain, they would earn a play-off. They drafted the out-of-favour Stanley Matthews into the side on the right, switching Finney to the left, and brought Milburn and Baily in for Bentley and Mannion — to no avail. They lost 1–0.

So Spain joined Uruguay, Olympic champions Sweden and Brazil in the final pool. Sweden's 3–2 victory over Italy had been the deciding factor in the group of

England's humiliating defeat by the part-timers of the United States was the main talking point back home, tending to obscure what was an awesome triumph for South American football.

Uruguay's keeper Maspoli goes up for the last Brazilian corner as English referee George Reader (far right) turns round to whistle for time.

three. Although the holders had been seriously weakened by the loss of eight internationals in the 1949 Superga air crash, their defeat at the hands of the Swedish amateurs was still a shock.

Brazil qualified through Group One, but not without a certain amount of anxiety. They easily took care of Mexico at the Maracana in the opening match of the tournament, but were held to a draw by the Swiss, whose second equalizer came two minutes from time. Brazil now had to beat Yugoslavia. They made several changes, stumbling on the effective inside-forward trio of Zizinho-Ademir-Jair, and ran out winners by 2–0.

Sensational Brazil

Having overcome their first-round nerves and settled on their best side, Brazil came out against Sweden and entertained the near-140,000 crowd to a sensational display of football. Sweden, whose performance in reaching the final pool was a wonderful tribute to their English coach George Raynor, were swamped 7–1 by the dazzling Brazilians, for whom the unstoppable Ademir scored four.

There was more joy for Brazil with the result from São Paulo, where Spain held Uruguay, now their biggest obstacle to success. And when Brazil put on another scintillating exhibition of attacking football for over 150,000 at the Maracana, beating Spain 6–1, there seemed to be no stopping them. Uruguay, meanwhile, managed to edge past the Swedes 3–2 in the last five minutes after twice being a goal down. But they would have to beat Brazil in the deciding match — in effect, the final of a competition designed not to have one.

Triumph for tactics

For Brazil to lose was unthinkable. Their overwhelming displays against Sweden and Spain had given them an aura of invincibility in the eyes of their millions of followers, who felt sure they would engulf Uruguay. Brazil's team manager Flavio Costa was wary, however, knowing Uruguay's propensity over the years for upsetting Brazil. He feared that his team would be overconfident, that the flamboyance they had shown against the European teams — as when Zizinho beat the Spanish keeper and then waited for him to get up so that he could beat him again — would be dangerous against Uruguay, who knew them too well.

A world record crowd of some 200,000 squeezed into the still unfinished Maracana on the big day, and the atmosphere was electric. From the start, Brazil's inside trio carved their way through the Uruguayan defence, but there was always someone there to frustrate them. The Uruguayan captain, Varela, once an inside-left and now a roaming centre-half of the old school, eschewed his attacking tendencies to bind his defence, while Roque Maspoli performed superbly in goal.

They kept the Brazilians at bay for 45 minutes, but two minutes after the break their defence was finally breached. Drawn out to cover danger on Brazil's left flank, they were caught out when the ball was suddenly switched, and right-winger Friaca came flying in to crack the ball first time into the net.

Now, surely, the floodgates would open, thought the fans. But Uruguay had already shown signs of aggression, having weathered the first-half storm, and Varela was beginning to move menacingly upfield. Brazil sensed danger, but their instinct was to attack, not to pull back and protect their lead — after all, Uruguay needed two goals.

They got the first midway through the second half. Appropriately it was Varela who started the move, sending Ghiggia away on the right. He then found Schiaffino, who had scored four against Bolivia, and he gave Barbosa no chance.

The Brazilians were demoralized. But worse was to follow. Perez made a resolute incursion upfield, and laid on a chance that Ghiggia took with relish. Uruguay held out for the remaining 10 minutes. It was a triumph for tactics and determination. And no one deserved more to receive the newly named Jules Rimet Trophy than Obdulio Varela, a hero among heroes.

FINAL SCORE

Group 1

Brazil	4	Mexico	0
Yugoslavia	3	Switzerland	0
Brazil	2	Switzerland	2
Yugoslavia	4	Mexico	1
Brazil	2	Yugoslavia	0
Switzerland	2	Mexico	1

	P	W	D	L	F	A	P
Brazil	3	2	1	0	8	2	5
Yugoslavia	3	2	0	1	7	3	4
Switzerland	3	1	1	1	4	6	3
Mexico	3	0	0	3	2	10	0

Group 2

England	2	Chile	0
Spain	3	United States	1
United States	1	England	0
Spain	2	Chile	0
Spain	1	England	0
Chile	5	United States	2

	P	W	D	L	F	A	P
Spain	3	3	0	0	6	1	6
England	3	1	0	2	2	2	2
Chile	3	1	0	2	5	6	2
USA	3	1	0	2	4	8	2

Group 3

Sweden	3	Italy	2
Sweden	2	Paraguay	2
Italy	2	Paraguay	0

	P	W	D	L	F	A	P
Sweden	2	1	1	0	5	4	3
Italy	2	1	0	1	4	3	2
Paraguay	2	0	1	1	2	4	1

Group 4

Uruguay	8	Bolivia	0

Final Pool

Brazil	7	Sweden	1
Uruguay	2	Spain	2
Brazil	6	Spain	1
Uruguay	3	Sweden	2
Sweden	3	Spain	1
Uruguay	2	Brazil	1

Deciding match: Maracana Stadium, Rio, 16 July 1950. Attendance 199,854

Uruguay: Maspoli, Gonzales M, Tejera, Gambetta, Varela, Andrade, Ghiggia, Perez, Miguez, Schiaffino, Moran
(Scorers: Schiaffino, Ghiggia)

Brazil: Barbosa, Augusto, Juvenal, Bauer, Danilo, Bogode, Friaca, Zizinho, Ademir, Jair, Chico
(Scorer: Friaca)

Leading scorers
9 Ademir (Brazil)
5 Schiaffino (Uruguay)
Basora (Spain)

Pegasus leave fans hoarse

THE WHOLE COUNTRY cheered when Pegasus beat Bishop Auckland 2–1 in the Amateur Cup final at Wembley. This was no disrespect to the mighty Bishops, playing in their 14th final. It was sheer admiration for the "new Corinthians", whose dramatic and romantic rise has captured the public imagination.

Formed in 1948 from graduates of Oxford and Cambridge Universities, Pegasus do not play in a league or have a ground of their own. To reach the final, they played seven away fixtures and came from behind to win five of them, sometimes perilously close to the end. At Wembley, in front of a record 100,000 crowd for an amateur game, they absorbed Bishop's pressure in the first half, and took the lead through Potts six minutes after the interval. Ten minutes from time they made sure with a goal from Tanner, although Bishop Auckland pulled one back before the end.

Never has there been a more popular victory in the competition's 57-year history. Pegasus embody all the traditions of true amateurism, good sportsmanship and fine team spirit, and their success has brought back to the game something of the romance and the glory of the early days of soccer.

Tanner (second from the right) puts Pegasus two up.

Push-and-run Spurs win first Championship

WHILE NEWCASTLE were winning the Cup at Wembley, just a few miles down the road Spurs were clinching the League title by beating Sheffield Wednesday 1–0. It was a nervy match, and Sheffield battled hard in their efforts to stave off relegation. But a goal from Channel Islander Len Duquemin just before the interval was enough to give Spurs the two points they needed to beat off Manchester United's challenge.

Playing the same push-and-run game that earned them promotion last season — ironically together with Wednesday — Spurs have hit the top echelon like a breath of fresh air. Their second successive title win is a tribute to manager Arthur Rowe. The goals have been shared around, with much of the inspiration coming from left-half Ron Burgess, right-back Alf Ramsey and inside-left Eddie Baily. But all the side have worked hard, none more so than right-half Billy Nicholson, who covered acres of ground every match in both defence and attack, and thoroughly earned an England cap, against Portugal.

Heroic 10-man England finally succumb to Scots

ENGLAND fought an heroic rearguard action for most of the game at Wembley after losing Wilf Mannion, and even took the lead. But in the end they could not resist the Scottish pressure any longer and lost a thrilling match 3–2.

England were struggling to hold the rampant Scots from the start. Billy Liddell on the left was dangerous every time he got the ball, but his crosses were being wasted. Then came the cruel blow for England. In the 13th minute, Mannion, dropping back to help his overworked defence, went up for the ball with Liddell and their heads cracked together. The Scot was able to play on, but Mannion was carried off on a stretcher.

It looked bad for England, but against the run of play they scored first through a breakaway. Finney, now at inside-right, and Mortensen carved out the opening, and Harold Hassall, on his international debut, cracked a tremendous shot past Cowan, high into the Scottish net. Scotland continued to press, however, and Lawrie Reilly set up an easy equalizer for Bobby Johnstone.

Scotland took the lead early in the second half, Johnstone returning the compliment for Reilly to score. Then Bert Williams, the player most responsible for keeping the score down, made his one mistake. He fumbled an apparently harmless cross, and Liddell swept the ball into the net.

That should have been the end for the 10 brave men, but they would not lie down. Matthews and especially Finney made some dangerous runs. And when Finney brought down a defence-splitting chip from Mortensen, ran on and coolly flicked the ball over the keeper, England were back in the game. A Mortensen drive flashed just wide of the post. But in the end Scotland were worthy winners.

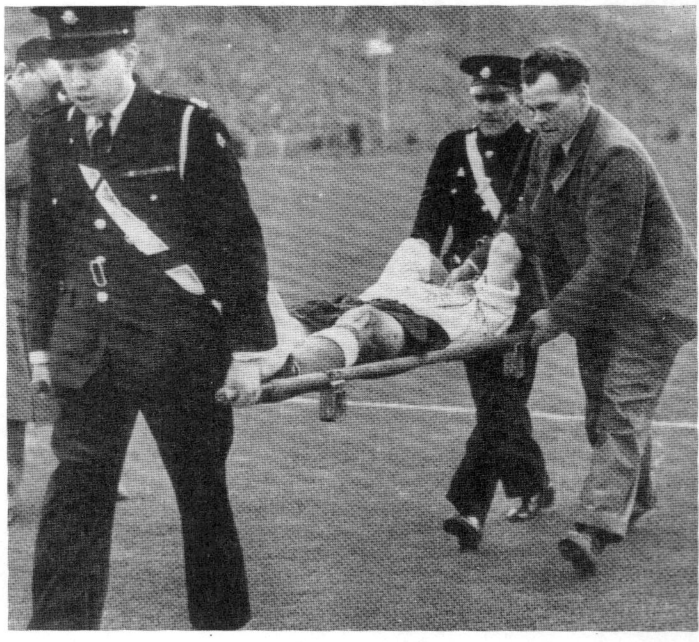

Mannion is carried off with a fractured cheek-bone.

Milburn and Mortensen rescue England

ELEVEN DAYS after spearheading opposing teams in the Cup final, Jackie Milburn and Stan Mortensen returned to Wembley and dramatically snatched victory out of Argentina's grasp.

In the first international between the two countries, played as part of the Festival of Britain, Argentina took an 18th-minute lead. From then on, it was all England, but they just could not penetrate Argentina's well-organized defensive screen. Milburn twice hit a post, but time began to run out, and England were in danger of losing at home for the first time to a team from outside the British Isles.

Then, with the Wembley roar spurring them on, England finally cracked it. Mortensen, who often claims to be a poor header of the ball, nodded a Finney corner home with 11 minutes to go, and then got above the defence to head a Ramsey free-kick down on to Milburn's foot for the winner.

Mortensen heads England's equalizer past Argentine keeper Rugilo.

Scotland lose home record

SCOTLAND lost their proud home record against foreign sides when Austria beat them 1–0 on a bone-hard ground at Hampden Park on 13 December. There can be no excuses for the Scots, who never seem to be able to produce the passion against Continental teams that they show against the "auld enemy" England. Scotland exhibited a marked lack of shooting power against the far from impressive Austrians — no "Wunderteam", this — and a goal from outside-right Ernst Melchior was enough to make history.

This was the first match between the two countries since the war. Austria humbled the Scots 5–0 in Vienna in 1931, and there have been two draws since. Scotland's withdrawal from the World Cup last year was narrow-minded and inexcusable. Perhaps this defeat will drive home the need to broaden their international outlook.

FOOTBALL FOCUS

- The two Divisions Three were increased to 24 clubs each.
- Arsenal centre-half Leslie Compton became the oldest British player to make his international debut when, at 38 years 2 months, he represented England against Wales on 15 November.
- Rangers took a back seat for a change in Scotland. They were runners-up in the League to Hibs, who lost in the League Cup final to Motherwell, who lost in the Cup final to Celtic — a chain of events that must have gone down well at Parkhead.
- Scotland, having lost their home record to Austria, were beaten 4-0 in Vienna in May, when Billy Steel became the first Scottish player to be sent off in an international.
- Alec Herd, 39,and his son David, just 17, played together in Stockport's last game of the season, a 2–0 win over Hartlepool.

FINAL SCORE

Football League
Division 1: Tottenham Hotspur
Top scorer: Stan Mortensen (Blackpool) 30
Division 2: Preston North End
Division 3S: Nottingham Forest
Division 3N: Rotherham United
Footballer of the Year: Harry Johnston (Blackpool)

FA Cup Final

Newcastle United	2	Blackpool	0

Scottish League
Division A: Hibernian
Top scorer: Lawrie Reilly (Hibernian) 22
Division B: Queen of the South

Scottish FA Cup Final

Celtic	1	Motherwell	0

Scottish League Cup Final

Motherwell	3	Hibernian	0

International Championship
Scotland, 6 pts

Stanley is magic, but it's Jackie's match

STANLEY MATTHEWS played his heart out for Blackpool and at times seemed to be taking on the whole Newcastle defence by himself. But the FA Cup final belongs to Jackie Milburn, whose two goals will be recalled for decades to come.

All in all, Newcastle were the better side. Blackpool's attack relied too much on Mortensen in the middle, the "maestro" on the right wing, and the driving force behind them, Harry Johnston, captain and Footballer of the Year. Milburn, England inside colleague and sometime rival of Mortensen, was the obvious Newcastle danger man, well supported by the explosive Bobby Mitchell on the left wing and at inside-right by the diminutive Ernie Taylor, a crafty box of tricks.

The first half was even, although Blackpool had the better chances. But they were playing a dangerous game at the back, and when Milburn beat their offside trap, only a fine save from Farm kept his shot out. The warning went unheeded, and five minutes into the second half, Milburn was put away again, by Chilean George Robledo. Racing through from half-way, he slotted the ball right-footed past the advancing Farm to keep up his record of scoring in every round.

Four minutes later, Newcastle were two up. Walker pushed the ball inside to Taylor on the edge of the box. The little schemer casually caressed the ball underfoot and then, without looking around, rolled it back to Milburn, who cracked it, left-footed this time, high into the net from an angle and some 25 yards out. The speed, simplicity and execution of the goal were breathtaking.

Blackpool came back strongly, and Matthews, who hasn't scored for over two years, uncharacteristically cut inside several times to shoot, despairing of the efforts of his colleagues. It was to no avail, however, and Newcastle defended well enough to survive the onslaught.

Milburn wheels away after pushing the ball past Farm to score his first goal.

To Newcastle the Cup – to Arsenal the glory

THE CRIES of "Lucky Arsenal", familiar since their triumphs in the thirties, were absent at Wembley on Saturday, when their gallant 10 men finally succumbed to the persistence of the Newcastle attack. The bad luck that had destroyed their Championship hopes followed Arsenal to Wembley, when right-back Walley Barnes badly injured a knee in the first half. Typical of Arsenal's spirit, he twice came back with his knee strapped up, but finally had to leave the field after 27 minutes.

Arsenal had been on top until then, with Doug Lishman giving the Newcastle defence a fright when his elegant overhead kick scraped a post. But as the game wore on, it seemed inevitable that Newcastle would score. Arsenal's walking wounded — Ray Daniel with his broken wrist in a cast, Lishman with a septic cut and Jimmy Logie with an internal haemorrhage — had to fight a desperate rearguard action.

Lishman's overhead effort just fails after two minutes at Wembley.

Skipper Joe Mercer played his greatest game, an unforgettable display of courage and captaincy. Daniel, a highly skilful centre-half, subdued last year's Wembley hero, Jackie Milburn. And Don Roper, a makeshift right-back, did a marvellous job on the elusive Bobby Mitchell. Indeed, Roper was lying on the ground injured when Mitchell finally broke through to put over the cross from which George Robledo headed the winner — off a post with only five minutes to go.

Newcastle are the first team this century to retain the Cup. Perhaps it was merciful that Arsenal were spared extra time. They won more friends in defeat than with all their triumphs of the past.

SOCCER SOUNDBITES

"We have won the Cup, but the glory is yours."

STAN SEYMOUR,
Newcastle director-manager to Arsenal after their brave display in the Cup final.

"Joe Mercer is the greatest player I have ever met in this game."

JOE HARVEY,
of his opposing Cup final captain (also his former wartime sergeant-major).

"Boys, I have never been so proud of you in victory as I am in defeat."

TOM WHITTAKER,
Arsenal manager.

Mission impossible

THAT ARSENAL failed in the first leg of their Herculean attempt to bring off the League and Cup "double" was not surprising. They needed to beat champions elect Manchester United by seven goals at Old Trafford, so it was a chance in fantasy only. In the event, an Arsenal side already disjointed by injuries and reduced to 10 men after only 24 minutes — they finished with nine — were beaten 6–1, with Jack Rowley scoring a hat-trick.

The League triumph is no more than United deserve, after finishing runners-up in four of the five seasons since the war. Johnny Carey, as ever, has been an inspirational leader, and with Allenby Chilton and Henry Cockburn provided a powerful springboard for United's supremacy. Rowley spearheaded the goals department with 30, while Stan Pearson chipped in with an invaluable 22. It is United's third League title, but their first for 41 years.

Gunners throw light on night football

The sight of things to come: floodlit football at Highbury.

THE FIRST official match under floodlighting since 1878 took place at Highbury on 19 September, when Arsenal entertained the Hapoel club of Tel Aviv in a friendly. A crowd of 44,000 saw the Gunners cruise to a 6–1 victory, but the important thing was that they saw it — very clearly, indeed.

It was Arsenal manager the late Herbert Chapman, back in the thirties, who advocated the use of floodlights. Impressed with what he had seen on the Continent, he had them built into the West Stand. But the FA banned them for use in official matches, because they feared that, if the idea caught on, "clubs would be drawn into spending too much money". Chapman's protégé Tom Whittaker, the current Arsenal manager, put on a literally brilliant show for Press and public at Highbury, and the verdict from each was a unanimous thumbs-up.

Lofthouse, the Lion of Vienna

NAT LOFTHOUSE'S two goals for England at the Prater Stadium, particularly his brave winner, earned him the nickname "Lion of Vienna". It was an important match, against Austria, with reputations at stake.

Austria had been slamming goals past European defences — eight against Belgium, seven Yugoslavia, six Eire — and had beaten Scotland home and away. Earlier in the season they had held England to a draw at Wembley. England, unbeaten in their last eight games, had just played out a most unconvincing 1-1 draw in Italy and looked a tired side. They were there for the taking. The match was billed in Vienna as the "Championship of Europe", and the city, still under post-war Allied occupation, was tense with expectation. There were some 2,000 British troops in the 60,000 crowd.

After 20 minutes of canny defence, England struck, with Lofthouse volleying home a Sewell cross. Seconds later, however, Froggatt brought Dienst down and Huber scored from the spot. England hit back immediately, and Sewell, with a feint and a shot, restored their lead. Nevertheless, Dienst managed to get away from Wright and put Austria level again just before the interval.

In the second half, Austria stepped up the pressure, and it became a physical game. The England defence worked overtime, with Merrick having an inspired game in goal. Austria were determined to win, but they left themselves wide open for a counter-attack, and this is what happened. Merrick leapt high to pluck a corner out of the air, and threw the ball out to Tom Finney. The England winger drew the only defender and put Lofthouse away on a lone 50-yard run. It was a duel between Lofthouse and the keeper, who came out to meet him. Lofthouse shot as they collided, and was out cold when the ball hit the net. There were only eight minutes left when he was carried off the field on a stretcher, but he returned to help England protect their lead. Although hobbling on the wing, he still managed to crash a shot against the post. A mass of khaki-clad servicemen invaded the field to carry off the England players at the end.

Nat Lofthouse, Lion of Vienna.

FOOTBALL FOCUS

- Wales, who shared the Home International Championship with England (both got five points), beat a Rest of the UK selection 3–2 at Cardiff on 5 December in a match to celebrate the Welsh FA's centenary.
- Derek Dooley scored 46 goals in 30 League games for Division Two champions Sheffield Wednesday.
- Billy Wright won his 42nd cap against Austria in Vienna to beat Bob Crompton's long-standing record for England.

FINAL SCORE

Football League
Division 1: Manchester United
Top scorer: George Robledo (Newcastle United) 33
Division 2: Sheffield Wednesday
Division 3S: Plymouth Argyle
Division 3N: Lincoln City
Footballer of the Year: Billy Wright (Wolverhampton Wanderers)

FA Cup Final
Newcastle United 1 Arsenal 0

Scottish League
Division A: Hibernian
Top scorer: Lawrie Reilly (Hibernian) 27
Division B: Clyde

Scottish FA Cup Final
Motherwell 4 Dundee 0

Scottish League Cup Final
Dundee 3 Rangers 2

International Championship
England, Wales, 5 pts

'Clockwork' Ocwirk makes Austrians tick

THE IMPRESSIVE Austrians earned a 2–2 draw with England at Wembley at the end of November in the long-awaited clash. Having beaten Scotland at Hampden last season — the first foreign side to win on Scottish soil — and then routed them 4–0 in Vienna, Austria seemed to be returning to their pre-war eminence, and were expected to challenge England's proud home record.

The match was not a disappointment. The head-on collision between the two soccer schools provided a fascinating comparison. Austria, their slow, close-passing style revolving around "centre-half" Ernst Ocwirk, rely on precision and positioning. England's traditional "third-back" game, with speed and close marking the basic virtues, was put to the test.

The tall Ocwirk, quickly dubbed "Clockwork" by the England fans, was a revelation. He is a centre-half of the old school, the hub of all his side's build-ups, a supremely gifted player with impeccable ball control and passing skills.

Because of injuries, England had been forced to chop and change their side, and they fielded a completely new right wing, Ivor Broadis of Manchester City inside and Arthur Milton of Arsenal on the flank. Broadis, nearly 29, was an experienced schemer, creative, fast and with a powerful shot. Milton, at 23, had rocketed into contention with no more than a dozen first-team appearances. Unfortunately the Wembley crowd did not see what he could do because Broadis starved him out of the game.

Austria scored first, from a superb long ball by Ocwirk to Melchior. Alf Ramsey equalized from the spot, and seven minutes from time placed an indirect free-kick, which the Austrians were still disputing, on to the head of the unmarked Nat Lofthouse to give England the lead. But Stojaspal scored a deserved equalizer two minutes later from a penalty for hands.

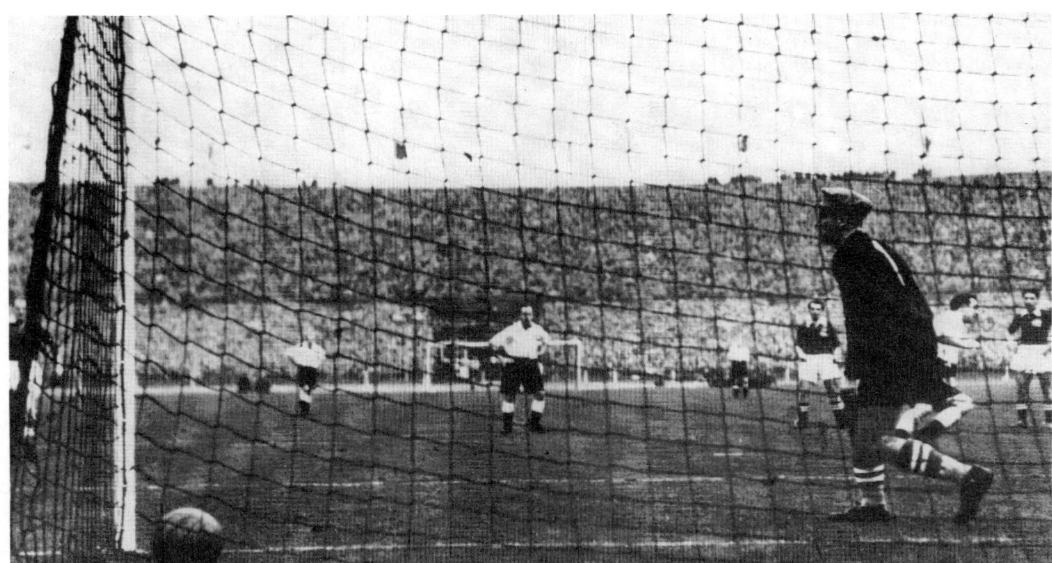

Ramsey equalizes from the penalty spot against the impressive Austrians.

Matthews gets his medal at last

WEMBLEY was the stage as the world's most famous footballer, Stanley Matthews, at last won the FA Cup medal that had eluded him for 20 years. After a dramatic finish in which he made Blackpool's winner for Bill Perry, Matthews went up to receive his medal from the newly crowned Queen Elizabeth II, who was only six when Stan first turned out for Stoke City.

Twice in three years (1948 and 1951) Matthews was on the losing side in classic finals, and for years the whole country has been behind the "Wizard of the Dribble" in his season-by-season quest for a winners' medal. When Bolton were 3–1 up after 55 minutes, it seemed Matthews would again be denied. But Bolton had played much of the game with left-half Eric Bell a passenger on the wing, and in the last quarter of the match, inspired by Matthews's irresistible runs along the wing, Blackpool began to overrun the Bolton defence.

With 22 minutes left, Stan Mortensen, who had scored in the first half, added a second, poking the ball in when keeper Stan Hanson fumbled a Matthews cross. The gallant Bolton defence then held out until the last minute of normal time before the equalizer came. Jackie Mudie was brought down outside the box as he fastened on to another Matthews centre, and Morty crashed the free-kick past the defensive wall.

The fans now knew the Cup was Blackpool's as extra time loomed. But it wasn't needed. In injury time, Matthews again jinked past his man and towards the touchline, cut in and laid the ball back invitingly into the path of left-winger Perry, and the South African swept it into the net from 10 yards.

Stan had his medal in a fairytale ending, but there were other heroes on the day, not least his England colleague Mortensen, who became the first man to score a hat-trick in a Wembley final. There was Bell, who tore a muscle after 20 minutes, yet courageously rose to head Bolton's third goal. And one can only feel sympathy for left-back Ralph Banks, who was increasingly lame and had to suffer being turned inside-out by the 38-year-old maestro. One wonders just how long the ageless wonder can continue to turn it on — days like this could keep him going for ever.

The "Wizard of the Dribble" gets his FA Cup-winners' medal at last.

Nail-biting finish as Arsenal win record seventh title

ARSENAL clinched the League Championship on Friday evening in a nerve-tingling match that they had to win in order to overtake Preston, who had already finished their programme. Pity poor Preston. When they beat Arsenal at Deepdale last Saturday, they gave themselves a chance of their first Championship since they won the first two inaugral League titles at the end of the 1880s. Burnley were Arsenal's opponents, and they gave the anxious 51,000 fans at Highbury a fright when they took the lead after only three minutes.

Fortunately for Arsenal, Alex Forbes, who played a blinder, chose the occasion to score his only goal of the season and put them on level terms. Lishman and Logie added further goals, and the crowd began to relax. Burnley pulled one back after the interval, however, and Arsenal's nerves began to show. But with Joe Mercer as calm as ever at the helm — what an Indian summer the old man's having! — Arsenal held out for a 3–2 win and the title, a record seventh, on goal average.

The Gunners and Preston had identical results — 21 wins, 12 draws and nine defeats — but Arsenal's goal average was 1.51 to North End's 1.41.

Jimmy Logie (8) scores Arsenal's crucial third goal in the title decider against Burnley.

Old-timer Sagar leaves his post after 24 years

LONG-STANDING Goodison Park fans found they had to acquire a new habit during the 1952–53 season. They had to look at the programme to see who was in goal for the Toffeemen. Ted Sagar retired in May after only one appearance in the season, bringing to an end the longest continuous spell any player has served with one club as a professional. Sagar joined Everton on 26 March 1929, so has completed 24 years' service and has just had his 43rd birthday.

As a youngster, Sagar had a trial with Hull City, who were so slow to offer him a contract that Everton nipped in. Sagar won a regular place in the first team in 1931, and has played in every season since, winning two League Championship and one Cup-winners' medal, a Second Division title medal, and four England caps. Not a big man, Sagar relied on skill and positioning, and was utterly fearless in diving at the feet of forwards. Despite losing a great part of his career to the war, he accumulated an Everton record of 465 League appearances.

Goalkeeper Ted Sagar hangs up his boots after his record spell of 24 years with Everton.

FOOTBALL FOCUS

- On Boxing Day at Hillsborough, three Wednesday players, Vince Kenny, Norman Curtis and Eddie Gannon, scored own goals. Their opponents West Bromwich gratefully accepted the Christmas presents and went home with a 5–4 win.

- In Huddersfield's 8–2 defeat of Everton in Division Two, Jimmy Glazzard scored five goals — all headers from crosses by winger Vic Metcalfe.

- Nat Lofthouse scored six goals for the Football League against the League of Ireland at Molineux on 24 September, a record for an Inter-League match.

- Irish international Charlie Tully scored direct from a corner for Celtic at Falkirk in the Cup on 28 February, but the goal was disallowed because some of the crowd had spilled on to the pitch. So Tully retook the corner and promptly scored again.

- Leicester City's Arthur Rowley, signed from Fulham two seasons earlier, scored a hat-trick in both League games against his former team.

- Amateur club Walthamstow Avenue beat two League clubs in the FA Cup before remarkably holding Manchester United to a 1–1 draw at Old Trafford in the fourth round. But they lost the replay 5–2 at Highbury.

Derek Dooley loses leg

DEREK DOOLEY, Sheffield Wednesday's exciting young centre-forward, on the brink of a great career, has had to have his right leg amputated. He broke it against Preston on 14 February, challenging the keeper for a fifty-fifty ball. A couple of days later, in Preston Royal Infirmary, with Dooley about to be discharged and getting used to the idea of missing the rest of the season, it was discovered that gangrene had set in. There was no alternative but to amputate.

Big and strong, but looking cumbersome and unpolished when he was establishing a place in the team last season, he cracked 46 goals in 30 games to lead Wednesday to promotion. With a fast-growing reputation for scoring goals from impossible situations, the 23-year-old had accrued 16 in 29 First Division games this season and was already in the running for an England cap. The whole football world now mourns the loss of a rising young star.

Dooley: a tragic end to a meteoric career.

FINAL SCORE

Football League
Division 1: Arsenal
Top scorer: Charlie Wayman (Preston North End) 24
Division 2: Sheffield United
Division 3S: Bristol Rovers
Division 3N: Oldham Athletic
Footballer of the Year: Nat Lofthouse (Bolton Wanderers)

FA Cup Final

Blackpool	4	Bolton Wanderers	3

Scottish League
Division A: Rangers
Top scorers: Charlie Fleming (East Fife), Lawrie Reilly (Hibernian) 30
Division B: Stirling Albion

Scottish FA Cup Final

Rangers	1	Aberdeen	1
Replay: Rangers	1	Aberdeen	0

Scottish League Cup Final

Dundee	2	Kilmarnock	0

International Championship
England, Scotland, 4 pts

Struth! Another 'double' for Rangers

RANGERS brought off the League and Cup "double" again, although it was a close call in both competitions. Centre-half George Young had to go in goal for 18 minutes of the Cup final when keeper George Niven was off injured. He played well enough for Rangers to draw 1–1 with Aberdeen, and they went on to win the replay 1–0.

They now needed three points from their remaining two fixtures to pip Hibs for the League title. A 3–1 win over Dundee three days after the replayed Cup final left them requiring a draw with Queen of the South at Dumfries. Thanks to a dramatic Willie Waddell equalizer in the 75th minute, they did it, just edging past Hibs on goal average.

What a catalogue of success manager Willie Struth, now in his 75th year, has compiled with the Gers since he took over as manager in 1920 — 18 Championships, 10 Cups and three League Cups. That is a record without equal in first-class football. Yet Struth had had little experience as a player. He was a stonemason and a professional runner before getting a job as trainer at Ibrox Park, becoming manager when the previous boss died in an accident. An inspired choice by the board!

Ramsey saves England from banquet blues

ENGLAND took on the Rest of Europe as part of the FA's 90th birthday celebrations. The Rest, an untried combination of stars from Austria, Germany, Italy, Spain, Sweden and Yugoslavia — the Hungarians, who come to Wembley next month, ominously withdrew their players — felt they had no chance. But it was England who played as if they'd never met before, and who were lucky in the end to escape with a draw.

When the teams came out on to the pitch, the biggest cheer was for Stanley Matthews, recalled to the side at 38. But Matthews apart, there was little to cheer the 97,000 fans. Inside-forwards Kubala of Spain and Vukas of Yugoslavia soon showed they were streets ahead of the labouring Englishmen in technique and tactics.

Eckersley finds the only way to stop Vukas is to bring him down, after just five minutes, and Kubala scores from the spot. But England are fighters, and Mortensen equalizes two minutes later. Boniperti of Italy scores twice — England 1 The Rest 3. Some Matthews magic gives England heart. Mullen takes advantage of a defensive lapse and pulls one back — half-time 2–3. Another Matthews dribble brings the crowd to its feet and he sets Mullen up for the equalizer. But still the Europeans control the game, and they take the lead when Kubala fires the ball in, with the England defence spread-eagled. England's hopes are waning, but Mortensen is brought down in the box. Up steps ice-cool Alf Ramsey to send substitute keeper Beara the wrong way for a last-minute equalizer — it's 4–4, England's home record is still intact, and the FA notaries can enjoy the celebratory banquet.

England's bastion breached by the magicians — Hungary win 6-3

IT HAD TO HAPPEN — England's proud undefeated home record against Continental invaders had to go sometime. All the signs were there. But it didn't just slip away, it was shattered. Those "Magic Magyars", unbeaten since May 1950, produced a truly wonderful display of football, the like of which has not been seen at Wembley since that legendary one-off performance by the Scots in 1928.

England did not play badly. But the Hungarians were in another class. Speedy, fluent, and with the confidence that comes with 20 wins in 23 games since their last defeat, they were superior in every aspect of the game. Indeed, led by the remarkable Ferenc Puskas — what a superb left foot he has — they seemed to be playing a different game altogether.

Puskas and the other inside-forward, the tall, elegant Sandor Kocsis, a brilliant header of the ball, spearheaded the attack, while Nandor Hidegkuti, the No. 9, foraged behind them. In the past, England have survived against cleverer Continental opposition because of their inability to shoot. Not this time, though. Hidegkuti dispelled any such delusions in the very first minute, slashing a 20-yarder past the bewildered Merrick. Bewilderment is perhaps the best word to describe the reactions of the England defence throughout the match. Time and again they were left gaping as Puskas and company ran rings round them.

Puskas (10) acclaims his exquisitely executed first goal.

Yet England equalized after 13 minutes, when Mortensen put Sewell through to score a classic goal. The hopes of 100,000 fans rose — only to be dashed a short time later in a seven-minute spell that surely marked the end of an era. First Hidegkuti scored from close in, then Puskas left Wright tackling thin air as he dragged the ball back with his studs and rifled it in from a narrow angle. The unstoppable Puskas then deflected a Bozsik free-kick into the net to put his side 4–1 up, before Mortensen pulled one back. The Hungarians continued to dominate after the interval. Bozsik — has there ever been a finer wing-half? — scored with a tremendous drive and Hidegkuti volleyed his third. It could have been more had these footballers from another planet not slackened in the last half-hour, and a Ramsey penalty was little consolation.

The English players knew they'd been given a lesson, and Billy Wright, their captain, summed it up when he said ruefully: "The Hungarians produced some of the finest, most brilliantly applied football it has ever been my privilege to see. The ball did precisely what they wanted . . . They were relentless. They were superb."

Billy Wright exchanges pennants with the deceptively podgy Puskas.

FINAL SCORE

Football League
Division 1: Wolverhampton Wanderers
Top scorer: Jimmy Glazzard (Huddersfield T) 29
Division 2: Leicester City
Division 3S: Ipswich Town
Division 3N: Port Vale
Footballer of the Year: Tom Finney (Preston NE)

FA Cup Final

West Brom	3	Preston North End	2

Scottish League
Division A: Celtic
Top scorer: Jimmy Wardhaugh (Hearts) 27
Division B: Motherwell

Scottish FA Cup Final

Celtic	2	Aberdeen	1

Scottish League Cup Final

East Fife	3	Partick Thistle	2

International Championship
England, 6 pts

Port Vale pull welcome mat from under Matthews's feet

WHEN CUP-HOLDERS Blackpool were drawn away to Port Vale in the fifth round, Stanley Matthews looked forward to a welcome return to the Potteries. They gave him a welcome all right — they cleverly forced him away from the drier areas on the wing into the middle, where he met mud as well as a massed defence. The tactics worked, and Vale won 2–0 to pull off a giant-killing act to rival Norwich's in the last round — a tribute to manager Freddie Steele, a long-time Stoke teammate of Matthews in the thirties!

Vale, who won 2–0 at First Division Cardiff in the last round, are set to visit a fellow Division Three side, Leyton Orient, in the last eight, so there will be a Third Division club in the semi-finals for only the second time (Millwall did it in 1937).

The Port Vale defence block a Matthews effort from close in.

Magyars dish out lesson No. 2

THE RETURN came too quickly for England to have absorbed the lesson they received at Wembley. Six months ago they were shown to be years behind the Hungarians in the very basics of football — control, technique, accuracy and movement. Now, at the People's Stadium in Budapest, they were given a second lesson in the arts of the game they introduced to the world.

This time, those "Magnificent Magyars" showed no mercy. Puskas, who scored twice, once again dictated their play and was the architect of their victory — 7–1, the heaviest defeat ever suffered by an English side. Only Merrick, Wright, Dickinson and Sewell kept their places from Wembley, while Hungary made just one change. It would not have mattered what combination was chosen to represent England; the result would have been the same. Perhaps England will finally learn from this defeat, and take note of the advances in the game that have been made outside the hidebound home countries.

On this form, Hungary are clear favourites for the next World Cup

Kocsis, completely unchallenged, about to hit Hungary's fourth goal.

Norwich do a 'Walsall' on Arsenal

LEAGUE CHAMPIONS Arsenal suffered their most humiliating Cup defeat since Walsall ruffled the pride of the great Herbert Chapman team in 1933, when Third Division Norwich City beat them at Highbury in the fourth round. At least Walsall had the decency to do the dirty on their own ground!

Nearly 55,000 turned up to see what they hoped would be a comfortable victory, especially after the 5–1 defeat of Villa in the third round. They were in for a rude awakening when Arsenal conceded a penalty in the second minute, but Jack Kelsey saved from Bobby Brennan. And although Arsenal took a second-half lead through Jimmy Logie, Norwich's reserve centre-forward Tom Johnston stunned the Arsenal faithful by scoring twice. The Gunners fired everything bar the kitchen sink at Norwich in the last 10 minutes without any luck. That's Cup football for you, as the old adage goes. "David" wins again!

Johnston (left) heads Norwich's winner past Dodgin, Wills and Kelsey.

FOOTBALL FOCUS

- Port Vale beat Orient 1–0 in the sixth round of the Cup, but lost 2–1 in the semi-finals to eventual winners WBA. However, in the League, they topped Division Three (N) by 11 points and set records for the fewest goals conceded (21) and the most games with a clean sheet (30), and a Division Three (N) record for fewest defeats (three).
- Former Scottish international winger Jimmy Delaney pulled off a unique treble when he won a Cup-winners' medal with Derry City in Northern Ireland, having already won a Scottish Cup medal with Celtic in 1937 and an FA Cup medal with Manchester United in 1948.
- Sam Bartram made his 500th League appearance for Charlton on 6 March in their Division One game with Portsmouth at the Valley, a record for any League club.

The world weeps for Hungary

The all-conquering 'Magic Magyars' were the popular favourites to win the 1954 World Cup in Switzerland. They had thrilled the world with their speedy, breathtakingly fluent football, and on the way to the final they scored 25 goals in four matches, including four each against Brazil and Uruguay. But they fell, controversially, at the last hurdle. And it is sad for the winners, a fine West German side, that the 1954 tournament will always be remembered as Hungary's World Cup.

THERE WERE 38 original entries, England and Scotland were again allowed to qualify from the Home Championship, and there were nine other groups. Brazil emerged without trouble from South America and, with holders Uruguay automatic finalists, Argentina again declined to enter.

A curious format

Yet again the format was changed. The 16 finalists were divided into four groups of four, but two seeded countries in each group would not play each other. Extra time would be played in group matches level at 90 minutes, and there would be play-offs if the second and third teams in a group finished level on points. The only sane decision was to revert to the knock-out system from the last eight onwards.

Hungary gave immediate confirmation of their strong favouritism by beating South Korea 9–0 and then West Germany 8–3. Sepp Herberger's gamble in playing a weakened side was derided by the 30,000 German fans who travelled to Basle to see the match. The German coach, however, was confident they could win a play-off, as indeed they did, 7–2 against Turkey, to earn a quarter-final against Yugoslavia rather than Brazil.

Stanley Matthews (left) was in fine form for England against Belgium.

Mixed British luck

Scotland, who condescended this time to play in their first World Cup as runners-up in the Home Championship, found themselves having to play Austria and Uruguay. They were a little unlucky to lose 1–0 to Austria, but their team manager Andy Beattie resigned and they were hammered out of the competition 7–0 by Uruguay, showing form worthy of world champions.

Meanwhile, England progressed through to the quarter-finals without setting the tournament alight. They took a 3–1 lead against Belgium, but lost it in the last 15 minutes, and were held 4–4. It did not matter, because they qualified by beating Switzerland 2–0 and heading their group. In Group One, Brazil and Yugoslavia both went through after playing out a 1–1 draw.

The Battle of Berne

It was unfortunate that arguably the two top teams of the competition, Hungary and Brazil, met so early. But what was expected to be a classic quarter-final between the best from Europe and South America turned out to be a most violent match and ended in a riot, with the fighting on the field carried on into the dressing-rooms and hundreds of spectators also involved.

Only three minutes after the start, Hidegkuti scored for Hungary despite having half his shorts ripped off. Five minutes later he crossed for Kocsis to head his eighth goal of the tournament. The Brazilians, instead of trying to play themselves back into the game, resorted to violence. The Hungarians began to retaliate, and the match degenerated into a battle, finishing at 4–2 to Hungary, and only nine players on either side, two Brazilians having been sent off along with the Hungarian captain Bozsik (Puskas did not play), and with Toth a virtual passenger on the wing.

Meanwhile, the West Germans were qualifying for the semi-finals with a 2–0 win over Yugoslavia. The previous day, the hosts Switzerland had lost a 3–0 lead in a record 12-goal classic, Austria emerging 7–5 victors, having been 5–3 up only 10 minutes after being three down!

England found themselves up against formidable opponents in the world champions. They were outplayed in the end, even though Uruguay had three players injured, and lost 4–2, Merrick's goalkeeping errors proving costly.

The goals flow

The "Battle of Berne" apart, the tournament so far had been a

How is it possible to lose a group match in the World Cup finals by eight goals to three and then beat the same nation in the final? Germany did it — and the Hungarians, so desperately unlucky, were the fall-guys.

Czibor opens the scoring for Hungary in the classic semi-final against Uruguay.

wonderful advertisement for exciting soccer, with plenty of goals. And they continued unabated in the semi-finals. The Austrian defence, so shaky in the Swiss match, proved no better against the Germans, who won a convincing and ominous 6–1 passage to the final.

If there were misgivings about the other semi-final, another clash between Europe and South America, they were soon dispelled, as Hungary and Uruguay put on one of the finest exhibitions of football ever seen. With 15 minutes to go, Hungary were two up through goals by Czibor and Hidegkuti, but Uruguay pulled them back, Schiaffino twice putting Hohberg in to score, the second with only three minutes to go. In extra time, the Hungarians, still without Puskas, called on all their resources, and Kocsis produced two more towering headers to put them in the final, and inflict on Uruguay their first ever defeat in the World Cup.

Sad end for Hungary

Puskas insisted on playing in the final, even though he was not 100 per cent fit. And it looked like his gamble had paid off when he followed up a blocked shot from Kocsis to put Hungary ahead after six minutes. Two minutes later, Czibor nipped in to take advantage of a defensive mistake and put them two up.

But the Germans did not crack. They came back immediately. Their captain and inside-left Fritz Walter hit a fast cross which Morlock, stretching out, converted at the near post. In the 18th minute, Rahn scored after a corner, and Germany were level. Hungary returned to the attack and some of their moves were breathtaking, but when German keeper Turek was beaten, Kohlmeyer popped up to save on the line.

The Germans began to come back into the game with a quarter of an hour to go, gaining strength from Hungary's inability to score. Bozsik made a rare mistake and Schaefer put Fritz Walter away. His cross was only half-cleared, and there was Rahn on hand to shoot home from 15 yards. With just five minutes to go, Puskas, who had almost faded from the game, suddenly latched on to a pass from Toth and cracked the ball past Turek. But the linesman's flag was up for offside. It was all over for the magnificent Magyars. West Germany were the new world champions.

WORLD CUP FOCUS

- Turkey enjoyed a curious qualification for the finals, drawn in a group of two with Spain. They lost 4–1 in Madrid, but won the return 1–0 in Istanbul. The two teams then met in Rome for a play-off. On receipt of a mysterious telegram, Spain left out their star player, Kubala, and could only draw 2–2. Lots were drawn out of a hat by a blind Italian boy, and Turkey were through to Switzerland.

- Inquiries into the so-called "Battle of Berne" took place, but, apart from reprimanding the guilty players, the international disciplinary committee left any punitive action to the respective national bodies. When Bozsik was asked later by the referee Arthur Ellis how he had been dealt with, he replied: "We don't punish Members of Parliament in Hungary."

Rahn (20) hits the winner for West Germany in the final.

FINAL SCORE

Group 1

Yugoslavia	1	France	0
Brazil	5	Mexico	0
France	3	Mexico	2
Brazil	1	Yugoslavia	1

	P	W	D	L	F	A	P
Brazil	2	1	1	0	6	1	3
Yugoslavia	2	1	1	0	2	1	3
France	2	1	0	1	3	3	2
Mexico	2	0	0	2	2	8	0

Group 2

Hungary	9	South Korea	0
West Germany	4	Turkey	1
Hungary	8	West Germany	3
Turkey	7	South Korea	0

	P	W	D	L	F	A	P
Hungary	2	2	0	0	17	3	4
Turkey	2	1	0	1	8	4	2
W Germany	2	1	0	1	7	9	2
South Korea	2	0	0	2	0	16	0

Play-off

West Germany	7	Turkey	2

Group 3

Austria	1	Scotland	0
Uruguay	2	Czechoslovakia	0
Austria	5	Czechoslovakia	0
Uruguay	7	Scotland	0

	P	W	D	L	F	A	P
Uruguay	2	2	0	0	9	0	4
Austria	2	2	0	0	6	0	4
Czech	2	0	0	2	0	7	0
Scotland	2	0	0	2	0	8	0

Group 4

England	4	Belgium	4
Switzerland	2	Italy	1
England	2	Switzerland	0
Italy	4	Belgium	1

	P	W	D	L	F	A	P
England	2	1	1	0	6	4	3
Italy	2	1	0	1	5	3	2
Switzerland	2	1	0	1	2	3	2
Belgium	2	0	1	1	5	8	1

Play-off

Switzerland	4	Italy	1

QUARTER-FINALS

Austria	7	Switzerland	5
Uruguay	4	England	2
West Germany	2	Yugoslavia	0
Hungary	4	Brazil	2

SEMI-FINALS

Hungary	4	Uruguay	2
West Germany	6	Austria	1

THIRD-PLACE MATCH

Austria	3	Uruguay	1

FINAL

West Germany	3	Hungary	2

Wankdorf Stadium, Berne, 4 July 1954. Attendance 60,000

West Germany: Turek, Posipal, Kohlmeyer, Eckel, Liebrich, Mai, Rahn, Morlock, Walter O, Walter F, Schaefer
(Scorers: Morlock, Rahn 2)
Hungary: Grosics, Buzansky, Lantos, Bozsik, Lorant, Zakarias, Czibor, Kocsis, Hidegkuti, Puskas, Toth
(Scorers: Puskas, Czibor)

Leading scorers
11 Kocsis (Hungary)
6 Hugi (Switzerland)
Morlock (West Germany)

Wolves restore English pride — Puskas and Co. beaten

WOLVES have done it again. Last month it was Moscow Spartak, beaten 4–0 under the Molineux floodlights with an unforgettable three-goal burst in the last three minutes. Now it's Honved, arguably the best club side in the world, studded with internationals and fielding five of the Hungarian side that so humiliated England 7–1 in May. The Hungarian Army club looked like emulating the national side when they went two up inside 15 minutes. But the Football League champions came storming back in the second half for a famous 3–2 victory to restore some of the lost English pride.

It was a case of déjà vu for home fans when Sandor "Golden Head" Kocsis gave Honved the lead after just 10 minutes with one of his inimitable headers. The inside-forward trio of Kocsis, Puskas and Machos were causing the Wolves defence all kinds of trouble, and when Machos scored a second after 14 minutes, it really did look as if another rout was on the cards. But Billy Wright was magnificent at the heart of the Wolves defence, inspiring his side by example. In the last year, the England captain has seen enough of Puskas and Co. to last him a lifetime. But he's not the sort of man to capitulate, and the Wolves side went in at half-time without conceding any further goals.

Roy Swinbourne celebrates his winning goal for Wolves.

Whatever manager Stan Cullis said to his men during the interval, it had a galvanizing effect. They stormed into the attack, and little Johnny Hancocks was brought down in the box. He took the kick himself and scored. Spurred on by the goal and by the roar of the 55,000 fans, Wolves began to take command, but it was 14 minutes from time before they got a deserved equalizer, Swinbourne heading in a Wilshaw cross.

The shouting had not died down when, two minutes later, Leslie Smith left two defenders in his wake as he cut the ball inside for Swinbourne again to lash it into the net on the run — a fitting winner for a fabulous game.

Newcastle take advantage as Cup jinx strikes again

Milburn opens the scoring with less than a minute gone. Not even Trautmann could stop his header.

MANCHESTER CITY right-back Jimmy Meadows injured knee ligaments and had to go off after just 20 minutes of the Cup final, leaving City to battle with 10 men for the rest of the match before Newcastle finally broke them down. If you think you've heard the story before, you're right. Look back three years to when Newcastle last won the Cup, and you will find that Arsenal's right-back Walley Barnes suffered the same injury at about the same time, no more than a few yards from the spot where Meadows fell. And the man whom both were trying to tackle was the same Bobby Mitchell, Newcastle's elusive outside-left.

It was a tragedy for Meadows, but the accident should not be allowed to detract from Newcastle's fine win, their third in five years. They were in front after only 50 seconds, through Milburn, and only brilliant goalkeeping by Bert Trautmann prevented them from increasing their lead. But Manchester City, despite their handicap, still managed some dangerous attacks, and drew level with a Johnstone header a minute before half-time.

After the interval, it was plain to see that both Milburn and White, Newcastle's right wing, were struggling with injuries, so this evened up matters. Their captain and right-half Jimmy Scoular was majestic in midfield, and Bob Stokoe ably looked after things at the back. But the Newcastle star was Mitchell, who really put makeshift right-back Spurdle through the mangle. Even the magnificent Trautmann had to give him best. Twice Scoular put Mitchell away with raking cross-field passes. Twice he shot, the first, from the narrowest of angles, surprising Trautmann at the near post. The second was parried, only for Hannah to lash in the rebound.

FOOTBALL FOCUS

- Tommy Briggs set a Second Division scoring record with seven goals in Blackburn's 8–3 win over Bristol Rovers on 5 February.
- Two pairs of brothers played for Wales against N.Ireland on 20 April at Belfast, John and Mel Charles and Len and Ivor Allchurch, John Charles scoring all their goals in a 3–2 win.
- Birmingham won a three-way tie for the Division Two title on goal average from Luton and Rotherham, helped by a record 16 goals in consecutive home games (7–2 against Port Vale and 9–1 against Liverpool) in mid-season.
- After their Wembley débâcle, Scotland beat Portugal and Austria, but lost 3–1 in Hungary, while England had a disastrous tour, losing in France and Portugal.
- Chelsea, who won their first League title, were scheduled to play Djurgarden of Sweden in the new European Cup next season, but withdrew on the advice of the Football League.

York battle in vain

Bottom (8) scores against Notts County to put York in the semi-finals.

WITH THE scalps of Blackpool and Spurs already under their belts, York City so very nearly became the first Third Division side to reach the FA Cup final when they took giants Newcastle to a semi-final replay. In the first match, at Hillsborough, they went ahead through Arthur Bottom, scorer of the goal that put Notts County out in the sixth round. And they kept Newcastle out with sterling defence until Keeble finally squeezed an equalizer. In the replay, at Roker Park, they were soon a goal down, scored by White, and, with centre-half Stewart going to the wing with a cut head, they looked down and out. But they still came at Newcastle until Keeble, again, finished them off in the last minute.

The extraordinary thing is that York did all this without a manager. When Jimmy McCormick resigned in September, he had built up a side around a nucleus of players signed from the proceeds of the sale of centre-forward David Dunmore to McCormick's former former club, Spurs. And when York beat Spurs 3–1 in the fifth round, Dunmore had sat and watched the upset as twelfth man!

FINAL SCORE

Football League
Division 1: Chelsea
Top scorer: Ronnie Allen (West Bromwich Albion) 27
Division 2: Birmingham City
Division 3S: Bristol City
Division 3N: Barnsley
Footballer of the Year: Don Revie (Manchester City)

FA Cup Final

Newcastle United	3	Manchester City	1

Scottish League
Division A: Aberdeen
Top scorer: Willie Bauld (Hearts) 21
Division B: Airdrieonians

Scottish FA Cup Final

Clyde	1	Celtic	1
Replay: Clyde	1	Celtic	0

Scottish League Cup Final

Hearts	4	Motherwell	2

International Championship
England, 6 pts

Matthews still magic at 40 — Scots downed 7–2!

SCOTLAND reached a new low at Wembley, annihilated 7–2 by the "auld enemy", their biggest defeat in the Home Championship and equalling their own record victory against England way back in 1878. They retained 10 of the team that lost 4–2 to Hungary at Hampden in December — regarded by some of the Scottish media as a "moral victory" because it was by a smaller margin than England's defeats by the "Magic Magyars"! With such thinking, it's sackcloth and ashes time for Scottish football. This side was outgunned in every department.

Without a win against Scotland at Wembley since 1934, England scored twice in the first eight minutes, after which no other result looked possible. Stanley Matthews, so often the scourge of the Scots, is still tormenting them at 40. He was unplayable, and created so many openings that England could have scored twice as many. Dennis Wilshaw scored four, Nat Lofthouse two (it should have been more). The other was notched by inside-right Don Revie, playing as a midfield schemer and aiding and abetting Matthews in the destruction of the Scots. Duncan Edwards of Manchester United, just 18 years 183 days old, made an impressive debut at left-half, while Jimmy Meadows and Ken Armstrong were also winning their first England caps.

But it was "old man" Matthews who won the honours again, and the Wembley crowd rose to applaud him off the field at the end of the game.

Dennis Wilshaw (10) jumps above Willie Cunningham and heads England's fifth goal against Scotland.

Manchester United win 11-goal thriller at Stamford Bridge

THE STAMFORD BRIDGE crowd went home with mixed feelings after watching an 11-goal thriller in which their side went desperately close to making the comeback of the season. Leading 3–2 at half-time, Manchester United were soon 5–2 up, and although Chelsea managed to pull one back, United restored their three-goal lead.

But Chelsea continued to pile on the pressure. Two more goals, and they were only one down with 12 minutes to go. But United held out for a 6–5 victory.

One Chelsea player will remember the match with particular pride. Seamus O'Connell, an amateur inside-left making his debut, scored a hat-trick.

Trautmann the hero: latest Cup final casualty plays on in spite of his broken neck

MANCHESTER CITY keeper Bert Trautmann played the last 15 minutes of the Cup final in great pain, not realizing his neck was broken. With his side two up, this latest victim of the "Wembley hoodoo" could have been excused for going off after a dive to save at the feet of Birmingham's Peter Murphy left him dazed and reeling. When the highly popular ex-German POW, newly elected Footballer of the Year, staggered to his feet, the fans burst out into a refrain of "For he's a jolly good fellow". He went up with his team-mates to collect his medal after their 3–1 victory, and it was only later that X-rays showed the fracture which could easily have been fatal.

This was a Cup final that had everything. Birmingham started as firm favourites after a dazzling Cup run that saw them reach Wembley without a single home tie, scoring 18 goals against two. Manchester City, by contrast, scraped through with single-goal victories in every round. And injuries forced a last-minute reshuffle of their team for the final. The out-of-favour Don Revie, dropped by both England and his club earlier in the season, was brought back from reserve-team football to play his deep-lying centre-forward role, and Bobby Johnstone was moved out to the right wing.

These controversial moves by manager Les McDowall proved to be match-winners. If Trautmann's heroics stole some of the headlines, Revie was the man of the match. He set up the first goal with a long cross-field ball to Roy Clarke from near half-way, was in the box for the return pass, and back-heeled the ball for Joe Hayes to score — this after only three minutes.

Birmingham equalized against the run of play after 15 minutes through Noel Kinsey. It was another 50 minutes before Jack Dyson restored Manchester's lead. And five minutes later the same player headed a long Trautmann clearance into the path of Johnstone, who beat the advancing Gil Merrick with ease to become the first man to score goals in successive Wembley finals.

The save that left Bert Trautmann with a broken neck... and a place in football folklore.

'Boom-Boom' Edwards stars as England beat world champions

NOT YET 20, Duncan Edwards, one of the "Busby Babes" who ran away with the Championship this season, turned the game around for England against West Germany in Berlin at the end of their summer tour. England were being overrun by the world champions when Edwards brought the ball out of defence, powered his way through the middle of the field, swerving past defender after defender, and unleashed an unstoppable shot from 25 yards.

This giant of a man, immediately nicknamed "Boom-Boom" by the spectators, has established his place as a tower of strength in the England side. After his 27th-minute wonder goal, England took control, and further goals by Grainger and Haynes midway through the second half wrapped it up before Fritz Walter scored a consolation five minutes before the end.

England powerhouse Duncan Edwards scored a great goal.

South American 'Real' king of the first European final

ARGENTINE-BORN Alfredo di Stefano orchestrated Real Madrid's thrilling victory over French club Reims in Paris in the first ever European Cup final. The No.9, a prolific goalscorer but not a centre-forward in the accepted sense, likes to dominate a game from one penalty area to another. With Reims two goals up, he illustrated this in the best possible fashion.

Beating two men in midfield, he put Marsal away, lost his markers by stopping, and then accelerated into the box to lash the return pass into the net. Di Stefano continued to be the driving force as Real equalized, fell behind again and then snatched two more goals for a brilliant 4–3 victory.

This first European Cup has been a marked success. With Chelsea refused entry by the short-sighted Football League, who did not look kindly on additions to the fixture list, Hibs of Scotland were Britain's only representatives, and they were beaten by Reims in the semi-finals.

Alfredo di Stefano led Real Madrid to victory.

Boston pitch Rams out at Baseball Ground

WHEN DERBY, the first post-war Cup-winners, dropped down to Division Three (North) last season for the first time in their history, they did not think they could sink any lower. But they have reached a new nadir — beaten in the second round of the FA Cup, beaten at home by a non-League side, and not just beaten, but thrashed 6–1.

There are a couple of instances of non-League giant-killers beating League opposition by similar scores before, but never away from home, and certainly not so illustrious a team as Derby, who are challenging for promotion. Boston United's feat must go down as one of the most sensational results in the Cup's long history.

The part-timers from the Midland League went ahead after 26 minutes, and were 3–1 up by half-time, Derby's only reply coming from a penalty scored by former Wolves and England star Jesse Pye. Any thoughts of a Derby comeback were snuffed out midway through the second half, when Boston hit three more in a 10-minute spell. Geoff Hazledine completed his hat-trick, and Ray Wilkins scored two. Both players were formerly with Derby, among seven in the side.

Derb's player-manager Ray Middleton, their goalkeeper, had picked up a "job lot" of five players at the end of last season when Derby had a relegation clear-out. They certainly came back to haunt the Rams.

England beat ball-juggling Brazilians at Wembley: Matthews stars again

AGELESS Stanley Matthews had a hand in three of England's goals as they beat the touring Brazilians 4–2 at Wembley in an extraordinary match packed with incident. Atyeo and Byrne both missed penalties. After French referee Marcel Guigue awarded one of these, a Brazilian player grabbed the ball and walked away with it, followed in single file by the referee, half the Brazilian team, and England captain Billy Wright — much to the crowd's amusement.

This was one of England's best victories. The Brazilians gave a wonderful display of ball-juggling skills, but they did not appear to have any kind of tactical plan. England were two up in five minutes. The first was begun and finished by players from the impressive young Manchester United side, the new League champions. Left-half Duncan Edwards found Matthews on the right. A square cross was touched forward by Johnny Haynes, and Tommy Taylor was at the far post to hit the ball home first time.

When outside-left Colin Grainger, making his England debut, scored the second, it looked as if Brazil were in for a thrashing. But they came back well, and drew level soon after the interval with goals by Paulinho and Didi. England, however, took control again, the halves Clayton, Wright and Edwards tackling hard and providing the springboard for their attacks. Taylor, proving a fine leader of the forward line, restored England's lead from close in, and Matthews, still delighting the crowd and bamboozling left-backs with his footwork under the new Wembley floodlights, put the ball on Grainger's head for England's fourth.

Both penalties were awarded for hands by Zozimo, and both were saved by Gilmar.

Sheffield United winger Colin Grainger (11) heads England's fourth on a memorable debut.

FOOTBALL FOCUS

- Tranmere centre-half Harold Bell finally missed a match in September after completing a record 401 consecutive League appearances from the start of the 1946–47 season.
- Wolves equalled the Division One away goalscoring record (set by Sunderland at Newcastle in December 1908) when they won 9–1 at Cardiff on 3 September.
- A last-minute equalizer by Johnny Haynes at Hampden gave England a 1–1 draw and ensured the first ever four-way tie for the Home International Championship.
- The first floodlit matches between League teams in first-class competitions were played, in a second-round Cup replay at Newcastle between Carlisle and Darlington on 28 November, and in the League between Portsmouth and Newcastle at Fratton Park on 22 February.
- Manchester United equalled the record margin of victory in Division One, finishing on 60 points, 11 ahead of Blackpool and Wolves.
- Arsenal were leading Blackpool 4–0 in a First Division match at Highbury on 17 December, when someone in the crowd blew a whistle. Dennis Evans, Arsenal's left-back, thought it was the referee blowing for time, and whacked the ball into his own net. Result: 4–1.

FINAL SCORE

Football League
Division 1: Manchester United
Top scorer: Nat Lofthouse (Bolton W) 32
Division 2: Sheffield Wednesday
Division 3S: Leyton Orient
Division 3N: Grimsby Town
Footballer of the Year: Bert Trautmann (Manchester City)

FA Cup Final

Manchester City	3	Birmingham City	1

Scottish League
Division A: Rangers
Top scorer: Jimmy Wardhaugh (Hearts)
Division B: Queen's Park

Scottish FA Cup Final

Hearts	3	Celtic	1

Scottish League Cup Final

Aberdeen	2	St Mirren	1

International Championship
Four-way tie on 3 pts

European Cup Final

Real Madrid	4	Reims	3

United still clear after classic with Spurs

A TREMENDOUS top-of-the-table clash at White Hart Lane between leaders Manchester United and nearest rivals Spurs finished even. Just three days after their second-leg European Cup match in Dortmund, where their magnificent rearguard action earned them a 0–0 draw to put them through to the quarter-finals, the "Busby Babes" travelled to North London to protect their two-point First Division lead.

United soon found themselves struggling and were two down in eight minutes. But their defence gradually stifled the Spurs threat, and they then took up the attack. Just before half-time, left-back Roger Byrne produced one of his long-distance dribbles, finishing with a shot that rattled the cross-bar, and Duncan Edwards smashed the rebound against a post. Immediately after the interval, outside-right Johnny Berry pulled one back for United, and they continued to pile on the pressure. Danny Blanchflower had a magnificent game for Spurs, and it looked like they were going to draw level with United at the top when, three minutes from the end, little Eddie Colman popped up to bang the ball into the net.

What an advertisement for football this match was, and who is going to stop the almost frighteningly mature "Busby Babes" from taking the title again?

United's Tommy Taylor fails to connect with goalkeeper Ted Ditchburn beaten.

Busby's boys take Europe by storm

THE Football League tried to stop them and failed. Poor Anderlecht tried to stop them, but it was like trying to stand up in the face of a tornado. Manchester United have made an immediate mark on the European Cup competition, and will go into the next round as feared and respected on the Continent as they are at home.

With the Old Trafford floodlights not yet ready, United played their preliminary-round, second-leg tie at Maine Road, starting with a two-goal lead from their match in Belgium. That had not been an easy game: Anderlecht missed a penalty just before Dennis Viollet scored the first, and Tommy Taylor gave United a somewhat flattering 2–0 scoreline. So no-one was prepared for the avalanche of goals in the return.

Viollet scored four, Taylor three, Whelan two and Berry one. It was a superb, flawless exhibition of football, and United did not let up for a moment. Man of the match David Pegg, the only forward not on the score-sheet, made more than half their goals. What price the Football League's advice now?

'Babes' meet their match in Madrid, but will be chasing again next season

MANCHESTER UNITED have been knocked out of the European Cup by Real Madrid, but they retained their League title and will be back next year for another tilt at the Champions' Cup.

What a fortnight this has been for the English champions. On 11 April, they held out for an hour in Madrid against the champions of Europe in the first leg of the semi-finals before succumbing 3–1 to Di Stefano and company. Then came four League matches in 10 days: on the 13th, a 2–0 win at Luton; the 19th (Good Friday), a 3–1 win at Burnley; and the 20th, the 4–0 victory over Sunderland at Old Trafford that clinched the League Championship for the second season running, before fielding seven reserves against Burnley on Easter Monday and still winning 2–0!

But now they have finally been eliminated from the European Cup, by surely the greatest club side in the world. Although United had come back from two down in the quarter-finals to beat Spanish champions Athletic Bilbao, Real Madrid were a different proposition. They took a 2–0 lead under the new Old Trafford floodlights, before United hit back through Taylor and young Bobby Charlton to make the aggregate score respectable. They were beaten by experience and a genius called Di Stefano, but their turn will surely come. Now their thoughts turn to the Cup and that elusive "double".

League champions Manchester United: back row, Bill Foulkes, Eddie Colman, Liam "Billy" Whelan, Ray Wood, Mark Jones, Duncan Edwards; front, Johnny Berry, Dennis Viollet, Roger Byrne (capt.), Tommy Taylor, David Pegg; insets, Bobby Charlton, Jackie Blanchflower.

Cutler wins argument with post before knocking out Wolves

BOURNEMOUTH brought off the shock of the fourth round of the Cup when they went to Molineux and beat mighty Wolves 1–0. Billy Wright and his men have conquered the best in Europe in a series of thrilling floodlit friendlies that gave impetus to the inception of the European Cup. So they were not expected to have any trouble with a Third Division side. But that's the romance of the Cup, as we hear it said year after year. The man who did the damage — in more ways than one — was left-winger Reg Cutler. First he collided with a goal-post, and the game had to be stopped for repairs — to the post! Then he scored the winning goal.

Under manager Freddie Cox, no stranger to Wembley, Bournemouth can cause one or two more surprises.

Play stops while post receives treatment at Molineux.

Villa rob United of 'double' as Wembley jinx strikes again

YET AGAIN we have had to witness the sight of a team struggling through most of a Cup final with only 10 men. This time it was no accident, but a foul charge by Aston Villa's Peter McParland on Ray Wood that left the Manchester United keeper concussed and with a broken cheek bone. This, after only six minutes, completely disrupted a United side who were bidding to become the first club to bring off the League and Cup "double" since Villa did it 60 years ago.

But for Wood's injury, United would almost certainly have achieved it. Centre-half Jackie Blanchflower went in goal — and played a blinder! Edwards went to centre-half, where he is perfectly at home, and was another United hero. But Whelan's dropping back to left-half left the forward line unbalanced and lacking his goalscoring power (he was United's leading League scorer with 26 goals). A groggy Wood returned for 10 minutes half an hour later, but only as nuisance value on the wing.

The reorganized Manchester side held out until midway through the second half, when two goals from outside-left McParland virtually killed their chances. With seven minutes to go, however, Taylor headed in an Edwards corner, and United brought Wood back into goal for a last desperate effort. But Villa's defence, admirably marshalled by Dugdale at centre-half, held out against all their opponents could do, and the Midlanders had won their record seventh FA Cup.

Villa captain and inside-left Johnny Dixon had an outstanding match, but their star was Irish international McParland, always the danger man, although his second goal was arguably offside. His performance, however, should not be allowed to whitewash the unforgivable foul that laid out the United keeper. Wood had already caught the ball from McParland's header and was standing still, some four yards from his goal-line, when the oncoming winger, who could easily have avoided him, crashed into him. At best, it was reckless and irresponsible. Yet the referee did not even caution McParland. Sadly, it left a nasty taste in the mouth.

Villa "villain" McParland crashes into United keeper Wood.

SOCCER SOUNDBITES

"I can still see young Colman running to collect the ball for a throw-in with only two or three minutes left."

MANCHESTER UNITED MANAGER MATT BUSBY,
on his side's keenness even when 10 goals up.

"Why don't they pick the whole side for England? The best teams from Hungary have never beaten us like this."

JEF MERMANS, ANDERLECHT CAPTAIN,
after their 10–0 defeat by Manchester United.

FINAL SCORE

Football League
Division 1: Manchester United
Top scorer: John Charles (Leeds United) 38
Division 2: Leicester City
Division 3S: Ipswich Town
Division 3N: Derby County
Footballer of the Year: Tom Finney (Preston North End)

FA Cup Final

Aston Villa	2	Manchester United	1

Scottish League
Division 1: Rangers
Top scorer: Hugh Baird (Airdrieonians) 33
Division 2: Clyde

Scottish FA Cup Final

Falkirk	1	Kilmarnock	1
Replay: Falkirk	2	Kilmarnock	1

Scottish League Cup Final

Celtic	0	Partick	0
Replay: Celtic	3	Partick Thistle	0

International Championship
England, 5 pts

European Cup Final

Real Madrid	2	Fiorentina	0

European Footballer of the Year 1956
Stanley Matthews (Blackpool & England)

FOOTBALL FOCUS

- Non-League Bedford Town drew 2–2 at Arsenal in the third round of the Cup and were leading 1–0 in the replay with seconds left, when Arsenal equalized and beat them 2–1 in extra time.

- Stoke outside-right Neville Coleman scored seven goals in their 8–0 win over Lincoln on 23 February, a League record for a winger and equalling the Division Two goalscoring record.

- All four Football League divisional champions scored more than 100 goals, for the first time since 1931–32.

- After their triumph at Molineux, Cup giant-killers Bournemouth beat Spurs 3–1 and were leading a 10-man Manchester United (Mark Jones had gone off injured) by 1–0 at Dean Court in the quarter-finals before two goals from Berry ended their adventures.

United bring out the best in Arsenal but remain supreme

Bobby Charlton (left) scores United's second goal.

IN PERHAPS the finest match seen at Highbury since the thirties, Manchester United emerged as winners by the odd goal in nine to stay in second place in the League, four points behind Wolves. The capacity 64,000 crowd gasped at the breathtaking football of the visitors as they took a first-half 3–0 lead. Edwards and Colman, in their different ways, dominated the midfield, and their wingers were running Arsenal ragged — no, not Berry and Pegg, but Morgans and Scanlon. There seems no end to the talent Mr Busby has nurtured at Old Trafford.

Edwards, Charlton and Taylor all scored to give United a seemingly impregnable lead. The ground was abuzz at half-time, marvelling at the magic conjured up by the "Busby Babes", looking to dominate English football for years to come. Even the Arsenal fans sat back, resigned to another exhibition in the second half, and possibly a thrashing.

But perhaps some of the magic rubbed off after the interval on what is frankly a mediocre Arsenal side. Galvanized into action by their captain Dave Bowen, they scored three goals in as many minutes. But the "Babes" brushed aside their challenge almost imperiously, as Viollet and Taylor made the score 5–3. Still Arsenal were not finished: Tapscott pulled a goal back, Groves nearly equalized — but United held out. The crowd rose to the masters and a team of artisans who, for one glorious afternoon, almost matched their magic.

FOOTBALL FOCUS

- Northern Ireland had their first win at Wembley (3–2) on 6 November, and on 15 January they beat Italy 2–1 in Belfast to qualify for the World Cup finals. All four home countries made it to Sweden.
- Hereford United equalled the record score for non-League clubs against League opposition in the FA Cup when they beat QPR (Division Three (South) 6–1 in the second round. First Division Newcastle lost 3–1 at home to Third Division Scunthorpe.
- Cardiff City (Division Two) won at Leeds (Division One) for the third season running in the FA Cup — in the same round (third) and by the same score (2–1) — the only difference being that they have swapped divisions since 1956!
- Hearts scored a record 132 goals in Scottish Division One, with a record goal difference (103).
- Sunderland were relegated for the first time, after an unbroken run in Division One since their election in 1890.
- While all the attention was focused on Manchester United, Wolves quietly won the League, and became the first club other than United to win the FA Youth Challenge Cup, coming back from a 5–1 first-leg deficit in the final to beat Chelsea 7–6 on aggregate.
- In his first season in Italy, John Charles led Juventus to the title and was the championship's leading goalscorer with 28 in 34 games.

'Busby Babes' in plane crash: the football world mourns

THE AIRCRAFT carrying the Manchester United football team, officials and journalists crashed on take-off at Munich Airport on 6 February. Over half the 40 aboard were killed, while many others are fighting for their lives in a Munich hospital.

The Elizabethan airliner had stopped to refuel on the way back from Belgrade, where United had drawn 3–3 with Red Star to earn a place in the European Cup semi-finals. Snow was falling as it prepared to take off for the third time, after two aborted attempts. It reached the point of no return, but failed to get off the ground and ploughed through the perimeter fence. It split in half, the port wing and part of the tail section hitting a house.

The dead include left-back and captain Roger Byrne, reserve left-back Geoff Bent, right-half Eddie Colman, centre-half Mark Jones, outside-left David Pegg, centre-forward Tommy Taylor and inside-right Liam "Billy" Whelan. Club secretary Walter Crickmer also was killed, along with team coach Bert Whalley and trainer Tom Curry. Several journalists also died, including former England goalkeeper Frank Swift.

Among the seriously injured are United manager Matt Busby, who is in a critical condition with a crushed chest, and England international Duncan Edwards, who is in a coma. Survivors with no more than minor injuries include Bobby Charlton, who was thrown from the plane still strapped to his seat, Dennis Viollet, Ken Morgans, Billy Foulkes and Harry Gregg. Johnny Berry and Jackie Blanchflower also survived but are thought unlikely to play again.

The whole country is in deep shock, and the football world mourns the tragic loss of so many young lives.

The wreck of the Elizabethan airliner lies on the Munich snow.

Bolton win the Cup: United's triumph was getting there

BOLTON were in a "no-win" situation from the start. Manchester United, shattered three months earlier by the Munich plane crash, had reached the Cup final on a wave of public sympathy and thanks largely to the inspirational play of Bobby Charlton, on to whose young shoulders all United's hopes have now been transferred. Five years ago, Bolton were in a similar position, when the weight of "neutral" support was behind Stanley Matthews and Blackpool. They lost that one, but this time they won — and they won well.

But United were also winners. Their remarkable resurgence after the tragedy, and their determination to succeed have won the hearts of the footballing world. Of the immediate survivors of the crash, Duncan Edwards hung on for two more weeks before he also died. Matt Busby miraculously clung to life, and was passed fit enough to attend the final. His assistant Jimmy Murphy, who missed the Belgrade trip only because he was managing the Welsh international side, had taken charge of the club and hastily drafted some experienced players into his team of reserves and the few Munich survivors. Berry and Blanchflower would never play again. But Charlton and Viollet had recovered from their injuries and, with Gregg and Foulkes, played in the final — the only four of the "Babes" to make it.

Nat Lofthouse scored for Bolton after three minutes. Then, early in the second half, a Charlton shot hit a post and bounced into goalkeeper Hopkinson's hands, Bolton raced away, and Lofthouse scored again, controversially charging Gregg into the net with the ball as he parried a shot.

In the end, perhaps, the result was not important. A Manchester win would not have brought the lost "Babes" back. What matters is that the club is alive, and that the spirit is still there.

Lofthouse, both feet off the ground, illegally charges Gregg over the line, but the referee awarded a goal.

Seven-goal Celtic crush rivals Rangers in major final

THE SCORELINE was sensational, Rangers 1 Celtic 7, in the Scottish League Cup final — the highest score in any major British final. It was a day when Celtic suddenly clicked. They led only 2–0 at half-time but had already struck the woodwork three times. Rangers, though, were completely demoralized, and Bobby Evans broke up their few attacks with ease. Neil Mochan, restored on the left wing, scored twice and was a permanent thorn in Rangers' right side. Billy McPhail, who hit a second-half hat-trick, had the beating of Valentine in the air and on the ground. And, it was highly appropriate that right-half Willie Fernie, the chief architect of Celtic's victory, should score their last goal, albeit from a penalty.

No praise is too much for Fernie. On this day, he was unplayable, a master craftsman who shrugged off all crude attempts to unsettle him without ever resorting to the physical himself. In front of him, he had the superb right-wing pair of Charlie Tully and inside-right Bobby Collins.

Inside-left Sammy Wilson opened the scoring after 23 minutes, and a brilliant solo effort from Mochan put Celtic in command before the second-half floodgates opened.

One could only feel sorry for Rangers' centre-half Johnny Valentine, who came from Queen's Park at the start of the season and has tried desparately to fill the gap left by the incomparable George Young. But he was out of his depth, and it will be a long time before he forgets the humiliation he suffered against the highly skilled McPhail. It will be even longer before the inconsolable Rangers fans are allowed to forget this quite extraordinary Old Firm thrashing.

SOCCER SOUNDBITES

"No team should be able to beat Rangers 7–1. It just should not be possible."

RANGERS FAN,
in utter disbelief as he left Hampden Park.

Cliff-hanger at Valley as Charlton climb back from the depths

CHARLTON BROUGHT OFF the most extraordinary comeback in League history when they beat Huddersfield 7–6 at the Valley in a Division Two match on 21 December. They were reduced to 10 men after 15 minutes when centre-half Derek Ufton broke a collar-bone, and were 2–0 down at half-time. Ten minutes later, the score was 1–5! But from this hopeless position they proceeded to score five goals in a sensational spell, as left-winger Johnny Summers ran riot. Five of their six goals at that stage had come from the right boot of the naturally left-footed Summers, and the other was made by him for centre-forward Johnny Ryan. Charlton allowed Huddersfield to draw level two minutes from time, but Summers wasn't finished yet: he made one final surge and put Ryan through for the winner with the last kick of the game.

FINAL SCORE

Football League
Division 1: Wolverhampton Wanderers
Top scorer: Bobby Smith (Tottenham H) 36
Division 2: West Ham United
Division 3S: Brighton & Hove Albion
Division 3N: Scunthorpe United
Footballer of the Year: Danny Blanchflower (Tottenham Hotspur)

FA Cup Final

Bolton Wanderers	2	Manchester United	0

Scottish League
Division 1: Hearts
Top scorer: Jimmy Wardhaugh, Jimmy Murray (both Hearts) 28
Division 2: Stirling Albion

Scottish FA Cup Final

Clyde	1	Hibernian	0

Scottish League Cup Final

Celtic	7	Rangers	1

International Championship
England, N.Ireland, 4 pts

European Cup Final

Real Madrid (after extra time)	3	AC Milan	2

Inter-Cities Fairs Cup (1955–58)
Final: Barcelona beat London 2-2, 6–0

European Footballer of the Year
1957 Alfredo di Stefano (Real Madrid & Spain)

Brazil conquer Europe

Brazil, when they finally settled down, gave Europe a lesson in tactics as well as in football. All their players displayed a complete mastery of the ball, and their stars entertained with outstanding skills, from Didi's midfield genius to Pele's precocious finishing. The home countries were pedestrian by comparison, light-years behind in technique, although Wales and Northern Ireland came out of their first World Cups covered in glory.

IN THE qualifying competition, England and Scotland did no more than was expected of them, but Northern Ireland, orchestrated by Danny Blanchflower, dramatically beat Italy 2–1 in Belfast to get through. Wales were at first eliminated in Czechoslovakia's group, but qualified by the back door. As country after country in the Asia/Africa region withdrew rather than face political outcasts Israel, someone had to play them for the place. Wales won the ballot of the second-placed teams and beat them twice.

In the finals, teams level on points for second place in their group were to replay two days before the quarter-finals, a "fate" that befell three of the home countries. Scotland did not even get that far, however, finishing bottom of their group with a single point.

Busby Babes missed

England, not really recovered from the loss of Edwards, Byrne and Taylor in the Munich air crash four months earlier, were in arguably the toughest group. They drew with the USSR after being two down. But Finney, who equalized from a penalty, was injured and took no further part. Against Brazil, their forward line was ineffective, but they drew 0–0 thanks to an excellent, well-organized defence in which Billy Wright and keeper Colin McDonald were outstanding.

Pele (third left) volleys Brazil's third goal in the final to complete a breathtaking solo effort.

England fielded an unchanged side against Austria, and struggled to earn a point after a colourless performance. Meanwhile, Brazil had found the right blend and their form, with the explosive Garrincha coming in at outside-right, Vava replacing Mazzola at centre-forward, and the 17-year-old Pele, recovered from injury, at inside-left. Didi, as usual, dictated the play from midfield, and the Soviets were lucky to keep the score to 2–0.

This left England and the USSR to play off. England made some changes, but not the one the Press and public were demanding — Bobby Charlton for Kevan in the middle. With Haynes still sadly out of sorts, England failed to score, and a single goal was enough for a somewhat fortunate Soviet victory.

British pride saved

Northern Ireland and Wales, for so long regarded as the "minnows" of British international football, excelled themselves in their first World Cup finals and restored some of Britain's lost pride. They both had world-class players in Danny Blanchflower and John Charles, who were huge influences on their respective teams, and there were no better goalkeepers than Jack Kelsey and, on his day, Ireland's Harry Gregg.

Ireland, astutely managed by former inside-forward Peter Doherty, had the skilful, scheming Jimmy McIlroy to link up with Blanchflower, and two dangerous wingers in Billy Bingham and Peter McParland, complemented by a group of players guaranteed to rise to the occasion in the green shirts. Two players who did so in their first match, against Czechoslovakia, were 5ft 5in Wilbur Cush, who headed the winner, and Gregg, who performed heroics in goal. But Ireland were outplayed by the otherwise disappointing Argentina side, and needed all Gregg's brilliance — and two McParland goals — to earn a draw with West Germany. This put them in a play-off, where they again had to beat the Czechs, sensational 6–1 victors over Argentina. With Gregg injured, the Irish were given no

Ungainly but effective, Just Fontaine (France) digs another one in against West Germany.

WORLD CUP QUOTES

"Our tactics are to equalize before the other side scores."

DANNY BLANCHFLOWER,
Northern Ireland captain.

'Here indeed was a match to remember — a clean, sporting struggle between two great teams, one worthy of the World Championships.'
ARTHUR DREWRY, PRESIDENT OF FIFA, of the World Cup final.

Peter McParland (centre) scores one of his two equalizers for Northern Ireland in their draw with West Germany.

chance of a repeat performance; yet they came back from a goal down, and two more goals from McParland, the second in extra time, saw them through to the quarter-finals, a magnificent achievement.

Wales, meanwhile, had been taking the same route, but with three draws. They held Hungary — a shadow of the great pre-Uprising side — with John Charles equalizing an early Bozsik strike with a towering header. They, in turn, were surprisingly held by the Mexicans. Sweden, still coached by Yorkshireman George Raynor and now professionals, had two wins in the bag, so fielded several reserves against Wales. But Kelsey had to be at his imperturbable best to earn a 0–0 draw.

Tichy gave Hungary a half-time lead in the play-off, but Wales, urged on by their captain and left-half Dave Bowen, produced one of the finest performances in their history. Shamefully, the Soviet referee ignored the brutal treatment being dished out to John Charles. But he returned limping after one particularly bad assault and crossed for Ivor Allchurch to equalize with a cracking 35-yard volley on the run. Terry Medwin then scored the winner after stealing the ball from a careless Grosics clearance-kick.

Pele scored his first World Cup goal against Wales in the quarter-finals. It was not one of his greatest, but it was enough to beat the Welsh, always struggling after their play-off, from which the battered John Charles did not recover in time. Only the brilliant Kelsey held the rampant Brazilians at bay, somehow keeping out all that Garrincha, Didi, Mazzola, Pele and Zagalo threw at him — until Pele's shot was deflected past him.

Northern Ireland, also exhausted from their play-off exertions, and with the injured Gregg back in goal because his replacement Norman Uprichard was in even poorer shape, were no match for the French. Raymond Kopa tormented them, and Just Fontaine added two more goals to what was already an impressive tally.

Numbers tell in semis

In both semi-finals, one side played much of the match with only 10 men, and the handicap proved too much for them. Against Brazil, France lost Jonquet, the hub of their defence, injured after 37 minutes. Fontaine — who else? — had equalized a Vava goal in the first 10 minutes, but no sooner had Jonquet gone than Didi put Brazil ahead with a 30-yard "banana" shot, and the precocious Pele scored a hat-trick in the second half.

Kurt Hamrin was both hero and villain in the other semi-final. He played the game of his life, and beat several defenders before scoring Sweden's third and clinching goal. But he had Juskowiak sent off for retaliation, and a subsequent foul by Parling left Fritz Walter a virtual passenger. Thus depleted, West Germany succumbed late on.

Four days later, in the match for third place, the Germans were destroyed by the wizardry of Kopa and the immaculate finishing of Fontaine, who scored four goals to bring his total for the finals to a record 13.

A joy to watch

It was a tribute to Raynor that his unfancied Sweden side reached the final at all. But any hopes that an early Liedholm goal stirred in the home fans were soon stifled as Brazil unleashed all their brilliance, to give the breathtaking display of football they had promised from the start of the tournament but never quite yet achieved. Vava scored twice, from identical Garrincha low crosses after dazzling right-wing runs, to give them a half-time lead. The third goal, scored by Pele, was sheer poetry, and not only confirmed Brazil as worthy winners, but was a celebration of their joyous football, their willingness to improvise and their supreme ball skills. The young inside-left — first capped a year earlier when not yet 17 — was closely marked in the box and standing with his back to goal, when he took a pass on his thigh, flicked the ball over his head with his foot, and turned past his marker to smash it on the volley into goal.

Brazil proceeded to stroll through the rest of the match. Zagalo scored a fourth, Simonsson snatched one for Sweden and then, right at the end, it was Pele appropriately who headed Brazil's fifth. They had triumphed in Europe, the first country to win the World Cup outside their own continent.

FINAL SCORE

Group 1

West Germany	3	Argentina	1
N.Ireland	1	Czechoslovakia	0
West Germany	2	Czechoslovakia	2
Argentina	3	N.Ireland	1
West Germany	2	N.Ireland	2
Czechoslovakia	6	Argentina	1

	P	W	D	L	F	A	P
W.Germany	3	1	2	0	7	5	4
Czech	3	1	1	1	8	4	3
N.Ireland	3	1	1	1	4	5	3
Argentina	3	1	0	2	5	10	2

Play-off

N.Ireland	2	Czechoslovakia	1

Group 2

Yugoslavia	1	Scotland	1
France	7	Paraguay	3
Paraguay	3	Scotland	2
Yugoslavia	3	France	2
France	2	Scotland	1
Paraguay	3	Yugoslavia	3

	P	W	D	L	F	A	P
France	3	2	0	1	11	7	4
Yugoslavia	3	1	2	0	7	6	4
Paraguay	3	1	1	1	9	12	3
Scotland	3	0	1	2	4	6	1

Group 3

Sweden	3	Mexico	0
Hungary	1	Wales	1
Mexico	1	Wales	1
Sweden	2	Hungary	1
Sweden	0	Wales	0
Hungary	4	Mexico	0

	P	W	D	L	F	A	P
Sweden	3	2	1	0	5	1	5
Wales	3	0	3	0	2	2	3
Hungary	3	1	1	1	6	3	3
Mexico	3	0	1	2	1	8	1

Play-off

Wales	2	Hungary	1

Group 4

USSR	2	England	2
Brazil	3	Austria	0
Brazil	0	England	0
USSR	2	Austria	0
Brazil	2	USSR	0
England	2	Austria	2

	P	W	D	L	F	A	P
Brazil	3	2	1	0	5	0	5
England	3	0	3	0	4	4	3
USSR	3	1	1	1	4	4	3
Austria	3	0	1	2	2	7	1

Play-off

USSR	1	England	0

QUARTER-FINALS

France	4	N.Ireland	0
West Germany	1	Yugoslavia	0
Sweden	2	USSR	0
Brazil	1	Wales	0

SEMI-FINALS

Brazil	5	France	2
Sweden	3	West Germany	1

THIRD-PLACE MATCH

France	6	West Germany	3

FINAL

Brazil	5	Sweden	2

Rasunda Stadium, Solna, Stockholm, 29 June 1958. Attendance 49,737

Brazil: Gylmar, Santos D, Santos N, Zito, Bellini, Orlando, Garrincha, Didi, Vava, Pele, Zagalo (Scorers: Vava (2), Pele (2), Zagalo)
Sweden: Svensson, Bergmark, Axbom, Borjesson, Gustavsson, Parling, Hamrin, Gren, Simonsson, Liedholm, Skoglund (Scorers: Liedholm, Simonsson)

LEADING SCORERS
13 Fontaine (France) 6 Pele (Brazil)
6 Rahn (West Germany)

Wright is the first football 'centurion'

BILLY WRIGHT, the England and Wolves captain and centre-half, became the world's first footballer to win 100 caps when he led England to victory over Scotland at Wembley on 11 April. It was his 85th game as skipper, and of the 100 matches, England have won 59 and drawn 22. He has made a record 65 consecutive appearances for England, and has missed only three of their 103 post-war matches.

A one-club man, and originally a right-half, Wright led Wolves to their second League title in five years last season, and is poised to make it three before the month is out. He won a Cup-winners' medal in 1949 and was voted Footballer of the Year in 1952.

He has been a wonderful ambassador for football, and it was highly appropriate that he should reach this soccer milestone at Wembley and with a win over Scotland (Bobby Charlton scored the only goal of the game).

Wright is chaired off the field by Ron Clayton (left) and Don Howe.

Hatters cage Canaries in a replay

LUTON FINALLY put a stop to Third Division Norwich's remarkable FA Cup run when they beat them 1–0 in the replayed semi-final at St Andrews, Birmingham. This season, managed by former Scottish international Archie Macaulay and skippered by Ron Ashman, the Canaries surpassed their giant-killing exploits of 1954, when they beat Arsenal at Highbury in the fourth round. They first hit the headlines in the third round, when they beat Manchester United 3–0 at Carrow Road. Another home tie saw them defeat Second Division Cardiff 3–2, and then they held Spurs 1–1 in the fifth round and won the home replay 1–0.

But their bravest performance came in their sixth-round tie at Bramall Lane, when keeper Ken Nethercott played the last half-hour with a dislocated shoulder. They were already a goal down, but they managed to keep Sheffield at a distance, equalized, and then won the replay 3–2. Norwich played well in the semi-final, but were out of luck, and Billy Bingham put an end to their dreams with the only goal.

Billy Bingham (far right) scores in the semi-final replay to put Norwich out of the Cup.

It's 10–4 and out for Everton as Spurs welcome new manager

THE SPURS players heard of the appointment of Bill Nicholson as manager in the dressing-room before the game. It was no surprise: he had been with Spurs since before the war, as player and latterly as coach. So it was nothing he said, no new tactical plan, that turned a potentially gritty battle between two sides in the relegation zone into the highest scoring match in the First Division this century.

Spurs had brought back little Tommy Harmer, dropped four matches earlier. Light as a feather, but on his day the trickiest schemer in the land, Harmer was behind nearly every Spurs move, and nearly every move seemed to lead to a goal. All Spurs' forwards scored: centre-forward and captain Bobby Smith (four), Alf Stokes (two), Terry Medwin, George Robb and Harmer, and centre-half Ryden, a passenger on the wing for the last 15 minutes, chipped in with the final goal to make the score 10–4. Jimmy Harris hit a hat-trick for Everton, and Bobby Collins scored the other. Stand-in Everton keeper Albert Dunlop is going to find it hard to hold his place, just as new Spurs manager Nicholson is going to be hard put to maintain his sensational start.

FOOTBALL FOCUS

- Denis Law, Huddersfield's inside-left, became Scotland's youngest international when he won his first cap at the age of 18 years 236 days against Wales in October, and he scored in their 3–0 win.
- Centre-forward Brian Clough is emulating his 1920s predecessor at Middlesbrough, George Camsell, leading the Division Two goalscorers (with 42 goals) for the second year running. It is the third season he has averaged a goal a game, and he has reached 100 League goals in quicker time than any player previously.
- Aston Villa, needing to win at West Brom on the last day of the season to be sure of staying in Division One, conceded a goal a minute from time when leading 1–0. Rivals Manchester City won their game, so Villa were relegated.

Tired England flop in New World, but Wright finishes his career on a high note

THE FA have been strongly criticized in many quarters for planning a 20,000 mile summer tour for England on top of a heavy League season. It was no surprise when they lost their first match 2–0 to world champions Brazil in Rio; under the circumstances, this was a creditable performance against Didi, Pele and company in front of 151,000 partisan fans in the great Maracana Stadium. But the rest of the Latin American trip was a disappointment. England lost 4–1 against Peru, whose players were individually more skilful — how England missed the injured Tom Finney on this tour! Jimmy Greaves, however, could be pleased with his performance and a goal in his first international.

There followed a frustrating 2–1 defeat in the sweltering heat and thin air of Mexico City to a Mexican side who did not possess the sophistication of the South Americans. But the tour ended on a high note, especially for Billy Wright, who retired from international football with 105 caps after this last match. It was in Los Angeles against the United States, who nine years earlier had humbled England in the World Cup finals. Wright, the only survivor from that débâcle, must have taken particular satisfaction in England's 8–1 victory.

Henrique stretches a leg to score Brazil's second goal against England.

Forest overcome Wembley 'hoodoo' to win Cup with 10 men

THAT WEMBLEY CUP final jinx struck again. Nottingham Forest right-winger Roy Dwight was carried off with a broken leg after 32 minutes, but Forest, two up at the time, defended stoutly and held out for a 2–1 victory over Luton.

Any other result would have been a travesty. For half an hour, Forest outplayed Luton with a display of confident, fast-moving football, the like of which we have not seen in a Cup final since the Manchester United-Blackpool game in 1948.

Luton, with experienced big-match players such as Billy Bingham, Allan Brown and Syd Owen in their side, started as favourites. Only three weeks ago they beat Forest 5–1 in the League. But they were two down in 14 minutes as Forest's fluent passing tore them apart. Dwight was the star of that brilliant early attack, slamming the ball in to put his side one up after great work from Stewart Imlach on the left. Four minutes later, Tom Wilson finished off another glorious move with a header. Forest were two up, and their keeper had not touched the ball.

Only Luton keeper Ron Baynham kept the score down, but it must surely have been a rout had not Dwight had a shinbone cracked in what seemed a harmless challenge with Brendan McNally. Now the sides were even. Forest continued to play the better football — the only football — but were gradually forced on the defensive as the spongy turf took its toll on their 10 men. David Pacey pulled one back after a corner, but Luton could not score again.

Luton are helpless as Dwight's shot finds the net.

FINAL SCORE

Football League
Division 1: Wolverhampton Wanderers
Top scorer: Jimmy Greaves (Chelsea) 32
Division 2: Sheffield Wednesday
Division 3: Plymouth Argyle
Division 4: Port Vale
Footballer of the Year: Syd Owen (Luton Town)

FA Cup Final
Nottingham Forest 2 Luton Town 1

Scottish League
Division 1: Rangers
Top scorer: Joe Baker (Hibernian) 25
Division 2: Ayr United

Scottish FA Cup Final
St Mirren 3 Aberdeen 1

Scottish League Cup Final
Hearts 5 Partick Thistle 1

International Championship
England, N.Ireland, 4 pts

European Cup Final
Real Madrid 2 Reims 0

European Footballer of the Year 1958
Raymond Kopa (Real Madrid & France)

Busby saves Quixall from Division Two and breaks British transfer record

MANCHESTER UNITED bought unsettled Sheffield Wednesday star Albert Quixall for a British record fee of £45,000 on 18 September. After a poor start to the season, Matt Busby stepped into the transfer market again when it became clear that his side, tragically depleted in the Munich air crash, still needed strengthening.

The fair-haired inside-forward won the first of his five England caps five years ago while still on National Service, but has not been picked since May 1955. Last season he played against United in their first match after Munich, when Wednesday lost 3–0. He later became captain, but Wednesday were relegated at the end of the season, and he made it clear that he did not relish playing in Division Two.

Quixall is the third player to figure in a record deal involving Wednesday in the last nine years. Eddie Quigley was sold to Preston for £26,000, and Jackie Sewell was bought from Notts County for £34,000.

Post-War heroes

THE POST-WAR period is often referred to as the "Golden Age of Football", with grounds up and down the country bursting at the seams every Saturday to see their sporting heroes perform. It was a time, still, of attacking football, and the fans went along to see goals and goalmouth incident, wingers who could beat their man and send in wicked crosses, centre-forwards who could put the ball in the net. If a Matthews or a Lawton were on the visitors' teamsheet, the gates were sure to be closed with thousands more locked out.

The goalscorers

Tommy Lawton stands out from the immediate post-war period in Britain as the complete centre-forward. It is remarkable that Everton should have found such a player to replace the "irreplaceable" Dixie Dean, although his best years, his early 20s, were consumed by the war, as were those of many contemporary heroes. After the war, with Chelsea and later with Third Division Notts County, Lawton continued to spearhead the England side, but he played as many wartime games as he did in peace, and his total haul was 47 goals in 46 internationals. He was fast, smooth, packed a powerful shot in both feet, and was supreme in the air.

After Lawton came Jackie Milburn, a converted winger, with a winger's speed and silky skills, an idol in the North-East, where he played for Newcastle and won Cup glory. Nat Lofthouse of Bolton made the position his own in the early fifties (30 goals in 33 games to set an England record), a brave battering ram of a leader, more in the Ted Drake mould. Often playing alongside one or other of these centre-forwards, or in place of them, was Blackpool's Stan Mortensen, and he also knew how to score — 23 in 25 England games, and the only man to score a Cup final hat-trick this century.

At international level, Scotland's football had declined, their ambitions still anachronistically rooted to beating the "auld enemy". Lawrie Reilly became their most capped centre-forward, with 38 appearances, and scored 22 goals. Only 5ft 7in, he was an all-round player with fast reflexes, and starred in the high-scoring Hibs forward line that dominated Scottish football for a while in the early fifties.

John Charles: equally effective at centre-half or centre-forward.

At the same time, the powerful Trevor Ford was scoring a Welsh record 23 goals in his 38 internationals. But directly behind him, on the field, was the man who became the biggest of all Welsh stars, John Charles, the "Gentle Giant", a master of aerial combat. There was no better centre-half in the game, but Leeds transformed him into a centre-forward, and when he took his powerful skills to Juventus in the mid-fifties he became the idol of Italian football.

In the early fifties, when it became increasingly obvious that the rest of the world had caught up with British football and were in the process of overtaking it, foreign stars suddenly became household names. Ferenc Puskas, the plumpish "Galloping Major" of the 1953 Hungarians, stamped his personality and his class on the Wembley turf, rifling the ball in from all angles with that remarkable left foot of his and demonstrating that his goalscoring feats — eventually 83 goals in 84 internationals for Hungary — could be reproduced at the highest level. The Magyars' other inside-forward, Sandor Kocsis, scored many of his 75 international goals (in 68 games) with elegant headers. "Golden Head", as he was known, ranked with Dean, Lawton and Charles in the air.

Wing wonders

A feature of post-war football was wing-play, as epitomized, above all, by Matthews and Finney. It was the classic duel, the winger and his opposing full-back. Stanley Matthews was over-simplified as the "one-trick wizard", because the back knew what he was going to do 90 per cent of the time — go past him on the outside — but somehow Matthews always seemed to be behind him before he could make his tackle. Tom Finney could play on either wing and, like Matthews, was beautifully balanced with a superb body swerve. Matthews spanned the war and was to play on into a fourth decade, and all the time he was the greatest draw in English football. Finney had a fine shot with either foot, and was a complete forward who scored 30 goals for England. Both, above all, had a wonderful temperament, and there were no finer sportsmen in the whole of football.

Scotland's wing heroes were Billy Liddell on the left and Willie Waddell on the right. Liddell of Liverpool was hard, fast and fair, with a ferocious shot, and his inspiration of both team and fans justified the name "Liddellpool" applied to the club in his day. He later moved to centre-forward and took his League tally to a club record 216 goals. Waddell of Rangers was in the same mould, and the pair first played for Scotland together

Ferenc Puskas of Hungary.

in 1942 at Hampden in a rare 5–4 wartime victory over England.

When Wolves developed their long-ball game in the early fifties, they had the wingers to play it in Hancocks and Mullen, always remembered as a pair. The tiny Johnny Hancocks on the right, with dynamite in his boots, perfectly complemented left-winger Jimmy Mullen, also a consistent scorer.

Schemers

The midfield general of post-war days was still called a schemer. He was the inside-forward who made the team tick, linking defence and attack with astute passes. Wilf Mannion of Middlesbrough took over the role for England from Raich Carter, and he too could score goals as well as make them. Blond and compactly built, he used his pace and ball control to go past defenders. He was an exciting player to watch, as was his contemporary, Len Shackleton, who won only five caps to Mannion's 26. "Shack", a footballing maverick forever at odds with authority, was considered "too good for the rest of the team" by the England selectors. He was a marvellous showman with a portfolio of tricks, and he entertained the crowds royally at Newcastle, where he scored six goals on his debut in 1946, and at Sunderland, where he spent most of his career.

Alfredo di Stefano: the master.

Danny Blanchflower: the "thinking man's footballer".

Other schemers overlooked by the selectors were those diminutive North London heroes Jimmy Logie of Arsenal, who won a solitary Scottish cap, and Tommy Harmer of Spurs, who played once for England "B" in 1952.

In the mid-fifties, Johnny Haynes made the England schemer position his own, despite playing for Second Division Fulham. Famed for his passing ability, he won 56 caps, latterly as captain, and scored 18 goals, too. But when it came to passing skills, Brazil's Didi had no equal, and keepers never got to grips with his famous "dry leaf" free-kick.

Of the scheming wing-halves, two were conspicuous by their talents in post-war football: Danny Blanchflower of Spurs and Northern Ireland, and Joszef Bozsik of Hungary and Honved. Blanchflower, known as the "thinking man's footballer", was a master tactician, never afraid to try something new, and a perfect distributor of the ball. His captaincy was an inspiration to both club and country. Bozsik was the general of the "Magic Magyars" and won a record 100 caps.

Unsung heroes

The men who perform the heroics at the back often do not get their fair share of the limelight, although wing-halves Joe Mercer (Arsenal) and Billy Wright (Wolves) were idolized by the fans, and Wright broke all records as captain of England, converting to centre-half in 1954. Perhaps the greatest centre-half of the period was John Charles — when he wasn't playing up front. All three were renowned for their sportsmanship and fair play.

Scotland, hitherto known for attacking football, could call on some of the finest defenders in their history in the post-war years. They began to turn defence into a fine art in the late 1940s, with the introduction of the so-called "Iron Curtains". George Young and Sammy Cox of Rangers were probably Scotland's best ever full-back pairing, with club-mate Willie Woodburn an outstanding centre-half. Young eventually took over as centre-half, and was a tower of strength for Rangers and Scotland.

Among the many fine post-war goalkeepers, Frank Swift of the huge hands continued his popular and spectacular wartime guardianship of the England goal until he retired in 1949. Jack Kelsey kept Wales and Arsenal in many a match when they were being outplayed — unflappable, courageous, making the difficult look easy. The German Bert Trautmann, who took over from Swift in the Manchester City goal, soon won the hearts of the fans, played over 500 League games and represented the Football League.

The masters

Two players stand out from this period as "total footballers" before the term was coined, not so much players who could play anywhere, but players whose territory was the whole pitch. Duncan Edwards was one of those rare masters of the game, already a legend at the age of 21 when he died in the Munich air crash. Nominally a left-half, he was back in defence or up in attack when he wasn't spraying passes to his team-mates, he had a sensational shot, and he was a model professional.

The other "master" was Alfredo di Stefano, the Argentinian who was nominally a centre-forward in Spain for Real Madrid in their five successive European Cup final victories. But he was more than that: he controlled the game, endlessly moving up and down the pitch from box to box, starting moves, finishing them, directing the pattern of the play. And he was a goalscoring genius who amassed 428 for Real in 510 games, including 49 in the European Cup. He was the undisputed "King of Football".

Stanley Matthews: the wizard.

England all wrong without Wright

WITH THE SAME SIDE that drew in Cardiff 11 days earlier, England lost 3–2 to Sweden, their first defeat by foreign opposition at Wembley since the Hungarians beat them there seven years ago. The World Cup finalists, even without those players who are with Italian clubs, were too good for an England side ably led by Ronnie Clayton, yet still unable to get used to the absence of the retired Billy Wright.

Centre-forward Brian Clough and left-winger Eddie Holliday of Second Division Middlesbrough were together in their second international outing, but the potentially lethal partnership of Clough and Jimmy Greaves again failed to click, and England's goals were scored by John Connelly and Bobby Charlton. Even so, the same side might still have won had keeper Eddie Hopkinson played up to anything like his normal form

Clough fires a great chance straight at the Swedish keeper.

FOOTBALL FOCUS

- Brian Clough scored all the Football League's goals in their 5–0 defeat of the Irish League in Belfast on 23 September and scored 39 League goals for Second Division Middlesbrough, but was dropped after just two appearances for England.
- St Mirren's Gerry Baker, brother of England centre-forward Joe, scored 10 goals in their 15–0 thrashing of Glasgow University on 30 January in the first round of the Scottish Cup.
- Former Arsenal star Cliff Holton, the League's leading scorer with 42 goals for Fourth Division Watford, became the first player ever to score hat-tricks on successive days, on 15 and 16 April in Easter wins over Chester (4–2) and Gateshead (5–0).
- Motherwell's Ian St John notched a hat-trick in two-and-a-half minutes on 15 August in a League Cup tie at Hibs.
- After being held 2–2 at Fourth Division Crewe in a fourth-round Cup tie, Spurs won the replay 13–2 at White Hart Lane.
- Wolves became the first Division One club to score 100 goals in three consecutive seasons.
- European champions Real Madrid won the first World Club Championship, beating the South American champions Penarol in a two-legged home-and-away tie.

Wembley final spoilt by injury again, and by boorish behaviour of some fans

THE 1960 FA CUP final will be remembered for the pre-match rows, for the disgraceful behaviour of the Blackburn fans, and for yet another serious injury that left one side struggling against impossible odds.

Poor Wolves — they won the Cup, but had to run the gauntlet of angry Blackburn fans when they attempted to parade it. The fans were upset for a number of reasons. Discontent at the club had been building up over the weeks before the final and, an hour before the kick-off, Derek Dougan, their popular but maverick Irish centre-forward, had put in a transfer request. The final had been a poor advertisement for football, and was made even worse by the accident to Blackburn left-back Dave Whelan, who broke a leg trying to tackle an opponent. Ironically Whelan had been in hospital on Cup final day the previous year, with knee trouble.

The accident occurred shortly before half-time, and just after Wolves had gone ahead with an own goal by Mick McGrath. Wolves played their usual long-ball game, and typically it was a winger, little Norman Deeley, who scored the two goals that wrapped the match up 3–0 in the last quarter. The booing and jeering they had to face from the Blackburn supporters, not to mention the rubbish thrown at the referee, was shameful. If anything good is to come out of this game, then surely it is time for substitutes to be allowed.

Wolves go one up as Blackburn's McGrath (right) puts through his own goal

Real Madrid are kings of Europe again as di Stefano and Puskas share seven goals in Hampden feast

THIS WAS SURELY the greatest club match ever played. A crowd of 127,621 packed into Hampden Park to see Eintracht Frankfurt take on the undisputed "Kings of Europe", Real Madrid, in the final of the European Cup.

Real, four times champions, have dominated the competition since its inception in 1955–56. The club have been transformed into a formidable force by the president and former player Santiago Bernabeu. After building a magnificent new stadium, he set about recruiting the best players in the world to fill it. First came the Argentinian Alfredo di Stefano, the virtuoso around whom the whole side revolves. Others who followed included the brilliant fleet-footed left-winger Francisco Gento, a Spaniard from Real Santander, the scheming Reims star Raymond Kopa, who had faced them in the first final, the Uruguayan Jose Santamaria, who became the kingpin of their defence; and the overweight Hungarian exile Ferenc Puskas.

Puskas played a part in last year's campaign, but this was his first final. He has struck up a magical partnership with di Stefano, and the two "generals" have blended perfectly. Against the unfortunate Germans, these two ageing stars rolled back the years and produced as breathtaking a display of attacking football and clinical finishing as has been seen in Britain since the Hungarians gave England a lesson in 1953 — when, remarkably, Puskas was also a central figure.

It cannot be said, either, that Eintracht were pushovers. They had put six goals past Rangers in both legs of their semi-final, so their reputation in Glasgow was sky-high. They, too, had a redoubtable duo of veterans in schemer Alfred Pfaff and right-winger Richard Kress. And it was Kress who burst through to put them ahead after 18 minutes.

This was not the first time Real had been down in a final, and typically it was di Stefano who replied, lashing home a cross from Brazilian outside-right Canario eight minutes later and then putting Real ahead after a mistake by the German defence. At this stage, the South American maestro was orchestrating the match, bestriding the pitch from box to box. Then Puskas took over the baton, rifling the ball in from the byline, and after the interval converting a penalty. He then completed his hat-trick with a header from a Gento cross after the flying winger had sprinted 50 yards with the ball, and scored his fourth with a delightful pivot from just inside the box.

The Frankfurt side emphasized their worth by scoring twice more, through Erwin Stein, but in between di Stefano again stamped his majesty on the game with an interpassing move out of defence that he finished off sublimely for his third and Real's seventh goal. At the end, the normally partisan Scottish crowd gave the Spanish side an ovation usually reserved for the victories of their own national team.

Di Stefano scores the first of his three goals against Eintracht at Hampden Park.

FINAL SCORE

Football League
Division 1: Burnley
Top scorer: Dennis Viollet (Manchester U) 32
Division 2: Aston Villa
Division 3: Southampton
Division 4: Walsall
Footballer of the Year: Bill Slater (Wolverhampton Wanderers)

FA Cup Final
Wolves 3 Blackburn Rovers 0

Scottish League
Division 1: Hearts
Top scorer: Joe Baker (Hibernian) 42
Division 2: St Johnstone

Scottish FA Cup Final
Rangers 2 Kilmarnock 0

Scottish League Cup Final
Hearts 2 Third Lanark 1

International Championship
England, Scotland, Wales, 4 pts

European Nations Cup Final
USSR 2 Yugoslavia 1
(after extra time)

European Cup Final
Real Madrid 7 Eintracht Frankfurt 3

Inter-Cities Fairs Cup Final
Barcelona beat Birmingham City 0–0, 4–1

European Footballer of the Year 1959
Alfredo di Stefano (Real Madrid & Spain)

World Club Championship
Real Madrid (Spain) beat Penarol (Uruguay) 0–0, 5–1

Dennis Viollet, Division One leading scorer.

USSR first European champions

A TOURNAMENT that started in 1958 ended with victory for the USSR. They won the first European Nations Cup when they beat Yugoslavia 2–1 in the final on 10 July in Paris. Once again the four home countries absented themselves from a major international competition, West Germany and Italy did not take part, and Spain withdrew for political reasons when drawn against the USSR in the second round.

The contest was played on a home-and-away basis until the semi-finals, played in France. The final was settled in extra time by a goal from Ponedelnik.

Burnley's title a triumph for football

AFTER A UNIQUE campaign in which they did not lead the table until their last game, Burnley found themselves needing to beat Manchester City to take the League title. They thrillingly won 2–1 at Maine Road, thus depriving leaders Wolves, who beat them 6–1 only five weeks ago, of a hat-trick of League titles.

If Burnley had drawn, Wolves would have been champions on goal average. Spurs were third, missing their chance when beaten 1–0 at home in two successive matches late on.

Burnley deserved their first Championship triumph since 1921 for playing pure football with the accent on attack. Their success stems from midfield, where captain and right-half Jimmy Adamson and inside-forward Jimmy McIlroy have been outstanding, setting up the chances for England right-winger John Connelly (20 goals), centre-forward Ray Pointer (19) and inside-forward Jim Robson (18). Left-back Alex Elder, not 19 until April, made a remarkable impression. Manager Harry Potts always sent the team out to "Play football and enjoy your game". They did so, and thousands of fans all over the country have enjoyed watching them.

'Slavery' abolished: players' strike off

SATURDAY'S threatened football strike has been called off as the Football League gave in to the demands of the Professional Footballers Association on Wednesday 18 January. In a meeting between the League and the PFA at the Ministry of Labour, the League agreed to scrap the contract binding players to their clubs for life — the so-called "slavery" contract. They abolished the £20 maximum wage a week ago, so this is another great victory for the PFA, led by their outspoken chairman, Jimmy Hill of Fulham.

It is also good news for George Eastham, who has been playing for Arsenal since November, but is taking former club Newcastle United to court on a "restraint of trade" charge for refusing him a transfer.

Arsenal's George Eastham, no longer a "slave".

Scots staggered by England's one over the eight

Spread-eagled Haffey dives in vain as another England goal hits the net.

SCOTLAND SUFFERED the most humiliating defeat in their history on Saturday when England, the "auld enemy", crushed them 9–3 at Wembley.

Celtic's Frank Haffey, called in because of injuries to two other keepers, had a nightmare match, but this should take nothing away from England's brilliant attacking performance, which is yet another vindication of team manager Walter Winterbottom's policy of keeping to a settled team. They have now won their last five games, scoring 32 goals, with 11 of them coming from Chelsea's prolific inside-right Jimmy Greaves, whose transfer to AC Milan has just been agreed. He had another outstanding game against Scotland, hitting three, while inside-left Johnny Haynes (Fulham) tore the defence to shreds with his devastating passing and scored twice. The other goals were scored by Bobby Smith (two), Bobby Robson and Bryan Douglas.

Spurs' record run halted, but who will catch them now?

AT LAST SPURS have shown signs of mortality, losing their first point of the season after 11 straight victories. Nobody could have predicted that Manchester City would be the team to spoil their 100 per cent record by holding them to a 1–1 draw, and at White Hart Lane, too, especially after their last two victories, 6–2 over Aston Villa and 4–0 over Wolves at Molineux.

Sheffield Wednesday are also still unbeaten, and are four points behind with a game in hand: not an unbridgeable gap. But the way Spurs have been playing and scoring — with 37 goals, almost twice as many as Wednesday — it is difficult to see them slipping.

FOOTBALL FOCUS

● As if there weren't enough fixtures in an already overcrowded programme, a new competition, the Football League Cup, was launched in 1960. Played on a knock-out basis, with two-legged ties from the semi-finals, it was somewhat devalued when five top clubs — Arsenal, Sheffield Wednesday, Spurs, WBA and Wolves — declined to take part.

● Not quite emulating his brother Gerry's 10-goal feat last season, Joe Baker scored nine for Hibs in their 15–1 win over Peebles Rovers in the second round of the Scottish Cup.

● Denis Law scored all six of Manchester City's goals in a fourth-round Cup tie at Luton, but they didn't count because the game was abandoned. He scored again when City lost the replay 3–1.

● The marvellous Real Madrid were finally beaten in the European Cup, by their great domestic rivals, Barcelona, in the first round. But the Spanish champions, with Hungarian exiles Kocsis and Czibor, lost to Portuguese side Benfica in the final. Burnley reached the quarter-finals, but lost 4–1 in Hamburg after taking the first leg 3–1.

● Spurs' outright Championship records included most wins (31) and most away wins (16).

● Peterborough United, elected to the League in 1960 after 12 times having the "old pals' act" slammed in their face, made a sensational debut, winning the Fourth Division and scoring a League record 134 goals, with centre-forward Terry Bly hitting a post-war record 52.

● The "lure of the lira" led some of Britain's leading players to Italy: Joe Baker (£73,000) and Denis Law (£100,000) to Turin, Jimmy Greaves (£80,000) to AC Milan, and Gerry Hitchens (£80,000) to Inter-Milan. Johnny Haynes stayed with Fulham and was rewarded by becoming England's first £100-a-week footballer.

Rangers restore Scots pride but fail in new Euro final

JUST FOUR DAYS after three of their stars shared the ignominy of Scotland's 9–3 Wembley defeat, Rangers went to Molineux where a draw with Wolves was sufficient to see them through to the final of the European Cup-Winners' Cup. There were 10 entries for this new competition, and Rangers, who last season reached the semi-finals of the European Cup, soon avenged their crushing defeat by a West German side — Eintracht Frankfurt — in the senior competition by thrashing Borussia Moenchengladbach 3–0 and 8–0 in the quarter-finals.

Rangers, whose close-season signing of the classy Jim Baxter from Raith Rovers has transformed them from a workman-like defensive team into a flair side committed to attack, won the League Cup and then, despite a crippling injury list, the Championship. The first British club to reach a European final, they could not, however, break down the Fiorentina defence at Ibrox, and the Italian side had no trouble protecting a two-goal lead in the return in Florence.

Team of the century Spurs complete the 'impossible double'

Leicester's defence is finally beaten by Smith (centre) as Jones (7) celebrates.

THEY SAID it couldn't be done again, the League and Cup "double". Many clubs have tried to emulate a feat previously accomplished by Preston and Aston Villa in the 1800s, when the fixtures were fewer and the competition not so intense. Some have been a whisker away from success when their luck ran out, as happened with Manchester United in 1957, when only an injury to their goalkeeper at Wembley deprived them of the honour. But it was Spurs' opponents Leicester City who suffered the Wembley "hoodoo", losing right-back Len Chalmers after only 18 minutes. It still took off-colour Spurs another 48 minutes to score, and in the end they ran out 2–0 winners.

Spurs made sure of the League Championship nearly three weeks ago, setting various records as they did so. When they beat Sheffield Wednesday 2–1 at White Hart Lane on 17 April, after going a goal down, the title was theirs. In a magnificent campaign, Spurs were never headed. They dropped only one point in their first 16 matches, before their first defeat — 2–1 to Wednesday. They finished up with 115 goals, the highest First Division total for 27 years, with Bobby Smith (28) and Les Allen (23) their leading scorers. And they equalled the points record of 66, set by Arsenal in 1931.

At Wembley, the mental strain on Tottenham showed. Manager Billy Nicholson's great team looked and played like jaded men, and Leicester were on top until Chalmers's unfortunate injury, incurred in a clash with Allen. Leicester were superb in defence, with young Gordon Banks outstanding in goal. But there was nothing he could do about the goals when they did eventually come. First Smith took a Dyson through-ball and for once beat the formidable Ian King to crash an unstoppable shot into the net. A few minutes later, Smith returned the compliment for Dyson to head Spurs' second and clinching goal.

Spurs will be remembered, however, not for their tense Cup final performance, but for the scintillating football they played week after week, a thrilling, attacking game in which every man played his part. The Cup final team — Brown, Baker, Henry, Blanchflower, Norman, Mackay, Jones, White, Smith, Allen and Dyson — were the eleven that had turned out regularly in the League, eight of them playing 40 or more games (of the others, only right-winger Terry Medwin played enough League games to win a medal). This mix — the great and the good — blended into arguably one of the finest English club sides of the century, and few of the record two-and-a-half million people who watched Spurs throughout the season would disagree.

FINAL SCORE

Football League
Division 1: Tottenham Hotspur
Top scorer: Jimmy Greaves (Chelsea) 41
Division 2: Ipswich Town
Division 3: Bury
Division 4: Peterborough United
Footballer of the Year: Danny Blanchflower (Tottenham Hotspur)

FA Cup Final
Tottenham Hotspur 2 Leicester City 0

League Cup Final
Aston Villa beat Rotherham United 0–2, 3–0

Scottish League
Division 1: Rangers
Top scorer: Alex Harley (Third Lanark) 42
Division 2: Stirling Albion

Scottish FA Cup Final
Dunfermline Athletic 0 Celtic 0
Replay: Dunfermline Athletic 2 Celtic 0

Scottish League Cup Final
Rangers 2 Kilmarnock 0

International Championship
England, 6 pts

European Cup Final
Benfica 3 Barcelona 2

Cup-Winners' Cup Final
Fiorentina beat Rangers 2–0, 2–1

Inter-Cities Fairs Cup Final
AS Roma beat Birmingham City 2–2, 2–0

European Footballer of the Year 1960
Luis Suarez (Barcelona & Spain)

World Club Championship
Penarol (Uruguay) beat Benfica (Portugal) 0–1, 5–0, 2–1

Terry Bly scored 52 goals for Fourth Division champions Peterborough.

'Ramsey's Rustics' are new League champions

IPSWICH MANAGER Alf Ramsey has worked a minor miracle in a corner of East Anglia, guiding his unfancied club to the League title in their first season in Division One. The pundits laughed when the former England right-back "strengthened" his collection of unknowns and discards after they won promotion — signing one new player. He paid a club record £12,000 for schemer Doug "Dixie" Moran from Falkirk. They would have to do more than that if they were to stay in the top echelon. Nobody dreamt they would win it.

But Ramsey has proved a remarkable motivator and strategist. Getting his players to believe in themselves and fulfil their potential as individuals, he also designed tactics to blend them into a formidable team. Ray Crawford (33 goals) and Ted Phillips (28) have been outstanding. And 33-year-old Jimmy Leadbetter, ostensibly a left-winger, has confused defences with his unorthodox positioning.

Ipswich made a poor start to the season, with only one point from their first three matches. But when they beat Burnley 6–2, people began to take notice. Burnley and Spurs proved to be their chief rivals, although both were involved in other competitions and suffered a pile-up of fixtures at the end of the season. When Ipswich lost 5–0 at Old Trafford on 7 April, however, they appeared to have shot their bolt. With five games left, they were a point behind Burnley, who had two games in hand and a far superior goal average. But Burnley, going for the "double", blew up and won only one of their last seven games. Ipswich continued to play fresh, fluent football, and took the title by three points.

League champions Ipswich, average age nearly 28, won the title at the first attempt.

Spurs provide a 'passport to paradise' for Greaves: £99,999 brings him back from Italy

BILL NICHOLSON, manager of Spurs, has brought off the coup of the season, bringing back homesick Jimmy Greaves from Italy, where England's prolific young goalscorer has not been able to settle down.

Greaves scored nine goals in 14 matches for AC Milan and made a hit with the fans, but the extremely strict discipline within the club and the defensive style of Italian football have been anathema to him. He was extremely unhappy about being prevented from playing for England as a disciplinary measure. Needless to say, he is delighted to be back home again.

Nicholson broke the British transfer record to get his man, but paid £99,999 to avoid saddling him with the title of Britain's first £100,000 footballer. With a third of the season gone, Spurs are chasing the European Cup as well as domestic honours, and Greaves, who last season became the youngest player to reach 100 League goals in England, while still only 21 years of age, will be an invaluable asset in their challenge on all fronts.

Night of the long shots

FERENC PUSKAS, the Hungarian star of Real Madrid's wonderful 1960 European Cup-winners, hit a first-half hat-trick in the final against holders Benfica in Amsterdam. But the Portuguese side staged a splendid comeback and emerged 5–3 winners in a match notable for goals scored from a distance.

The evergreen Puskas is tubbier now but still was recognisable as the "Galloping Major", at least in the first period, when he ran half the length of the pitch after being put away by di Stefano to score one of his goals. He hit a typical long-range piledriver for another, then Aguas and Cavem, with another power-drive, put Benfica level before Puskas completed his hat-trick. During the interval, Bela Guttmann, Benfica's wily Hungarian coach, produced the tactics to negate the ageing di Stefano and isolate Puskas. Coluna equalized with another long shot, a 30-yarder.

Then the 20-year-old prodigy Eusebio took charge, scoring from the penalty spot after being pulled down, and thundering a tapped free-kick from Coluna into the net via a hapless defender.

FOOTBALL FOCUS

- Prolific scorer Brian Clough — 197 goals in 213 League games — left Middlesbrough for Sunderland in a £45,000 transfer at the start of the season, and scored 29 goals in 34 matches for the club, who missed promotion by a point.
- A record crowd for a friendly match, 104,493, saw Eintracht Frankfurt beat Glasgow Rangers 3–2 at Hampden Park on 17 October.
- Stanley Matthews, at 46, left Blackpool in October. But he did not retire. He went back to Stoke for a nominal £2,500 fee and trebled their gates in Division Two.
- The Italian League beat the Scottish League 2–0 at Hampden on 1 November — with the help of Denis Law (Scotland), John Charles (Wales) and Gerry Hitchens (England).
- Three players scored hat-tricks for Wrexham in their 10–1 Fourth Division defeat of Hartlepool on 3 March — Ron Barnes, Roy Ambler and Wyn Davies.
- Accrington Stanley resigned from the League on 6 March, because of financial difficulties, and their Division Four results were expunged.
- Former England captain Billy Wright took over from George Swindin as manager of Arsenal in March.
- England suffered their first defeat at Hampden Park for 25 years when Scotland won 2–0, a fine comeback after their Wembley débâcle last season.

Stanley Matthews, 46, back in the Potteries.

Spurs retain Cup at Wembley: not a stretcher in sight

TOTTENHAM HOTSPUR beat Burnley 3–1 at Wembley to retain the FA Cup in a match for once not marred by the sight of an injured player being carried off or hobbling helplessly on the wing. Spurs, who blew their chances of another League and Cup "double" at Easter, and Burnley, who let the Championship slip out of their grasp in the closing stages, put on a show befitting teams finishing third and second respectively in the table. But it was not a memorable match in that Spurs never really seemed to be in danger of losing it.

Burnley, after their disappointing form of late in the League, played well, but without that spark, that belief in themselves that might have turned the game. And their confidence was jarred after only three minutes, when Spurs took the lead. Jimmy Greaves, so glad to be back on English soil after his early-season misery in Milan, came out bursting with enthusiasm. He latched on to a Smith flick-on, overran the ball, but as the Burnley defence were putting on the brakes, cleverly slotted it past them inside the far post.

Oozing confidence now, Spurs put together some fine, flowing moves. But Burnley, with the classy Adamson and McIlroy — Footballer of the Year and runner-up, respectively — in midfield, managed to come back into the game. They equalized five minutes after half-time, when Jimmy Robson converted a near-post cross for the 100th Cup final goal in Wembley history. But Spurs hit back immediately through a thumping Smith shot, and Blanchflower sealed it with a late penalty after Cummings had handled with goalkeeper Blacklaw beaten.

Tottenham beat Euro champs but lose semi

Spurs go a goal down and effectively give Benfica a three-goal start.

AFTER A NIGHT full of drama and passion at White Hart Lane, Spurs just failed to pull back their 3–1 first-leg deficit in the European Cup semi-final against holders Benfica. In Lisbon, they paid the price of fielding an uncharacteristically defensive formation, and gave away two early goals.

The atmosphere at White Hart Lane was electric, and the roar of the 65,000 crowd would have done Hampden or Wembley proud. But Benfica, strengthened since last season by the addition of Simoes and the amazing Eusebio up front, began like true champions and Aguas scored after 15 minutes to put them 4–1 up overall. Undaunted, Spurs came roaring back, and the dynamic Mackay hit a post. Then they had what looked like a perfectly good goal disallowed when the speed of Greaves beat that of the linesman's eye.

The pace did not slacken thereafter. First Smith scored for Spurs, then Aguas hit their bar, on the stroke of half-time. Four minutes after the interval, Cruz brought down White, and Blanchflower coolly sent Costa Pereira the wrong way from the penalty spot — 3–4 now, and Mackay was driving Spurs on, seemingly at the heart of their every move.

Did Germano handle Medwin's header? The referee waved play on. Mackay made one last surge through the binding mud and smashed a shot past the keeper... and against the crossbar. It just was not Spurs' night.

FINAL SCORE

Football League
Division 1: Ipswich Town
Top scorer: Ray Crawford (Ipswich Town) 33
Division 2: Liverpool
Division 3: Portsmouth
Division 4: Millwall
Footballer of the Year: Jimmy Adamson (Burnley)

FA Cup Final

Tottenham Hotspur	3	Burnley	1

League Cup Final
Norwich City beat Rochdale 3–0, 1–0

Scottish League
Division 1: Dundee
Top scorer: Alan Gilzean (Dundee) 24
Division 2: Clyde

Scottish FA Cup Final

Rangers	2	St Mirren	0

Scottish League Cup Final

Rangers	1	Hearts	1
Replay: Rangers	3	Hearts	1

International Championship
Scotland, 6 pts

European Cup Final

Benfica	5	Real Madrid	3

Cup-Winners' Cup Final

Atletico Madrid	1	Fiorentina	1
Replay: Atletico	3	Fiorentina	0

Inter-Cities Fairs Cup Final
Valencia beat Barcelona 6–2, 1–1

European Footballer of the Year 1961
Omar Sivori (Juventus & Italy)

World Club Championship
Santos (Brazil) beat Benfica (Portugal) 3–2, 5–2

SOCCER SOUNDBITES

"The men who got us into the First Division will prove themselves good enough to keep us there."

Understatement of the season by Ipswich manager
ALF RAMSEY.

A World Cup to forget

What was expected to be a soccer feast, a showpiece for football artistry, turned out to be a defence-ridden scrap where the fear of failure dominated and onfield violence was the norm. The pressure on teams in the early stages has become too great, and some of the scenes transmitted by television to millions of viewers around the world warranted an "X" rating. Brazil deservedly retained the trophy, but rarely reached the heights of 1958, and it was sad that injury deprived the fans of Pele for all but their first two matches. That other master of the game, Spain's Alfredo di Stefano, was unable to play at all.

UNLIKE LAST TIME, only England of the home countries qualified for Chile. The choice of host country had lain between Argentina and Chile. The former looked set to get the vote until, paradoxically, Chile was hit by a series of devastating earthquakes in mid-1960. FIFA awarded them the 1962 finals after a plea from Carlos Dittborn, president of their FA: "We have nothing: that is why we must have the World Cup."

Chile, an impoverished nation, nevertheless built a magnificent National Stadium in Santiago, but there were only three other venues. The organization was competent, but high admission prices resulted in poor gates at all venues except the capital. In the group matches, goal difference was to count, obviating the need for play-offs.

Early casualties

After just two days of matches, with each team having played once, the World Cup image was severely blemished. After another full round, it had become tarnished beyond repair. With teams desperate not to make an early exit, the "casualty count" had mounted to nearly 50, including four players in hospital with fractures. In addition, Bulgaria had lost their centre-forward and outside-right, Spain their two full-backs, and four players had been sent off.

In an attempt to check the savagery, the World Cup organizing committee called the 16 team managers together to warn them and to impress upon the players that such violence would not be tolerated. But they let the guilty players off lightly.

Greaves scores from close in against Argentina, and Charlton (11) joins in the celebration.

Chile-Italy débâcle

Chile had made a good start in Group 2, beating Switzerland 3–1. But the match that really hit the headlines — for all the wrong reasons — was their second game, against Italy. Two Italian journalists in Chile had written insulting, patronizing articles about the country and, by the time the two teams met, the atmosphere between them was hostile and potentially violent. Italy were soon riled by the spitting Chileans. Chile's outside-left Leonel Sanchez, who had scored a glorious solo goal against the Swiss, was involved in a private kicking match with Italy's Giorgio Ferrini behind the back of English referee Ken Aston. Then Landa kicked Ferrini, who was seen kicking back and ordered off. It took eight minutes, several Italian officials and a squad of policemen to persuade him to leave the field!

Ken Aston sends off Italy's Ferrini in the infamous game with Chile.

Italy, notoriously defensive anyway with their catenaccio system, retreated even more. Players of both sides were to be seen rolling around in feigned agony after nearly every tackle. Sanchez broke Maschio's nose with a left hook clearly seen on television but missed by a linesman almost on top of the incident. A few minutes before half-time, Sanchez was fouled by Mario David and knocked him down, too, but amid scenes of furore involving police, photographers and officials the referee took no action. Just before half-time David aimed a kick at Sanchez and was sent off. Even so, Chile needed another half-hour to score against nine man; they eventually won 2–0.

The immediate result of this most disgraceful episode in the history of the World Cup was the suspension of Ferrini for one game and the "severe admonishment" of David and Sanchez. These so-called punishments arguably left FIFA as guilty as the teams who perpetrated the incidents and the officials who failed to control them.

Back to the football

Football had largely been forgotten. But there was little of it to stir the blood, anyway. In Group 3, at the charming coastal resort of Vina del Mar, Pele treated the meagre crowds to some of his magic before hobbling out of the tournament. Against Mexico, he made Brazil's first for Zagalo, then went on a spectacular dribble half the length of the pitch before scoring with a cracking shot. He pulled a muscle early on against Czechoslovakia, and was replaced against Spain by Amarildo, the "White Pele".

The Spain-Brazil match was one of the highlights of the finals. The Spanish team manager Helenio Herrera dropped inside-forwards Luis del Sol and Luis

There were some moments of Chile's World Cup that we should all like to forget, but at least the best team won, and there were some signs of sportsmanship if you looked hard enough.

Zito (19) heads Brazil's second goal in the World Cup final in Santiago.

Suarez, the captain, both of whom had been signed by Italian clubs in world record transfers. Ageing Hungarian exile Puskas was still playing well and Gento was on the wing, but the other Real star, di Stefano, had been ruled out by injury before the start. Puskas made a first-half goal for Adelardo, but two fine goals late on from the 22-year-old Amarildo gave Brazil victory and eliminated Spain.

England's 'progress'

England never settled down in Chile, but they managed to struggle through to the quarter-finals, despite losing the first match, against Hungary. No longer the "Magic Magyars" of the early fifties, Hungary were nevertheless a workmanlike side and won 2–1, a Flowers penalty being the only consolation for an uninspired England.

With Inter-Milan's Gerry Hitchens struggling to get to grips with England's football, he was replaced against Argentina by the untried Alan Peacock of Middlesbrough, and it was Peacock's header, handled as it was crossing the line, that gave Flowers the opportunity for another successful spot-kick. Charlton and Greaves also scored in a fine, and surprising, victory. A deadly dull goalless draw with Bulgaria was then enough to see them through.

Brazil proved too good for England at Vina del Mar in a game that restored some of the World Cup's lost reputation for open, attacking football. Knocks to inside-forwards Didi and Amarildo limited their efficiency, but right-winger Garrincha was Brazil's star. Time and again he sent the England defence the wrong way with his swerve, explosive acceleration and ball control. But it was with a header that he opened the scoring after half an hour, popping up to convert Zagalo's corner.

England were in danger of cracking, but suddenly they were back on terms. Greaves headed a Haynes free-kick against a post, and Hitchens, back for the injured Peacock, knocked the ball in. Soon after the interval, however, Springett failed to hold a vicious Garrincha free-kick, and Vava nodded the ball home. On the hour, Garrincha made sure with a dipping, swinging, curling 25-yarder that left Springett gasping.

Chile inspired

The shock of the quarter-finals was the USSR's 2–1 defeat by Chile, who were inspired by the fanatical support of the whole country. It was a sad day for the normally impeccable Lev Yashin in the Soviet goal, who perhaps should have stopped both Chile's long-range efforts.

The biggest crowd of the finals — 76,594 at the National Stadium — saw Chile's progress halted at last by Brazil, in particular by Garrincha, who scored twice and made one of Vava's two in a 4–2 victory. He was then sent off for a retaliatory push after being sworn at, spat upon and pushed. In the other semi-final, only 6,000 turned up to watch Czechoslovakia emerge 3–1 victors over Yugoslavia.

Brazil retain the cup

FIFA allowed Garrincha to compete in the final, a welcome decision after some of their earlier judgements. But Brazil found themselves a goal down for the second final running, when Masopust, Czechoslovakia's attacking left-half, ran on to a defence-splitting Scherer pass and left-footed the ball past Gylmar. Their lead was short-lived, however, as Amarildo scored a stunning equalizer, taking the ball to the left byline, drawing the keeper to the near post, and then hitting a swerving shot round him just inside the far post.

The counter-attacking Czechs held their own against the still-adventurous Brazilians until the 69th minute, when again it was Amarildo who pierced their defence with Pele-like skills on the left and crossed for Zito to head in. Another eight minutes, and it was all over — the hapless Schroif, blinded by the sun, fumbled a speculative Djalma Santos lob, and Vava pounced to put the loose ball away. Brazil were now level with Italy and Uruguay with two World Cups to their credit.

FINAL SCORE

Group 1

Uruguay	2	Colombia	1
USSR	2	Yugoslavia	0
Yugoslavia	3	Uruguay	1
USSR	4	Colombia	4
USSR	2	Uruguay	1
Yugoslavia	5	Colombia	0

	P	W	D	L	F	A	P
USSR	3	2	1	0	8	5	5
Yugoslavia	3	2	0	1	8	3	4
Uruguay	3	1	0	2	4	6	2
Colombia	3	0	1	2	5	11	1

Group 2

Chile	3	Switzerland	1
West Germany	0	Italy	0
Chile	2	Italy	0
West Germany	2	Switzerland	1
West Germany	2	Chile	0
Italy	3	Switzerland	0

	P	W	D	L	F	A	P
W.Germany	3	2	1	0	4	1	5
Chile	3	2	0	1	5	3	4
Italy	3	1	1	1	3	2	3
Switzerland	3	0	0	3	2	8	0

Group 3

Brazil	2	Mexico	0
Czechoslovakia	1	Spain	0
Brazil	0	Czechoslovakia	0
Spain	1	Mexico	0
Brazil	2	Spain	1
Mexico	3	Czechoslovakia	1

	P	W	D	L	F	A	P
Brazil	3	2	1	0	4	1	5
Czech	3	1	1	1	2	3	3
Mexico	3	1	0	2	3	4	2
Spain	3	1	0	2	2	3	2

Group 4

Argentina	1	Bulgaria	0
Hungary	2	England	1
England	3	Argentina	1
Hungary	6	Bulgaria	1
Hungary	0	Argentina	0
England	0	Bulgaria	0

	P	W	D	L	F	A	P
Hungary	3	2	1	0	8	2	5
England	3	1	1	1	4	3	3
Argentina	3	1	1	1	2	3	3
Bulgaria	3	0	1	2	1	7	1

QUARTER-FINALS

Yugoslavia	1	West Germany	0
Chile	2	USSR	1
Brazil	3	England	1
Czechoslovakia	1	Hungary	0

SEMI-FINALS

Czechoslovakia	3	Yugoslavia	1
Brazil	4	Chile	2

THIRD-PLACE MATCH

Chile	1	Yugoslavia	0

FINAL

Brazil	3	Czechoslovakia	1

National Stadium, Santiago, 17 June 1962. Attendance 68,679

Brazil: Gylmar, Santos D, Santos N, Zito, Mauro, Zozimo, Garrincha, Didi, Vava, Amarildo, Zagalo (Scorers: Amarildo, Zito, Vava)
Czechoslovakia: Schroif, Tichy, Novak, Pluskal, Popluhar, Masopust, Pospichal, Scherer, Kadraba, Kvasnak, Jelinek (Scorer: Masopust)

Leading scorers
4 Albert (Hungary) Garrincha (Brazil) Ivanov (USSR) Jerkovic (Yugoslavia) Sanchez (Chile) Vava (Brazil)

End of the big freeze: soccer back to normal at last

AT LAST, on 16 March, it has been possible to play a complete programme of League football. The "big freeze" started on 22 December, and has played havoc with League and Cup competitions throughout the country. This has been the worst winter in football history, even worse than 1946–1947.

Only three third-round FA Cup ties out of 32 were played on the day they were scheduled for, 5 January. Fourteen of them were postponed 10 or more times, the Lincoln-Coventry game 15 times! The replayed Blackburn-Middlesbrough tie was not completed until 11 March. Only four Football League fixtures were completed on 5 January, and five on 2 February. The following week there were seven League fixtures but the whole Scottish League programme was frozen off. Bolton Wanderers went the longest period without a match in League history, from their 1–0 win over Spurs at Burnden Park on 8 December to their 3–2 defeat at Arsenal on 16 February.

The Football Pools were affected, of course, and for three consecutive Saturdays in January the coupons were declared void. Then the companies came up with the idea of a special panel of "experts" — four former players and a referee — to determine the likely "results" of matches not played. The panel sat for four Saturdays, some of the decisions causing much controversy.

All manner of ideas and devices were tried to beat the freeze — flame-throwers at Bloomfield Road, a tar-burner at Stamford Bridge, a hot-air tent at Filbert Street, a Danish snow-shifting tractor at St Andrews, and 80 tons of sand at Wrexham's Racecourse Ground — but the clubs were fighting a losing battle, and the season will now have to be extended to almost the end of May.

Birmingham use a snow-shifting tractor at St Andrews.

'Cheque-book champions': Everton clinch League title

EVERTON CLINCHED their sixth League title in front of 60,000 delirious fans at Goodison Park on Saturday 11 May when they beat Fulham 4–1. Of the leading clubs in Division One, Everton are the only one to have finished their programme, but no other team can catch them now. Spurs lost their last slender chance when they went down 1–0 at Manchester City.

Already Everton are being called "cheque-book champions", but it has been money well spent. After forking out some £175,000 on five players last season, new manager Harry Catterick completed the "jigsaw" during this season's big freeze, with left-half Tony Kay (£60,000 from Sheffield Wednesday) and right-winger Alex Scott (£40,000 from Rangers).

Although they lost their pre-freeze lead, Everton went back to the top of the table when they beat Spurs 1–0 on 20 April, and have stayed there to the end. Against Fulham, inside-left and captain Roy Vernon scored a hat-trick to make him leading scorer with 24 goals, above centre-forward Alex Young (22). Although it is invidious to pick out names from this side of stars, the brilliantly creative Young and centre-half Brian Labone have been outstanding.

Manager Harry Catterick with his Championship-winning Everton team.

A 5–2 rout in France emphasizes magnitude of Ramsey's task

IF ENGLAND'S new manager Alf Ramsey thought life was going to be easier with England than with Ipswich, he suffered a rude awakening in Paris. England, in his charge for the first time, lost 5–2 to France and go out of the European Nations Cup in the first round.

When Walter Winterbottom resigned after the 1962 World Cup, it was decided to appoint a full-time team manager for the first time. Ramsey, who worked a minor miracle at Ipswich, accepted the post on the understanding that he would have sole responsibility for team selection. He was charged with building a team capable of winning the World Cup when England host the finals in three years' time.

Ramsey introduced only one new cap, Ron Henry of Spurs, in his first team selection, and made few changes. But England's performance was disjointed, and Springett had a poor game in goal. They pulled back from a 3-0 half-time deficit with headers from Bobby Smith and Bobby Tambling, but their revival was short-lived. Defeat in France is a setback. But at least Ramsey knows the magnitude of the task that lies ahead.

FOOTBALL FOCUS

● Before the start of the season, Denis Law returned to Manchester — United this time — for a British record £115,000 from Torino, who also sold Joe Baker to Arsenal for £70,000. Law starred for United in their Cup final triumph, although they went close to relegation.

● Fulham's Johnny Haynes was badly hurt in a car crash on 23 August and was out of action for most of the season.

● Chelsea achieved the win they needed against Portsmouth to take them into Division One, and at 7–0 it was their biggest since the 1910–11 season. At the other end of the table, Charlton won 2–1 at Walsall to go ahead of them on goal average and stay up.

● In a momentous High Court decision on 4 July 1963, in George Eastham v Newcastle United FC and others, Mr Justice Wilberforce declared that the regulations of the Football League in relation to the retention and transfer of professional footballers were in "unreasonable restraint of trade".

Glory, glory night as Spurs win Cup-Winners' Cup

SPURS BECAME the first British side to win a European trophy when they whipped Atletico Madrid 5–1 in Rotterdam on 15 May in the final of the Cup-Winners Cup. What another "glory, glory" night this was for their fans, out in force in Holland to see them take on the holders. Spurs suffered a blow before the game, when the dynamic Dave Mackay failed a fitness test. But inspired by their captain, Danny Blanchflower, and with Cliff Jones unstoppable on the right wing, they took a two-goal half-time lead through Greaves and White. The match, however, was to belong to left-winger Terry Dyson. Content usually to play a supporting role to his more illustrious team-mates, the little Yorkshireman has never served Spurs better.

Match-winner Terry Dyson shows the trophy to the fans.

Two minutes after the interval, Henry fisted out a goalbound shot, and Collar scored from the spot. For 20 minutes, Spurs needed all their fight and resolve to prevent the revitalized Spaniards from forcing an equalizer. Then Dyson, already proving a handful on the wing, took the match by the scruff of the neck. First he curled in a shot that the keeper could not prevent crossing the line. Then he centred for Greaves to score. And finally he burst 25 yards down the middle and hammered the ball into the net, a glorious climax to a glorious victory.

Stoke up! Maestro's first goal of the season clinches promotion

STOKE CITY beat Luton Town 2–0 at the Victoria Ground on 18 May to clinch promotion and the Second Division title, while sending Luton down to Division Three. With a great sense of occasion, Stanley Matthews chose to score his first goal of the season, Stoke's second. What an inspiration the ageing maestro has been to his old club, in his first full season since rejoining them. Those 48-year-old legs have seen him through more than 30 League games, and were prominent again last week when Stoke won 1–0 at Chelsea to set up this climax.

But Chelsea, after their stirring 1–0 victory at Roker Park, are favourites to join Stoke in Division One next year. That was Sunderland's last game, and they finished a point behind Stoke. Chelsea, a further two points behind, but with a superior goal average, now need to beat Portsmouth in their last game on Tuesday to go up.

Matthews's 48-year-old legs elude those of Chelsea's Eddie McCreadie, 23, at Stamford Bridge.

FINAL SCORE

Football League
Division 1: Everton
Top scorer: Jimmy Greaves (Tottenham Hotspur) 37
Division 2: Stoke City
Division 3: Northampton Town
Division 4: Brentford
Footballer of the Year: Stanley Matthews (Stoke City)

FA Cup Final

Manchester United	3	Leicester City	1

League Cup Final
Birmingham City beat Aston Villa 3–1, 0–0

Scottish League
Division 1: Rangers
Top scorer: Jimmy Millar (Rangers) 27
Division 2: St Johnstone

Scottish FA Cup Final

Rangers	1	Celtic	1
Replay: Rangers	3	Celtic	0

Scottish League Cup Final

Hearts	1	Kilmarnock	0

International Championship
Scotland, 6 pts

European Cup Final

AC Milan	2	Benfica	1

Cup-Winners' Cup Final

Tottenham Hotspur	5	Atletico Madrid	1

Inter-Cities Fairs Cup Final
Valencia beat Dynamo Zagreb 2–1, 2–0

European Footballer of the Year 1962
Josef Masopust (Dukla Prague & Czechoslovakia)

World Club Championship
Santos (Brazil) beat AC Milan (Italy) 2–4, 4–2, 1–0

England on top of the world after 100 years

Law beats Banks to score for the World XI.

ENGLAND BEAT a Rest of the World XI 2–1 at Wembley on 23 October in a match to celebrate the centenary of the Football Association. A crowd of 100,000 turned up to see world stars such as di Stefano, Puskas, Gento, Raymond Kopa, Lev Yashin, Djalma Santos and Eusebio — the World XI were allowed to use 16 players in all — and they were not disappointed. They were treated to a feast of football from both sides.

For England, Greaves was in exceptional form, and the two Scots in the World XI, Law and Baxter, were thoroughly at home in such illustrious company. All the goals came in the last 20 minutes. Terry Paine shot England ahead after a Greaves effort was blocked. Then Law combined with Puskas and di Stefano to put the Rest level.

England went close when Bobby Charlton thundered a shot against the base of the post and Greaves scraped the bar, then finally produced the winner with seven minutes remaining. Goalkeeper Soskic, who had replaced Yashin for the second half, could not hold another Charlton thunderbolt, and Greaves, as ever, was at hand to crack the ball home.

Danny Boy bows out

DANNY BLANCHFLOWER, 38, announced that he will be retiring from football at the end of the season when his contract with Spurs expires. He was dropped from the first team in November and later aggravated a knee injury playing for the reserves. Last month Bill Nicholson paid Fulham £72,500 for Alan Mullery, a British record for a half-back, to take over from Blanchflower.

Blanchflower, who made his League debut for Barnsley in 1949, cost Spurs a then club record of £30,000 when they bought him from Aston Villa in 1954, arguably the best money they ever spent. A constructive right-half, he led them to this century's first League and Cup "double" in 1961 and to the first British success in Europe last season, when they won the Cup-Winners' Cup. He also played the last of his record 56 Irish internationals last season.

A cultured footballer with a cultured mind (which he has never been afraid to speak!), he has not always seen eye to eye with management. But he has been a supreme leader for both club and country, a master tactician, respected and revered by those he has played with.

Rangers reign supreme in Scotland: Cup gives them the 'treble'

A CROWD OF nearly 121,000 at Hampden Park saw Rangers climax another record season with two goals in the last minute to beat Dundee 3–1 in the Cup and clinch the domestic "treble". In a hugely entertaining match played to the almost continuous roar of the crowd, Rangers took the lead in 66 minutes through Millar, but Cameron hooked in a spectacular equalizer within a minute. Millar, again, and Brand took advantage of Henderson's nippiness on either wing to provide the dramatic climax.

Having already won the League Cup, with Jim Forrest scoring four goals in the final, and the League Championship, Rangers emulated their own "treble" feat of 15 years ago, the only other time it has been done. They will carry Scotland's colours again next season in the European Cup, the only competition they entered and failed to win, having suffered a 6–0 thrashing by Real in Madrid.

Greaves (right) pounces to hit England's winner past Eyzaguirre and Soskic.

Top stars in betting scandal: England internationals accused of match fixing

DISCLOSURES IN *The People* newspaper have revealed a widespread bribery scandal in English football, with money paid to players for "fixing" matches for betting purposes.

Among the footballers so far named are three Sheffield Wednesday players: England internationals Peter Swan and Tony Kay (now with Everton) and David "Bronco" Layne. It is alleged that they took part in arranging the outcome of a Sheffield Wednesday First Division game, one which they lost 2–0 at Ipswich in December 1962. Further revelations are expected to be made.

Mackay breaks leg as United knock Spurs out of Europe

SPURS SUFFERED a double blow at Old Trafford on 10 December. Not only did Manchester United beat them 4–1 to win their European Cup-Winners' Cup tie 4–3, but Dave Mackay was carried off to hospital with a broken leg after only eight minutes. The Cup-holders battled bravely with 10 men, and remained ahead on aggregate until the last 13 minutes.

It was a night of high emotion, a game of tremendous action, played sportingly throughout. Spurs, with a 2–0 lead from White Hart Lane, almost made it three when Smith put his point-blank header straight at Gaskell from Mackay's early cross. This was, in retrospect, the turning point of the tie. For, only a minute later, David Herd pulled the all-important early goal back for United. David Sadler beat Spurs keeper Brown to a loose ball, crossed it from the bye-line, and there was Herd flying in with a diving header.

So when Mackay was carried off, Spurs' lead had been reduced to just one goal and, soon after the interval, Herd scored again to level the scores.

This should have spelt the end for Spurs. But they immediately went onto the attack. They broke through on the left with John White, who floated a perfect cross for Jimmy Greaves to score with a rare header. So they were in front again.

They held out until Charlton latched on to a floated Crerand pass and smashed a volley home, and then, with only two minutes remaining, the same player lashed in the winner from another Crerand pass to provide the game with a dramatic climax — but you had to feel sorry for Spurs.

FOOTBALL FOCUS

- England beat Northern Ireland 8–3 on 20 November in the first international at Wembley played entirely under lights.
- There was a First Division goal glut on Boxing Day, when 66 goals were scored in 10 games. Fulham beat Ipswich Town by 10–1, and leaders Blackburn won 8–2 at West Ham.
- Oxford United, in only their second season since being elected to the League, beat Blackburn 3–1 to become the first Fourth Division side to reach the quarter-finals of the FA Cup. Earlier, non-League Bedford Town won 2-1 at Second Division Newcastle in the third round.
- Jim Fryatt of Bradford PA scored the fastest goal on record on 25 April against Tranmere Rovers, timed by the referee's watch at four seconds.
- England beat USA 10–0 in New York on 27 May, but lost 5–1 to Brazil three days later in Rio.
- On 25 May, the blackest day in football history, more than 300 died in Lima during riots after a Peruvian goal against Argentina was disallowed.

Rioting at Lima leads to 300 deaths.

Bold Boyce hits West Ham's Cup-winner in injury time

The ball is tantalizingly over the line for Hurst's goal.

IN THE MOST exciting FA Cup final since the "Matthews match" 11 years ago, West Ham twice came from behind to beat Second Division Preston 3–2, with Ron Boyce scoring the winner in the second minute of time added on for stoppages.

It became clear from the start that this was not going to be a walk-over for the First Division side. Preston matched them in skills, and scored first, after 10 minutes. Howard Kendall, at 17 years 345 days the youngest ever FA Cup-finalist, started the move, Dawson's shot was only parried, and Holden forced the ball in. West Ham, despite looking nervous, equalized immediately. Skipper Bobby Moore stole the ball and moved upfield before finding Byrne, who put 18-year-old John Sissons away on a fine run, finishing with a shot past Kelly.

Undaunted, Preston continued to have the better of the game in the first half, controlling the midfield in which young Kendall was prominent. They deservedly regained the lead five minutes before half-time when Dawson headed in from a corner.

Manager Ron Greenwood changed West Ham's tactics at the interval, and they began to erode Preston's midfield superiority. Eventually a Hurst header hit the bar, rebounded against Kelly, and rolled slowly over the line. So the Hammers were level with 38 minutes left.

Both teams were tiring, but not Hurst, who went on one last powerful run through the middle before slipping the ball out to Brabrook on the right. The former England winger cut in before floating a centre to the far post for Boyce to head the ball back into the opposite corner for the dramatic winner.

FINAL SCORE

Football League
Division 1: Liverpool
Top scorer: Jimmy Greaves (Tottenham Hotspur) 35
Division 2: Leeds United
Division 3: Coventry City
Division 4: Gillingham
Footballer of the Year: Bobby Moore (West Ham United)

FA Cup Final
West Ham United 3 Preston North End 2

League Cup Final
Leicester City beat Stoke City 1–1, 3–2

Scottish League
Division 1: Rangers
Top scorer: Alan Gilzean (Dundee) 32
Division 2: Morton

Scottish FA Cup Final
Rangers 3 Dundee 1

Scottish League Cup Final
Rangers 5 Morton 0

International Championship
England, N. Ireland, Scotland, 4 pts

European Cup Final
Inter-Milan 3 Real Madrid 1

Cup-Winners' Cup Final
Sporting Lisbon 3 MTK Budapest 3
Replay: Lisbon 1 MTK Budapest 0

Inter-Cities Fairs Cup Final
Real Zaragoza 2 Valencia 1

European Footballer of the Year 1963
Lev Yashin (Moscow Dynamo & USSR)

World Club Championship
Inter-Milan (Italy) beat Independiente (Argentina) 0–1, 2–0, 1–0

Farewell Sir Stan: England maestro retires at 50

INTERNATIONAL footballers past and present paid tribute to Sir Stanley Matthews at Stoke on Wednesday night, 28 April, in a special benefit match to celebrate his retirement. The ageless maestro was knighted in the New Year, the first footballer to be so honoured. He played his last first-class match on 6 February, five days after his 50th birthday, when he helped Stoke beat Fulham 3–1.

It is incredible to think that Matthews made his League debut for Stoke in March 1932 at the age of 17 — 33 years ago. The remarkable career of the "Wizard of the Dribble" for Stoke, Blackpool and England (54 caps) is now part of football folklore. He showed all his familiar tricks on the right wing in his farewell match against an International XI that included Alfredo di Stefano, Ferenc Puskas, Lev Yashin and Josef Masopust, and he was carried off shoulder-high in triumph at the end.

Sir Stan on the shoulders of Yashin (left) and Puskas.

John White killed by lightning

JOHN WHITE, the Spurs and Scotland inside-forward, was struck by lightning and killed while playing golf on 21 July. His wife had dropped him at the Crews Hill club, Enfield, and he had just driven off the first tee when it started raining. He took shelter under a line of oak trees, and was seen sitting under one by golfers running for the clubhouse. There was a single flash of lightning, and White's body was found later by two groundsmen.

White's tragic death at 27 is a terrible blow to his family, to Spurs and to football as a whole. His frail physique belied the strength in his legs, and although he was known best for his defence-splitting passes, he also had a fierce shot. He earned the nickname the "Ghost of White Hart Lane" for his uncanny ability to drift unseen into dangerous positions. His midfield partnership with Danny Blanchflower was at the heart of Spurs' "double" triumph in 1961 and their later successes in domestic and European cups. He won 22 international caps, and will be sorely missed by both club and country.

Footballers jailed for match-fixing: internationals Kay and Swan among those found guilty

TEN PROFESSIONAL footballers were found guilty at Nottingham Assizes on 26 January of "fixing" match results. They were all sent to prison. Aberdeen-born Jimmy Gauld, an inside-forward who played for Charlton, Everton, Plymouth, Swindon and Mansfield between 1955 and 1960, was sentenced to four years with £5,000 costs, while the others received terms of between four and 15 months.

After years of rumours, Gauld, who was found to be at the centre of the conspiracy, decided last April to "tell all" to a Sunday paper, for which he received £7,000. The evidence for these articles was later handed to the Director of Public Prosecutions. Among those jailed are former England players, centre-half Peter Swan (Sheffield Wednesday) and left-half Tony Kay (Everton, formerly with Wednesday), along with David Layne (Wednesday) and former Celtic and Scottish Under-23 keeper Dick Beattie, who also played for Portsmouth and Peterborough. The Football Association are to obtain transcripts of the court proceedings before deciding what action they will take.

Agony of Dave Mackay: breaks leg again in comeback match

SPURS AND SCOTLAND left-half Dave Mackay has broken his leg again in his comeback match after nine gritty months spent regaining fitness. Playing for the reserves against Shrewsbury Reserves at White Hart Lane on 14 September, he suddenly spun agonizingly to the ground just outside the opposition penalty area, clutching the same left leg that he broke against Manchester United in the European Cup-Winners' Cup.

There are no stouter hearts in football than the fearless midfield dynamo, inspiration of all his colleagues. But he will need all his courage, only two months from his 30th birthday, to come back again from such a devastating blow.

Mackay goes down in agony, clutching his broken leg.

Hammers triumphant in Wembley classic

BOBBY MOORE climbed the Wembley stairs to collect another trophy, little more than a year after leading West Ham to FA Cup victory, when the Hammers beat Munich 1860 by 2–0 in the final of the European Cup-Winners' Cup. With both sides going out from the start to play attacking football, the 100,000 crowd enjoyed one of the finest matches ever seen at Wembley Stadium. And it was played in a highly sporting manner throughout.

West Ham's triumph is the perfect tribute to manager Ron Greenwood's belief in positive, stylish football, and Wembley was the ideal setting for it. With the inexperienced Alan Sealey and Brian Dear replacing injured England international forwards Brabrook and Byrne, the Hammers fans could be excused for feeling apprehensive. But both newcomers blended in seamlessly from the start, and it was Sealey who scored both goals, in the 69th and 71st minutes, to bring the trophy to England for the second time.

Sealey (right) celebrates his second goal with Martin Peters.

Extra-time drama as Liverpool lift Cup: Leeds suffer second let-down in a week

LIVERPOOL BEAT Leeds 2–1 at Wembley in the FA Cup final, all the goals coming in extra time. For Leeds, still in with a chance of the "double" only a week ago, it was their second disappointment in six days. On Monday, while they drew 3–3 at Birmingham, Manchester United beat Arsenal 3–1 to pip them for the League title on goal average.

Liverpool thoroughly deserved their first Cup win. The football, although not in itself remarkable, was played in a highly-charged emotional atmosphere, and the passionate singing of the Liverpool fans, before, during and after the match, will be the abiding memory of the occasion. Leeds, in their first final, started as favourites, but could not get their attack going, although they defended superbly. There was, fortunately, none of the unpleasantness too frequently associated with Leeds teams this season.

For Liverpool, Stevenson was outstanding in the middle, and Tommy Smith, playing as an extra centre-half, helped them win midfield control. After three minutes of extra time, Liverpool finally found a way through when Hunt stooped low to head in a cross from Byrne, later found to have played 115 minutes with a broken collar-bone. This setback would have finished most sides, especially in the heavy rain and on the energy-sapping Wembley turf, but not Don Revie's men. Charlton, stealing up into attack, nodded down a Hunter lob, and there was the dynamic Bremner, still full of fire, to hit an unstoppable volley.

Liverpool were stunned, but they too are fighters, and with nine minutes left St John met a Callaghan cross with his head to flash it past Sprake. The refrains of "Ee-ay-addio, we won the Cup" seemed to go on for ever.

St John powers a header into the Leeds goal for the winner.

FOOTBALL FOCUS

- Portsmouth and England wing-half Jimmy Dickinson retired with a record 764 League appearances for his only club. He made his League debut in 1946, won two Championship medals and played 48 times for England.
- Shrewsbury player-manager Arthur Rowley hung up his boots in February with a British record of 434 League goals to his name. He made his debut in 1946 and scored his goals with West Brom (four), Fulham (27), Leicester (251) and Shrewsbury (152) in a total of 619 matches.
- The players found guilty in the courts of match-fixing were suspended for life by the FA in April.
- Kilmarnock needed to win by two clear goals at Hearts in the last match of the season to pip them on goal average for the title. They did just that, and claimed their first Scottish Championship.

FINAL SCORE

Football League
Division 1: Manchester United
Top scorer: Jimmy Greaves (Tottenham Hotspur), Andy McEvoy (Blackburn) 29
Division 2: Newcastle United
Division 3: Carlisle United
Division 4: Brighton & Hove Albion
Footballer of the Year: Bobby Collins (Leeds U)

FA Cup Final

Liverpool	2	Leeds United	1

(after extra time)

League Cup Final
Chelsea beat Leicester City 3–2, 0–0

Scottish League
Division 1: Kilmarnock
Top scorer: Jim Forrest (Rangers) 30
Division 2: Stirling Albion
Footballer of the Year: Billy McNeill (Celtic)

Scottish FA Cup Final

Celtic	3	Dunfermline Ath	2

Scottish League Cup Final

Rangers	2	Celtic	1

International Championship
England, 5 pts

European Cup Final

Inter-Milan	1	Benfica	0

Cup-Winners' Cup Final

West Ham United	2	Munich 1860	0

Inter-Cities Fairs Cup Final

Ferencvaros	1	Juventus	0

European Footballer of the Year 1964
Denis Law (Manchester United & Scotland)

World Club Championship
Inter-Milan (Italy) beat Independiente (Argentina) 3–0, 0–0

'El Beatle' gives Benfica a hard day's night

MANCHESTER UNITED went to Lisbon with a slender one-goal lead for the second leg of their quarter-final European Cup tie against Benfica, twice winners of the trophy and twice runners-up in the last five years. The Portuguese champions had a formidable home record in Europe and had been quite happy to come away from Old Trafford with a 3–2 defeat. United, up against the likes of Eusebio, Coluna and Germano, would have their work cut out to gain the draw they needed to take them through to the semi-finals in this, their first year back in the competition since the Munich air crash in 1958.

Manager Matt Busby told his side to play a holding game for the first 20 minutes, but George Best, as Busby joked after the game, "must have had cotton wool in his ears". The young Irishman with the Beatle hairstyle proceeded to take Benfica's defence apart, and put United two up in only 12 minutes. Best, not yet 20 but already capped 12 times by Northern Ireland, and a major force in United's title-winning side last year, has just about every skill in the game. His first goal was a perfectly timed header from a Dunne free-kick. It stunned the crowd to silence. The second, a swerving, jinking run right through the Benfica defence to slide the ball past Costa Pereira in goal, had them gasping in astonishment.

Hardly had the crowd recovered their breath from this onslaught than left-winger John Connelly scored a third to put United 6–2 up on aggregate. Benfica tried to salvage some of their self-respect in the second half, but their main striking force Eusebio was being well held by the ungainly Stiles, and their only consolation was a Brennan back-pass that beat his own keeper. Then, in the last few minutes, Law put wing-half Crerand through for the fourth, and Bobby Charlton went on one of his majestic solo runs from his own half before slamming the ball wide of the keeper. The final tally was 5–1 — what a scoreline! In Benfica's own Stadium of Light! This was one of the finest team performances by a side away from home in European competition. But the Portuguese have already singled out one hero — brilliant George Best or, as they now call him in Portugal, "El Beatle".

George Best, "El Beatle", with United fans.

Liverpool clinch League: Arsenal's record equalled

LIVERPOOL WON the League easing up, finishing their programme with a draw at Nottingham Forest on 10 May after clinching the title 10 days earlier, when they beat Chelsea 2–1 at Anfield. In between, however, they lost in the European Cup-Winners' Cup final to Borussia Dortmund.

Under Bill Shankly's shrewd guidance, Liverpool have emerged as arguably England's leading side, and certainly the most consistent, with their third major honour in three years. They finished on 61 points, six ahead of runners-up Leeds, and have equalled Arsenal's record of seven League titles. They have also set a record by winning the Championship using the remarkable total of only 14 players — virtually 12, as two players made only four appearances between them, one of them in the last match.

A well-balanced side with a strong defence, in which Tommy Smith and skipper Ron Yeats serve as twin stoppers, Liverpool conceded only 34 goals. Roger Hunt was their top scorer for the fifth season running, with 30 League goals, and he and Ian St John have enjoyed excellent service from wingers Peter Thompson and Ian Callaghan, the latter ever-present, as he was in the title-winning side of two years ago. Liverpool took over at the top on 27 November, and were never headed after that.

Liverpool, the FA Cup-holders, went out at home to Chelsea in the third round this time, but atoned for that lapse in champion style.

A jubilant Liverpool acclaim Roger Hunt's second goal against Chelsea, knowing the title is theirs.

FOOTBALL FOCUS

- On the first day of the season, 21 August, Charlton's Keith Peacock became the first player to come on as substitute, against Bolton at Burnden Park in Division Two, under the new rule allowing one substitute for an injured player.
- When Frank Saul was sent off against Burnley at Turf Moor on 4 December, it marked the end of a proud and probably unique record for Spurs, who had not had a player dismissed in a League match since 27 October 1928.
- The Italian FA, satisfied that Roma had actively encouraged the crowd disorder in the Fairs Cup tie against Chelsea, fined them a derisory £500, although the Fairs Cup committee banned them from participation for three years. Chelsea and Leeds were both knocked out in semi-final play-offs.
- Billy Wright has been unable to repeat his onfield success in the managerial chair, and parted company with Arsenal at the end of the season to take up a career in television.

More violence in the 'Not Fairs' Cup

THE VIOLENT Leeds-Valencia clash in the third round of the Inter-Cities Fairs Cup on 2 February at Elland Road provided yet another reason for branding this season's competition the "Not Fairs" Cup. At the unedifying sight of Jack Charlton furiously chasing an opponent round the pitch, the police went on to intervene and the referee ordered both sides to their dressing-rooms for a 10-minute cooling-off period. Charlton stayed off, and two Valencia players were also dismissed from a scandalous game that finished 1–1.

This season's tournament has been marked by a series of violent incidents. Leeds suffered a terrible blow in the first round, in Italy against Torino, when a tackle from Poletti broke captain Bobby Collins's thigh. But the most scandalous tie was the Chelsea-Roma first-round clash, in which Eddie McCreadie was sent off in the Stamford Bridge brawl (won 4–1 by Chelsea) for retaliating, and in the return, won 1–0 by Roma, the crowd, fired up by the Italian Press, pelted Chelsea with an avalanche of rubble and rubbish and stoned their coach as it left the stadium.

World Cup found: unearthed by dog in a London front garden

A WEEK AFTER it was stolen when on show at a stamp exhibition in Westminster, the World Cup has been found by a dog out for a walk with his owner. The little black and white mongrel, called Pickles, has saved the embarrassment not only of the Football Association but of the whole country.

Londoner David Corbett was walking Pickles in Norwood, a South London suburb, when the dog disappeared into a front garden. Mr Corbett found him digging up a brown paper parcel, and was astonished to find it contained the Jules Rimet Trophy. Mr Corbett stands to gain a considerable reward, and no doubt there will also be some juicy bones for the four-legged hero.

Hero Pickles, World Cup saviour.

Double by Trebilcock sparks Everton Cup comeback

OUTSIDERS Sheffield Wednesday almost had the Cup in their grasp at Wembley, but defensive errors in the last half-hour allowed Everton to complete a thrilling comeback. The Everton hero, with two goals, was 21-year-old Mike Trebilcock, a surprise replacement up front for their experienced and expensive top scorer, Fred Pickering.

Everton, who reached Wembley without conceding a goal in seven matches, found themselves one down in four minutes to Wednesday, who had reached the final without a single home draw. Centre-forward Jim McCalliog, a Chelsea discard and the brains behind the constantly switching Wednesday attack, fired in a shot that was deflected past the helpless Gordon West. Wednesday went further ahead after 57 minutes through Dave Ford. But Trebilcock flashed a half-volley past Springett in the next minute to make it 2–1.

The first of the errors came five minutes later, when a poor headed clearance by Wednesday's inexperienced centre-half Sam Ellis, a stand-in for the injured Vic Mobley, let Trebilcock in for another chance which he gladly accepted. Everton's third goal was a personal tragedy for another defender, Gerry Young, who failed to control a harmless-looking punt, and left-winger Temple, with a clear run on goal, slipped the ball past Springett for a dramatic winner.

Trebilcock (8) wheels away after beating Springett for Everton's equaliser.

FINAL SCORE

Football League
Division 1: Liverpool
Top scorer: Roger Hunt (Liverpool) 30
Division 2: Manchester City
Division 3: Hull City
Division 4: Doncaster Rovers
Footballer of the Year: Bobby Charlton (Manchester United)

FA Cup Final

Everton	3	Sheffield Wed	2

League Cup Final
WBA beat West Ham United 1–2, 4–1

Scottish League
Division 1: Celtic
Top scorer: Joe McBride (Celtic), Alex Ferguson (Dunfermline Athletic) 31
Division 2: Ayr United
Footballer of the Year: John Greig (Rangers)

Scottish FA Cup Final

Rangers	0	Celtic	0
Replay: Rangers	1	Celtic	0

Scottish League Cup Final

Celtic	2	Rangers	1

International Championship
England, 5 pts

European Cup Final

Real Madrid	2	Partizan Belgrade	1

Cup-Winners' Cup Final

Borussia Dortmund	2	Liverpool	1

(after extra time)

Inter-Cities Fairs Cup Final
Barcelona beat Real Zaragoza 0–1, 4–2

European Footballer of the Year 1965
Eusebio (Benfica & Portugal)

World Club Championship
Penarol (Uruguay) beat Real Madrid (Spain) 2–0, 2–0

The Boys of '66

When Alf Ramsey took over as manager of the England team on 1 May 1963, he gave an interview to a local reporter in Ipswich, where he was ending a successful eight-year spell with Ipswich Town. "England will win the World Cup in 1966," said Ramsey. This remark came to haunt him over the next three years as he tried to mould an England team that would have at least a sporting chance.

RAMSEY SOON sorted out his defence, giving caps to George Cohen, Jack Charlton and Nobby Stiles. With Gordon Banks, Ray Wilson and skipper Bobby Moore, he had a firm base. Bobby Charlton and Jimmy Greaves were established up front. The rest was to come very late, with Martin Peters who, Ramsey said, was "ten years ahead of his time", and Alan Ball staking a midfield claim. However, it was among the wingers that the manager had his big problems. Among those tried were Peter Thompson, Bobby Tambling, Gordon Harris, Alan Hinton, Terry Paine, Ian Callaghan and John Connelly, the last three all playing in early World Cup matches. But by the quarter-finals Ramsey had dispensed with wingers altogether, and Geoff Hurst finally came into his own as a replacement for the injured Greaves. Ramsey's team of "wingless wonders" was complete.

The demise of Brazil

Brazil, the holders, were the firm favourites when the finals began on 11 July. Their group, played in the north-west, was the strongest, including also Hungary and Portugal. Pele scored the first goal of the tournament as Brazil beat Bulgaria 2–0 at Goodison Park, but vicious tackling virtually put him out of the competition. He was unable to play against Hungary, who won a marvellous match 3–1, Brazil's first World Cup defeat since Hungary, again, beat them in the "Battle of Berne" in 1954. Brazil then needed to beat Portugal, but the returning Pele was literally and disgracefully kicked out of it again, Eusebio was inspired, and Brazil went down, and out, 3–1.

England's matches were all at Wembley. The opener was a dreadful goalless stalemate with Uruguay. But England got under way in their second match, a great individual effort by Bobby Charlton, climaxed with a 20-yard drive, setting them on their way to a 2–0 win over Mexico. The game with France, also won 2–0, with both goals by Roger Hunt on his 28th birthday, brought trouble when Stiles perpetrated such a bad foul (ignored by the referee) that FA Council members suggested he should be left out of the team thereafter. Ramsey threatened to resign if he could not pick the players he wanted, and the FA Council backed down. England qualified with Uruguay.

The greatest shock came in Group 4 at Middlesbrough. The defensive Italians, needing only a draw with the mysterious North Koreans to be virtually certain of going through, contrived to lose 1–0, and were eliminated. Pak Doo Ik was the unlikely name on the scoresheet. The efficient West Germans and talented Argentinians were too good for Spain and Switzerland in Group 2 and also went through.

The Rattin incident

England's quarter-final with Argentina proved explosive. For the first time, England played without wingers, using a 4–4–2 combination in which the front men were Hunt, with three goals already to his credit, and Hurst. Despite a penchant for petty fouling, for which many were booked, the Argentinians played well and looked the more likely winners until their outstanding skipper Antonio Rattin intervened when the referee was booking yet another of his teammates. He appeared to be abusing the referee and, already booked once, was sent off. But he refused to go, and it took 10 minutes and the deployment of several officials before he went.

Thirteen minutes from the end, England finally scored — a glancing header from Hurst. The referee was escorted off the pitch with a heavy police guard. Ramsey physically prevented Cohen swapping shirts with an opponent and, after more disgraceful behaviour from the Argentinians in the dressing-rooms, likened them to "animals", a justifiable but perhaps imprudent remark.

There was a sensation of a different kind at Goodison, and nobody could believe the intermediate scoreline flashed around the country, "North Korea 3 Portugal 0". Eusebio finally pulled his team together and scored four (two penalties) as Portugal recovered to win 5–3.

The Uruguayans, a goal down to West Germany and smarting after having a penalty appeal for handball turned down, proceeded to lose their heads. They had two men sent off, and three late goals gave the Germans a 4–0 victory when, in the first half, Uruguay had been the better side. The USSR caught Hungary on an off day and won the fourth semi-final place.

A classic semi-final

England's semi-final with Portugal was a classic match of good, clean, sporting football. Nearly an hour had gone by before the referee blew for the first foul. Stiles managed to keep Eusebio reasonably quiet, while Bobby Charlton was finding more space for his forays from midfield to the Portuguese penalty area. In the 31st minute, Pereira, the Portuguese keeper, dashed to the edge of the box to beat Hunt to a through-ball, but it ricocheted to Charlton, following up, and he side-footed it in from outside the area.

Ten minutes from time, Charlton scored a great second, running on to a ball pulled back by Hurst to hammer it into the far corner. It is an indication of the sportsmanship of this match that the Portuguese players congratulated Charlton — one shook his hand — as he trotted back to the centre circle. Shortly afterwards, Jack Charlton fisted the ball out from under the bar, and Eusebio scored from the spot — the first goal Banks had conceded in the tournament. Portugal pressed for the remaining seven minutes, to no avail.

West Germany beat the USSR in the other semi-final, in a match that turned on an incident just before half-time. The Soviets' Chislenko seemed to be badly fouled, but the referee did not

‘And there are some people on the pitch. They think it’s all over... IT IS NOW!’ **KENNETH WOLSTENHOLME** — the famous lines of his World Cup final commentary as Geoff Hurst scored in the 120th minute.

England skipper Bobby Moore holds the Jules Rimet Trophy aloft after a pulsating final.

blow, and West Germany carried on to open the scoring. On the resumption, the incensed Chislenko kicked the first German he came across, and was sent off. West Germany won 2–1.

A late equalizer

The final opened badly for England when, after 13 minutes, Haller scored from an attempted Wilson clearance. Six minutes later, however, the West Ham connection registered an equalizer as Moore’s free-kick was headed in by Hurst. With 12 minutes left in the game, a Hurst shot was blocked and the third West Ham finalist, Martin Peters, slammed the ball in. England seemed to be home.

But the Germans scored an equalizer in the dying seconds. A disputed free-kick against Jack Charlton found its way across the England goal — arguably via a German hand — and Weber netted from close in. Thirty gruelling minutes of extra time were now necessary.

The disputed goal

Of all World Cup controversies, England’s goal after 10 minutes of extra time remains one of the biggest. Ball, with typical energy, chased a forlorn long ball towards the right-hand corner flag, caught it and pulled it back to the ever-available Hurst near the angle of the six-yard box. Hurst turned and hooked the ball past Tilkowski on to the underside of the bar. The ball bounced down almost straight, but then bounced up and out of goal. The inrushing Hunt, instead of trying to put it in, wheeled round with his arm aloft, convinced that the ball had crossed the line. Charlton thought that it had, too. Weber headed it away behind the goal.

There was a heart-stopping delay while Swiss referee Gottfried Dienst consulted his Soviet linesman, Tofik Bakhramov, who signalled towards the centre spot. England led 3–2. The goal is still argued about today, and film evidence, while inconclusive, veers towards the German view that the ball did not cross the line. But in the last minute, Moore, cool as ever under pressure, floated a long clearance to Hurst, who ran on and hit a fabulous fourth for his hat-trick. England had won 4–2. Ramsey’s prophecy was fulfilled. And the country that gave football to the world had finally won the World Cup.

FINAL SCORE

Group 1

England	0	Uruguay	0
France	1	Mexico	1
Uruguay	2	France	1
England	2	Mexico	0
Uruguay	0	Mexico	0
England	2	France	0

	P	W	D	L	F	A	P
England	3	2	1	0	4	0	5
Uruguay	3	1	2	0	2	1	4
Mexico	3	0	2	1	1	3	2
France	3	0	1	2	2	5	1

Group 2

West Germany	5	Switzerland	0
Argentina	2	Spain	1
Spain	2	Switzerland	1
Argentina	0	West Germany	0
Argentina	2	Switzerland	0
West Germany	2	Spain	1

	P	W	D	L	F	A	P
W.Germany	3	2	1	0	7	1	5
Argentina	3	2	1	0	4	1	5
Spain	3	1	0	2	4	5	2
Switzerland	3	0	0	3	1	9	0

Group 3

Brazil	2	Bulgaria	0
Portugal	3	Hungary	1
Hungary	3	Brazil	1
Portugal	3	Bulgaria	0
Portugal	3	Brazil	1
Hungary	3	Bulgaria	1

	P	W	D	L	F	A	P
Portugal	3	3	0	0	9	2	6
Hungary	3	2	0	1	7	5	4
Brazil	3	1	0	2	4	6	2
Bulgaria	3	0	0	3	1	8	0

Group 4

USSR	3	North Korea	0
Italy	2	Chile	0
Chile	1	North Korea	1
USSR	1	Italy	0
North Korea	1	Italy	0
USSR	2	Chile	1

	P	W	D	L	F	A	P
USSR	3	3	0	0	6	1	6
North Korea	3	1	1	1	2	4	3
Italy	3	1	0	2	2	2	2
Chile	3	0	1	2	2	5	1

QUARTER-FINALS

England	1	Argentina	0
West Germany	4	Uruguay	0
Portugal	5	North Korea	3
USSR	2	Hungary	1

SEMI-FINALS

West Germany	2	USSR	1
England	2	Portugal	1

THIRD-PLACE MATCH

Portugal	2	USSR	1

FINAL

England	4	West Germany	2

(after extra time)

Wembley, 30 July 1966. Attendance 93,000

England: Banks, Cohen, Wilson, Stiles, Charlton J, Moore, Ball, Hurst, Hunt, Charlton R, Peters (Scorers: Hurst (3), Peters)

West Germany: Tilkowski, Hottges, Schnellinger, Beckenbauer, Schulz, Weber, Held, Haller, Seeler, Overath, Emmerich (Scorers: Haller, Weber)

Leading scorers 9 Eusebio (Portugal) 5 Haller (West Germany) 4 Beckenbauer (West Germany) Hurst (England) Porkujan (USSR)

League Cup comes to Wembley: QPR win thriller

THE FOOTBALL League Cup has come alive. The first Wembley final of this unpopular and largely unwanted competition could not have made a better impact, as Third Division Queen's Park Rangers came back in the last half-hour from two down to beat the holders West Bromwich 3–2.

Known as "Hardaker's Horror" after Alan Hardaker, the Football League secretary whose brainchild it was in 1960, the League Cup has only recently been contested, somewhat reluctantly, by all the League's leading teams. The glamour of Wembley — and a 30,000 allocation of tickets to each of the competing clubs — drew a crowd of 97,952, which was some 28,000 more than the aggregate attendance of any of the previous finals.

It was no surprise when West Bromwich went into an early lead, and it was thanks largely to QPR's veteran left-back Jim Langley that they were only two up at the break, both goals being scored by former Rangers left-winger Clive Clark. But a half-time pep-talk from wily manager Alec Stock sent QPR out a new team. After 18 minutes, Roger Morgan headed them back into the game. Twelve minutes later, the inspirational Rodney Marsh picked the ball up on the halfway line, jinked his way through the defence and struck a low shot in off a post.

Now Rangers were on top, and they piled on the pressure, although the winner was a controversial goal scored by winger Mark Lazarus after West Brom keeper Dick Sheppard had lost the ball in a collision with QPR centre-half Ron Hunt. Sadly, QPR will not be able to take advantage of the new League Cup "carrot" of qualification for the Fairs Cup — which is open only to First Division clubs — but they will be more concerned with their bid for promotion.

Morgan (right, white strip) heads QPR's first, watched by team-mate Marsh (centre).

Scottish shock of the century: Berwick beat Rangers in Cup!

IT WAS A CASE OF "Jock the Giant-killer" at Shielfield Park, where a jubilant, if incredulous, record 13,365 crowd saw Berwick Rangers knock mighty Glasgow Rangers out of the Scottish FA Cup in the first round. The Berwick hero was Jock Wallace, their goalkeeper-manager, who kept the marauding Rangers forwards at bay with a string of spectacular saves after Sammy Reid had put Berwick ahead in the 32nd minute.

Berwick, the only club in the Scottish League whose ground is in England, have never finished higher than eighth in Division Two. But they have enjoyed previous giant-killing fame in the Cup. In 1953–54, two years before they were elected to the League, they beat Ayr 5–1 and First Division Dundee 3–0 before losing to Rangers 4–0 in the quarter-finals. And three years ago they reached the semi-finals of the League Cup before Rangers, again, beat them 3–1.

This time they got their revenge over the Cup-holders, the team that have won the trophy four times in the last five years. It is arguably the most sensational result in the history of Scottish soccer.

Rangers keeper Martin cannot believe that Berwick have scored.

Celtic 'Kings of Europe': grand slam for Jock Stein's men

Chalmers (hoops, right) turns away after deflecting the ball past Sarti.

CELTIC'S stirring victory in Lisbon over Inter-Milan in the final of the European Cup is a triumph for attacking football over the ultra-defensive Italian style that has been threatening to suffocate the game on the Continent. Former captain Jock Stein has worked wonders since he took charge at Parkhead two years ago. First he transformed the ailing club into the best team in Scotland, and now they have proved themselves truly "Kings of Europe".

No British side had even reached the final before, but Celtic went into the match brimful of confidence, having cleaned up at home in League, Cup and League Cup — their first domestic "treble". Now they were going for the "grand slam". But the 12,000 fans who travelled to Portugal to lend their vociferous support to the "Bhoys" were briefly silenced after only eight minutes when Mazzola converted a penalty.

This was the signal for Inter to retreat into their shell, and for the rest of the game it was Celtic's attack against the formidable Italian defence. Tricky right-winger Jimmy Johnstone proceeded to give Burgnich a trying time, and Bobby Murdoch put himself majestically in control of the midfield. But Celtic's greatest threat was their overlapping backs, Jim Craig and particularly Tommy Gemmell on the left.

With Sarti performing heroics in goal, and Auld and Gemmell both hitting the bar, it was well into the second half before Celtic broke the Italians down. Gemmell fed Murdoch, who switched play to the right. Craig cut the ball back across field for the advancing Gemmell to take it in his stride and hammer it past Sarti from 25 yards. Six minutes from time, the heroic Gemmell moved up again on the left and squared the ball to Murdoch, who drove the ball low into the crowded penalty area. As Sarti moved to cover it, Steve Chalmers deflected it past him for the winner.

What a climax! That was Celtic's 200th goal of the season, in 64 games, and they had won everything they entered. But above all, they had won the battle for the attacking game.

FOOTBALL FOCUS

- England's Alan Ball moved from Blackpool to Everton for £110,000 in August, the first £100,000 transfer between British clubs.
- Billy Ferguson (Linfield) became the first Irish footballer to be sent off in an international, and the first ever player in the Home International Championship, when N.Ireland lost 2–0 to England in Belfast on 22 October.
- England manager Alf Ramsey was knighted in the New Year's honours list.
- Blackpool beat Newcastle 6–0 on 22 October in a Division One match, not an unusual result except that it was their only home win. Needless to say, they finished bottom of the table.
- England lost their first game since winning the World Cup, on 15 April at Wembley, 3–2 to Scotland, whose delirious fans regarded it as their own World Championship and proceeded to invade the pitch at the end and cut out pieces of turf.
- Rangers just failed to make it a Scottish double in Europe when they lost the Cup-Winners' Cup final 1–0 to Bayern Munich in extra time.

FINAL SCORE

Football League
Division 1: Manchester United
Top scorer: Ron Davies (Southampton) 37
Division 2: Coventry City
Division 3: Queen's Park Rangers
Division 4: Stockport County
Footballer of the Year: Jack Charlton (Leeds United)

FA Cup Final
Tottenham Hotspur 2 Chelsea 1

League Cup Final
QPR 3 WBA 2

Scottish League
Division 1: Celtic
Top scorer: Steve Chalmers (Celtic) 21
Division 2: Morton
Footballer of the Year: Ronnie Simpson (Celtic)

Scottish FA Cup Final
Celtic 2 Aberdeen 0

Scottish League Cup Final
Celtic 1 Rangers 0

International Championship
Scotland, 5 pts

European Cup Final
Celtic 2 Inter-Milan 1

Cup-Winners' Cup Final
Bayern Munich 1 Rangers 0
(after extra time)

Inter-Cities Fairs Cup Final
Dynamo Zagreb beat Leeds United 2–0, 0–0

European Footballer of the Year 1966
Bobby Charlton (Manchester United & England)

World Club Championship
Racing Club (Argentina) beat Celtic 0–1, 2–1, 1–0

Cockerels coast through Cockney final

IN THE FIRST all-London FA Cup final this century, Spurs enjoyed a much easier victory over Chelsea than the final 2–1 scoreline suggests. It was their third Cup win in the sixties, but only two men remained from their previous success in 1962 — Dave Mackay and Jimmy Greaves. Bill Nicholson has built another fine footballing side after the break-up of the "double" team, the heart of which was wrenched out with the retirement of Blanchflower, the tragic death of White and the serious injuries to Mackay. But Mackay's undoubted courage has never been better demonstrated than by his double comeback, and it was entirely appropriate that he should lead the new Spurs to their latest triumph.

Spurs seemed to stroll through the match, always in control, individually and collectively superior to a Chelsea side they never allowed into the game. Up front, Greaves and Gilzean were always dangerous; at the back England was dominant. Chelsea's few threats came from Charlie Cooke's exciting but erratic dribbling.

Spurs went ahead on the stroke of half-time when Mullery broke down the middle and his shot was blocked to Robertson, who swept it in past Bonetti. Saul put them two up midway through the second half with a spectacular hook shot on the turn. Tambling's goal for Chelsea four minutes from time never threatened to disturb the result of the match.

Six sent off in World Club brawl

IN A MATCH that should never have been played, four men from Celtic and two from Racing Club (Argentina) were sent off in a play-off for the so-called World Club Championship. This abomination of a competition reached its nadir in Montevideo as Celtic clearly decided to get their retaliation in first. There is no excuse for Celtic's behaviour, tried though they must have been after their experience in Buenos Aires three days earlier.

For a start, the format of the competition between the respective champions of Europe and South America is flawed, the winner being decided not by aggregate goals but by games won. This is the fourth time in the eight years since its inception that a third match has been necessary. Celtic won the first leg, at Hampden Park on 18 October, with a header from their captain, Billy McNeill. Then in Buenos Aires on 1 November, they came up against the same bitter atmosphere of intimidation that faced Inter-Milan both inside and outside the stadium two years ago. Keeper Ronnie Simpson was struck by a missile from the crowd before the game began and had to be replaced by Fallon. Celtic led by a Gemmell penalty but, with their little right-winger Jimmy Johnstone bearing the brunt of persistently savage treatment, they succumbed to two goals from Racing, and the tie went into a decider.

The play-off was sheer carnage, with each side perpetrating atrocious acts. At times, police had to go on to the pitch to break up the fighting. The referee warned the captains that if the savagery continued, he would start sending players off. Johnstone, who had to wash the spittle out of his hair during the interval, was one of the Celtic players expelled, although Auld refused to go. A Cardenas goal after 57 minutes won the game for Racing. Celtic have fined their players £250 each. The Racing players each received a new car.

Celtic's John Hughes was sent off for this foul on Racing's keeper.

Luck of the Irish: Jennings scores

NOT TOO MANY FA Charity Shield matches are memorable games. But Spurs' Irish international keeper Pat Jennings will remember the one against Manchester United at Old Trafford on 12 August. Moving to the edge of his area, he sent a mighty punt upfield, well into the United half. The ball sailed over the Spurs forwards and United defenders, and swirled in the high wind. United keeper Alex Stepney was back-pedalling furiously, but there was nothing he could do as the ball bounced over his head and into the goal.

Jennings was not sure if it counted at first, but it did (it's the goal-kick that cannot be scored from), and it helped Spurs to a 3–3 draw. Another memorable moment in the match was a magnificent overhead kick by Denis Law that sent the ball flashing past Jennings into the Spurs net. It brought the 63,000 crowd to its feet, but they gasped again when the referee disallowed the goal, for some obscure reason. Jennings is an outstanding keeper, but he had more than his share of luck in this game.

SOCCER SOUNDBITES

"I couldn't believe it. I wasn't even sure it counted in the laws of the game."

PAT JENNINGS
on his goal in the FA Charity Shield game.

England make their point in needle match with Scotland

THE SCOTLAND-ENGLAND clash at Hampden on 24 February was a real needle match. England needed only to draw to earn qualification for the Nations Cup — now called the European Football Championships — which was based this time on the aggregate of this and last season's Home Championship. Scotland desperately wanted to win, not only for European qualification, but to confirm last season's victory over the world champions, which had been devalued by injuries to the England team.

Fortunately, the bitterness built up between the two camps did not spill over on to the field. England controlled the match, despite the brilliant runs of Chelsea's Charlie Cooke for Scotland, who badly missed the unfit Law and Baxter. England, without Stiles, Cohen and Jack Charlton, went ahead through Peters. And although Hughes equalized in the 39th minute, Scotland finished relieved that England's overall superiority was not translated into an avalanche of goals. The 1–1 draw takes England through to the quarter-finals of the European Championships, and a two-legged tie with Spain.

John Hughes (right) heads past Banks to put Scotland level.

Sad Rangers booed off after first defeat

THE FANS of Glasgow Rangers are certainly hard to please. The scene is Ibrox, on 27 April, where Rangers complete their League programme. They go to the game unbeaten, with 61 points out of a possible 66. But they lose 3–2 as Aberdeen score a last-minute goal, and their own supporters jeer and whistle them off the pitch.

This might sound incomprehensible, but Rangers have just handed deadly rivals Celtic the title on a plate. It has been a strange season for Rangers, who went ahead in the League when they beat Celtic 1–0 on 16 September (Celtic's only defeat) and promptly sacked their manager Scot Symon, who had brought them 15 major honours in 13 years. Knocked out of the League Cup, the Scottish Cup and the Fairs Cup, Rangers just had to succeed in the League. But the unthinkable has happened. Celtic, who would have had to fight for a result in three days' time at Dunfermline, recent winners of the Cup, are currently level on points with a far superior goal average. Only a 16–0 defeat will hand the title to Rangers now!

FOOTBALL FOCUS

- The International Board introduced a rule limiting keepers to four steps while in possession of the ball before releasing it into play.
- Martin Chivers moved from Southampton to Spurs in January for a British record fee of £125,000, exceeded in June by Allan Clarke's £150,000 move from Fulham to Leicester.
- Bobby Charlton scored his 45th goal for England in the 3–1 win over Sweden at Wembley on 22 May, to go ahead of Jimmy Greaves as England's all-time leading scorer.
- Cardiff's valiant effort in the Cup-Winners' Cup continued in the semi-finals, where they drew 1–1 in Hamburg before going down 3–2 at home — and they avoided relegation to Division Three!
- With a few minutes to go on the last day of the season, Keith Bradley turned a cross past his own keeper at Villa Park, giving QPR the win they needed to beat Blackpool on goal average for the second promotion place to Division One.

Mercer's men pride of Manchester after last-day drama

MANCHESTER CITY have pipped rivals United at the post and are the new League champions. A stirring 4–3 victory at Newcastle while United lost 2–1 at home to Stoke has put them two points clear, with Liverpool, who beat Forest 6–1 and still have a game to play, a further point behind.

United were five points ahead at one time, but have found the strain of the European Cup too much. With two games left, City were ahead on goal average, and Leeds were a point behind with a game in hand. Leeds blew their chances, however, losing their unbeaten home record in their last home match, 2–1 to Liverpool.

When City persuaded old pro Joe Mercer to come out of semi-retirement to take the helm in 1965, they were at their lowest ebb, having finished 11th in Division Two. In his first week, Mercer signed Malcolm Allison as coach and assistant manager, and in their first season together they took City back to Division One. Mercer's shrewd buys have included Francis Lee (£60,000), Colin Bell (£45,000) and Mike Summerbee (£35,000), but it was local product Neil Young who led the scoring with 19 goals. Veteran Tony Book, a bargain at £13,500, has made an inspirational captain. Full-back Book was wellknown to Allison, who managed him at Bath and Plymouth, his previous clubs, and he was City's only ever-present in the League.

United can still go on to win the European Cup, but for now City are the toast of Manchester.

Joe Mercer, with the Championship trophy, and Allison (left).

Russian revenge for Cardiff, 23 years after

WELSH CLUBS, who have a relatively easy qualification for the European Cup-Winners' Cup, are looked down upon by the teams from England and Scotland. But this season, Cardiff, languishing in the lower regions of the English Second Division, excelled themselves in Europe and put their more illustrious neighbours to shame.

While Spurs and Aberdeen were being knocked out in the second round, Cardiff beat Dutch side NAC Breda to progress to the quarter-finals, in which they have now accounted for Moscow Torpedo. Not that this should come as such a surprise, for Cardiff previously showed their fighting qualities when they knocked out holders Sporting Lisbon in the 1964-65 tournament.

Cardiff won their home leg against Moscow 1–0 through a Barrie Jones goal. Manager Jimmy Scoular, a redoubtable Cup fighter himself with Newcastle in the fifties, prepared the side well for their long trip to Tashkent, where the second leg was being played because of the severe Muscovite winter. They received a warm welcome from their Uzbek hosts, and held Torpedo to a single goal. It was an astounding performance in such a foreign environment. But thanks to Scoular's experience and attention to detail, the team were completely relaxed and not in the least overawed.

Now, remarkably, with five reserves in the side, including centre-half Ritchie Morgan making his first-team debut, they have won the play-off, which took place at Augsburg, West Germany on 3 April. Again there was only one goal in it, scored three minutes before half-time by reserve centre-forward Norman Dean after 19-year-old John Toshack had brilliantly nodded the ball down.

Victory against a Moscow side is all the sweeter for Cardiff, whose older fans remember their 10–1 thrashing at the hands of Dynamo just after the war. But now they must get back to the more mundane task of avoiding relegation before taking on Hamburg and Uwe Seeler in the semi-finals.

Magic in Madrid takes United through to Euro final

MANCHESTER UNITED took their slender 1–0 lead to Spain for the second leg of the European Cup semi-final with Real Madrid and found themselves trailing 3–2 on aggregate at half-time. But they staged a courageous recovery against the six-times champions and won the tie 4–3.

Pirri put Real level overall after 32 minutes, and then, just before half-time, Gento scored a second. Zoco put one in his own net for United, but Amancio restored Real's aggregate lead. United went in at the break thoroughly shaken: Real were rampant and bursting for more, the crowd's noise intimidating. But Matt Busby gently encouraged his players in the interval, and told David Sadler to move up into attack. United went out and held their own, and it was Sadler who scored with some 15 minutes left to even up the tie.

Then came a typical piece of magic from George Best, who had scored United's home goal. He left the Real defence floundering as he took the ball to the right-hand byline and pulled it back for centre-back Bill Foulkes, of all people, to turn one of his rare goals into the net for the winner. The crowd were stunned, and United are in the final at last.

The vital goal in the first leg, scored by Best (centre).

Sadler (10) scores and has an hypnotic effect on the Real defence.

Errant Husband's miss is the turning point in Cup final

Astle's extra-time winner sails into the net.

WEST BROMWICH, equalling Newcastle's record of appearing in 10 finals, won the Cup in the third minute of extra time with a goal by Jeff Astle. But the additional period would not have been necessary had Jim Husband taken an easy chance five minutes from the end of normal time.

It was not an adventurous final, with the first half dominated by spoiling tactics. Ball was his usual industrious self for Everton, and Hope a live wire for Albion. Everton had the edge of the goalless 90 minutes, and should have won when a cross from Morrissey found Husband unmarked six yards out. But he somehow contrived to head the ball over the bar.

Astle's winner was spectacular. Kendall's foul tackle disturbed his momentum as he advanced towards the box, but when his right-foot drive cannoned back off Harvey, he smashed the rebound with his weaker left foot 20 yards into the far corner of the net. Astle, who had scored in every round so far, had done little else in the final, thanks to Everton stopper Brian Labone, but Albion could not have asked for more.

FINAL SCORE

EUROPEAN CHAMPIONSHIPS 1968

QUARTER-FINALS

England v Spain 1–0, 2–1
Bulgaria v Italy 3–2, 0–2
France v Yugoslavia 1–1, 1–5
Hungary v USSR 2–0, 0–3

Last four in Italy:

SEMI-FINALS

Yugoslavia	1	England	0
Italy	0	USSR	0

(Italy won toss)

THIRD-PLACE MATCH

England	2	USSR	0

FINAL

Italy	1	Yugoslavia	1

(after extra time)
Rome, 8 June 1968. Attendance 75,000

Italy: Zoff, Burgnich, Facchetti, Ferrini, Guarneri, Castano, Domenghini, Juliano, Anastasi, Lodetti, Prati
(Scorer: Domenghini)
Yugoslavia: Pantelic, Fazlagic, Damjanovic, Pavlovic, Paunovic, Holcer, Petkovic, Acimovic, Musemic, Trivic, Dzajic
(Scorer: Dzajic)

FINAL REPLAY

Italy	2	Yugoslavia	0

Rome, 10 June 1968. Attendance 60,000

Italy: Zoff, Burgnich, Facchetti, Rosato, Guarneri, Salvadore, Domenghini, Mazzola, Anastasi, De Sisti, Riva
(Scorers: Riva, Anastasi)
Yugoslavia: Pantelic, Fazlagic, Damjanovic, Pavlovic, Paunovic, Holcer, Hosic, Acimovic, Musemic, Trivic, Dzajic

Busby: from tragedy to triumph as United win European glory

WHEN MATT BUSBY lay fighting for his life in a Munich hospital 10 years ago, his magnificent young team decimated, his dreams of European glory smashed, who would have thought he would have the physical strength and mental fortitude not only to recover from these great personal blows, but to start all over again. But at Wembley, on 29 May, in a night charged with emotion, his third great Manchester United side beat Benfica 4–1 after extra time to win the European Cup, the first English club to do so.

The win was also a personal triumph for Bobby Charlton, a survivor of the Munich air crash who has become a national hero. He captained United and scored two goals. His first, a rare headed effort, put United ahead eight minutes into the second half. Continued United pressure failed to extend their lead, however, as the chances made on the left by John Aston, playing a blinder, went begging. With nine minutes left, Graca scored, and Benfica were transformed. Eusebio came bursting through in the last minute, but Stepney was there heroically to block his fearsome shot.

Three minutes into extra time, Kidd flicked on a Stepney punt and Best pounced. Steering the ball skilfully away from a couple of tackles, he made for goal with a panicking defence in hot pursuit. He was the coolest man in the stadium as he drew the keeper and slid the ball into the net. There could only be one result now. Kidd, on his 19th birthday, headed a third and then made the fourth for Charlton. Yes, United had won the European Cup: Busby's dream was fulfilled. Nothing could make up for Munich, but here at last was a tribute to those who perished there.

Busby, with — at last — a dream fulfilled.

Kidd leaps in celebration of his goal, along with Best (centre).

FINAL SCORE

Football League
Division 1: Manchester City
Top scorer: George Best (Manchester United), Ron Davies (Southampton) 28
Division 2: Ipswich Town
Division 3: Oxford United
Division 4: Luton Town
Footballer of the Year: George Best (Man U)

FA Cup Final
WBA 1 Everton 0
(after extra time)

League Cup Final
Leeds United 1 Arsenal 0

Scottish League
Division 1: Celtic
Top scorer: Bobby Lennox (Celtic) 32
Division 2: St Mirren
Footballer of the Year: Gordon Wallace (Raith R)

Scottish FA Cup Final
Dunfermline Athletic 3 Hearts 1

Scottish League Cup Final
Celtic 5 Dundee 3

International Championship
England, 5 pts

European Cup Final
Manchester United 4 Benfica 1
(after extra time)

Cup-Winners' Cup Final
AC Milan 2 SV Hamburg 0

Inter-Cities Fairs Cup Final
Leeds United beat Ferencvaros 1–0, 0–0

European Footballer of the Year 1967
Florian Albert (Ferencvaros & Hungary)

Leading European Scorer (Golden Boot)
Eusebio (Benfica) 43

World Club Championship
Estudiantes (Argentina) beat Manchester United (England) 1–0, 1–1

Mullery the first England player to be sent off

IT WAS A black day for the world champions in Florence on 5 June, when a ruthless Yugoslavia beat them 1–0. Not only did this end England's hopes of winning their first European Football Championships, but it is the first time an England player has been sent off in a full international.

Alan Mullery was the culprit, kicking at an opponent who had just hit him with a late tackle, and who leapt up from his display of horizontal theatricals as soon as the Spurs wing-half left. Mullery, perhaps, was paying for Norman Hunter's crippling tackle that put Osim out of what was a vicious game. A beautifully volleyed late goal by star outside-left Dragan Dzajic settled the issue.

Argentinians win world clubbing championship

MANCHESTER UNITED were again victims of South American violence in the return leg of the so-called World Club Championship at Old Trafford on 16 October. In the first leg last month in Buenos Aires, which they lost 1–0, they bit the bullet and allowed the wild men of Estudiantes to trample all over them. Charlton needed three stitches after being hacked down, while Stiles, a marked man from the start, was back-headed in the face, and was later sent off for dissent.

Estudiantes went ahead after only five minutes in the return. Law had to be substituted after getting the "stud treatment" from the keeper. And Best, hit, kicked, fouled and spat upon, was sent off along with Medina for fighting. Morgan equalized, but United failed to score again, which is perhaps a blessing in disguise.

Medina of Estudiantes departs in tears after he and Best are sent off.

Sir Matt to hand over the reins

SIR MATT BUSBY of Manchester United announced on 14 January that he is to relinquish his job as team manager and will become general manager of the club that he has served for 23 years. Knighted after United's European Cup triumph last season, Sir Matt is the League's longest-serving manager. He was a wing-half with Manchester City, playing in the FA Cup finals of 1933 and 1934, later joined Liverpool, won one full cap, and captained Scotland later in wartime.

Busby took over at United straight after the war and built three great sides, all renowned for playing an attacking, entertaining brand of football that has had the crowds flocking to Old Trafford in droves. Busby has always moulded the outstanding products of his vast scouting network and excellent youth policy with astute buys, and has never been afraid to allow individual flair its full rein.

When his first side, post-war winners of League and Cup under the captaincy of Johnny Carey, got too old, he built another. These, with an average age of 22 and nicknamed the "Busby Babes", were twice League champions and potentially the greatest English club side of all before they were tragically broken up in the Munich air disaster, which took the lives of Duncan Edwards and several other outstanding young footballers. Almost at death's door himself, Busby fought back, took up the reins again and began rebuilding his beloved United. With Munich survivor Bobby Charlton, the young genius George Best, and the irrepressible Denis Law, brought back from Italian football, they won the League again, and then last year fulfilled Busby's dream by winning the European Cup.

Now Sir Matt can relax and look back on a quarter-century of achievement during which he has remained a modest, compassionate man loved and admired throughout the game.

Sir Matt Busby, a father figure of football.

Six of the best for Hurst — well, five anyway

WEST HAM thrashed Sunderland 8–0 at Upton Park on 19 October, and World Cup hero Geoff Hurst scored six of them, so equalling Vic Watson's club record for a League game, set in 1929. The last individual six in a League match was scored by Bert Lister for Oldham against Southport in Division Four six years ago.

Hurst, who hit a hat-trick in each half, completed the scoring in 75 minutes. Perhaps it's just as well he failed to equal Ted Drake's First Division record of seven, scored for Arsenal at Villa Park in 1935, as he later admitted putting the first of his goals in with a hand as he dived on the blindside of the referee.

Hurst dives to put the first past Sunderland's Montgomery — with his hand, as he was later to admit.

Derby's Dave in back four is the real Mackay

THEY SAID Dave Mackay was finished, that age and injury had slowed him down and that he would never recapture the barnstorming form of his halcyon days as a wing-half with Tottenham and Scotland. But, relishing his new role in the back four, he has used his head to save his legs, and has led Derby to promotion from Division Two, clinched with their 5–1 win over Bolton on 5 April in front of 30,000 delighted fans at the Baseball Ground.

Mackay, joint Footballer of the Year with Manchester City's equally inspirational veteran captain Tony Book, has been the key factor in a side shaped by manager Brian Clough that should be a credit to the First Division next season.

With a sound defence and a free-scoring attack, Derby had seven points to spare over their nearest rivals at the finish.

'Treble' in three weeks for rampant Bhoys

CELTIC COMPLETED their second domestic "treble" in three years when they thrashed Rangers 4–0 in the Scottish Cup final at Hampden on 26 April. It was their second thumping Cup win, having beaten Hibs 6–2 in the League Cup three weeks earlier. They had already clinched the League on 21 April, when a late goal by Tommy Gemmell earned them a 2–2 draw at Kilmarnock.

A fire at Hampden Park that damaged a stand put the League Cup final back, but 74,000 saw the demolition of Hibs, in which Lennox hit a hat-trick. In the quarter-finals, Celtic had enjoyed 10–0 and 4–2 wins over Hamilton, and had twice beaten Rangers in the qualifying group. But neither Glasgow club could match last season's record in the League; despite beating Celtic twice, which might have been decisive in any other season, Rangers dropped points all over the place and allowed their rivals a smooth passage in the end.

The "grand slam" eluded the Bhoys this season, although they held AC Milan to a goalless draw at the San Siro in the quarter-finals of the European Cup. But they were without the injured Lennox in the return and never recovered from an early Prati goal. Still, some say this is a better Celtic side than the so-called "Lisbon Lions" of two years ago. They are a more mature side now, and Jock Stein has further strengthened his squad. If their performance in the Cup final against a Rangers side who had beaten Aberdeen 6–1 in the semis is anything to go by, they will certainly continue to reign supreme in Scotland for the foreseeable future.

Chalmers (hoops) scores Celtic's fourth goal in the Cup final.

Piracy at Wembley as jolly Rogers plunders Arsenal

THIRD DIVISION Swindon shocked Arsenal at Wembley in the final of the League Cup, and winger Don Rogers was their hero. His two buccaneering goals in extra time finished off the flu-stricken Gunners, who were all at sea in the heavy mud.

Arsenal, who lost narrowly to Leeds in last year's final, have been enjoying a good season and giving away few goals. But several of their players were suffering from the after-effects of the flu epidemic. Swindon went to Wembley unfancied but confident: they had accounted for two First and two Second Division sides to get there.

For most of the first half, Arsenal were in control, and only the fine form of Peter Downsborough in goal kept Swindon in the game. But 10 minutes before the interval, Ian Ure made a hash of a back-pass to keeper Bob Wilson, and Roger Smart was left with a simple tap-in. In the second half, Arsenal put Downsborough under real pressure with nine corners in a 10-minute spell. They finally equalized with four minutes left, when the persistent Bobby Gould forced Downsborough into his only error.

If anyone thought this was the signal for Arsenal to take charge in extra time, they were mistaken. The mud and the flu had taken their toll, and Arsenal had given their all. From the restart, Swindon looked and played like the stronger team, and began to tear huge gaps in the Arsenal defence. The inevitable goal came seconds before the break, Rogers cracking the ball in after a corner. He finished it off with a flourish in the last minute, racing over the half-way line on to a pass from Smart and waltzing round Wilson to plant the ball into the unguarded net. As a Third Division side, Swindon don't qualify for Europe, but they are in a good position to emulate QPR's feat of two seasons ago, and win promotion to go with the unexpected silverware they collected at Wembley.

The Arsenal defence is beaten as Swindon's second goal finds the net.

Leeds set new League marks

A GOAL by Johnny Giles five minutes from the end of their last League match on 30 April against Nottingham Forest gave Leeds a 1–0 win and the two points they needed to set a new First Division record. Leeds's first League title has been a long time in coming, but they did it in no uncertain manner, with only two defeats — another League record for 22-club divisions.

Their 67 points beats by one the long-standing mark, set first by Arsenal in 1931, when the Gunners scored 127 goals — almost twice Leeds's tally of 66. Leeds, indeed, become only the fifth club to win the Championship with more points than goals; they have scored fewer than any title-winning team since before the off-side law change in 1925.

Don Revie has assembled an enormously powerful side, strong in every department and with a team spirit that borders at times on the fanatical. But they were building up a reputation as the "nearly men" — beaten Cup-finalists in 1965 and Fairs Cup-finalists in 1966, and League runners-up in those years, too — until last season's double success of League Cup and Fairs Cup.

When Revie took charge at Elland Road eight years ago, Leeds were an unfashionable, struggling Second Division side. With very little recourse to the transfer market, he developed the considerable raw talent available, knitted it into a team and made the players believe in themselves. They won promotion in 1964 and were beaten only on goal average for the League title the following year.

Only three players in the title-winning side cost money — Johnny Giles (£35,000) from Manchester United, England outside-left Mike O'Grady (£30,000) from Huddersfield, and striker Mick Jones (£100,000) from Sheffield United — a tribute to Revie's scouting system and youth policy, which unearthed and brought on the Scottish wingers Peter Lorimer and Eddie Gray. Other products of the youth scheme include Welsh international keeper Gary Sprake and the versatile Paul Madeley.

Giles, who moved in from the wing when Bobby Collins broke a thigh, has been a key figure as a midfield schemer, striking up a formidable partnership with the dynamic Billy Bremner. Revie also transformed Jack Charlton from a solid club centre-half to a World Cup-winner, and the fierce-tackling Norman Hunter into another England international. With Paul Reaney and Terry Cooper behind them, Leeds conceded only 26 goals, fewer than any previous champions in a 42-match season, although runners-up Liverpool beat that by two.

Mick Jones was top scorer with only 14 League goals. Critics of Leeds label them as destructive and defensive, but only two clubs in the First Division scored more goals this season. Leeds's finest accolade came in their penultimate match, at Anfield, where a 0–0 draw put them out of Liverpool's reach and clinched the League title for them. At the end of the game, they did a lap of honour and were cheered generously by the fans on the Kop.

Giles (centre) and Bremner (above), the midfield heart of Leeds United's title-winning side.

FOOTBALL FOCUS

- Scottish club Dunfermline beat West Bromwich in the quarter-finals of the European Cup-Winners' Cup, and only narrowly lost to eventual winners Slovan Bratislava in the semis.
- Rangers broke the transfer record between Scottish clubs by a massive £40,000 when they signed striker Colin Stein from Hibs for £100,000 at the end of October.
- Tommy Docherty managed three clubs in six weeks: he resigned from Rotherham on 6 November to take over at QPR, but walked out on them a month later after a row with the chairman, and he became Aston Villa's manager on 18 December.
- League Cup-winners Swindon and FA Cup-finalists Leicester will meet next season in the Second Division, after Swindon duly won promotion and Leicester were unable to stave off relegation.
- Northampton have completed a remarkable cycle of promotion and relegation in the 1960s, going from Division Four in 1960 to Division One in 1965, and now back again to Division Four in 1969.
- After years of struggling to stay in Division One, Fulham have gone straight down to Division Three in two seasons.
- Champions Leeds broke the British transfer record in June when they signed striker Allan Clarke from Leicester for £165,000.

Magpies steal a march on Hungarians

NEWCASTLE UNITED, the club who got into the Fairs Cup although finishing only 10th in the First Division last season, have confounded everyone and won it. They went to Budapest with a 3–0 lead from the first leg of the final and proceeded to beat Ujpest Dozsa again, this time by 3–2.

Newcastle's "back-door" qualification came about because of the "one city, one team" rule in the Fairs Cup (which precluded Everton, Spurs and Arsenal); the increase in England's entry to four clubs; and the participation of Manchester United and West Bromwich, respectively, in the Champions' Cup and the Cup-Winners' Cup. While Liverpool and Chelsea went out of the competition on the toss of a coin, and Leeds lost both quarter-final legs to Ujpest, Newcastle were accounting for Feyenoord, Sporting Lisbon, Real Zaragoza, Vitoria Setubal and, in the semis, Glasgow Rangers.

Skipper Bobby Moncur was their hero in the first leg of the final, at St James's Park. A defensive wing-half, he went up to help his forwards, who had been battering vainly at the Ujpest defence, and scored after 63 minutes — his first goal in seven years at the club. No doubt flushed with success, he scored again nine minutes later, and Scott made it 3–0 six minutes from the end.

The return was no foregone conclusion. Newcastle did not have a good away record, and the Hungarian side were a different proposition on their own pitch, with the great Ferenc Bene in their side. And it was Bene who pulled a goal back after 20 minutes; Gorocs scored a second before half-time, and Ujpest looked as if they were going to run away with it. But again Moncur intervened, scoring his third goal of the final a minute after the interval with a volley from Sinclair's cross. Danish international Ben Arentoft soon scored a second, and teenage substitute Alan Foggon made it 3–2 after 67 minutes. It was an extraordinary result, 6–2 on aggregate, and a performance to rank with United's FA Cup feats of the fifties.

Moncur (left) breaks the ice for Newcastle in the first leg.

Tired England fade in Rio

ENGLAND'S June tour included a trip to Mexico for a taste of the conditions they will experience in next year's World Cup. They found the heat and altitude of Mexico City a little too much of a handicap in the end, and could only draw 0–0 with Mexico in the Aztec Stadium, where the World Cup final will be played.

Two days later, and 2,000 feet lower, an England XI cruised to a 4–0 victory over a Mexican XI in Guadalajara, where England will play their group matches. England then moved on to Montevideo and beat Uruguay 2–1.

The big test was reserved for their last match, against Brazil and Pele in Rio. England went ahead in the first half through Colin Bell, who was first to the ball when a Peters cross hit a defender. Tommy Wright tripped Gerson in the box, but Gordon Banks managed to save Carlos Alberto's spot-kick.

England continued to play well until they began to tire late in the second half. Tostao equalized for Brazil 10 minutes from time and, two minutes later, laid one on a plate for Jairzinho to score the winner. Nevertheless, it was by no means an unsuccessful tour, and both Sir Alf Ramsey and the England team will have learnt a lot to hold them in good stead for the World Cup in a year's time.

FINAL SCORE

Football League
Division 1: Leeds United
Top scorer: Jimmy Greaves (Tottenham H) 27
Division 2: Derby County
Division 3: Watford
Division 4: Doncaster Rovers
Footballers of the Year: Tony Book (Manchester City) and Dave Mackay (Derby County)

FA Cup Final

Manchester City	1	Leicester City	0

League Cup Final

Swindon Town	3	Arsenal	1

(after extra time)

Scottish League
Division 1: Celtic
Top scorer: Kenny Cameron (Dundee United) 26
Division 2: Motherwell
Footballer of the Year: Bobby Murdoch (Celtic)

Scottish FA Cup Final

Celtic	4	Rangers	0

Scottish League Cup Final

Celtic	6	Hibernian	2

International Championship
England, 6 pts

European Cup Final

AC Milan	4	Ajax Amsterdam	1

Cup-Winners' Cup Final

Slovan Bratislava	3	Barcelona	2

Inter-Cities Fairs Cup Final
Newcastle United beat Ujpest Dozsa 3–0, 3–2

European Footballer of the Year 1968
George Best (Manchester United & N Ireland)

World Club Championship
AC Milan (Italy) beat Estudiantes (Argentina) 3–0, 1–2

Leading European Scorer (Golden Boot)
Petar, Jekov (CSKA Sofia) 36

Joint Footballers of the Year, Dave Mackay (left) and Tony Book.

Six of the Best on bad boy's return

GEORGE BEST, the man you just can't keep out of the news, equalled the FA Cup scoring record on 7 February with six goals in Manchester United's 8–2 fifth-round victory at Northampton. Coming back from a month's suspension, controversially imposed as punishment for a petulant incident, he treated the 22,000 fans at the County Ground to a rare exhibition of all the skills in the game. He scored with his head, with flashing shots, and by dribbling round the keeper, sending the hapless Book the wrong way with the merest shrug of his shoulder.

Northampton, who were in the First Division only four years ago, have a reputation as Cup fighters. But this time Goliath gave David a rare thrashing. Kidd scored the other United goals, while McNeil and Large were on target for the Cobblers. (United favourite Denis Law scored six goals in the Cup at Luton in 1961 for local rivals Manchester City, but the match was abandoned and the records expunged... and City lost the replay.)

Bad boy Best heads the first of his six goals against Northampton.

Leeds go down fighting: great run comes to an end at Goodison

LEEDS'S RECORD unbeaten run in the First Division finally came to an end on 30 August when League leaders Everton beat them 3–2 at Goodison. Three goals down soon after the interval, Leeds threw everything at Everton and clawed two back. But it was not quite enough.

Leeds's last defeat was 5–1 at Burnley on 19 October 1968, after which they went 28 games unbeaten to take the League title with a record number of points and, with another six games this season, they took their unbeaten League run to 34 matches.

In the first half, Leeds looked anything but champions as Everton ran them ragged, with left-winger John Morrissey in particular giving the normally solid Paul Reaney a roasting. They deserved more than goals from Jimmy Husband and Joe Royle to show for their dominance at half-time. Royle was giving Jack Charlton the run-around, superior both in the air and on the ground. Only Billy Bremner and Norman Hunter prevented a Leeds thrashing.

And it was the never-say-die Bremner who brought Leeds back into the game after Royle had given Everton a 3–0 lead four minutes after half-time. He chested in a Johnny Giles corner after 62 minutes, and wrested the initiative from the home side. An Allan Clarke goal then gave Leeds 15 minutes in which to equalize. But Everton held out. They have dropped only one point in seven matches this season, but Leeds demonstrated that they will not be giving up their title without a struggle.

Sucks to Leeds as Toffeemen take title

EVERTON MADE sure of the League title on 1 April when they beat West Bromwich 2–0 at Goodison for their third win of the Easter holidays, while their only challengers, Leeds, were losing the first leg of their European Cup semi-final to Celtic at Elland Road. Leeds, last season's champions with a record total of 67 points, also lost at home to struggling Southampton on Saturday, their first home defeat in the League, and were thrashed 4–1 at Derby on Monday. They can no longer catch Everton.

The pile-up of fixtures caused by their marathon Cup semi-final with Manchester United and their involvement in the European Cup has proved too much for Leeds. They took over the League leadership from Everton in mid-January, but the Toffeemen regained it two months later, and now need to win their two remaining matches away from home to equal Leeds's points record.

More history for Celtic

CELTIC WROTE another page of Scottish football history at Hampden on 25 October when they won their fifth successive League Cup. But all credit must go to their opponents, lowly St Johnstone, not only for holding the Bhoys to a single goal, but for reaching the final in the first place. With Ayr United forcing Celtic to a replay in the semi-finals, this has been quite a tournament for the provincial clubs.

Manager Jock Stein dropped Tommy Gemmell for the final, after he had been sent off playing for Scotland against Germany, and Celtic were also without the injured Bobby Lennox and suspended Willie Wallace. But when they took an early lead through Bertie Auld, another huge Celtic score in the League Cup final looked on the cards. In the end, however, they had to settle for 1–0.

Celtic's Auld hits the only goal.

The happy Highbury days are here again

Radford climbs high to head Arsenal's second goal.

IN AN EMOTION-PACKED night at Highbury on 28 April, Arsenal came back from a 3–1 first-leg deficit to win the European Fairs Cup, their first major honour for 17 years. Goals by Kelly, Radford and Sammels gave them a 3–0 victory over Belgian club Anderlecht on the night, but the all-important goal was scored last week by young substitute Ray Kennedy, with a header five minutes from the end that gave Arsenal a lifeline when they looked down and out.

It was right-half Eddie Kelly, another 18-year-old, who ignited Arsenal at Highbury, flicking the ball up with his left foot and blasting it in with his right from the edge of the box to give them a 26th-minute lead. Arsenal, playing their 18th cup-tie of a gruelling season, now needed one goal to put them ahead on the "away goals" rule, and John Radford got it with a soaring header from Bob McNab's cross with 18 minutes left. A minute later, John Sammels swept a long Charlie George pass in with a crisp cross-shot to seal a glorious evening for the Gunners.

Dons dash Celtic's hopes of another grand slam

CELTIC'S HOPES of another grand slam of domestic and European titles were ended abruptly at Hampden when Aberdeen brought off a shock 3–1 Cup final victory. Celtic, League Cup winners, runaway champions again and going into the home leg of their European Cup semi-final with Leeds on Wednesday with a 1–0 lead, were the hottest favourites in years to retain the Cup. But, perhaps like Leeds in England, involvement in so many competitions has proved too much for them this season, and their heads went down after a couple of early setbacks in the final.

Aberdeen's hero was young outside-right Derek McKay, virtually unknown until an influenza epidemic forced a drastic reshuffle in the Dons' side. They brought the 20-year-old Dundee reject into the side for the quarter-final against Falkirk, he scored the winner and has not looked back since. Aberdeen's first goal in the final resulted from a McKay cross that hit a defender's hand. The referee awarded a hotly disputed penalty, and Joe Harper scored from the spot. When Bobby Lennox had a goal ruled out a few minutes later, Celtic seemed to lose heart. But with almost an hour left, it was still anybody's game — until the last hectic seven minutes. First McKay smashed the ball in after a fine run by Jim Forrest. Then Lennox scored for Celtic with only two minutes to go. But McKay then raced upfield again for a spectacular clincher, and the Dons had won their first Cup triumph for 23 years.

Leeds beaten by own success as Celtic reach Euro final

LEEDS UNITED, held to a draw by Chelsea in Saturday's strength-sapping Cup final on the heavily sanded Wembley pitch, went out of the European Cup to Celtic 3–1 on aggregate. Celtic had a 1–0 cushion from the first leg of the semi-final, at Elland Road, the goal scored after 90 seconds by George Connelly. The return was played at Hampden in front of 134,000 impassioned fans, most of whom were knocked back after 13 minutes when Billy Bremner scored with a thundering shot from outside the box.

Both teams had suffered from a congestion of fixtures because of their involvement in three competitions — Leeds had played seven Cup ties in 32 days, and fielded a reserve side in the League after they finally gave up chasing Everton. It was Celtic who proved the stronger at Hampden, with Murdoch and Auld wresting the vital midfield control from Bremner and Giles. Two minutes after the interval, John Hughes, who had come in for the injured Wallace, headed an Auld cross past Sprake to put Celtic ahead again on aggregate.

Shortly afterwards, Sprake was injured and had to be replaced by David Harvey, whose first chore was to pick the ball out of the net. Jimmy Johnstone, who had given Cooper such a torrid time in the first leg, was at it again. He beat man after man on the left before laying the ball into Murdoch's path for the big man to crack it into goal. The best of Scotland had beaten the best of England.

Murdoch scores the second goal to give Celtic their 3–1 aggregate victory.

Webb the unlikely hero as Chelsea finally conquer Leeds

DAVID WEBB put the humiliation of Wembley behind him to score Chelsea's extra-time winner in the Cup final replay and leave poor Leeds with nothing to show for a magnificent season's effort. Webb was turned inside-out by Leeds winger Eddie Gray in the 2–2 draw at Wembley 18 days ago that necessitated the first replayed Cup final since 1912. Switching places with Ron Harris for the Old Trafford return, he was less vulnerable in the centre of defence and finished up as Chelsea's hero.

It is perhaps hard to feel sorry for Leeds, whose superb play has earned them universal admiration, but whose gamesmanship and "win at all costs" attitude has won them few friends. In Chelsea they found a team that gave as good as they got, and this resulted in two bitterly fought games, especially the replay, where a repeat of Mr Jennings's weak refereeing allowed players from both sides to get away with a series of unpleasant fouls.

For Chelsea, it has been an uphill battle all the way. At Wembley, on that terrible surface, Peter Houseman equalized Jack Charlton's headed goal in the first half, but they looked finished when Mick Jones scored a second for Leeds six minutes from time. However, only two minutes later, Ian Hutchinson headed them level again from a John Hollins cross.

In the first half at Old Trafford, Chelsea keeper Peter Bonetti needed prolonged treatment after being laid out by a late charge from Jones, and had not fully recovered when the Leeds striker scored a brilliant goal after racing through the Chelsea defence. Chelsea equalized — for the third time in the tie — with a spectacular goal 12 minutes from time. Charlie Cooke sent the ball through the Leeds defence for Peter Osgood, coming up fast on the blind side, to score with a diving header. The climax came a minute before the extra-time break. Hutchinson took a mighty throw on the left, it was deflected to the far post as the heads went up, and there was Webb to bundle it into goal with head and shoulder.

Jones (right) hits No.2 for Leeds at Wembley past Bonetti's dive.

Webb heads Chelsea's winner in the replay.

Second Cup for Manchester City

WHILE CHELSEA were winning the FA Cup at Old Trafford, the other half of Manchester was celebrating victory in another knockout competition — Manchester City 2 Gornik Zabrze 1 in the European Cup-Winners' Cup final in Vienna. This climaxes another fine season for City, who won the Football League Cup only last month. In that competition, they enjoyed three home ties, beating Liverpool, Everton and QPR, before accounting for rivals United in the semis and WBA in the final. And it was at Maine Road where they laid the foundations for the European triumph.

They won all four of their home legs, the last with an impressive display of attacking football to beat West German side Schalke 04 by 5–1 after losing the away leg 1–0. They continued to play fluent football in the final, and Neil Young gave them an early lead after a shot from the elusive Francis Lee hit a post. Two minutes before the interval, Lee scored from a penalty after the Polish keeper, Kostka, had brought Young down when he was clean through. Gornik scored 20 minutes from time, through Ozlizlo, but City held out for a well-merited victory, to follow Spurs and West Ham, the previous English winners of the trophy.

Neil Young (right) moves in to score City's first.

Bobby Moore is freed: theft charges dropped

THE AFFAIR of the emerald bracelet is over. The accusations of theft against England captain Bobby Moore have been withdrawn and he has been freed from house arrest in Colombia. He is now on his way to join the rest of the international squad in Mexico.

The incident was said to have taken place after England beat Colombia 4–0 in the first match of their World Cup acclimatization tour, when Moore and Bobby Charlton visited the Green Fire jewellery shop in their hotel. The team went on to Ecuador, winning 2–0, but en route for Mexico City they stopped again in Bogota, where Moore was arrested.

Salesgirl Clara Padilla, who made the allegations, claimed that she had only just recognized the England captain. Now, four days from England's opening World Cup match with Romania, she has retracted them, claiming she was confused. The Colombian Press denounced the accusations from the start as a national scandal, citing several recent attempts at framing foreign celebrities for the purpose of extortion. But Moore, who had denied even seeing the bracelet in question, was ordered to remain in Bogota pending further investigations.

Not surprisingly, the whole squalid affair has unsettled the England squad and disrupted their captain's training. Moore will need all his unshakeable temperament to put this behind him.

FOOTBALL FOCUS

● The great Pele scored his 1,000th first-class goal from a penalty in Santos's 2–1 win over Vasco da Gama at the Maracana Stadium on 20 November. The goal, which had been eagerly awaited for some weeks, sparked wild scenes of rejoicing throughout Rio de Janeiro.

● Martin Peters cost Tottenham Hotspur an estimated £200,000 (including, sadly, a makeweight Jimmy Greaves in part exchange) when Spurs signed him from West Ham United in March, a British record.

● Bobby Charlton made his 100th appearance for England at Wembley on 21 April against Northern Ireland, the World Cup holders last home game before defending their title. Charlton, team captain for the match, scored England's third goal in a 3–1 win. Charlton later passed Billy Wright's record of 105 caps in the World Cup quarter-final match against West Germany.

● The goalless draw between Scotland and England at Hampden on 25 April was the first in the series since the very first match, also at Hampden, in 1872.

● How are the mighty fallen! Last century's League and Cup "double" winners, Aston Villa and Preston, both suffered the ignominy of being relegated to Division Three for the first time in their history. Sunderland and Sheffield Wednesday went down to Division Two, and Bradford Park Avenue were voted out of the League to make way for Cambridge United.

Pele (right) scores from the spot — his 1,000th career goal.

Favourites Celtic fall to Feyenoord

CELTIC FAILED to repeat their European Cup triumph of three years ago when they surprisingly went down 2–1 to Dutch team Feyenoord after extra time in the final in Milan. Celtic, perhaps overconfident after their semi-final victory against Leeds, were not the same side, and the Rotterdam team deserved to win.

Feyenoord, who beat holders AC Milan in the second round, employed a sweeper, the skilful Rinus Israël, in a form of catenaccio that was not, like the Italian method, purely defensive. But most critically, they marked the dangerous Jimmy Johnstone out of the game.

Celtic scored first, after 30 minutes, when left-back Tommy Gemmell provided a repeat of his piledriver in the 1967 final, after Bobby Murdoch had back-heeled a free-kick. But Israël moved up from defence to head an equalizer only two minutes later. As the game progressed it got faster and better, with the Dutch side taking charge. It went into extra time and, four minutes from the end, Billy McNeill handled a lob. The referee waved play on and the Swede Ove Kindvall beat Celtic keeper Evan Williams with ease. So Celtic failed to make it a grand slam for British clubs in Europe.

The Celtic defence is aghast as Israël (third from right) equalizes.

FINAL SCORE

Football League
Division 1: Everton
Top scorer: Jeff Astle (West Bromwich Albion) 25
Division 2: Huddersfield Town
Division 3: Leyton Orient
Division 4: Chesterfield
Footballer of the Year: Billy Bremner (Leeds United)

FA Cup Final

Chelsea	2	Leeds United	2
(after extra time)			
Replay: Chelsea	2	Leeds United	1
(after extra time)			

League Cup Final

Manchester City	2	WBA	1

Scottish League
Division 1: Celtic
Top scorer: Colin Stein (Rangers) 24
Division 2: Falkirk
Footballer of the Year: Pat Stanton (Hibernian)

Scottish FA Cup Final

Aberdeen	3	Celtic	1

Scottish League Cup Final

Celtic	1	St Johnstone	0

International Championship
England, Scotland, Wales, 4 pts

European Cup Final

Feyenoord	2	Celtic	1
(after extra time)			

Cup-Winners' Cup Final

Manchester City	2	Gornik Zabrze	1

Inter-Cities Fairs Cup Final
Arsenal beat Anderlecht 1-3, 3-0

European Footaller of the Year 1969
Gianni Rivera (AC Milan & Italy)

Leading European Scorer (Golden Boot)
Gerd Muller (Bayern Munich) 38

World Club Championship
Feyenoord (Holland) beat Estudiantes (Argentina) 2-2, 1-0

Brilliant Brazilians

Mexico was a controversial choice to host the 1970 World Cup, and the distressed condition of some of the athletes in the Olympic Games held there two years earlier did nothing to help the Mexican cause. But in the event the finals not only provided thrilling competition and splendid entertainment, but there was little of the negativity and thuggery that blighted football in the sixties. Brazil, with the incomparable Pele, raised the game to new heights and were universally popular winners. And England, who did not give up their hold on the trophy without a fight, took part in two unforgettable matches.

A RECORD 71 countries entered the 1970 World Cup, but none had a more eventful passage to Mexico than El Salvador from the Concacaf zone. They played 10 games before qualifying, and one win over the neighbouring Honduras sparked off a two-week war between the mutually antagonistic countries. By contrast, Brazil qualified effortlessly from South America, winning all six matches and scoring 23 goals (Tostao nine, Pele six, Jairzinho four) to two. With England exempt as holders, West Germany were the most impressive European qualifiers, dropping only one point. Gerd Muller scored 10 of their 20 goals, and they mauled Cyprus 12–0 in one game. The Germans conceded only three, all to Scotland, who were eliminated.

Banks's save

England and Brazil were drawn in the same group, played out in Guadalajara — without the severe altitude problem of Mexico City, but with an appalling 98 degrees of torrid heat. Nevertheless, the clash of the two favourites, after they had both won their opening matches, produced a classic encounter, won 1–0 by the South Americans but remembered for evermore for one Banks save from Pele.

Pele after scoring in the final, with Tostao (left) and Jairzinho.

England were on top early on, and both Peters and Lee missed chances. Then Jairzinho powered past Cooper to the byline and crossed the ball from the corner of the penalty box to the far post, where the leaping Pele unleashed a perfect downward header towards the empty net. The crowd's roar to acclaim a goal was stifled as Banks appeared, seemingly from nowhere, but from the other side of his goal, to paw the ball up and over the bar. England took heart from this reprieve, but in the end it was to no avail, as Brazil got on top in the second half and Tostao and Pele made a goal for Jairzinho. Nevertheless, England had done enough — with Moore, despite his recent problems in Colombia, outstanding — to hope that the two might meet again in the final.

West Germany were impressive qualifiers in Leon, apart from an initial hiccup against Morocco, with Muller hitting two hat-tricks. The Soviet Union looked dangerous in Group One, coping well with the problems of Mexico City and going through with the host country. Italy scored just one goal in Group Two, but typically conceded none and finished top.

It could be said that England lost their quarter-final with West Germany because Banks, arguably the best keeper in the world, couldn't hold his drink — the bottle of Mexican beer, that is, that left him weak and groggy. This attack of "Montezuma's revenge" crucially kept him out of the game in Leon. It was another epic encounter between the teams who contested the 1966 final. England, playing their best football so far, deservedly went two up in 50 minutes with goals from Mullery and Peters, both from crosses by right-back Newton. But early in the second half they started back-pedalling and lost the initiative. Beckenbauer cleverly broke through and pulled one back for the Germans. Ramsey — now Sir Alf — put Bell on for Bobby Charlton, and Hunter for Peters, but Seeler equalized with a freakish back-header.

England went into extra time looking tired, but the excellent Hurst soon had the ball in the net from Lee's pull-back — yet had it disallowed for no apparent reason. Inevitably it was Muller who scored the winner, volleying in from close range. Pity poor Bonetti, without a competitive match for more than a month.

The goals flow

It was in the quarter-finals that the goals began to flow — 17 in four matches. Only in the Uruguay-USSR game was there a paucity, Uruguay's winner coming in extra time, just three minutes away from the iniquitous drawing of lots. Brazil and Peru — the surprise of the tournament — put on a dazzling show at Guadalajara, with Brazil's shaky keeper Felix almost letting the Peruvians back into the game before Brazil won 4–2. In Toluca, against Mexico, Italy conceded their first goal of the finals, but after a lucky, deflected equalizer, their attack was seen at last, and they won 4–1 with second-half goals from Riva (two) and substitute Rivera.

The two semi-finals had more goals, thrills aplenty and exhibition stuff from Pele, 12 years after he first exploded on to the World Cup scene as a 17-year-old in Sweden. Intent, as always, not only on winning but

Against all the odds and most of the predictions, the heat and altitude of Mexico produced the most memorable World Cup of all — thanks largely to those brilliant ball-playing Brazilians, who restored faith in international competition.

on entertaining with his efforts to score the unique goal, Pele had already had one remarkable near miss against Czechoslovakia, with a shot from the centre circle. In the 3–1 win over Uruguay, he will always be remembered for the dummy that transfixed keeper Mazurkiewicz to the spot before he hooked the ball just wide.

The other semi became a thriller in extra time, not because of any pretensions of open football, rather for sheer fatigue. Boninsegna had given Italy the lead in the ninth minute, and his team-mates closed up shop in the second half, unwisely allowing West Germany to take control of midfield. But, after battering away incessantly at the Italian goal, it was not until injury time that they equalized, when left-back Schnellinger suddenly arrived to convert Grabowski's cross. The Germans began extra time with a distinct disadvantage, Beckenbauer having been cynically hacked down and playing with an arm strapped to his side as they had used their substitutes. Both sides scored twice more before Rivera, on as substitute for the third match running, gave the Italians a 4–3 victory.

Pele and Bobby Moore after the England-Brazil match.

A beautiful finale

Brazil did not disappoint the hundreds of millions of television fans around the world who were glued to their sets in the expectation of seeing a triumph for adventurous football. With arguably the most inventive and deadly attacking force seen in modern times, Brazil knew no other way to play, although they dared not fall back on defence with Felix as their last line. Indeed, it was a bad defensive error that allowed Italy back into the game after Pele had put his side ahead with one of his power-headers, his fourth goal of the finals. A casual back-heel from Clodoaldo put Brazil in trouble, and a mad rush from Felix allowed Boninsegna to find the unguarded net.

In the second half, with Clodoaldo and particularly Gerson taking control of the midfield, Brazil mounted attack after attack. Rivelino had a swerving shot parried by Albertosi and then crashed a drive on to the bar with his rarely employed right foot. After 65 minutes, Gerson unleashed a left-foot drive from outside the box to put them ahead, and then lifted a 50-yard pass which Pele nodded down for Jairzinho to run in and maintain his record of scoring in every game.

The last 20 minutes were sheer magic, a celebration of the beautiful Brazilian game, climaxed with an exhibition goal. It was started by Clodoaldo in his own half, who beat five men as he sambaed upfield, carried on by Rivelino, Jairzinho and Pele, before it was finished off in spectacular fashion by right-back and captain Carlos Alberto. It was Brazil's World Cup and, appropriately, as the first three-time winners, they kept the Jules Rimet Trophy.

An open-mouthed crowd watch Banks save Pele's (left) header.

FINAL SCORE

Group 1

Mexico	0	USSR	0
Belgium	3	El Salvador	0
USSR	4	Belgium	1
Mexico	4	El Salvador	0
USSR	2	El Salvador	0
Mexico	1	Belgium	0

	P	W	D	L	F	A	P
USSR	3	2	1	0	6	1	5
Mexico	3	2	1	0	5	0	5
Belgium	3	1	0	2	4	5	2
El Salvador	3	0	0	3	0	9	0

Group 2

Uruguay	2	Israel	0
Italy	1	Sweden	0
Italy	0	Uruguay	0
Israel	1	Sweden	1
Sweden	1	Uruguay	0
Israel	0	Italy	0

	P	W	D	L	F	A	P
Italy	3	1	2	0	1	0	4
Uruguay	3	1	1	1	2	1	3
Sweden	3	1	1	1	2	2	3
Israel	3	0	2	1	1	3	2

Group 3

England	1	Romania	0
Brazil	4	Czechoslovakia	1
Romania	2	Czechoslovakia	1
Brazil	1	England	0
Brazil	3	Romania	2
England	1	Czechoslovakia	0

	P	W	D	L	F	A	P
Brazil	3	3	0	0	8	3	6
England	3	2	0	1	2	1	4
Romania	3	1	0	2	4	5	2
Czech	3	0	0	3	2	7	0

Group 4

Peru	3	Bulgaria	2
West Germany	2	Morocco	1
Peru	3	Morocco	0
West Germany	5	Bulgaria	2
West Germany	3	Peru	1
Bulgaria	1	Morocco	1

	P	W	D	L	F	A	P
W. Germany	3	3	0	0	10	4	6
Peru	3	2	0	1	7	5	4
Bulgaria	3	0	1	2	5	9	1
Morocco	3	0	1	2	2	6	1

QUARTER-FINALS

Uruguay	1	USSR	0
Italy	4	Mexico	1
Brazil	4	Peru	2
West Germany	3	England	2

SEMI-FINALS

Italy (after extra time)	4	West Germany	3
Brazil	3	Uruguay	1

THIRD-PLACE MATCH

West Germany	1	Uruguay	0

FINAL

Brazil	4	Italy	1

Aztec Stadium, Mexico City, 21 June 1970. Attendance 107,000

Brazil: Felix, Carlos Alberto, Brito, Piazza, Everaldo, Clodoaldo, Gerson, Jairzinho, Tostao, Pele, Rivelino (Scorers: Pele, Gerson, Jairzinho, Carlos Alberto)

Italy: Albertosi, Burgnich, Facchetti, Cera, Rosato, Bertini (Juliano), Riva, Domenghini, Mazzola, De Sisti, Boninsegna (Rivera) (Scorer: Boninsegna)

Leading scorers

10 Muller (West Germany) 7 Jairzinho (Brazil) 5 Cubillas (Peru)

Mighty Leeds crash in Cup to 'Grandad's Army' from Colchester

FOURTH DIVISION Colchester 3 First Division leaders Leeds 2! There has been plenty of giant-killing in the FA Cup before, but this remarkable result from the fifth round at little Layer Road beggars belief. Mighty Leeds, the most talented, resolute, battle-hardened, ruthlessly efficient outfit in the land, would surely not succumb to a collection of veterans and rejects labelled "Grandad's Army"? But they did.

Colchester's "trump card" was centre-forward Ray Crawford, who led the First Division scorers 10 years ago with Ipswich and played twice for England. Manager Dick Graham had rescued him from non-League football. Five of his team-mates were also over 30, but instead of being overawed, Colchester gambled on all-out attack. They ruffled Leeds, and Crawford put them in front with a header after 18 minutes. Before Leeds could recover, Crawford scored again, hooking the ball in while on the ground. Gasps of disbelief were heard at grounds around the country as the half-time score was flashed up.

Without any thought of sitting on their lead, Colchester came out after the interval playing inspired football, and Dave Simmons swept through to head past goalkeeper Gary Sprake and put them 3–0 up. But with 35 minutes left, they began to tire, and Leeds at last began to play the cultured football they are famous for. Norman Hunter and Johnny Giles pulled goals back. There was 15 minutes left, but the "no-hopers" found another hero in keeper Graham Smith. Time and again Leeds broke through, but the brilliant Smith was always there to frustrate them. By the end of the match, "Grandad's Army" were panting and creaking. But they were in the sixth round of the Cup.

SOCCER SOUNDBITES

"I always play well against Leeds. I always score goals against Jack Charlton."

The prophetic **RAY CRAWFORD** (speaking from a long memory), before Colchester shocked Leeds in the Cup.

Crawford swivels to hook the ball past Sprake, Reaney and Charlton.

From spoiler to scorer: it's another Storey

PETER STOREY'S reputation has been built up as a midfield spoiler, a ruthless destroyer, the "iron man" of Arsenal's defence. But every dog has his day, and Storey's came at Hillsborough in the FA Cup semi-final against Stoke. It did not start out that way, as Denis Smith blocked an attempted Storey clearance for the ball to sail into Arsenal's net. John Ritchie then took advantage of a poor Charlie George back-pass to put Stoke deservedly two up at half-time. Soon after the interval, though, Storey struck back with probably the finest goal he will ever score. He is not known for his shooting, but when the ball came out to him on the edge of the box, he took off and hit the sweetest of right-foot volleys past Gordon Banks.

Stoke, however, held out, and with the match going into injury time, Arsenal's hopes of the "double" appeared to be shattered. Then, with one last attack, they won a disputed corner — Banks claimed he was pushed. Frank McLintock's header was bound for the net when John Mahoney dived full length to push it aside — no dispute about the penalty. George had gone off injured, so Storey — the other penalty-taker, not because of any dead-ball ability, but for his ice-cool temperament — strode up to take the spot-kick against the world's best keeper. It was not a particularly good kick, but he sent Banks the wrong way, and had kept Arsenal in the Cup.

Mahoney (left) handles and referee Partridge awards a last-gasp penalty — for Storey to take.

Offside rumpus leads to riot at Leeds: chairman and Revie condone pitch invasion

A CONTROVERSIAL referee's decision at Elland Road on 17 April sparked some of the most deplorable scenes witnessed on any football ground in Britain. They were started by a mass protest of the Leeds players, who jostled the referee after West Bromwich Albion's second goal. Some 30 or 40 angry fans raced on to the field, and the players found themselves obliged to protect the referee, Ray Tinkler, while a linesman was hit on the head with a stone. It took the police five minutes and 32 arrests to clear the pitch.

The dispute occurred 20 minutes into the second half, with Albion already a goal up. Albion's Tony Brown blocked a Hunter pass, and followed the ball as it rebounded into the Leeds half. The linesman flagged because Colin Suggett was in an offside position near the centre circle. But the referee decided he was not interfering with play and allowed Brown to continue. Brown took the ball on, then released it to Jeff Astle, who scored with ease. Many referees would have blown for offside, but it was by no means a clear-cut decision. It certainly did not warrant the continued protests of the Leeds players or the comments of the disappointed Leeds chairman and manager Don Revie after the match, condoning the pitch invasion.

Leeds scored just before the end, and Albion won 2–1, their first away victory for 16 months. On the day, they were the better team, but Leeds appear to believe they have a divine right to win, and they have an appalling habit of whingeing, on and off the field, whenever a decision goes against them. They were at one time seven points clear in Division One, but Arsenal's win over Newcastle takes them above Leeds on goal average, with two games in hand.

As Billy Bremner (in white, left) remonstrates with the referee, police and fans grapple on the Elland Road pitch.

Arsenal beat Spurs for first leg of 'double'

THE CULMINATION of a remarkable League campaign saw Arsenal get the result they needed at White Hart Lane to snatch the title from Leeds by a single point. Arsenal went into the match needing a win or a goalless draw to clinch their eighth Championship. Defeat or a scoring draw would give Leeds the title, so tight was the situation at the top. And Spurs, well behind in third place, were out to stop their North London rivals emulating their "double" season of 10 years ago.

The match, played before a capacity crowd with another 20,000 locked out, provided a nail-biting night for Arsenal fans. They did not go on the defensive, and had marginally the better of a fast, exciting struggle, but it was two minutes from time before Ray Kennedy headed them into the lead. This could have been Arsenal's undoing, because a Spurs goal at this stage would still have deprived them of the title. And it needed all Bob Wilson's courage and sharpness in the dying seconds to dive into a forest of legs and grab the ball as Spurs threatened to score.

Arsenal's triumph has been a team effort, with the occasional injection of flair from the mercurial Charlie George just when it was needed. Frank McLintock's conversion to centre-half has been a major factor in Arsenal's season, his class and his unflappable leadership knitting the side together and providing an example for the youngsters. Kennedy, in his first full season, has forged a fine twin spearhead with John Radford and finished top scorer with 20 League goals. One more match, against Liverpool on Saturday, now stands between Arsenal and the "double".

Bob Wilson jumps for joy at the final whistle: Arsenal are champions.

SOCCER SOUNDBITES

"I don't blame them at all. The referee's decision in allowing West Bromwich's second goal was diabolical."

Leeds manager **DON REVIE** on the reaction of his team's fans.

"I am not blaming the spectators. There was every justification for it."

ALDERMAN PERCY WOODWARD, Leeds chairman.

"You have cost us a lot of money."

UNNAMED LEEDS PLAYER to referee Tinkler as the injured linesman was being treated.

Another Ibrox disaster: worst day in British football

SIXTY-SIX PEOPLE were killed in a terrible crush at Ibrox Park, as the New Year's fixture between Rangers and Celtic was coming to a close. About another 200 were injured. The disaster occurred when crush-barriers collapsed on a staircase leading out of the ground. With Celtic leading 1–0 and only a minute or two left, thousands of spectators began to make their way out from the terraces. Suddenly, there was a tremendous roar as Colin Stein snatched a last-gasp equalizer for Rangers. Hundreds of fans on the wide staircase turned to try to get back into the ground. As they met others still streaming out, the tubular steel barriers buckled, and hundreds of people began to fall. Most of the victims died through suffocation as they were swept down and piled on top of each other.

Ibrox was the scene of a similar tragedy in April 1902, when part of a new stand collapsed at the Scotland-England international. And 10 years ago, two people were killed and several injured when crush barriers collapsed during a Rangers-Celtic match.

'Double' joy for Arsenal, as they come from behind again

ARSENAL COMPLETED the "double" in dramatic fashion at Wembley, coming from behind, as they have all season, to beat Liverpool 2–1. They made enough chances to have won comfortably, but the game had gone into extra time when Heighway broke away on the left and put Liverpool into the lead within two minutes.

Against a Liverpool defence that had given away a record low 24 League goals and only one in the Cup, it looked all up for Arsenal now. But they refused to panic, and Kelly, who had gone on in the second half for Storey, took advantage of a rare defensive lapse to push the ball goalwards and Graham, the man of the match, might just have touched it in. Whoever scored, it was Arsenal's equalizer, just before the change-around. And it was George who stole the headlines again with a scorching winner from Radford's pass eight minutes from time.

For Arsenal's captain McLintock, Footballer of the Year, it was a first Cup-winner's medal after four fruitless trips to Wembley. Wilson and all-purpose winger Armstrong played in all 64 of Arsenal's competitive matches this term, McLintock, Kennedy and Rice all but one. England internationals McNab, Radford and newly capped Storey missed only two. Arsenal's feat is the result of a tremendous team performance, with a great deal of credit going to manager Bertie Mee, their former physiotherapist, and coach Don Howe.

They survived away draws in every round, and came from behind in the semi-final and final. At times they played brilliant, powerful football, but often had to rely on sheer professionalism and team spirit to survive. Above all, they have finally laid to rest the ghost of the great Arsenal sides of the past.

Charlie George hits the winner from the edge of the box.

Best penalized for robbing Banks of England

Banks tries, but fails, to stop Best from heading in.

AN ORIGINAL scoring attempt by George Best in Northern Ireland's match against England at Belfast was disallowed by a referee who was almost as embarrassed as the England keeper. As the visitors' No.1, Gordon Banks, released the ball to punt it upfield, Best, with the perfect timing that characterizes all his play, flicked the ball up and over Banks's head and headed it into goal. The referee disallowed the score, presumably for "foot up", but Best had not even touched the keeper. England were outplayed in the first half, and their late winner by Allan Clarke was an injustice to an Irish side for whom Best, Derek Dougan and a solid defence were outstanding.

FOOTBALL FOCUS

- Barnet became the fifth non-League club to beat League opposition 6–1 in the Cup when they thrashed Newport County of Division Four by that score.
- The Scottish League have introduced "goal difference" instead of "goal average" to determine League positions when clubs are equal on points.
- Rangers ended the most barren period in their history, four years without a major trophy, when they beat Celtic 1–0 in the final of the Scottish League Cup, the goal scored by Derek Johnstone, at 16 the youngest player ever to appear in a final.
- Leeds's 64 points in Division One was the highest ever obtained by the runners-up. The FA fined them £750 and ordered their ground to be closed for the first four matches of next season as a result of the pitch invasion in April.
- Celtic brought off the Cup and League "double" for the third time in five seasons, and equalled their own early-1900s record of six League titles in a row.
- Bolton and Blackburn, founder members of the League, were both relegated to Division Three for the first time.
- Jimmy Greaves (44 goals, 57 caps) and Jimmy Armfield (43 caps, 15 times England captain) retired at the end of the season.

Chelsea beat the old masters in Athens

Chelsea captain Ron Harris with the trophy.

CHELSEA BEAT mighty Real Madrid in Athens to take the European Cup-Winners' Cup in the replayed final, the fourth English side to do so. Real Madrid may not be the force of old, but this was their ninth European final and they are still formidable Cup fighters. Chelsea owe their success largely to the motivation of Charlie Cooke in midfield, the brilliance of Peter Bonetti in goal, and the determination that won them the FA Cup last season despite being outplayed. They also had to overcome injury problems.

In the semi-final, without strikers Hutchinson and Osgood, they beat holders Manchester City, themselves severely depleted by injuries, 1–0 in each leg to avenge an earlier defeat by City in the FA Cup. They looked to have won the final at the first attempt, with an Osgood goal before he went off injured, but Zoco equalized for Real in the dying moments when Dempsey mis-kicked, and it was Chelsea who had to hold out in extra time.

Dempsey made amends in the replay, slamming the ball in when his first headed attempt had been saved, and Osgood put Chelsea two up before again having to go off. Cooke, in at right-half for the injured Hollins, had another fine game and, although Fleitas scored for Real with 15 minutes to go, they could not get past Bonetti again. Chelsea's triumph climaxed a remarkable season for London clubs, after Tottenham's League Cup and Arsenal's "double".

Consolation for Leeds at the last

LEEDS HAD TO wait until 3 June before they finally won a trophy at the end of a gruelling season in which they had again played the bridesmaid. They held Juventus to a 1–1 draw at Elland Road, which was enough to give them the Fairs Cup on the away goals rule, having drawn 2–2 in Turin five days earlier. It was somewhat of an anti-climax after the stirring semi-final with Liverpool, in which a single goal at Anfield by Bremner, returning after a long spell off through injury, decided the tie. This put Leeds into their third Fairs Cup final, although they must have been relieved that holders Arsenal had been knocked out by Cologne in the quarter-finals.

Eddie Gray dislocated a shoulder in the first leg of the final, before it was abandoned in torrential rain. Leeds twice had to come back in the replay, with goals from Madeley and, 13 minutes from time, substitute Bates. An early goal from Clarke in the return was equalized by the expensive Anastasi, but Leeds's disciplined defence denied Juventus any more, and the Italians, who had not been beaten in any of their 12 games in the competition, had lost on the technicality.

The Fairs Cup, now won for the fourth year running by an English club, will be succeeded next season by the UEFA Cup.

Mick Bates (left) scores a vital equalizer in Turin.

FINAL SCORE

Football League
Division 1: Arsenal
Top scorer: Tony Brown (WBA) 28
Division 2: Leicester City
Division 3: Preston North End
Division 4: Notts County
Footballer of the Year: Frank McLintock (Arsenal)

FA Cup Final

Arsenal	2	Liverpool	1
(after extra time)			

League Cup Final

Tottenham Hotspur	2	Aston Villa	0

Scottish League
Division 1: Celtic
Top scorer: Harry Hood (Celtic) 22
Division 2: Partick Thistle
Footballer of the Year: Martin Buchan (Aberdeen)

Scottish FA Cup Final

Celtic	1	Rangers	1
Replay: Celtic	2	Rangers	1

Scottish League Cup Final

Rangers	1	Celtic	0

International Championship
England, 5 pts

European Cup Final

Ajax Amsterdam	2	Panathinaikos	0

Cup-Winners' Cup Final

Chelsea	1	Real Madrid	1
(after extra time)			
Replay: Chelsea	2	Real Madrid	1
(after extra time)			

Inter-Cities Fairs Cup Final
Leeds United beat Juventus 2–2, 1–1 (on away goals)

European Footballer of the Year 1970
Gerd Muller (Bayern Munich & West Germany)

Leading European Scorer (Golden Boot)
Josip Skoblar (Marseille) 44

World Club Championship
Nacional (Uruguay) beat Panathinaikos (Greece) 1–1, 2–1

Radford and George in classic giant-killing act

IT WAS NOT the Arsenal pair, but non-League Hereford's Ron Radford and substitute Ricky George who made the headlines, completing the giant-killing of First Division Newcastle in the third-round FA Cup replay.

The drama started in early January, at St James's Park, where the Southern League side held Newcastle to a 2–2 draw. A month and half a dozen postponements later, 15,000 fans packed into the little Edgar Street ground for the return. Newcastle did everything but score; Malcolm Macdonald should have done, at least twice. But Fred Potter in the Hereford goal made some breathtaking saves and, when he was beaten, the woodwork came to the rescue.

As Newcastle's confidence began to wane, Hereford took charge, and it was against the run of play that Macdonald put the Magpies ahead with 10 minutes left. But three minutes later, Radford won a tackle in midfield, strode on through the mud and hit a blinding 30-yarder past the startled Iam McFaul in Newcastle's goal. In extra time, Radford pushed the ball through for George to score the winner amid a tumult of sound.

Whatever happens now when they entertain First Division West Ham United in the fourth round on Wednesday, Hereford have made their point, and it would be a travesty of justice if they are not playing League football next season.

Newcastle keeper McFaul is too late to stop George's winner for Hereford.

Celtic stung by Thistle

CELTIC, IN THEIR eighth consecutive League Cup final, lost 4–1 to unfancied Partick Thistle in the biggest upset for years in Scottish football. It may seem out of place to talk about giant-killing when a mid-table First Division side win a Cup final, but this really was a sensational result. Celtic, admittedly without their influential captain Billy McNeill, have been riding high in domestic and European football for several years now, while Partick have to go back more than 50 years for their only previous honour, the Cup in 1921.

A friendly, popular Glasgow club with a reputation for entertaining play and unpredictability, Partick demonstrated both when they went into a 4–0 lead in just 37 minutes. They attacked Celtic from the start, with strikers Frank Coulston and Jimmy Bone to the fore and Denis McQuade and Bobby Lawrie creating problems on the flanks. But even when skipper Alex Rae scored after nine minutes and Lawrie put Partick two up after 15, the Celtic fans were not unduly worried. Then Celtic winger Jimmy Johnstone had to go off injured and was substituted by full-back Jim Craig. Thistle continued to play glorious stuff, and further goals by McQuade and Bone to one by Dalglish produced a scoreline greeted with utter disbelief around the country.

Brave Moore in goal, but Stoke win marathon

STOKE FINALLY settled this epic tie in the second play-off at Old Trafford, beating West Ham 3–2 to go through to the League Cup final at Wembley. The Hammers can consider themselves desperately unlucky to go out, and it is a pity, after four fine games, that there had to be a loser.

West Ham won the first leg 2–1 at Stoke, but Stoke equalized at Upton Park and took the tie into extra time. With three minutes left, Banks made a brilliant penalty save from World Cup colleague Geoff Hurst, who had scored from the spot in the first tie. The first play-off at Hillsborough was full of all good things except goals. So seven weeks after the first game, the fourth and, ultimately, deciding fixture took place on 26 January.

There was early drama as West Ham keeper Bobby Ferguson had to go off. When he returned 20 minutes later, the saga had taken some more dramatic turns. Bobby Moore had gone in goal and saved a penalty from Bernard, who followed up to score. Then 10-man West Ham (they had gambled on Ferguson's return) carried the game to Stoke and took the lead, with goals by Bonds and Brooking. Stoke seemed to play better against the full West Ham side. Dobing equalized and, shortly after the interval, Conroy put them in front again. The Hammers came storming back, but finally had to admit defeat, after 420 minutes.

Moore parries Bernard's penalty, only to be beaten by a second shot from the rebound.

England need to rebuild from the rubble of humiliation

ENGLAND WERE outclassed by West Germany at Wembley in the first leg of their European Championship quarter-final, although it was late in the game before the Germans translated their superiority into a 3–1 victory.

Nothing could symbolize more poignantly England's decline since their 1966 World Cup triumph than the withdrawal of Geoff Hurst in the 58th minute. As the hat-trick hero of England's 4–2 victory six years ago walked sadly to the bench, we were witnessing the end of an era.

West Germany have blossomed since then, and they humbled England with a side still in the early stages of preparation for the 1974 World Cup. Beckenbauer has brought a new meaning to the term "sweeper", commanding the middle of the pitch in front of his defenders as well as behind them. The fleet-footed Günter Netzer was a revelation as a midfield general. With the eager Hoeness and the powerful Wimmer also outstanding, England's midfield of Ball, Bell and Peters were rendered ineffective.

Agony for Banks as Netzer (out of picture) converts a penalty.

Hoeness put the Germans ahead after 27 minutes. But England kept plugging away, and Lee popped home a flattering equalizer with 13 minutes to go. In the last six minutes, however, Banks could not stop a Netzer penalty, given away by Moore, and Muller scored a third.

Boosting England's morale for the return in two weeks' time is manager Ramsey's immediate task, but it pales into insignificance when compared with the long hard grind of rebuilding English soccer.

Triumphant Leeds set for 'double'

LEEDS DESERVEDLY beat Arsenal 1–0 at Wembley in the 100th FA Cup final, although the match was not the best advertisement for English soccer. The two sides knew each other too well and, with the emphasis on stopping the other team playing, there was a surfeit of fouls. Four players were booked, McNab and George for Arsenal, Bremner and Hunter for Leeds. But the only serious injury was when Leeds striker Mick Jones dislocated an elbow in a last-minute collision with Arsenal keeper Geoff Barnett. He will be missed when Leeds go for the second leg of the "double" at Molineux, in a match senselessly scheduled by the Football League for two days after the Cup final.

Allan Clarke scored the winner after 54 minutes with a fine lunging header from a Jones cross. Hunter and Charlton completely subdued the threat of Radford and George, although the latter did provide one moment of magic when he hooked the ball fiercely on to the bar. And, in the first half Alan Ball hit a perfect volley that Reaney instinctively cleared off the line. Apart from those two efforts, however, it was mostly Leeds.

Banks and Eastham inspire Stoke to first major trophy

ON THEIR FIRST ever visit to Wembley, Stoke beat Chelsea 2–1 in the League Cup Final to win their first major honour in 109 years. Two players who are familiar with the Wembley turf, however, had a big say in Stoke's triumph: their senior citizens George Eastham and Gordon Banks. Eastham, 35, scored the winner, his first goal in 18 months. And Banks, 34, made two late saves that demonstrated why he is still one of the world's greatest keepers.

Credit must also go to Terry Conroy, whose brave one-man raids kept Stoke in the game when Chelsea were threatening to crush them. He also scored the first goal, a header after five minutes, and made the cross that led to their winner.

But Chelsea must be wondering how they lost a match they had controlled for so long, with Hudson and Hollins dominating the midfield. The answer lies in the iron grip of the unflappable Smith and Bloor over Chelsea's front line. Osgood had a mixed match, cautioned and lucky not to be sent off after a couple of bad fouls, and then scoring an extraordinary equalizer just before half-time, when he hooked the ball in while on the ground.

After 73 minutes, Ritchie headed down a cross from Conroy, and although Bonetti parried Greenhoff's shot, he could do nothing about Eastham's follow-up. Chelsea rallied, but Banks had an answer to everything.

Eastham (right) hits Stoke's winning goal.

Derby win League in Majorca as Leeds and Liverpool slip

IN A MOST extraordinary finish to the title race, Derby County have won their first Championship thanks to Leeds's defeat at Wolves and Liverpool's failure to beat Arsenal at Highbury. Having seen Derby complete their programme with a 1–0 win over Liverpool, which took them to the top of the table on 58 points, Brian Clough took his team on holiday. He had brought them from near bottom of the Second Division in just five years, but had not expected success so soon.

Even allowing for their Cup exertions two days earlier, Leeds were expected to get the point they needed at Wolves. That they did not was down largely to bad luck. First, Wolves played their best football of the season, and their keeper Phil Parkes made some world-class saves. Second, Leeds had two penalty appeals turned down after blatant handling offences by defenders. Third, they had to play a heavily strapped Eddie Gray and Allan Clarke dosed up with pain-killing injections. And finally, when they got back into the game in the last minutes, a Lorimer header hit the bar.

Munro scored for Wolves three minutes before half-time when Giles muffed a clearance, and Dougan added a second after 67 minutes. Leeds drew on all their resources to pull one back — typically through Bremner — before Clarke had to be substituted by Yorath. But Parkes, and the cross-bar, kept their last efforts out, and Leeds had to be content with finishing League runners-up for the fifth time in eight seasons.

At Highbury, meanwhile, the night was just as electric, the drama as poignant, although Liverpool could only snatch the title if Leeds lost. A young Liverpool side with only one defeat in their last 16 matches had not played for a week and were fresh. Arsenal, of course, had been at Wembley two days earlier, which was hard to believe given the effort put in by such as McLintock, Ball, Rice and Storey.

Again, it was a marvellous match, one of the best seen at Highbury all season. Hughes struck the Arsenal bar after 17 minutes with a 30-yard volley, and Keegan, having a brilliant game on the right, put the rebound inches wide with an overhead kick. But Liverpool's unluckiest moment came two minutes from time when, with their fans chanting "Leeds are losing", they had a goal from Toshack disallowed for a marginal offside.

By such narrow decisions are Championships won and lost. But Derby are worthy champions. It is perhaps unfair to pick out individuals, but McFarland and Todd at the back, Gemmill in midfield, and Hector, O'Hare and Hinton up front were all major contributors to their success.

Reaney (left) and keeper Harvey fail to stop Munro scoring for Wolves.

● Chelsea broke all records in the Cup-Winners' Cup with a first-round massacre of Luxembourg's Jeunesse Hautcharage 13–0 at Stamford Bridge for a 21–0 aggregate score. Peter Osgood scored eight goals in the tie.

● Ted MacDougall set a scoring record for the FA Cup proper on 20 November when he hit nine against non-League Margate, three more than the previous best, in Bournemouth's 11–0 first-round win.

● Giant-killers Hereford continued their Cup progress in the fourth round, holding West Ham to a 0–0 draw before going down 3–1 at Upton Park, and were duly elected to the League in place of Barrow, albeit by only one vote.

● Arsenal reached the Cup final for the second season running without a single home draw.

● Leeds cancelled the proposed transfer of Asa Hartford from West Brom when a medical uncovered a "hole-in-the-heart" condition, although this did not stop the player from winning his first caps for Scotland.

● Rangers were banned from European competition for a year as a result of their fans' behaviour in Barcelona.

Dixie Deans's hat-trick atones for penalty miss

DIXIE DEANS, the Scot with the famous football name — well, nearly — scored a Cup-final hat-trick in Celtic's 6–1 demolition of Hibs, and so made up for the penalty miss that sealed the Bhoys' elimination from the European Cup last month. Deans, signed from Motherwell as part of Celtic's rebuilding programme, was the unfortunate individual whose effort in the ridiculous penalty shoot-out at Parkhead, after two goalless semi-final draws, was the only one of the 10 not converted.

Hibs were overwhelmed at Hampden, and Deans took his goals brilliantly. Skipper McNeill and Lou Macari (two) scored the others. With a transitional side this season, Jock Stein has guided Celtic to their second consecutive League and Cup "double", and he has high hopes of further success in Europe next season.

Dixie Deans heads past Hibernian goalkeeper Jim Herriot to score Celtic's second goal.

Spurs win first UEFA Cup in all-England final

SPURS, PIONEERS of English success on the Continent, became the first English club to win two different European competitions when they held off a brave rally by Wolves and carried off the UEFA Cup at White Hart Lane. With a 2–1 lead from the first leg at Molineux a fortnight ago, the 1–1 draw was enough to win them the new trophy.

So England's domination of the Fairs/UEFA competition continues, despite holders Leeds's shock defeat in the first round. They had a 2–0 lead over Lierse from the first leg in Belgium, but, because of fixture congestion at home, fielded a virtual reserve side at Elland Road and lost 4–0.

Chivers scored two breakaway goals for Spurs at Molineux, sandwiching McCalliog's effort for Wolves. Skipper Mullery, the man Spurs called in from the cold last month — he was on loan with Fulham — scored with a spectacular header from Peters's free-kick to increase Spurs' lead in the return and, with Perryman, ensured his team's grip on midfield. But, five minutes from the interval, Wolves pulled a goal back when Wagstaffe hit a fierce 20-yarder in off a post. Wolves staged a late rally, but they could not get past Jennings.

Action from the second leg at White Hart Lane.

FINAL SCORE

Football League
Division 1: Derby County
Top scorer: Francis Lee (Manchester City) 33
Division 2: Norwich City
Division 3: Aston Villa
Division 4: Grimsby Town
Footballer of the Year: Gordon Banks (Stoke City)

FA Cup Final

Leeds United	1	Arsenal	0

League Cup Final

Stoke City	2	Chelsea	1

Scottish League
Division 1: Celtic
Top scorer: Joe Harper (Aberdeen) 33
Division 2: Dumbarton
Footballer of the Year: Dave Smith (Rangers)

Scottish FA Cup Final

Celtic	6	Hibernian	1

Scottish League Cup Final

Partick Thistle	4	Celtic	1

International Championship
England, Scotland, 4 pts

European Cup Final

Ajax Amsterdam	2	Inter-Milan	0

Cup-Winners' Cup Final

Rangers	3	Moscow Dynamo	2

UEFA Cup Final
Tottenham Hotspur beat Wolverhampton Wanderers 2–1, 1–1

European Footballer of the Year 1971
Johan Cruyff (Ajax Amsterdam & Holland)

Leading European Footballer of the Year (Golden Boot)
Gerd Muller (Bayern Munich)

World Club Championship
Ajax Amsterdam (Holland) beat Independiente (Argentina) 1–1, 3–0

Best quits at 26; flies off to Spain

GEORGE BEST, who failed to turn up to play for Northern Ireland at Hampden last week, has announced that he is quitting soccer. At 26, the wayward genius, arguably the most talented British footballer of all time, spoke to a Sunday newspaper of his premature retirement from the game before flying off to Spain. Best, who was Manchester United's leading scorer again this season with 18 goals in 40 League games, described himself as a mental and physical wreck and confessed to having done nothing but drink for the last year.

No other footballer has had to live with the off-field pressures that Best, with his pop-star lifestyle, has faced. If this is the end of his career, rather than just another escapade, it will be a sad loss to the game he has enriched with his unique skills.

Rangers fans out of control as they win Cup-Winners' Cup

Johnston celebrates Rangers' third goal — or is he trying to hold the crowd back?

RANGERS' FINE 3–2 victory over Moscow Dynamo in the final of the European Cup-Winners' Cup in Barcelona was marred by the disgraceful, puerile behaviour of their fans, who invaded the pitch at every opportunity.

Some 20,000 Rangers fans had flown from Glasgow to support their heroes and, as they overflowed on to the pitch, the players had to leave the field three times before the game could start. Each Rangers goal — from Colin Stein in 24 minutes, Willie Johnston in 40 and 49 minutes — was the signal for a pitch invasion.

John Greig was outstanding for Rangers: he seemed to be everywhere at once. But they appeared to relax when 3–0 up, and Dynamo scored on the hour and then three minutes from the end, through Estrekov and Makovikov. Scottish supporters were grateful to Peter McCloy for some brave saves that ensured victory.

The final pitch invasion at the end developed into a riot, as club-wielding police battled with Glasgow fans throwing broken seats and bottles. Many fans and police were injured, and there were several arrests. As the crowd finally streamed out, they continued their behaviour, bringing further violence to the streets of Barcelona.

FINAL SCORE

EUROPEAN CHAMPIONSHIP 1972

QUARTER-FINALS
England v West Germany 1–3, 0–0
Italy v Belgium 0–0, 1–2
Hungary v Romania 1–1, 2–2, 2–1
Yugoslavia v USSR 0–0, 0–3

Last four in Belgium:

SEMI-FINALS

USSR	1	Hungary	0
West Germany	2	Belgium	1

THIRD-PLACE MATCH

Belgium	2	Hungary	1

FINAL

West Germany	3	USSR	0

Brussels, 18 June 1972. Attendance 43,437

West Germany: Maier, Hottges, Schwarzenbeck, Beckenbauer, Breitner, Hoeness, Wimmer, Netzer, Heynckes, Muller, Kremers (Scorers: Muller 2, Wimmer)
USSR: Rudakov, Dzodzuashvili, Khurtsilava, Kaplichny, Istomin, Troshkin, Kolotov, Baidachni, Konkov (Dolmatov), Banishevski (Kozinkievits), Onishenko

Clough outbursts upset League: Derby warned

LEAGUE CHAMPIONS Derby County could face severe disciplinary action from the Football League if they cannot persuade their manager, the outspoken Brian Clough, to modify his criticisms of the football establishment. Club chairman Sam Longson reluctantly revealed as much on the return flight from Sarajevo, after Derby had withstood substantial provocation in beating Zeljeznicar in the European Cup with a display that was a credit to British football. Longson was apparently sent for and told that Clough is not entitled to make comments about matters not concerning Derby!

Clough has, of course, been a major critic of England manager Sir Alf Ramsey. He has also made caustic remarks about the two-year ban from international football imposed on Colin Todd, the Derby defender.

This is merely the background to the failure of the Derby board and their manager to reach an amicable agreement over his new contract. Clough, who won't be gagged, reckons they are still "a million miles apart". One cannot blame him. He is totally involved in football, and perfectly entitled to speak about it, even if he does ruffle a few feathers. Clough's abrasive personality might irritate a lot of people, but the other side of the coin was demonstrated after the Zeljeznicar game, when he insisted his players meet the tiny knot of County fans who had travelled to the match.

Clough: a man who refuses to be gagged.

Jennings thwarts League leaders with two penalty saves

SPURS WON A rare point at Anfield on 31 March, thanks largely to a brilliant display from keeper Pat Jennings, who saved two penalties. Jennings played a blinder: apart from the penalty saves — from Keegan (38 minutes) and Smith (85) — he also stopped a six-yard shot from Cormack and a point-blank header from Hall. Even the 70th-minute goal that beat him was a mishit by Keegan into the ground, the ball sailing over Jennings's head.

Spurs had gone in front with a fine goal by Gilzean after 21 minutes. Neither penalty was well struck, although Jennings's huge presence in goal must have been daunting to the taker. But the loss of a point was not as serious to the League leaders as was first thought after this pre-lunch game. By tea-time, Arsenal and Leeds had both lost, and Liverpool remain strong favourites for the title. They also are in the UEFA Cup semi-final... and face Spurs again.

Jennings gets down to save his second penalty, this one from Tommy Smith.

SOCCER SOUNDBITES

"These people have come 2,000 miles to see you. Go and shake their hands and thank them."

BRIAN CLOUGH
to his players, referring to the Derby fans staying in the same hotel in Yugoslavia.

"Are your players aware of the rules?"

FIFA OBSERVER,
before the Derby-Zeljeznicar match.

"Are you?"

BRIAN CLOUGH,
in reply.

Banks hurt in crash: may lose sight of eye

ENGLAND KEEPER Gordon Banks was involved in a road accident on 22 October, when his car and a van met in a head-on collision. Surgeons are fighting to save the sight of his right eye, damaged by pieces of glass from his shattered windscreen. Although nearly 35, he recently signed a six-year contract with Stoke and still figures in Sir Alf Ramsey's plans for the 1974 World Cup. His uncanny anticipation and lightning reflexes have made him arguably the greatest goalkeeper in the history of soccer, and if his career is cut short now it will be a sad loss to the game.

Hibs' revenge as Celtic lose again

CELTIC LOST in the League Cup final for the third season running, as Hibs extracted their revenge for the 6–1 drubbing in last season's Scottish Cup final. Hibs won 2–1, with all the goals coming in the second half. Skipper Pat Stanton put Hibs ahead in the 60th minute and then laid on their second six minutes later for Jim O'Rourke, the "overnight success" who has been with Hibs for 10 years. Celtic's sole reply came from Kenny Dalglish after 71 minutes.

All over bar the shouting: eighth title for Liverpool

WITH THEIR FINE 2–0 victory over Leeds at Anfield on Easter Monday, 23 April, and Arsenal's failure to win at Southampton, Liverpool have, to all intents and purposes, won the Championship. Leeds can no longer catch them, while Arsenal would have to win their last two matches (at West Ham and Leeds), and Liverpool lose their home game with Leicester — all by substantial margins — for the London side to overtake them. Full celebrations must wait until Saturday, but they were already partying on the Kop when Keegan clinched the match five minutes from time, after Cormack had put Liverpool in front on 47 minutes. Don Revie, manager of Cup-finalists Leeds, who have again failed to achieve the cherished "double", conceded that Liverpool were the better side on the day. Liverpool manager Bill Shankly, in turn, was overjoyed at his team's display. He built up a great side in the mid-sixties, and this one looks even better. He has bought particularly well: Ray Clemence, Alex Lindsay, Larry Lloyd, Emlyn Hughes and Kevin Keegan were virtually unknown when he plucked them from the lower divisions. Hughes has been outstanding this season, a dynamic midfielder for Liverpool, yet now an established left-back for England. Keegan and Clemence both won their first England caps.

Liverpool's success is based above all on a blend of skill, power and sheer determination Every member of the side shows a tremendous work-rate, constantly running and challenging. They took over the League leadership from Everton on 23 September and, apart from one brief period in February, stayed there.

Keegan scores to clinch the match, and another Championship for Liverpool.

Bobby Charlton retires: end of an era at Old Trafford

WHEN Bobby Charlton played his last game for Manchester United at Stamford Bridge on 28 April, it marked the end of a great era. With Denis Law and Tony Dunne moving on, and the defection again of George Best (although he has had talks with manager Docherty and is contemplating yet another comeback), United's great side of the sixties has all but disappeared.

It has been a traumatic season for the Red Devils, who seem to have lost the "devil" altogether. That Charlton finished top scorer with six goals speaks volumes. But he had the consolation of helping the club avoid relegation, for they failed to win any of their first nine games and did not finally climb out of the bottom two until March. Tommy Docherty, who took over as manager from Frank O'Farrell in December, will have a monumental job next season to revive United's fading fortunes.

Charlton, of course, is a last link with the "Busby Babes". He carried the mantle of that long-lamented side, and won just about every honour in the game. Above all, he won universal respect and admiration, as a sportsman as well as a footballer.

While Bobby was being saluted by the Chelsea crowd, his brother Jack of Leeds limped off the Southampton pitch with a hamstring injury in what could be his last competitive match before moving on to management.

Bobby Charlton: retiring from football.

England celebrate Moore's century and shatter Scotland's centenary

SCOTLAND'S CENTENARY celebrations became an icy nightmare on the evening of 14 February, as England humiliated them 5–0 at Hampden, their biggest victory there since 1888. The result was a fitting tribute to England skipper Bobby Moore, making his 100th international appearance, and must have cheered up Alf Ramsey, who was criticized after England's dismal goalless draw with Wales last month. But it was a dreadful baptism for Willie Ormond, Scotland's new team manager.

Scotland, as if bent on demonstrating the type of game that became a tradition in their great years, started out with some beautiful football, stroking the ball around between themselves for the first five minutes. Yet 10 minutes later they were 3–0 down! Channon hit a 20-yarder that Lorimer deflected into goal. Channon then sent Clarke away for the second, and scored the third with a half-volley from a Chivers throw.

Scotland's defence could not cope with either the frosty surface or the lively England attack. They were frequently torn apart by the nimble running of Clarke, Chivers and Channon, the outstanding forward of the match. There was positive intent in midfield, too, dominated by Ball, Peters and Bell. The 48,000 crowd jeered Scotland throughout the second half, and further goals from Chivers and Clarke did not improve their mood.

Double save of the season: 'Monty' the hero as Sunderland win the Cup

SUNDERLAND BECAME the first Division Two side to win the FA Cup for 42 years when they beat Leeds 1–0 at Wembley, and at the end manager Bob Stokoe ran on to the field straight into the arms of keeper Jim Montgomery. For "Monty" had made a double save midway through the second half that denied Leeds when an equalizer seemed inevitable, with one of the most remarkable pieces of goalkeeping ever seen.

Before the match, Sunderland were given no chance. Leeds were the Cup-holders, had finished third in the League and were in the final of the European Cup-Winners' Cup. They were a mean side and had seen it all before. Sunderland, though, had a tremendous Wearside following and, as their Cup run progressed, they became infected by the fanaticism of a wonderful crowd. And the manner in which they had beaten Arsenal in the semi-final should have been a warning.

At Wembley, they matched Leeds in spirit and showed no little skill. But it was still a shock when they took the lead through Ian Porterfield in the 32nd minute from their first corner. Leeds proceeded to grind away at Sunderland, yet the individual flair that might have made the breakthrough appears to have been sacrificed in this side for the sake of "professionalism".

It seemed, however, that they had finally cracked the Sunderland defence after 65 minutes. Right-back Reaney crossed a long ball to the far post where his partner Cherry had stolen up on the blind side. It looked a certain score as Cherry launched himself at the ball, met it perfectly with his head, and sent it hurtling towards the opposite corner of the goal. Montgomery, whose handling of the ball hitherto had been far from perfect, twisted in mid-air to parry the ball, but only on to the lethal right foot of Peter Lorimer. From six yards out, the Leeds winger lashed the ball towards the invitingly unguarded net, but somehow "Monty" managed to lift himself up and deflect the ball on to the bar and eventual safety.

This miracle reprieve gave his team-mates fresh heart, and planted the seeds of doubt in their opponents. With Horswill, a talented and impudent slip of a lad, and the intelligent Porterfield continuing to subdue Bremner and Giles, Sunderland firmly retained midfield control. So although the tremendous effort of Hughes, Halom and Tueart in the first hour began to take its toll of stamina in the closing stages, Sunderland never really looked like surrendering the initiative. And as Leeds desperately overreached themselves in the tense final minutes, Sunderland counter-attacked and very nearly scored again, with Harvey making a splendid save from Halom.

Sunderland's victory was the most popular at Wembley since the "Matthews final" 20 years ago, not so much because they were the underdogs, but because they emphasized, by beating Leeds, the apostles of cold efficiency, that there is no substitute, even in the commercial world of modern soccer, for flair, imagination and spirit.

"Monty" parries Cherry's power-header to Lorimer (7).

Superb Rangers end seven-year itch

Alfie Conn (on ground) scores Rangers' second goal.

GLASGOW RANGERS brought their centenary celebrations to a perfect climax by beating Celtic 3–2 in one of the most exciting Cup finals seen at Hampden for years. Dalglish put Celtic ahead after 24 minutes with a fine shot from a Deans pass, and 10 minutes later Parlane equalized, heading in a MacDonald cross. Conn put Rangers ahead only seconds after the interval, but Celtic fought back and, six minutes later, after Greig handled in the box, Footballer of the Year George Connelly equalized from the spot.

It was Rangers, however, who continued to attack with more panache, and Forsyth forced in the winner after a Derek Johnstone header had struck a post and run along the line.

FOOTBALL FOCUS

- Derby paid Leicester a record British fee of £225,000 for full-back David Nish in August, and he won his first England cap in May.
- Johnny Giles made a record-equalling fifth Cup final appearance at Wembley (one for Man Utd, four for Leeds).
- Huddersfield were relegated for the second year running, and will play in Division Three for the first time.
- The first official women's international in Britain took place at Cappielow Park (Morton), England beating Scotland 3–2.
- Ajax Amsterdam won the European Cup for the third consecutive season.

Lesson for Liverpool, but they bravely take trophy

LIVERPOOL WERE ominously outplayed in Moenchengladbach but, although Borussia pulled back two of the three-goal deficit from the first leg, Bill Shankly's team staged a fine rearguard action to take the UEFA Cup final 3–2 on aggregate. The Reds certainly needed those three Anfield goals — from Keegan (two) and Lloyd — as they were given a first-half football lesson by a brilliant Borussia side, who flowed as beautifully as West Germany at Wembley last year. The Liverpool defence and midfield were rent constantly as Netzer, Danner and Wimmer swept with geometric precision towards their goal.

Twice Rupp, a stocky nuisance of a centre-forward, made goals for Heynckes, after 30 and 40 minutes, and Liverpool's terrible anxiety was revealed when Hughes was booked for a crude foul on Vogts and Lawler pulled down Netzer.

Yet Liverpool, in the second half, with defeat staring them in the face, drew on all their resources of character as Smith, their indomitable captain, drove them forward. They seldom looked like scoring, but at least they kept the now tiring Germans away from their penalty area, and brought their first European trophy back to Anfield. But the performance of the Germans gave a salutary message, not only for Liverpool but for English soccer at large. Last night was no cause for celebration.

Lloyd (left) scores the all-important third goal in the first leg.

Heart-break again for Leeds as Milan steal Cup

IT WAS FLOODLIGHT robbery in Salonika as Leeds lost the Cup-Winners' Cup final to a team they outplayed. Usually cast as the villains of calculated efficiency and gamesmanship, Leeds went down to an early Milan goal of dubious origin and a string of baffling refereeing decisions that negated their all-out efforts to score.

As a heavy thunderstorm rolled around the stadium, Leeds were caught cold by Milan — and the first dubious decision — after only four minutes. Greek referee Christos Michas ruled that Madeley had impeded Bigon 20 yards out, and Chiarugi's free-kick was deflected off the Leeds wall past Harvey. Thereafter Leeds, without Bremner, Giles, Clarke and Eddie Gray because of injury or suspension, managed something like 30 goal attempts, while Harvey was barely troubled. Vecchi, in Milan's goal, superbly kept out a series of shots and headers, particularly from Jordan, Jones, the tenacious Lorimer, and those hard-working midfield operators Madeley and Bates.

But if Vecchi was the Milan hero, referee Michas ran him close. After 25 minutes he ignored Anquilletti's blatant trip on Jones in the box, which occurred right under his nose. Twice more, in the second half, he took no action over penalty offences, first when Zignoli handled Lorimer's cross, and then when Jones was pushed by Sabadini. The Greeks in the 45,000 crowd clearly showed their disapproval of the home-based referee, and began chanting for Leeds.

The game blew up in the closing stages when Rivera, pretty anonymous until now, chopped Hunter down as he attempted to break through on the left. Hunter retaliated, and scuffles broke out between two groups of players near the touchline, as a result of which Hunter and Sogliano were sent off.

At the end, the crowd left no doubts as to where their sympathy lay, shouting "Shame, shame" at the victorious Italians and singing the praises of the English side from outside the main stand: "Ole, ole, Leeds, ole" — some small consolation for Don Revie's men after they had lost their third trophy at the end of a heart-breaking season.

The free-kick goal by Chiarugi that gave AC Milan the Cup-Winners' Cup.

FINAL SCORE

Football League
Division 1: Liverpool
Top scorer: Bryan Robson (West Ham) 28
Division 2: Burnley
Division 3: Bolton Wanderers
Division 4: Southport
Footballer of the Year: Pat Jennings (Tottenham Hotspur)

FA Cup Final
Sunderland 1 Leeds United 0

League Cup Final
Tottenham Hotspur 1 Norwich City 0

Scottish League
Division 1: Celtic
Top scorer: Alan Gordon (Hibernian) 27
Division 2: Clyde
Footballer of the Year: George Connelly (Celtic)

Scottish FA Cup Final
Rangers 3 Celtic 2

Scottish League Cup Final
Hibernian 2 Celtic 1

International Championship
England, 6 pts

European Cup Final
Ajax Amsterdam 1 Juventus 0

Cup-Winners' Cup Final
AC Milan 1 Leeds United 0

UEFA Cup Final
Liverpool beat B Moenchengladbach 3–0, 0–2

European Footballer of the Year 1972
Franz Beckenbauer (Bayern Munich & West Germany)

Leading European Scorer (Golden Boot)
Eusebio (Benfica) 40

World Club Championship
Independiente (Argentina) 1 Juventus (Italy) 0

Polish 'clown' denies England World Cup chance

ON A NIGHT of missed chances and extraordinary saves from Jan Tomaszewski, the Polish keeper labelled a "clown" on TV by Brian Clough, England saw their World Cup hopes disappear at Wembley last night. They stumbled exhausted and heart-broken out of the competition after a 90-minute all-out assault had failed to break down Poland's grim determination.

On the pitch where, some seven years ago, they had won the trophy, Sir Alf Ramsey's men played with a spirit that deserved a better fate. But no one can deny that Poland's overall performances in the competition, after a disastrous defeat in their opening match against Wales, make them worthy of qualification. And at Wembley they fought a magnificent rear-guard action before the most partisan crowd gathered there since the 1966 World Cup final.

The plain and unpalatable fact is that England moved boldly on to the offensive in this tournament when it was too late. Had they produced just a little of this attacking zeal against Wales at Wembley last March and Poland at Chorzow in June, they might not now have found themselves out in the cold. It can be fairly argued that Ramsey's overcaution in selection and tactics in recent years has been the major cause of this failure. Indeed, it became clear last night that England have become so used to playing with predominantly defensive efficiency that they could not switch smoothly enough into forward gear to overcome such stubborn opponents.

With Peters, Bell and Currie dominating the midfield from the early stages, and Channon leading the front line with dash, they launched and sustained an almighty assault on the Polish barrier, creating chance after chance. But it was Poland who scored first, after 58 minutes, when Hunter was uncharacteristically caught in possession by the flying winger Gadocha, who raced away and crossed for Domarski to shoot under Shilton's dive.

England equalized six minutes later, Clarke converting a borderline penalty. But they could not beat Tomaszewski again.

SOCCER SOUNDBITES

"I have never seen a better performance at Wembley by a visiting goalkeeper."

SIR ALF RAMSEY,
on Jan Tomaszewski, the architect of England's failure.

The end in sight for England after Domarski had scored.

Sub Jordan books Scotland's final place

SCOTLAND, SKILLED and tenacious on a night of fierce tension, reached the finals of the World Cup for the third time when they beat Czechoslovakia 2–1 at Hampden on 26 September. Leeds striker Joe Jordan became the hero of the 100,000 crowd when, six minutes after replacing Kenny Dalglish, he headed the 70th-minute winner from Willie Morgan's centre. Scotland, having beaten Denmark twice, cannot now be overhauled, no matter what happens in their final game, the return against the Czechs.

A goal behind after 33 minutes, when Nehoda took advantage of a right-wing breakaway, Scotland maintained their formidable pressure with neat, skilful football. They were rewarded when Jim Holton, the Manchester United centre-half, headed the equalizer in the 40th minute from a corner by Tommy Hutchison. Only a series of notable saves by the agile Viktor and rugged defensive work denied the Scots further goals.

David Hay, one of five Celtic men in the reshaped team, worked splendidly in midfield alongside Billy Bremner, while up front Denis Law, recalled after a 15-month absence for his 51st cap, and Coventry's Hutchison caused the Czechs continual problems. Morgan, Dalglish and even full-back Danny McGrain used the spaces on the flanks well. The first of many free-kicks was awarded after only 45 seconds, and the referee eventually booked two Czechs for scything fouls on the lively Bremner.

Jordan's header is Scotland's passport to the World Cup.

Clough: outspoken... outrageous... and out!

AFTER AN ORGY of allegations between himself and the board, Brian Clough, together with his partner Peter Taylor, have resigned from Derby County. The chief bone of contention has been Clough's outspoken comments on TV and in newspaper articles, and the club feared expulsion from the League. The last straw came when in his ghosted newspaper column he accused some of his England players of "cheating" by not giving 100 per cent because of their preoccupation with tonight's World Cup match against Poland.

From the moment Clough began to receive payment for his opinions, some public sympathy was lost, and unforgiving critics have accused him of being deliberately controversial. But in Derby, the club's supporters began demonstrating in Clough's favour and are seeking a showdown with the club.

Late strike ends Wolves' famine

JOHN RICHARDS'S goal in the 84th minute of an ultimately exciting League Cup final earned Wolves their first major success for 14 years. A solid, down-to-earth performance was just good enough to overcome the brittle skills of their more purposeful opponents from Manchester City.

The sensible and direct Midlanders dominated the first half and should have had more to show for their efforts at the interval than the 43rd-minute goal Ken Hibbitt scored with a mishit shot from Geoff Palmer's cross. But City improved immensely in the second half, wrested midfield control from Mike Bailey, and deservedly equalized on the hour with a powerful shot from Colin Bell.

Then, shortly after Bell had hammered the ball against the bar, Richards stepped in with his match-winner at the other end. Inexperienced reserve keeper Gary Pierce, who was told only on Thursday that he would be playing, contributed substantially to Wolves' victory with a series of agile saves when City threatened to take control after the break.

The one sour note was the churlish behaviour of Rodney Marsh, who left the arena without accompanying his team-mates to collect his loser's tankard or join in the applause for the winners. In contrast, team-mate Denis Law gave his shirt to Francis Munro, a fellow Scot who had beaten him all afternoon.

Richards (9) lands the killer blow for Wolves.

Bristol City put Leeds out of Cup

BRISTOL CITY, seventh from bottom of the Second Division, succeeded where the First Division elite have failed on 29 occasions this season. They defeated hitherto unbeaten Leeds, the League leaders and Cup favourites, in this hard-fought fifth-round FA Cup replay at Elland Road by 1–0, and richly deserved to do so.

Full of confidence and effort, and showing no little skill, Bristol were full value for a victory that earns them their first quarter-final place for 53 years and a home tie with League champions Liverpool. The decisive, splendidly taken goal came in the 23rd minute from Don Gillies, 22, their Scottish striker.

A well-conceived move, it began, as much did, with Gerry Gow in midfield, and Keith Fear then held off Bremner before feeding Gillies just inside the box. Gillies evaded a challenge from Hunter and shot past the unsighted Harvey.

SOCCER SOUNDBITES

"I'm not even thinking about what changes Leeds may make... Imagine a side that can bring in three internationals."

ALAN DICKS,
Bristol City manager, on Leeds's injury "problems" for the replay.

Leeds land League at Liverpool — without playing!

LEEDS FIND themselves in the improbable position of having long-time rivals Arsenal to thank for finally clinching them the League Championship, as Ray Kennedy's goal at Anfield inflicted Liverpool's only home defeat of the season and meant they could no longer catch Leeds.

It is ironic that Leeds should win their second title in six years by sitting on their backsides, after missing so many honours when their fate was in their own hands. But no one can deny their right to be called champions. They have led the table from the start, winning their first seven matches. They beat Sheffield United's all-time record of 23 opening games without defeat, and just failed to equal Burnley's undefeated run when they were beaten 3–2 at Stoke in their 30th match, on 23 February.

Before this defeat, they were nine points ahead of second-placed Liverpool. But the Leeds nerves began to jangle as Liverpool's refusal to give up saw their lead gradually eroded when they hit a run of three defeats in March: 1–0 at Anfield, amazingly 4–1 at home to Burnley, and 3–1 at West Ham. This left Liverpool only four points behind with three games in hand; but their involvement in the Cup, with a semi-final replay, proved too much and, as Leeds recovered, so Liverpool began to falter.

Leeds have been at the top of English soccer, or thereabouts, for the past decade, although they have not won the rewards they felt they deserved — five times League runners-up in those 10 years. Most of the side who won the League for the first time in 1969 are still there, although Harvey has replaced Sprake in goal, Cherry has come in for Cooper and McQueen for Charlton. Clarke and Jordan have reinforced the front line, although Mick Jones leads their League scorers with 14.

Above all, Billy Bremner has been the driving force behind their success, a tremendous all-round footballer and an inspiring captain. If he would only cut out the gamesmanship and stop whining at the referee, he would be the perfect player.

Manager Don Revie, too, deserves considerable praise for his astute buying and blending.

Shabby dismissal Ramsey's 'reward' after 11 years

THE FA'S DECISION to sack Sir Alf Ramsey apparently came out of the blue to the England manager who, according to associates, was badly shaken. It was obvious that there was considerable disenchantment about England's failure to reach the World Cup finals, and speculation has been rife concerning a possible successor. But even if the FA were in a desperate hurry to get rid of a faithful servant, they might at least have allowed him the opportunity to resign.

Coventry general manager Joe Mercer has been appointed caretaker-manager, but has made it clear that, at 60, he does not want the job permanently. Whoever succeeds Ramsey will still be obliged to accept that international matches are rarely granted priority over club fixtures, and will be frequently deprived of players for spurious reasons. It is a tribute to Ramsey's ability that he overcame such obstacles often enough to guide England to 69 victories and 27 draws in 113 matches.

Perhaps the satisfaction of leading England to their only World Cup triumph, a knighthood and an assured place in soccer history, as both player and manager, will be some compensation for the disappointments and, now, the bitterness of summary dismissal.

Sir Alf Ramsey in happier days.

Black day at Old Trafford: United go down as fans shame club

HUNDREDS OF young Manchester United fans shamed the great club's reputation as they invaded the pitch four minutes before full time, and in the end the referee had to abandon the game against Manchester City. United needed to win this match if they were to stand any chance of First Division survival.

The trouble started when Denis Law, not long ago an idol of Old Trafford, cheekily back-heeled the ball into their net after 82 minutes, virtually condemning them to the Second Division. Some 400 hooligans invaded the pitch and, although it was cleared this time, a few minutes later a much larger and more determined invasion was launched from the Stretford End, and on police advice the referee abandoned the game.

The first thing the League have to decide is whether to allow the result to stand. United are relegated anyway, as both Birmingham and West Ham won the necessary points to stay up. More important, a disciplinary commission will have to determine what penalty if any to impose on United. A recent precedent is the similarly frightening episode at St James's Park during Newcastle's FA Cup quarter-final against Forest. Following an FA investigation, Newcastle were last week ordered to play any home FA Cup ties next season on opponents' grounds.

At the time, the commission emphasized that Newcastle could have done little to prevent the riot. The same conclusion may be reached about the Old Trafford pitch invasions. But the fact remains that British soccer fans are now among the most violent, unsporting partisans in Europe.

SOCCER SOUNDBITES

"The way things are going, the FA and the League will have to be thinking in terms of fences."

SIR MATT BUSBY.

Liverpool's red army take Wembley by storm

LIVERPOOL'S HANDSOME 3–0 victory over Newcastle at Wembley in the FA Cup final has established them as entertainers of the highest class. Since Bill Shankly became manager in December 1959, Liverpool have won the Second Division title, three League Championships, the UEFA Cup, and now their second FA Cup. Yet beyond Merseyside they have been regarded, without warmth, as a ruthlessly efficient machine.

The third team that Shankly has patiently built at Anfield do not deserve to be damned with such faint praise. Their virtuoso performance during the second half at Wembley was sweet music indeed to those who had begun to despair of the future of English soccer. They played so well that the much-vaunted Newcastle side simply could not live with them. Kevin Keegan emerged as the popular hero with two beautifully taken goals, but they were a triumph of superb teamwork. Smith made the first goal, in the 57th minute, with a cross that Keegan chested down and then drove with a flourish into the net.

Two-goal Keegan tries an overhead kick.

With Hall, Callaghan and Cormack denying their opponents midfield possession, Liverpool boldly mounted wave after wave of attacks and moved further ahead in the 74th minute, when Toshack headed on a long pass and Heighway, bringing the ball under control, changed direction and placed it wide of McFaul. The third goal, two minutes from time and scored by Keegan, was the culmination of nearly a dozen passes and left Newcastle gaping.

Baton charge clears fans as Spurs lose UEFA Cup final

TOTTENHAM, FACING an uphill battle after their 2–2 draw at White Hart Lane in the first leg, lost for the first time in a Cup final when Dutch champions Feyenoord took the UEFA Cup with goals by Rijsbergen and Ressel before a 67,000 crowd in Rotterdam.

The team failed with dignity, but the occasion was made deplorable by the hooligan element among their supporters, who wrecked part of one end of the ground and flung chair backs at Dutch fans. They ignored public address appeals by Spurs chairman Sidney Wale and manager Bill Nicholson, who called them a disgrace to Britain. The trouble subsided only when a force of baton-wielding police finally charged among the rioters and appeared to clear all the Spurs supporters from the stadium.

On the pitch, Spurs found the strength and skill of Feyenoord totally daunting, and with England striker Chivers rarely a threat they never looked likely to score the crucial away goals that might have continued England's six-year run of success in this competition. The first Dutch goal, in the 41st minute, was the result of a collector's piece — an error by keeper Jennings. The second, six minutes from time, was made by a dazzling run and pass by substitute Boskamp. So Spurs, on the pitch where they earned glory in 1963 by becoming the first British club to win a European trophy, trailed sadly away, shamed utterly by their so-called admirers.

On another night of shame for British clubs in Europe, Dutch police break up the rioting Spurs rabble.

FOOTBALL FOCUS

- Three up/three down promotion and relegation was introduced between Divisions One and Two and between Two and Three.
- Johan Cruyff of Ajax signed for Barcelona in August for a world record £922,300, about £400,000 of which he pocketed himself.
- Three Notts County players missed the same penalty at Portsmouth on 22 September (two had to be retaken because of encroachment), but County won 2–1.
- Trevor Hockey (Aston Villa) became the first Welsh player to be sent off in an international, on 26 September in Poland.
- Sunday soccer was launched in England on 6 January with four FA Cup ties, the first being Cambridge v Oldham (2–2) at 11 am, and the gates were all high.
- Beaten Cup-finalists Newcastle enjoyed an extraordinary passage to Wembley. They needed replays in the third and fourth rounds after being held at home by amateurs Hendon and Fourth Division Scunthorpe. At home to Forest in the sixth round, the crowd invaded the pitch after United went 3–1 down when Lyall scored from the spot, and the referee took the players off. When they returned, with 10 men (Pat Howard had been dismissed for protesting at the penalty decision), Newcastle proceeded to win 4–3. The FA ordered the match to be played again, at Goodison Park: they drew 0–0 and then won the replay (also at Goodison) 1–0.
- Exeter, with nine players unfit, risked expulsion from the League by refusing to turn up for their fixture at Scunthorpe on 2 April. For this unprecedented action, the League fined them £5,000 and awarded Scunthorpe both points.
- Third Division Plymouth beat three Division One sides away in the League Cup — Burnley, QPR and Birmingham — before losing to Manchester City in the semi-finals.
- Jack Charlton guided Middlesbrough to the Division Two title in his first season as manager, and with 65 points they had a 15-point margin over the next club, a League record.
- Celtic won their ninth consecutive League title in Scotland, and achieved another League and Cup "double".
- Crystal Palace went down to Division Three, relegated for the second season running.
- Sir Stanley Rous was succeeded as president of FIFA by Brazil's Joao Havelange before the start of the 1974 World Cup.

Johan Cruyff, £400,000 signing-on fee from Barcelona.

FINAL SCORE

Football League
Division 1: Leeds United
Top scorer: Mick Channon (Southampton) 21
Division 2: Middlesbrough
Division 3: Oldham Athletic
Division 4: Peterborough United
Footballer of the Year: Ian Callaghan (Liverpool)

FA Cup Final
Liverpool 3 Newcastle United 0

League Cup Final
Wolves 2 Manchester City 1

Scottish League
Division 1: Celtic
Top scorer: Dixie Deans (Celtic) 24
Division 2: Airdrieonians
Footballers of the Year: Scottish World Cup Squad

Scottish FA Cup Final
Celtic 3 Dundee United 0

Scottish League Cup Final
Dundee 1 Celtic 0

International Championship
England, Scotland, 4 pts

European Cup Final
Bayern Munich 1 Atletico Madrid 1
Replay: B. Munich 4 Atletico Madrid 0

Cup-Winners' Cup Final
FC Magdeburg 2 AC Milan 0

UEFA Cup Final
Feyenoord beat Tottenham Hotspur 2–2, 2–0

European Footballer of the Year 1973
Johan Cruyff (Ajax, Barcelona & Holland)

Leading European Scorer (Golden Boot)
Hector Yazalde (Sporting Lisbon) 46

World Club Championship
Atletico Madrid (Spain) beat Independiente (Argentina) 0–1, 2–0

Total football

Holland won the hearts of the footballing world in West Germany, even if they did not win the World Cup. Playing an attacking brand of soccer dubbed "total football", they replaced Brazil as the "people's favourites" and excitingly stormed their way to the final, where they lost to the talented but less charismatic home nation.

GOAL DIFFERENCE was brought into play in the qualifying competition, cutting down on play-offs, although Sweden and Yugoslavia both needed one before eliminating Austria and Spain respectively. Belgium were the unluckiest non-qualifier, going out undefeated and without conceding a goal. They held Holland to two goalless draws, but massive Dutch victories over Norway and Iceland — they scored 24 goals in those four games — saw them through. The Soviet Union had to play off with Chile for a finals place but after drawing 0–0 in Moscow, they refused to play in Santiago for political reasons and were eliminated. Australia, East Germany, Haiti and Zaïre all qualified for the first time.

Scotland's Joe Jordan outjumps Zaïre as Denis Law watches.

Behind the scenes

Before the World Cup got underway, it was almost overwhelmed by commercialism and greed, politics and power struggles, all of which provided a tense background as the teams prepared to do battle. With tight security necessary after the tragic terrorist activities at the Munich Olympics in 1972, the atmosphere was grim and unfriendly — and it rained throughout most of the tournament.

There was considerable unrest in both the Dutch and the West German camps, with players threatening to go on strike in rows over pay and bonuses. Everywhere, players seemed to have their hands out — for interviews, for having their pictures taken, or for wearing a certain manufacturer's product. The Scots fell out with their football boot company and erased its symbols with black boot polish.

Three days before the tournament began, Sir Stanley Rous was "ousted" as president of FIFA by the Brazilian millionaire Joao Havelange, who was said to have spent a fortune on canvassing support, and there were rumours of a possible European breakaway from the world governing body.

Neeskens scores from the spot in the sensational opening to the final.

The format of the competition had been changed again, with the top two teams of the four groups in Round One going through to Groups A and B, the winners of these to play the final.

Scotland, managed by Willie Ormond, who had taken over when Tommy Docherty went to Manchester United half-way through the qualifying competition, and captained by Billy Bremner, put their internal squabbles behind them and went out with their colours flying. It was unfortunate that their first match was with Zaïre, as caution kept their win down to two goals. Yugoslavia proceeded to thrash the Africans 9–0, so for Scotland to be certain of going through, they had to beat Yugoslavia. A draw would let Brazil in, provided they beat Zaïre by more than two.

Yugoslavia took the lead against Scotland in Frankfurt with only eight minutes left. But Hutchison, who had replaced the ineffective Dalglish midway through the second half, made the equalizer for Jordan just before the end. All eyes turned to the electronic scoreboard to see how Brazil were faring in Gelsenkirchen. Alas for Scotland, Brazil scored their crucial third goal 10 minutes from time, and so avoided the toss of a coin. It was a shoddy performance from Brazil, which must have saddened the watching Pele.

WORLD CUP QUOTES

"The World Cup is on a disaster course. The players have become money-mad."

JOAO SALDANHA,
former Brazilian manager.

"Great game!? You know what that was? Two Third Division teams trying to kick each other to death, that's what it was."

Liverpool manager
BILL SHANKLY,
on the Scotland-Brazil goalless draw.

Cruyff was in the German box in a flash, brought down, and Neeskens's spot-kick into the back of the net put Holland one up in the final before a West German player had touched the ball.

East Germany caused a stir in Round One when they beat West Germany 1–0, but the favourites were already sure of going through, and there was a feeling that they wanted to avoid Holland in the second round. The Dutch were very impressive, with the two Johans, Cruyff and Neeskens, outstanding. Cruyff had taken over from Pele as the world's acknowledged No.1, and he soon stamped his authority on this tournament.

Poland were a revelation in Group Four, with Lato and Szarmach up front capitalizing on the midfield mastery of Deyna. They toppled first Argentina and then Italy, who were eliminated.

The big two emerge

The results of the second round groups were clear-cut — both Holland and West Germany won all their matches, beating Brazil and Poland, respectively, in last-match "deciders". Holland's "total football" was wonderful to watch, with all their outfield players capable of switching into attack or defence. West Germany, the European champions, found their true form at last: while not as versatile as the Dutch, they had, under Helmut Schoen, thrown off the defensive shackles that for so long blighted the European game.

With wingers — the flying Hoeness on the right and the tricky Grabowski on the left — to feed the master goal-poacher Muller in the centre, Overath and Bonhof controlling midfield, and skipper Beckenbauer majestically leading them in his "attacking sweeper" role, the Germans opened up in Group B. But it was the all-purpose Breitner, nominally a left-back, who ignited them with the opening goal against Yugoslavia. Then, in appalling conditions, they produced a superb display against Sweden, before being brought down to earth again by the splendid Poles, on an even more atrocious pitch. Only keeper Maier redeemed them before Muller scored the late winner, although Tomaszewski did save a penalty from Hoeness.

Meanwhile, Cruyff and Co. were sweeping aside Argentina, East Germany and World Cup-holders Brazil, scoring eight goals without conceding one, and setting up a mouth-watering final.

A tale of two penalties

While not the classic of optimistic expectations, the 1974 World Cup final had the most dramatic opening, with a penalty for Holland before a German had touched the ball. Cruyff picked the ball up in his own half and was racing into the West German box before they knew it. Only the fleet-footed Hoeness had any chance of catching him, and that's exactly what he did — unfairly inside the area. Neeskens scored from the spot-kick.

There was no doubt about the foul, although not every referee would have had the courage of Jack Taylor to give such an early penalty against the Germans in Munich's Olympic Stadium. Whether this had a subconscious effect on his later decision is hard to say, but he awarded a borderline penalty against the Dutch after 25 minutes, when Holzenbein went down, also after a fine run into the box. Breitner equalized from the spot.

Vogts was booked for persistent fouling after only four minutes, and Neeskens was lucky to get away unpunished for two crude tackles on Hoeness. But Van Hanegem was shown the yellow card for an off-the-ball push on Muller, spotted by a linesman, and Neeskens, too, was finally cautioned. Soon after, two minutes before half-time, Bonhof got through the Dutch defence and squared a short pass to Muller, who cleverly swivelled and scored a typical, opportunist goal.

Cruyff, obviously unhappy with the way the decisions were going, and mindful no doubt of West Germany's notorious propensity for "conning" referees, had words with Jack Taylor as they walked off at the interval, was booked and, indeed, lucky not to be sent off. The second half was nearly all Holland, and West Germany had to withstand tremendous pressure. And although there is the feeling that the better team lost, the Germans — especially Vogts, who did a wonderful job in minimizing the effectiveness of Cruyff — must be applauded for their spirited and intelligent performance.

Muller (13) hits West Germany's winner in the final.

FINAL SCORE

First round

Group 1

West Germany	1	Chile	0
East Germany	2	Australia	0
West Germany	3	Australia	0
East Germany	1	Chile	1
Chile	0	Australia	0
East Germany	1	West Germany	0

	P	W	D	L	F	A	P
E. Germany	3	2	1	0	4	1	5
W. Germany	3	2	0	1	4	1	4
Chile	3	0	2	1	1	2	2
Australia	3	0	1	2	0	5	1

Group 2

Brazil	0	Yugoslavia	0
Scotland	2	Zaïre	0
Brazil	0	Scotland	0
Yugoslavia	9	Zaïre	0
Scotland	1	Yugoslavia	1
Brazil	3	Zaïre	0

	P	W	D	L	F	A	P
Yugoslavia	3	1	2	0	10	1	4
Brazil	3	1	2	0	3	0	4
Scotland	3	1	2	0	3	1	4
Zaïre	3	0	0	3	0	14	0

Group 3

Holland	2	Uruguay	0
Sweden	0	Bulgaria	0
Holland	0	Sweden	0
Uruguay	1	Bulgaria	1
Holland	4	Bulgaria	1
Sweden	3	Uruguay	0

	P	W	D	L	F	A	P
Holland	3	2	1	0	6	1	5
Sweden	3	1	2	0	3	0	4
Bulgaria	3	0	2	1	2	5	2
Uruguay	3	0	1	2	1	6	1

Group 4

Poland	3	Argentina	2
Italy	3	Haiti	1
Italy	1	Argentina	1
Poland	7	Haiti	0
Poland	2	Italy	1
Argentina	4	Haiti	1

	P	W	D	L	F	A	P
Poland	3	3	0	0	12	3	6
Argentina	3	1	1	1	7	5	3
Italy	3	1	1	1	5	4	3
Haiti	3	0	0	3	2	14	0

Second round

Group A

Holland	4	Argentina	0
Brazil	1	East Germany	0
Holland	2	East Germany	0
Brazil	2	Argentina	1
Holland	2	Brazil	0
East Germany	1	Argentina	1

	P	W	D	L	F	A	P
Holland	3	3	0	0	8	0	6
Brazil	3	2	0	1	3	3	4
E. Germany	3	0	1	2	1	4	1
Argentina	3	0	1	2	2	7	1

Group B

West Germany	2	Yugoslavia	0
Poland	1	Sweden	0
Poland	2	Yugoslavia	1
West Germany	4	Sweden	2
West Germany	1	Poland	0
Sweden	2	Yugoslavia	1

	P	W	D	L	F	A	P
W. Germany	3	3	0	0	7	2	6
Poland	3	2	0	1	3	2	4
Sweden	3	1	0	2	4	6	2
Yugoslavia	3	0	0	3	2	6	0

THIRD-PLACE MATCH

Poland	1	Brazil	0

FINAL

West Germany	2	Holland	1

Olympic Stadium, Munich, 7 July 1974. Attendance 77,833

West Germany: Maier, Vogts, Schwarzenbeck, Beckenbauer, Breitner, Hoeness, Bonhof, Overath, Grabowski, Muller, Holzenbein (Scorers: Breitner pen, Muller)
Holland: Jongbloed, Suurbier, Rijsbergen (De Jong), Haan, Krol, Jansen, Neeskens, Van Hanegem, Rep, Cruyff, Rensenbrink (Van der Kerkhof R (Scorer: Neeskens pen)

Leading scorers
7 Lato (Poland)
5 Szarmach (Poland)
Neeskens (Holland)

Shankly drops a bombshell: to retire as Liverpool chief

BILL SHANKLY, 58, probably the most popular figure in League soccer, caused the first major surprise of the close season by deciding to retire after 15 years in command at Anfield. His standing down comes barely a week after Don Revie's departure from Elland Road to become manager of England. So now Leeds, the champions, and Liverpool, the runners-up and Cup-winners, both face the prospect of starting the season with a new man in charge.

The club directors reluctantly accepted Mr Shankly's decision to end his illustrious career. He wants some relief from the strain of managing a club that has rarely been out of the limelight during his association with them. He took over at Anfield in December 1959, and two-and-a-half years later guided them to promotion. Since then, they have won the League three times, the Cup twice and the UEFA Cup once — with three outstanding teams.

He achieved all this with a blend of toughness, knowledge and a sharp wit that made him the most quotable and quoted manager in British soccer. He developed those qualities as the son of a Lanarkshire miner in the bleak late twenties, as a top-class wing-half with Carlisle and Preston (capped five times for Scotland), and as the industrious manager of Carlisle, Grimsby, Workington and Huddersfield. How many future managers will serve so long, hard and sound an apprenticeship, or achieve success so consistently, while remaining so human a character?

Bill Shankly, celebrating with the Championship trophy.

Disgrace of Bremner and Keegan: sent off in Wembley showpiece

THE JOINT DISGRACE of Billy Bremner and Kevin Keegan in becoming the first British players to be sent off at Wembley was only a part of the ugliness of a shabby Charity Shield match. If the season's traditional opener, between the country's two leading teams, held at Wembley and televised live for the first time, is an example of what's to come, then we might just as well forget about it. The match had everything — sly, niggling fouls, outrageous tackles, unseemly off-the-ball scuffles, and a major flare-up. Why the two players, dismissed after an hour by a too-patient referee for fighting, felt they were hard done by and compounded their ignominy by flinging their shirts on to the Wembley track, is a mystery. Mr Matthewson had no alternative but to issue marching orders.

For the record, Boersma scored for Liverpool in the 20th minute, and Cherry headed Leeds's equalizer in the 70th. They each scored from their first five penalties, and keeper Harvey, inexplicably asked by Leeds to take their sixth, hit it over the bar. Callaghan then gleefully thumped home the winning penalty for Liverpool. But no one was the winner in this travesty of a match, and "charity" was nowhere to be seen.

Keegan and Bremner: shameful performance.

Revie confirmed as new England manager

DON REVIE WAS confirmed as Sir Alf Ramsey's successor on 4 July on a five-year contract, and his first job as England supremo was to fly out to Munich to watch the World Cup final between West Germany and Holland. His main task, of course, will be to build an England squad capable of coping with the likes of those two countries in the European Championships, and eventually challenging for the 1978 World Cup.

Success in Europe could well depend on the outcome of England's first qualifying tie, against Czechoslovakia at Wembley in October. And unless arrangements are made for an earlier get-together, he will meet his players for the first time only four days before that game. In other words, he has inherited all Ramsey's old problems; for he knows only too well the reluctance of clubs to release players for England duty except when it is absolutely essential: nobody was less co-operative than he.

Revie's qualifications for the job are excellent. A gifted inside-forward who won six England caps while with Manchester City, he lifted Leeds from Division Two to being the most feared side in the land, with major successes at home and in Europe. But the FA must have given serious thought to some aspects of Leeds's "tactics".

SOCCER SOUNDBITES

"I made the first move. They did not contact me. I fancied being England manager."

DON REVIE,
after his appointment.

Clough's reign at Leeds ends after 43 days

BRIAN CLOUGH'S short, uneasy association with Leeds ended abruptly on 12 September following a four-hour meeting at the club between him, his solicitor, and chairman Manny Cussins. A terse statement gave no indication as to why he was leaving.

His departure from Elland Road, however, only 43 days after he was appointed manager of the League champions in succession to Don Revie, further emphasizes the increasing power now wielded in League soccer by First Division players. One has to conclude that the main reason for his leaving is that the players didn't want him. At all events, yesterday's meeting came less than 24 hours after the senior squad were reported to have passed a vote of no confidence in their new boss shortly before the midweek League Cup tie at Huddersfield.

Mr Clough can scarcely have expected the players to love him, since he had been highly critical of Leeds as a team, and had singled out several individuals for attack, in print and on television, during his days as manager of Derby. Moreover, his recent purchase of John McGovern and John O'Hare, from Derby, while no reflection on the players personally, is unlikely to have improved dressing-room harmony.

According to Leeds, Mr Clough will receive a "reasonably substantial" golden handshake. He will need it, as Brighton, apparently, have no intention of withdrawing their writ against him for breach of contract.

SOCCER SOUNDBITES

"The Leeds United club and the happiness of the Leeds United players must come first."

MANNY CUSSINS,
Leeds chairman, commenting on the sudden departure of manager Brian Clough.

Nicholson resigns: players getting too difficult

SPURS CHIEF Bill Nicholson, 54, has resigned after 38 years with the club as player and manager. Although this has come as a shock to the outside world, apparently his disenchantment with the modern game — the modern player, in particular — has been building up. He stressed that his resignation had nothing to do with Spurs' poor start to the season — their worst for 62 years — and that, if Spurs had won the UEFA Cup last season, he would have gone then. He and the board, who tried to dissuade him, emphasized that he would not be retiring, but would stay on to help a new manager in some capacity if required.

As a player, Nicholson made over 300 League appearances for Spurs, and was a key member of the Championship-winning team of 1951, as well as winning one England cap and scoring with his first kick. He then guided them to the first League and Cup "double" this century, in 1961; two more FA Cups, the Cup-Winners' Cup in 1963, when Spurs were the first British club to win a European trophy; and the UEFA Cup in 1972.

Contractual problems and transfer requests have perhaps precipitated Mr Nicholson's decision, but it is his disaffection with the attitude of players that is the root cause, particularly the illegal demands that had become the norm from players who might have joined the club. He complained that the club were defeated over two transfers because they refused to break the regulations, and that the problem of under-the-counter payments had affected all of his negotiations in the past two seasons. Spurs chairman Sidney Wale claimed that the "going rate" for joining a London club was a demand for seven to 10 thousand pounds tax-free.

The thought is surely bound to strike someone that, if Mr Nicholson is no longer to be Spurs manager, there should be a place for him in the administration of the game, which has a desperate need for his unique brand of honesty.

SOCCER SOUNDBITES

"Players have become impossible. They talk all the time about security, but are not prepared to work for it. I am abused by players when they come to see me. There is no longer respect."

BILL NICHOLSON.

Nicholson: 38 years with Spurs.

Leeds beat Guy at last: non-Leaguers out

WIMBLEDON'S CUP exploits have come to an end at last, in the replayed fourth round tie with Leeds at Selhurst Park. Keeper Dickie Guy, who played a blinder at Burnley in the third round, when Wimbledon became the first post-war non-League side to beat a First Division club away, and saved a Peter Lorimer penalty eight minutes from time at Elland Road to take this tie to a replay, was finally beaten — but not by a Leeds player. Mighty Leeds needed an own goal by Dave Bassett to take them through in the end.

Dickie Guy, Wimbledon's goalkeeping hero, in action.

West Ham's Taylor-made win in Cockney final

IT WAS NOT A fairy-tale ending for Fulham at Wembley, as they went down 2–0 to West Ham in this Cockney Cup final. While most neutrals were behind the Second Division side, eager to pay homage to the grand old masters Bobby Moore and Alan Mullery, and manager Alec Stock, it was young Alan Taylor who won the glory with two goals after an hour of an otherwise unmemorable match.

It was more a case of Fulham losing the Cup, as Peter Mellor, the brave, agile giant of a keeper who had done so much to put them into the final, failed to hold shots from Jennings and Paddon, and the quicksilver Taylor was there to pounce. This was Taylor's third consecutive Cup double, after scoring all West Ham's goals in the sixth round at Arsenal and the semi-final replay with Ipswich — in his first season with the club.

After another Wembley anti-climax, it was a poignant moment when Moore and Mullery, in the twilight of their careers, slowly walked off the pitch they have graced for so many years, one arm around the other's shoulders, the other hand clutching a losers' medal. Sadder, though, was the sight of the young West Ham supporters' manic invasion of the pitch, ending in a crude attempt to taunt the disappointed Fulham fans and stripping the last vestiges of the old standards from the Cup final, which had already dispensed with "Abide with Me", the traditional Wembley hymn.

Bobby Moore (centre) is consoled by his former West Ham colleagues.

Second 'non-playing' title for Derby

DERBY HAVE WON their second League title in four seasons — again without having to kick a ball. In 1972, under Brian Clough, they were in Spain when their challengers failed to catch them. They didn't leave the country this time, as they still had a match to play, but Ipswich's failure to win at Maine Road means that Dave Mackay's men have done it.

In a season during which the First Division lead changed hands a record 21 times, Derby took over for the first time only on 9 April, and have seen off the challenges of Liverpool, Ipswich and Everton. It was good to see centre-half Roy McFarland back for the last few matches after his long injury, although young Peter Daniel has been a splendid replacement. Despite the forward power of Kevin Hector, Roger Davies and Francis Lee, midfielder Bruce Rioch is leading scorer with 15. Colin Todd was the players' choice as Footballer of the Year, and skipper Archie Gemmill also had a fine season. Above all, their success is a wonderful tribute to Mackay, who had the unenviable task of following in the footsteps of Brian Clough — and did so.

Derby County: 1975 League Champions.

Wembley scoring record for five-goal Macdonald

MALCOLM MACDONALD, the Newcastle marksman who thought his brief international career had ended when he was twice passed over by Don Revie, put his name firmly in the record books on 16 April by becoming the first player to score five goals in a Wembley international. His feat equals the England goalscoring record, and only Willie Hall in 1938 has also hit five for England this century.

Cyprus, admittedly, were weak opponents. Yet if Macdonald and the equally industrious Keegan had not gone foraging for themselves, England's goal difference in Group One of the European Championships might not now look so healthy — and this could be an important factor in deciding whether England reach the quarter-finals next year.

It all looked too easy when Macdonald headed Hudson's free-kick in after only two minutes. And although Keegan made a second for him after 35 minutes, frustration began to set in. We did not see the midfield smoothness that Hudson, Ball and Bell demonstrated in the Wembley win over West Germany last month. But another three headers in the second half gave England a comfortable 5–0 victory and Macdonald an indisputable claim on the match ball.

Macdonald, five-goal hero.

Leeds deprived of Euro glory again as fans compound misery

Riot squad in action, Parisian style, as Leeds fans turn ugly.

LEEDS'S VERY real hopes of European Cup glory, as they outplayed Bayern Munich for most of the final in Paris, turned into a nightmare as two late strikes by the Cup-holders plunged them to defeat and their so-called fans again disgraced themselves on the Continent.

Leeds forced the Germans on to the defensive when Swedish World Cup star Andersson was carried off after a clash with Yorath early on, and Bayern had to make another first-half substitution when Uli Hoeness limped off. Beckenbauer was twice lucky not to be penalized in the box, for handball and then a trip on Clarke, and Giles, Bremner, Lorimer and Jordan continued to keep Leeds on top in the second half. But the turning point came after 66 minutes, when Lorimer smashed the ball past Maier, only to have his effort disallowed for offside against his team-mates. The Leeds fans erupted violently at this decision, and the rioting became worse six minutes later, when Roth scored from a Bayern breakaway. Gerd Muller, who had spent much of his time helping out a beleaguered defence, then sealed Leeds's fate nine minutes from the end.

The hooligans continued their deplorable and menacing behaviour after the final whistle, as a result of which Leeds have been banned from Europe for three years.

Keegan back after England walk-out

AS DAVID JOHNSON of Ipswich was making a dream debut for England, scoring both goals and salvaging a draw with Wales at Wembley, Kevin Keegan, the Liverpool striker, was disappearing from the national team's Hertfordshire headquarters, the third player to take French leave from England in the last year. Manager Don Revie had left Keegan out of the Home International Championship match after the goalless draw in Northern Ireland.

This follows a pattern set by QPR forward Stan Bowles, who walked out on the England squad a year ago as they prepared for the match against Scotland, and continued by Ipswich defender Kevin Beattie, who went to his parents' home in Carlisle last December instead of reporting to an England Under-23 squad meeting in Manchester.

However, Keegan returned to the fold the next day and, after a heart-to-heart talk with Revie, was back in the side to face Scotland at Wembley. The Scots, badly missing their Leeds contingent, were well and truly thrashed 5–1, so England, after two unconvincing performances, have won the Home Championship.

FOOTBALL FOCUS

- Keegan and Bremner received unprecedented punishments for "bringing the game into disrepute" in the Charity Shield — a fine of £500 and suspension for what amounted to 11 matches.
- Bobby Charlton, as Preston player-manager, returned to football, albeit in Division Three, and scored 10 times in League and Cup, taking his League goals above the 200 mark.
- It was third time lucky for manager Ron Saunders, reaching his third League Cup final running, with different clubs — Norwich, Manchester City, and now Aston Villa, who gave him his first success.
- Wales went top of their European Championship qualifying group with the aid of a double over Hungary, following a 2–0 home victory on 30 October by sensationally winning 2–1 in Budapest on 16 April, Hungary's first post-war home defeat in a competitive match.
- Celtic's League supremacy in Scotland (nine wins in a row) came to an end, and skipper Billy McNeill retired after leading them to victory in the Cup (their seventh successive final). In a reorganization of Scottish football next season, there will be a Premier League of 10 clubs and a First and a Second Division of 14 clubs each.

FINAL SCORE

Football League
Division 1: Derby County
Top scorer: Malcolm Macdonald (Newcastle United) 21
Division 2: Manchester United
Division 3: Blackburn Rovers
Division 4: Mansfield Town
Footballer of the Year: Alan Mullery (Fulham)

FA Cup Final
West Ham United 2 Fulham 0

League Cup Final
Aston Villa 1 Norwich City 0

Scottish League
Division 1: Rangers
Top scorer: Andy Gray (Dundee United), Willie Pettigrew (Motherwell) 20
Division 2: Falkirk
Footballer of the Year: Sandy Jardine (Rangers)

Scottish FA Cup Final
Celtic 3 Airdrieonians 1

Scottish League Cup Final
Celtic 6 Hibernian 3

International Championship
England, 4 pts

European Cup Final
Bayern Munich 2 Leeds United 0

Cup-Winners' Cup Final
Dynamo Kiev 3 Ferencvaros 0

UEFA Cup Final
Borussia Moenchengladbach beat Twente Enschede 0–0, 5–1

European Footballer of the Year 1974
Johan Cruyff (Barcelona & Holland)

Leading European Scorer (Golden Boot)
Dudu Georgescu (Dinamo Bucharest) 33

World Club Championship
Competition not held

Doyle carts off another medal as he inspires City to Wembley win

WHEN MIKE DOYLE looks back on his fourth appearance at Wembley for Manchester City, he may well conclude that this was the afternoon on which he reached the peak of an illustrious one-club career that has brought him every major prize domestic soccer can offer. During City's 2–1 League Cup victory over Newcastle, Doyle scaled heights rarely attained by players even in more glamorous competitions. As marshal of defence, instigator of counter-attacks, crucial contributor to the all-important opening goal and, above all, as a calm, authoritative captain, this elegant footballer gave a superb performance — comparable with that of Franz Beckenbauer when West Germany beat England at Wembley four years ago. Even so, City did not control the game as firmly as they should have, after a carefully rehearsed move enabled Doyle to head down a free-kick for Peter Barnes to score in the 12th minute. As they sat back, somewhat complacently, Newcastle equalized in the 34th minute when Alan Gowling finished off one of the slickest moves of the match.

The winning goal came seconds after the interval, when Dennis Tueart scored with a spectacular bicycle-kick after Tommy Booth had headed a cross back into the middle. Newcastle staged a grandstand finish, but Doyle made sure City stayed ahead to the final whistle.

Tueart goes horizontal to hit City's winner.

Liverpool pip QPR for title after fright from Wolves

LIVERPOOL WON the League Championship for a record ninth time amid tumultuous scenes at Molineux, when they came back from a goal down at half-time to win 3–1 and consign Wolves at the same time to Second Division football next season. And QPR's 10-day wait, as they sat on top of the table with a one-point lead, ended in disappointment. They fought a brave fight all season, and took 27 points from their last 15 games, but Liverpool dropped only one point in their last nine, and their total of 60 points was good enough.

Wolves had to win to stand a chance of staying up, and took the lead through Kindon after 12 minutes. Keegan and Heighway began to open up the Wolves defence but, as the minutes continued to go by, one's mind went back to 1972 when Leeds were thwarted at Molineux in a similar situation. But Bob Paisley brought Fairclough on for Case in the 65th minute and, 12 minutes later, Keegan powered the ball in from Toshack's nod down. That would have been enough to give Liverpool the title, but in the last five minutes Toshack and Kennedy made sure.

SOCCER SOUNDBITES

"Bill Shankly set such a high standard. Liverpool have been geared to this sort of thing for 15 years. I have just helped things along."

BOB PAISLEY,
Liverpool's ever-modest manager.

Bradford rise from sick beds to give Canaries dose of own medicine

FIRST DIVISION NORWICH, so often the giant-killers of the past, went down 2–1 at home to Bradford City, who become the third Division Four side to reach the quarter-finals of the FA Cup. Barely back off their sick beds after influenza had twice been the cause of postponements, Bradford were about to sink to their knees from exhaustion when Billy McGinley blocked a clearance and scored the winner two minutes from time in what was their only attack of the second half.

Bradford defended magnificently throughout, rode their luck, and scored with their only two chances. They took a brief lead six minutes from half-time with a solo effort from diminutive left-winger Don Hutchins, which was soon equalized by Martin Peters's header. Near the end, Norwich hit the woodwork twice and had a goal disallowed, before Bradford got their shock winner.

Wreckers on the rampage again

WITH THE SEASON only two weeks old, hooligans have already plunged the game into an abyss of despond. In one of the blackest days for British football to date, behaviour at grounds in various parts of the country plumbed new depths. The Chelsea following in the Second Division match at Luton sparked off violent scenes when they swarmed on to the pitch after their team had gone three down in the second half. They attacked players, police and stewards — one steward was knifed, another had his nose broken — and play was suspended for five minutes. Luton keeper Barber, who was earlier pelted with coins, was punched on the back of the head. The violence continued after the match, in the Luton streets and on the trains back to London, as the rampaging hooligans left a trail of vandalized cars, shops and railway carriages in their wake.

More than 100 Chelsea fans were arrested, and other black spots included Ibrox (60 arrests) and Stoke, where 50 of Manchester United's thugs were apprehended. The so-called "English disease" is still spreading and getting more virulent. Implementation of the findings of the government working party on crowd behaviour published a month ago cannot come soon enough, but it will be a massive and expensive task.

Bremner is one of six given life ban by Scotland

THE LONG, COLOURFUL, often controversial international career of Billy Bremner, captain of Scotland and Leeds, came to a sad and ignominious, if not entirely unpredictable, end in Glasgow on 8 September, when the Scottish selectors decided that he and four others should never play for their country again. The others banned following an investigation of alleged misconduct after last week's European Championship qualifier in Copenhagen were Joe Harper (Hibs), Pat McCluskey (Celtic), and Willie Young and Arthur Graham (Aberdeen). Bremner, 32, has won 54 Scottish caps, one fewer than Denis Law's record.

All five players were said to be involved in incidents at a Copenhagen night club and in the squad's hotel later. Bremner vehemently denied the charges over the weekend, but the committee accepted detailed reports of officials without calling on the players concerned. It was obvious that the committee, conscious of the current concern over hooliganism, would take a hard line.

Stokes fires Saints to stun Red Devils

SECOND DIVISION Southampton stunned hot favourites Manchester United at Wembley with a late goal from Bobby Stokes to win the first major honour in their 91-year history. Not since 1939, when Portsmouth also ridiculed the odds by defeating Wolves, has the South of England had so much to shout about on Cup final day. And the last time Southampton reached the Cup final, in 1902, they were in the Southern League and had the immortal C.B.Fry in their team.

United, who 10 days earlier still had hopes of the "double", failed to play up to their high standards, with the exception of Martin Buchan, their elegant captain, and his partner in central defence, Brian Greenhoff. They also failed utterly to prove that the reintroduction of a pair of conventional wingers is the answer to English soccer's prayers, and Tommy Docherty ultimately abandoned the policy by pulling off Gordon Hill after 66 ineffective minutes and replacing him with David McCreery.

Southampton, whose confidence had been growing as McCalliog gradually took midfield control away from the quietly fading Macari and Daly, now sensed their opponents were seriously worried, and pushed forward even more purposefully, with the eager Stokes, the surprisingly industrious Osgood and the fleet-footed Channon frequently harassing United's defence and testing the watchful Stepney.

At last, seven minutes from time, Stokes raced on to a beautifully judged through-pass from McCalliog and calmly placed a low, firm, left-foot shot wide of the diving keeper, fulfilling a prediction last week by jubilant manager Lawrie McMenemy that he would score the winner at Wembley.

SOCCER SOUNDBITES

"This is the first time that the Cup final will be played at Hillsborough... The other semi-final is a bit of a joke, really."

TOMMY DOCHERTY,
Manchester United manager, after his side were drawn to play Derby in the semi-finals, with Southampton facing Third Division Crystal Palace.

Stepney is left down and out by Stokes's winner for Southampton.

Hearts broken as Rangers clinch 'treble'

FOR THE THIRD TIME in their history, Rangers completed the "treble" when they beat Hearts 3–1 in the Scottish Cup final at Hampden. With the inaugural Premier League title and the League Cup already won, they rammed home their superiority from the start. They took only 41 seconds to find the back of Hearts' net: Jim Jeffries fouled Derek Johnstone and, from Tommy McLean's free-kick, the tall Johnstone outjumped the Hearts defence to head strongly in.

After such a great start, Rangers' victory never looked in doubt. Chances were missed by both sides, however, before they increased their lead just before half-time through Alex MacDonald, who shot home through a ruck of players following a corner. Continuous Rangers pressure brought them their third goal — and Johnstone's second — in the 81st minute and, a couple of minutes later, Graham Shaw tapped in Hearts' consolation.

Hearts' keeper Cruickshank is beaten by Johnstone (out of picture).

Revival raises Anfield hopes for return

A MAGNIFICENT second-half comeback enabled Liverpool to wipe out Bruges's early two-goal advantage and gain a narrow but richly deserved win in the first leg of the UEFA Cup final at Anfield on 28 April. Three goals in five hectic minutes accounted for the surprised Belgians and, after one of Liverpool's most remarkable performances in 12 successive years of European competition, they have high hopes of aggregate victory in the return in three weeks' time.

The 50,000 crowd, stunned to silence as Lambert and Cools scored after five and 12 minutes, almost raised the roof when Liverpool, ever resolute, hit back on the hour. The atmosphere was electric, reminiscent of Anfield's most memorable European nights, as Liverpool attacked their favourite Kop end in the second half. They drew level with a splendid 20-yarder from the busy Kennedy, after Keegan and Heighway had linked up on the left, and a simple tap-in from substitute Case after Kennedy, put through by Keegan, had driven the ball against the far post. They then rounded off the revival when Keegan scored from the spot after Heighway was brought down.

Keegan scores from the spot to give Liverpool a first-leg lead.

Dutch double and Holland trip contribute to Hammers' downfall in Belgium

Holland (far right) gives West Ham a first-half lead against Anderlecht.

WEST HAM FAILED to repeat their Cup-Winners' Cup triumph of 11 years ago at Wembley, as this time they were the "away" side, and Anderlecht beat them 4–2 in Brussels. Yet they might have defeated the Belgians, but for a defensive error just before the interval that lost them the initiative of a goal lead. Dutch World Cup star Robert Rensenbrink was outstanding for Anderlecht.

West Ham appeared in command after taking the lead with a goal by Pat Holland in the 29th minute. Then, three minutes before half-time, a misjudged back-pass from Frank Lampard left keeper Mervyn Day stranded, and Ressel pushed the ball inside for Rensenbrink to score easily.

Soon after the interval, Rensenbrink put Van der Elst through to give Anderlecht the lead, although the Hammers fought back with skill and courage and equalized in the 66th minute, when the tireless Trevor Brooking worked his way to the left byline and curled a centre into the goalmouth for "Pop" Robson to head in off a post. But West Ham never looked in charge in the second half, and Rensenbrink and fellow Dutchman Ari Haan began to launch quick counter-attacks. In one of these, Holland brought down Rensenbrink, who scored from the spot.

Anderlecht, now playing beautiful football, made sure of victory a few minutes from the end, when Rensenbrink, again, found Van der Elst with a long through-pass, and the little winger rounded John McDowell and Day before popping the ball into the net.

FINAL SCORE

EUROPEAN CHAMPIONSHIP 1976

QUARTER-FINALS

Spain v West Germany 1–1, 0–2
Holland v Belgium 5–0, 2–1
Czechoslovakia v USSR 2–0, 2–2
Yugoslavia v Wales 2–0, 1–1

Last four in Yugoslavia

SEMI-FINALS

Czechoslovakia	3	Holland	1
(after extra time)			
West Germany	4	Yugoslavia	2

THIRD-PLACE MATCH

Holland	3	Yugoslavia	2

FINAL

Czechoslovakia	2	West Germany	2
(after extra time)			

Czechoslovakia won 5–3 on penalties
Belgrade, 20 June 1976. Attendance 45,000

Czechoslovakia: Viktor, Dobias (Vesely F), Pivarnik, Ondrus, Capkovic, Gogh, Moder, Panenka, Svehlik (Jurkemik), Masny, Nehoda (Scorers: Svehlik, Dobias)
West Germany: Maier, Vogts, Beckenbauer, Schwarzenbeck, Dietz, Bonhof, Wimmer (Flohe), Muller D, Beer (Bongartz), Hoeness, Holzenbein (Scorers: Muller, Holzenbein)

FOOTBALL FOCUS

- Bobby Charlton resigned as Preston manager on 21 August over a dispute with the directors about transfers.
- Aston Villa defender Chris Nicholl scored all four goals in their 2–2 draw with Leicester on 20 March!
- Real Madrid achieved a remarkable comeback against Derby County (for whom Charlie George scored four goals in the two legs) in the second round of the European Cup, returning from 4–1 down in the first leg, to take the second 5–1 after extra time. But they lost in the semis to Bayern Munich, who went on to win their third successive trophy by beating St. Etienne 1–0 at Hampden Park.
- Two of England's top strikers signed for Belgian clubs, Duncan McKenzie (£250,000) went to Anderlecht from Leeds, and Roger Davies (£130,000) to Bruges from Derby.
- The Football League arrived in the 20th century on 4 June, when they decided to replace the antediluvian goal average system for determining League positions by goal difference from next season.
- Jimmy Hill, managing director of Coventry City, signed a long-term contract to be Saudi Arabia's London-based soccer supremo, appointing coaches, officials and administrators.

The goal that won Bayern Munich their third European Cup.

SOCCER SOUNDBITES

"I refuse to have players at the club that I don't want... If they [the directors] want to have somebody to carry out their decisions, they can get anyone to do that!"

BOBBY CHARLTON,
on resigning from Preston.

"I have become increasingly disillusioned with the way English football is heading. I am sad and frustrated by some of the trends in the game."

MALCOLM ALLISON,
on resigning from Crystal Palace.

Liverpool's Cup as battered red wall stands firm

LIVERPOOL, England's newly confirmed champions, completed a magnificent double in the Olympia Stadium on 19 May, when their second-leg 1–1 draw against Bruges, who had also won their national championship, was enough to give them the UEFA Cup for the second time in four years. Their task in this hard-fought final was never easy but, after Kevin Keegan had equalized an early penalty, Liverpool's formidable defence stood firm.

After the two goals had been scored in a hectic opening 15 minutes, Liverpool set out to contain a series of Bruges attacks, absorb the pressure, and break quickly from the back when their rare chances came. It was such a break that enabled them to hit back after Raoul Lambert's penalty, conceded for a Smith handball. Neal was fouled on the edge of the Bruges box, Hughes tapped the free-kick to Keegan, and the newly elected Footballer of the Year lashed a right-foot shot into goal from 18 yards.

The defence performed valiantly, with heads, bodies and legs blocking a succession of shots and headers and, although Jensen in the Bruges goal had little to do, Keegan's control and pace kept their defence on the alert. Clemence was lucky to see a tremendous shot from Lambert hit a post soon after the interval, but he made a vital stop from Van Gool four minutes from time that saved Liverpool from defeat.

Keegan (arm raised) celebrates his crucial goal.

FINAL SCORE

Football League
Division 1: Liverpool
Top scorer: Ted MacDougall (Norwich City) 23
Division 2: Sunderland
Division 3: Hereford United
Division 4: Lincoln City
Footballer of the Year: Kevin Keegan (Liverpool)

FA Cup Final
Southampton 1 Manchester United 0

League Cup Final
Manchester City 2 Newcastle United 1

Scottish League
Premier Division: Rangers
Top scorer: Kenny Dalglish (Celtic) 24
Division 1: Partick Thistle
Division 2: Clydebank
Footballer of the Year: John Greig (Rangers)

Scottish FA Cup Final
Rangers 3 Hearts 1

Scottish League Cup Final
Rangers 1 Celtic 0

International Championship
Scotland, 6 pts

European Cup Final
Bayern Munich 1 St Etienne 0

Cup-Winners' Cup Final
Anderlecht 4 West Ham United 2

UEFA Cup Final
Liverpool beat FC Bruges 3–2, 1–1

European Footballer of the Year 1975
Oleg Blokhin (Dynamo Kiev & USSR)

Leading European Scorer (Golden Boot)
Sotiris Kaiafas (Omonia Nicosia) 39

World Club Championship
Bayern Munich (West Germany) beat Cruzeiro (Brazil) 2–0, 0–0

Czechs annex European prize: Germans pay the penalty

IN A DRAMATIC European Championship final in Belgrade, Czechoslovakia won the trophy for the first time when they defeated the holders and World Cup champions West Germany on penalties. The Germans, those marvellous survivors, had fought back from a 2–0 deficit, their equalizer coming in the last seconds of normal time. There was no further scoring in extra time, and it was a travesty of a fine game — and a splendid tournament — that it should have to be settled by the iniquitous penalty shoot-out.

Czechoslovakia matched the Germans in every department, and bewildered them with a series of cross-field movements, with Masny their constant inspiration. Their attacking football paid dividends after only eight minutes, when Svehlik drove the ball into an open goal with Maier stranded. In the 26th minute, a Masny free-kick was blocked to Dobias, who scored from 25 yards.

The Germans, who had been two down in the semi-finals too, replied immediately, when Dieter Muller, the hat-trick hero against Yugoslavia, scored with an acrobatic volley. The football remained of the highest standard, in keeping with the rest of the matches in Yugoslavia, and it seemed that Czechoslovakia were home and dry, before Holzenbein stunned everyone by heading in a Bonhof corner to take the match into extra time. There were no more goals, and eventually the unfortunate Uli Hoeness drove his penalty high and wide, leaving Panenka to win the game for Czechoslovakia.

Panenka turns after hitting the decisive Czech penalty.

England World Cup hopes crash in Rome

ENGLAND FLEW HOME from Rome beaten for the first time in the current World Cup qualifying tournament and with their hopes of reaching the finals in Argentina in 1978 flickering only faintly. The sad fact is that England played as well as they were able, but could never match the liquid skills of the Italian master craftsmen. That is even more depressing than the 2–0 scoreline.

To prevent Italy lining up in the last 16, Don Revie's men almost certainly will have to win the return match, preferably by three clear goals, because the other nations in the group, Finland and Luxembourg, are merely making up the numbers.

Italy's first goal came after 36 minutes, following a foul on Causio just outside England's penalty box. Causio tapped the ball to Antognoni, who drove it at the England wall and got a crucial deflection off Keegan's body. A rout seemed on, but Italy allowed England back into the game — at least until 12 minutes from time, when they sealed victory with a brilliant second goal. Causio found Benetti on the left and, as his low cross came over, Bettega launched himself at it to head past Clemence in goal.

Bettega's spectacular header clinches the game for Italy.

Dutch masters put shaky England on canvas

IT WAS ONLY a friendly, but England's hopes of lifting their sagging morale following last autumn's World Cup defeat by Italy were soon shattered at Wembley on 9 February, when Holland, playing smooth, attacking football, moved into a two-goal lead before half-time and stayed in control throughout.

The Dutch masters quickly took charge in midfield, where Greenhoff alone, before he was injured and replaced by Todd after 34 minutes, offered England much prospect of success, and soon Revie's defenders were under heavy pressure. This was turned into goals by Jan Peters, who scored in the 30th and 39th minute, the first set up by Cruyff and Neeskens, the second by new cap Hovencamp.

Cruyff, indeed, seemed to be everywhere, and Madeley ultimately gave up trying to mark him. England tried to get back into the game, with Bowles and Francis spearheading one or two purposeful looking raids, although Keegan was having a quiet time for him. The attack received little help from midfield, however, and Holland soon reassumed complete control. Their performance was "the best at Wembley since the Hungarians in 1953", according to England manager Don Revie.

Record for super Bowles as QPR spill Cologne

QUEEN'S PARK RANGERS, at their scintillating best, took another impressive stride towards a major trophy in their first European season with the demolition of Cologne in the UEFA Cup third round, first leg at Loftus Road. Goals by Don Givens, David Webb and Stan Bowles took their tally to 22 in five UEFA matches so far, and Bowles, who has now collected 10 of them, broke the British joint record of Dennis Viollet, Denis Law and Derek Dougan for European goals in one season.

For the first time, QPR met worthy opposition, and they will not underestimate the Germans in the return leg, for they played attractive football throughout, and Parkes had to make three outstanding saves from Mueller in the second half. But with Rangers playing their exciting brand of attacking football, and Bowles at his most impudent, Rangers forced Cologne on to the defensive and struck with two goals just before the interval, both set up by Thomas and McLintock. Bowles crowned a splendid QPR performance with a superb goal 15 minutes from the end. Picking up the ball just outside the box, he dribbled round three defenders, walked up to the keeper Schumacher and coolly rounded him before slipping the ball into the net.

Little goals mean a lot as Villa end marathon

AFTER AN EPIC 5½-hour battle, Aston Villa finally won the League Cup when Brian Little scored the second of his goals in the last minutes of extra time to beat Everton 3–2 in this second replay at Old Trafford. Compared with the somewhat tame afternoon at Wembley in the first match in March, and the replay at Hillsborough, the atmosphere was electric. Both teams also played with much more endeavour, but, alas, the football was no better.

Everton seemed to be moving towards victory with a 38th-minute goal by Latchford, when there was suddenly a flurry of goals. First Nicholl equalized 10 minutes from time with a ferocious 35-yard left-foot drive, and then Little ran at the Everton defence and lashed the ball home a minute later to give Villa the lead. Everton, stunned as they were, came back and drew level again through Lyons, who headed in after a corner.

So the match went into extra time again and, just as a penalty decider looked ominously certain, Little burst through the tired Everton defence to convert a centre and produce a fitting climax to a thrilling match.

Little's late winner ends marathon final.

Jack Charlton joins the exodus of managers

JACK CHARLTON'S resignation from Middlesbrough on 21 April completes a flurry of managerial drop-outs in the Football League over the last couple of days. Like his erstwhile team-mate at Leeds, Johnny Giles, who resigned from West Bromwich Albion the day before, Charlton will leave at the end of the season. Two other managers, however, did not just go — they were pushed. Tony Waiters was sacked at Plymouth, while Stockport have decided to part company with Eddie Quigley for reasons of economy.

Charlton has become increasingly disenchanted at the lack of enthusiasm shown by local supporters after he guided the team to Division One in his first season, 1973–74. This season, Middlesbrough were top in October, but have since slumped to mid-table.

At West Bromwich, chairman Bert Millichip tried to make player-manager Giles change his mind. Giles, who also had taken his club into the First Division, has made no secret of the fact that the insecurity of football management disturbs him, but emphasized that he had no disagreement with anyone at the club. He will have done the game a service if his comments cause directors throughout the country to reflect: in the last 10 months, 33 League clubs have changed managers. "The job should come with a health warning," says Giles.

Jack Charlton: disenchanted.

SOCCER SOUNDBITES

"We are on the crest of a slump."

JACK CHARLTON,
a few days before resigning from Middlesbrough.

"Football, and management, are precarious professions. There is so much fear in the game, it spreads like the plague."

JOHNNY GILES,
on resigning from West Brom.

Old Firm double for Conn as Lynch hangs one on Rangers

CELTIC HAD TO FIGHT all the way to beat Rangers in the Scottish Cup final at Hampden — so completing their League and Cup "double" — with their goal coming from a penalty by Andy Lynch in the 20th minute, after Johnstone had handled a chip from Celtic skipper Dalglish. And ex-Spurs star Alfie Conn made history by becoming the first player to win Cup medals with both Old Firm clubs. He won his medal with Rangers when they beat Celtic 3–2 in the final in 1973. Now, after a spell with Spurs, he's done it for Celtic, too.

Rangers' finishing was poor, with their twin strikers Parlane and Johnstone out of touch. Celtic had more trouble from Robertson, the Rangers substitute, who twice went close to equalizing near the end.

In the rain, the game deteriorated into a succession of fouls. The poor attendance, 54,000, the lowest for more than 50 years, was due partly to the miserable weather, but mainly to live television.

Celtic's history-making Alfie Conn in the thick of the action.

Fans to be caged next season after increased rowdiness

THERE WAS A disturbing end to the League season on many grounds, and fans at Stamford Bridge at least will be fenced in behind iron railings next season. There was even trouble at Anfield, where Liverpool played safely for a goalless draw with West Ham to make sure of retaining their League title, but were prevented from celebrating by hordes of young fans.

Hooligans purporting to be fêting the success of Wolves and Chelsea in the Second Division and of Brighton in the Third, and lamenting Tottenham's departure from the First, staged much uglier demonstrations. Chelsea's chairman Brian Mears was so disturbed by the wild behaviour at Stamford Bridge that he has already given orders for iron fences to be erected all round the ground next season. One celebration not marred by fans was that of Nottingham Forest, who won the third promotion place to Division One when Bolton lost at home to Wolves. Champagne must have been flowing in Forest's Majorca hotel — the same one in which their boss Brian Clough celebrated five years ago when his Derby County team won the League, thanks that time also to a Wolves victory!

An all-too-typical scene of soccer in the Seventies — a pitch invasion at Stamford Bridge.

Liverpool's 'treble' chance dashed: United's bold football triumphs

MANCHESTER UNITED beat Liverpool 2–1 at Wembley in a Cup final that went some way towards restoring faith, not only in football but in the behaviour of the fans. Champions Liverpool, their "treble" dreams shattered, will have a difficult task picking themselves up for Wednesday's European Cup final in Rome.

Sanity and sportsmanship came back to soccer on Saturday, with "Abide with Me" rendered with soul-stirring passion at the start, and the much-maligned United fans chanting "Liverpool, Liverpool" to salute their beaten rivals at the end.

United manager Tommy Docherty deserves great credit for not abandoning their policy of bold football after last year's Wembley defeat and failure in Europe this season. His response to those setbacks was to buy another attacking player, Jimmy Greenhoff, elder brother of Brian. And it was Jimmy who played a crucial part in taking United to the final, with the opening goal in the semi-final against Leeds, his former club. Greenhoff also scored the winner at Wembley — a fluke, as he admitted later. Trying to get out of the way of a Lou Macari shot (which was going wide), he deflected the ball over keeper Clemence and into goal. All the goals were crammed into a flurry of activity between the 50th and 55th minutes. Stuart Pearson had opened the scoring for United, racing through to hammer the ball in after Jimmy Greenhoff, again, had flicked it over Emlyn Hughes.

Macari and (behind him) Greenhoff celebrate their joint effort.

Two minutes later, Liverpool responded like true champions. Case, the game's outstanding player, controlled a centre on his thigh, turned and then drove one of the best Cup final goals for years into the roof of the net.

Ray Kennedy came closest to equalizing when he hammered a shot against the bar late on, but Liverpool had spurned their best chances in the first half, and United went on to win the most sporting, skilful and exciting final seen at Wembley for many a year.

Night of triumph for Paisley and Co.

LIVERPOOL'S 13 consecutive seasons of campaigning in European competitions reached a memorable climax at the Olympic Stadium in Rome on 25 May, when they won the major trophy, the European Cup, with one of the most distinguished performances of their long history. The League champions swept Borussia Moenchengladbach to decisive defeat with the smoothly skilled, intelligent football we had come to believe was now a Continental monopoly.

Any doubts as to the effect of Saturday's disappointing Wembley visit on Bob Paisley's men were allayed in the first quarter of an hour. With Case, Kennedy, Callaghan and in particular McDermott using the ball proficiently and running alertly into space, Liverpool soon commanded midfield. And Liverpool's front line of Keegan and Heighway looked much sharper than at Wembley.

It was no surprise when they took the lead after 28 minutes. McDermott spotted a gap, raced through it on to Heighway's perfectly timed pass, and hit the ball hard and low into the far corner of the net. But Liverpool lapsed into carelessness six minutes into the second half, and Simonsen pounced on Case's misplaced pass, sped into the box and lashed a fierce shot past Clemence.

For 10 minutes, Liverpool lost their composure as Borussia, sensing they could steal victory, pushed forward eagerly. Appropriately, however, it was Tommy Smith, making his farewell appearance for the club, who came to the rescue. Due to retire at the end of the season, he was brought back into the team only a couple of months ago when Phil Thompson was injured. As two defenders followed Keegan, Smith moved into the vacated space to head a corner from Heighway forcefully into the net. Then, seven minutes from time, Keegan, who was also playing his last match in Liverpool colours before leaving for Hamburg, and who had led Vogts a merry dance all evening, went on a determined run into the box. Vogts could only pull him down, and Neal scored emphatically from the spot. At last Liverpool had translated their undoubted domestic domination into supremacy in Europe.

Footballer of the Year Emlyn Hughes received the trophy, to spark a night of prolonged — but thankfully well-behaved — celebrations among the thousands of supporters who had travelled to cheer the team.

Case (8) watches as Smith heads the all-important second goal.

Fans take Wembley turf... and gloss off Scottish victory

WHATEVER PLEASURE Scotland got from winning a dreadful match was spoilt by the hordes of their puerile, drunken fans who invaded the Wembley pitch at the end to celebrate by breaking both sets of goal-posts, ripping out the nets, and cutting out pieces of turf to take home as trophies of their triumph.

At least the Scots had the consolation of retaining the Home Championship. But England will have gained nothing from this hard, ill-tempered, disagreeable match of low technical and tactical quality other than a severe dent in their morale prior to their upcoming tour of South America. Scotland gave a competent, spirited performance, and achieved a merited 2–1 victory thanks largely to McGrain's polished defensive and attacking football, the midfield industry of Hartford, Masson's precise placing of the dead ball, the persistence of Dalglish and Macari, and the commanding presence of McQueen. England lost chiefly because they were overwhelmed in midfield, even before the departure of the injured Brian Greenhoff.

Scotland took control in the 42nd minute when McQueen headed home Masson's free-kick. Despite the loss of Jordan immediately afterwards, they remained on top, and Dalglish popped in No.2 in the 63rd minute. Three minutes from the end, Channon scored England's belated goal from a penalty after Francis was brought down. Then came the invasion.

SOCCER SOUNDBITES

"Another afternoon of British rubbish."

Disenchanted voice in the
WEMBLEY PRESS BOX.

Dalglish (left) beats Neal and Hughes to score Scotland's second.

Scottish fans disgrace themselves on the Wembley turf.

FINAL SCORE

Football League
Division 1: Liverpool
Top scorer: Andy Gray (Aston Villa), Malcolm Macdonald (Arsenal) 25
Division 2: Wolverhampton Wanderers
Division 3: Mansfield Town
Division 4: Cambridge United
Footballer of the Year: Emlyn Hughes (Liverpool)

FA Cup Final

Manchester United	2	Liverpool	1

League Cup Final

Aston Villa	0	Everton	0
Replay: Aston Villa (after extra time)	1	Everton	1
Replay: Aston Villa (after extra time)	3	Everton	2

Scottish League
Premier Division: Celtic
Top scorer: Willie Pettigrew (Motherwell) 21
Division 1: St Mirren
Division 2: Stirling Albion
Footballer of the Year: Danny McGrain (Celtic)

Scottish FA Cup Final

Celtic	1	Rangers	0

Scottish League Cup Final

Aberdeen (after extra time)	2	Celtic	1

International Championship
Scotland, 5 pts

European Cup Final

Liverpool	3	B Moenchengladbach	1

Cup-Winners' Cup Final

SV Hamburg	2	Anderlecht	0

UEFA Cup Final
Juventus beat Athletic Bilbao 1–0, 1–2 on away goals

European Footballer of the Year 1976
Franz Beckenbauer (Bayern Munich & West Germany)

Leading European Scorer (Golden Boot)
Dudu Georgescu (Dinamo Bucharest) 47

World Club Championship
Boca Juniors (Arg) beat Borussia Moenchengladbach (W.Ger) 2–2, 3–0

FOOTBALL FOCUS

- George Best scored within 71 seconds of his debut for Fulham on 9 September and, on 2 October, the day red and yellow cards were introduced in the Football League, became one of the first players to receive a red card, sent off at Southampton for foul and abusive language.
- Republic of Ireland manager Johnny Giles awarded himself a record 48th cap on 30 March, and his side beat France 1–0 in Dublin in a World Cup qualifier.
- Bobby Moore played his 1,000th and last first-class game in Fulham's match at Blackburn, on 14 May, before retiring.
- Ex-England winger Terry Paine retired at the end of the season with a record 824 Football League appearances to his name, 713 for Southampton and 111 for Hereford.
- Wales beat England 1–0 in the Home Championship on 31 May, their first ever win at Wembley.
- Liverpool's Kevin Keegan signed for Hamburg on 3 June for £500,000, a record for a British club.
- Renowned Cup fighters Wimbledon of the Southern League were elected to the League in place of Workington, who finished bottom of Division Four.

Terry Paine of Hereford acknowledges the applause of his former club-mates at the Dell as he embarks on his 806th League appearance in his last season.

Revie defects to Middle East: FA read about it in papers

NOT ONLY HAS Don Revie resigned as England manager, as announced on 12 July in a national newspaper, but he has agreed to work in the United Arab Emirates for the next four years at a tax-free £60,000 a year plus bonuses — a contract he presumably negotiated while still England manager.

Don Revie: deserts to desert.

Revie, formerly an outstanding club manager with Leeds, had a mediocre record as national supremo with only 14 wins in 29 internationals during his three years at the helm. He was expected to remain in the post at least until the last World Cup qualifying match against Italy in November, even though it would need something out of the ordinary — Luxembourg drawing in Italy — for England to reach Argentina. Meanwhile, there is inevitable speculation as to Revie's successor. But Revie's tenure of office has been a cautionary tale for current aspirants, as he has discovered a vast gulf between the day-to-day running of a League club and the management of the national team.

SOCCER SOUNDBITES

"Don Revie's decision doesn't surprise me in the slightest. Now I only hope he can quickly learn how to call out bingo numbers in Arabic."

ALAN HARDAKER,
Football League secretary.

"The committee unanimously deplores the action of Don Revie... and the FA is taking legal advice."

TED CROKER,
FA secretary.

Revie accused of match-fixing attempts

NEW ALLEGATIONS have emerged of an attempt to "fix" the Wolves-Leeds League match in 1972, a game Leeds needed only to draw to complete the "double". They were made in an article in the Daily Mirror on 6 September, which also dealt with the rise of Don Revie, the former Leeds and England manager, now based in Dubai. The article alleged that a former Wolves and Leeds player acted as middleman in an unsuccessful attempt to guarantee Leeds at least the point they needed. An earlier investigation by the League failed to substantiate similar claims, and League secretary Mr Alan Hardaker said the only thing new to him was the name of the supposed go-between.

Further accusations have been made in the Mirror and the Sunday People concerning other attempts on the part of Mr Revie — and Leeds captain Billy Bremner — to affect the results of matches, and the names of several witnesses have been published. Both Revie and Bremner have denied all allegations, but the FA have ordered a top-level inquiry.

Dalglish to Anfield for record £400,000

LIVERPOOL HAVE kept faith with their supporters by spending a large proportion of the £500,000 they received for Kevin Keegan to purchase Kenny Dalglish, the pride of Celtic and Scotland, as his replacement. The League and European champions indicated, when reluctantly agreeing to release Keegan last May, that they would reinvest the largest sum ever received by a League club as soon as the right player became available. They kept their word on 10 August by paying a British record fee of £400,000 to persuade Celtic to allow Dalglish, 27, to move to Anfield.

Although expensive, this signing could be the shrewdest move Bob Paisley has made since becoming manager just over two years ago. Liverpool needed an outstanding footballer to replace a player of Keegan's ability and charisma. Like Keegan, the personable Scot can play up front or in midfield. Indeed, in Scotland, he is considered a better player than England's captain in the deeper position and at least his equal further forward.

That record-breaking style: Dalglish (centre) in action for Celtic.

Docherty sacked for breaking 'moral code'

TWENTY-FOUR HOURS after Manchester United chairman Louis Edwards declared that reports of the impending departure of their manager were "nonsense", Tommy Docherty has been sacked. Docherty, 49, has paid the penalty for having a love affair with the wife of club physiotherapist Laurie Brown. He has been held to have breached his contract, presumably on the grounds that he has brought the club's reputation into disrepute.

At a Press conference two weeks ago, after news of the liaison had broken, Docherty said he thought that he and Mr Brown could still work amicably together. The club obviously thought otherwise. Docherty, only six weeks after steering United to victory in the FA Cup, is understandably shattered at what he described as an "abrupt" dismissal. He brought post-Busby success to the club after Wilf McGuinness and Frank O'Farrell had tried and failed.

Caretaker Greenwood gets England supremo job

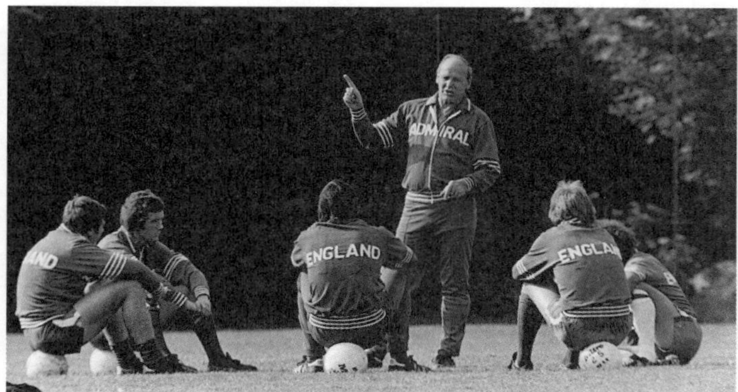

Ron Greenwood: new England supremo.

RON GREENWOOD, who has been managing the England side on a temporary basis since last August, has been made supremo, with a contract until July 1980, coinciding with the end of the European Championship. Depending, presumably, on how England fare in Europe, he is likely to be asked to stay on and see them through to the next World Cup.

Greenwood, 55, was chosen for the job above Brian Clough — the popular choice — Ipswich manager Bobby Robson, and Lawrie McMenemy of Southampton. West Ham have said they will not be seeking compensation for the loss of Mr Greenwood's services, and John Lyall will take over as manager of the club — only their fourth in 46 years.

As manager of the London club, Greenwood gained a reputation for producing teams that were always a delight to watch, playing attractive, attacking football.

SOCCER SOUNDBITES

"He has got people believing in themselves and talking to each other. The family atmosphere had gone, but he has brought it back."

EMLYN HUGHES,
England captain, on Ron Greenwood's appointment.

Manchester fans on rampage in France

MANCHESTER UNITED fans fought pitched battles with French police and spectators on the terraces of the Geoffroy-Guichard Stadium in St Etienne on 14 September. At least a dozen fans lay injured on the field as fists, boots and bottles flew before the start of United's European Cup-Winners' Cup first leg match with St Etienne.

The trouble began on the terraces behind one of the goals, where most of the visiting fans were packed among thousands of Frenchmen. Dozens of frightened spectators climbed over the 15ft fences on to the pitch, and a reserve match in progress had to be abandoned.

Riot police climbed in among the feuding fans and, using fists and batons, drove a wedge between them. When neither side showed any real signs of giving up, the police ran headlong at the United contingent, driving dozens of them out of the ground and others into a corner where they could be arrested and taken off for questioning. Some spectators said later that St Etienne supporters had started the trouble by throwing bread and bottles at United fans. Order was restored after 20 minutes of chaos. For the record, the match was drawn 1–1. But there followed a night of violence, as Manchester supporters went on a rampage through the streets of the town, smashing windows and ransacking shops, and threatening passers-by. Several further arrests were made.

United go down fighting — in the nicest sense

IT WAS MANCHESTER United who did the fighting at Old Trafford on 2 November in the return leg of their second-round Cup-Winners' Cup tie with Porto, instead of their notorious fans. But United, having been kicked out of the tournament after the appalling behaviour of their following at St Etienne, and then reinstated after being ordered to play the second leg at faraway Plymouth, are finally out of the competition. They put up a magnificent battle to try to claw their way back from a 4–0 deficit, but in the end it proved too much and they went down 6–5 on aggregate.

They went in at half-time 3–1 up, with goals from Coppell, Murca (og) and Nicholl, but Porto's away goal meant that United had to win by five. Coppell made it 4–1, but Porto's striker, Seninho, scored his second goal five minutes from time, and another Murca own goal was immaterial. However, United's display of bold, attacking football did much to repair the damage inflicted on their pride in Portugal two weeks ago.

Pele's farewell

A TEARFUL PELE bade farewell to competitive soccer on 1 October, ending his 22-year career in an exhibition match watched by 77,000 people in Giants' Stadium, New Jersey. Pele, 36, shared his talents between the two teams taking part. He played the first half — and scored, with a stunning free-kick — for the New York Cosmos, and finished the game in a final reunion with Santos of Brazil, for whom he had scored 1,090 goals in 1,114 games before retiring in 1974.

Pele, perhaps the greatest player of all time, came back in 1975, signing a lucrative contract with the American club, and helped them win the NASL title this year.

Late penalty is Scots' passport to Argentina

SCOTLAND'S 2–0 victory over Wales at neutral Anfield made sure of their qualification for next summer's World Cup in Argentina. The Welsh played the better football and created the better chances, but with a team half-composed of players from outside the First Division, they could not sustain the effort. It was 12 minutes from time, however, before Scotland broke the deadlock, skipper Don Masson (QPR) scoring from a penalty awarded for a handling offence — a decision that TV playbacks indicated was wrong. The Scots in the crowd were celebrating before Dalglish, on his home turf, made sure with a glancing header three minutes before the end.

Scotland skipper Don Masson scores the hotly disputed penalty.

Burns, Woods raise Forest: champions beaten in League Cup

CHAMPIONSHIP LEADERS Nottingham Forest won the League Cup for the first time when they beat Liverpool 1–0 in the replayed final at Old Trafford. After a goalless draw at Wembley, it took a second-half penalty to separate the teams. But whereas Forest fought a two-hour rear-guard action on Saturday, they created more chances and gave Liverpool more trouble in the first 20 minutes here than in the whole game at Wembley, and Withe and Woodcock were both profligate early on.

But Liverpool came back, and it was Dalglish's turn to squander an opportunity. Forest began the second half by pushing forward again, and as O'Hare moved on to a fine through-pass from Woodcock, he was brought down from behind by Thompson. Liverpool claimed it was outside the box, but the referee awarded a penalty, and Robertson put his kick out of Clemence's reach.

Liverpool, like true champions, immediately forged upfield, and three minutes later McDermott, who had a goal disallowed on Saturday, broke through to put the ball in the net again, but was adjudged to have handled.

Forest held out, and 18-year-old Chris Woods played another blinder in goal. As Cup-tied Peter Shilton's deputy, he has still to make his League debut! Having lost his skipper, John McGovern, injured in the second half at Wembley, manager Brian Clough played a master card in making "wild man" Kenny Burns captain. He was an inspiration to his team, who scored 24 goals during the competition, and conceded only five.

Robertson strokes his spot-kick wide of Clemence.

FOOTBALL FOCUS

- York City, who slumped from Division Two to Division Four in successive seasons, finished third from bottom and had to seek re-election.
- Three spectacular debuts during the season: Tony Woodcock (Nottingham Forest) and Peter Ward (Brighton) both scored hat-tricks on their first appearances for England Under-21s, and Colin Lee scored four on his debut for Spurs, when they beat Bristol Rovers 9–0 in Division Two on 22 October. Forest, of course, won the League and League Cup, while Spurs edged Brighton out of promotion to Division One on goal difference.
- Manchester United signed Scottish international defender Gordon McQueen from Leeds on 9 February for £495,000, a record deal between two English clubs.
- England fielded six Liverpool players plus their former star Kevin Keegan against Switzerland at Wembley on 7 September, but could only draw 0–0. This was the highest number of players from one club in an English team since 1934, when seven Arsenal men played against Italy at Highbury.

Blyth spirit too much for Potters

BLYTH SPARTANS of the Northern League earned a place in the fifth round of the FA Cup with a shock victory over Second Division Stoke at the Victoria Ground. A goal down with 13 minutes to go, they equalized and then scored a winner less than two minutes from time.

An upset looked likely as early as the 10th minute, when Stoke keeper Jones fumbled a corner and Terry Johnson easily scored from close range. But Stoke came back early in the second half with two goals in two minutes, from Busby and Crooks, which should have done for the non-Leaguers. But now it was Blyth's turn to come storming back: Guthrie's free-kick was deflected on to a post, Shoulder headed on to the other post and Carney bundled the ball in. It was another free-kick from Guthrie that led to the winner. It rebounded to Johnson, and from 15 yards out the centre-forward coolly slotted the ball into goal. So Blyth are the first non-League club to reach the fifth round since Colchester and Yeovil in the late 1940s.

Forest clinch title with four games to play

ANOTHER FINE performance from Peter Shilton helped earn Nottingham Forest a goalless draw at Coventry, and the point they needed to clinch their first League Championship with four games still to play. Brian Clough's controversial £250,000 purchase in September from Stoke, a club record and also the highest fee ever paid for a goalkeeper, has been justified many times over this season, and against a dominant Coventry side Shilton emphasized just what an asset a great keeper is to a team. Clough also bought the tempestuous Kenny Burns, the player nobody wanted, from Birmingham for £150,000 — and transformed him into the newly elected Footballer of the Year.

Mr Clough and his assistant Peter Taylor have brought off the League and League Cup double in their first season after promotion. In doing so, they have denied mighty Liverpool a hat-trick of League titles, and Clough, who guided Derby to League success in 1972, joins the immortal Herbert Chapman, the only other manager to win the Championship with two clubs.

Happy Rangers do the 'treble'

RANGERS' DOMINATION of Scottish football is complete once again. Their 2–1 victory over Aberdeen in the Scottish Cup final at Hampden gave the Ibrox club a clean sweep of the three domestic honours for the second time in three seasons.

Aberdeen had very little to offer, and Rangers' total superiority was rewarded by goals from Alex MacDonald (33 minutes) and Derek Johnstone (58), who scored in every round. The Dons made a bold late attempt to salvage the game, but could not break through until Ritchie scored four minutes from time.

The sponsor's £100 cheque for the man of the match went, almost inevitably, to gifted midfielder Robert Russell who, in his first season as a senior, has been astonishingly successful, even by Rangers' standards. For veteran skipper John Greig, in his 18th season, it was his sixth Scottish Cup-winners' medal, to go with five Championship and four League Cup gongs.

Liverpool kings of Europe again

LIVERPOOL HAVE WON the European Cup in successive seasons, and although they did not attain the high standard of football that defeated Borussia in Rome last year, their 1–0 defeat of Bruges was a patient, soundly professional performance, capped by a coolly taken goal by Kenny Dalglish in the 66th minute.

The Belgians, without their key forwards Lambert and Courant, could have been forgiven for thinking they had gone to Anfield by mistake when they emerged from the Wembley tunnel to a seething mass of red and a wall of sound from what was one massive Kop. But it took Liverpool some time to get into their stride. Eventually, Kennedy, McDermott and Souness began to get a grip in midfield, and Jensen in the Bruges goal was kept much busier than Clemence. Just before the interval, Hansen for Liverpool and Ku for Bruges headed just over the bar.

Both managers made tactical substitutions in the second half, Paisley sending on Heighway for Case to boost Liverpool's attack. Within a minute, Heighway touched the ball back to McDermott, who found Dalglish; he then exchanged passes with fellow Scot Souness, splitting the Bruges defence wide open, before gently chipping the ball over Jensen's dive. The Belgians then threw everything into attack and, indeed, Thompson, Liverpool's outstanding defender, had to clear the ball off the line. But Bruges had left their offensive too late.

Dalglish chips the keeper for Liverpool's winning goal.

Wembley 'walk-over' for Ipswich

THE 1–0 SCORELINE hardly suggests a walk-over, but Ipswich's triumph over favourites Arsenal in the FA Cup final was comprehensive in all but goals. Indeed, after the first 10 minutes, when Arsenal's initial flourish petered out, it was all Ipswich. Mariner struck the bar, Wark twice hammered fierce shots against a post, and Jennings atoned for his otherwise uncertain performance with the save of the match, from a Burley header.

Arsenal's gamble of playing Sunderland, clearly not match fit, and Brady, obviously not recovered from an ankle injury and replaced by Rix in the 65th minute, did not come off. Wark, the epitome of power and determination, Talbot, as industrious as ever, and Osborne, rising nobly to the occasion, quickly established control in midfield, where Hudson failed miserably to take up the burden. So, with Woods and Geddis torturing Arsenal on the flanks, Mariner tore the centre of Arsenal's defence apart. Yet there were only 14 minutes left when Geddis crossed low and hard into Arsenal's goalmouth, Young could not clear properly, and Osborne shot in. Justice, there is no doubt, had been done.

Osborne celebrates after driving a low shot past the Arsenal defence for the only goal of the match.

FINAL SCORE

Football League
Division 1: Nottingham Forest
Top scorer: Bob Latchford (Everton) 30
Division 2: Bolton Wanderers
Division 3: Wrexham
Division 4: Watford
Footballer of the Year: Kenny Burns (Nottingham Forest)

FA Cup Final

Ipswich Town	1	Arsenal	0

League Cup Final

Nottingham Forest	0	Liverpool	0
(after extra time)			
Replay: N. Forest	1	Liverpool	0

Scottish League
Premier League: Rangers
Top scorer: Derek Johnstone (Rangers) 25
Division 1: Morton
Division 2: Clyde
Footballer of the Year: Derek Johnstone (Rangers)

Scottish FA Cup Final

Rangers	2	Aberdeen	1

Scottish League Cup Final

Rangers	2	Celtic	1

International Championship
England, 6 pts

European Cup Final

Liverpool	1	FC Bruges	0

Cup-Winners' Cup Final

Anderlecht	4	Austria/WAC	0

UEFA Cup Final
PSV Eindhoven beat Bastia 0–0, 3–0

European Footballer of the Year 1977
Allan Simonsen (Borussia Moenchengladbach & Denmark)

Leading European Scorer (Golden Boot)
Hans Krankl (Rapid Vienna) 41

World Club Championship
Competition not held

Argentina at last

Argentina was a controversial choice to host the World Cup in view of the military coup there in 1976 and the state of the country. Such was the football that, in the end, neutral observers did not really care who won or lost. They were just glad it was all over. There were very few heroes on the pitch, and the world game had degenerated sadly since the heady days of 1970. It is easy to blame the poor refereeing for not controlling the violence on the field, and the inadequate laws for failing to punish the "tactical" fouls that are part and parcel of the game today. It is almost impossible for truly skilful players to operate in such an environment and, for that, considerable blame must attach to the managers and coaches, too.

FOR THE FIRST time, the number of World Cup entries exceeded 100, although six of the 106 withdrew without taking part. Only Scotland of the home countries qualified for the finals, but such was their performance, on and off the field, that they could be excused for wishing they had not.

England's early 2–0 defeat in Italy was demoralizing, and their preparations were not helped by the resignation midway through the qualifying tournament of their manager, Don Revie. Even when they reversed the Italian result at Wembley, their other wins had not provided enough goals, and Italy needed only to beat Luxembourg in Rome.

Among the qualifiers, Iran and Tunisia were making their first appearances in the finals.

Scotland's own goals

Scotland's World Cup campaign was a catalogue of catastrophes. All kinds of stories emanated from their camp before they even took the field — tales of players living it up, wrangles, as usual, over bonuses, complaints by the Mexicans about noise. Manager Ally MacLeod had acquired an almost messianic reputation among the Scottish fans and media before the finals, but was hampered by his lack of knowledge of international football, his opponents and even his own players, and no team could have gone out less prepared for their first match, against Peru. Despite taking an early lead through Jordan, they were pegged back by half-time and, after Masson had a penalty saved, the veteran Cubillas hit two viciously swerving, long-range shots past Rough for a 3–1 win. To add insult to injury, Willie Johnston failed a drug test — he had been taking stimulants — and was sent home in disgrace.

Iran proceeded to humiliate Scotland further, holding them to a draw after giving them an own goal just before half-time. This left the Scots needing to beat Holland by three clear goals to survive — and, all credit to them, they very nearly did. With Souness belatedly coming into the side and giving it more bite, Scotland came back from a goal down to put three past the Dutch, the last, from Archie Gemmill, the best of the tournament, as he beat man after man in a confined space before chipping in. But Holland scored again four minutes later, and Scotland made a sad exit, all the more depressing for what might have been had they gone better prepared.

Gemmill (dark shirt) finishes off his brilliant run against Holland.

Weak refereeing

Argentina won their first two matches, against Hungary and France, 2–1, helped by favourable decisions from weak referees intimidated by the crowd. The Hungarians had two players sent off, albeit deservedly, in the last four minutes — but what provocation striker Andres Torocsik suffered before he finally blew up. With a strong referee, Mr Klein of Israel, Italy beat the hosts 1–0, but both teams had by then qualified for the second round.

Poland came through strongly in Group Two, after drawing 0–0 with world champions West Germany. The Germans demolished Mexico 6–0, but scraped through with a goalless draw against the splendid Tunisians, when a defeat would have sent them out.

The matches in Group Three were the closest, with never more than a goal in it, and Austria were quickly through after beating Spain and Sweden. Brazil toiled to two lack-lustre draws, in the first of which Welsh referee Clive Thomas blew for time a split-second before the ball entered the Swedish goal for what would have been the Brazilian winner. They then beat a lukewarm Austria to go through to Round Two.

Europe v S. America

As things turned out, Group A was bound to produce a European finalist, and the odds were on a South American finalist emerging from Group B, unless Poland could spring a surprise. But the biggest shock of the second round was the elimination of West Germany, who failed to win any of their three matches.

Without Beckenbauer, who had "retired" to play in the United States, and with rumours of unrest in their camp, the Germans failed to produce their usual spirited performances, and hard-fought draws with Italy and Holland virtually put paid to their chances of retaining the Cup. But it was still a bombshell when

Controversy and Argentina are never far apart at World Cup time, and 1978 was no exception. They played some of the best football in the finals, but would they have won the competition away from home?

A section of the excited Argentinian crowd at the final.

they lost to Austria, a side whom the rapidly improving Dutch had thrashed 5–1. Ruud Krol was the dominating figure for Holland in the absence of that other famous retiree, Cruyff, although they were aided by weak refereeing in their victory over Italy.

The contentious issue in Group B was the planning that allowed Argentina to start their last match after Brazil's had ended, so they knew exactly what they had to do. Brazil had emerged from the shambles of their early matches with good wins against Peru and Poland, although the goalless draw with Argentina was featureless apart from the fouling.

Eventually, Argentina kicked off knowing they needed to beat Peru by better than 4–1 to reach the final, and the Peruvian defence looked suspiciously vulnerable as they allowed their hosts to make raid after raid and run in six goals without reply.

A flawed final

Before the start of the final, Argentina were inexcusably allowed to get away with two pieces of gamesmanship. They kept Holland — and the rest of the world — waiting for five minutes before they came out, and they made a calculated, unwarranted fuss about the protection on Rene Van der Kerkhof's injured arm, which he had worn in previous rounds. Having allowed these pieces of nonsense, Sergio Gonella, the compromise selection as referee, proceeded to give as ineffectual a performance as had been seen in what was one of the worst refereed World Cups for some years. With an average of one free-kick every 90 seconds, the final was no worse than some of the earlier games, and the Dutch were penalized more than twice as much as the host country. While it is probably fair to say that Argentina would not have won this World Cup had it been held anywhere else, this does not excuse Holland's tacky display.

The chief reason, however, for the Dutch defeat was their failure to take the chances they made. Although they had world-class goalscoring wingers in Rep and Rensenbrink, they missed not having a true central striker against the best opposition. Argentina had the best player in the tournament — and he was voted so — in Mario Kempes, and his partnership with Luque up front was decisive. Little Ardiles was a revelation in midfield, at the heart of every move. And skipper Passarella, when he wasn't engaged in skulduggery, was a superb defender.

Kempes put Argentina in front after 38 minutes, and it looked to be enough until substitute Dirk Nanninga rose to head an equalizer from Rene Van der Kerkhof's cross eight minutes from time. The Dutch almost stole the Cup when Rensenbrink hit a post, but the game went into extra time. Before the break, Kempes broke through and just managed to keep control and stab the ball past Jongbloed. It was all Argentina now, and Bertoni clinched it five minutes from the end of extra time after a lovely one-two with Kempes.

So Argentina had won at last, 48 years after they reached the first World Cup final, in Uruguay. It was a particularly sweet triumph for manager Cesar Menotti, who kept faith with an attacking style alien to most club football in the country, despite constant criticism from all sides.

Bertoni (right) scores the World Cup clincher in extra time.

FINAL SCORE

FIRST ROUND

Group 1

Italy	2	France	1
Argentina	2	Hungary	1
Italy	3	Hungary	1
Argentina	2	France	1
Argentina	0	Italy	1
France	3	Hungary	1

	P	W	D	L	F	A	P
Italy	3	3	0	0	6	2	6
Argentina	3	2	0	1	4	3	4
France	3	1	0	2	5	5	2
Hungary	3	0	0	3	3	8	0

Group 2

Poland	0	West Germany	0
Tunisia	3	Mexico	1
West Germany	6	Mexico	0
Poland	1	Tunisia	0
Poland	3	Mexico	1
West Germany	0	Tunisia	0

	P	W	D	L	F	A	P
Poland	3	2	1	0	4	1	5
W. Germany	3	1	2	0	6	0	4
Tunisia	3	1	1	1	3	2	3
Mexico	3	0	0	3	2	12	0

Group 3

Sweden	1	Brazil	1
Austria	2	Spain	1
Austria	1	Sweden	0
Spain	0	Brazil	0
Brazil	1	Austria	0
Spain	1	Sweden	0

	P	W	D	L	F	A	P
Austria	3	2	0	1	3	2	4
Brazil	3	1	2	0	2	1	4
Spain	3	1	1	1	2	2	3
Sweden	3	0	1	2	1	3	1

Group 4

Peru	3	Scotland	1
Holland	3	Iran	0
Iran	1	Scotland	1
Holland	0	Peru	0
Peru	4	Iran	1
Scotland	3	Holland	2

	P	W	D	L	F	A	P
Peru	3	2	1	0	7	2	5
Holland	3	1	1	1	5	3	3
Scotland	3	1	1	1	5	6	3
Iran	3	0	1	2	2	8	1

SECOND ROUND

Group A

Holland	5	Austria	1
West Germany	0	Italy	0
Holland	2	West Germany	2
Italy	1	Austria	0
Holland	2	Italy	1
Austria	3	West Germany	2

	P	W	D	L	F	A	P
Holland	3	2	1	0	9	4	5
Italy	3	1	1	1	2	2	3
W. Germany	3	0	2	1	4	5	2
Austria	3	1	0	2	4	8	2

Group B

Brazil	3	Peru	0
Argentina	2	Poland	0
Argentina	0	Brazil	0
Poland	1	Peru	0
Brazil	3	Poland	1
Argentina	6	Peru	0

	P	W	D	L	F	A	P
Argentina	3	2	1	0	8	0	5
Brazil	3	2	1	0	6	1	5
Poland	3	1	0	2	2	5	2
Peru	3	0	0	3	0	10	0

THIRD-PLACE MATCH

Brazil	2	Italy	1

FINAL

Argentina	3	Holland	1

(after extra time)

River Plate Stadium, Buenos Aires, 25 June 1978. Attendance 77,260

Argentina: Fillol, Olguin, Galvan, Passarella, Tarantini, Ardiles (Larrosa), Gallego, Kempes, Bertoni, Luque, Ortiz (Houseman)
(Scorers: Kempes 2, Bertoni)
Holland: Jongbloed, Poortvliet, Krol, Brandts, Jansen (Suurbier), Neeskens, Haan, Van der Kerkhof W, Van der Kerkhof R, Rep (Nanninga), Rensenbrink (Scorer: Nanninga)

Leading scorers

6 Kempes (Argentina)
5 Cubillas (Peru)
Rensenbrink (Holland)

Tottenham's South American coup

ON 10 JULY, just 15 days after Argentina's triumph over Holland in the World Cup final, Spurs manager Keith Burkinshaw brought off a sensational coup by signing two of their squad. Osvaldo Ardiles, the small, wiry midfielder from Huracan, was for many the most influential of the Argentinian team. The powerful Ricardo Villa, a wide midfield player from Racing Club, made only two appearances in the finals as a substitute but has a growing reputation in his own country. It appears that the two players, both 25, came as a "package" and the cost was in the region of £750,000, including agents' fees, signing-on fees, and a small percentage to the Argentinian FA.

Mr Burkinshaw was alerted to the fact that several of the successful Argentina side were up for sale by Sheffield United manager Harry Haslam, who has an Argentinian coach and had established links with agents in the country. While Second Division Sheffield could not afford to buy players of such quality, Burkinshaw was eager to strengthen his newly promoted side, and wasted no time in boarding a plane to Buenos Aires.

Argentinian stars Villa (left) and Ardiles: in Spurs' starting line-up.

Spurs go down to record defeat at Anfield

LIVERPOOL'S SEVEN-GOAL demolition of Tottenham on 2 September — the biggest defeat in the Londoners' 70-year membership of the League — suggests that the European Cup-holders are poised to achieve new heights in their illustrious post-war history. Manager Bob Paisley described the humiliation of Spurs, who included their £1 million new signings Ardiles, Villa and John Lacy, as "almost frightening at times".

Spurs have not won at Anfield for 66 years, and on Saturday Liverpool's Clemence was stretched by only one shot, from Lacy, who at the other end was hard pressed to provide the solidity at centre-back for which Fulham were recently paid so handsomely. But few teams could have withstood this onslaught, and Spurs deserve honourable mention because the avalanche never provoked spoiling tactics.

Daines was powerless to prevent all but Liverpool's fifth goal, which passed through his legs, and he made several excellent saves. Certainly, Dalglish might have at least doubled the goals he collected in the 10th and 22nd minutes. After the retirement of his captain Hughes, with a knee injury, Dalglish moved back into midfield, and two of his thrusts from there provided goals for substitute Johnson. Ray Kennedy had scored a third goal before half-time, and Neal made it 6–0 from a penalty. The best was saved till last, a high-speed, five-man move finished off by a spectacular header from McDermott, after a run of 60 yards.

Liverpool top the table, having won their first four games, with a goal record of 16–2. They have reached awesome form in time for this season's first defence of the European Cup. They meet Nottingham Forest, who have drawn all four of their League matches so far this season, in the first-round, first-leg match at the City Ground.

Forest end Liverpool's European reign

IN A PULSATING match at Anfield on 27 September, Nottingham Forest resisted everything Liverpool threw at them and emerged into the second round of the European Cup. Protecting the 2–0 first-leg lead Birtles and Barrett had given them a fortnight earlier, Forest stood firm as the European champions and League leaders drove forward with tremendous determination, sometimes flinging nine men into attack in their efforts to reduce the gap. But McGovern, Gemmill and Bowyer did an excellent holding job in midfield to restrain McDermott and Souness, and Lloyd and Burns somehow held on in the back line. Behind them, Shilton was calmness personified.

In a last effort, manager Paisley put on strikers Fairclough and Johnson for McDermott and Case, but they failed to make any impact and the result was, for Forest, a glorious goalless draw.

Viv Anderson (left) and Liverpool's Ray Kennedy in action.

Clough makes Trevor Francis the first £1m player

BIRMINGHAM and England striker Trevor Francis became Britain's first £1 million footballer on 9 February, when Brian Clough signed him for Nottingham Forest. This doubles the transfer record between British clubs, set last December when West Brom paid Middlesbrough £500,000 for David Mills.

When VAT, the contribution to the Football League Provident Fund and Francis's five-per-cent cut are added, Forest have committed themselves to paying £1,180,000. No other club had shown any inclination to approach the unprecedented figure Birmingham were demanding for Francis, 24, who first burst on to the scene with them as a prodigy of 16. He developed into an England player, though not a regular member of the team, but has suffered from Birmingham's repeated struggles to avoid relegation.

The fact that Forest have been able to find such a vast amount is, according to Mr Clough, due to good management. He claimed they would be able to pay a similar sum again if the right player became available.

Million-pound man Francis.

FA won't turn blind eye to Nelson

SAMMY NELSON, Arsenal's Northern Ireland international left-back, has been suspended for two weeks by his club and fined two weeks' wages for lowering his shorts in front of the crowd after equalizing in the 1–1 draw against Coventry at Highbury on 3 April. He also seems certain to be charged by the FA with bringing the game into disrepute. Nelson's gesture came after he had been barracked by the crowd for putting the ball into his own goal in the first half. The player is extremely contrite about his behaviour, and the only charitable thing that can be said is that it appeared to be entirely out of character.

Nelson finds a new way of celebrating!

Forest regain touch and retain League Cup

NOTTINGHAM FOREST will line up against Grasshoppers in the second leg of their European Cup quarter-final in Zurich on Wednesday with the comforting knowledge that they have regained the elusive touch of true champions. Forest left Wembley after beating Southampton 3–2, with the League Cup securely in their grasp for the second season in succession, after a second-half performance of the highest quality had swept away the doubts and inhibitions accumulated during the long, cold, frustrating winter.

When searching for the hero of Forest's victory, look no further than their manager, Brian Clough, whose few well-chosen words during the interval transformed a witless, dissident team, seemingly tottering towards defeat, into aggressive, conquering heroes. The star who caught the eye on the field was young Garry Birtles, a £5,000 bargain from neighbouring Long Eaton, who is in his first season of senior football. He scored two goals and had two disallowed for offside, one of them a borderline decision.

Birtles pounced on an error by the hesitant Nicholl in the 50th minute to equalize Peach's 17th-minute goal and, in effect, provide the base for Forest's victory. The goal inspired Gemmill and McGovern to take command in midfield from the previously dominating Ball, Holmes and Williams, and produce some of the most devastating attacking soccer seen at Wembley for years. Southampton's defence, who had conceded only two goals in their last eight games, was torn apart. They were outrageously fortunate to survive until the 78th minute, but then Birtles shook off a challenge by Nicholl and planted the newly styled red and white ball firmly past the diving Gennoe. Woodcock, who had so ably supported Birtles, added a third in the 82nd minute. Holmes volleyed home a defiant 15-yarder just before the end, but Southampton never really looked like saving the game.

Birtles scores to put Forest ahead in the League Cup final.

Brady sets up Arsenal's amazing Cup climax

WITH A MINUTE to go at Wembley, and Manchester United still on a high after sensationally scoring twice in two minutes to pull back their half-time deficit, Arsenal's Liam Brady collected the ball in his own half. As the elusive Irishman began to run with it, euphoria turned to panic in the United ranks. It seemed half the Manchester side were crowding round, jockeying back, fearful of the educated left foot that had tormented them all afternoon. Just when it seemed he was running into a cul-de-sac, Brady released the ball without breaking stride, and there was Graham Rix clear on the left. Over came a long, outswinging centre, above the defence and out of the reach of young Bailey in goal, for Alan Sunderland at the far post to hit into the empty net.

Three goals in four minutes: never has there been such a climax to an FA Cup final, and there must have been thousands who missed it, streaming out before the end with Arsenal apparently coasting to a comfortable victory. The player inadvertently responsible for this late avalanche of action was Arsenal substitute Steve Walford. He was sent on by manager Terry Neill for David Price five minutes from time, a decision that seemed to destroy Arsenal's concentration, perhaps persuading them that their task was complete.

Sunderland wheels away after hitting the winner, with Walford (left) in attendance.

Whether or not Arsenal dropped their guard, Jordan swept Coppell's free-kick back into the middle for McQueen to score in the 86th minute, and two minutes later Sammy McIlroy took a pass from Coppell, wriggled past O'Leary and Walford, and struck the equalizer out of Jennings's reach. What had been a predictable match, after Arsenal gained in confidence and took control early on, was transformed into a thriller, a game that will be talked about for years to come.

Brady was the jewel in an otherwise moderate Arsenal side, striding away in the 12th minute to instigate the move that Talbot finished off and, two minutes from half-time, accelerating to beat Albiston and Buchan before crossing perfectly for Stapleton to head powerfully down and into goal. It was wholly appropriate that it was then Brady, head and shoulders the man of the match, who should pick Arsenal up again and make the decider.

FOOTBALL FOCUS

- The International Board abolished the "played-onside" clause from the offside law before the start of the season. A ball deflected by an opponent will no longer put a player onside.

- Viv Anderson, the 22-year-old Forest full-back, became the first black footballer to represent England in a full international when he played against Czechoslovakia at Wembley on 29 November.

- When Forest lost 2–0 at Liverpool on 9 December, it was their first League defeat for one year and 13 days — a run of 42 games.

- The FA imposed a 10-year ban on Don Revie, dating from his unscheduled departure from England in July 1977, for "bringing the game into disrepute". Apparently, after he signed a contract with the United Arab Emirates in secret, he offered to resign his England post and asked for £50,000 tax-free compensation.

Liverpool break Leeds and their record

WHEN LIVERPOOL went to Elland Road on 17 May for their last match of the League season, they had sewn up the title nine days before and had 66 points, one fewer than the First Division record set by Leeds 10 year earlier. If Leeds, in fifth place, harboured any ideas that they might preserve their record, they were dispelled pretty quickly as the Reds began to show their devastating finishing power.

Johnson drove home their first goal after 21 minutes, and Case hammered in number two four minutes before half-time. Liverpool gave Leeds little scope for attack and, 10 minutes after the interval, Johnson made it three with a powerful header. That was the end of the scoring.

Dalglish, who had a hand in all three goals, finished as the Reds' leading League scorer with 21. They conceded an all-time Football League low of 16 goals in 42 matches, an extraordinary achievement. In amassing their record 68 points, they lost only four matches, none at Anfield, where they dropped only two points and boasted a goal record of 51–4. They led the table from start to finish, dropping just one point in their first 11 games, and used only 15 players in winning their record 11th Championship.

Dalglish, ever present again, and leading scorer for Liverpool.

SOCCER SOUNDBITES

"Tonight we practised everything we ever preached in the game. There was no dissent from the players, no shady tackling. We worked tremendously hard and gave a performance that everyone connected with the club can be proud of."

BRIAN CLOUGH,
Forest manager, after their semi-final triumph in Cologne.

"No way would Francis have played if the others [Gemmill and O'Neill] had been fully fit."

CLOUGH,
after the final.

"I have been with him [Brian Clough] longer than any other player, but don't ask me to define his success. I can only say he makes you want to play for him."

JOHN MCGOVERN,
Forest's captain.

Million-pound Francis inspires fairy-tale Forest triumph

Francis ducks into his match-winning header against Malmo.

MILLION-POUND striker Trevor Francis, eligible to play for Forest in the European Cup for the first time, was drafted in to play on the right wing against Malmö in the final in Munich, and he scored the only goal. What's more, he scored it with his head, a part of his anatomy he normally uses purely for outwitting the opposition, rather than for making physical contact with the ball.

Forest came to the final as strong favourites. They had done all the hard work in getting there: going through a baptism of fire against Liverpool, winners for the last two years; comfortably beating Puskas's AEK Athens 7–2 on aggregate and Grasshoppers of Zurich 5–2; and magnificently coming through against Cologne in the semi-finals, where they recovered from two down to 3–3 at home and then won in Germany with a goal from play-anywhere Ian Bowyer.

Archie Gemmill was still unavailable for the final, as was Forest's other influential midfield player Martin O'Neill, but the Swedes, managed by Englishman Bob Houghton, also had two important players ruled out by injury. After a nervy start, Forest began to put together some inventive, exciting attacking moves, with Francis the main inspiration. And it was Francis who scored just before half-time with a beautifully worked goal. Robertson beat two men on the left, and curled a cross over Malmö's defence to the far post, where Francis, after a 30-yard sprint, headed in. With McGovern giving a real captain's performance in midfield, Francis continuing to dominate out on the right, and Robertson causing all sorts of problems on the other flank, Forest remained firmly in charge after the interval.

Forest's triumph is nothing short of a fairy-tale, a remarkable rise for a team just scraping out of England's Second Division only two years ago and now champions of Europe. Above all, it is a tribute to the astute management and motivation of Brian Clough and Peter Taylor.

Ten-man Celtic snatch League title from Rangers

IN A THRILLING, late finish to the Scottish Championship race, Rangers needed at least a draw with Celtic at Parkhead to have a chance of the title. But Celtic, who went a goal down and then had John Doyle sent off, staged a fighting recovery and won 4–2.

Rangers were still leading with McDonald's goal 23 minutes from time. But in a finish to rival that of the FA Cup final, Aitken equalized and McCluskey put Celtic ahead. Back came Rangers with a goal from Russell to draw level again. But in the last five minutes, Jackson put the ball into his own net and McLeod scored Celtic's fourth for a dramatic victory.

Five points behind now, Rangers' last two matches are academic as far as the title is concerned, and they can only hope for consolation in their second Cup final replay with Hibs in a week's time.

This is not a vintage Celtic team — they have scored only 61 goals in their 36 league games, divided between 17 players — but they have shown great spirit, inspired by Aitken and McGrain in defence and Burns in midfield. They won nine and drew one of their last 11 matches: Champion form indeed.

FINAL SCORE

Football League
Division 1: Liverpool
Top scorer: Frank Worthington (Bolton Wanderers) 24
Division 2: Crystal Palace
Division 3: Shrewsbury Town
Division 4: Reading
Footballer of the Year: Kenny Dalglish (Liverpool)

FA Cup Final

Arsenal	3	Manchester United	2

League Cup Final

Nottingham Forest	3	Southampton	2

Scottish League
Premier Division: Celtic
Top scorer: Andy Ritchie (Morton) 22
Division 1: Dundee
Division 2: Berwick Rangers
Footballer of the Year: Andy Ritchie (Morton)

Scottish FA Cup Final

Rangers	0	Hibernian	0
Replay: Rangers	0	Hibernian	0
Replay: Rangers	3	Hibernian	2

Scottish League Cup Final

Rangers	2	Aberdeen	1

International Championship
England, 5 pts

European Cup Final

Nottingham Forest	1	Malmö	0

Cup-Winners' Cup Final

Barcelona	4	Fortuna Düsseldorf	3

(after extra time)

UEFA Cup Final
Borussia Moenchengladbach beat Red Star Belgrade 1–1, 1–0

European Footballer of the Year 1978
Kevin Keegan (SV Hamburg & England)

Leading European Scorer (Golden Boot)
Kees Kist (AZ 67 Alkmaar) 34

World Club Championship
Olimpia (Paraguay) beat Malmö (Sweden) 1–0, 2–1

Stars of the 60s and 70s

WITH THE ABOLITION of the maximum wage in England and the new freedom of contract established in the early sixties, soccer stars began to enjoy a new, higher status in society. No longer were they the slaves of their clubs, revered by the fans but unable to earn wages commensurate with their fame and their special talents. Now the leading soccer stars could take their place along with their counterparts in other branches of the sports and entertainment industry, such as golfers, boxers and film actors.

The previous situation could not, of course, have been allowed to continue. But this new-found wealth and freedom did not have an entirely benign effect on the game. Money became too big a factor, for both club and player, leading to the "win at all costs" attitude that began to creep into the game in the late sixties, and to the loss of loyalty as players became mercenaries, moving from club to club for the signing-on fees or abroad for vast fortunes.

Pele (Santos and Brazil).

Pele versus Best

Two players stand out in this period above all others — Pele of Brazil and George Best of Northern Ireland — and they always figure in any discussion about the greatest footballers. Of course, it is an impossible argument, but the case for these two is mighty powerful.

Pele first showed his precocious talents to the world in the 1958 World Cup, and as a great goalscorer — 1,217 in 1,254 games — and a scorer of great goals, in a career spanning 18 years, he surely has no peer. His feats are legendary. He would take the ball through defences as if they were not there, beating man after man with acceleration and ball control, even rebounding the ball from defenders' legs. There is a plaque in Rio's Maracana Stadium commemorating "The most beautiful goal ever seen", when for Santos in March 1961 he beat every man in the Fluminense team before putting the ball in their net. His shooting and heading, his telepathic passing and positional play, were supreme. Everything he did, he did beautifully. And he played with such joy, such an obvious love for the game, in the manner and spirit in which it should be played.

How can you compare Best with such a paragon? He never enjoyed the international success of Pele — but how could he, playing for a country where talent was so thin on the ground? Also, he allowed the pressures of fame and fortune to get to him, and his career was cut short by "drink, dames and decadence". Yet anyone who saw Best play when he was at his peak — and he gave Manchester United six or seven marvellous years — will say there was none better. He had every gift in the game, and was always a joy to watch, poetry in motion, with perfect balance, co-ordination and timing. He could dribble and shoot with either foot, and though not a striker scored more than his share of goals. And he was a brilliant ball-winner, anticipating or tackling as well as any defender. Whether on the wing or coming through the middle, he was, at his best, almost impossible to dispossess without fouling, a "tactic" opponents regularly used. It was one of the game's great scandals that it was Best who too often was penalized for retaliating, suspended for "bringing the game into disrepute", when the authorities should have answered that charge for their negligence in allowing such talent to be stifled so unfairly.

Old Trafford riches

It is extraordinary that alongside Best at Old Trafford were two other world stars — Bobby Charlton and Denis Law — and all three were voted European Footballer of the Year in the sixties, a wonderful story of an Englishman, a Scotsman and an Irishman. Bobby Charlton was a striker who became a midfield player, a withdrawn centre-forward, while Law trod the opposite path. Charlton, with a swerving run and a thunderbolt shot in either foot, scored a record 49 goals for England in 106 internationals. He became a national hero, the most popular footballer in the land, for his sportsmanship as well as his skills, loved and respected throughout the world. The spring-heeled Law possessed a midfield command comparable with that of the great Di Stefano, before he became an out-and-out striker, cobra-like in the goalmouth as he struck with head or foot. Law scored a record 30 goals for Scotland in 55 internationals, and his impish smile and triumphant salute were unforgettable symbols of soccer in the sixties.

Global audiences

With the growth of televised football and the proliferation of international country and club competition, football followers around the world could enjoy, on a regular basis, the skills of the best footballers in Europe and South America. While

George Best (Manchester United and Northern Ireland).

Gerd Muller (Bayern Munich and West Germany).

England could boast Bobby Charlton and Bobby Moore in the 1966 World Cup, Portugal had Eusebio, the "Black Panther", a graceful mover with an explosive shot, the leading goalscorer in the finals and outstanding for Benfica in European club competition.

Pele, literally kicked out of the 1966 World Cup, came back in 1970, when the world was also treated to the silky skills of Tostao, another superb Brazilian ball artist, almost too small and light to be the excellent target man he was. Jairzinho took over Garrincha's role in earlier World Cups as the fast, direct winger with a penchant for goals. And Gerson commanded the midfield, as did Beckenbauer for West Germany and Jim Baxter all too briefly for Scotland.

Missed opportunity

Some stars never paraded their talents in World Cups, from lack of opportunity or of form and fitness at the right time. Jimmy Greaves was England's most prolific post-war goalscorer, six times leading the First Division for Chelsea or Spurs, perhaps the best snapper-up of chances there ever has been. Playing for Scotland in World Cups could be damaging to one's career. Kenny Dalglish rarely produced the form for his country that electrified Celtic and Liverpool fans, although he equalled Law's record of 30 goals, scored in 102 internationals. Dave Mackay's World Cup record was negligible, but for Spurs he was a dynamic left-half, an inspirational midfield dynamo with a barrel chest and a ferocious tackle, equally good in defence and attack. Smaller, but with similar skills and stamina, Billy Bremner was the inspiration of the almost all-conquering Leeds side of the period, a great battler for Scotland, too, but he missed his chance of World Cup fame in 1974, in front of the Yugoslavian goal.

Small is beautiful

As in all eras, size did not matter in the sixties and seventies, particularly in midfield. The tiny Bremner was partnered at Leeds by another small man, Republic of Ireland international Johnny Giles, a fine reader of the game, a master tactician with passing ability to match his ideas. Liam Brady, another Irishman, of Arsenal and Juventus, worked wonders as a midfield general with his educated left foot. And England's Alan Ball and the Argentinian Ossie Ardiles were small wonders of boundless energy and stamina as they brought their team-mates into the game with their give-and-go passing.

Up front, too, some of the best strikers were small. Greaves, Law and Tostao were joined in that department by Gerd Muller and Kevin Keegan, whose low centre of gravity kept them stable in tight situations. Both were stocky, mobile with immensely powerful thighs. Muller stuck to goalscoring and scored so many vital ones for West Germany that one wonders if they would have won anything without him — 68 goals in only 62 internationals, including a record 14 in two World Cups. Keegan was an all-round player, who lifted every team he played for, notably England, Liverpool, Hamburg, Southampton and Newcastle, and was loved by fans everywhere for his honest application as well as his talent.

Tall men with grace

Goalkeepers need to be tall, but they also need courage, and the greatest of the period, mostly British, could not be faulted on that score. England were blessed with Gordon Banks, Ray Clemence and Peter Shilton, Northern Ireland with Pat Jennings. Their only rival, perhaps, was Lev Yashin of the Soviet Union. All of them inspired confidence in others. If they made a rare mistake, it merited headlines.

"Tall and elegant" would describe Bobby Moore and Franz Beckenbauer, master tacticians and captains of England and West Germany respectively, often in opposition, always with more time than anyone else, and always perfect gentlemen.

Best of the seventies

The world star of the seventies, who took over that mantle from Pele and Best, was the mercurial Dutchman Johan Cruyff, a "total footballer" in the teams that gave the world "total football", the highly successful Ajax club of the early seventies and the Dutch team that so nearly won the 1974 World Cup. Cruyff was all over the field, darting along the wings, picking a ball up in defence and spearing into his opponents' penalty box with it the very next moment. As a captain. he lacked the calm temperament of a Moore or a Beckenbauer, but he imposed himself on a game, and was a sublime finisher. His inventiveness and at times sheer cheek captured the imagination of soccer fans everywhere, and he certainly put his country on the footballing map.

Liam Brady (Arsenal and Republic of Ireland).

McMenemy lands Keegan coup for Southampton

LAWRIE MCMENEMY, the persuasive manager of modest Southampton, pulled off the first truly big European transfer coup of the eighties on 11 February by talking Kevin Keegan into an agreement that will take him to the Dell when he leaves Hamburg in the summer. Mr McMenemy, having invited the Press to a hotel near Romsey to meet "someone who will play a big part in Southampton's future", then produced the little man who has become the hottest property in European soccer since leaving Liverpool three years ago.

Once Keegan had announced that he would be quitting the Bundesliga at the end of the season, it was generally assumed that not even the richest English clubs would be able to compete with their Continental counterparts for Keegan's expensive services. But Mr McMenemy, alive to the fact that fees between clubs from EEC countries are restricted to £500,000, eventually persuaded Hamburg to accept £400,000, a fraction of the current British record for the man twice voted European Footballer of the Year.

Kevin Keegan: a bargain buy for Southampton.

Harlow add up Cup success

JOHN MACKENZIE, 25, a company accountant, was the toast of Isthmian League part-timers Harlow as his goal in the third-round replay with Leicester created the season's first major Cup giant-killing act. Amid amazing scenes of jubilation, the like of which the Sports Centre ground has never seen before, he shocked the 1,600 Leicester fans and sent the home crowd wild when he struck Micky Mann's free-kick through a ruck of players two minutes before half-time.

The Second Division promotion hopefuls will rue the chances they missed on Saturday before Harlow's Neil Prosser equalized in the last minute. Harlow were now familiar with Leicester's policy of pumping high balls into the heart of their defence, and it foundered on the height and strength of Vic Clarke and Tony Gough. Harlow's best ever attendance of 9,723 will savour the night for a long time.

Aberdeen are 'Terrorized'

DUNDEE UNITED, the "Terrors", won their first major honour on 12 December, when they beat Aberdeen 3–0 in the replayed final of the Scottish League Cup. The Dons, who beat both Celtic and Rangers twice on their way to the final, were hot favourites when the teams met at Hampden Park, but Dundee United held them to a goalless draw against the run of play. Four days later, in the replay at Dens Park, home of their neighbours Dundee, Jim McLean's young Terrors dominated the Dons, and Willie Pettigrew set them on the way to victory with a goal in 15 minutes. He headed another midway through the second half, and Paul Sturrock then made it three.

Rocketing transfers: Daley and Gray fetch £1.5m each

THE BRITISH TRANSFER record was shattered on 5 September when Manchester City manager Malcolm Allison paid Wolves £1,437,500 for England B midfielder Steve Daley — but the new figure did not last for long. While Daley was completing his transfer forms at Maine Road, Aston Villa's Scottish international striker Andy Gray was on his way to Molineux to finalize details of his £1,469,000 transfer with Wolves manager John Barnwell. This is almost 10 times the club's previous record fee.

Revie: criticised for outrageous disloyalty.

Hollow victory for Revie

THE FA, ORDERED by the High Court to lift their 10-year ban on Don Revie, are unlikely to take any further action against the former England manager, although Mr Justice Cantley found him guilty of bringing the game into disrepute. FA secretary Ted Croker, interpreting the judge's remarks as a total justification of the charge they had brought, felt that the door was still open for further disciplinary proceedings, but that the FA, rather than be accused of vindictiveness, would take no further action.

Mr Justice Cantley's decision to lift the ban was made "with regret", as statements by FA chairman Sir Harold Thompson, made before presiding over the commission, raised a "real likelihood of bias". Mr Revie can now take up a consultancy, worth £90,000 over nine years, with former club Leeds United, and there is naturally speculation that he might return there as manager when his tax-free £340,000 contract with the United Arab Emirates ends in 18 months' time. Whether there will be a rush for his services then is another matter.

SOCCER SOUNDBITES

"A sensational, outrageous example of disloyalty, breach of duty, discourtesy and selfishness."

MR JUSTICE CANTLEY,
on Don Revie's conduct.

Gray day for Shilton: blunder gives Wolves League Cup

A HORRENDOUS Peter Shilton blunder cost Nottingham Forest the chance to make it a hat-trick of League Cups at Wembley, and allowed Andy Gray of Wolves to stroll through for the easiest goal he'll ever score. When Peter Daniel floated a long, high pass to the edge of the Forest area and David Needham shaped to chest the ball clear, Shilton came out and ran straight into his centre-back. As they staggered apart, both Andy Gray and the ball went through the gap, and the £1.5 million striker walked it into the empty net.

Overall, Wolves just about deserved to win. The first half was one of stupefying boredom. But after the interval, the advantage started to creep Forest's way, until the fateful defensive misunderstanding in the 67th minute. Kenny Burns was splendid throughout for Forest, but Viv Anderson, who was cautioned for a dreadful foul on John Richards in the sixth minute, was subsequently lucky not to be sent off. Daniel was Wolves' best player, and it was appropriate that he should have had a hand in their goal. It also was consolation for Gray, injured when Villa won the trophy four years ago.

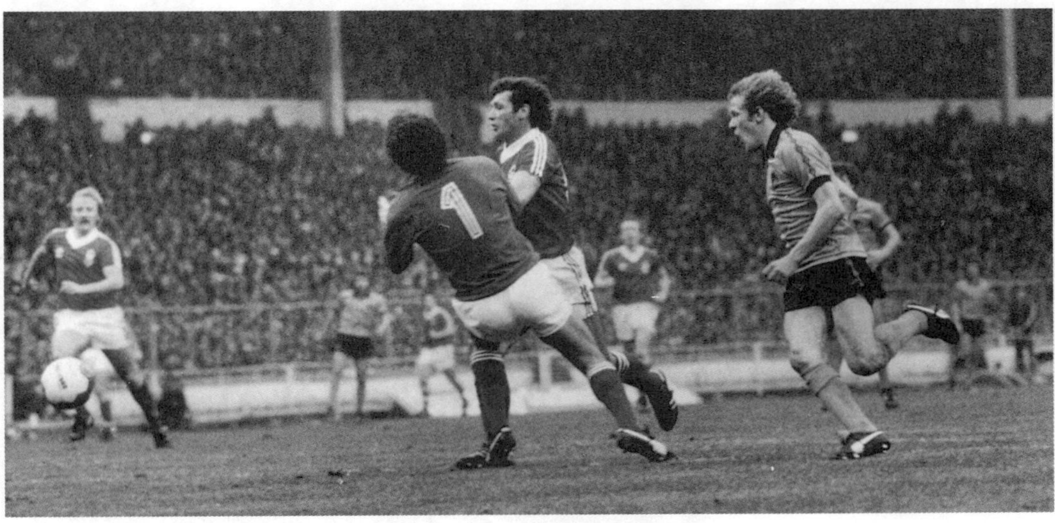

Gray (right) about to pounce, with Needham and Shilton stranded.

SOCCER SOUNDBITES

"I did call, but David didn't hear my shout. You can't hear anything at Wembley."

PETER SHILTON,
taking the blame for Wolves' goal.

Arsenal make third final: Liverpool's 'double' hopes shattered

ARSENAL AT LAST ended the marathon FA Cup semi-final with Liverpool at Coventry on 1 May with a goal by Brian Talbot that earned them a record-breaking third consecutive Cup final appearance and shattered their opponents' hopes of completing the "double". The decisive goal came in the 12th minute following an uncharacteristic error by Ray Kennedy, himself a "double" champion with Arsenal nine years ago. He trod on the ball just outside his six-yard box, and it ran to Stapleton, who put it neatly into the centre for Talbot to head home.

What a cliff-hanger this saga has been! The two sides, however, must be thoroughly sick of each other by now. After a goalless draw at Hillsborough, Sunderland equalized Fairclough's goal in the first replay at Villa Park; Dalglish responded with an injury-time equalizer in the second replay after Sunderland had put Arsenal ahead in 15 seconds, and now Arsenal have settled the issue after four games and seven hours — plus a 1–1 League draw at Anfield in between.

Rix and Brady did an excellent job in midfield for Arsenal at Highfield Road, and the Gunners thoroughly earned the right to meet fellow Londoners, Second Division West Ham, at Wembley on Saturday week.

Avi's strange afternoon out

AVI COHEN WAS obliged to wait until the last Saturday of the League season to play his first senior game in front of the Liverpool crowd, but enough was packed into it to last him for years. After all, it is not every day of the week that an Israeli international makes his home debut in the Football League on the afternoon that his club win the Championship. Nor have many footballers from any country opened their account with an own goal and then balanced the books by scoring for their own side, at the same end, 25 minutes later.

Cohen's first goal put Aston Villa level in the 25th minute, wiping out the lead Johnson had snatched in the fourth. But five minutes after half-time, the Israeli left-back drove a low cross from Dalglish into the far corner of Villa's net, to restore Liverpool's lead and put his wavering team-mates back on course for their fourth Championship in five years.

From that moment, Bob Paisley's men played the highly skilled, attacking football with which they had opened up the substantial mid-season points gap that, ultimately, proved a valuable insurance against Manchester United's late challenge. Further goals by Johnson and Ray Kennedy brought the game — and the season — to a rousing climax.

Cooper the penalty pooper

IPSWICH KEEPER Paul Cooper saved another two penalties on 29 March, in the 1–1 draw with Derby at Portman Road, making his season's tally eight in 10 penalty attempts. He attributes his success to 90 per cent luck and 10 per cent research into the habits of penalty takers. Barry Powell had a 14 out of 14 record before Cooper ended it, and it was only Gerry Daly's second miss in nine attempts. Derby needed a win — they are in grave danger of relegation.

Brian Talbot rises to settle the marathon.

Hammers outsmart Gunners at Wembley

Arsenal are stunned, West Ham jubilant, as Brooking (on ground, right) scores West Ham's winner.

WEST HAM TOOK a leaf out of Arsenal's book at Wembley to win the FA Cup for the second time in six years, this time as an unfancied Second Division side. They stole an early goal, a Trevor Brooking header in the 13th minute, and then sat back to employ the contain-and-counter-attack policy that has been the hallmark of Arsenal's game in their long Cup campaign.

West Ham's shrewd manager John Lyall had had ample time to study Arsenal in combat during their marathon semi-final against Liverpool, which seemed to have left the Gunners mentally and physically drained. He pulled Stuart Pearson back into midfield, adding to the flair of the interceptions and counter-thrusts of Brooking, Devonshire, Allen and Pike.

The West Ham goal came when a misdirected Pearson shot from an angle found the rarely used head of Brooking, who reacted quickly to score from close in. The other talking point was Willie Young's trip on 17-year-old Paul Allen — the youngest player to appear in an FA Cup final — just outside the box, as he was clear and likely to double the margin.

Penalty choker for Arsenal in European shoot-out

Rix's penalty is saved, and Arsenal lose their second final in five days.

IN THE FIRST major Cup final to be decided on penalties, Arsenal lost the European Cup-Winners' Cup to Valencia without conceding a goal in regular play in the final. Defences were on top throughout the match, although Brady made several threatening runs for Arsenal. The Spaniards were disappointing, and more was expected of the Argentinian Mario Kempes and the German Rainer Bonhof.

With no goals scored in 120 minutes, Kempes missed the first penalty and then Brady, of all people, threw away Arsenal's advantage. It went into sudden death after the next eight successful kicks. Then Arias scored for Valencia, and their keeper Pereira saved from Rix. No match should be decided in this fashion, let alone a Cup final, and it's high time the authorities came up with a more acceptable method.

FINAL SCORE

Football League
Division 1: Liverpool
Top scorer: Phil Boyer (Southampton) 23
Division 2: Leicester City
Division 3: Grimsby Town
Division 4: Huddersfield Town
Footballer of the Year: Terry McDermott (Liverpool)

FA Cup Final
West Ham United 1 Arsenal 0

League Cup Final
Wolves 1 Nottingham Forest 0

Scottish League
Premier Division: Aberdeen
Top scorer: Doug Somner (St Mirren) 25
Division 1: Hearts
Division 2: Falkirk
Footballer of the Year: Gordon Strachan (Aberdeen)

Scottish FA Cup Final
Celtic 1 Rangers 0
(after extra time)

Scottish League Cup Final
Dundee United 0 Aberdeen 0
Replay: Dundee U 3 Aberdeen 0

International Championship
Northern Ireland, 5 pts

European Cup Final
Nottingham Forest 1 SV Hamburg 0

Cup-Winners' Cup Final
Valencia 0 Arsenal 0
(after extra time)
Valencia won 5–4 on penalties

UEFA Cup Final
Eintracht Frankfurt beat Borussia Moenchengladbach 2–3, 1–0 on away goals

European Footballer of the Year 1979
Kevin Keegan (SV Hamburg & England)

Leading European Scorer (Golden Boot)
Erwin Van Den Bergh (Lierse) 39

World Club Championship
Nacional (Uruguay) 1 Nottingham Forest 0

FOOTBALL FOCUS

- Non-League Harlow, the FA Cup giant-killers, bravely went out at Watford in the fourth round 4–3, after taking a half-time lead and then going behind 4–1.
- Arsenal played 70 first-class games in the season, in League, FA Cup, League Cup, European Cup-Winners' Cup and Charity Shield.
- Colin Garwood finished as leading scorer for both Portsmouth (17 goals in 24 games) and Aldershot (10 in 16) in Division Four.
- As the result of a bribery scandal in Italy, AC Milan were demoted to the Second Division, club president Felici Colombo banned for life, and international Paolo Rossi of Perugia suspended for three years.

Shilton the hero as Forest retain European Cup

PETER SHILTON put his League Cup final blunder a long way behind him with a masterful performance in Madrid to help Nottingham Forest proudly retain the European Cup. For the second consecutive season, a single goal — this time scored by John Robertson in the 21st minute against Hamburg — was enough to earn Forest the most coveted trophy in club football. But let no one imagine Brian Clough's men were allowed as comfortable a passage to victory as against Malmö last year. This time the boot was on the other foot, as they battled to prevent Kevin Keegan and his spirited colleagues taking home the Cup for the first time.

It was indeed a great tactical triumph for Mr Clough and his partner, Peter Taylor, and they were given an even warmer reception than the team when they were persuaded to take a bow on the pitch at the end. Burns was superb in central defence, and Lloyd a dependable partner. Skipper McGovern and O'Neill, brave, skilful and selfless, also deserve great credit for intercepting, tackling and generally scuffling to great effect in amongst the determined Hamburg forwards. The industrious Bowyer and 18-year-old Mills did a highly efficient job in midfield, too. And Birtles ran himself into the ground as a lone raider.

In the absence of Francis and Bowles, Forest were forced to employ a hyper-defensive policy, and rely on quick breaks to snatch a goal. The decisive, four-man move was started by Frankie Gray, breaking quickly out of defence, and finished by Robertson with a 20-yarder hammered in off the far post.

SOCCER SOUNDBITES

"The odds were stacked against us... It was one of the best 90 minutes we have ever had, absolutely marvellous."

An emotional
BRIAN CLOUGH,
after the match.

Robertson lets fly for the Forest winner against Hamburg in Madrid.

Belgium fail — what a lot of Hrubesch!

WEST GERMANY re-established themselves as a leading soccer power when they beat Belgium 2–1 in Rome, their third consecutive European Championship final over eight years and their second success. Two goals by Horst Hrubesch, the big blond striker, who has been playing alongside Kevin Keegan for Hamburg, were just enough to earn this young German side the triumph they deserved.

After two weeks of rubbish — boring football and poor refereeing — the Championship at last produced a match with thrills, drama and no little skill. During the first half-hour, the Germans played the most inventive football seen in the competition. Newcomer Bernd Schuster was a revelation in the West German midfield, which was disrupted when the splendid Hans-Peter Briegel had to go off in the second half, following which there was a period when the West Germans looked uncertain and their 10th-minute lead vulnerable. After 70 minutes, Belgium equalized from a disputed penalty: Van der Elst looked a foot outside the box when Stielike brought him down, but he was clean through, so justice was done when Vandereycken scored from the spot. Then, with three minutes left, Hrubesch rose above the rest to head Muller's corner into the net.

The new group format for the finals was not a success. Belgium went through to the final at the expense of host country Italy because they scored more goals. Italy's only goal in their three matches — struck late on by Marco Tardelli when he took time off from shackling Keegan — was enough to beat England, who had a disappointing tournament. Ron Greenwood's boys will have to show more imagination if they are to stand a chance in the 1982 World Cup in Spain.

Oh Brotherston! Noel's vital goal

A BEAUTIFULLY TAKEN goal by Noel Brotherston after 23 minutes against Wales brought Northern Ireland their first outright British International Championship since 1914. With the Championship taking place over nine days, the Irish success in Cardiff can be measured against England's 4–1 defeat there six days earlier. It also renders the coming Scotland-England clash irrelevant as far as the title is concerned. The Irish drew 1–1 at Wembley.

If the Championship is to be taken seriously, however, one would expect more than 13,000 to turn up for the deciding match. There were 24,000 at Wrexham when England played there, and 92,000 at Wembley to see England beat Argentina 3–1 in a friendly four days earlier. So what price the Home Championship now?

FINAL SCORE

EUROPEAN CHAMPIONSHIP 1980

Group 1

West Germany	1	Czechoslovakia	0
Holland	1	Greece	0
West Germany	3	Holland	2
Czechoslovakia	3	Greece	1
West Germany	0	Greece	0
Holland	1	Czechoslovakia	1

	P	W	D	L	F	A	P
W. Germany	3	2	1	0	4	2	5
Czech.	3	1	1	1	4	3	3
Holland	3	1	1	1	4	4	3
Greece	3	0	1	2	1	4	1

Group 2

England	1	Belgium	1
Italy	0	Spain	0
Italy	1	England	0
Belgium	2	Spain	1
England	2	Spain	1
Belgium	0	Italy	0

	P	W	D	L	F	A	P
Belgium	3	1	2	0	3	2	4
Italy	3	1	2	0	1	0	4
England	3	1	1	1	3	3	3
Spain	3	0	1	2	2	4	1

THIRD-PLACE MATCH

Italy	1	Czechoslovakia	1

Italy won 9–8 on penalties

FINAL

West Germany	2	Belgium	1

Rome, 22 June 1980. Attendance 47,864

West Germany: Schumacher, Briegel (Cullmann), Forster K, Dietz, Schuster, Rummenigge K-H, Hrubesch, Muller H, Allofs, Stielike, Kaltz (Scorer: Hrubesch 2)
Belgium: Pfaff, Gerets, Millecamps, Meeuws, Renquin, Cools, Vandereycken, Van Moer, Mommens, Van der Elst, Ceulemans (Scorer: Vandereycken pen)

Eerie silence greets Hammers' super victory

WEST HAM'S SPLENDID 5–1 victory over Castilla of Spain on 1 October to come back from their 3–1 first-leg deficit in the Cup-Winners' Cup was greeted by an eerie silence from the Upton Park terraces. This was because the match was played behind closed doors — West Ham's punishment for their followers' disgraceful, drunken behaviour at the Bernabeu Stadium in Madrid two weeks earlier. UEFA also imposed a heavy fine on the club, although West Ham had done everything in their power to prevent trouble in Madrid.

They made tickets available only to registered supporters, who were photographed and their passport numbers noted. And skipper Billy Bonds wrote to each ticket-holder stressing the need for sensible behaviour. But there was nothing the club could do about the so-called fans who travelled independently and bought their tickets in Spain or from other sources.

At Upton Park, the Hammers treated the 300 or so officials present to a splendid display, taking an overall lead with three goals before half-time. Castilla scored after the interval, and took the game into extra time, but two more goals by David Cross to complete his hat-trick put West Ham through to the second round 6–4 on aggregate.

No crowd trouble at Upton Park as West Ham play Castilla behind closed doors.

Jack Charlton reduced to tears by rioting Wednesday fans

SOCCER'S REPUTATION was done further damage at Oldham on 6 September when the behaviour of Sheffield Wednesday followers brought a 29-minute stoppage and tears of frustration to the eyes of manager Jack Charlton, who pleaded unsuccessfully for restraint and was struck by a missile for his pains. The crowd rioted after Wednesday striker Terry Curran had been sent off following a clash with Simon Stainrod. In the ensuing uproar, 20 people, including police, were injured. Fans hurled concrete, bricks, coins — anything they could find. They scaled six-foot barriers and carried their fight on to the pitch. Nine people were arrested.

There was violence at another Second Division match, Chelsea v West Ham at Stamford Bridge, where fighting broke out on the terraces. Forty-two people were arrested and two policemen injured.

A distressed Jack Charlton at Oldham.

Three points for a win from next season

AT A SPECIAL meeting of the Football League at Solihull on 9 February, a number of resolutions were passed arising out of football's "blueprint for the future". From next season, there will be three points for a win (still one for a draw); six matches will be allowed each weekend on Fridays or Sundays; no official (director or secretary) may be involved in the management or administration of more than one club; there will be a transfer embargo on clubs which have payments outstanding from other deals; and — this only a "gentlemen's agreement" — no club is to hire another League club's manager during the season.

Proposals rejected include the reduction of the "majority vote" from three-quarters to two-thirds, and an extension of the half-time interval to 15 minutes.

The "blueprint" was originally drawn up as a charter, "Soccer — The Fight for Survival", by a study group of club secretaries and managers last August. There are still a number of proposals requiring further discussion.

Allen and Sansom in swap deal

ARSENAL AND CRYSTAL Palace did the biggest exchange deal in the history of British soccer on 13 August, when striker Clive Allen — only 62 days on Arsenal's books — and reserve goalkeeper Paul Barron moved to Selhurst Park, and England left-back Kenny Sansom went to Highbury. For the second time in two months, since he left QPR for Arsenal, the 19-year-old Allen has been valued at £1.2 million, and his personal signing-on fees for the two deals add up to an estimated £100,000, without his having kicked a ball in competition. Sansom is valued at £1 million, and Palace have paid £400,000 for Barron, kept out of the Arsenal first team by the evergreen Pat Jennings.

Spending in the transfer market has now reached a staggering £14 million in three months since Cup final day, covering 72 major deals and including two other £1 million transfers, Ian Wallace from Coventry to Forest and Paul Goddard from QPR to West Ham.

Villa transistor champions

ASTON VILLA FANS, with the news of Ipswich's demise at Middlesbrough coming through on their transistor radios, celebrated their Championship triumph at Highbury on 2 May with a benign pitch invasion and a 2–0 defeat! With their thoughts on Ayresome Park, where their only challengers Ipswich were vainly trying to stay in the title race, Villa's nerves were stretched too tightly. So instead of playing the skilful, highly efficient attacking football that has earned them the title, they meekly surrendered control to Arsenal, who looked more like Championship material and clinched their place in the UEFA Cup next season.

Nevertheless, Villa have done enough this season to earn their first League title since 1910. In Cowans, Mortimer and Des Bremner, they possess a formidable midfield unit of well-balanced skill, power and drive. Further forward, Withe, a target-man who scores, Shaw, a young striker of great potential, and Morley, a genuine winger, emphasize Villa's ability to wreck opposing defences. Villa have used only 14 players, with seven of them ever-present.

There was a festival atmosphere before the start, with Highbury guest Pele saluting all parts of the 57,000 crowd and helping release hundreds of balloons. There were also hundreds of police to keep the peace, and at the end form a barrier between the 16,000 Villa supporters and the Arsenal North Bank fans who were allowed to converge on the pitch. Thankfully, it turned out to be a friendly invasion.

Skipper Dennis Mortimer and manager Ron Saunders celebrate in Birmingham.

Anarchy at Luton as mob run Wylde

THANK GOODNESS Luton look like missing promotion to the First Division. Their players may be good enough: their supporters certainly are not. The disgraceful scenes at Kenilworth Road on Saturday, when young fans invaded the pitch three minutes from time in an obvious attempt to get the game called off, were sickening. Fortunately, the police stayed calm, the referee took the players off the pitch for 10 minutes, and Oldham were able to complete a creditable 2–1 victory.

The trouble started an hour earlier, with a reckless tackle by Oldham's Rodger Wylde on Luton back Kirk Stephens. Even Oldham's manager Jimmy Frizzell later admitted that he had seen players sent off for less. The situation wasn't helped when the Luton scoreboard flashed "Send him off". Wylde was the subject of continuing abuse from the crowd, who were incensed still further when he scored two goals. When the referee restarted the match after the pitch was cleared, he advised Mr Frizzell to leave Wylde in the dressing-room but, to his credit, the Oldham manager insisted on sending the player back on, albeit with the warning to stay near the tunnel. Once anarchy takes over from the referee's whistle, football is dead. It looked very sick at Luton.

First League Cup success for Liverpool

LIVERPOOL FINALLY WON the League Cup, the only domestic competition that had eluded them, in a highly entertaining replay at Villa Park. Smartly taken goals by Kenny Dalglish and Alan Hansen helped them recover from Paul Goddard's early blow and take control against West Ham. If the final at Wembley was a great disappointment, the replay made up for it, with Liverpool putting on one of the finest displays of the season.

Most of the thrills at Wembley were crammed into the last three minutes of extra time: a highly disputed goal, when Alan Kennedy hammered a poor clearance past Parkes as Sammy Lee was lying on the ground in an offside position; and West Ham's equalizer, a Ray Stewart penalty with the last kick of the match after McDermott had handled with goalkeeper Clemence beaten.

At Villa Park, West Ham, runaway leaders of the Second Division, scored in their first serious attack, after nine minutes, when Goddard headed in Neighbour's cross at the near post. But Liverpool maintained the control they had exerted before this setback, with Lee outstanding in midfield. The nippy Rush, brought into the attack for only his second full game, drove Lee's free-kick against the angle and Ray Kennedy headed on to the bar.

Then came the goals, after 25 and 28 minutes. First, Dalglish burst past a lunging Bonds from McDermott's shrewd pass and hooked the ball past Parkes with consummate skill. Then Hansen headed home Case's corner at the far post, the ball clipping Bonds on the way. West Ham improved in the second half, with Brooking and Devonshire coming more into the game. But it was a brave effort on the Hammers' part to keep their defeat down to a single goal, with Liverpool playing such commanding football.

Liverpool's disputed goal in the 1-1 draw at Wembley.

Villa the Spurs hero in Cup replay

RICARDO VILLA, who left the pitch in tears on Saturday after being substituted in the 100th FA Cup final, returned to Wembley to score twice and earn Tottenham victory in a hard, exciting replay. After the bearded Argentinian had given Spurs an early lead, Manchester City fought back to equalize, then move in front. But a goal from Crooks and a sensational winner from Villa maintained Spurs' record of never losing a domestic Cup final.

When Villa was substituted by young Garry Brooke midway through the second half in the first match, with Spurs a goal down, he must have thought his season was over. But Hutchison, who had scored City's goal, deflected a Hoddle chip into his own net to afford Spurs a replay. Manager Keith Burkinshaw showed great courage in keeping faith with Villa for the return, and the Argentinian repaid him by sweeping a loose ball into the net after only seven minutes. Young Steve MacKenzie equalized for City three minutes later with a spectacular volley from 22 yards out, and they went ahead after the interval when Reeves converted a penalty. Spurs were regretting their earlier misses now, but they continued to play good football and press forward, with the other Argentinian, Ardiles, and Hoddle running the midfield.

It was a typical piece of Hoddle flair that led to their equalizer after 70 minutes, as he flicked the ball up and over the advancing City defence for Archibald to lay on Crooks's goal. The dramatic winner came seven minutes later. Villa got the ball on the left and began to run powerfully at the City defence. They held off, but he beat one man after another before cutting inside and hammering the ball past Corrigan. It was a fitting climax for what had become a classic Cup final.

Villa (5) evades Caton's last-ditch tackle to score the dramatic winner.

FOOTBALL FOCUS

● John Trollope made his 765th League appearance for Swindon on 18 October, beating the record for one club set 15 years ago by Portsmouth's Jimmy Dickinson. Full-back Trollope, 37, had relinquished his first-team place two seasons earlier to take charge of the youth team. He finally retired in November after five more games.

● The FA ended the red and yellow card system for dismissals and cautions with effect from 19 January, a decision unpopular with most referees.

● Ipswich gained a 1-2-3 in the PFA's Player of the Year poll, with John Wark winning it from Frans Thijssen (the Football Writers' Footballer of the Year) and Paul Mariner — a Scotsman, a Dutchman and an Englishman!

● Exeter were the Cup giant-killers of the season, reaching the quarter-finals despite being drawn away in five of their six rounds. The mid-table Third Division side drew at First Division Leicester in the fourth round and beat them 3–1 in the replay, with a hat-trick by Tony Kellow, who scored 33 goals during the season. They then drew at St James's Park before thrashing Second Division Newcastle 4–0 at their own St James Park! But they finally fell 2–0 to Spurs at White Hart Lane.

● Leicester, who were later relegated, won 2–1 at Anfield on 31 January to inflict Liverpool's first home defeat for three years 10 days, covering 85 League, FA Cup, League Cup and European matches.

● Arbroath, in Scotland's Division Two, won fewer home matches (three) and more away matches (10) than any other club in the division. They finished ninth of 14.

Battling Ipswich win UEFA Cup

WHEN IPSWICH took a 3–0 lead over AZ 67 Alkmaar to Holland in the final of the UEFA Cup, their travelling fans could not be confident of the outcome, bearing in mind their team's tendency in previous campaigns to collapse in the away leg, a failing that had twice proved almost fatal earlier this season. But they had recently produced good away results, particularly in the quarter-finals, when they went to France and beat St Etienne 4–1 despite an early Johnny Rep goal that had taken the home side's tally in the competition to 23–0.

AZ were the new Dutch champions, but a cracking 20-yard volley in four minutes from one of Holland's own stars, Frans Thijssen, gave Ipswich a dream start and meant AZ had to score at least five. They did score two, before John Wark got a priceless goal back for Town. Not only did it virtually ensure victory for Ipswich, but it was Wark's record-equalling 14th European goal of the season. AZ refused to surrender and scored twice more, but Ipswich thoroughly deserved their overall 5–4 triumph.

John Wark (right) scores his all-important 14th European goal of the season.

Third European Cup for Liverpool

LIVERPOOL MADE SURE the European Cup will remain in England for the fifth successive year when they earned their third victory in the competition with a spectacular goal from left-back Alan Kennedy in the 81st minute at the Parc des Princes. This equals the record of Spain (1956-60), whose five wins were all recorded by Real Madrid, Liverpool's 1–0 victims in Paris. Another triumph for the club was the behaviour of their 12,000 travelling fans, who took the Paris police by surprise by giving them no trouble.

The match was a highly interesting, if not over-exciting, battle of wits between two teams searching for openings and intent on offering their opponents as few opportunities as possible. Both managers gambled by bringing back players following long lay-offs: Liverpool's Dalglish after a month with ankle ligament trouble, and Real's English international Laurie Cunningham after six months with a foot injury. Cunningham caused Liverpool most trouble, but the Reds did most of the pressing, even if their goal attempts were mostly from long range.

The breakthrough came from a Ray Kennedy throw-in on the left. There seemed little danger when his namesake Alan chested the ball down in Real's penalty area, but Cortes took a wild swing at it, and Kennedy brushed past him and from a narrow angle slammed the ball past Real's keeper.

Liverpool skipper Phil Thompson with the European Cup.

FINAL SCORE

Football League
Division 1: Aston Villa
Top scorer: Steve Archibald (Tottenham Hotspur), Peter Withe (Aston Villa) 20
Division 2: West Ham United
Division 3: Rotherham United
Division 4: Southend United
Footballer of the Year: Frans Thijssen (Ipswich Town)

FA Cup Final

Tottenham Hotspur	1	Manchester City	1
(after extra time)			
Replay: Tottenham H.	3	Manchester City	2

League Cup Final

Liverpool	1	West Ham United	1
(after extra time)			
Replay: Liverpool	2	West Ham United	1

Scottish League
Premier Division: Celtic
Top scorer: Francis McGarvey (Celtic) 23
Division 1: Hibernian
Division 2: Queen's Park
Footballer of the Year: Alan Rough (Partick Thistle)

Scottish FA Cup Final

Rangers	0	Dundee United	0
Replay: Rangers	4	Dundee United	1

Scottish League Cup Final

Dundee United	3	Dundee	0

International Championship
Not completed

European Cup Final

Liverpool	1	Real Madrid	0

Cup-Winners' Cup Final

Dynamo Tbilisi	2	Carl Zeiss Jena	1

UEFA Cup Final
Ipswich Town beat AZ 67 Alkmaar 3–0, 2–4

European Footballer of the Year 1981
Karl-Heinz Rummenigge (Bayern Munich & West Germany)

Leading European Scorer (Golden Boot)
Georgi Slavkov (Trakia Plovdiv) 31

World Club Championship

Flamengo (Brazil)	3	Liverpool (England)	0

England booked for Spain — and not as tourists

Brooking's second goal stays where he placed it.

AFTER THEIR STIRRING 3–1 victory in Hungary on 6 June, England will begin their holidays knowing that they now have excellent prospects of visiting Spain next summer, not in the widely predicted role of tourists, but as one of the 24 World Cup finalists. There is still hard work to do in Oslo in September and against Hungary two months later, when the qualifying competition will be completed at Wembley. But success in Budapest — those who saw it will remember it as a famous victory — has put England back on the course from which the defeats in Romania and Switzerland had blown them.

There is a long way to go yet but, having come so perilously close to disaster, they are unlikely to lose their way again. Victory in Hungary was a major achievement for England after their recent run of failures, especially the defeat in Basle a week ago, which saw strident calls for Ron Greenwood's resignation. Against the Magyars, Mr Greenwood opted for experience, and the "old guard" simply closed their ears to the awesome noise of the Nep Stadium and played with a maturity their opponents could not match.

Though it was predominantly an admirable all-round team effort, Thompson and Brooking emerged as the heroes. Thompson held the defence together with an assurance that even the gifted Torocsik and powerful Kiss could not shake. Brooking exploited the space allowed him to engineer the dismantling of Hungary's nervous defence — and scored two goals into the bargain.

The first came in the 19th minute, when he hooked the ball home after a delightful move with Neal, Coppell and McDermott. Hungary equalized on the stroke of half-time through Garaba, but Brooking put England firmly back on top on the hour with a spectacular left-foot shot that left the ball jammed between the net and back stanchion. And, as the Hungarian spirit sagged, Keegan made it 3–1, converting a penalty after being brought down by Garaba.

England now have seven points from six matches, with a goal difference of plus five. Romania have six points from five games, Hungary five from four.

Shankly: soccer's true folk hero

FORMER LIVERPOOL manager Bill Shankly died on 29 September, aged 67, following a heart attack. In the world of professional football, "Shanks" was unique, a folk hero to the core.

He will best be remembered as the driving force behind Liverpool FC. In 15 glorious years as manager at Anfield, he made them into one of the world's most famous and respected clubs. A Second Division title, three League Championships, two FA Cups and one UEFA Cup remain as monuments to Shankly's magnificent work at Liverpool, where he built two great sides before his retirement in July 1974. And he laid the foundations for Bob Paisley, his eager lieutenant, to go on to even greater success.

Bill Shankly, idol of the Kop.

But the admiration which football people have for Shankly goes far beyond the Merseyside boundaries. He was born in the Ayrshire mining village of Glenbuck into a footballing family. He made his mark at Preston as a tenacious, dedicated wing-half, helping the club to the FA Cup final in 1937 (lost) and 1938 (won), and would have won more than his five Scottish caps but for the war. He turned to management in the late forties, with Carlisle, Grimsby, Workington and Huddersfield, before the call from Liverpool came in 1959. After signing men such as Ian St John and Ron Yeats, he took the slumbering giant back into Division One and on the road to 18 successive seasons in European competition.

A tremendous motivator of men, Shankly filled his teams with inspiration, and helped turn promising players such as Kevin Keegan — recruited from lowly Scunthorpe — into great ones. One of Shankly's greatest attributes was his judgment in the trnsfer market: few of his signings turned out wrong. He also became the idol of the Kop, developing a closer relationship with supporters than probably any other manager in history.

"Shanks" had a sharp, dry and sometimes abrasive wit, but was a soft, warm-hearted man. Impulsive and loquacious words poured from him in a crisp Scottish accent, and his countless quips have become part of soccer folklore.

SOCCER SOUNDBITES

"I have only felt like this once before, and that was when my father died, because Bill was like a second father to me."

KEVIN KEEGAN.

"He was a great man. His motivation could move mountains."

RON YEATS.

"Football is not a matter of life and death — it's much more important."

BILL SHANKLY.

England and Northern Ireland book tickets to Spain

ENGLAND'S WORLD CUP qualification campaign, so often teetering on the brink of disaster during the past year, finally ended in triumph at Wembley on 18 November when Ron Greenwood's men beat Hungary 1–0 and were assured by the crowd that they would not be walking alone in Spain next summer. Indeed, with Northern Ireland beating Israel by the same score in Belfast, and Scotland already qualified, they will be joined there by two other home countries. Wales, however, who lost 3–0 to the USSR, will only make it to the finals if their conquerors win in Czechoslovakia in the remaining match in Group Three.

Long after the players had disappeared down the Wembley tunnel, following the narrow but clear victory over Hungary, the fans were singing, cheering and waving their flags to celebrate England's right to feature in the finals for the first time since Mexico in 1970.

Although Greenwood said that "there was no great euphoria in the dressing room after the match — just gratitude that we had managed to get through", England had produced their best performance of the competition to wipe out all memory of their failures against Romania, Switzerland and, latterly, their almost catastrophic defeat in Oslo. Fortunately for England, Switzerland had subsequently taken three points off Romania; otherwise, England might have been out of the running instead of needing just to draw with Hungary. Although there was only Mariner's 16th-minute goal to separate the teams at the end, England produced an exhilarating performance, with Martin doing well alongside Thompson at the centre of the defence, and Robson, Brooking and Keegan in scintillating form in midfield. This display must encourage the belief that their journey to Spain next summer will not be a waste of time.

Malcolm Macdonald: first paid director

MALCOLM MACDONALD, the Fulham manager and former England striker, became the first paid director of a Football League club on 19 November, within minutes of an FA decision to approve the innovation at an Extraordinary General Meeting. As soon as the members decided to permit one paid director per club, by 522 votes to 28, Ernie Clay, the Fulham chairman and chief shareholder, told Mr Macdonald that the job was his. He will have responsibility for controlling the football side of the club's activities.

Fulham manager, and new paid director, Malcolm Macdonald.

SOCCER SOUNDBITES

"Now the gate is open for the game to be run by people with the necessary football knowledge and experience."

ERNIE CLAY,
Fulham chairman, speaking after Malcolm Macdonald's appointment.

Liverpool home with the Milk

LIVERPOOL LEFT IT late in defence of the League Cup — now the Milk Cup, sponsored by the Milk Marketing Board. They were trailing Spurs at Wembley to an 11th-minute Archibald goal until the 87th minute, when Ronnie Whelan snatched a dramatic equalizer. Only two minutes earlier, Archibald had missed a chance to clinch the match for Spurs. Now, in extra time, they were visibly wilting, and in the second period Dalglish coolly set up a second for the 20-year-old Whelan, who has established himself in the side this season as a goalscoring midfielder in place of Ray Kennedy, and Rush scored a third in the last minute. So Tottenham's "grand slam" dreams of a clean sweep at home and a European trophy are now shattered. Both sides have important European matches on Wednesday, and both will be challenging strongly for the Championship if they can capitalize on all those games in hand.

Keeper Bruce Grobbelaar leads Liverpool in a victory song, with last season's League Cup and their newly won Milk Cup: Top (l-r) Dalglish, Lawrenson, Lee, Rush, Grobbelaar, Hansen, McDermott, Thompson; crouched (l-r) Whelan, Johnson, Souness, Alan Kennedy, Neal.

Roberts hat-trick knocks Southampton off the top

Keegan finds a way to stop Roberts scoring.

SPURS PAID Weymouth £30,000 for Graham Roberts and converted him from a non-League striker into a central defender last season. He showed he had not lost his striking ability when he was drafted into the side on 20 March to replace the injured Ardiles against Southampton, his home-town team, and one of the League clubs that had rejected him. He scored three goals, and was unlucky not to get two or three more, as Spurs knocked the leaders off their perch with a 3–2 win at White Hart Lane. Southampton, indeed, only woke up when they were two down, but the scoreline flattered them.

Spurs, who reached the semi-finals of the Cup-Winners' Cup on Wednesday and are in the FA Cup semis, too, are still in with a good shout for the League. They are seven points behind new leaders Swansea, but have five games in hand — worth three points a time now, if they can win them!

Brazil 5 Southampton 3

AT FIRST SIGHT, the scoreline does not look so bad for First Division leaders Southampton, but the five goals against them were scored by Alan Brazil of Ipswich, and not the country of the same name. They stay top, but their challengers have played fewer games, and Ipswich are among them, six points adrift with five games in hand.

A series of setbacks for Ipswich over the last two weeks, including exits from both domestic Cup competitions, saw Brazil dropped before the 4–0 League defeat at Anfield. But he wasn't out for long and, boosted by his recall to the Scottish squad, he has now produced the deadliest exhibition of finishing seen in Division One since Roger Davies scored five for Derby against Luton seven years ago. He hit a first-half hat-trick and scored his fifth four minutes from time. But it was not a one-man show, and Brazil was the first to acknowledge the debt he owed to co-striker Mich D'Avray, deputizing for the injured Mariner, who made four of the goals. On the other side, strikers Keegan and Channon could do little more than stand and admire.

Brazil celebrates another goal.

SOCCER SOUNDBITES

"I wish that man would go back to Brazil, or wherever it is he comes from."

IVAN KATALINIC,
Southampton's Yugoslav goalkeeper.

Classy extra-time win for Dons

Strachan (left) slots in goal number three for Aberdeen in extra time.

ABERDEEN BEAT Rangers in the Scottish Cup final at Hampden 4–1 after extra time, breaking the hold that the "Old Firm" have had on the trophy since the Dons last won it in 1970. Indeed, Rangers had not lost a final to any club but Celtic since 1929 — and they have been in a few!

Rangers took the lead with a John MacDonald goal after 15 minutes, one of the best of their entire season's output. Aberdeen equalized 18 minutes later with a swerving shot from centre-back Alex McLeish, who shared the Aberdeen honours with fellow redhead and World Cup colleague Gordon Strachan, as they took control of the match in the second half. But they failed to translate their class and superiority into goals until extra time, when they ran Rangers ragged and McGhee, Strachan and Cooper all scored.

It was a fitting reward for Alex Ferguson's men, who so narrowly missed catching Celtic in the League after winning 15 of their last 16 matches.

FOOTBALL FOCUS

● FIFA's technical committee have expressed concern about the "excessive demonstrative attitude of some players and teams when a goal is scored". They felt that "the scorer should be congratulated by the team captain or the player who made the pass, but the exultant outbursts of several players at once jumping on top of each other, kissing and embracing, should be banned from the football pitch", and recommended that national associations should curb such behaviour.

● Before the transfer market slumped, with the deepening financial crisis in football, several more huge transfers took place, including Justin Fashanu from Norwich to Nottingham Forest for £1 million and Trevor Francis from Forest to Man City for £1.2 million. But the "last of the big spenders" proved to be new Man Utd manager Ron Atkinson, who bought John Gidman and Remi Moses for nearly £0.5 million each; Frank Stapleton, a "steal" at the tribunal valuation of £1.1 million; and then broke the British record by paying £1.7 million for Bryan Robson from West Brom.

● The international referees' committee, in answer to a question from the Swiss FA regarding a goal-kick in which the ball touched the referee in the penalty area before passing out of the area, agreed by a majority of votes that the referee should be considered as "air" and that the ball was in play.

● Glenn Hoddle scored from the spot with only the sixth penalty awarded in an FA Cup final (all successful) to give Spurs a 1–0 win in the replay against Second Division QPR.

QPR captain Tony Currie brings Graham Roberts down in the box for Spurs' winning Cup final penalty.

Liverpool soar to majestic heights

ALL-CONQUERING Liverpool won their 13th League title, their fifth in seven seasons, when they beat Spurs 3–1 at Anfield on 15 May. Manager Bob Paisley, who has guided them to these successes, as well as three European Cups, a UEFA Cup win and two League Cups, rates this latest triumph as the greatest. Liverpool were languishing in mid-table at the turn of the year but, despite Paisley's rebuilding the side during the season, they came with a late run — 11 straight wins from 9 March to 1 May — and inexorably caught and passed all their rivals.

The turning point came shortly after the decision had been taken — in the famous Anfield Boot Room — to give Ray Kennedy's midfield job to young Irish international Ronnie Whelan and to confirm Ian Rush as Dalglish's front-line partner. The timing of the changes and, later, the employment of Australian Craig Johnston in place of McDermott, were crucial. Bruce Grobbelaar, too, settled in after a shaky start as Clemence's replacement in goal, and central defender Mark Lawrenson was another success story — although these two had an unfortunate match when Liverpool went out of the European Cup in the semi-finals to CSKA Sofia. It was a Grobbelaar error that conceded a late equalizer, and Lawrenson became the first Liverpool player to be sent off in 18 successive years of European competition.

But that was Liverpool's only real setback in another triumphant season, and they can't be expected to win everything — or can they?

Villa make it six in a row for England in European Cup

ASTON VILLA, WITH only two seasons of UEFA Cup experience in Europe, started as underdogs in the European Cup final against Bayern Munich in Rotterdam. But they pulled off a famous 1–0 victory over the three-times champions with a 67th-minute goal from Peter Withe, to ensure that Europe's premier trophy stayed in England for a record sixth successive season. Their triumph was even more remarkable in that it was achieved a mere 103 days after Tony Barton took over as manager from Ron Saunders, and 81 minutes after reserve keeper Nigel Spink had taken over in goal for only his second senior game for the club (the first was in December 1979!).

Spink, indeed, was Villa's hero. Going on for Jimmy Rimmer, who found a neck injury sustained in training too much of a handicap, he rose to the occasion magnificently, coming to Villa's rescue with a series of astonishingly confident saves when they were in danger of being overwhelmed. He was called into action soon after reaching the pitch to defy close-range efforts by Durnberger and Rummenigge. Then, when Bayern — the last Continental club to win the trophy before Liverpool ushered in the age of English supremacy — applied increasingly heavy pressure after the interval, his keen eyes, safe hands and instinctive agility stood between the Germans and victory.

This is not to belittle the performances of Spink's colleagues. Cowans and Mortimer, with commendably efficient displays in midfield, refused to allow Breitner to control the game. The combative Evans and calm McNaught, though sometimes outsmarted by Bayern's slick football, refused to bow the knee to the persistent Rummenigge and Hoeness. And, having spoilt many a promising move early on, Shaw, Morley and Withe ultimately produced the most telling strike of the night: Shaw conjured up a piece of skill on the left and fed left-winger Morley, who worked his own brand of magic, turning his man inside-out before sending a low centre across goal which Withe gleefully converted.

Withe scores the goal that won Villa the European Cup.

Nigel Spink: heroics as substitute keeper.

Sending-off proposed for 'professional foul'

AT AN Extraordinary General Meeting of the Football League, the clubs agreed in principle the proposals put forward in May by the Busby Advisory Committee. The committee, under the chairmanship of Sir Matt Busby and including Bobby Charlton and Jimmy Hill, had come up with a series of revolutionary and far-reaching suggestions, and the League recommended that the FA be asked to put those requiring law changes to the International Football Association board. Although there was no intent expressed to go it alone if FIFA refused permission to experiment, it was agreed that some of the proposals could be implemented by instructing referees on the interpretation of the laws.

Thus if the key proposal — that the so-called "professional" or "tactical" foul committed outside the penalty area be punishable by a penalty kick, if it prevented a likely goal — were rejected, referees could still be instructed to send the offender off, as provided for in the laws (presumably for "serious" foul play). In the same way, throwing in from the wrong place could be treated as a foul throw (i.e., a ball improperly thrown in).

FIFA's reactions will not be known until later on this summer, but the ruling body are unlikely to allow any unilateral experiments, having already warned that English football would be ostracized unless it "continued to abide by international rules".

FINAL SCORE

Football League
Division 1: Liverpool
Top scorer: Kevin Keegan (Southampton) 26
Division 2: Luton Town
Division 3: Burnley
Division 4: Sheffield United
Footballer of the Year: Steve Perryman (Tottenham Hotspur)

FA Cup Final

Spurs	1	QPR	1
(after extra time)			
Replay: Spurs	1	QPR	0

League Cup Final

Liverpool	3	Spurs	1
(after extra time)			

Scottish League
Premier Division: Celtic
Top scorer: George McCluskey (Celtic) 21
Division 1: Motherwell
Division 2: Clyde
Footballer of the Year: Paul Sturrock (Dundee United)

Scottish FA Cup Final

Aberdeen	4	Rangers	1
(after extra time)			

Scottish League Cup Final

Rangers	2	Dundee United	1

International Championship
England, 6 pts

European Cup Final

Aston Villa	1	Bayern Munich	0

Cup-Winners' Cup Final

Barcelona	2	Standard Liège	1

UEFA Cup Final
IFK Gothenburg beat SV Hamburg 1–0, 3–0

European Footballer of the Year 1981
Karl-Heinz Rummenigge (Bayern Munich & West Germany)

Leading European Scorer (Golden Boot)
Wim Kieft (Ajax Amsterdam) 32

World Club Championship

Penarol (Uruguay)	2	Aston Villa (England)	0

Restored Italian master

The increase from 16 to 24 entrants did not improve the World Cup, played in Spain, and the second-phase format was a failure. Italy were lucky to survive the first round, but suddenly came alive, as striker Paolo Rossi, recently restored to football after a two-year suspension for his part in a bribery scandal, rediscovered his scoring skills. England, after a bright start, and conceding only one goal, lost the art of scoring and went out like a damp squib.

Rossi, Italy's goalscoring hero.

THE HOME COUNTRIES took advantage of the extra qualifying places, and three got through to the finals, Scotland and Northern Ireland from the same group. England just muddled through. European champions West Germany qualified ominously well, with eight straight wins and 33 goals against three.

The first phase of the finals — six groups of four, with two going through from each — threw up a handful of surprises. Holders Argentina lost to Belgium in the opening match, and Algeria made a sensational World Cup debut, beating West Germany 2–1. They beat Chile, too, but were scandalously prevented from going through when West Germany and Austria contrived the result of their match, the last of the group.

England got a wonderful start, skipper Bryan Robson scoring against France in 27 seconds, a World Cup record, and they won their three matches. Brazil were the only other side to take six points, with displays of exciting, attacking football not seen since the days of Pele, Gerson, Tostao and company.

Scotland scored first against the Brazilians, a cracking goal from right-back David Narey. But, with Zico, Socrates, Cerezo and Falcao the elegant masters of midfield, knocking the ball about as if they were on a training session, Brazil crushed the brave Scots 4–1. This left Scotland needing to beat the Soviet Union to go through to the next phase. They could only draw, and went out on goal difference for the third World Cup running.

Viva Zapata

Although Honduras gave an excellent account of themselves in Group 5, with draws against Spain and Northern Ireland, the allocation of a second finals places to the Central and North American zone was looking a little sick when El Salvador went down to a record defeat, 10–1 against Hungary. Ramirez Zapata, their scorer, was El Salvador's hero.

Robson (16) scores in 27 seconds against France.

New Zealand, making their World Cup debut, fared little better, although the two goals they scored against a criminally careless Scotland proved the Scots' downfall. Cameroon were expected to be the chopping-blocks of Group 1, but nobody could beat them. With their captain Thomas N'Kono an inspiration in goal and Roger Milla a dangerous striker, it was only inexperience that let them down. Had they taken their chances, Italy would have made a shock early exit.

The finest performance from an unfancied side in the first phase belonged to Northern Ireland. With a squad largely recruited from the lower reaches of the Football League, and a string of poor results behind them, they not only qualified from Group 5, they won it. They beat hosts Spain with a Gerry Armstrong goal just before the interval, and, despite having Mal Donaghy harshly sent off half an hour from the end, kept the Spaniards at bay.

Favourites depart

Both remaining South American countries, World Cup holders Argentina and favourites Brazil, were in the same group. Italy, despite their pitiful start to the competition, were not overawed, and set out against Argentina in typically cynical fashion, intent on stopping Maradona and company come what may. The first half was a disgrace to football, with the Italians the chief culprits along with the referee and the inappropriately named Gentile clobbering Maradona if he so much as thought of going for the ball. Having softened up the opposition, the Italians began to play the ball in the second half, and won 2–1.

Maradona took his frustration out on Brazil, and he was sent off for blatantly kicking Batista, but not before the Brazilians had scored three delightful goals. But Brazil lacked a competent central striker, and that is the department that finally gave Italy the edge when the two sides met in the decider, a wonderful match.

Paolo Rossi, hitherto struggling to find his form, was suddenly back to his old, sharp self. Twice he scored, typical opportunist goals, and twice the Brazilians came back, with magnificent efforts from Socrates and Falcao. But Rossi completed his hat-trick with 16 minutes to go, and the best side in the competition were out.

British exit

Northern Ireland's bubble was burst by France, who were beginning to play some lovely football and outclassed them 4–1. England were drawn with their old rivals West Germany in Madrid, but the game disappointed the 75,000 crowd in the magnificent Bernabeu Stadium. It was mostly tight and negative and, although England made the better chances, they were content with a 0–0 draw after Rummenigge erupted a 25-yarder onto the bar near the end.

When the Germans beat Spain, England needed a good win against the hosts (2–1 would have meant drawing lots). They were far superior to Spain, but just could

Brazil and France played the best football, England and Cameroon were undefeated, but Italy, thanks to the revival of Rossi, won their third World Cup.

not score. Ron Greenwood brought Keegan and Brooking — neither fully recovered from injury — off the bench after 63 minutes for their first taste of World Cup football in a desperate attempt to add penetration. But sadly they missed the easiest chances of the game, which at their sharpest they would probably have put away. The game ended goalless, and England — unbeaten — were out.

Italy had no trouble beating Poland — without the suspended Boniek, their star player — in the first semi-final. A goal in each half from Rossi saw to that. The every opportunity. Even the scandalous foul by German keeper Schumacher on substitute Battiston — for which he went unpunished and the Frenchman was carried off — did not stop their flow. But it was not until the first period of extra time that the French attack earned their reward, with brilliant goals from defender Tresor and from Giresse. But then they allowed the Germans back into the game. The half-fit Rummenigge, used only in spells, had not long been on the field, but scored an opportunist goal, and then Fischer

Platini remonstrates with the referee after Battiston is felled.

second semi, between France and West Germany, produced one of the most memorable matches in World Cup history. There could have been few neutral observers not willing the French to win, as they put on a dazzling performance that rivalled the Brazilians in inventiveness and sheer footballing artistry. Platini and Giresse were magically creative in midfield, where anchorman Tigana was the perfect foil. On the wing, Rocheteau — the "French George Best" — was always dangerous.

The first half was packed with incident and good football, and Platini equalized an early Littbarski goal with a penalty. It continued in the same vein in the second half, with the French on top, often leaving four or five men upfield, with backs Bossis and Amoros breaking forward at equalized with a spectacular overhead kick. Unfortunately this wonderful game went to penalties, where football is always the loser, and Hrubesch eventually put West Germany in the final.

Bearzot's triumph

The final, for the most part, was not a good advertisement for football, following the pattern of so many of the earlier matches — fouls, spoiling tactics, gamesmanship and incompetent refereeing. For almost an hour, it was a war of attrition. Italy's Cabrini shot wide from a first-half penalty, the first such miss in a World Cup final, and then Rossi put them ahead from close-in after 57 minutes. Only then did they show the skill and flair manager Enzo Bearzot had almost despaired of bringing out. Crucified over many months in the Italian Press for the team's poor results, he had long been frustrated in his attempts to harness their talent into adventurous attacking football, alien as that was to their negative domestic game. Tardelli and then Altobelli scored to make the game safe before Breitner scored a late goal for the by-now well-beaten Germans.

FINAL SCORE

FIRST ROUND

Group 1

Italy	0	Poland	0
Peru	0	Cameroon	0
Italy	1	Peru	1
Poland	0	Cameroon	0
Poland	5	Peru	1
Italy	1	Cameroon	1

	P	W	D	L	F	A	P
Poland	3	1	2	0	5	1	4
Italy	3	0	3	0	2	2	3
Cameroon	3	0	3	0	1	1	3
Peru	3	0	2	1	2	6	2

Group 2

Algeria	2	West Germany	1
Austria	1	Chile	0
West Germany	4	Chile	1
Austria	2	Algeria	0
Algeria	3	Chile	2
West Germany	1	Austria	0

	P	W	D	L	F	A	P
W. Germany	3	2	0	1	6	3	4
Austria	3	2	0	1	3	1	4
Algeria	3	2	0	1	5	5	4
Chile	3	0	0	3	3	8	0

Group 3

Belgium	1	Argentina	0
Hungary	10	El Salvador	1
Argentina	4	Hungary	1
Belgium	1	El Salvador	0
Belgium	1	Hungary	1
Argentina	2	El Salvador	0

	P	W	D	L	F	A	P
Belgium	3	2	1	0	3	1	5
Argentina	3	2	0	1	6	2	4
Hungary	3	1	1	1	12	6	3
El Salvador	3	0	0	3	1	13	0

Group 4

England	3	France	1
Czechoslovakia	1	Kuwait	1
England	2	Czechoslovakia	0
France	4	Kuwait	1
France	1	Czechoslovakia	1
England	1	Kuwait	0

	P	W	D	L	F	A	P
England	3	3	0	0	6	1	6
France	3	1	1	1	6	5	3
Czech.	3	0	2	1	2	4	2
Kuwait	3	0	1	2	2	6	1

Group 5

Spain	1	Honduras	1
Yugoslavia	0	Northern Ireland	0
Spain	2	Yugoslavia	1
Northern Ireland	1	Honduras	1
Yugoslavia	1	Honduras	0
Northern Ireland	1	Spain	0

	P	W	D	L	F	A	P
N. Ireland	3	1	2	0	2	1	4
Spain	3	1	1	1	3	3	3
Yugoslavia	3	1	1	1	2	2	3
Honduras	3	0	2	1	2	3	2

Group 6

Brazil	2	USSR	1
Scotland	5	New Zealand	2
Brazil	4	Scotland	1
USSR	3	New Zealand	0
USSR	2	Scotland	2
Brazil	4	New Zealand	0

	P	W	D	L	F	A	P
Brazil	3	3	0	0	10	2	6
USSR	3	1	1	1	6	4	3
Scotland	3	1	1	1	8	8	3
N. Zealand	3	0	0	3	2	12	0

SECOND ROUND

Group A

Poland	3	Belgium	0
USSR	1	Belgium	0
Poland	0	USSR	0

	P	W	D	L	F	A	P
Poland	2	1	1	0	3	0	3
USSR	2	1	1	0	1	0	3
Belgium	2	0	0	2	0	4	0

Group B

West Germany	0	England	0
West Germany	2	Spain	1
England	0	Spain	0

	P	W	D	L	F	A	P
W. Germany	2	1	1	0	2	1	3
England	2	0	2	0	0	0	2
Spain	2	0	1	1	1	2	1

Group C

Italy	2	Argentina	1
Brazil	3	Argentina	1
Italy	3	Brazil	2

	P	W	D	L	F	A	P
Italy	2	2	0	0	5	3	4
Brazil	2	1	0	1	5	4	2
Argentina	2	0	0	2	2	5	0

Group D

France	1	Austria	0
Northern Ireland	2	Austria	2
France	4	Northern Ireland	1

	P	W	D	L	F	A	P
France	2	2	0	0	5	1	4
Austria	2	0	1	1	2	3	1
N. Ireland	2	0	1	1	3	6	1

SEMI-FINALS

Italy	2	Poland	0
West Germany	3	France	3

(after extra time)

West Germany won 5–4 on penalties

THIRD-PLACE MATCH

Poland	3	France	2

FINAL

Italy	3	West Germany	1

Santiago Bernabeu Stadium, Madrid, 11 July 1982. Attendance 90,000

Italy: Zoff, Gentile, Collovati, Scirea, Cabrini, Conti, Oriali, Bergomi, Tardelli, Rossi, Graziani (Altobelli, Causio)
(Scorers: Rossi, Tardelli, Altobelli)
West Germany: Schumacher, Kaltz, Forster K-H, Stielike, Forster B, Briegel, Breitner, Dremmler (Hrubesch), Littbarski, Fischer, Rummenigge (Muller)
(Scorer: Breitner)

Leading scorers
6 Rossi (Italy)
5 Rummenigge (W.Germany)
4 Boniek (Poland)
Zico (Brazil)

Bobby Robson is new England supremo

BOBBY ROBSON was appointed England team manager on 7 July for a five-year term, and is the second Ipswich manager in 19 years to take charge of the national team. Like Sir Alf Ramsey before him, he has brought considerable success to the East Anglian club and will leave somewhat reluctantly a job that he has relished.

As an inside-forward, Mr Robson made his debut for Fulham in 1950, clocked up 584 League appearances in two spells with the London club and one with West Bromwich, and played 20 times for England, including the 1958 and 1962 World Cups, scoring four goals. Now, at 49, he takes over from the retiring Ron Greenwood an England squad who promised more in the World Cup in Spain than they ultimately achieved. And, as no candidate for entry into the squad will have played more than three League games before England meet Denmark in Copenhagen in their opening European Championship fixture, he will be unlikely to make any startling changes as he begins his first task of building a team initially for Europe and, in the longer term, for the 1986 World Cup.

Robson, hoping to emulate Sir Alf Ramsey.

Fifty scored in First Division goal feast

Watford's hero Luther Blissett (8) scores one of his four goals.

IT IS A LONG TIME since the First Division enjoyed such a feast of goals, 50 in the 11 matches played on Saturday 25 September. Eight teams scored four or more. Ipswich, finally recovering it seems from the loss of manager Bobby Robson to the England team, took themselves off the bottom of the table with their first win of the season: 6–0 away to Notts County. But pride of place must go to newly promoted Watford, who went third in the table with their 8–0 thrashing of Sunderland, which equalled the club's record defeat, suffered at West Ham in 1968.

This was a majestic performance by any yardstick. They were so completely in control that they could have had at least 12; apart from a number of outstanding saves by Chris Turner, they struck the woodwork four times. Luther Blissett, the man of the match, scored four, with two each for Ross Jenkins and Nigel Callaghan.

There was another eight-goal match: Stoke 4 Luton 4. But this game was notable chiefly for the controversial sending-off of Stoke keeper Peter Fox, which highlighted the confusion and inconsistency surrounding the new FA ruling on "professional fouls". With Stoke leading 2–1, a free-kick by Watson rebounded off referee Mr G.J.Napthene, and ran loose. Fox raced out of his area to chest down an awkwardly bouncing ball, but it eluded him. He turned and tried to smother it on the edge of the box, but Paul Walsh rounded him and drove the ball home. The referee disallowed the goal and awarded Luton a free-kick just outside the area. Then, after consulting a linesman, he sent Fox off. Subsequent TV inquests confirmed that Fox, who left the field in a distraught state, had been harshly treated, since it was not clear what his offence had been. He did not appear to handle outside the area or, indeed, impede Walsh.

The sob story of the day came from the Third Division, where Reading's Kerry Dixon became one of the few players in history to score four goals and still finish on the losing side. Doncaster won 7–5!

International Board make yet another boob

THE INTERNATIONAL Football Association board have blocked the Football League's attempts to introduce a number of experimental rules for the 1982-83 season, because they feared that it could "confuse the rest of the world". The changes, proposed initially by the Busby Committee, and including the introduction of penalty-kicks for certain fouls outside the penalty area, the banning of passing to the keeper from outside the box, and a variation of the offside law, were rejected at the laws meeting in Madrid.

The board expressed interest in one of the proposals, that is, relaxing the offside rule from goalkeepers' clearances, and have promised to discuss it again next summer. They have introduced one new rule, to tighten up on time-wasting by goalkeepers. In future, a keeper may take no more than four steps, from the moment the ball comes under his control, before releasing it. Unfortunately, however, they have not felt the need to define the term "under his control", so confusion is guaranteed to reign as soon as the season starts. This is typical of the utterances spewed forth annually by the International Board, whose inability to write plain English is matched only by their complete ignorance of the game of football.

FA create handball chaos

THE HANDBALL controversy raged on in late October as the FA repeatedly threw the game into confusion. First they instructed referees that, contrary to edict they had handed down at the start of the season, deliberate handball should not now be considered "serious foul play" meriting dismissal, but should be dealt with by a caution under "ungentlemanly conduct".

That brought immediate protest from the referees, so the League obtained confirmation from the FA that the officials still had discretion to "treat handling as a sending-off offence, in appropriate situations". Now the FA have announced that they have deleted specific references to handball from their interpretation of foul play, and it is up to the referee to decide what is, in his opinion, serious foul play.

In other words, it is up to the referees to decide how the laws should be interpreted — which is what they appeared to be doing until they were told not to a week earlier! Let us hope that the FA now keep quiet and allow referees to get on with their campaign to combat the cheating that has turned so many former fans against the game.

Clubs reject Chester Report

THE SECOND REPORT compiled by Sir Norman Chester for the Football League was published on 28 March. The main proposals were: a reduction of the First Division to 20 clubs, with an increase in Division Two to 24 and the amalgamation of Divisions Two and Three, plus some newcomers, into four regional sections with 16 clubs in each; clubs most frequently seen on TV to receive a larger share of the money; the League's constitution to be changed so that only a three-fifths majority would be needed to approve changes instead of the present three-quarters.

A month later, however, the clubs rejected their last chance to come to terms with reality, and decided to take the long and painful road of natural wastage to restructure the League. The other proposals are to be put forward at the annual League meeting in June.

One proposal that is likely to meet with approval, certainly among the big clubs, is that all gate receipts should be retained by the home club, instead of being shared out with the visitors, as now.

Paisley leads final procession in triumph

BOB PAISLEY'S 12th and last visit to Wembley in charge of Liverpool ended wholly appropriately with his becoming the first manager to lead his men in triumph up the steps to the Royal Box after their 2–1 victory over Manchester United in the Milk Cup final. Even dyed-in-the-wool traditionalists will not fault the team's decision to accord their boss an honour no other manager has enjoyed since English soccer set up its playing headquarters at this stadium 60 years ago.

This was Liverpool's third League/Milk Cup win in a row, but all of the sympathy and most of the admiration went to Manchester United at the end of an eventful but undistinguished game. United found themselves without both central defenders with the score at 1–1 and 14 minutes of normal time left. They were desperately unlucky to lose Kevin Moran with a twisted ankle after 69 minutes and then, 10 minutes later, to see Gordon McQueen reduced by cramp and hamstring problems to a hobbling passenger. Yet, having established a 12th-minute lead through Norman Whiteside's beautifully struck goal, they let Liverpool off the hook. Six minutes after Moran's injury, Liverpool equalized when Alan Kennedy hit a swerving 25-yarder that Bailey saw too late to save.

Even so, it was a controversial "professional foul" by keeper Bruce Grobbelaar in the last minute of normal time that kept Liverpool in the game, but should have seen their keeper out of it. He deliberately body-checked the injured McQueen, who had broken away on the right, but was merely cautioned by referee George Courtney — an outrageous decision to those in the crowd who drew a parallel between Grobbelaar's action and the assault of West Germany's Schumacher on Battiston of France during last year's World Cup. According to Mr Courtney, he did not feel that McQueen had a scoring opportunity!

The burden of extra time was always going to be too much for United's heroic, beleaguered garrison, and they were finally forced to submit to Ronnie Whelan's spectacular dipping shot after nine minutes. Sadly, Liverpool lost more friends with their blatant and persistent time-wasting, which reached a ludicrous climax when Dalglish booted the ball towards the tunnel.

Manchester United goalkeeper Bailey is left grounded by Whelan's winner for Liverpool.

Dons graduate in Europe

ABERDEEN BEAT Real Madrid 2–1 in Gothenburg in the final of the Cup-Winners' Cup, thanks to an extra-time goal by substitute John Hewitt, to win their first European trophy. Fierce and driving rain throughout the afternoon meant a soaking for Aberdeen's vast army of supporters, but they were soon cheering the opening goal. McLeish met Strachan's corner with a powerful downward header and, when the ball was deflected by a Madrid defender, Black pounced to score from close range. It was no more than Black deserved, for he had struck the cross-bar three minutes earlier with a fierce volley from another of Strachan's crosses.

Aberdeen, in their first European final compared with Real's 11th, looked happier in the difficult conditions until a defensive lapse led to Real's equalizer after 14 minutes. McLeish sent his back-pass well short of Leighton, who brought down Santillana in the box, and Juanito scored from the spot. Miller, an industrious captain, and McLeish nipped further danger in the bud, and Aberdeen got on top in the second half, with strong runs from Strachan and Simpson and some promising raids on the left from Weir.

Black took a painful kick and was replaced by Hewitt in the 87th minute, and it was the substitute who scored the winner with a spectacular goal midway through the second period of extra time. Weir won the ball with a timely tackle in his own half and jinked his way forward before sending McGhee away on the left with a perfectly weighted chip. McGhee then beat his man on the outside and crossed to the near post, where Hewitt met the ball at the end of a 70-yard run to place a conclusive header into the net.

The Dons, astutely managed by Alex Ferguson, won eight and drew two of their 11 games in the competition, scoring 25 goals and conceding only six. In effect, they have qualified for next year's tournament twice, for they won the Scottish Cup as well earlier this season.

Hewitt turns away after his extra-time winner for the Dons.

Little Terrors win League glory

DUNDEE UNITED, the "Terrors", are at it again. Having won their first major honour, the Scottish League Cup, only three years ago, and retained it the following season, they have now won the Scottish League. Manager Jim McLean has nursed the club through a record-breaking season with a nucleus of only 12 players. In a dramatic run-in, they won their last six matches to overtake champions Celtic and, in a heart-stopping finale, held off the challenge of both Celtic and Aberdeen, fresh from their European triumph, who both finished a point behind. Celtic demonstrated on the last day that they would not relinquish their title readily by beating arch rivals Rangers 4–2 at Ibrox despite being 2–0 down at half-time, and Aberdeen could do no more than beat Hibs 5–0 at Pittodrie.

But United, who many thought might have faltered in their final Tayside derby match with Dundee at Dens Park, did nothing of the kind. They won 2–1, to earn themselves premier billing in Scottish soccer for the first time in their 74-year history. They equalled Celtic's Premier League record of 56 points, and both clubs scored a record 90 goals.

Dundee United players chair manager Jim McLean in triumph after clinching the Championship.

Camera company to sponsor League as TV talks fail

FROM NEXT SEASON, England's premier football competition will be known as the Canon Football League. The Japanese-owned Canon UK, manufacturers of cameras and business equipment, and the Football League have announced a £3 million sponsorship deal spread over three years. Each year £496,000 will be distributed to the clubs, with another £214,000 in prize money for the leading teams in each division and additional monthly and seasonal awards for the clubs scoring most goals.

This is the biggest sponsorship deal in British sport, but is contingent on TV coverage and could be thrown into confusion if the League fail to reach an agreement with the television companies for screening matches next season. The League have just rejected a package of £5.4 million for two seasons, which included limited shirt advertising and four live matches each weekend. Both the BBC and ITV have now withdrawn all previous offers in disgust.

SOCCER SOUNDBITES

"The Football League are strangling themselves to death. They have shown this with the Chester Report and the television negotiations. They are in chaos."

Joint **BBC-ITV** statement.

Brighton's leading man fluffs the punch line

IN THE MOST absorbing FA Cup final for years, Brighton threw off the depression of their recent relegation and the disappointment of skipper Steve Foster's suspension, to frighten the life out of Manchester United with a dramatic late equalizer, only for Gordon Smith to miss the chance of a lifetime to score the winner in the last seconds of extra time. Curiously, Smith had been on the losing side in the Scottish League Cup final earlier in the season, when on loan to Rangers.

With four goals, unremitting effort, no little subtlety, and constant changes of fortune, all of it on a soggy pitch that sucked at the players' legs, this was a game to remember. In the end, Brighton, the underdogs, proved every bit a match for the more talented and experienced team that had finished third in Division One. They took the lead as early as the 14th minute with a far-post header from Smith, and stayed in front without undue difficulty until half-time. The turning point came soon after the interval with the only blot on the match, a reckless, vicious tackle by young Norman Whiteside on Brighton's Chris Ramsey that crippled the right-back.

He played on briefly on one leg, but was unable to make an effective challenge when Duxbury's cross was headed on by Whiteside for Stapleton to plant in the net a minute later. Ramsey was replaced by substitute Gerry Ryan, but the end for Brighton seemed nigh in the 72nd minute when Muhren at last produced a long, defence-wrecking pass, and Wilkins sent a classic left-foot shot curling beyond Moseley's reach.

Then Gary Stevens, a Herculean figure who rose above even Bryan Robson in terms of achievement on the day, copied the attacking forays of the absent Foster to such good effect that he equalized with only three minutes of normal time remaining. He controlled a pass flicked on by Grealish from Case's corner, and directed it powerfully past Bailey from 10 yards.

The miss of the match came, understandably, in the last moments of extra time, an inhuman demand on this bog of a pitch. Mike Robinson rolled the ball carefully into the path of Smith in the box, when the two strikers were through and opposed by only one defender. But the tiring Scot delayed his shot and then struck it weakly at the grateful Bailey, who smothered it as he came out. It is a miss that will haunt Smith for ever if Brighton lose the replay.

Stevens (second right) hits Brighton's late equalizer.

SOCCER SOUNDBITES

"I wasn't expecting a pass from Robbo. Robbo never passes."

GORDON SMITH,
Brighton striker, on his crucial miss.

FOOTBALL FOCUS

- A Football League plan to allow two substitutes next season, as in international matches and Scottish and European club competitions, was rejected by the clubs, who felt they could not afford a "13th man".

- In their final League match of the season, Manchester City, second in the Division One table in November, were relegated when Luton substitute Raddy Antic scored in the 86th minute at Maine Road — a match Luton had to win to stay up themselves.

- Liverpool killed off their challengers for the title, their 14th Championship win, so early that, even though they took only two points from their last seven games, they still won by 11 points from nearest challengers Watford.

- Aberdeen became the first club apart from Celtic and Rangers to retain the Scottish FA Cup this century, with a goal from young striker Eric Black four minutes from the end of extra time. So Rangers had lost in both domestic Cup finals.

Black heads Aberdeen's Cup-winner against Rangers.

FINAL SCORE

Football League
Division 1: Liverpool
Top scorer: Luther Blissett (Watford) 27
Division 2: Queen's Park Rangers
Division 3: Portsmouth
Division 4: Wimbledon
Footballer of the Year: Kenny Dalglish (Liverpool)

FA Cup Final
Manchester United 2 Brighton & Hove A 2
(after extra time)
Replay: Man United 4 Brighton & Hove A 0

League Cup Final
Liverpool 2 Manchester United 1
(after extra time)

Scottish League
Premier Division: Dundee United
Top scorer: Charlie Nicholas (Celtic) 29
Division 1: St Johnstone
Division 2: Brechin City
Footballer of the Year: Charlie Nicholas (Celtic)

Scottish FA Cup Final
Aberdeen 1 Rangers 0
(after extra time)

Scottish League Cup Final
Celtic 2 Rangers 1

International Championship
England, 5 pts

European Cup Final
SV Hamburg 1 Juventus 0

Cup-Winners' Cup Final
Aberdeen 2 Real Madrid 1
(after extra time)

UEFA Cup Final
Anderlecht beat Benfica 1–0, 1–1

European Footballer of the Year 1982
Paolo Rossi (Juventus & Italy)

Leading European Scorer (Golden Boot)
Francisco Gomes (Porto) 36

World Club Championship
Gremio (Brazil) 2 SV Hamburg (W. Germany) 1
(after extra time)

England pay penalty as Denmark squeeze home at Wembley

ENGLAND'S PROSPECTS of reaching next year's European Championship finals took a nosedive at Wembley on 21 September, when Allan Simonsen earned Denmark their first victory in nine matches between the countries with a 38th-minute penalty. England gave their customary slovenly early-autumn performance, and were lucky not to be more than one goal down at half-time, the penalty having occurred when Neal handled the ball. In the second half, the Danes clung to their lead, and an England team sorely missing the injured Bryan Robson just could not break down a well-organized defence, so ably marshalled by Morten Olsen. Failure to beat Greece last March has now assumed disastrous proportions.

The decider: Simonsen scores from the penalty spot.

Historic Irish victory in Hamburg

NORTHERN IRELAND'S prestige in world football was raised to new heights on 16 November by their shock, but deserved, 1–0 victory over West Germany in a European Championship qualifier in Hamburg. It was one of their finest performances, and West Germany's first home defeat in nine years. Pat Jennings, aged 38, made three remarkable saves from Waas, Rummenigge and Matthaus, giving arguably his finest display in 102 appearances. Manager Billy Bingham achieved a tactical triumph, as the Irish back four stamped their authority on the game. Norman Whiteside scored their goal in the 50th minute, and they were unlucky not to score two more in quick breakaways near the finish.

Despite now having completed the double over West Germany, the Irish chances of qualifying for the finals are slim, as the Germans have only to win their final match with Albania to overtake them on goal difference.

Ireland have taken 11 points from their eight games, but the 1–0 defeat by Turkey in Ankara on October 16 has proved a vital blow. England's hopes have disappeared completely, even though they won 4–0 in Luxembourg, because Denmark won 2–0 in Greece.

Déjà vu for Arsenal, as Walsall humble them again

HUNDREDS OF ARSENAL supporters demanded manager Terry Neill's resignation after Arsenal's Milk Cup humiliation at the hands of Third Division Walsall at Highbury on 29 November. The fans laid siege to the ground's main entrance for almost 45 minutes after Walsall had swept aside a disgraceful Arsenal effort with some exhilarating attacking football.

Fifty years after the famous FA Cup giant-killing act at Fellows Park, when Walsall last toppled the Gunners, Ally Brown, 32, the former West Brom and Crystal Palace striker, helped them repeat the feat with a goal five minutes from time. Arsenal had gone ahead against the run of play in the 31st minute, when Nicholas put Robson through. But Walsall, riding high in Division Three with only one defeat in their last 15 matches, equalized in the 61st minute when Brown raced clear of the offside trap, hammered the ball against keeper Jennings, and pushed the rebound through for Ross to score. And Chris Whyte, who had a nightmare evening, then missed his kick completely to let Brown through for the winner.

Walsall manager Alan Buckley felt some of his side's football would have done justice to the First Division. Arsenal's, however, did not, and Neill can thank the seemingly ageless Jennings, who made some brilliant stops, for saving him from even greater embarrassment.

Holders make an early Cup exit at Bournemouth

MANCHESTER UNITED'S dismissal from both domestic Cup competitions by Third Division opponents in the space of 19 days indicates a serious flaw in the make-up of the men claiming to be the second best in the land, and this 2–0 defeat at Bournemouth must rank as one of the biggest surprises in the FA Cup's long history.

Failure at Oxford in a Milk Cup fourth-round second replay could be excused in a competition twice won at Wembley by Third Division challengers. But the collapse at Dean Court, in their first defence of the FA Cup they won last May, leaves a big question mark against United. The truth is that both Oxford and Bournemouth earned their victories by out-thinking and ultimately outplaying them, as well as outrunning and outgaming them.

Bournemouth went ahead on the hour, when Bailey misfielded a corner and Trevor Morgan nodded the ball back for Milton Graham to score. Then Robson failed to clear La Ronde's long free-kick, and Ian Thompson got number two. Admittedly, United were without McQueen and Moran, their central defence, and the loss of Albiston at half-time forced them to make further positional changes; but a team of their stature — 10 of the men on duty at Bournemouth are full internationals — should be able to take such setbacks in their stride.

Souness shot decides

LIVERPOOL WON THE Milk Cup for keeps when a solitary goal from Graeme Souness floored luckless Everton in a thrilling replay at Maine Road and earned them a record fourth consecutive triumph in the competition. It cannot be long, however, before Everton lose their label as second-class soccer citizens on Merseyside, for they were desperately unlucky not to win at Wembley, where they enjoyed the better of the play in the goalless draw, although they never quite managed to exploit the possession won by their skill and endeavour in the replay.

In both games, Everton had the outstanding midfielder in Peter Reid, despite the opposition of such accomplished footballers as Souness, Lee, Whelan and Johnston. Ably assisted by Richardson, he was in command for long periods, and gave Everton every chance to clinch the trophy. Yet they rarely created any clear-cut opportunities.

In contrast, Liverpool always looked dangerous when they broke out of defence. And it was a typical counter-attack, pressed home with speed and power, that brought them the crucial goal in the 21st minute of the return. Souness began the four-man move with a pass to Neal, and completed it himself by collecting a cross from the same player and shooting past Southall into the corner of the net.

As Everton tired towards the end, Liverpool took control, and would have won by more if Rush had not left his shooting boots in the dressing-room for once. But it would have been unjust had they won by more than a single goal.

Liverpool hat-trick down to continuity

LIVERPOOL BECAME only the third club in the history of the League, after Huddersfield in the twenties and Arsenal in the thirties, to achieve a hat-trick of Championships when they drew 0–0 at Notts County on 12 May. Their latest triumph emphasizes that careful planning and continuity of management are essential requirements for consistent success in modern League soccer. While other clubs have changed managers with distasteful and expensive frequency, Liverpool have quietly kept matters in the family, promoting Bob Paisley when Bill Shankly retired and, 12 months ago, appointing Joe Fagan to maintain that line of succession. And Mr Fagan has quietly gone about his job, too, with two major honours under his belt already and the European Cup final coming up at the end of the month.

Typical of the way the club works is the purchase of men such as John Wark, shrewdly signed from Ipswich a couple of months ago when the Anfield midfield unit was beginning to show occasional signs of faltering. Wark, who has missed only a handful of games through injury over the last 10 years and rarely turns in a bad performance, provided the extra touch needed during the tiring closing weeks. Players like him — and Lee, Hansen, Neal and Kennedy — provide essential support for the more gifted football of Souness, Lawrenson, Dalglish, Rush and Whelan. For anyone who has lost count, this was Liverpool's 15th Championship.

Sweet compensation for the spilt Milk

EVERTON RETURNED to Wembley to beat Watford 2–0 in the final of the FA Cup, their first trophy since 1970, and rich consolation for having lost to their Merseyside rivals Liverpool in the final of the Milk Cup two months earlier.

As always seemed likely, the redoubtable Everton defence proved strong enough — if only just at times — to hold Watford's rampant attack in check. At the other end, however, Watford were undone by the inexperience of their youthful back four and the fallibility of Steve Sherwood, although Everton's second goal, scored in the 41st minute when Andy Gray patently headed the ball out of his hands, would surely have been disallowed by nine out of ten referees. This virtually killed Watford off, for they had gone one down only four minutes earlier, when a bad clearance and poor marking allowed Sharp to shoot in unchallenged from 10 yards.

But Watford were not outplayed, and they gave the lie to their reputation for kick-and-rush, up-and-under football. Most of the progress they made in the first half was by subtle diagonal passing, intelligent use of set-pieces, and sheer individual brilliance. But for the brilliance of Southall in goal, Watford would have made much more of a game of it.

Andy Gray makes contact with Sherwood's hands for the controversial second goal.

Parks the Spurs hero in Euro shoot-out

TOTTENHAM spectacularly survived the emotional torture of a penalty shoot-out in the second leg of the UEFA Cup final against Anderlecht, when Keith Burkinshaw's fairy-tale farewell to White Hart Lane surpassed even the most extravagant expectations. And the two most important saves of Tony Parks's fledgling career ensured that the UEFA Cup will nestle in Spurs' trophy cabinet as a sparkling reminder of the nerve-shredding climax to Mr Burkinshaw's reign as manager.

After the 1–1 draw in Belgium, Cup-holders Anderlecht came to White Hart Lane determined not to give up the trophy without a fight. And they seemed capable of protecting their 60th-minute goal by Alex Czerniatinski before acting skipper Graham Roberts stormed through for a dramatic equalizer in the 83rd minute, after substitute Ardiles had hit the bar, to take the game into extra time and then to the penalty decider.

Parks, the understudy whose hopes at the start of the season went little further than the occasional first-team game, saved the first penalty from Olsen. But then, at 4–3, Danny Thomas missed Spurs' fifth spot-kick to give Anderlecht another chance. Parks, however, kept his nerve and beat out the penalty from Icelandic striker Gudjohnsen — before being swallowed up in the jubilant congratulations of his delirious team-mates.

Tony Parks smothers Anderlecht's fifth penalty to give Spurs the UEFA Cup.

Rome falls to all-conquering Reds

Alan Kennedy sends Roma's keeper the wrong way.

LIVERPOOL RETURNED home from Rome triumphantly as European Cup-winners for the fourth time, after becoming the second English club on consecutive Wednesdays to win a European final on penalties. And it was Alan Kennedy who, for the second time in successive finals, won the Cup for his team.

Liverpool, with the extreme disadvantage of playing in their opponents' back yard, took control of the game with a 14th-minute goal resulting from a double defensive error. The scorer, Phil Neal, was the only survivor of their first European Cup success on the same pitch seven years ago. But the Reds became uncharacteristically sloppy, and Pruzzo headed an equalizer just before half-time. With no further score at the end of 120 minutes, Nicol, who had come on for the tiring Johnston, hit the first kick way over the bar. Roma scored from their first penalty; Neal levelled the score; and then Conti, one of Italy's World Cup heroes, blasted his shot even higher than Nicol's. Roma's next miss, by Graziani, was at 3–2 down, leaving Kennedy to make history and settle the first penalty shoot-out in the 28-year history of the Champions' Cup.

Ireland win the last Home Championship

A GOAL OF STUNNING quality by England's Tony Woodcock against Scotland brought down the curtain on the final British International Championship at Hampden Park in May. But the 1–1 draw it produced provided Northern Ireland with only their third win in the Championship, which has been staged continuously, apart from the war years, since the 1883–84 season.

All four countries finished on three points for only the second time in history. In 1955–56, the title was shared; but this time goal difference counted, in Northern Ireland's favour, their 2–0 win over Scotland in Belfast last December being decisive. Wales finished second, completing an ironic twist to the story of how the oldest soccer competition in the world met its end. For it was England and Scotland who had decided to withdraw, because they felt the ailing Championship had outlived its usefulness and were deaf to all protests by the other FAs, who feared economic ruin as a result of losing their annual fixtures with the two major British nations.

Woodcock (9) scores for England after holding off the determined Miller on a run from the touchline.

FOOTBALL FOCUS

- A £10 million take-over bid for Manchester United by a consortium headed by millionaire publisher Robert Maxwell, chairman of Oxford United, fell through in mid-February after two weeks' negotiations.
- Aberdeen became only the second club this century, after Rangers, to win the Scottish FA Cup three times in a row, remarkably each one after extra time.
- England won the fourth European Under-21 Championship, beating Spain in the two-legged final in May, 1–0 in Seville and 2–0 at Bramall Lane.
- To qualify for the European Championship, Spain needed to beat Malta by 11 clear goals and, despite missing a penalty, they won 12–1 and so pipped Holland on goals scored — 24 to eight compared with 22 to six by the Dutch.
- Third Division sides reached the semi-finals of both the Milk Cup and FA Cup. Walsall held Liverpool to a 2–2 draw at Anfield in the Milk Cup before losing the second leg at home 2–0. Plymouth lost 1–0 to Watford in the FA Cup.
- Kenny Dalglish became only the third player to register a century of League goals in both Scotland and England, with Celtic and Liverpool.

Barnes goes native in Brazil

Barnes (11) wheels away after scoring his sensational goal in the Maracana Stadium.

AFTER A FAIRLY wretched second season under the management of Bobby Robson, England — who failed to qualify for the European Championship, lost miserably to Wales in the last Home International Championship and were beaten 2–0 at Wembley by the USSR — gained a measure of consolation by beating Brazil in Brazil for the first time ever. Although they subsequently lost to Uruguay and only drew with Chile in their South American tour, the game in Rio will be remembered for their second goal, scored by winger John Barnes. Taking the ball on a mazy run on the left in which he beat man after man, he cut in and waltzed right through Brazil's central defence before planting the ball in the net. The crowd of 56,000 rose as one to acknowledge a goal of such brilliance that even their own favourite Pele would have been proud of it.

French lesson good for the game

FRANCE SCORED A major triumph for the future of soccer at the Parc des Princes in Paris, overcoming fierce Spanish resistance to win the European Championship for the first time. Under the enlightened management of Michel Hidalgo, the French have remained in the forefront of the move away from the sterile, defensive school of soccer — despite cruel setbacks — and the manner of their victory should be a lesson to the rest of Europe.

Second-half goals from Platini — a free-kick that squirmed out of the otherwise reliable Arconada's arms — and a solo effort from Bellone in the last minute saw France through in a disappointing final. But they had done enough in the rest of the competition to demonstrate the skill and imagination that has made them Europe's leading team over the past two years. Michel Platini scored in every match, a record nine goals in all, including the only goal of the crucial game with the talented Danes and hat-tricks against Yugoslavia and Belgium.

The finals produced some of the most fluent and exciting football seen anywhere for years and, as well as France, Denmark and Portugal were outstanding. The French success will surely advance the cause of those trying to turn soccer back into a game which players and spectators can enjoy. World champions Italy failed miserably to qualify, winning only the last of their eight group matches (at home to Cyprus!), and West Germany's team manager Jupp Derwall resigned after his side's poor showing in the finals, with Franz Beckenbauer expected to take over the squad.

FINAL SCORE

Football League
Division 1: Liverpool
Top scorer: Ian Rush (Liverpool) 32
Division 2: Chelsea
Division 3: Oxford United
Division 4: York City
Footballer of the Year: Ian Rush (Liverpool)

FA Cup Final
Everton 2 Watford 0

League Cup Final
Liverpool 0 Everton 0
(after extra time)
Replay: Liverpool 1 Everton 0

Scottish League
Premier Division: Aberdeen
Top scorer: Brian McClair (Celtic) 23
Division 1: Morton
Division 2: Forfar Athletic
Footballer of the Year: Willie Miller (Aberdeen)

Scottish FA Cup Final
Aberdeen 2 Celtic 1
(after extra time)

Scottish League Cup Final
Rangers 3 Celtic 2
(after extra time)

International Championship
Northern Ireland, 3 pts

European Cup Final
Liverpool 1 AS Roma 1
(after extra time)
Liverpool won 4–2 on penalties

Cup-Winners' Cup Final
Juventus 2 Porto 1

UEFA Cup Final
Tottenham Hotspur beat `Anderlecht 1–1, 1–1
4–3 on penalties

European Footballer of the Year 1983
Michel Platini (Juventus & France)

Leading European Scorer (Golden Boot)
Ian Rush (Liverpool) 32

World Club Championship
Independiente (Argentina) 1 Liverpool (England) 0

FINAL SCORE

EUROPEAN CHAMPIONSHIP 1984

Group 1

France	1	Denmark	0
Belgium	2	Yugoslavia	0
France	5	Belgium	0
Denmark	5	Yugoslavia	0
France	3	Yugoslavia	2
Denmark	3	Belgium	2

	P	W	D	L	F	A	P
France	3	3	0	0	9	2	6
Denmark	3	2	0	1	8	3	4
Belgium	3	1	0	2	4	8	2
Yugoslavia	3	0	0	3	2	10	0

Group 2

West Germany	0	Portugal	0
Spain	1	Romania	1
Spain	1	Portugal	1
West Germany	2	Romania	1
Spain	1	West Germany	0
Portugal	1	Romania	0

	P	W	D	L	F	A	P
Spain	3	1	2	0	3	2	4
Portugal	3	1	2	0	2	1	4
W. Germany	3	1	1	1	2	2	3
Romania	3	0	1	2	2	4	1

SEMI-FINALS
France 3 Portugal 2
Denmark 1 Spain 1
Spain won 5–4 on penalties

FINAL
France 2 Spain 0

Paris, 27 June 1984. Attendance 80,000.

France: Bats, Battiston (Amoros), Le Roux, Bossis, Domergue, Giresse, Platini, Tigana, Fernandez, Lacombe (Genghini), Bellone (Scorers: Platini, Bellone)
Spain: Arconada, Urquiaga, Salva (Roberto), Gallego, Camacho, Francisco, Julio Alberto (Sarabia), Senor, Victor, Carrasco, Santillana

Turkey roasted by Robson's raiders

ENGLAND BEAT TURKEY 8–0 in Istanbul on 14 November, their biggest away victory in the World Cup since they won 9–0 in Luxembourg 24 years ago. They go top of Group 3 and establish themselves as firm favourites to qualify next autumn.

Turkey might not be a leading European soccer power, but they have never been so humiliated in front of their own fervent supporters. Bobby Robson's plan to start out tight and score in the first 20 minutes — to quell both the crowd and their opponents — worked to perfection. Indeed, England were two up in 17 minutes, as Bryan Robson scored the first of his three and Woodcock the first of his pair. Robson scored his second after Williams hit a post and England went in 3–0 up at half-time.

Bobby Robson, right-half in that rout of Luxembourg, geed his men up during the interval, and they put another five past the hapless Turks, Barnes contributing two and Anderson, Robson and Woodcock one each. Even allowing for the dreadful state of Turkey's game, England's football was a delight to watch and a much-needed confidence-booster after the trials of last season.

Odd spot: England used a "W" formation — Withe, Williams, Woodcock, Wright and Wilkins were all in the team.

Bryan Robson (right) heads his first in the rout of Turkey.

Hooligans compound Celtic's misery

CELTIC WENT DOWN 1–0 to Rapid Vienna at Old Trafford on 12 December, going out of the Cup-Winners' Cup and completing a miserable second round tie. They had already paid dearly for two bottles thrown on their Parkhead pitch last month, when they had their stirring 3–0 win — and overall 4–3 victory — annulled by UEFA and were ordered to replay the match at another, distant venue. Unfortunately, this did not stop the hooligan element from travelling, and just two among the 51,500 who followed them to Manchester have now put the club's long-term European future in jeopardy.

Midway through the second half, one of those two idiots raced onto the pitch and attacked Rapid's goalkeeper, Feurer. The other kicked Pacult, the Austrian goalscorer, as he was leaving the pitch at the final whistle.

On the pitch, Celtic never looked like repeating their Parkhead performance, and it was soon evident they were going out. UEFA have already fined them £4,000, and they may well decide now to suspend them from European competition for some time to come.

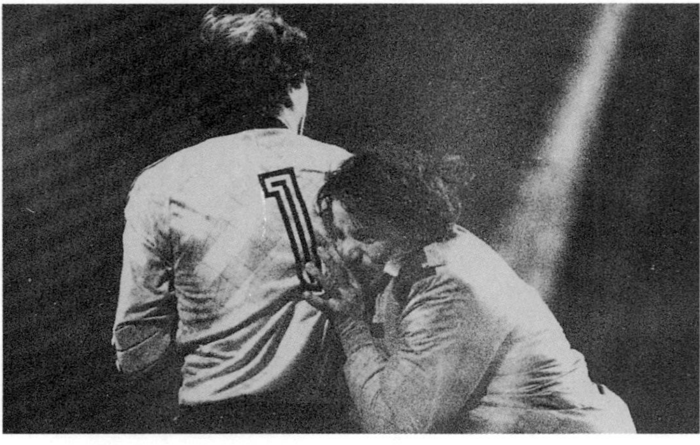

A crazed Celtic fan attacks Rapid keeper Herbert Feurer.

Bates loses faith after battle of Stamford Bridge

THE SECOND LEG of Chelsea's Milk Cup semi-final with Sunderland was a travesty of a match, with violence on the field, pitch invasions and even attacks on players. The result, a 3–2 win for Sunderland to give them a 5–2 aggregate score, seemed irrelevant on such a night of mayhem. When hooligans invaded the pitch after Sunderland's second goal, Chelsea chairman Ken Bates, his faith in the Chelsea fans shattered, offered to concede the tie.

Clive Walker, the winger who left Stamford Bridge to rebuild his career in the North-East, triggered the sadly predictable scenes when he returned to score the goals that put paid to Chelsea's chances. David Speedie, who was eventually sent off five minutes from time when he succumbed to the manic atmosphere in which seven players were booked, had brought the sense of excitement to fever pitch when he scored after only six minutes, reducing Chelsea's deficit to a single goal. But Walker scored for Sunderland before the interval, and killed the tie as a contest with his second after 71 minutes.

That proved the signal for a disgraceful demonstration by Chelsea's violent fringe. Referee Alan Gunn was forced to usher the teams into the centre circle while mounted police charged the invaders. The officers subsequently became targets for seats, staves, bottles and other missiles. And Walker's former team-mates had to come to his rescue when one hooligan tried to attack him.

The trouble started among supporters who were in the £6 seats, and Mr Bates has said that he will close that section of the East Stand for the rest of the season. But Chelsea must now brace themselves for a full-scale official enquiry.

SOCCER SOUNDBITES

"We need more action from the government to help curb these hooligans."

KEN BATES,
Chelsea chairman

Luton pitch a battleground as fans run amok

BRIAN STEIN'S 31st-minute goal decided a chaotic FA Cup quarter-final at Kenilworth Road on 13 March, which, during the last 10 minutes, was as close to being abandoned in disgrace as a match could be. There had already been a 25-minute hold-up soon after the start, caused by overcrowded Millwall supporters spilling onto the pitch. Then, during the last 10 minutes, several hundred so-called fans of the South London club, who had been marauding along the touchline, twice broke through police cordons and careered about on the pitch. Only the battling courage of the couple of dozen police who could be spared to move to that part of the ground prevented the situation getting completely out of hand. And only the determination to finish the match of referee David Hutchinson — a police inspector — enabled matters to be kept under control.

But after the referee and players bolted for the dressing-rooms at the final whistle, the pitch became a battleground. With the police no longer standing in their way, the trouble-makers went for the seated enclosure and ripped out dozens of seats. Incredible scenes ensued, with hooligans attacking police with ripped-out seats, and the police regrouping to win the battle with a series of baton charges and the use of dogs. Police and Millwall supporters from other parts of the ground joined in. There was complete chaos as police, stewards and innocent bystanders were led away for treatment. The rioting Millwall fans, who had caused damage in the town before the game, continued to do so when they finally left the ground.

FA chairman Mr Bert Millichip considered the events "probably the worst in the long catalogue that has blighted our game over the last 20 years". He was resigned to the fact that the Luton riots had now ruined the FA campaign to stage the 1988 European Championship finals in England.

Third time lucky for Canaries

SINCE WINNING the League's knock-out competition 23 years ago, when the two-legged final attracted as much attention as a local hospital tournament, Norwich have twice lost at Wembley. But they beat Sunderland 1–0 in the Milk Cup final on 24 March, and deserved their narrow win.

The match was decided in three crucial minutes at the start of the second half, when Norwich scored and Sunderland missed a penalty. Veteran ex-England striker Mick Channon mishit a shot which eventually fell to Asa Hartford, another old soldier, and his first-time effort was deflected past Turner in the Sunderland goal by the luckless Chisholm. Three minutes later, a determined Sunderland attack forced a handling offence from Van Wyk, but Walker's spot kick clipped the wrong side of a post. They never got a better chance.

Keeper Chris Turner is beaten by the deflected shot.

Dons clinch Premier title

A 1–1 DRAW with Celtic at Pittodrie was enough for Aberdeen to retain their Premier League title in Scotland with two matches remaining. Despite the loss of Strachan, Rougvie and McGhee in transfer deals worth £1.13 million, the Dons have led from start to finish after dropping only one point in their first eight fixtures. They spent only £140,000, on Frank McDougall from St Mirren and Tommy McQueen from Clyde, and McDougall in particular, their top League scorer with 22 goals, has proved an excellent investment. This is now the third League title in six seasons for Alex Ferguson's men, who show no signs of relinquishing their new-found predominance north of the border.

Aberdeen skipper Willie Miller celebrates a rare goal, but one that clinched the Scottish League title.

Oxford graduate to First Division

OXFORD UNITED confirmed their promotion to Division One on 24 April with a nervous 1–0 victory over Shrewsbury at the Manor Ground. But while thousands of fans celebrated the historic achievement, their colourful chairman, Robert Maxwell, hurled another verbal volley at the local council on the subject of Oxford's cramped ground. He accused the Oxford City Council of cheating and lying for 30 years, and demanded financial help to bring the ground up to First Division standard or to find a new ground.

Formerly Headington United, Oxford were elected to the League only 23 years ago, and have now gone from Third to First Division in two seasons.

Wales take big step to Mexico

WITH THEIR comprehensive 3–0 victory over Spain at Wrexham on 30 April, Wales threw Group 7 of the European World Cup qualifying competition wide open, and took a big step nearer to the finals in Mexico next year. With just their home fixture with Scotland to come in September, they now lead by two points from the Scots and Spain, who both have two games left.

The match was a hard-fought, bruising clash with no quarter given. Although Wales dominated the first half territorially, they were well contained by the experienced Spanish defence and had to wait until just before the interval for their first goal. And then it was a gift for Ian Rush after a terrible mix-up between the keeper Arconada and two defenders. The strength of the lively Mark Hughes began to stretch the Spanish defence, and he produced a supreme piece of skill to put Wales two up after 54 minutes with a spectacular scissors kick. The striking pair combined four minutes from the end for the third Welsh goal, Hughes putting Rush through the middle for the sort of chance the Liverpool man relishes and rarely wastes.

Hughes (left) and Phillips celebrate victory.

First leg of treble for Toffeemen

EVERTON REAPED the richly deserved reward for a magnificent season's work when a 2–0 victory over QPR in front of a season's best crowd of 50,514 at Goodison secured the Football League title for the eighth time, and with five games still to play. Though the season had once looked like producing the closest struggle for many years, Everton have settled the issue emphatically with five games to spare. Now they can concentrate on completing a unique treble, by taking the European Cup-Winners' Cup and retaining the FA Cup, with those finals coming up in the next 12 days.

Such an outstanding achievement would allow them to mingle once again, without embarrassment, with rivals Liverpool, who, since Everton last won the title in 1970, have amassed eight Championships and four European Cups. To accomplish their objective, the new champions will have to play with the commendable consistency that has taken them through their last 27 League games without defeat, outlasting Manchester United and Spurs and holding off Liverpool's late challenge.

Yet it would be wrong do describe Everton simply as an efficient team. Like Liverpool they have an abundance of individual talent, including Neville Southall, the Footballer of the Year, and Peter Reid, the PFA choice. Southall, whose keeping is now in the Shilton class, and Kevin Ratcliffe, one of Britain's most accomplished centre-backs, have formed, with Derek Mountfield, Gary Stevens and Pat Van Den Hauwe, the League's soundest defence. During the last eight months, Trevor Steven, Reid, Paul Bracewell and Kevin Sheedy have become as formidable a midfield unit as Liverpool possessed in the heyday of Graeme Souness. And despite the loss of Adrian Heath, potentially their most dangerous forward, through injury in December, Everton have scored more goals than any of their rivals, with substantial contributions from the Scottish pair Andy Gray and Graeme Sharp.

Goals, however, come from a wide range of positions, such is Everton's fluency and finishing power. They have scored in 35 of their 37 League games so far. The man responsible for bringing together these players and quietly and firmly building them into a team of true Championship quality is Howard Kendall, who, remarkably, has achieved this distinction while still in his thirties.

Big hand for Pat Jennings — and a handsome cheque, too

THE KEEPER WITH reputedly the largest hands in football — they have certainly appeared so to opposing strikers over the last 23 years — was given a big hand, and hand-out, when a crowd of 25,000 turned out for his testimonial at Highbury on 8 May. Jennings, 40 next month and no longer an Arsenal regular, earned around £100,000 from the match between his current club and North London rivals Spurs, for whom he played a record 472 League games. He went on to play another 237 for Arsenal, who paid Spurs a mere £40,000 for him in 1977.

In an unblemished career, the 110-cap Irish international keeper, who still figures in Northern Ireland's World Cup plans, has set a marvellous example for young players, and has been admired and respected by team-mates and opponents alike for his fine sportsmanship and healthy attitude to the game.

Deserved applause for goalkeeper Pat Jennings: a model professional.

Fifty dead in Bradford fire inferno

MORE THAN 50 soccer fans were feared killed when fire swept through the main stand at Bradford City's ground during the match with Lincoln City on 11 May. It was estimated that there were between 3,500 and 4,000 people in the stand when fire broke out and suddenly turned into a raging inferno. The number of injured may exceed 200 and the death toll is expected to rise.

The dramatic scenes were seen on the news by millions of television viewers, as the match, in which Bradford City were celebrating their newly won promotion to the Second Division, was being recorded. It was a terrifying sight, with fans — some with clothes and hair alight — scrambling over the barriers at the front of the stand, their escape fortunately unimpeded because the ground has no anti-vandal security fences. The fire horror was made worse because a strong breeze swept flames along the stand and the roof collapsed in a billowing cloud of smoke.

Fire and smoke engulf Bradford's main stand: the tragedy was over in minutes.

The wooden structure, erected at the Valley Parade ground in 1909, was apparently underlaid with litter accumulated over the years, and this is thought to have acted as a tinder-box, ignited possibly by a carelessly discarded cigarette end or lit match. As with so many struggling clubs, it is inevitable that safety standards are lower in their old stands than would be considered adequate for a new stadium. Indeed, in recent years fire has destroyed or severely damaged stands at Bristol Rovers, Brighton, Brentford and Norwich, but until Bradford there had been no loss of life. Now there will almost certainly be a demand by fire chiefs for significant improvements in standards. And as FA chairman Bert Millichip has pointed out, that will probably mean the end for some clubs.

Teenager killed at Birmingham as Leeds fans go on rampage

VALLEY PARADE was not the only ground where tragedy struck on the last Saturday of the season. In violence at the Birmingham-Leeds clash at St Andrews, apparently initiated by hooligans from Leeds, a stretch of 12-foot high retaining wall collapsed, killing a teenage fan and injuring others.

Earlier in the day Leeds fans had wrecked a public house in the city centre, and the violence at the match started when Birmingham scored just before half-time. Angry Leeds fans tore up advertising hoardings, seats and cushions, and began hurling them at police. As mounted police and scores of officers in riot gear went in to restore order, about 200 City fans dashed onto the pitch, and for more than half an hour police struggled to break up violent clashes.

Police put the injury toll at over 150, including a police officer said to be in a serious condition. There were 125 arrests.

Rapid exit as Everton land second leg of treble

Andy Gray celebrates his goal in the Cup-Winners' Cup final.

EVERTON'S MAGNIFICENT season and their quest for a remarkable treble continued in style in Rotterdam on 15 May, when Howard Kendall's talented team became the seventh British winners of the Cup-Winners' Cup, beating Rapid Vienna in the final. Second-half goals by three men who have made outstanding contributions throughout the campaign — Andy Gray, Trevor Steven and Kevin Sheedy — brought a European trophy to Goodison for the first time.

Backed by a highly vocal travelling army of about 20,000 supporters in the Feyenoord Stadium, the League champions dominated throughout. But their failure to translate their complete control of the first half into goals gave their fans some cause for anxiety. They relaxed when Sharp intercepted a poor back pass in the 58th minute and laid on Gray's goal. And when Steven hooked the ball in after a corner 15 minutes later, they were jubilant. Krankl rounded the largely unemployed Southall to pull one back for the Austrians, but Everton struck back two minutes later when Sharp enabled Sheedy to clinch the match.

History created and crushed at Wembley

A TRULY HEROIC performance by Manchester United on a warm, oppressive afternoon at Wembley deprived Everton of their remarkable "treble" and redeemed an FA Cup final that had failed almost completely to realize its rich promise. What changed the whole character of the contest was the controversial sending-off of Kevin Moran, one of United's central defenders, 12 minutes from the end of normal time for committing what is known in the business as a "professional foul" on Everton's Peter Reid.

Moran having gained, in the 104th Cup final, the dubious distinction of being the first player to be sent off in any one of them, United were compelled to play with 10 men. But it was no backs-to-the-wall triumph. They responded by lifting their game to such a level of industry and inspiration that it came as no surprise when Norman Whiteside, their young Irish international, was able to score the winning goal.

Whiteside's scorching winner for Manchester United.

The incident that paradoxically turned the match came when Reid intercepted a pass by McGrath and broke forward, with Gray and Sharp unmarked to his left and right. Moran swept his feet from under him — a foul, but no worse than one by Ratcliffe on Stapleton a little earlier, for which the Everton captain was not even cautioned. Under pressure from FIFA, the FA has long abandoned its campaign to eradicate the "professional foul" by sending off offenders, so it was a surprise to everyone when referee Peter Willis pointed to the dressing-rooms. Nevertheless, Moran's initial frenzied refusal to accept the decision was as outrageous a sight as seen at Wembley since the scandalous exhibition of Argentina's Rattin in the 1966 World Cup. And, however much sympathy one may have for the Manchester United player, this sort of behaviour must never be condoned.

The sending-off had a galvanizing effect on United, who twice went close in the remaining 12 minutes of normal time, and continued in the same vein for the extra 30 minutes. The winning goal came after five minutes of the second period. Hughes, who seemed to gain in strength as the game wore on, found Whiteside in the right. The youngster carried the ball forward, mesmerized Van Den Hauwe by feinting to shoot, and then did so, curling the ball past Southall and just inside the far post.

In the end, one's sympathy must be with Everton, because surely now it has been proved beyond doubt that a sending-off is no compensation for a lost opportunity. Only when FIFA appreciate this, perhaps by studying the report of the Busby Committee, instead of petulantly ignoring it, will the "professional foul" be eradicated from the game.

FOOTBALL FOCUS

- The Scottish League Cup, now sponsored by Skol despite the ban on alcohol at Scottish grounds, was organized on a straight knock-out basis until the two-legged semi-finals this season.
- QPR had a chastening experience in the UEFA Cup, They took a 6–2 first-leg lead from their home tie (played at Highbury because of QPR's synthetic pitch) into the second round against Partizan Belgrade, were beaten 4–0 in Yugoslavia and lost on the away goals rule.
- The two Milk Cup finalists, Norwich and Sunderland, were both relegated to Division Two at the end of the season.
- England went down 1–0 to Scotland, their first defeat at Hampden Park since 1976, in the inaugural match for the Sir Stanley Rous Cup on 25 May.

Moran has to be restrained by team-mates when he refuses to go.

Chinese fans on rampage after defeat

SQUADS OF baton-wielding police were drafted onto the streets of Peking to disperse thousands of rioting soccer fans after China lost their World Cup qualifier 2–1 to Hong Kong on 19 May. In scenes reminiscent of the Maoist Cultural Revolution, gangs of youths turned on foreigners as well as Chinese, attacking the cars of foreign correspondents and a diplomat. The 80,000 crowd at the Workers' Stadium had jeered the Hong Kong side throughout the match, and the visitors needed police protection when they left.

Forty killed in European Cup final riot

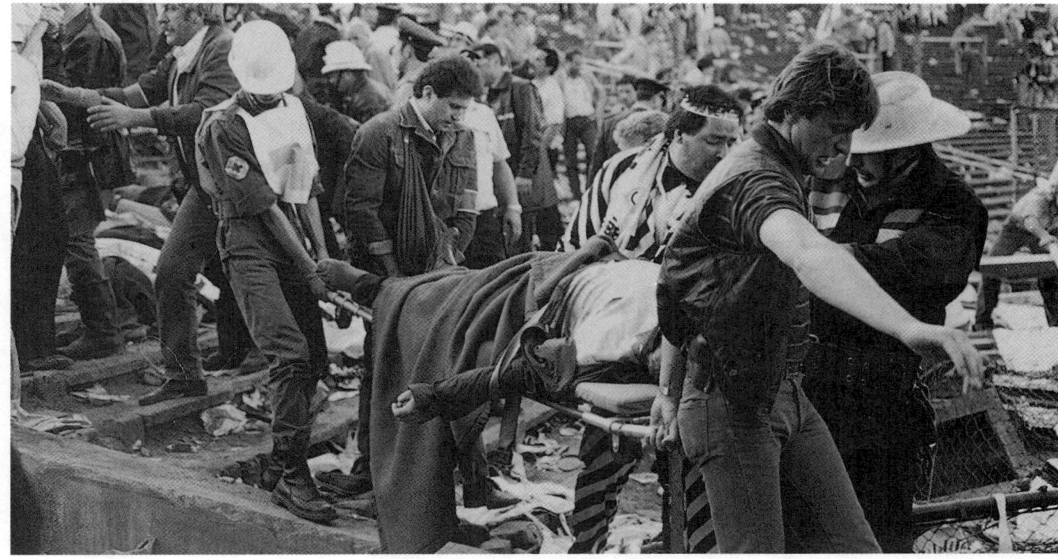

Heysel Stadium, Brussels, a horrifying scene of carnage as bodies are carried away.

ABOUT 40 PEOPLE were killed — many of them trampled to death — when a wall and a safety defence collapsed during rioting by Liverpool and Juventus fans before the European Cup final in Brussels on 29 May. More than 350 people were injured, and most of the casualties were Italians. Although Juventus fans throwing fireworks and other missiles at the police at one end were the first troublemakers, Liverpool fans charging into some Italians and causing the wall to collapse were apparently responsible for the disaster. Bodies were piled high in two tents outside the main gates of the stadium as helicopters and ambulances carried the injured people to hospitals. The match was eventually played to prevent escalation of the trouble, as police seemed helpless to control the problem.

The deaths were the hideous climax to a night of rioting during which fans, many of them drunk, had used flagpoles and metal torn from safety barriers as weapons, and had fireworks, bottles and cans and pieces of concrete. Events that led to the tragically fatal incident began when Liverpool supporters started to hurl cans and bottles at Juventus fans separated from them only by a wire fence. A few of the Liverpool mob encroached into a section of the terracing occupied by Italians, an action that the authorities of the antiquated Heysel Stadium had not anticipated despite previous football violence. As soon as the Belgian police charged forward in battle formation, hundreds of Liverpool fans swarmed out of their area to join in. According to witnesses, many Italians tried to climb over a wire perimeter fence and a wall, and dozens of them fell 40 feet from the back of the terracing when the wall collapsed under them.

In the dressing-rooms, the players were not officially told about the deaths, and, with the police still making pathetic and half-hearted attempts to restore order, the game began 85 minutes late. As professionals, the players went through the motions, but few people felt that the match — won 1–0 by Juventus with a Platini penalty — had any significance.

The violence continues as the Belgian police are helpless in the face of rioting Juventus fans.

SOCCER SOUNDBITES

"We were trying to pull people out, but idiots were still pushing. I've finished with Liverpool until those idiot supporters go away."

An innocent and distressed LIVERPOOL FAN caught up in the tragedy.

"There is no doubt that the Liverpool fans started the trouble. They are animals."

Another LIVERPOOL SUPPORTER.

"... like a sickening sight from the Middle Ages."

NEWS REPORTER on American TV.

FINAL SCORE

Football League
Division 1: Everton
Top scorer: Kerry Dixon (Chelsea), Gary Lineker (Leicester City) 24
Division 2: Oxford United
Division 3: Bradford City
Division 4: Chesterfield
Footballer of the Year: Neville Southall (Everton)

FA Cup Final

Manchester United	1	Everton	0

(after extra time)

League Cup Final

Norwich City	1	Sunderland	0

Scottish League
Premier Division: Aberdeen
Top scorer: Frank McDougall (Aberdeen) 22
Division 1: Motherwell
Division 2: Montrose
Footballer of the Year: Hamish McAlpine (Dundee United)

Scottish FA Cup Final

Celtic	2	Dundee United	1

Scottish League Cup Final

Rangers	1	Dundee United	0

European Cup Final

Juventus	1	Liverpool	0

Cup-Winners' Cup Final

Everton	3	Rapid Vienna	1

UEFA Cup Final
Real Madrid beat Videoton 3–0, 0–1

European Footballer of the Year 1984
Michel Platini (Juventus & France)

Leading European Scorer (Golden Boot)
Francisco Gomez (Porto) 39

World Club Championship
Juventus (Italy) 2 Argentinos Juniors (Argentina) 2
Juventus won 4–2 on penalties

POST-HEYSEL DIARY

30 May All British clubs banned from playing in Belgium.
31 May FA withdraws all English clubs from Europe for a year; 38 confirmed dead; Brussels fire officers disclose that Heysel Stadium had not been given full safety check since early 1930s and condemn it as inadequate for major international matches.
2 Jun UEFA place indefinite ban on all English clubs in Europe.
6 Jun FIFA ban all English clubs from playing clubs from other countries.
13 Jun FIFA ban on English clubs to include friendlies.
20 Jun UEFA ban Liverpool for three years.
21 Jun Liverpool to appeal against UEFA sentence, which is now understood to mean any three years in which they qualify for European competition after ban on other clubs is lifted.
6 Jul Belgian parliamentary investigation committee reports that politicians, police and soccer chiefs must all take part of blame.

French lesson for Bobby Robson

FRANCE BEAT URUGUAY 2–0 in the inaugural Intercontinental Cup match for the Artemio Franchi Trophy in Paris on 21 August, and in doing so offered England supremo Bobby Robson a memorable insight into the sumptuous standards required of credible World Cup candidates. A superb victory over the South American champions fuelled Gallic optimism that a romantic European Championship triumph will be surpassed in Mexico next summer. France's performance on a balmy evening embodied the qualities which make them Europe's most attractive side — instinctive skill, technical excellence and a gritty refusal to be intimidated.

The Uruguayans, whose team featured just four of the side that defeated England in Montevideo last summer, revealed little of their undoubted flair, and reverted to the darker principles of the South American game. But by a delicious irony, Toure — the target for the Uruguayans' most concerted assaults — sealed the victory with his first goal in international football.

The young forward stepped inside Diogo's lunge before continuing his run into the penalty box and hooking Giresse's delicate pass over the Uruguayan keeper to put France two up after 55 minutes.

Almost immediately, Platini hit a post with a typical curling shot. But for once, France's inspirational captain was not their most influential figure — an honour due to Giresse, his tiny lieutenant. It was the Bordeaux midfielder who signalled a performance of rare quality within three minutes of the start, when he picked out Platini, who put Rocheteau through for their first goal. From that moment on, envy and admiration must have been the major emotions felt by the watching Mr Robson, and virtually every other onlooker.

Gallic style: Platini (right) threads a pass through the Uruguay defence.

The lady is not amused

THE FOOTBALL LEAGUE has again disappointed the Prime Minister with its latest 10-point plan for curbing soccer violence. Mrs Thatcher may not be kicking the proposals into the stand, but she is known to be "deeply unimpressed" by what has been put forward.

Regarding the League's first proposal, individual club membership schemes for supporters — which rejects the national identity-card plan as unworkable — she believes that football organizations are showing a total lack of imagination. She says that she has been misrepresented, and that she has not argued for a national computerized membership scheme by the start of next season, but that membership cards introduced by individual clubs should be compatible, so that it could be developed gradually on a national scale — and this, in her view, could increase support for soccer.

The Prime Minister is opposed to the proposal that the executive boxes and viewing restaurants at grounds should be exempt from the alcohol ban, though she does favour more morning kick-offs, more all-ticket games, backing for the new Public Order Act giving police greater powers of arrest, and more closed-circuit television. But many of these items are already agreed.

Mrs Thatcher rejects the other major League proposals that the policing of grounds should be met by the government and that there should be a reduction in the pools Betting Duty by 2.5 per cent, equivalent to £20 million, and that this should go to improvements. What is seen as an attempt by the League to negotiate for more government funds — when high transfer fees are still being paid — is regarded as "totally unacceptable".

FIFA lift embargo on English clubs

BRITISH CLUBS may now play abroad, outside Europe, according to the latest FIFA edict of 11 July, amending their blanket ban of five weeks earlier. Their decision has been greeted by English clubs with a mixture of enthusiasm and chagrin, however.

While Spurs and Norwich, whose chairmen are getting together straight away, are amongst several clubs already interested in setting up a lucrative tournament in Saudi Arabia, others are frustrated that the timing of FIFA's ban, and now its removal, has not left sufficient time for foreign pre-season tours — originally planned and then cancelled — to be rearranged.

The six clubs denied their places in the European competitions — Everton, Liverpool, Spurs, Manchester United, Southampton and Norwich — are the ones most likely to make attempts to play abroad. Norwich chairman Sir Arthur South envisages not only the chance to make the money they are banned from making in Europe, but also the opportunity to show the European authorities that they can take supporters abroad who will behave themselves.

FIFA also spelt out that they would be keeping a watchful eye on English efforts to cure hooliganism, and they highlighted the current lack of agreement that appears to exist between the government and the clubs as to who is most responsible for spectator behaviour.

Death of Jock Stein

JOCK STEIN WAS truly a giant of British football, the most successful club manager in the history of the game. He became Scotland manager after the debacle of the 1978 World Cup, but will be remembered most for his remarkable reign at Celtic. He took over at Parkhead in 1965, and in 11 seasons (he missed 1975–76 after a near-fatal car crash), they won the League title 10 times, the Cup seven and the League Cup six. At the same time, in nine seasons of European Cup competition, Celtic became, in 1967, the first British club to win the trophy. Their 2–1 triumph over Inter Milan was a reward for Stein's philosophy of all-out attacking football.

Stein's rise from obscurity is like a fairy story. As a player, he was on the point of quitting the game and returning to the pits after an undistinguished career with Albion Rovers and non-League football when Celtic signed him as a reserve centre-half. Because of injury to the regular stopper, he found himself straight in the first team — and he never looked back.

In 1954, he captained Celtic to their first League and Cup double for 40 years. The next year, an ankle injury ended his playing career, and he coached Celtic for five years before becoming manager of Dunfermline, saving them from relegation and then taking them to their 1961 FA Cup victory over Celtic. After a brief spell with Hibs, he returned to Celtic and glory. Their "grand slam" in 1967 was unique, and he achieved it with a side that cost virtually nothing. Stein retired in 1977, but was persuaded to make a comeback with Leeds a year later. Then, after less than seven weeks, and before signing a contract, the call came from Scotland.

Jock Stein was a simple, straightforward man, completely dedicated to football. He possessed a vast knowledge of the game, and had an exceptional ability to bring out the best in his players. His death was a terrible loss to the Scots, but he will also be missed by all who love the game.

SOCCER SOUNDBITES

"The best place to defend is in the other side's penalty box."

JOCK STEIN

Jock Stein, a giant of British football, collapses just minutes before the final whistle at Ninian Park, Cardiff.

Manager's death mars Scots' late rescue

MOMENTS AFTER watching his side snatch a late equalizer at Ninian Park on 10 September to keep their hopes of qualification for the World Cup very much alive, Jock Stein, Scotland's supremo, collapsed and died of a heart attack.

Stein, who was 62, had survived a heart attack eight years ago. His death was a tragic end to a match that had virtually put paid to Welsh chances of going to Mexico but had paved the way for Scotland.

The draw puts the Scots above Wales on goal difference. But if Spain win the remaining match in Group 7 — which they should, at home to Iceland, having previously beaten them in Reykjavic — they will qualify as of right, leaving Scotland with the not too arduous task of playing off with the winner of the Oceania group for the last qualifying place. If Spain do not win, however, Scotland automatically qualify, and Wales play off.

With these simple permutations in their minds, the teams walked out to tumultuous applause from the 38,000 crowd, and the opening minutes brought intensely physical exchanges between the famed Welsh strikers Hughes and Rush and Scottish centre-back McLeish, with free-kicks going both ways — against Hughes and McLeish. Hughes soon stamped his class on the match, however, when he superbly struck in a low Nicholas cross, on the turn, after just 14 minutes.

The referee awards the penalty that dims Welsh World Cup hopes.

With so much at stake, the match continued to be physical. Following their defeat at Hampden by the Welsh last March, Scotland had made six changes, with Gough and McLeish attempting to close-mark Hughes and Rush and with Miller acting as sweeper. As the second half wore on, Scotland stepped up the pressure, but the award of a penalty against Phillips for hands with just 10 minutes left was perhaps a little harsh — especiaaly since a disputed penalty eight years ago also gave Scotland a World Cup finals place, and again at the expense of Wales.

Davie Cooper, who had come on as substitute for Strachan, converted it. So Scotland take a very large step towards Mexico — tragically, however, without Jock Stein.

Jennings the Great seals Mexico place

NORTHERN IRELAND clinched a place among the 24 World Cup finalists with a disciplined defensive performance against England that earned them the point sufficient to offset Romania's victory in Turkey and book their trip to Mexico. Thousands of delighted Irishmen at Wembley on 13 November will claim success was wholly merited. Rightly, they will point to the sensible football their team played to contain and frustrate England in this goalless draw — and to world-class goalkeeping by Pat Jennings in the closing minutes. If the Romanians take a look at the video of this match, they may well conclude that they are not going to Mexico because of the gross incompetence of an England side who had already booked their passage. The crowd began to chant "It's a fix", especially after one terrible Kerry Dixon miss, but England gave the lie to any such accusations when they swarmed round the penalty box in the closing stages and gave the Irish back four a hard time.

But Jennings, this great goalkeeper who has not played a senior club match for a year, was equal to their best efforts. Moving with the speed of a man half his 40 years, he blocked one shot from Dixon that had been deflected and then, a few minutes from the end, leapt across his area to tip over a close-range header from the same player. The sight of the venerable Jennings turning cartwheels on the Wembley turf at the final whistle confirmed that, once again, Northern Ireland had defied logic.

Jennings defies the England attack yet again.

Liverpool hooligans will not learn

A BRICK AND AEROSOL attack on Manchester United players before their game at Anfield on 9 February was the first serious outbreak of hooliganism at a football ground this season, although there have been incidents away from football stadiums. It is sickening, in view of their part in the Heysel tragedy, that Liverpool fans are again the ones involved. Predictably, in view of the bad blood between both clubs, it happened when it did.

Aerosol sprays were aimed at the United players as they disembarked from their coach, and a brick was thrown at a window. Although most of the players were affected by the spray, which left their eyes burning and throats spluttering, they soon recovered on getting treatment and it did not appear to affect their performance. The 1–1 draw was not enough to take them back on top above Everton, but they stay ahead of Liverpool, who are now without a home League victory over United in six League meetings.

SOCCER SOUNDBITES

"How could I take the job if I was told I could not sign a Catholic? I'm married to one."

GRAEME SOUNESS,
on signing for Rangers as player-manager.

Live soccer returns to TV

ON 20 DECEMBER, the long-running battle between the League and the television companies was finally settled — only two weeks after the announcement regretting that 15 months' negotiations had broken down irretrievably. As soon as the £1.3 million deal was done with the League, to cover the rest of the season, ITV and the BBC were then able to agree similar terms over the same period with the FA. Viewers can expect live telecasts of four League games, both Milk Cup semi-finals and the final, as well as four FA Cup ties plus semi-finals and final.

Rangers make catholic choice

GRAEME SOUNESS, Scotland's World Cup captain, signed as player-manager for Glasgow Rangers on 8 April and promised that sectarianism was out. The Sampdoria midfielder, who left Liverpool for the Italian club for £700,000 two seasons ago, will take over from the departing Jock Wallace, but will play out the rest of the season with Sampdoria, who are understood to be receiving a £300,000 fee.

Souness's brief, a daunting one for a man in his first managerial post, is to restore the club's prestige; Rangers have finished out of the top two places in the Premier Division for the last six seasons.

Souness, taking over at Rangers.

Distinction for Oxford

OXFORD UNITED achieved the distinction of winning the Milk Cup for the first time when they beat QPR 3–0 at Wembley for the most decisive victory in the final of this competition since it became a one-off match.

Though this was a commendable all-round team performance by the underdogs, 20th in the First Division, the key figure in a resounding triumph was Trevor Hebberd. This skilful, thoughtful former Southampton midfielder played a crucial part in the three goals that upset the odds in favour of a Rangers victory. After an exceptionally dull first half-hour, Oxford, with Hebberd, Phillips and Houghton working smoothly in midfield, began to undermine QPR's confidence. They deservedly took the lead five minutes before the break when Aldridge laid on a simple goal for Hebberd on the edge of the six-yard box.

Once in front, Oxford took complete control. Rangers simply did not show a glimpse of their usual form. Houghton played a defence-splitting one-two with Hebberd after 51 minutes and ran on to score the second goal. Aldridge, usually a lethal striker, missed a couple, before Hebberd put him through again with four minutes left. And, although his shot was beaten out, Charles followed up to score. Now Oxford must quickly return to earth and resume the grim business of trying to hang on to the First Division status they have enjoyed for less than a season.

Man of the Match Hebberd (left) shoots Oxford's first goal.

Broken Hearts 'Kidded' out of title

POOR, SAD HEARTS, they were so close to their first League title since 1960, when a Dundee substitute wrecked their dreams on the last day of the season. A week earlier, with only two teams still in the race, Celtic needed maximum points from their last three games and for Hearts to lose. Even then, they would have to make up the goal difference. But the unbelievable happened. Celtic won their two matches in hand, and it all hinged on the last day's action. They finished in magnificent style, winning 5–0 at St Mirren. At Dens Park, Hearts were not finding it easy against Dundee, but with eight minutes left the 0–0 scoreline would have been enough to give them the title. Then along came Dundee substitute Kidd to prise the title from their grasp with a goal in the 83rd minute, and kill them off completely with another in the 87th. Now Hearts must pick themselves up for the FA Cup final with Aberdeen in a week's time.

Albert Kidd (centre) celebrates his triumph and Hearts' misery.

Luton to ban away fans

LUTON ARE TO TAKE unilateral steps to keep visitors' supporters from Kenilworth Road. Understandably determined to avoid the disgraceful, costly riots suffered during Millwall's Cup visit last season, they announced their plans on 29 April. They will consider withdrawing from the FA Cup and the newly sponsored League Cup (by Littlewoods), or play on opponents' or neutral grounds, if the governing bodies insist on away supporters being allocated tickets.

All supporters attending Kenilworth Road will have to have bought a £1 membership card, with a magnetic code to be scanned in computer-controlled turnstiles costing £250,000. Card-holders must sign a good behaviour pledge, and the computer will reject stolen cards or those belonging to blacklisted members.

Luton chairman David Evans claims the club's novel scheme has the backing of the Prime Minister, the government, the police, local council and residents.

More power for big clubs

FIRST DIVISION CLUBS were granted a significant increase in power at a Football League Extraordinary Meeting on 28 April, making the threatened formation of a breakaway "super league" unlikely now. Resistance from the lower divisions to the 10-point plan sponsored by the leading clubs collapsed in less than 30 minutes, as compromise was reached over the crucial issue of voting. The majority required for constitutional changes was reduced from 75 per cent to 66, and First Division clubs will have one and a half votes each, Second Division clubs one each, with Third and Fourth sharing eight votes between them.

A major reform is the reduction in size of the First Division from 22 to 20 clubs (with the Second to be increased to 24), with end-of-season play-offs over the next two seasons for some promotion and relegation places in the League. Other proposals accepted give the First Division clubs larger shares in gate receipts and TV and sponsorship money.

It's Liverpool, d'ye Ken!

LIVERPOOL WON THE League Championship for the eighth time in 11 seasons when they beat Chelsea 1–0 at Stamford Bridge on 3 May, with a typically nerveless, smothering performance and a marvellous goal scored fittingly by player-manager Kenny Dalglish. In a game they had to win, Dalglish's single, first-half strike proved just enough to account for Chelsea, render meaningless the heroics elsewhere of West Ham and Everton, and take the title back to Anfield at the end of the scorer's first season in charge.

Dalglish would be the first to acknowledge that he owes much of his astonishing success to the strength of the squad he inherited from Bob Paisley and Joe Fagan. There was abundant proof of that at Stamford Bridge. The failure of Jan Molby, Liverpool's influential Danish international midfielder, to recover from a stomach ailment merely meant the reintroduction of Mark Lawrenson, the gifted Irish international who is regarded by many as the best defender in Europe!

Liverpool came up the finishing straight like the thoroughbreds they are, with 11 victories and one draw in their last 12 matches. Everton, who led for much of the season, fought all the way to retain their title before coming unstuck last Wednesday at Oxford. And West Ham, too, strung together six wins in 15 days, including the sensational 8–1 drubbing of Newcastle, but could not quite make up the leeway. Most extraordinary, however, was the slump of Manchester United, who won their first 10 matches, just failing to equal Spurs' long-standing record when they drew at Luton.

Liverpool were 10 points behind United at that time, and later 11 points behind leaders Everton. But, as so many teams have found to their dismay over the last dozen years or so, you discount Liverpool at your peril, and sure enough they snatched another League title. Kenny Dalglish is the first player-manager to accomplish such a remarkable feat, and history, with the FA Cup final coming up next Saturday, is still beckoning him vigorously.

Dalglish celebrates his title-winning goal.

Hero Hewitt the Heartbreaker

ABERDEEN, WITH AS clinical a performance as they've ever produced, beat Hearts 3–0 at Hampden in the 101st Scottish FA Cup final, and in doing so they completed the most depressing and shattering eight days in the history of Heart of Midlothian Football Club. It was, indeed, heartbreaking for the 40,000 fans of the Edinburgh club, nearly two-thirds of the attendance, having seen the League title snatched from their grasp only seven days earlier.

The player chiefly responsible this time was Man of the Match John Hewitt, who struck a severe body blow as early as the sixth minute, when he weaved his way beyond three defenders in the box before unleashing a low drive into the corner of the net. Hearts, who were never three goals inferior to the Dons, proceeded to miss two great chances to level the match before the second, killer goal came in the 49th minute. Hewitt, again, found himself on his own when MacDougall dummied Weir's cross, and tucked the ball away. With 15 minutes left substitute Stark stooped to head a third from another Weir cross. For Alex Ferguson's men, it was a second Cup of the season. For Hearts, it all ended in tears. They had three men booked, and their captain Walter Kidd, who had been cautioned in the first half, was sent off in the 77th minute for throwing the ball at an opponent in sheer frustration.

Stark (12) wraps it up for Aberdeen with number three.

FOOTBALL FOCUS

- "Double" winners Liverpool won the FA Cup final with only one player born in England — and he was Republic of Ireland international Mark Lawrenson, born in Preston!
- Reading, who won the Third Division title, created a League record by winning their first 13 games.
- Kenny Dalglish, not content with his club triumphs, became the first Scot to win 100 caps.
- Pat Jennings came out of partial retirement to rejoin Spurs as extra cover, and was signed on a non-contract basis for Everton, after the transfer deadline, as cover in the Cup when Neville Southall was injured. So he found himself in the unique position of being eligible for Spurs in the League and Everton in the Cup. In the event, he played for neither, but represented Northern Ireland in the 1986 World Cup, playing his 119th and last game (a world record) against Brazil on his 41st birthday.

Double-take: Rush job makes Dalglish's day

IN THE FIRST-EVER all-Merseyside FA Cup final, Liverpool beat Everton 3–1 at Wembley to become only the third club this century to complete the "double". It is an extraordinary achievement for Kenny Dalglish, in his first season as player-manager, to bring off what his illustrious predecessors had failed to do in all Liverpool's years of supremacy.

Yet in a thrilling match of curious shifts and changes, Liverpool at one time looked to be on the point of taking a heavy beating from their old rivals. But Rush came to the rescue with two typical pieces of finishing.

Rarely have Liverpool been so outplayed as they were for the best part of an hour. Grobbelaar was having one of his more eccentric games, and it was no surprise when Footballer of the Year Gary Lineker gave Everton the lead after 28 minutes, from an exquisite Reid through-pass.

What saved the day for Liverpool was a magnificent save by Grobbelaar from Sharp, and the determination of Jan Molby, their bulky Danish international, to stamp his influence on the game. Freeing himself from the dominance of Reid and Bracewell, no easy task in itself, he constructed Liverpool's first two goals and also contributed to their third. He provided an angled pass for Rush to score Liverpool's unexpected equalizer after 57 minutes, and six minutes later a low cross was missed by Dalglish but converted eagerly at the far post by the Australian Craig Johnston.

And it was Molby who, six minutes from the end, sent Liverpool forward with a searching pass from midfield for Whelan. The Irishman floated the ball across the penalty area to the unmarked Welshman Rush, who drove it firmly into the net — and beyond all hope for Everton.

Man of the Match Molby strides majestically through the Everton defence.

'El Tel' pays the penalty

WHEN TERRY VENABLES was chaired off the field by his players at the end of the dramatic European Cup semi-final second leg, in which Barcelona had overcome a 3–0 deficit to beat Gothenburg on penalties, it seemed as if the hard part had been accomplished. "El Tel's" men had beaten European champions Juventus in the quarter-finals, and before that had survived two close ties on the away goals rule. Now only the unheralded Steaua Bucharest stood between them and the title that had eluded them for a quarter of a century — and the final was being played in Spain.

But it was not to be. Steaua, a team of soldiers from the Romanian capital, beat the odds-on favourites in a bizarre shoot-out after a goalless draw in Seville, and so became the first Eastern Bloc holders of the European Cup.

In a close, exciting two-hour battle, the Romanians never really threatened Barcelona's goal. During the final stages, the Spaniards always looked likely to snatch victory — Steve Archibald missed a golden opportunity 10 minutes from normal time — and Steaua had to hang on grimly.

So for the second time in three years, this illustrious competition was reduced to a penalty decider. The crowd were ecstatic when Urruti saved the first spot-kick, but Steaua's Ducadam matched him, and they both saved the next one, too. Then Lacatus put the Romanians ahead, Ducadam saved his third penalty, Balint put Steaua two up, and the amazing Ducadam saved from Marcos — four out of four penalty stops, a unique feat in a major final. It was all over, and the desperately disappointed crowd sportingly applauded the victors off the field.

Helmut Ducadam makes his fourth and match-winning penalty save.

FINAL SCORE

Football League
Division 1: Liverpool
Top scorer: Gary Lineker (Everton) 30
Division 2: Norwich City
Division 3: Reading
Division 4: Swindon Town
Footballer of the Year: Gary Lineker (Everton)

FA Cup Final

Liverpool	3	Everton	1

League Cup Final

Oxford United	3	QPR	0

Scottish League
Premier Division: Celtic
Top scorer: Ally McCoist (Rangers) 24
Division 1: Hamilton Academical
Division 2: Dunfermline Athletic
Footballer of the Year: Sandy Jardine (Heart of Midlothian)

Scottish FA Cup Final

Aberdeen	3	Heart of Midlothian	0

Scottish League Cup Final

Aberdeen	3	Hibernian	0

European Cup Final

Steaua Bucharest	0	Barcelona	0

Steaua won 2–0 on penalties

Cup-Winners Cup Final

Dynamo Kiev	3	Atlético Madrid	0

UEFA Cup Final
Real Madrid beat Cologne 5–1, 0–2

European Footballer of the Year 1985
Michel Platini (Juventus & France)

Leading European Scorer (Golden Boot)
Marco Van Basten (Ajax Amsterdam) 37

World Club Championship
River Plate (Argentina) 1 Steaua Bucharest (Romania) 0

Maradona wins World Cup single-handed

THE ABIDING memories of the 1986 World Cup will be the magic of Diego Maradona (not to mention his sleight of hand), dazzling displays of fluent attacking football from France, Brazil, Denmark and the USSR, and a thrilling final in which the artistry of Argentina prevailed over the courage and discipline of West Germany.

It was arguably the best World Cup since the finals were last held in Mexico, in 1970 — remarkably so in view of the unwieldy format of the competition, the trying climatic conditions and the glaring inadequacy of the onfield officials. Football triumphed despite all these obstacles: a testimony to the game's enduring capacity to entertain.

Unpromising start

The 1986 World Cup was a juggernaut of a competition. There were 52 matches in all, played over a period of a month. It required two weeks and 36 matches to eliminate just eight of the 24 teams. Yet so tight was the timetable that three of the quarter-finals had to be decided on penalties, regarded by just about everyone as a terribly unsatisfactory way to determine a result. To accommodate television scheduling, matches were played in the hottest part of the day — in one centre, Monterrey, in appalling conditions of heat and humidity. Referees were drawn from many more countries than in previous competitions, which resulted in inconsistent and at times confusing decision-making by the officials.

Robson's choice

England played their first three matches in Monterrey, in Group F. The "Group of the Sleeping", the locals called it, because of the dearth of goals and the boring football served up in the first four matches. At that stage, England were in very great danger of going out of the competition. They had no goals and only one point. Against Morocco, they had lost their captain, Bryan Robson, injured, and their vice-captain, Ray Wilkins, sent off for throwing the ball at the referee.

To be sure of qualifying for the last 16, England needed to beat Poland in their last group match. They did so, arguably because manager Bobby Robson was now forced to make the changes that most of his critics had been advocating. Hitherto, he had persisted with his lion-hearted namesake Bryan, even though the England skipper had to play in a shoulder harness and could not possibly give anywhere near 100 per cent. And Wilkins had forgotten how to attack. Now supremo Robson had to replace them: he also dropped Waddle, and fielded a 4–4–2 line-up, with the splendid Beardsley replacing Hateley as Lineker's partner, and Reid and Hodge coming in to strengthen the midfield. The new formation clicked, Lineker scored a hat-trick inside 35 minutes, and England had survived.

In the knock-out stage, England again demonstrated how well they can play when they go into battle with the correct tactics. They chalked up another 3–0 win, against Paraguay, and Lineker scored another two. Morocco, for their remarkable achievement of heading the group, above three European nations, earned the dubious reward of another match in Monterrey, with West Germany for opponents. Courageously as they played, they were beaten by a fine free-kick from Matthaus two minutes from time.

Burruchaga (left) watches the World Cup winner on its way.

Bryan Robson in agony after dislocating his shoulder against Morocco.

Scotland lose bottle

Scotland were the underdogs in the toughest group, pitted against South American champions Uruguay and two of Europe's strongest teams, West Germany and Denmark. In their first two matches, against the latter two, they earned many friends and plenty of praise, but no luck and no points. Then, when suddenly an opportunity to progress was handed to Scotland on a plate, they, in the modern idiom, "lost their bottle". Playing against a Uruguayan side reduced to 10 men after a sending-off in the first minute, they disintegrated into amateurishness, failed to score, and were eliminated.

Argentina's progress

Argentina played football worthy of champions. They won their group, and then beat the talented but flawed Uruguayans. But their quarter-final win against England was devalued because of the nature of their first goal, propelled into the net by the hand of Maradona. He later made amends, however, taking the ball in a mazy, irresistible run before slotting it past Shilton.

It was Maradona, too, who masterminded his country's semi-final win over Belgium, the surprise packet of that half of the last 16. By that time, the main European threats, Denmark and the USSR, had been eliminated. The Soviets, the most sporting of all the teams on view, had opened up in their group with a comprehensive victory over Hungary. But against Belgium, a

Maradona, the world's greatest footballing talent in the 1980s, scored one of the greatest World Cup goals against England, but sadly will be remembered more for the one he fisted in.

Lineker scores his second against Paraguay.

combination of fine defending, at least one dubious decision, and the ability of the Belgians to surge out of defence in brilliant breakaways, led to their downfall after extra time.

Belgium proceeded to repeat their performance against Spain in the quarter-finals, prevailing this time on penalties. The Spaniards had knocked out Denmark 5–1 in the second round but, with due respect to Spain, the Danes were a great loss to the tournament and would have graced the later rounds. Against Spain, they were shaken by giving away a silly equalizer, and crumbled in the second half.

The finest match

In the other half of the knock-out stage, two of the best sides of the tournament, Brazil and France, clashed in the quarter-finals. Brazil, despite initial problems, were gradually justifying their rating as favourites, while European champions France had seen off reigning world champions Italy with an outstanding exhibition of mature football. The meeting of these most fancied teams from either side of the Atlantic produced a match of exquisite football, full of skill and imagination, worthy of a final. Many experts described it as the finest game they had ever seen, and it was a travesty that it had to be decided on penalties.

It was again a loss for the tournament as a whole when the victors of this classic, France, then came unstuck in the semi-finals against their bête noire, West Germany. For although the Germans outplayed them on the day, most neutral observers, having witnessed the heights France were capable of reaching, would rather have seen them in the final.

It was also sad to see in this tournament the last of some of the world's great footballers: Zico, Platini, Socrates, Karl-Heinz Rummenigge and, of course, Pat Jennings, who finished up with a world record 119 international caps. Happily, we were still able to enjoy the fabulous skills of Platini and Socrates, and Jennings went out in a blaze of sentimental glory against Brazil on his 41st birthday (although he didn't thank debutant right-back Josimar for the 25-yard "birthday present" that was Brazil's third goal). Injuries, however, prevented both Zico and Rummenigge from doing themselves justice.

The Maradona show

Above all others, individually, was Diego Maradona. It would not be fair to say he carried his team, but he made all the difference. He inspired them, he prompted, he directed their play, and he was always capable of turning a match with one brilliant thrust. He also scored five goals — four of them legal. Some of the treatment he had to endure was scandalous, but this time he kept his temper.

In the final, Argentina went two up from Maradona-inspired attacks: the excellent central defender José Luis Brown, of Irish ancestry, headed in from a free-kick after 22 minutes, and Valdano raced in from the left to score 11 minutes after the interval. The Germans then mounted one of their famous last-ditch comebacks, with 17 minutes left and Argentina seemingly cruising to victory. Rummenigge and Völler both scored after corners.

Argentina were devastated by this sudden turn-around. But in their moment of crisis, with six minutes to go and the Germans pressing hard for the winner, Maradona made his final contribution to a tournament he had dominated. Catching the Germans on the break, he set Jorge Burruchaga free with a beautifully timed pass, and the young Nantes midfielder ran through, calmly drew Schumacher, and then planted the most important goal of his life into the far corner — the goal that won the 1986 World Cup.

FINAL SCORE

FIRST ROUND

Group A

Bulgaria	1	Italy	1
Argentina	3	South Korea	1
Italy	1	Argentina	1
South Korea	1	Bulgaria	1
Argentina	2	Bulgaria	0
Italy	3	South Korea	2

	P	W	D	L	F	A	P
Argentina	3	2	1	0	6	2	5
Italy	3	1	2	0	5	4	4
Bulgaria	3	0	2	1	2	4	2
S. Korea	3	0	1	2	4	7	1

Group B

Mexico	2	Belgium	1
Paraguay	1	Iraq	0
Mexico	1	Paraguay	1
Belgium	2	Iraq	1
Mexico	1	Iraq	0
Paraguay	2	Belgium	2

	P	W	D	L	F	A	P
Mexico	3	2	1	0	4	2	5
Paraguay	3	1	2	0	4	3	4
Belgium	3	1	1	1	5	5	3
Iraq	3	0	0	3	1	4	0

Group C

France	1	Canada	0
USSR	6	Hungary	0
France	1	USSR	1
Hungary	2	Canada	0
France	3	Hungary	0
USSR	2	Canada	0

	P	W	D	L	F	A	P
USSR	3	2	1	0	9	1	5
France	3	2	1	0	5	1	5
Hungary	3	1	0	2	2	9	2
Canada	3	0	0	3	0	5	0

Group D

Brazil	1	Spain	0
Algeria	1	Northern Ireland	1
Brazil	1	Algeria	0
Spain	2	Northern Ireland	1
Spain	3	Algeria	0
Brazil	3	Northern Ireland	0

	P	W	D	L	F	A	P
Brazil	3	3	0	0	5	0	6
Spain	3	2	0	1	5	2	4
N. Ireland	3	0	1	2	2	6	1
Algeria	3	0	1	2	1	5	1

Group E

Denmark	1	Scotland	0
Uruguay	1	West Germany	1
Denmark	6	Uruguay	1
West Germany	2	Scotland	1
Denmark	2	West Germany	0
Scotland	0	Uruguay	0

	P	W	D	L	F	A	P
Denmark	3	3	0	0	9	1	6
W. Germany	3	1	1	1	3	4	3
Uruguay	3	0	2	1	2	7	2
Scotland	3	0	1	2	1	3	1

Group F

Morocco	0	Poland	0
Portugal	1	England	0
England	0	Morocco	0
Poland	1	Portugal	0
England	3	Poland	0
Morocco	3	Portugal	1

	P	W	D	L	F	A	P
Morocco	3	1	2	0	3	1	4
England	3	1	1	1	3	1	3
Poland	3	1	1	1	1	3	3
Portugal	3	1	0	2	2	4	2

SECOND ROUND

Belgium	4	USSR	3
Mexico	2	Bulgaria	0
Argentina	1	Uruguay	0
Brazil	4	Poland	0
France	2	Italy	0
West Germany	1	Morocco	0
Spain	5	Denmark	1
England	3	Paraguay	0

QUARTER-FINALS

Brazil 1 France 1
(aet) France won 4–3 on penalties
West Germany 0 Mexico 0
(aet) West Germany won 4–1 on penalties
Argentina 2 England 1
Belgium 1 Spain 1
(aet) Belgium won 5–4 on penalties

SEMI-FINALS

Argentina	2	Belgium	0
West Germany	2	France	0

THIRD-PLACE MATCH

France 4 Belgium 2

FINAL

Argentina 3 West Germany 2

Aztec Stadium, Mexico City, 29 June 1986. Attendance 114,590

Argentina: Pumpido, Cuciuffo, Brown, Ruggeri, Olarticoechea, Giusti, Batista, Burruchaga (Trobbiani), Enrique, Maradona, Valdano (Scorers: Brown, Valdano, Burruchaga)
West Germany: Schumacher, Berthold, Briegel, Jakobs, Forster, Eder, Brehme, Matthaus, Allofs (Völler), Magath (Hoeness), Rummenigge (Scorers: Rummenigge, Völler)

Leading scorers
6 Lineker (England)
5 Butragueno (Spain), Maradona (Argentina), Careca (Brazil)

Divine intervention is the verdict

FIFA HAVE gone on record to defend what appeared to many to be the World Cup finals' most brazen piece of gamesmanship — Diego Maradona's "Hand of God" goal against England. In the July issue of *FIFA News*, the official publication of the world's governing body, an exonerating article exclaims that "Diego Maradona's football in Mexico was honest".

For the monthly publication to have stated that Maradona's strong, skilful and imaginative play throughout the 30 gripping days had proved him to be the world's most accomplished player, would have brooked no argument. But for there to be not an inkling of official disquiet over such a crucial and controversial goal – which shocked millions of TV viewers throughout the world – must come as a great surprise to many football supporters in England.

The crucial moment, as Maradona scores against England in Mexico.

New boss sent off in first match

THE HOMECOMING of Graeme Souness, the local boy who made good, ended in disgrace. Back in his native Edinburgh as new player-manager for Rangers, Souness was sent off in the 37th minute against Hibs, and not even a subsequent public apology could smooth things over.

Scotland's World Cup captain set the poorest of examples to his own players and fans alike with a lunging tackle on George McCluskey that put the Hibs striker out of the game. Coming after a caution for a late challenge on Kirkwood, there was only one punishment.

Shameful scenes then followed as the other players became involved in a punch-up before the game continued, with tempers flying high and nine bookings. So the dawning of a new age for Rangers got off to a nightmare start, culminating in a 2–1 defeat.

Ferry brawl a setback for English clubs

A FULL-SCALE battle between over 100 Manchester United and West Ham supporters on a ferry taking them to the Continent for pre-season friendlies has struck a critical blow to England's chances of returning to European club competition. Sealink Ferries admitted they made a grave error in relaxing their unwritten rule not to carry football supporters, against police advice, and that they did not realize they were rival fans.

During the trip, which had to turn round after 2.5 hours of the eight-hour journey between Harwich and the Hook of Holland, hooligans fought with knives, bottles and fire hoses. When the ship returned to Harwich, 14 arrests were made, and four people were taken to hospital with stab wounds, while others had injuries caused by broken glass, kicks and punches. Most accounts agreed that there were about 100 Manchester fans and 30 West Ham fans, described as well dressed and older. With no police on board, the Dutch crew members were unable to stop the brawling, and it was decided to turn around when some of the 2,000 passengers became alarmed.

'English fans worse': UEFA chief

UEFA PRESIDENT Jacques George, speaking after an executive committee meeting in September, said that the behaviour of English fans had worsened. Although the meeting did not touch on the indefinite European ban on English clubs, he told the Press that he did not see how the ban could be lifted. The condition for doing so was improved behaviour of English fans, and this patently had not happened. He added that the ban would not be officially discussed until some time next year.

Lineker bonanza

BARCELONA'S close-season signing of Everton and England striker Gary Lineker is reported to have cost Terry Venables's club £4,262,000, a new Spanish record. Lineker, the leading World Cup scorer in Mexico with six goals, will bank some £1.5 million over the six years of his contract — excluding wages and match bonuses!

He will receive this signing-on fee at the rate of £243,000 a year, or £4,672 a week. He will also collect a basic wage of £150 a week plus a match bonus that could bring in about £800 a week.

Lineker, born in November 1960, played for his local club, Leicester City, for several seasons before joining Everton for £800,000 in July 1985. He has since added 11 caps to the seven he gained with Leicester, and seems sure to be a key figure for years to come.

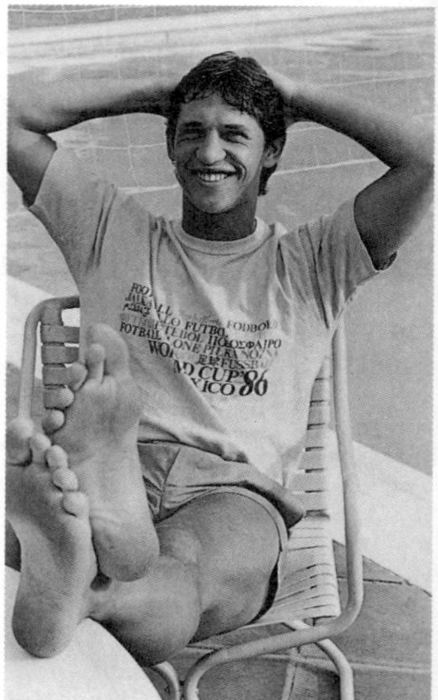
Gary Lineker, from riches to riches.

'Skolars', but no gentlemen

RANGERS BEAT CELTIC 2–1 in the Skol Cup on 26 October with a penalty eight minutes from time — their 14th success in this competition and their first trophy under Graeme Souness. But a crowd of almost 75,000 at Hampden saw an unsavoury end to a poor final, in which Celtic's Mo Johnston was sent off and nine other players booked.

Following a tame first half, the game was brought to life when Durrant put Rangers ahead in the 62nd minute and McClair equalized eight minutes later. Meanwhile the referee had booked five Celtic players and one from Rangers, all for bad tackles. He took two other Celtic names for protesting a penalty after 82 minutes, which was converted by Cooper. Two minutes from time, an off-the-ball incident between Munro and Johnston resulted in a booking for the Rangers player and the dismissal of Johnston, who had already been cautioned. In the ensuing chaos, it appeared that Celtic's Shepherd had also been sent off, but he remained on the field.

It can only be hoped that these scenes are not going to be repeated when the two sides meet again at Parkhead on Saturday in a League match.

Celtic's Maurice Johnston gets his marching orders.

FA back Luton in fight against hooligans

LUTON, FORCED TO withdraw from the Littlewoods Cup after refusing to compromise over their ban on visiting supporters, have received more than adequate compensation by being permitted to operate their membership scheme during FA Cup ties. The FA's admirably sensible decision came 48 hours after the League had told Luton they could be reinstated in the Littlewoods Cup only if they agreed to lift their restriction on fans of visiting clubs or play their home ties on their opponents' or neutral grounds.

Leeds fans cause new fire at Bradford

THERE SEEMS TO BE no depths to which the Leeds hooligan element won't stoop. Their latest, almost unthinkable act of vandalism has been to cause a mobile fish-and-chip shop at Valley Parade to turn over and catch fire, leading hundreds of spectators, mindful of last year's 56-death disaster, to take refuge on the pitch. The incident occurred on 20 September, after Bradford City had taken a 2–0 second-half lead. The match was held up for 20 minutes.

FA chairman Bert Millichip said that the club would not be punished for yet another instance of their supporters' hooliganism, but that he will press for serious consideration to reimpose the ban preventing Leeds supporters from being admitted to away matches.

FA gag Bobby Robson

ENGLAND MANAGER Bobby Robson has been banned by his employers, the FA, from writing his column in a national newspaper. Robson has been contributing his ghosted articles to the Sunday Mirror since he took over as England supremo four years ago. FA chairman Bert Millichip explained that he did not feel it appropriate that Robson should work exclusively for one newspaper, and that the England manager should be freely available to all the media, without payment for his views.

In a diary of the World Cup finals this summer, in his book *So Near and Yet So Far*, Mr Robson confesses he lied to the English Press about the extent of a leg injury sustained by England captain Bryan Robson, and disguised the fact that he had dislocated his suspect shoulder again. Although the FA embargo on Robson's newspaper articles has nothing to do with the publication of his book — indeed, the FA appear to be taking a surprisingly tolerant view of his revelations — other passages led one commentator to suggest that the FA might not have been quite so ready to extend his contract had they read his book first.

Clough pans Forest fans

NOTTINGHAM FOREST manager Brian Clough was furious with the club's fans for their treatment of Arsenal's Charlie Nicholas during the League match at the City Ground on 27 September, which Forest won 1–0. A few thousand in the crowd of 25,371 chanted abuse at the Arsenal striker throughout the match, and especially when he was carried off on a stretcher after an hour with a badly gashed knee. Mr Clough showed his disgust with gestures as he leapt out of his touchline dugout to remonstrate with the fans. And when the same section chanted Mr Clough's name in admiration, he refused to accept the tribute.

Mr Clough is clearly prepared to stand up and be counted — which is what everyone in and around the football world needs to do if the worst standards being displayed by the minority are not to hold sway and continue to damage the sport's image.

Brian Clough remonstrates with the Forest fans.

Atkinson latest victim of vain search for new Busby

RON ATKINSON, the most colourful showman in British football, has paid the traditional penalty for lack of success, and after five years as manager of Manchester United makes way for Alex Ferguson, the Aberdeen boss. The definition of "success" at Old Trafford is not the same as at most other clubs, as Mr Atkinson's predecessor Dave Sexton found when he was booted out after United were losing Cup finalists in 1979 and League runners-up in 1980.

Atkinson's "sin" was his failure to produce more than two FA Cup triumphs in his five years and a final League position that did not vary from third or fourth. This time last year, United were top of the League and unbeaten after 15 matches. Now they have only 13 points from 13 matches.

United and their customers understandably still hunger for the glory of Championship and European Cup, which they last enjoyed in the 1960s, when Matt Busby was in charge, and Charlton, Best and Law ruled on the pitch. Mr Atkinson didn't deliver the goods, so he had to go. It's a hard life, but a man of his energy, talents, knowledge and realistic attitude to league soccer is not likely to be out of work any longer than he chooses.

"Big Ron" Atkinson (right) with Everton's Howard Kendall.

Rangers and Borussia face UEFA wrath over bruising clash

GLASGOW RANGERS went out in the third round of the UEFA Cup on 10 December on the away goals rule when they could only draw 0–0 with Borussia in Moenchengladbach. And both sides are to be reported to UEFA after their bruising clash, screened live across West Germany, in which six players were booked and two Rangers players were sent off.

Belgian referee Alexis Ponnet revealed that he almost sent off another Rangers player, Ally Dawson, but felt it was too early in the game. The two who received their marching orders were full-back Stuart Munro, for kicking an opponent after the ball had gone, and winger Davie Cooper, for a second bookable offence.

Dawson's early crude kick at Michael Frontzeck had set the tone for a game in which player-manager Graeme Souness was accused of a "brutal tackle" on Thomas Krisp. In a "counter action", Rangers are to report the referee, who explained that he showed Cooper the second yellow card for calling him a "dirty German", whereas the Scottish international claimed he had merely, and supposedly innocently, inquired if Mr Ponnet was allowed to book Germans.

Wolves at bottom of pack

THE DISMISSAL OF Wolves in the first round of the FA Cup by non-League Chorley marks a new low in the fortunes of this once-great club, and is a grim warning to others caught in soccer's vicious circle of escalating costs and declining income. "It was the most humiliating night in the history of the club," confessed Graham Turner, Wolves' 12th manager since Stan Cullis was sacked in the early 1960s.

Relegated three times in as many years after Derek Dougan's last-ditch rescue act in 1982, Wolves, once the scourge of Europe, not only suffered the indignity of inclusion in the first-round draw, but were held 1–1 by the non-Leaguers, playing their home tie at Bolton's ground, and then 1–1 again under the floodlights of Molineux — where, in their halcyon days of the mid-1950s, they saw off the likes of Honved and Spartak Moscow. Surely, with a third chance, again at Burnden Park, they would finish off those upstarts from the Multipart League? No, they were humiliated by three goals to nil, and clearly are in their greatest crisis.

A dismal Wolves go through the motions against non-League Chorley.

Dutch catch 'English disease'

SOCCER HOOLIGANISM, justly described as the "English disease", has not vanished from Europe simply because English League clubs have been banished. Supporters of Dutch club Feyenoord ran amok in Moenchengladbach on 22 October, before, during and after their UEFA Cup tie with local side Borussia. Reporting "one of the worst outbreaks of soccer violence seen in West Germany", police said Dutch fans had fought with local citizens, plundered shops, started a fire in a bar, wrecked furniture in others and overturned cars. They made 71 arrests. Sounds all too depressingly familiar!

Charlie is my darling: part 2

SIXTEEN YEARS after Charlie George shattered Liverpool with an extra-time winner for Arsenal at Wembley in the FA Cup, another Charlie — Nicholas, this time — scored two to enable Arsenal to snatch the Littlewoods Cup from the Merseysiders, again after they had taken the lead. In doing so, Nicholas also ended one of football's most captivating legends — that Liverpool had never lost when Ian Rush scored. The Welsh star could point to 144 games that bore this out. But on the day that he wanted to leave British football with another memory before his much-publicized departure to Italy in return for the £3 million paid by Juventus, that particular myth was blown.

Arsenal's last Wembley appearance, in the 1980 FA Cup final, had coincided with Rush's £300,000 transfer to Anfield from Chester, and in the years between he has won virtually all there is to win in club competition. From the start it looked as if he was ready to deliver another trophy, as his terrific cunning and acceleration around the box began to unsettle the Arsenal defence.

Sure enough, when the breakthrough came in the 23rd minute, it was Rush who got the goal, clinically finishing a move put together by Molby and McMahon, who were looking ominously in control of the midfield, and giving goalkeeper Lukic no chance. At this stage, Arsenal looked like being torn apart. They had started very much as underdogs, having slipped from first in the League in January with a run of nine matches without a win and only one goal. But their gutsy comebacks against Spurs in the semi-finals must have given them a boost, and as Paul Davis began to assert himself in midfield, so the pattern of the game changed. And as soon as Nicholas scored in the 29th minute after a goalmouth scramble, it seemed that Wembley had decided that the inconsistent and unsettled Scot — a Highbury favourite who had not recaptured his Celtic goalscoring form of four years ago — was going to be the hero of the first Littlewoods Cup final, and not Rush.

Kenny Dalglish put himself on in the 72nd minute, but he could not upset the control that Davis, Rocastle and Williams were now exerting in midfield. Then Perry Groves went on for Quinn, and the first thing he did was leave Gillespie tackling thin air on the touchline, race into the box, and cross to the unmarked Nicholas. The Scot appeared to miscue his shot slightly, and Whelan diverted the ball beyond the fingertips of Grobbelaar. But the record books gave the goal to Nicholas, and that's how the fairy-tale should end.

Charlie Nicholas (10) scores Arsenal's winning goal.

Charlie Nicholas (visible through the netting) turns away in triumph after equalizing for Arsenal.

England lose 8–3 in Berne: the message is 'keep away'

ENGLAND'S DREAMS of a rapid return to European club football after their two-year exile were quickly shattered in Berne on 10 March. The 11-man UEFA executive committee voted 8–3 in favour of retaining the ban, imposed after the horror of the Heysel Stadium disaster in May 1985. They issued a terse 12-line communique, which left League president Philip Carter "dreadfully disappointed", but in no doubt as to the message.

After a 90-minute plea to the committee by Mr Carter and FA chairman Bert Millichip, in which they outlined the improvements in crowd control in England, there were hopes, if not of a return, then of at least some criteria for clubs to fulfil. But the statement removed any glimmer of hope of a reprieve for clubs, players and genuine supporters, and concluded: "The situation will be reviewed during 1988."

In other words, "Don't call us, we'll call you".

League block QPR-Fulham merger

THE FOOTBALL LEAGUE management committee have called off the proposed merger between Queen's Park Rangers and Fulham and appealed for someone to buy the name of the Third Division club from Marler Estates, the owners of Craven Cottage.

The League refuse to accept that Fulham, who were bought by Marler from club chairman Ernie Clay for £9 million last year, need to go out of business despite attracting all-time low attendances. They will not allow the registrations of any Fulham players to be transferred to the new club, who were to be retained as Queen's Park Rangers, though the League do admit they have no power to prevent Fulham from going into liquidation.

The situation cannot help the club to succeed on the field, irrespective of what happens in boardrooms and banks.

Finally, a sky-blue heaven

COVENTRY CITY, upsetting all the odds, beat Tottenham 3–2 at Wembley to win the FA Cup in their first final, and earn their first major honour since their election to the League in 1919. They carried off the trophy with an extra-time own goal after an absorbing and thrilling a final as has been seen for some years. A goal down almost before they had time to take in the twin towers, the Sky Blues twice hit back to equalize. Their achievement in going on to win was a massive tribute to the transformation effected by the partnership of managing director George Curtis and chief coach John Sillett at Highfield Road.

Spurs, successful in all seven of their previous FA Cup finals, made the perfect start, taking the lead after only two minutes, almost inevitably through Clive Allen. But Bennett put Coventry level seven minutes later, spinning and scoring from close range.

With Hoddle's party tricks and Waddle's incisive running regularly threatening to tear Coventry apart, Spurs took a deserved lead again four minutes before the interval, when a flighted Hoddle free-kick was deflected by Kilcline past his own keeper. Houchen, however, put Coventry on terms again after 62 minutes, with a diving header from a pass that the increasingly influential Bennett curled beautifully behind the Spurs defence.

The winner came early in extra time when Mabbutt deflected a driven McGrath cross in a looping arc over Clemence's straining fingers into the goal — and the history books.

Keith Houchen heads a spectacular second equalizer for Coventry.

Big Mac indigestible on Wearside

LAWRIE MCMENEMY finally resigned his Sunderland job on 16 April after a season of recriminations and sniping, and a financial crisis at the club that forced him to take a huge cut in salary. The former Southampton manager, who brought great prosperity and success to the south coast club, never got off the ground on Wearside. He was hailed as a messiah when he arrived at Sunderland 22 months ago, but from the start was under the intense pressure of being expected to restore the club to their former glories in the top echelon.

After all, he appeared to be the perfect manager they had been seeking for 20 years, a man of the North-East, steeped in tradition, who could feel the footballing pulse of the area. Despite his charisma and his public appeal, however, Mr McMenemy, 50, could not find the magic formula on the field, and he leaves Roker Park with Sunderland closer to the Third Division than the First.

Lawrie McMenemy (left): failed to deliver.

Ten years for Chelsea soccer thugs

TWO RINGLEADERS of a gang of Chelsea football hooligans who plotted a six-year campaign of soccer violence at grounds across the country were each jailed for 10 years at Inner London Crown Court on 11 May. Three other members of the mob, known as the "Chelsea Headhunters", were sentenced to a total of 18 years for their part in the violent outbreaks that left many victims scarred for life.

Judge Shindler QC, whose hobbies listed in Who's Who include watching soccer, told the five they were "ruthless, violent and nasty" men who used football as an excuse or a platform for violence.

The five, who were trapped by "Operation Own Goal", in which six undercover officers infiltrated the gang, were convicted at the end of an 18-week trial costing £3 million. They had a total of 32 previous convictions, almost all for violence and threatening behaviour, several associated with soccer.

Violence in Italy is no surprise

SOCCER HOOLIGANISM, still referred to in much of Europe as the "English disease", is painfully rife elsewhere on the Continent, as the Italian police will bear out after serious disturbances sparked by results at the top and bottom of their First Division.

Supporters of leaders Napoli went on a rampage in historic Verona after their team's shock 3–0 defeat, and there were 38 arrests. And after Sampdoria's win at Ascoli that virtually condemned the home side to relegation, it was an hour before the visitors could leave their dressing-room. In battles outside the stadium, several police were injured, and a bus carrying Sampdoria fans was damaged by stones.

These events are most unlikely to come as any surprise, however, to anyone who witnessed the monstrous behaviour of the Juventus fans during the Heysel Stadium disaster in Brussels two years ago.

Vintage Porto are the pride of Portugal

PORTO REPAIRED the recently tarnished image of Portuguese football with a thrilling comeback against Bayern Munich in the European Cup final to win the country's first trophy for 25 years. In the Prater Stadium, Vienna, packed with 60,000 enthralled fans, Porto wiped away the bitter memories of the financial wranglings and dissension that marred Portugal's World Cup campaign. They gave a display of tenacity and rare skill matched by exhilarating pace, epitomized by the talented Futre. And they clawed their way back into the match in three remarkable second-half minutes. With Bayern Munich, a goal up through a Kogl diving header in the 25th minute, seemingly cruising towards their fourth European Cup success, Porto conjured up an equalizer by their little-known Algerian winger Rabah Madjer, whose only claim to fame was a goal scored for his country in their 1982 World Cup triumph over West Germany. His goal against Bayern came in the 77th minute, when he took the German defence by surprise with a delightful back-heel into the net.

The celebrations were so boisterous that the Algerian limped away in need of treatment, and only just returned in time to play a part in Porto's winner. He sprinted past the tiring Winkelhofer, such an influence in the first half, before crossing a beautiful pass to the far post, where the unmarked substitute Juary volleyed home gleefully. The shocked West German champions never recovered.

Bayern keeper Pfaff can't prevent Juary from scoring Porto's winner.

FOOTBALL FOCUS

- The Rous Cup took the form of a three-cornered tournament this season, and was won by Brazil, who drew with England at Wembley and beat Scotland at Hampden Park.
- Scarborough, champions of the GM Vauxhall Conference, became the first club to win automatic promotion to the Football League.
- The Football League have agreed to allow two substitutes per team in the coming season.
- Because of two technical irregularities in the applications, 26 Liverpool fans won High Court orders in April blocking their extradition to Belgium to face manslaughter charges arising from the 1985 Heysel disaster.
- Promotion and relegation play-offs took place at the end of the season, in which Division One was reduced by one club to 21 and Division Two increased to 23. The last promotion place in each division was contested by the three clubs just below the automatic promotion spots and the club in the division above just above the automatic relegation spots. The four clubs played home-and-away semi-finals and finals.

Cup-tired Dundee United in vain fight-back

DUNDEE UNITED became the latest British team to be unable to overcome the difficulties of mounting a double cup campaign when they were beaten on aggregate goals by Gothenburg in the UEFA Cup final. Just four days after losing the Scottish FA Cup final against St Mirren, they found it impossible to defeat the highly efficient Swedish side at Tannadice Park. Rarely were they able to reproduce the passion and determination that had helped them overcome the formidable talents of Barcelona and Borussia Moenchengladbach in previous rounds.

United's hopes of crowning what had been an exciting and exhausting season by becoming the first Scottish club to win the UEFA Cup all but disappeared after 22 minutes. For that's how long it took Lennard Nilsson to score the crucial away goal to add to the Pettersson winner in the first leg a fortnight ago. Now United needed three goals. When they got one of them, on the hour, through Clark, they suddenly shook off the weariness of the 66 games they have played this season, and Clark's ability in the air gave Hysen an uncomfortable time. Indeed, he found Gallacher with a header just six yards out, but he could not keep his shot down. The ball flew over the bar, and with it went United's hopes.

Dundee's Clark is inconsolable.

FINAL SCORE

Football League
Division 1: Everton
Top scorer: Clive Allen (Tottenham Hotspur) 33
Division 2: Derby County
Division 3: Bournemouth
Division 4: Northampton Town
Footballer of the Year: Clive Allen (Tottenham Hotspur)

FA Cup Final
Coventry City 3 Tottenham H 2
(after extra time)

League Cup Final
Arsenal 2 Liverpool 1

Scottish League
Premier Division: Rangers
Top scorer: Brian McClair (Celtic) 35
Division 1: Morton
Division 2: Meadowbank Thistle
Footballer of the Year: Brian McClair (Celtic)

Scottish FA Cup Final
St Mirren 1 Dundee United 0
(after extra time)

Scottish League Cup Final
Rangers 2 Celtic 1

European Cup Final
Porto 2 Bayern Munich 1

Cup-Winners' Cup Final
Ajax Amsterdam 1 Lokomotiv Leipzig 0

UEFA Cup Final
IFK Gothenburg beat Dundee United 1–0, 1–1

European Footballer of the Year 1986
Igor Belanov (Dynamo Kiev & USSR)

Leading European Scorer (Golden Boot)
Rodion Camataru (Dinamo Bucharest) 44

World Club Championship
Porto (Portugal) 2 Penarol (Uruguay) 1
(after extra time)

England double scorer Robson challenges Maradona.

League win hands down

THE FOOTBALL League launched their centenary season in just about the best way possible before a crowd of 61,000 at Wembley on 8 August. Their representative side beat the impressive array of talent from around the world, assembled by Barcelona manager Terry Venables, by 3–0 in an interesting, if not wildly exciting, game. The goals were scored by Bryan Robson, who got the first and last, and Norman Whiteside, one of a horde of substitutes introduced in the second half, six by the League and seven by the Rest.

Before the start, the players were introduced to the crowd individually, American Super Bowl style, and predictably Diego Maradona emerged to a storm of booing, while the loudest cheers were reserved for another World star, Gary Lineker of Barcelona and England. The presentation of the players to the guest of honour was hardly routine, either. The celebrity in question, the legendary Pele, was genuinely moved by the experience, and stopped to embrace players in the line-ups.

The star of the show was not Maradona, the best player in the world at the moment and costing the League around £1,000 a minute for his appearance, but his predecessor in that role, the now retired Frenchman Michel Platini. While Maradona looked short of full match fitness, Platini stroked the ball around magnificently. Despite Robson's two goals, the pick of the League team was Neil Webb, the young Nottingham Forest midfield player. His adventurous, imaginative play did his prospects of winning his first full cap no harm at all.

Robson scored the first goal after 23 minutes, a far-post header from a long Sansom centre. The second goal, in 59 minutes, was an all-Irish affair, made by the Republic's Liam Brady for the North's Whiteside, while the third goal, which finished the contest two minutes from time, was an all-Manchester United production — made by Whiteside for Robson.

Barclays bank on fans in new deal

THE FOOTBALL League erased the nightmare of the ill-conceived Today newspaper sponsorship by unveiling, on 13 August, that £4.5 million backing for the next three years would be undertaken by Barclays Bank. Amid the delight at the speed with which they have managed to attract a major sponsor, League president Philip Carter warned of the threat to the deal posed by hooligans. Barclays chairman John Quinton confirmed that the Bank would have a get-out clause, as they would not wish to be associated with anything that "led to blood running in the streets".

Hopefully, much of the money will go to ensure that those smaller clubs in need of financial assistance will stay viable.

Silent Souness suspended

GLASGOW RANGERS player-manager Graeme Souness gave his impression of a petulant schoolboy when, with the inevitable "minder" in tow, he emerged from the Scottish FA headquarters on 24 September with his five-match suspension. All media questions were ignored as he thrust his hands into his pockets, whistled softly to himself and stared resolutely at the ground. No doubt his ghost-writer will soon be apprised of his views on the punishment, but he should consider himself lucky that the disciplinary committee took the easy option and dealt with him as a player rather than a manager.

His third dismissal in 14 months was for an offence committed in the impassioned environment of last month's "old firm" match against Celtic — a foul against opposing striker Billy Stark — and was compounded by his subsequent verbal abuse of the match referee.

Logic suggests that Souness should be basking in the glory of last season's League and Cup double. Instead, angered by insults — either real or imagined — he has adopted a hostile stance that overshadows the good things, such as regular capacity crowds, despite some erratic League results, and this week's arrival in the Skol Cup final.

Roast Turkey on England's menu again

HAVING ROASTED Turkey 8–0 in Istanbul three years ago, in a World Cup qualifier, England staged a repeat performance for the Wembley fans on 14 October. The unquenchable thirst of Gary Lineker for international goals, the rejuvenated talents of John Barnes and the youthful promise of Neil Webb emphatically atoned for the miserable performance in the goalless draw in Izmir last year. The goals, four in each half, came from Barnes (two), Lineker (three), Robson, Beardsley and Webb, entertaining the meagre 42,000 crowd. But they are irrelevant in the context of qualifying for West Germany, as Yugoslavia's 3–0 demolition of Northern Ireland in Sarajevo means England must earn at least a draw when they go to Belgrade next month if they are to be sure of reaching the European finals.

Lineker (left) and Barnes: five goals between them against Turkey.

Spurs in Vale of anguish

Walker opens the scoring for Port Vale.

PROUD PORT VALE capped Tottenham's miserable season with the first major FA Cup upset, producing a memorable 2–1 fourth-round victory that was surprisingly easier than the scoreline would suggest.

Everything went wrong for Spurs on an occasion Port Vale will never forget, as they took full advantage of the Londoners' apathy. Ray Walker, a £12,000 buy from Aston Villa, sparked off Vale's win with a superbly hit 25-yard drive in the 12th minute from Phil Sproson's defence-splitting pass, and 12 minutes later he returned the compliment for Sproson to add a second. As might be expected, Vale went onto the defensive in the second half, and Spurs pulled one back in the 64th minute when Neil Ruddock went up into the attack and atoned for earlier defensive gaffes by heading in from Waddle's free-kick, but it was to no avail.

Tottenham de-Pleated

DAVID PLEAT RESIGNED on 23 October after 17 months as Tottenham manager, following allegations in a national newspaper concerning his private life. It came on the day the newspaper published a second set of allegations that Mr Pleat had been questioned by the police about a kerb-crawling incident. The initial revelations in The Sun last June referred to incidents said to have occurred during his reign at Luton. At the time, Spurs chairman Irving Scholar stood by Mr Pleat. This time, however, the club presumably felt they had to protect their good name.

It is sad for Mr Pleat, who always appeared to have the ideal credentials for managing the fortunes of a club like Spurs or, ultimately, even his country. He joined Spurs on the dismissal of Peter Shreeves in the summer of 1986, and took them to the FA Cup final in his first season. Tottenham are expected to go for ex-Barcelona manager and their former star Terry Venables, at present on holiday in the United States, to take over from Mr Pleat.

England throw down gauntlet to Europe's best

ENGLAND FULFILLED the hopes not only of their much-criticized manager, Bobby Robson, but of the entire footballing nation with one of their finest performances, when they beat Yugoslavia 4–1 in Belgrade on 11 November to clinch their place in the European Championship finals. The systematic, skilful destruction of a highly-rated Yugoslav team will have sent shock waves through Europe, and already the bookmakers have made them second favourites, behind West Germany, the host country.

Needing a point to be sure of joining the seven other finalists, England achieved that and more in the space of 24 invigorating minutes. In that time, Peter Beardsley, John Barnes, Bryan Robson and Tony Adams scored the goals that stunned Yugoslavia and left 60,000 partisan fans howling derision at their own team. But for later generosity in front of goal and the bravery of substitute keeper Radaca, who replaced the unfortunate Ravnic, Yugoslavia might have been more embarrassed before they gained a consolation goal 10 minutes from time, by Katanec. It was the only goal England conceded in their six matches, having scored 19.

They will be joined in West Germany by the Republic of Ireland, who have to thank Scotland, out of it themselves, for winning in Bulgaria to secure their place. Wales, however, missed several chances before finally going down 2–0 in Czechoslovakia, so Denmark qualify from Group 6.

Tony Adams (5) scores goal number four.

Sharp's the word for Toffeemen, with a Cup hat-trick

AFTER CALLING ON every ounce of courage, determination and experience merely to stay alive in the first three matches of their FA Cup third-round thriller with Sheffield Wednesday, Everton took an unbelievable and unbreakable grip on the third replay in 45 minutes of dominant football. There had rarely been anything to choose between the two in-form First Division teams in the previous encounters, which had all ended 1–1, so a packed Hillsborough watched in utter disbelief as, after seven hours, the rampant League champions secured another Goodison game — this time against Middlesbrough, on Saturday — with five well-taken goals, all scored in the first half.

Leading scorer Graeme Sharp was the chief assassin for the Toffeemen, with three goals past Hodge, a former Everton goalkeeper, and the others were scored by Heath and Snodin. Wednesday were left to reflect that it might have been so different had Colin West taken an outstanding chance after only 20 seconds.

Everton spoil 'pool party

WAYNE CLARKE, whose elder brother Allan helped to write Leeds's unbeaten 29-match run at the start of the 1973–74 season into the record books, guaranteed that it would not be obliterated by Liverpool at Goodison Park on Sunday, 20 March. Fuelled by local pride, and bolstered by an atmosphere resembling that of an FA Cup final, Everton, for the second time this season, demonstrated that, brilliant as Kenny Dalglish's side may be, they are not invincible. Clarke's 14th-minute goal, watched by Allan, ended a magnificent run that began on a sunlit afternoon at Highbury last August, and had by the dark days of this winter laid waste to the challenge offered by the rest of the First Division.

Everton knew this was the last chance they had of making any impact on a season in which they will almost certainly be called on to pack up the Championship trophy and send it across Stanley Park to Anfield. They went out for an early lead, they got it, and they defended it efficiently, if sometimes desperately, for the remainder of the game.

It will be a great consolation to Everton and their supporters, who milled onto the pitch to celebrate the final whistle, that, with this victory and October's win in the Littlewoods Cup at Anfield, they have inflicted the only two defeats thus far in Liverpool's all-conquering season.

Keeping it in the family: Wayne Clarke scores to end Liverpool's great run.

Court convictions follow on-field trouble: Woods and Butcher guilty

RANGERS AND ENGLAND soccer stars Chris Woods and Terry Butcher were found guilty on 15 April at a Glasgow Sheriff Court of disorderly conduct and breach of the peace on the field of play. The two players were fined, Woods £500 and Butcher £250. Another Rangers and England player, Graham Roberts, walked free on a not proven verdict, while Scottish striker Frank McAvennie, the only Celtic player to be charged as a result of the goalmouth fracas at a Rangers-Celtic game last October, was found not guilty.

The Glasgow police clearly detected a connection between trouble on the pitch and subsequent violence on the terraces; consequently, they had every right to prosecute. Shrewsbury magistrates had taken a similar view 24 hours earlier, when Swindon's Chris Kamara was fined £1,200, and ordered to pay £250 compensation, for causing grievous bodily harm to Shrewsbury striker Jim Melrose in a Second Division match last February.

The conviction of the two England footballers will further damage their country's reputation abroad, which has been badly tarnished by a list of previous incidents.

Ferguson claims refs are intimidated at Anfield

AFTER MANCHESTER United's epic recovery at Anfield to draw 3–3 with 10 men, manager Alex Ferguson launched a ferocious attack on the effect of referees of the "intimidating" Anfield atmosphere. His comments, while conducting an interview on local radio, sparked a harsh verbal exchange with Liverpool manager Kenny Dalglish. Mr Ferguson, clearly upset by the sending-off of defender Colin Gibson for a foul on Nicol, his second bookable offence, reckoned Steve McMahon was getting away with committing the same fouls all afternoon.

"I can now understand why clubs come away from here having to bite their tongues, knowing they have been done by referees," he said. "I am not getting at this referee. It is the whole intimidating atmosphere and the monopoly Liverpool have enjoyed here for years that gets to them eventually." At one stage, Mr Dalglish, who was carrying his six-week-old daughter, suggested the interviewer would get more sense if he spoke to the baby, to which Mr Ferguson responded with a couple of well-chosen words. All this should not detract, however, from an enthralling match in which Liverpool seemed to have restored normal service after losing only their second League match two days earlier at Forest. They shrugged off the effects of conceding a second-minute goal to Robson, and 45 minutes later were 3–1 up, with goals from Beardsley, Gillespie and McMahon.

United's Paul McGrath (centre) clears from Peter Beardsley.

When Gibson was sent off after an hour, there seemed very little chance that United would avert a thrashing, let alone preserve their eight-year run without defeat at Anfield. But they came storming back with a second goal from Robson after 65 minutes and a coolly taken equalizer from Strachan 12 minutes later. Liverpool, who would have sewn up their 17th title had they won their two Easter matches, will now have to wait a little longer.

Luton hit Littlewoods jackpot

BRIAN STEIN ADDED to Wembley's endless tradition of romance and high drama as Luton produced a most remarkable finish to the Littlewoods Cup final. Only 14 seconds separated Arsenal from extra time when Stein scored to write himself into the stadium's folklore and give Luton their first major trophy in their 98-year history. But if you're looking for a hero, then surely Luton's stand-in keeper Andy Dibble must be the prime candidate. Not only did he have a brilliant match, keeping Arsenal at bay when they were very much on top, but he saved Winterburn's penalty kick when Luton were 2–1 down with less than 10 minutes left.

That was the turning point of the game, or at least a critical one. For this was a game full of twists, of ifs and buts, and meaningful substitutions. Luton, complete underdogs — more so than Arsenal were last year when they shocked Liverpool — took the lead against a surprisingly hesitant Arsenal after only 13 minutes. And they nobly protected it until Hayes, going on after an hour for last year's galvanizing substitute Groves, soon scrambled Smith's cross in. Then Smith scored and Arsenal hit bar and post as they began to overpower tiring Luton. And when Rocastle escaped Johnson's clutches for once and was brought down by Donaghy in the box, Luton were looking dead and buried.

But Luton, who had gambled on the inexperience of Black and the rustiness of Hill and Preece, found new spirit and an untapped reservoir of stamina from Dibble's magnificent save. Caesar, like his Roman namesake, was caught unawares, in front of goal, and Wilson took advantage to equalize. The amazing Ricky Hill, in his first game since breaking a leg on Boxing Day, drove Luton forward. Ashley Grimes, who had gone on for Preece after 76 minutes, took the ball down the right and somehow contrived to cross it with the outside of his left foot, surprising Arsenal so that Stein could rifle the ball in.

It was a breathtaking finish, and left Luton nurturing a dream of possible European competition, while Arsenal are still searching for a route out of Liverpool's shadow.

Dibble makes his crucial penalty save from Winterburn.

Wimbledon's Cup in safe keeping

WIMBLEDON CAUSED the biggest FA Cup final upset since Sunderland beat Leeds 15 years ago when they gave an extraordinary display of defiance against League champions Liverpool and beat them 1–0. A Southern League club only 11 years ago, they were meant to be the whipping boys as the Merseysiders went looking for their second League and Cup "double" in three years. But they rarely allowed their opponents the space to play their fluent, attacking football, and when Liverpool did get through, brave Dave Beasant was there to thwart them, with some remarkable stops in the first half and a penalty save — the first ever in a Wembley FA Cup final — in the second. Oddly enough, 29-year-old Beasant lives within sight of the famous twin towers.

He played a true captain's part as the unpretentious South London club snatched a goal in the 36th minute — a Sanchez header from Wise's free-kick — and then denied Liverpool the space they needed to break down their stubborn defence. They frustrated Liverpool without resorting to much of the rough stuff that has become their stock in trade. True, Vinny Jones did clatter into Steve McMahon early in the game, but that was the only nasty tackle. There were no real excuses for Liverpool, although they could point to the incident in the first half when the referee blew for a foul on Beardsley before he recovered to chip the ball over Beasant into the net.

As in the Littlewoods Cup, the crisis for the underdogs was the penalty. Beasant, at 6ft 4in, is a daunting obstacle. But Aldridge, the League's leading scorer, had successfully converted 11 penalties this season. He stroked the ball low and firmly towards the inside of Beasant's left-hand post, but the keeper launched his huge frame sideways and clawed the ball away. This was after 61 minutes, and there was still much to do. Liverpool rang the changes, bringing on Johnston and Molby for Aldridge and Spackman in a desperate attempt to find a way through. But they could not raise their game enough to deprive Wimbledon of the most wonderful moment in their short history as a Football League club.

Beasant reaches out to paw Aldridge's penalty to safety.

Jubilant Irish leave England huge task

JACK CHARLTON, who helped England conquer the footballing world 22 years ago, has almost guaranteed that they will not this season be crowned champions of Europe. In Stuttgart, the team he created provided the Republic of Ireland with their most glorious, and unexpected, triumph and left England struggling to stay in the European Championship.

Ray Houghton, a Scot by birth and a footballer moulded by Liverpool, headed England towards defeat in the sixth minute of their opening match in Group 2. Houghton's goal, his first in 16 internationals and only the second headed goal of his career, was enough to beat England. Their failure to equalize, despite constant pressure, was due to a combination of Bonner's heroics in goal and Lineker's uncharacteristic failure to convert the chances that his nose for an opening made for him.

As Bonner made one more acrobatic save in the dying minutes from late substitute Hateley, the massive Irish contingent began to celebrate in and around the ground, and England were left to reflect on their afternoon of missed opportunity. They cannot feel confident about their prospects against Holland and the USSR.

Houghton heads the Republic's shock winner against England.

Chelsea go down fighting

A SINGLE GOAL at Stamford Bridge against Middlesbrough was not enough to keep Chelsea in the First Division as they lost the play-off final on aggregate. But more serious to English football as a whole is the damage their rioting fans might have done to the cause of England's return to European club competition. While English fans in Lausanne were passing the "Swiss test", in the knowledge that any misbehaviour at the friendly which England won 1–0 might result in their team being replaced in the European Championship by Yugoslavia, Chelsea's thugs were destroying all the goodwill built up over the past season.

The initial pitch invasion, according to Chelsea chairman Ken Bates, was of Middlesbrough fans wishing to congratulate their team. But the so-called Chelsea supporters needed no encouragement, and a rampaging mob swarmed onto the field. Innocent fans were beaten up, ambulancemen were attacked with stones and bottles, one policeman was knocked unconscious and another taken to hospital. In all, there were 102 arrests.

Sad scenes at Stamford Bridge.

FOOTBALL FOCUS

- New Huddersfield manager Malcolm Macdonald saw his team trounced 10–1 by Manchester City at Maine Road on 7 November, with three players scoring hat-tricks: Paul Stewart, Tony Adcock and David White. It was a record defeat for Huddersfield, who were relegated at the end of the season.
- The Scottish League (Skol) Cup final was settled on penalties for the first time on 25 October, when Rangers and Aberdeen finished level at 3–3 after extra time. Rangers won the shoot-out 5–3.
- Rangers signed 33-year-old Trevor Francis from Italian club Atalanta on 5 August to bring their complement of English players up to seven.
- Southampton's Alan Shearer, at 17 years 240 days, became the youngest player ever to score a First Division hat-trick, in their 4–2 defeat of Arsenal on 9 April.
- On 5 September, Third Division Chesterfield, the only side in the League not yet to have conceded a goal after five games, visited Gillingham and went down 10–0.

FINAL SCORE

Football League
Division 1: Liverpool
Top scorer: John Aldridge (Liverpool) 26
Division 2: Millwall
Division 3: Sunderland
Division 4: Wolverhampton Wanderers
Footballer of the Year: John Barnes (Liverpool)

FA Cup Final
Wimbledon 1 Liverpool 0

League Cup Final
Luton Town 3 Arsenal 2

Scottish League
Premier Division: Celtic
Top scorer: Tommy Coyne (Dundee) 33
Division 1: Hamilton Academical
Division 2: Ayr United
Footballer of the Year: Paul McStay (Celtic)

Scottish FA Cup Final
Celtic 2 Dundee United 1

Scottish League Cup Final
Rangers 3 Aberdeen 3
(after extra time)
Rangers won 5–3 on penalties

European Cup Final
PSV Eindhoven 0 Benfica 0
(after extra time)
PSV Eindhoven won 6–5 on penalties

Cup-Winners' Cup Final
Mechelen 1 Ajax Amsterdam 0

UEFA Cup Final
Bayer Leverkusen beat Espanol 0–3, 3–0
Bayer Leverkusen won 3–2 on penalties

European Footballer of the Year 1987
Ruud Gullit (AC Milan & Holland)

Leading European Scorer (Golden Boot)
Tanju Colak (Galatasaray) 39

World Club Championship
Nacional (Uruguay) 2 PSV Eindhoven 2
Nacional won 7–6 on penalties

Dutch are the masters of Europe

SOCCER SOUNDBITES

"Both teams played football of the future, and they deserved to be in the European Championship final."

RINUS MICHELS,
Holland's manager.

TWO SUPERB GOALS by Gullit and Van Basten, and a penalty save by Van Breukelen, gave Holland the 2–0 victory they so richly deserved in the European Championship final against the USSR. Holland's triumph, won by playing entertaining and exciting football, is a tribute to their retiring supremo Rinus Michels. Having avenged their 1974 World Cup final defeat by Germany, when Michels was also in charge, with their splendid win in the semi-final at Hamburg, Holland returned to the Olympic Stadium at Munich to exorcize that memory completely.

Marco van Basten, who travelled to Germany as a reluctant substitute and played only 33 minutes in the opening match when they lost to the Soviets, confirmed himself as player of the tournament. Having stunned England with a hat-trick and scored Holland's last-gasp winner against the Germans, he turned in another dazzling performance. After 33 minutes, he headed a cross back into the centre for his Milan team-mate Ruud Gullit to strike a perfect header past Soviet keeper Dassayev.

Then, eight minutes into the second half, he produced the crowning moment of the Championship, a masterpiece of a goal. Arnold Muhren, the former Ipswich and Manchester United midfield star giving a fine display to mark his international swan-song, swung over a long cross, beyond the far post, and there was Van Basten to strike the most perfect right-foot volley from the narrowest of angles past the startled Dassayev.

It could have developed into an exhibition, but the Soviets raised their game and threw themselves into the attack. Belanov flicked the ball onto a post in a goalmouth scramble, and then Van Breukelen recklessly and unnecessarily dived across an opponent to concede a penalty after 57 minutes. But the former Nottingham Forest keeper made amends by blocking Belanov's spot-kick. The crisis was over, and Holland, somewhat unlucky losers in the World Cup finals of both 1974 and 1978, marched on to their first major triumph in international football.

Ruud Gullit's header puts Holland in front.

Van Basten's breath-taking volley clinches the Championship.

FINAL SCORE

EUROPEAN CHAMPIONSHIP 1988

Group 1

West Germany	1	Italy	1
Spain	3	Denmark	2
West Germany	2	Denmark	0
Italy	1	Spain	0
West Germany	2	Spain	0
Italy	2	Denmark	0

	P	W	D	L	F	A	P
W. Germany	3	2	1	0	5	1	5
Italy	3	2	1	0	4	1	5
Spain	3	1	0	2	3	5	2
Denmark	3	0	0	3	2	7	0

Group 2

Rep. Ireland	1	England	0
USSR	1	Holland	0
Holland	3	England	1
Rep. Ireland	1	USSR	1
Holland	1	Rep. Ireland	0
USSR	3	England	1

	P	W	D	L	F	A	P
USSR	3	2	1	0	5	2	5
Holland	3	2	0	1	4	2	4
Rep. Ireland	3	1	1	1	2	2	3
England	3	0	0	3	2	7	0

SEMI-FINALS

Holland	2	West Germany	1
USSR	2	Italy	0

FINAL

Holland	2	USSR	0

Munich, 25 June 1988. Attendance 72,308.

Holland: Van Breukelen, Van Aerle, Van Tiggelen, Wouters, Koeman R, Rijkaard, Vanenburg, Gullit, Van Basten, Muhren, Koeman E (Scorers: Gullit, Van Basten)
USSR: Dassayev, Khidiatulin, Aleinikov, Mikhailichenko, Litovchenko, Demianenko, Belanov, Gotsmanov (Baltacha), Protasov (Pasulko), Zavarov, Rats

England face total ban from foreign football

FOLLOWING VIOLENT clashes between German, Dutch and English fans on 15 June in Dusseldorf, where Holland beat England 3–1 to put them out of the European Championship, and further disturbances the next night in Frankfurt involving German and English mobs, the FA have withdrawn their request to UEFA for the return of English clubs to European competition. At the same time, after an emergency Downing Street "summit" on soccer hooliganism, Home Secretary Douglas Hurd announced a draconian five-point plan to crack down on soccer hooliganism, which incorporates a possible withdrawal of the England team from international matches, including the World Cup. Other proposed measures are powers for the courts to confiscate passports, a membership card scheme for all football supporters — Prime Minister Margaret Thatcher is a strong supporter of this idea — a review of the licensing laws and increased police intelligence gathering.

With over 200 English fans detained in Germany after the disgraceful scenes of violence, the FA decided to act quickly and pre-empt a possible worldwide ban. They felt, anyway, that there was little chance, in the current climate, of the three-year club ban being lifted, and they did not want to prejudice any further the very existence of the national side. They have also cancelled England's scheduled trip to Italy in September.

On the football front, England manager Bobby Robson is ignoring the hysterical demands from certain quarters for his resignation, and is even money with the bookmakers to remain in charge for start of the World Cup qualifying competition — that is, if England are not thrown out of it. Meanwhile, the Republic of Ireland's supremo, Jack Charlton, will return to a hero's welcome whether or not his team qualify for the European semi-finals in their last match, against Holland.

Modern superstars

Gullit — one of the modern-day Dutch masters.

GIANLUIGI LENTINI cost AC Milan £13 million when they signed him from Torino in 1992. The sum, which set a new world transfer record, is said to include his wages over three years. With endorsements and bonuses (Milan players made £200,000 apiece for winning the 1993 Italian league title), the 23-year-old son of a bricklayer earns in excess of £1 million a year. This shy, modest young man has helped Milan to dominate Italian football and excel in Europe, but he has a long way to go before he can be compared with the likes of Di Stefano, Cruyff, Platini, Rummenigge and other European giants of yesteryear. He has yet to establish a regular place in Italy's national side. And although he played his part in Milan's successful defence of the Italian championship, it was not the leading part. Whereas in Turin he had a free role and could move around the field, at Milan he must subjugate his talents to the overall tactics, and that means playing a wide midfield role. Anyone who saw him in the 1993 European Cup final will know that he has a fast, direct style, which enables him to beat his man on the outside, and he is an excellent crosser of the ball from difficult positions. But, like so many of today's high-priced stars, he did not stamp his authority on the game.

Gallery of stars

Milan's industrialist owner Silvio Berlusconi looks on Lentini as an investment. He stockpiles footballers like others might collect works of art. In 1992, Milan also bought striker Jean-Pierre Papin for £10 million from Marseille, and midfielders Stefano Eranio from Genoa for £5 million and Dejan Savicevic from Red Star Belgrade for £4 million. Add these to previous expensive foreign acquisitions — the Dutch trio of Ruud Gullit, Marco Van Basten and Frank Rijkaard — and established native talent such as Baresi, De Napoli, Donadoni and Maldini, and you have a whole team of superstars. Yet they cannot all play at once: because of Italian restrictions on the number of foreign players permitted in a team, some of Milan's most costly stars regularly find themselves on the substitutes' bench or even out of the side altogether

Platt — outstanding English talent.

Platini — Europe's best in the eighties.

(there is no reserve-team football in Italy). Papin, for example, played for less than an hour in his first game after signing for Milan, and then found himself — the European Footballer of the Year — sitting in the stand for the next three.

Team of all talents

How do the individuals in this team of all the talents compare with earlier stars? Ruud Gullit, as a striker or midfield general, must rank with the greats, a "total footballer" with commanding skills on the ground and in the air. Marco Van Basten, too, stands with the best, a complete striker, oozing class, a scorer of spectacular goals and European Footballer of the Year for the third time in 1992. Papin is a hard worker, the scorer of opportunist, and often brilliant, goals. With some of Milan's foreign stars about to move on, Lentini might well establish himself in a more commanding role; but judgement must be reserved until then. Paolo Maldini has developed into a cultured full-back. And the Italian side found they could not do without the highly skilful Franco Baresi in defence, recalling him after he retired from international football.

Where the money is

Most of the world's best footballers now gravitate to Italy, where the big money is — and has been for more than 40 years. Juventus are always among the big spenders, and they in turn paid £8 million for midfield star Roberto Baggio in 1990 and £12 million for striker Gianluca Vialli in 1992. In the "second division" as far as such fees are concerned come English players, who are rated around the £5–6 million mark: Paul Gascoigne, David Platt and Trevor Steven, for example, all midfielders. Steven, like winger Chris Waddle, played in France, where there are also two or three clubs such as Marseille and Monaco with money to burn.

Best Britons

British strikers who cost from £2.5 to £3 million or more — Ian Rush, Mark Hughes and Gary Lineker — had less than successful spells on the Continent, but have been among the top stars for both club and country at home. Lineker (England) and Rush (Wales), both master finishers, have scored prolifically at all levels, while Hughes (Wales) never scores a dull goal. Wingmen John Barnes and Chris Waddle have entertained domestic crowds with their dribbling skills, but have not been the most reliable performers in the England side.

Maradona — the master.

Of all contemporary British players, Gascoigne stands out as the one with true star quality, possessed of a certain juvenile charisma, and at his best an inspiration to England, the one man with the ability and inventiveness to raise the side above the ordinary. Bryan Robson, his predecessor, was a marvellous all-round midfielder for England in the 1980s, a ball-winner, a fine passer of the ball, and at his most dangerous when stealing into the box on a long run from deep in his own half. Despite his unfortunate record of injuries, he has been a wonderful captain for both England and Manchester United.

Germany and France

West Germany have been the most consistent national side in recent times, with success based on determination, graft and a considerable amount of skill. Karl-Heinz Rummenigge was a first-rate attacking player, classy, fast and a superb finisher, twice European Footballer of the Year in the early 1980s, an accolade also accorded his fellow-countryman Lothar Matthaus in 1990 and to Frenchman Michel Platini three times (1983–85). The complete modern footballer, a creative midfield dynamo, Matthaus captained the Germans to a World Cup triumph and helped both Bayern Munich and Inter Milan to domestic honours.

But the outstanding European footballer of the decade is Platini, captain of France, cornerstone of the fine Juventus side of the mid-eighties. A commanding midfield general of great vision and wonderful passing ability, he also possessed a deadly shot, especially from free-kicks, and was a prolific scorer. With the creative Giresse and anchorman Tigana, he formed a brilliant midfield in the French side who won the 1984 European Championship.

The little master

Above Platini, however, as the world star of the 1980s, the only player who deserves to be mentioned in the same breath as Pele, Best, Di Stefano and Puskas, is the controversial Argentinian Diego Maradona — controversial because of his temperamental behaviour and his involvement with drugs, but no less than a genius on the field. Despite being predominantly left-footed, Maradona could do virtually anything with the ball. Short but stocky, with enormously powerful legs, he would go on mazy runs, wriggling past defenders, spurting between them, sending them the wrong way, and creating panic whenever he had the ball. He controlled his teams' build-ups, playing lots of one-twos with his colleagues before making a final, defence-splitting pass or going for goal himself.

Crowds everywhere flocked to see Maradona. He led Argentina to World Cup victory in 1986 and then took a very ordinary side through to the final in 1990. He had gone to Europe while still very young, and had a short spell with Barcelona before joining unfashionable Napoli in 1984 for a world record £6.9 million. He inspired them to their first Italian championship, repaying his transfer fee in no time, and was idolized by the whole city. It is a pity that his treatment on the field, the lack of protection which a player of his undoubted genius often suffers, gave him a cynical approach to the game, and that the trappings of wealth and fame led to his fall from grace off the field.

Future stars

Where will the next Maradona come from, the next Platini or Gullit? Out of Africa, could be the answer. Many African stars have already won fame playing in Europe, among them Roger Milla of Cameroon and the spectacular Ghanaian Abede Pele, who helped Marseille to beat Milan in the 1993 European Cup.

In Britain, all eyes are on young Ryan Giggs of Manchester United. Carefully nursed along by his club, he gained his first Welsh cap in October 1991, six weeks before his 18th birthday, and helped United win the 1992–93 Premier League Championship. With his ability to glide past a man on either side, his stylish body swerve and shooting, he is already being compared at Old Trafford with George Best — and you can't ask more than that of a teenager.

Lentini — record transfer.

Giggs — one for the future.

Spurs break transfer record for Gascoigne

PAUL GASCOIGNE, 21, became England's first £2 million footballer when he signed for Tottenham from Newcastle United on 7 July. The previous record fee paid by a British club was the £1.9 million Liverpool shelled out for Peter Beardsley last summer, also from Newcastle. But the fee pales in comparison with the world record £5.5 million AC Milan paid for Dutch star Ruud Gullit last year.

The signing of Gascoigne — who has yet to win a full cap — brings Terry Venables's spending since he took over at White Hart Lane in November to £6.5 million, including £1.7 million for Paul Stewart, signed earlier in the summer from Manchester City, and substantial sums for Paul Walsh, Terry Fenwick and Bobby Mimms. Gascoigne, the PFA Young Player of the Year, has deliberated over his future for months and, although Manchester United made a late attempt to sign him, he decided to join the new-look Tottenham.

Paul Gascoigne, first £2m British signing.

End of TV saga as clubs at last agree to a £44m deal

PFA SECRETARY Gordon Taylor emerged as peacemaker in the long-running television saga, which ended on 8 August when the Football League chairmen agreed to accept the £11 million a year deal from ITV. By dropping the PFA claim from 10 to 5 per cent, giving them £550,000 a year from the deal, still more than double their previous share, Mr Taylor has made it possible for the two sides to reach an agreement. Of the remaining £10,450,000, the First Division will get £7,837,500 and the Second Division £1,306,250, with the same amount being shared by the Third and Fourth.

SOCCER SOUNDBITES

"I'm disappointed that the priority today was football finance other than a solution to football hooliganism."

Sports Minister
COLIN MOYNIHAN,
who arrived at the League meeting to explain the proposals for a national membership scheme and was left waiting for an hour.

Butcher fined £500 for damaging door

ENGLAND CENTRE-BACK Terry Butcher was in trouble again in Scotland, fined £500 by the Scottish FA on 7 November for bringing the game into disrepute. The latest distasteful chapter in Butcher's two-year stint as captain of Rangers arises from an incident following Rangers' 2–1 defeat by Aberdeen last month. He was asked, at an hour-long appearance, how the referee's dressing-room door at Pittodrie came to be damaged. After the hearing, an SFA spokesman said that Butcher had caused the damage by kicking the door. Although the episode had been witnessed by officers of the Grampian Police, who later interviewed the former Ipswich defender, they decided not to take any further action. Butcher was angered in the Aberdeen game by Neal Simpson's tackle on Iain Durrant, which has ended the Scottish international's interest in the season.

Rush back to Anfield

KENNY DALGLISH pulled off the transfer coup of the decade on 18 August when he brought Ian Rush back from Italy, after allowing him to go to Juventus 12 months ago for £3.2 million. No details of the fee or the length of his new contract have been disclosed, but according to Italian sources Liverpool have paid £2.8 million for their 26-year-old Welsh striker, beating the British record fee of £2.5 million paid by Everton for West Ham's Tony Cottee last month.

Juventus decided to let Rush go because they have exceeded their permitted quota of three "imports", and Rush, who has never settled down with the Italian culture and language and has struggled in Italian football, needed no persuasion. So the deal was completed, quietly and without fuss, in five days. This was possible only because of the special relationship that has built up between the two clubs since the tragic events at the Heysel Stadium in 1985. Rush was at pains to praise Juventus for the way they treat non-Italian players, and insisted his spell in Turin, during which he scored 14 goals, had been much more enjoyable than some reports had indicated.

Ian Rush: struggled in Italian football.

European ban lifted... conditionally

THE RETURN OF English clubs to European competition for the 1990-91 season was announced by UEFA on 11 April, but with important conditions. Nearly four years after the Heysel Stadium tragedy that resulted in the ban, UEFA have agreed to end the exile provided that the British government supports a readmission. Their return will also depend on the behaviour of English fans in Italy should the national side qualify to play in the fnals of the 1990 World Cup.

Reaction within the game was muted. The authorities are in a dilemna: they are faced with a measure they desperately do not want — the Football Spectators Bill, which includes a membership card scheme, a condition demanded by the government if they are going to sanction the return — to gain something they desperately do want, European football.

Sealey blunder hands Cup to father and son

LES SEALEY, LUTON'S extrovert and erratic goalkeeper, will probably never be able to explain what possessed him in the 55th minute of the Littlewoods Cup final at Wembley. Whatever his excuse, there is no denying that his rash action in bringing down Steve Hodge and conceding a penalty tilted the balance of the match in favour of the Clough family. Suddenly, Nottingham Forest, running rapidly out of ideas, were handed the most comfortable route to winning the Cup, and so collecting their first domestic trophy of the decade.

Nigel Clough, calmness personified, took one pace and stroked the ball into the centre of the net — and the course of the game changed there and then. Luton, watched by Andy Dibble, the keeper whose penalty save turned the match in their favour last year, became the second successive holders to reach Wembley again but fail to retain their trophy. It was such a terrible waste, for until that moment Luton had outthought a Forest side who had spent the first half struggling to come to terms with Harford and Wegerle. Harford's height was unsettling for Terry Wilson and Walker, and Luton capitalized on it. After 36 minutes of inconclusive sparring, Danny Wilson sent over a perfect cross following a corner, and Harford barely needed to lift himself off the turf to head Luton in front.

Before the penalty. Luton squandered three chances to increase their lead. After it, two further Forest goals in the 70th and 76th minutes put the match out of their reach. First Clough robbed the disappointing Black to find Gaynor, from whose devastating long pass Webb put Forest in front. And it was Gaynor again, on the right, who cut past the Luton defence to cross for Clough's second.

Forest manager Brian Clough, restored to his touchline seat after the FA ban, was always destined to dominate this final. He was a model of good behaviour during the match, but in trying to avoid the spotlight he inevitably attracted even more publicity. Having accepted the cheers and applause of the adoring Forest fans, he promptly disappeared down the tunnel to become the first winning manager at Wembley to miss the presentation of the trophy to his team.

Neil Webb scores goal number two past Les Sealey.

Clough in trouble over clash with fans

Brian Clough: personal crusade against hooligans.

NOTTINGHAM FOREST manager Brian Clough could face police action after allegedly taking the law into his own hands to deal with fans who invaded the pitch after Forest's 5–2 defeat of QPR in the Littlewoods Cup on 18 January. Investigations may be carried further if any of the four home supporters allegedly manhandled makes an official complaint. The FA immediately ordered an inquiry, which could result in a lengthy touchline ban.

This latest incident in a career of controversy has almost certainly put paid to any ambitions Mr Clough might still have had of becoming England manager. Millions of television viewers watched in astonishment as he appeared to punch and grab fans running onto the City Ground to celebrate Forest's victory. He has led a personal crusade against hooligans in the past that has been warmly applauded. He made a citizen's arrest at a Forest game two years' ago, and has remonstrated with his club's fans when they have used obscene chants. In a statement afterwards, he said the the incident was "regrettable", but the action had been taken with the right motive.

Ninety-four fans killed in semi-final horror

NINETY-FOUR FOOTBALL fans, including several children, were killed and about 150 seriously injured at Sheffield on 15 April in Europe's worst soccer tragedy. A senior police officer had ordered a gate to be opened, allowing fans to surge into the Hillsborough ground, and thousands of supporters were crushed on an overcrowded terrace at the FA Cup semi-final between Liverpool and Nottingham Forest.

The dead and injured, who were crowded at the Liverpool end of the ground for the capacity all-ticket game, were buried under falling bodies when hundreds of fans poured into the ground as the game was kicking off. Several children died after being crushed against the security fence, where they had been sent to get a good view. Fans tore down advertising hoardings and perimeter boards and used them as makeshift stretchers until the arrival of the ambulance services.

Apparently, Liverpool fans, frustrated at the time it was taking to get into the Leppings Lane entrance to the ground, began to push towards the turnstiles about ten minutes before kick-off.

To ease the crush, the police opened a big metal gate and the fans surged in. They poured through the the narrow, dark 30-yard tunnel in the centre of the stand, which offered them their first glimpse of the pitch. They careered into the central pens, crushing those at the front, although there was room to accommodate the latecomers in pens to either side. Those unaware of people dying at the front of the terraces pushed forward for a better view of the action. As they did so, more were trampled underfoot and crushed into the perimeter fencing at the bottom of the terraces, which had been put there to prevent hooligans from invading the pitch. Because of the perimeter fencing, few of the spectators could get out, although some managed to climb over the fencing or get through a narrow escape gate onto the pitch. Their plight was not immediately realized by the police inside the ground, but as soon as it was, a policeman ran onto the pitch to get the match stopped, some six minutes after it kicked off. Ten minutes later, the first ambulance arrived.

So for the third time in four years — after the Bradford fire and the Heysel Stadium disaster — the football authorities are left with the onerous task of restoring confidence in the flagging fortunes of Britain's national sport. One thing is clear. In the next few years, football must change its priorities and break away from what Graham Kelly, the Football Association chief executive, describes as "the ritual of standing on the terraces". In simple terms, that means a move towards all-seater stadiums — and quickly.

Makeshift stretchers are used to carry the victims away.

Fans caught in the crush are helped to safety by those in the upper tier of the Leppings Lane Stand.

Liverpool fans jailed for Heysel manslaughter

THE VERDICTS of the long-drawn-out trial in Brussels relating to the Heysel Stadium disaster of 1985 were given on 28 April. Fourteen of the 24 Liverpool fans were found guilty of manslaughter and sentenced to three years' imprisonment, with half of each term suspended. They were also each fined £1,000, with a further three months' jail in default. The cases against the other 10 were dismissed because of insufficient evidence. The accused had spent up to eight months in prison in England and Belgium while awaiting trial, and this will have to be deducted from their sentences. After the verdicts, the guilty were given a fortnight to appeal and allowed to go home.

There did not appear to be any arrangements for the fans to return to serve what remained of their sentences after proceedings described by many involved as a farce, and there was even more confusion to follow when the judges tried to deal with compensation claims totalling up to £10 million lodged by families of those who died in the riot. The court approved a mixture of claims ranging from about £1,500 to £300,000, but it was unclear who would be required to pay compensation.

The judges cleared the Belgian state, Brussels city authorities and UEFA of negligence. UEFA president Jacques Georges, Mayor Herve Brouhon and various other officials also went without censure.

Liverpool's Cup triumph a final tribute

LIVERPOOL DID AT Wembley what they had made up their minds to do 35 days ago, and won the FA Cup as a final tribute to the fans who had died so tragically at Hillsborough following their team. Winning the Cup had become an obsession at Anfield, where the players had immersed themselves totally and selflessly in the mourning for the dead. And the sense of achievement that manager Kenny Dalglish felt at the final whistle was clear for all to see.

With all the earlier doubts as to whether the competition should have been abandoned, or perhaps the Cup presented to Liverpool, it turned out to be the most dramatic final since the Arsenal-Manchester United epic 10 years ago. In this second all-Merseyside clash in four years, Liverpool eventually beat Everton 3–2, but not without some heart-stopping moments and the dramatic intervention of Ian Rush in extra time.

Just when Liverpool appeared to be coasting to victory on the strength of John Aldridge's fourth-minute goal, Everton equalized through midfielder Stuart McCall, one of their substitutes, in the last minute. Rush, the striker who has been searching for his form ever since he returned from Juventus, had gone on for Aldridge, his lookalike, after 72 minutes. And after four minutes of extra time, he showed the doubters that he had lost none of his predatory skills, by controlling a centre from Nicol, turning Ratcliffe quite beautifully and driving the ball into the far corner of the goal.

McCall's second equalizer, eight minutes later, was just as thrilling. When Hansen headed out a Ratcliffe free-kick, McCall volleyed the ball straight back and into the Liverpool net from some 25 yards. But this time, Everton's elation lasted only two minutes. Barnes floated the ball into the centre, and with the subtlest of flicks Rush directed it with his head into the far corner for his second goal, and his fourth in two finals against his Merseyside neighbours.

It was a blow that crushed Everton, and Liverpool would have won handsomely but for Southall's extraordinary saves to deny Houghton, Rush, Barnes and Beardsley. But Liverpool had completed their mission and the first half of what could be a historic and emotional double.

Liverpool substitute Rush scores his second, and winning, goal against Everton.

'Exile' Lineker sets up Barcelona victory

BARCELONA OFFERED Gary Lineker one solitary, meaningful opportunity to remind Europe of his talents in Berne on 10 May, and with it he helped Barcelona win the Cup-Winners' Cup final, their first European trophy in seven barren years. The England goal-poacher has spent a frustrating season in the Catalan city, and once again he was exiled on the right wing by coach Johan Cruyff.

After four minutes on a wet Swiss evening, it was hard to argue with the decision, though, as Lineker left his Sampdoria marker Pari in a tangled, confused heap on the floor, raced clear and, with considerable poise, delivered the crucial pass. The ball travelled perfectly to Roberto, who redirected it to the head of Salinas to score the goal that really decided this contest of Latin styles.

But from then on, when it seemed that Lineker offered the simplest route to their third triumph in this competition, Barcelona ignored him. So they made hard work of a night which should have been a comfortable stroll against a side missing their most accomplished defenders. Eventually, Barcelona clinched the trophy with a second goal, scored in the 79th minute by their substitute full-back Rekarte.

Lineker will not be fooled, however, that this victory will provide him with another year at Barcelona. Mr Cruyff has made it quite clear that they intend to replace him this summer.

Stevens' slip denies Rangers treble

WHILE MERSEYSIDE was battling it out at Wembley, Hampden was hosting another Old Firm episode, with Celtic beating Rangers 1–0 to deny them another domestic treble. Graeme Souness has spent more than £10 million on imported talent — much of it from England — but at the end of the day it was home-grown skills in the shape of Joe Miller that returned the silverware to the East End of Glasgow.

Wee Joe swooped on a disastrous back-pass by England's Gary Stevens four minutes from half-time, and Peter Shilton's understudy Chris Woods was left virtually a spectator as he clipped the ball into the net. As it turned out, that was all that separated the teams, but without doubt Celtic deserved their victory. Even the presence as a second-half substitute of player-manager Souness failed to lift the Ibrox outfit. In the end, the defeat was too much to handle even for veterans such as Terry Butcher, who, like several of his colleagues, wept openly at the final whistle.

Rangers had won the League title by six points from Aberdeen, and beat the Dons 3–2 in a Skol Cup final that was far more exciting than the clash with Celtic. Even though Rangers slipped up at the last hurdle, their domination of the domestic game in Scotland is now so great, and their resources seemingly unlimited, that many people fear for the future of the game in Scotland.

Gunners break Anfield hearts in title decider

IN THE MOST DRAMATIC finish to a Championship race since the formation of the Football League 101 years ago, Arsenal went to Anfield for the last game of a traumatic season and scored the two-goal victory they needed to wrest the title from Liverpool. The game was played on 26 May, in a season extended because of the Hillsborough tragedy. And the crucial second goal, scored by 21-year-old midfielder Michael Thomas, came a minute into injury time.

Thomas broke the hearts of the Liverpool team and their fans when, fed by Alan Smith, he burst through, held off a double challenge and flicked the ball wide of the advancing Grobbelaar. In doing so, he brought to an end Liverpool's remarkable efforts to retain the title they had won nine times in the last 13 years and their hopes of a second League and Cup "double" in four years.

Liverpool had incurred a daunting backlog of fixtures after Hillsborough, and it says much for their courage and professionalism that they were able to put the events of that fateful day behind them, go on to win the Cup, and continue a charge up the First Division table that had seen them close from 19 points behind Arsenal at the end of February to three points in front. Arsenal, on the other hand, had faltered on the run-in, and from being hot favourites were now facing a formidable task. Not only were Liverpool unbeaten since early January, but Arsenal had not won at Anfield for nearly 15 years.

But George Graham's team were undaunted. They reverted to the sweeper system, which allowed them to push their full-backs further forward, and Dixon and Winterburn denied Barnes and Houghton space, driving them deeper into less dangerous positions. With the central back three of O'Leary, Bould and Adams performing tremendously against first Aldridge and Rush and then Aldridge and Beardsley, Arsenal seemed capable of containing Liverpool, who needed only to draw, or lose by one goal, to take the title. But it was not until the 52nd minute that they broke through, Smith heading in a Winterburn free-kick.

Thomas (right) scores the last, historic, goal of the season.

The crowd sensed they were witnessing a little slice of footballing history. Only once before in this century have the top two teams fought out a Championship decider in the last game, and that was in 1952, when Arsenal went to Old Trafford needing to win by seven goals — and lost 6–1. Now, however, they were in with a chance. The 40,000 fans and millions more watching on live television held their breath as Thomas raced through, agonizingly delaying his shot until he could see the whites of the keeper's eyes...

The quality and courage of Arsenal's performance was recognized by the sporting Liverpool fans even in their state of disappointment, as they gave George Graham and his men a standing ovation at the final whistle.

Dutch duo turn on style for Milan

RUUD GULLIT AND Marco van Basten, who last summer helped Holland to conquer Europe, repeated the feat at club level with AC Milan, who beat Steaua Bucharest 4–0 in Barcelona in one of the most spectacular performances seen in a European Cup final for years. Within 46 minutes, the superb skills of this pair of Dutch masters had guaranteed that Milan's 20-year wait for the return of Europe's biggest club prize was over. But it was the style in which they achieved their resounding victory that captivated the fans.

For Gullit, it was a marvellous personal triumph. Five weeks ago he seemed to have little chance of playing, when he was carried off in the 5–0 dismantling of Real Madrid in the semi-final second leg, with a knee injury that required cartilage surgery. He was only 60 per cent fit when he took the field in Barcelona, and had to go off after 59 minutes, but by then the damage was done, and the Dutch duo had shared four goals. The Romanian Army team, surprise winners of the trophy three years ago — when they beat Barcelona on penalties — never reproduced that form. They failed miserably to come to terms with Gullit, who not only scored twice but also hit a post and won everything in the air. Panic spread through the Bucharest defence whenever the ball approached the front pair. Van Basten's second goal, just after the interval, was his 10th of the competition, made for him by Frank Rijkaard, Milan's third great Dutchman.

Gullit (centre) opens the scoring for AC Milan.

Gullit went off to a standing ovation. Had he been fully fit, he and his Milan colleagues might have rivalled the Puskas-Di Stefano show for Real Madrid in the 1960 final.

Lineker puts England in Pole position

ENGLAND'S 3–0 VICTORY over Poland at Wembley in a World Cup qualifier edges them considerably closer to the finals in Italy next summer. It was a long time in coming, and all the while thoughts went back to the Polish visit that frustrated England's World Cup ambitions in 1973. The hero that night for Poland was giant keeper Jan Tomaszewski, but it was fortunate for England that his 6ft 5in protegé, Jaroslav Bako, never threatened to emulate the feats of his mentor. On the contrary, Bako displayed a notable lack of judgement throughout, and committed the crudest of body-checks on Gary Lineker early on, for which he was lucky to be only booked. Players have been dismissed — even at Wembley — for lesser offences.

Lineker, who made a name for himself by scoring all three of England's goals against Poland in the last World Cup, got the vital first-half opener at Wembley, following up to score when his first attempt was blocked. And he helped make the other two, late in the second half, starting the moves that led to Barnes's clean far-post volley and then Webb's clinching goal seven minutes from time.

A job well done: Neil Webb (4) scores England's third goal.

FINAL SCORE

Football League
Division 1: Arsenal
Top scorer: Alan Smith (Arsenal) 23
Division 2: Chelsea
Division 3: Wolverhampton Wanderers
Division 4: Rotherham United
Footballer of the Year: Steve Nicol (Liverpool)

FA Cup Final
Liverpool 3 Everton 2
(after extra time)

League Cup Final
Nottingham Forest 3 Luton Town 1

Scottish League
Premier Division: Rangers
Top scorer: Charlie Nicholas (Aberdeen), Mark McGhee (Celtic) 16
Division 1: Dunfermline Athletic
Division 2: Albion Rovers
Footballer of the Year: Richard Gough (Rangers)

Scottish FA Cup Final
Celtic 1 Rangers 0

Scottish League Cup Final
Rangers 3 Aberdeen 2

European Cup Final
AC Milan 4 Steaua Bucharest 0

Cup-Winners' Cup Final
Barcelona 2 Sampdoria 0

UEFA Cup Final
Napoli beat Stuttgart 2–1, 3–3

European Footballer of the Year 1988
Marco van Basten (AC Milan & Holland)

Leading European Scorer (Golden Boot)
Dorin Mateut (Dinamo Bucharest) 43

World Club Championship
AC Milan (Italy) 1 Atletico Nacional (Colombia) 0
(after extra time)

FOOTBALL FOCUS

- On 26 May, while Arsenal were celebrating their first League triumph for 18 years and Sir Matt Busby his 80th birthday, former Leeds and England manager Don Revie, 61, died after suffering for two years from the incurable motor neurone disease.

- After rejecting a more lucrative move to Monaco, Gary Lineker returned to England on 20 June to join Tottenham on a mere £5,000 a week. The £1.5 million deal with Barcelona included midfielder Nayim, who had been on loan to Spurs.

- Goalkeeper Peter Shilton set a new record for England when he won his 109th cap, against Denmark on 7 June, passing Bobby Moore's total.

- Three brothers — Danny, Rodney and Ray Wallace — appeared for Southampton at the Dell on 22 October, the first time that this has happened in the First Division since Middlesbrough's Carr brothers 68 years ago.

- The format of the end-of-season play-offs was changed this season, so that the ordeal was confined only to teams seeking promotion. In each of the lower divisions, the four clubs just below the automatic promotion places played off for the remaining one in two-legged, home-and-away semi-finals and finals.

- On 1 May Wolves earned promotion to the Second Division by beating Bristol City 2–0, with both goals coming from Steve Bull. Counting all competitions, Bull has now scored exactly 100 goals in two seasons, 48 this time to go with 52 in 1987–88, and despite playing in a lower division he seems likely to gain his first England cap before long.

Palace Wright for Division One

CRYSTAL PALACE strode triumphantly into Division One amid amazing scenes when Ian Wright scored a stunning winner three minutes from the end of time in the second leg of their promotion play-off at Selhurst Park. Wright's carefully placed header capped a magnificent performance from Steve Coppell's team as they clawed back Blackburn's two-goal advantage from the first leg.

In a contest that could not be bettered as a sporting spectacle, Palace remained true to their season-long philosophy and gambled on attack. It was daring, painfully exciting, but above all successful. In the frenzied atmosphere, Palace benefited from an early break, when the prolific Wright scrambled home his first goal after Pardew's cross had caused havoc. Only the heroics of central defender Hendry kept Blackburn from disintegrating, but they stayed ahead on aggregate until just after the interval. Atkins needlessly brought down McGoldrick, and Madden converted the penalty to set up the eventual dramatic finish.

Ian Wright (left) celebrates his promotion-winning goal.

Liverpool go one over the eight at Aldridge farewell party

ANFIELD HAS STAGED some extraordinary matches in its long and glittering history, but few could rival the "farewell party" laid on for departing striker John Aldridge against Crystal Palace on 12 September. Amid amazing scenes as Liverpool achieved their record First Division win of 9–0, Aldridge left the substitutes' bench in the 69th minute to collect his "present".

The prolific Republic of Ireland striker, who with some reluctance was due to complete his £1 million move to Spanish club Real Sociedad the next day, had dreamed of leaving Anfield with another goal to remember. Manager Kenny Dalglish, with a great sense of theatre, decided the moment for that dream to come true was when, with their lead at 5–0, Whelan had been fouled in the penalty area. He replaced Beardsley with Aldridge, who jogged straight to the penalty spot to a standing ovation, and promptly sent Suckling the wrong way with his kick. The Kop went wild. At the final whistle, Aldridge raced to the cheering Kop, pulled off his shirt and boots and threw them to the fans among whom he used to stand. His co-stars on the Liverpool scoresheet, the first time in Football League history that eight players had scored for one team in a single match, were Nicol (two), McMahon, Rush, Gillespie, Beardsley, Barnes and Hysen. It was an awesome performance by a side deprived of the title last season by dint of goals scored, and takes them to the top of the table, above Millwall. The First Division tends to shudder when Liverpool edge in front in the dark days of December. For them to go to the front in the light nights of September is extremely ominous.

John Aldridge: scoring from the spot in his emotional farewell.

Mo Jo crosses the great divide

Maurice Johnston: Rangers' first big-name Catholic.

MAURICE JOHNSTON, who refused to join his former club Celtic in a £1.2 million transfer in June, surprised British football by signing for Glasgow Rangers from Nantes on 10 July in a £1.5 million deal. The fact that the 27-year-old Scottish international striker, who has 28 caps and once played for Watford, turned his back on Celtic to join their arch-rivals Rangers is enough to cause a stir. But inevitably the main talking point is his faith — he is the first high-profile Catholic player signed by the Ibrox club. When player-manager Graeme Souness took over at Rangers three years ago, he vowed that religion would be irrelevant if he thought a player was good enough, and he has kept his word as he takes his spending at Ibrox to £11 million.

The reaction of Rangers supporters to the signing of Johnston remains to be seen. One thing is certain, however: he will not be popular with the Celtic fans, who saw him paraded at Hampden at the Cup final before their deal with Nantes fell through. He will have to show great character, as well as skill, if he is to succeed.

SOCCER SOUNDBITES

"I have never been so nervous in my life as when I ran on to take that penalty."

JOHN ALDRIDGE,
on the goal that put Liverpool 6–0 up.

Waddle in surprise £4.5m move to France

OLYMPIQUE MARSEILLE made Spurs an offer they could not refuse — £4.5 million for Chris Waddle — which makes the England striker-cum-winger the third most expensive player in the world. Having rejected Marseille's original bid of £3 million for the Tottenham favourite, manager Terry Venables felt the new offer was too good to turn down for a player approaching his 29th birthday, while it would also be unfair to deny the former Newcastle forward the chance to become a millionaire.

Aware that losing Waddle would weaken Spurs, not to mention upsetting the fans, who had come to idolize a player many White Hart Lane supporters initially booed, Mr Venables promised that the windfall would be used to strengthen the team. However, while no one would doubt Waddle's value in the First Division, it is perhaps surprising that Marseille were willing to pay so much for a player who has never quite established himself at international level, despite his 44 England caps.

Waddle: millionaire status.

Celtic hit five but still go out

Dziekanowski acclaims one of his four goals — but it was despair for Celtic at the finish.

FOUR GOALS BY their Polish international striker Dariusz Dziekanowski and one by his partner Andy Walker were still not enough to give Celtic victory in a remarkable European Cup-Winners' Cup tie against Partizan Belgrade on 27 September at Parkhead. Unfortunately, a leaky Celtic defence, not aided by the team's impatience to pull back from the 2–1 deficit incurred in the first leg, allowed the Yugoslavs four away goals. As a result, the final 6–6 aggregate score broke down in favour of Partizan.

Never can the 50,000 fans at Parkhead have been through such a night of roller-coaster emotions, as their hopes dipped and then soared with every goal that went in. A first-leg 2–1 away defeat is not a bad result in Europe, but Partizan snatched back that precious away goal after only eight minutes, and Celtic were two goals to the bad. But then Dziekanowski came into the picture, and levelled the overall scores with two opportunist goals, the second just after half-time. At three-all on aggregate and no advantage to either side, now was the time for Celtic to heed the words of manager Billy McNeill and be patient. Five minutes later, however, Partizan scored again, which meant Celtic had to win the match by two clear goals. They soon got one of them, with Dziekanowski's hat-trick, but let Partizan in again — 3–3 on the night. Now the irrepressible Dziekanowski made a goal for Walker, and, with the crowd at fever pitch, hit his fourth with nine minutes to go and made the score 5–3 to Celtic, 6–5 on aggregate.

Oh, the anticlimax, though, when, with the crowd baying for the final whistle, Celtic's defence was split wide open again, and Scepovic scored within 90 seconds of the finish. Sadly, the fans drooped off. The scriptwriter had written an unhappy ending to one of the most amazing games in Celtic's history.

Proud Irish drink to Charlton

THE REPUBLIC of Ireland's 3–0 victory over Northern Ireland in Dublin on 11 October ensured their place in the World Cup finals for the first time — barring the extraordinary twin circumstances of defeat in Malta and a large Hungarian victory in Spain as their qualifying group ends. It is fairly safe to say, then, that the Free State will not wait another month before toasting manager Jack Charlton's outstanding achievement in bringing them such unprecedented success.

A sporting match was played in front of a benign crowd, who put the seedier world of English football to shame as they applauded the opposition from the start. Irish fans had been drinking in city-centre pubs since 7.30 am, but that did not turn them into crazed hooligans. After an anxious start in which the North could have taken the lead, Whelan settled the Republic down with a goal shortly before half-time. Goals from Cascarino and Houghton within 10 minutes of the interval put the result beyond doubt, and the celebrations began.

United takeover collapses

PROPERTY DEALER Michael Knighton finally abandoned his dreams of owning Manchester United on 11 October, after long-drawn-out and at times acrimonious negotiations, by agreeing to cancel his £20 million takeover deal. He accused the Press of creating "a Frankenstein that has got out of control" in the image they projected of him, although it would be most unlikely for members of the fourth estate to confuse the good doctor with his creation in that way.

Admittedly, the Press did not treat the boyishly enthusiastic Mr Knighton too reverently when he appeared on the Old Trafford scene in an explosion of razzmatazz. Weeks of speculation about his ability to complete the deal soured his relationship with the Old Trafford board, and at one stage chairman Martin Edwards took out a temporary injunction preventing Mr Knighton from showing financial details of the club to his advisors.

The takeover appeared to be back on course, however, a few days earlier, until the sudden announcement that Mr Knighton had withdrawn his option to buy Mr Edwards's shares in return for a seat on the board as a non-executive director.

Michael Knighton does a turn at Old Trafford in August.

Taylor Report attacks 'squalid' state of soccer clubs

Hillsborough 1989: chaos and confusion as the dead and dying are laid on the pitch.

LORD JUSTICE TAYLOR'S final report on the Hillsborough disaster was published on 29 January, and featured an ultimatum to the clubs to improve the "squalid" conditions at their grounds and clean up their tarnished image. Acting immediately on the report's recommendations, the government announced that terracing would be banned from all First and Second Division stadiums by August 1994 and in all designated Football League grounds by 1999. The report said crowd behaviour could be linked to the low standard of accommodation at soccer grounds, and that the country's national sport was blighted by old grounds, poor facilities, hooliganism, poor leadership, and fans caged and penned, treated sometimes more like "prisoners of war" than people helping to support a multi-million-pound industry.

The government stressed that the football industry would be responsible for cleaning up its act, and that the bulk of the funds needed for the switch to all-seater stadiums would have to be raised by the clubs. The government would not step in to finance safety measures, despite warnings from MPs that many Third and Fourth Division clubs, and possibly others higher up the scale, would be bankrupted by the cost. The government accepted the rejection of the proposed National Membership Scheme on the grounds of safety and effectiveness.

In all, the 104-page report submitted 76 recommendations to "promote better and safer conditions" at sports grounds. These also included the removal of "prison-type" perimeter fences, the reduction in their height, and more clearly marked gates which should be left unlocked; a review of police operations at grounds, better communications between police and emergency services; the introduction of electronic tagging to keep offenders away from grounds; and the creation of new offences of throwing a missile, chanting obscene or racialist abuse, and invading the pitch without reasonable excuse. It should also be an offence to sell tickets on match day without the club's authority.

For all it should do to improve safety, however, Lord Justice Taylor's report is not entirely satisfactory. While he denies that seating is a panacea, the emphasis he places on it may convince some people otherwise, although hooligans in seats have been known to tear them out to use as weapons. The report criticizes police failure to control the crowd outside Hillsborough, but the behaviour of that crowd has escaped proper analysis. The evidence is that thousands of people, some the worse for drink, created the crush at the Leppings Lane end, provoked by the failure of the FA to administer this fixture properly. And the government must remember that improving safety and eradicating hooliganism inside grounds is only the start. They will need to devise a strategy to combat hooliganism if and when it is shifted away from football.

Lord Justice Taylor said that it is a "depressing and chastening" thought that his report is the ninth official report covering football ground safety and control. Previous investigations had followed deaths at the stadiums of Bradford, Bolton and Ibrox, and the first Cup final at Wembley, in 1923, when miraculously nobody was killed. It is "astounding" that after eight such reports, "95 people could die from overcrowding before the very eyes of those controlling the event".

SOCCER SOUNDBITES

"The years of patching up grounds, of having periodic disasters and narrowly avoiding many others by muddling through on a wing and a prayer, must be over."

LORD JUSTICE TAYLOR

McCoist puts Scotland through

A GOAL JUST BEFORE half-time by Ally McCoist against Norway on 15 November settled Scotland's nerves and took his country on a tidal wave of national fervour through to their fifth successive World Cup finals. With just a draw with Norway needed to put themselves out of reach of France, Scotland's policy of going for a win paid off, and McCoist sent the 64,000 Hampden crowd into raptures when he ran onto a perceptive Malpas through pass and flicked it delightfully over Thorstvedt to put them ahead. It was just as well, because it gave them the luxury of allowing Norway to score a minute from time, when Leighton misjudged a speculative Johnson drive from 45 yards. So Scotland join England and the Republic of Ireland in Italy for the 1990 World Cup.

Ally McCoist celebrates after scoring against Norway.

Palace find 10-goal improvement to beat Liverpool

THE FA CUP semi-final at Villa Park between Crystal Palace and Liverpool was a memorable match for several reasons, not least of which was the result — a 4–3 win for Palace over the team that had humiliated them 9–0 in the League earlier in the season. It was also the best, the most thrilling semi-final seen for years, and the highest scoring one since Manchester United beat Fulham 5–3 in a replay 32 years earlier. And it was played on a Sunday at noon, to accommodate the BBC, who were transmitting both semi-finals live.

Liverpool, the Cup-holders, were riding high again at the top of the First Division, and were the hottest of favourites to beat relegation-troubled Palace. Not that they were taking this game lightly after defeat by Wimbledon in the 1988 final. And they had the best of starts, as Ian Rush glided onto a McMahon pass and beat Nigel Martyn after 14 minutes. But Liverpool, without a replacement striker, had to reshuffle their side when Rush went off shortly afterwards with bruised ribs, and again when they lost centre-back Gary Gillespie at half-time with a groin strain.

Even so, with Palace missing their star striker Wright and Liverpool in firm control, there was no hint of the rush of goals to come after the interval. However, Palace came storming out in the second half and Mark Bright volleyed in a rebound to put them level after just 16 seconds. Now it was Palace's turn to get on top, and they took a deserved lead after 70 minutes when defender Gary O'Reilly scored from close in — his first goal of the season.

If any Palace fans thought this was enough to beat Liverpool, they were in for a rude awakening 11 minutes later, when McMahon equalized and then Barnes scored from the spot after Pemberton foolishly tripped Staunton in the area. Now, it certainly looked like a third final running for Liverpool. Yet Palace, remarkably, after such a crushing double blow, pulled themselves together and, with two minutes left, Andy Gray headed in, with the normally rock-like Liverpool defence in complete disarray. With Palace now rampant, only the cross-bar saved Liverpool before the whistle. The winner came four minutes into the second period, when Liverpool, not for the first time, were found wanting at a set-piece. Central defender Andy Thorn flicked on a near-post corner, and Alan Pardew came in to head Palace into their first final.

A bitter moment for Liverpool as Gray heads a late equalizer.

Souness banned for breaching ban!

THE GRAEME SOUNESS saga continued in Scotland when the Scottish FA imposed a record £5,000 fine on the voluble Rangers manager in May and extended his touchline ban to the end of the 1991–92 season.

Rangers immediately condemned these latest punishments as "draconian" and the use of TV evidence as "deplorable". However, they admitted that he was clearly caught shouting to his players on the pitch from the tunnel area in the League game against Hearts on 17 February. This was in breach of a previous ban, imposed by the Scottish FA along with a £2,000 fine a year ago, for failing to adhere to a previous ban during the Cup semi-final with St Johnstone at Parkhead in April 1989.

Oldham fantastic on plastic: West Ham hammered

UNFASHIONABLE Oldham moved to the brink of their first Wembley appearance with an irresistible display of attacking football to beat fellow Division Two club West Ham 6–0 in the first leg of their Littlewoods League Cup semi-final on the notorious Boundary Park plastic pitch. Oldham have put together an unbeaten run of 32 matches on their artificial surface, and this performance at least equalled their victories over Arsenal and Southampton on the way to what will surely be a place in the final on 29 April.

West Ham were turned into a shambles as Oldham moved the ball around at speed. Oldham's inspiration was Andy Ritchie, their bargain £50,000 buy from Leeds. He scored two to take his Littlewoods tally this season to 10, and has scored in every round.

Andy Ritchie: hot stuff on plastic.

Wright lights up final, but 'Sparky' earns United a replay

Manchester United's Lee Martin (3) scores the only goal in the replay.

A DRAMATIC LATE introduction of the partially fit Ian Wright into the game brought Crystal Palace within seven minutes of winning the FA Cup on their first appearance in the final, but Mark "Sparky" Hughes intervened to earn Manchester United a replay.

Wright has twice broken a leg this season, and his achievement in getting fit enough to claim a seat on the Palace substitutes bench was no small miracle in itself. Manager Steve Coppell gambled on leaving him there for 69 minutes, but when he unleashed the striker he lit up a hitherto undistinguished match.

Bryan Robson had equalized an early O'Reilly goal in the first half, and Hughes had put United ahead after 62 minutes. Wright's two goals were gems in a sea of mediocrity, the first coming with his first significant touch as he destroyed £3 million worth of reputations only three minutes after going on. Both Pallister and Phelan were left floundering as Wright came bursting through from the left and slashed the ball past Leighton in goal. Two minutes into extra time, he scored another superb goal, stealing in at the far post to volley Salako's fine centre into the roof of the net.

But Manchester were not to be denied by Wright's spring-heeled heroics. In the exhausting last period, class began to tell. Ince, Webb, Phelan, Wallace and Hughes, a large part of the £13 million it has cost to build this United team, all came into their own as men capable of deciding the issue. And no United player was more influential than their remarkable captain, Robson, who carried his team along with the sheer force of his intensely competitive nature. United might have scored three times before Webb and Wallace split Palace down the middle and Hughes beat Martyn to earn them a replay.

Wright (partially hidden, left) beats Leighton to put Palace 3–2 ahead in extra time in the first match.

League give police veto on high-risk fixtures

AFTER THE WEEKEND of violence in early May by Leeds supporters in Bournemouth, the Football League, who had insisted, against police advice, that the fixture went on as scheduled, were shamed into giving police the power to veto future fixtures likely to produce a repeat performance.

Leeds's 1–0 win at Dean Court, on the last day of the League season, clinched their promotion and the Second Division title, while at the same time condemned Bournemouth to relegation. More than 5,000 Leeds supporters made the trip, although fewer than half had been allocated tickets. There was violence in the town on the previous night, with nine injuries and 19 arrests. More than an hour before the kick-off, police in riot gear had to charge a huge crowd of Leeds fans, who began pelting them with cans and stones. Cars and shop windows were smashed, and two public houses near the seafront extensively damaged. Amid calls for Leeds to forfeit their place in Division One next season, Bournemouth chairman Jim Nolan demanded the Yorkshire club be made to pay for the orgy of violence that resulted in 104 arrests.

Home Secretary Mr David Waddington has delivered strong public and private rebukes to the Football League for ignoring police requests to reschedule the match from the Bank Holiday weekend. The initial requests were made as early as last June, when the fixtures were first published. Dorset police have accused the League of arrogance, naivety and high-handedness, and of ignoring the lessons of Hillsborough.

FOOTBALL FOCUS

- Sheffield Wednesday, bottom of Division One, won 8–0 at Aldershot on 3 October, a record League Cup away victory, after being held 0–0 at home in the first leg.
- FIFA decided, in the light of the Hillsborough disaster, that all World Cup spectators must be seated, starting with the qualifying competitions for the 1994 finals.
- Second Division Oldham enjoyed unprecedented success in both Cup competitions, reaching their first FA Cup semi-final since 1913 (losing 2–1 to Manchester United after a 3–3 draw) and their first League Cup final (losing 1–0 to Nottingham Forest).
- Frank Stapleton set an individual record for the Republic of Ireland when he scored his 20th goal in their 3–0 win in Malta on 2 June.
- UEFA decreed that only four foreigners will be allowed in any team in European club competitions next season, and that English, Scottish, Welsh and Irish players will be classed as foreigners if they play for a club not of their home country. Players signed before 3 May 1988 will be exempt for a transitional period.

Aberdeen win the Cup in sudden death shoot-out after goalless bore

WHILE MANCHESTER United manager Alex Ferguson was in the end happy to earn a replay in the English Cup final, he was astonished to learn after the match of the FA's decision to settle the replay if necessary by penalties. He also heard that his old club Aberdeen had won the Cup north of the border in a penalty shoot-out, so perhaps that was a good omen.

The Scottish FA had decreed last summer that, in the light of a busy pre-World Cup programme, their Cup, newly sponsored by Tennents, would not even have the luxury of a replay. Perhaps it was just as well, because the match between Aberdeen and Celtic, winners for the last two years, was mostly a shapeless, scrappy affair. And with the game goalless after 120 minutes, it then took 20 penalty kicks to produce a result.

Celtic missed their first, Aberdeen their fourth, so it went to sudden death. After four more successful conversions each, Aberdeen's Dutch keeper Theo Snelders leapt to his left to save Anton Rogan's kick, and Brian Irvine stepped up to settle the issue by making it 9–8 to Aberdeen — a memorable score for an otherwise eminently forgettable final.

Snelders makes the vital save.

SOCCER SOUNDBITES

"Penalty shoot-outs have nothing to do with football. It's like shooting poor wee ducks at a fairground."

ALEX SMITH,
Aberdeen manager, after his team's victory.

England manager Robson to go Dutch after World Cup

AT A HASTILY CALLED Press conference at Lancaster Gate on 24 May, England manager Bobby Robson announced he would be leaving his job after the World Cup to take over as manager of Dutch club PSV Eindhoven. A furious Mr Robson had planned to make the announcement in Sardinia the following Monday as England prepared for the World Cup finals, but a front-page story in a tabloid newspaper reporting that he was to quit because of an alleged affair with a woman 13 years ago brought matters to a head.

Mr Robson explained that he was leaving because he did not think there was still a job with the FA, having more or less been told by FA chairman Bert Millichip that it was unlikely his contract would be renewed unless England won the World Cup. That is why he accepted PSV's offer.

A puzzling aspect of the FA's stance, if they wanted to get rid of Mr Robson, is why they did not do so after England's disastrous showing in the 1988 European Championship — a logical time for him to go. Instead they chose to defy a vicious, counter-productive campaign carried out by certain tabloid newspapers demanding that he be removed from his post. He repaid them by steering England to the World Cup finals for the second time in his eight-year reign, and FA chief executive Graham Kelly paid due tribute to his achievements. One was left wondering why, if they rated him so highly, they were not prepared to renew his contract.

Robson: highly regarded but allowed to go.

Rise and fall of Swindon Town

ON 28 MAY, Swindon Town won promotion to Division One when they beat Sunderland 1–0 in the final of the play-offs, held at Wembley for the first time, in front of a 72,873 crowd. Ten days later, after the club admitted to 35 charges involving irregular payments to eight players going back to 1985, the Football League relegated them two divisions, to Division Three, as well as ordering them to pay as yet unspecified amounts in compensation to six clubs who suffered financially because of Swindon's dealings. After an appeal, the FA cut Swindon's punishment, allowing them to stay in the Second Division.

FINAL SCORE

Football League
Division 1: Liverpool
Top scorer: Gary Lineker (Tottenham Hotspur) 24
Division 2: Leeds United
Division 3: Bristol Rovers
Division 4: Exeter City
Footballer of the Year: John Barnes (Liverpool)

FA Cup Final
Manchester United 3 Crystal Palace 3
(after extra time)
Replay: Man United 1 Crystal Palace 0

League Cup Final
Nottingham Forest 1 Oldham Athletic 0

Scottish League
Premier Division: Rangers
Top scorer: John Robertson (Heart of Midlothian) 17
Division 1: St Johnstone
Division 2: Brechin City
Footballer of the Year: Alex McLeish (Aberdeen)

Scottish FA Cup Final
Aberdeen 0 Celtic 0
(after extra time)
Aberdeen won 9–8 on penalties

Scottish League Cup Final
Aberdeen 2 Rangers 1
(after extra time)

European Cup Final
AC Milan 1 Benfica 0

Cup-Winners' Cup Final
Sampdoria 2 Anderlecht 0
(after extra time)

UEFA Cup Final
Juventus beat Fiorentina 3–1, 0–0

European Footballer of the Year 1989
Marco van Basten (AC Milan & Holland)

Leading European Scorer (Golden Boot)
Hugo Sanchez (Real Madrid),
Hristo Stoichkov (CSKA Sofia) 38

World Club Championship
AC Milan (Italy) 3 Olimpia (Paraguay) 0

Paying the penalty

The best thing about Italia '90 was Pavarotti. His singing of excerpts from Puccini, beamed out live on giant TV screens during the opening ceremony, will be remembered long after what football was served up by the 24 teams has been forgotten. This ailing competition, transmitted to countless millions around the world in a blaze of grandiose hype, was just about the worst imaginable advertisement for football. Fear and greed bedevilled the tournament, stifling adventure and squeezing the joy out of the occasion. Some would say, it was the referees' repeatedly flourished red and yellow cards that provided most of the colour.

"Gazza" injects a little light relief against Belgium.

THE ONLY RECORDS broken in Italy were unwanted ones. A total of 164 yellow and 16 red cards displayed by the referees meant that there was an average of over three bookings a match, with nearly one dismissal every three games.

Some of the most exciting football was played by Cameroon, the first African nation to reach the World Cup quarter-finals. They approached their games with a refreshing naivety, but their propensity for cynically hacking opponents down in full flight does not bode well for third-world football.

Never has there been a World Cup so devoid of star quality. There were some great names on view, but most of them appeared to have left their skills at home — or rapidly had the stuffing knocked out of them. Diego Maradona, still arguably the world's best player, worked hard to guide what was a shadow of the 1986 champion side to the final, but all too rare were the glimpses of his footballing genius. He was, however, the most fouled player in the tournament. The Dutch stars were equally disappointing, showing none of the commanding style that made Holland such exciting and popular European champions in 1988.

Sensational opening

World Cup '90 opened sensationally, with defending champions Argentina going down to Cameroon. The Africans, despite their unbeaten performance in the 1982 World Cup, were given no hope, but they beat an unrecognizable Argentina side 1–0, despite finishing up with nine men.

Hosts Italy, the favourites, were unrecognizable, too. They actually played creative, attacking football — until they came near goal. It needed a strike from inspirational substitute "Toto" Schillaci in the 78th minute, four minutes after he went on, to beat a thoroughly outplayed Austria in their first match. Vialli was one star who did enhance his reputation as Italy went on to win their three group matches. They were the only side not to concede a goal in the first round, although they struggled to beat the United States.

West Germany qualified with ease, and were top scorers in the first round with 10 goals — three more than the total scored in England's group. England muddled through once more, with Bobby Robson inexplicably imposing on them a sweeper system which they had never practised before. They got through by beating Egypt 1–0 in the only match not drawn. Had the overcautious North African side equalized, all four teams would have finished with identical records. As it turned out, Holland and the Republic of Ireland joined England in the next round.

Scotland, in their seventh World Cup finals, preserved their record of never getting past the first round. They added another inglorious chapter to their history of humiliating defeats when they lost 1–0 to Costa Rica. And although they beat Sweden — everyone did — they were subsequently undone by a late Brazilian goal, and put out of the tournament. Brazil, although they won their three matches, were not even a poor imitation of their exciting sides of yesteryear.

David O'Leary's penalty for the Republic of Ireland against Romania.

England rely on luck

England's progress to the semi-finals, their best World Cup showing apart from 1966, was down to the creative inspiration of Paul Gascoigne, the opportunism of David Platt and Gary Lineker, and no little luck, although they played some good football. Belgium hardly deserved to be beaten in a splendid, hard-fought second-round match, but Platt scored a spectacular winning goal in the last minute of extra time, getting behind the Belgian defence to hook home a Gascoigne free-kick. Platt also put England ahead against Cameroon, before England found themselves in serious trouble, 2–1 down with eight minutes to go. But Gascoigne drove them forward, and twice Lineker was brought down in the box, each time converting the spot-kick.

Elsewhere there had been some more thrills and even one or two games of good football. Jack Charlton's achievement in getting the Republic of Ireland to the quarter-finals was monumental. They were not pleasing to watch, but they performed heroically. Substitute David O'Leary clinched a penalty shoot-out against Romania, although they then went out gallantly to a single goal against the Italians.

The best match of the tournament was the last-16 clash between old rivals West Germany and Holland, made even more

In soccer's sick showpiece, both semi-finals were decided on penalties, before a sterile final, with two Argentina players sent off, was decided by the only goal, a late West German penalty.

Brehme scores... a fitting way to end the 1990 World Cup.

combative by the fact that three Dutch stars played for AC Milan and three Germans for Inter. Indeed, the Rijkaard-Völler confrontation proved rather too belligerent, and the two sides were left with 10 men after 21 minutes. Nevertheless, the match was a classic, with the much-fouled Matthaus and particularly Klinsmann outstanding for West Germany in their 2–1 win.

The Germans were less convincing against Czechoslovakia, but deserved to go through, while Argentina were positively struggling. Brazil should have thrashed them before a brilliant Maradona pass was expertly converted by Caniggia for the only goal of the game. Then, in the quarter-finals, after Yugoslavia's Sabanadzovic was sent off, they were held for an hour and a half by 10 men before finally winning on penalties.

Now, it was penalties all the way. In the first semi-final, Maradona, playing on his home ground in Napoli, inspired Argentina to a gritty performance against Italy, who had their poorest game of the finals. Halfway through the second half, Caniggia equalized Schillaci's early goal, and Argentina then held out despite losing Giusti, sent off, for the second period of extra time. They went through to the final again after keeper Goycochea made two fine saves in the penalty decider. But they would be without the cautioned Caniggia and Olarticoechea for the final, as well as Giusti.

England played their best football in the semi-final, and neither they nor West Germany deserved to lose. Gascoigne again was the driving force, never afraid to run at the German defence or try something new. Shilton was desperately unlucky when a Brehme shot from a free-kick was deflected over him, but Lineker equalized 10 minutes from the end. Gazza's famous tears flowed after he was booked for a silly foul and he knew he would miss the final. But Pearce and Waddle missed their penalties, and England were not in it — their consolation, the fair play award.

Veteran Roger Milla, a World Cup hit for Cameroon.

A squalid finale

Franz Beckenbauer became the first man to manage and captain World Cup-winning sides when West Germany beat Argentina 1–0 in Rome thanks to a Brehme penalty six minutes from the end. There is very little else to say about the final, except that the team who most consistently played the best football in Italy won it. Like the whole tournament, it was high in drama, low in football. The Germans dominated the match, but could not finish their chances. Monzon became the first player ever sent off in a World Cup final, for a bad foul on Klinsmann after 64 minutes; but the 84th-minute penalty, for a challenge on Völler by Sensini, was less clear-cut. When Dezotti was also expelled two minutes later for forcefully trying to retrieve the ball from a time-wasting opponent, his teammates went mad, and Maradona was booked for dissent. It was a fitting ending to a World Cup most people wanted to forget.

FINAL SCORE

FIRST ROUND

Group A

Italy	1	Austria	0
Czechoslovakia	5	United States	1
Italy	1	United States	0
Czechoslovakia	1	Austria	0
Austria	2	United States	1
Italy	2	Czechoslovakia	0

	P	W	D	L	F	A	P
Italy	3	3	0	0	4	0	6
Czech.	3	2	0	1	6	3	4
Austria	3	1	0	2	2	3	2
US	3	0	0	3	2	8	0

Group B

Cameroon	1	Argentina	0
Romania	2	USSR	0
Argentina	2	USSR	0
Cameroon	2	Romania	1
USSR	4	Cameroon	0
Romania	1	Argentina	1

	P	W	D	L	F	A	P
Cameroon	3	2	0	1	3	5	4
Romania	3	1	1	1	4	3	3
Argentina	3	1	1	1	3	2	3
USSR	3	1	0	2	4	4	2

Group C

Brazil	2	Sweden	1
Costa Rica	1	Scotland	0
Brazil	1	Costa Rica	0
Scotland	2	Sweden	1
Brazil	1	Scotland	0
Costa Rica	2	Sweden	1

	P	W	D	L	F	A	P
Brazil	3	3	0	0	4	1	6
Costa Riva	3	2	0	1	3	2	4
Scotland	3	1	0	2	2	3	2
Sweden	3	0	0	3	3	6	0

Group D

Colombia	2	UAE	0
West Germany	4	Yugoslavia	1
Yugoslavia	1	Colombia	0
West Germany	5	UAE	1
Yugoslavia	4	UAE	1
West Germany	1	Colombia	1

	P	W	D	L	F	A	P
W. Germany	3	2	1	0	10	3	5
Yugoslavia	3	2	0	1	6	5	4
Colombia	3	1	1	1	3	2	3
UAE	3	0	0	3	2	11	0

Group E

Belgium	2	South Korea	0
Uruguay	0	Spain	0
Spain	3	South Korea	1
Belgium	3	Uruguay	1
Spain	2	Belgium	1
Uruguay	1	South Korea	0

	P	W	D	L	F	A	P
Spain	3	2	1	0	5	2	5
Belgium	3	2	0	1	6	3	4
Uruguay	3	1	1	1	2	3	3
S. Korea	3	0	0	3	1	6	0

Group F

England	1	Rep. of Ireland	1
Holland	1	Egypt	1
England	0	Holland	0
Rep. of Ireland	0	Egypt	0
England	1	Egypt	0
Rep. of Ireland	1	Holland	1

	P	W	D	L	F	A	P
England	3	1	2	0	2	1	4
Rep. Ireland	3	0	3	0	2	2	3
Holland	3	0	3	0	2	2	3
Egypt	3	0	2	1	1	2	2

SECOND ROUND

Cameroon 2 Colombia 1
(after extra time)
Czechoslovakia 4 Costa Rica 1
Argentina 1 Brazil 0
West Germany 2 Holland 1
Rep. of Ireland 0 Romania 0
(after extra time)
Rep. of Ireland won 5–4 on penalties
Italy 2 Uruguay 0
Yugoslavia 2 Spain 1
(after extra time)
England 1 Belgium 0
(after extra time)

QUARTER-FINALS

Argentina 0 Yugoslavia 0
(after extra time)
Argentina won 3–2 on penalties
Italy 1 Rep. of Ireland 0
West Germany 1 Czechoslovakia 0
England 3 Cameroon 2
(after extra time)

SEMI-FINALS

Argentina 1 Italy 1
(after extra time)
Argentina won 4–3 on penalties
West Germany 1 England 1
(after extra time)
West Germany won 4–3 on penalties

THIRD-PLACE MATCH

Italy 2 England 1

FINAL

West Germany 1 Argentina 0

Stadio Olimpico, Rome, 8 July 1990.
Attendance 73,603

West Germany: Illgner, Berthold (Reuter), Kohler, Augenthaler, Buchwald, Brehme, Littbarski, Hassler, Matthaus, Völler, Klinsmann
(Scorer: Brehme pen.)
Argentina: Goycochea, Lorenzo, Serrizuela, Sensini, Ruggeri (Monzon), Simon, Basualdo, Burruchaga (Calderon), Maradona, Troglio, Dezotti

Leading scorers
6 Schillaci (Italy)
5 Skuhravy (Czechoslovakia)
4 Lineker (England), Matthaus (West Germany), Michel (Spain), Milla (Cameroon)

Arsenal suffer at the Sharpe end

WHEN MANCHESTER United arrived at Highbury for a fourth-round Rumbelows (League) Cup tie on 28 November, Arsenal had conceded only two goals at home all season. The Gunners were unbeaten, and still challenging Liverpool for the First Division leadership. When United left a shell-shocked Arsenal Stadium, Arsenal had conceded a further six goals and were out of the Rumbelows Cup.

Manchester put on a performance that night reminiscent of the Busby Babes of the fifties. And, indeed, it was a relative "babe" who stole the show, 19-year-old Lee Sharpe, recently converted from a full-back to a winger. After Clayton Blackmore had put United ahead in the first minute and Mark Hughes had finished a move started by Sharpe, the youngster scored the goal of the game himself, cutting in from the left and curling a superb 25-yarder over Seaman. It was hard to believe that United were without their captain, Bryan Robson, as they went in 3–0 up at half-time. Arsenal also found it somewhat mind-boggling, because they had shared the play.

After the interval, Arsenal came back at United with two goals from Smith. But in their eagerness to find an equalizer, they left gaps at the back. This was fatal with Sharpe in such dazzling form, and in the last 20 minutes United carved their way through the Arsenal defence in a series of lightning breaks. Sharpe scored two more to complete his hat-trick and Danny Wallace completed the rout at 6–2. This was Arsenal's first defeat of the season and their heaviest home defeat for 70 years, and a warning to the rest that United are getting it together.

Sharpe heads Manchester United into a 4–2 lead.

Gunners find brawl pointless and costly

ARSENAL, UNBEATEN but desperately trying to stay in touch with runaway First Division leaders Liverpool, suffered a major setback on 12 November when an FA disciplinary committee docked them two points for their part in the disgraceful brawl at Old Trafford on 20 October. Manchester United had one point deducted, and both clubs were fined £50,000, as the FA decided to get tough, especially in view of Arsenal's poor recent disciplinary record. They were involved in a similar brawl last season at Highbury with Norwich, for which they were fined £20,000 and the visitors £50,000, and were lucky to get away with another deplorable incident soon afterwards, at Villa Park, with their protests transgressing the limits of reasonable behaviour towards the referee.

Now they find themselves eight points behind a relentless Liverpool side who have dropped only two points in their 12 matches. Arsenal, who beat United 1–0, may find the loss of those two hard-earned points breaking their grip on Liverpool's coat-tails.

Sharpe leaves the Arsenal defence gaping as he completes his hat-trick.

FAR-out herOES

THE FAROES ARE a group of islands in the far North Atlantic, somewhere between the northern tip of Scotland and Iceland. They are part of the Kingdom of Denmark, but are self-governing in most matters, including, it seems, football. On 12 September 1990, they made their debut in the European Championship, in Group 4 of the qualifying competition. It was a home match with Austria, played in Landskrona, Sweden, because UEFA would not permit them to play on any of their own 12 suitable artificial pitches. Only 1,544 people turned up to see the game, but they witnessed a little piece of soccer history, arguably the most incredible result in international soccer: Faroe Islands 1 Austria 0.

How this team of part-timers, all amateurs — electricians, clerks, sheep-farmers, and the like — beat a nation of the standing of Austria, no longer a major European power but still good enough to reach the 1990 World Cup finals, is a mystery. Certainly the Austrian team manager Josef Hickersberger could not explain it, as he returned to Vienna to hand in his resignation. But a goal after 61 minutes from Torkil Nielsen, who works in a timber shop, won the Faroes the game, and made him into a folk hero back home, where the 47,000 islanders turned their bleak, remote habitat into one big celebration party.

After all, they were the only country in the world with a 100 percent record in major international competition.

Dalglish walks alone: Anfield stunned

KENNY DALGLISH suddenly resigned his Anfield job on Friday, 22 February, after nearly 14 years of unrivalled success as player and manager of Liverpool. With Liverpool leading the League and having just drawn an epic fifth-round FA Cup replay with neighbours Everton 4–4, the outside world had no inkling of what was going on in Mr Dalglish's mind, and nor did the Anfield board until the day before.

At a routine meeting on Thursday morning, Mr Dalglish, 40 next month, told his colleagues that he could go on no longer, the stress had become too much. For the next 10 hours, the board did everything within their power to persuade him to stay, perhaps to wait until the end of the season, or even take a sabbatical. But Mr Dalglish would not change his mind. At a Press conference the following morning, he struggled to explain why he was leaving the most successful club in Britain. It was not a sudden decision, but he had to make it because the pressure he was putting himself under — through his desire to be successful — had become too much to bear.

The immediate reaction at Liverpool — from the players, the Anfield staff and the fans — was utter disbelief. An idol of the Kop since he joined Liverpool in 1977 and achieved the seemingly impossible by replacing Kevin Keegan, Dalglish enjoyed remarkable success as a player. He won three European Cup medals and seven Championship medals (the last two as player-manager) to add to the four won with Celtic in Scotland. He scored over 100 goals in both Scotland and England, won a record 102 Scottish caps and equalled Denis Law's record of 30 goals for Scotland. Taking over as Liverpool manager at a very difficult time, straight after the Heysel disaster, he kept them at the top of English football, continuing the unprecedented run of success established by Shankly, Paisley and Fagan, and achieving something even his illustrious predecessors failed to manage — the League and Cup double in 1986. He retired from the playing side in 1989, and guided Liverpool to another League title last season.

This marks the end of an era at Anfield. As coach Ronnie Moran takes over as caretaker-manager, the question on everyone's lips must be: Are we seeing the beginning of the end of Liverpool's supremacy in English football?

Goodbye to Anfield: Dalglish announces his decision to resign the Liverpool job.

SOCCER SOUNDBITES

"Watching Kenny Dalglish walk out of Anfield was the saddest moment of my life."

PETER ROBINSON,
Liverpool chief executive.

Arsenal win battle of the giants

ONLY FOUR DAYS after their sensational home defeat by Manchester United in the Rumbelows Cup, Arsenal took on and comprehensively beat League leaders Liverpool 3–0 at Highbury. It was truly a battle of the giants, between two sides unbeaten in the League after 14 matches.

It was a vital match for Arsenal, after their midweek humiliation, and defeat would have left them trailing by nine points. Manager George Graham brought in O'Leary for only his second start of the season, and he played a superb game as sweeper, shoring up the shell-shocked Arsenal defence. Liverpool manager Kenny Dalglish, however, made a puzzling selection, aimed, it seems, to protect their six-point lead rather than exploit any Arsenal uncertainty. It failed miserably.

Arsenal took the lead in the 20th minute, when Merson scrambled in a header after Thomas twice had the Liverpool defence in a panic. Then, four minutes after the interval, a delightful Merson pass set left-winger Limpar away. The Swedish international, in his first season in English football, has, rightly or wrongly, earned a reputation for diving. So when he burst between Gillespie and Ablett and went crashing to the turf, Liverpool were most unhappy to see the referee pointing to the spot. Those who have been defeated by such decisions at Anfield over the years, however, will have little sympathy for Dalglish's men.

Dixon converted the penalty, and Smith rounded off Arsenal's victory near the end after the ubiquitous Merson had opened up the Liverpool defence with a slick back-heel. Now Arsenal had moved up within striking distance of the champions and the title race was really on.

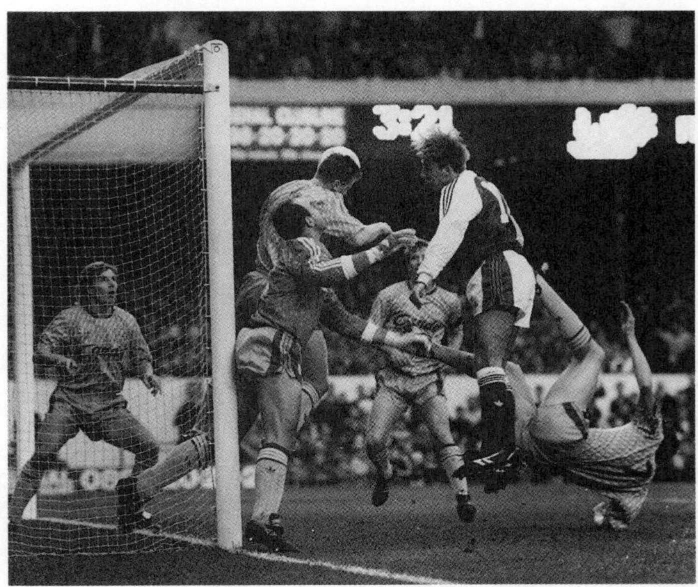

Merson heads Arsenal into the lead with the Liverpool defence in disarray, as they were to be so often.

Gascoigne the Spur: Arsenal semi-detached at Wembley

PAUL GASCOIGNE, back after a stomach operation only 34 days earlier, made a hero's appearance in the first FA Cup semi-final ever held at Wembley, and scored what his manager described as "one of the best goals ever seen there" to inspire Spurs to a famous 3–1 triumph over North London rivals Arsenal.

After a midweek run-out in the League, Gascoigne was surely not even half fit, and he played for just 61 minutes, but this will always be known as "Gazza's match". It took him only 10 minutes to respond to manager Venables's challenge to prove he is the most talented footballer of his generation. First he scored his goal, an audacious, sensational 35-yard free-kick that flashed past the ruin of Arsenal's defensive wall and the groping fingers of Seaman into the top corner of the net. With the adrenalin pumping, Gascoigne was everywhere, collecting every ball from his keeper, running at defenders, wanting to take every free-kick. In the 10th minute, an exhilarating exchange of passes with Paul Allen stretched the Arsenal defence to breaking point, Smith could not provide a defender's clearance and Lineker pounced on the error to put Spurs two up. With Stewart and Samways working feverishly in midfield, Spurs retained the initiative until just before half-time, when Smith rose to a Dixon cross from the right and powered a header past Thorstvedt. The League leaders, beaten only twice all season, came out in the second half determined to continue their comeback. And with Gascoigne soon going off, it was left to the brave Thorstvedt and his crossbar to keep Spurs ahead.

Gascoigne elated after his fifth-minute wonder goal.

Then came the killer blow, from Lineker who, along with Gascoigne, has so often seemed little more than collateral in Tottenham's financial confusion this season. Picking the ball up in the centre-circle, he took it forward unchallenged before hitting a speculative shot, the sort Seaman has been saving with ease all season. But the keeper, still perhaps unnerved by Gazza's early thunderbolt, merely helped it into the net. Spurs were in their ninth FA Cup final, and Arsenal's dreams of the double were in tatters.

Blackmore and Bruce revive Busby years

MANCHESTER UNITED added another memorable chapter to their proud European history when they overcame Montpellier 2–0 in France on 19 March to reach the last four of the Cup-Winners' Cup 3–1 on aggregate. Their triumph over the highly rated French side, who had already eliminated former European champions PSV Eindhoven and Steaua Bucharest from this season's competition, will stand alongside any of those in recent years.

United had seemed doomed to failure in this quarter-final, after conceding a precious away goal to the well-organized Frenchmen at Old Trafford a fortnight earlier. But Montpellier, with a formidable home record, could not make up their minds whether to protect their advantage or go for a straight victory. United took the decision out of their hands with goals either side of the interval, the first from a free-kick by the unsung Clayton Blackmore, which squirmed out of Barrabe's hands, the second after Blackmore was fouled, Steve Bruce converting the penalty.

To win now, Montpellier needed three goals, and they never looked like getting one of them.

Robson (7) bursts through the Montpellier defence.

Crisis at Spurs: world record bid for Gazza

ITALIAN CLUB LAZIO confirmed on 15 March that they had made a world record bid of £8.5 million for Tottenham's England star Paul Gascoigne, and claimed they had been given an option to buy. As Gascoigne left hospital after a stomach muscle operation, he was briefed on the position with the Roman club. His chief concern, now, is to get fit in time for the FA Cup semi-final with Arsenal in a month's time at Wembley.

Gascoigne, born in May 1967, developed at Newcastle and is now one of the few British players with a genuine chance of being rated world-class. His departure for Italy seems a foregone conclusion.

With Spurs in deep financial crisis, it looks like they will have to sell their most valuable asset if they are not to go under. Manager Terry Venables was meanwhile desperately trying to put together the necessary finance to complete the £20 million takeover of the club, but there was little evidence that his group had the money in place.

Tenth title for Arsenal: Liverpool capitulate

Anders Limpar: provided Arsenal with flair... and goals.

ARSENAL CELEBRATED their 10th League title at Highbury on the evening of 6 May — clinched when Liverpool lost 2–1 at Nottingham Forest in the afternoon — with a 3–1 win over Manchester United. That was appropriate, for United had been their opponents in two traumatic matches earlier in the season, when Arsenal had been docked two points for their part in the brawl at Old Trafford and then suffered that humiliating 2–6 Rumbelows Cup exit at Highbury. All this was forgotten, however, when Alan Smith put his hat-trick past United, with the Arsenal crowd celebrating a record-breaking season. And five days later, again at Highbury, when George Graham collected his Barclays Manager of the Season award, the Gunners gave an exhibition, in their 6–1 demolition of Coventry, full of imagination and flair that had often been missing during their season-long battle with Liverpool for the title.

Arsenal lost only one of their 38 League games — the fewest in the history of the League except for Preston's unbeaten season 102 years ago, when they played only 22 matches in the League's first season. They went a club record 24 matches unbeaten, before losing that game, 2–1 at Stamford Bridge to Chelsea on 2 February. David Seaman, their close-season £1.3 million signing from QPR, was ever-present, conceding only 18 League goals. Also ever-present in their back four were Dixon, Winterburn and Bould, and skipper Tony Adams returned with great courage after the shame of his mid-season "rest" (a spell in prison for a drink-drive offence) to lead them immediately to a crucial victory at Anfield in early March. Alan Smith led their scorers, and the League's with 23 goals, and the inspirational Merson chipped in with 13. Kevin Campbell scored eight of his nine goals in a vital 10 matches when he came into the side late in the season. But perhaps the most popular character with the fans was Anders Limpar, the impish Swedish international, who treated them to three of his always spectacular 11 goals in that last "exhibition" match against Coventry.

Souness takes over at Anfield

FORMER LIVERPOOL star and Glasgow Rangers manager Graeme Souness was confirmed as Liverpool's new manager on 16 April in succession to Kenny Dalglish. Caretaker manager Ronnie Moran had made it clear that he did not want to be considered for the job on a permanent basis. Mr Souness, 37, spent seven seasons at Anfield under Bob Paisley, during which Liverpool won three European Cups, five Championships and four League Cups. After two years in Italy with Sampdoria, he went to Rangers as player-manager, was sent off after 37 minutes of his debut match against Hibs in August 1986 and, despite frequently falling foul with the Scottish FA, has guided the Glasgow club to three Championships and four League Cups. He leaves Rangers on top of the League again, but very unhappy at losing him. He joins Liverpool, possibly at a watershed in their fortunes, second in the table, but trailing Arsenal now by five points. He has signed a five-year contract at Anfield worth around £350,000 a year, said to be £100,000 more than he was earning in Scotland.

Mr Souness's first job will be to prepare Liverpool for their next match, at home to Norwich, and in the longer term to produce a side capable of cashing in on the club's imminent return to Europe after their six-year ban following the Heysel disaster.

Souness comes out for his first match in charge of Liverpool.

SOCCER SOUNDBITES

"I believe he is making the biggest mistake of his life. Time will tell."

DAVID MURRAY,
Rangers chairman, on Souness's move.

Wednesday's Wembley win

SHEFFIELD WEDNESDAY surprised Manchester United 1–0 in the Rumbelows (League) Cup final, but, satisfying as this must have been for manager Ron Atkinson, sacked by United four years ago, he gained more pleasure 17 days later when Wednesday clinched their return to Division One at the first time of asking.

At Wembley, it was Irish international John Sheridan who won the match for Wednesday after 37 minutes, with a volleyed goal of such quality that it was out of place in a lack-lustre League Cup final newly sponsored by Rumbelows. Nevertheless, it gave Sheffield their first major domestic trophy for 56 years.

Manchester manager Alex Ferguson was left to lament that his side could beat Liverpool and Arsenal — inflicting their first defeats of the season — and win at Elland Road ("perhaps the most intimidating venue in Europe") on the way to the final, and then go out to a Second Division side.

Maxwell the hero in Scottish Cup thriller

MOTHERWELL AND Dundee United, two lesser lights on the Scottish scene, produced a fitting climax to the Scottish season — a seven-goal thriller, in which the heroics of Motherwell's injured keeper Ally Maxwell and a goal from their "super sub" Steve Kirk tipped the balance.

This was the sixth Scottish FA Cup final for both clubs, but only Motherwell had won the Cup before, in 1952. Poor Jim McLean, Dundee United's long-serving — and long-suffering — manager, had seen them lose five finals during his 20 years in charge, and now it was his younger brother Tommy who became the latest manager to upstage him.

There is no denying Motherwell deserved to win, and would probably have had a smoother passage but for Maxwell's injury, sustained in a collision soon after the interval, which left him with bruised ribs, double vision and nausea. They had taken a first-half lead, and an undamaged Maxwell would surely have saved United's equalizer, which passed under his body in the 55th minute.

Motherwell came storming back with two quick goals, but United soon pulled one back, and a last-minute equalizer by Jackson, who just beat the struggling Maxwell to a huge punt from his own keeper, took the match into extra time. Substitute Steve Kirk, who had moved off the bench to score three times before in Motherwell's Cup run, kept up his record with a header after five minutes. After that it was up to Maxwell, and although he could see two balls, he always stopped the right one.

Super sub Kirk (extreme left) heads the extra-time winner for Motherwell.

● Wayward 30-year-old fading star Diego Maradona, who brought Napoli unprecedented success and wealth since his record transfer in 1984, tested positive for cocaine in a random dope test following an Italian Serie A game on 17 March, and was banned from professional soccer for 15 months.

● Torquay became the first club to win promotion on penalties, beating Blackpool 5–4 after their play-off final was drawn 2–2, to earn a place in Division Three.

● Two international "giants" were slain on 5 June in European Championship qualifiers, world champions West Germany losing to an Ian Rush goal for Wales at Cardiff Arms Park and Italy going down 2–1 in Norway.

Barcelona reject Hughes gives them the old one-two

MARK HUGHES, rescued from a nightmare with Barcelona by Alex Ferguson three years ago, rewarded Manchester United by scoring the goals that won them the European Cup-Winners' Cup in Rotterdam, when they beat his old Spanish club 2–1 on a memorable night for English football. Maybe it was not a great game. But United won it well, and in so doing they have restored English football, at the first opportunity, to its pre-Heysel standing. And their fans, some two-thirds of the 45,000 crowd in the bleak, concrete bowl of the De Kuip Stadium, played their part to perfection, deliriously happy but, as they rightly declared themselves, "the best behaved supporters in the land". It was indeed fitting, and a great relief, that this was the night United's "Red Army", responsible for some notorious incidents in the past, had signed a disarmament treaty.

On the field, Bryan Robson was immense. He may no longer be needed by England manager Graham Taylor, but he typified everything that is good about the English game. Ably assisted by the bullish Hughes, he drove United forward in wave after wave of attacks that shook Barcelona out of their stride and finally broke them. The first goal came after 68 minutes, when Bruce headed a Robson free-kick into goal. Hughes ran on to give it a nudge, but generously insisted after that Bruce's effort had crossed the line. There was no doubt who scored the second, as Hughes, confirming his reputation as a scorer of "great goals", raced free, took the ball wide of the keeper and spectacularly belted the ball into the net from the narrowest of angles.

A typical Ronald Koeman free-kick ignored the defensive wall and beat the brave Sealey, playing despite a knee injury, to give United an anxious last 10 minutes, not least Ferguson, who emulates Mr Cruyff by winning this competition with different sides.

Brian McLair (left) and Bryan Robson with the Cup-Winners' Cup.

Spurs shatter Clough's dream despite Gazza's shattered knee

"GAZZAMANIA" TOOK on a new meaning at Wembley, when Spurs met Nottingham Forest in the FA Cup final. Not the hype and the spin-off industry surrounding England World Cup star Paul Gascoigne since his famous tearful exit in Italy, but the mental aberration that sent him rampaging around the pitch like a whirling dervish in the first 15 minutes, almost handing the Cup to Forest and finishing up with a self-inflicted injury that could seriously damage his career.

If this really was Gascoigne's last game for Spurs — although his serious knee-ligament injury might yet prejudice his pending transfer to Lazio — it was a singularly inglorious one. In a misguided attempt to live up to his media image as the "cheeky chappie superman" who would win this game on his own and maybe deliver Spurs from the hands of the receivers into the bargain, Gascoigne's first contribution was to catch Forest's Garry Parker on the chest with a follow-through straight out of the manual of kick-boxing. Escaping a yellow card for this was his first miracle of the afternoon, and an indictment of the kind of misguidedly lenient refereeing so often seen in Cup finals. A caution at this stage might have prevented the excesses that followed, but the overactive Gascoigne continued to hog centre stage, arms flailing about, until he once more overstepped the mark with an appalling scything tackle — rather a kick — on Gary Charles just outside the Spurs box. Although the Forest right-back soon recovered from the foul, it left the perpetrator writhing, seemingly in an attempt to avoid punishment. He did so, from an extraordinarily tolerant referee, whose main concern appeared to be to avoid controversy at all costs. As it turned out, Gascoigne was badly hurt, and, to add insult to injury, Stuart Pearce scored from the free-kick.

So Gazza the superman was carried off, which, paradoxically, turned out well for Spurs, because not only could they replace him, with Nayim, but they were now able to get down to playing football. This they did, to excellent effect. Paul Stewart was outstanding in midfield and scored a fine equalizer, too, but not before Lineker had a goal disallowed and a penalty saved, by Mark Crossley, who had brought him down and was another player lucky to escape a card of some colour. Stewart's goal came in the 55th minute, a right-foot cross-shot after being set free by the tireless Paul Allen.

Spurs were very much on top, with Forest tactically bereft of ideas, so it came as a shock at the end of 90 minutes when Brian Clough took his eccentricity too far and a leaf out of Paul Gascoigne's book of crass stupidity by exchanging pleasantries with a young policeman when his young team were crying out for his managerial advice. It was Terry Venables who won the tactical battle hands down, and no surprise when Spurs scored the winning goal in extra time, courtesy of the unfortunate defender Des Walker, who headed a corner into his own net. But this was in keeping with the madness of the day.

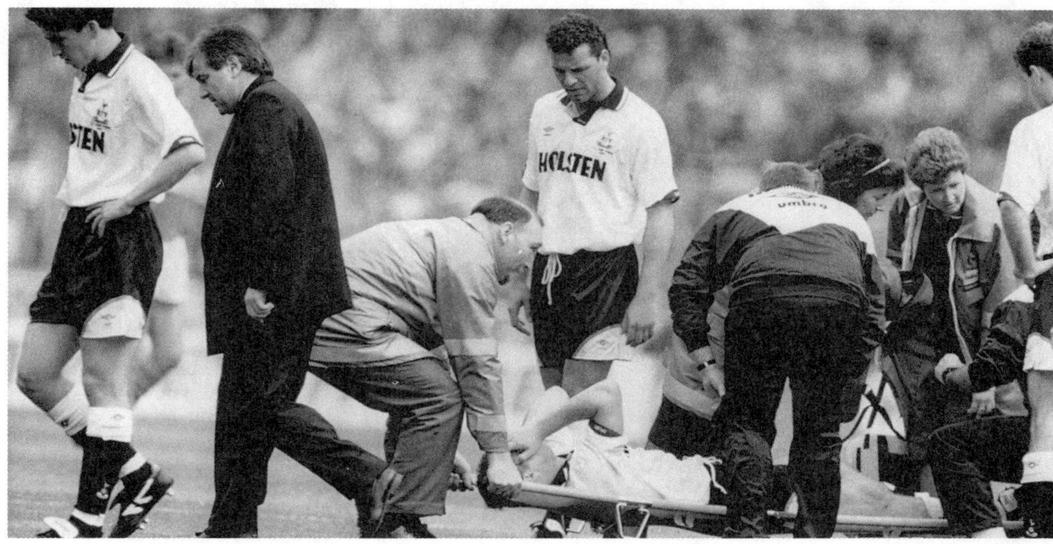

Paul Gascoigne is put on a stretcher and carried off after 15 minutes of lunacy.

Des Walker (4) heads into his own net for Spurs' winner.

FINAL SCORE

Football League
Division 1: Arsenal
Top scorer: Alan Smith (Arsenal) 23
Division 2: Oldham Athletic
Division 3: Cambridge United
Division 4: Darlington
Footballer of the Year: Gordon Strachan (Leeds United)

FA Cup Final
Tottenham Hotspur 2 Nottingham Forest 1
(after extra time)

League Cup Final
Sheffield Wed 1 Manchester United 0

Scottish League
Premier Division: Rangers
Top scorer: Tommy Coyne (Celtic) 18
Division 1: Falkirk
Division 2: Stirling Albion
Footballer of the Year: Maurice Malpas (Dundee United)

Scottish FA Cup Final
Motherwell 4 Dundee United 3
(after extra time)

Scottish League Cup Final
Rangers 2 Celtic 1
(after extra time)

European Cup Final
Red Star Belgrade 0 Marseille 0
(aet) Red Star won 5–3 on penalties

Cup-Winners' Cup Final
Manchester United 2 Barcelona 1

UEFA Cup Final
Inter Milan beat Roma 2–0, 0–1

European Footballer of the Year 1990
Lothar Matthaus (Inter Milan & West Germany)

Leading European Scorer (Golden Boot)
Darko Pancev (Red Star Belgrade) 34

World Club Championship
Red Star Belgrade (Yugoslavia) 3 Colo Colo (Chile) 0

The 'professional foul'

THE TERM "Professional foul" is a euphemism for an offence committed in order to gain an advantage. The phrase has entered the language, bestowing on the word "professional" the meaning "intentional", with regard to the breaking of rules. Tom Stoppard wrote a play built round the concept. And administrators of the game have tried for years to banish it, without success.

There should, of course, be no place for such a phenomenon in any self-respecting sport. For a similar offence in rugby, the referee is empowered to award the other side a try. In snooker, a "miss" is given. But it still exists in football because the law-makers have not the wit to find a punishment that fits the crime.

The solution

One of the problems in soccer is that the law-makers are caught up in a web of their own making. By some historical accident, a penalty-kick may be given only if an offence is committed inside a box measuring 44 yards by 18 yards called the penalty area. The penalty-kick was originally introduced in 1891 as the result of new attitudes creeping into the game since the advent of professionalism. Matters came to a head after an incident in the last eight of the FA Cup, when Notts County full-back Hendry punched a goal-bound Stoke effort off his own line with his keeper beaten. The resultant free-kick on the line was easily smothered, and Stoke lost the game 1–0. The first penalty area was bounded by a line drawn right across the field 12 yards from the goal-line. The present penalty area was introduced in 1902. These were rules brought in by the International Football Association Board (IFAB) at meetings held in hired rooms in public houses; they were not brought down from Mt Sinai on tablets of stone. So why is it that a penalty-kick may be awarded only for offences committed in a certain area of the pitch? Surely it is the seriousness of an offence in relation to the play that should determine the form of punishment.

If referees were empowered to award a penalty-kick for an offence wherever it occurred, it would stamp out the "professional foul" at a stroke. This remedy was suggested by the Busby Committee in 1982, proposed by the Football Association, and rejected by FIFA. But the usual argument against it, that it is impossibly subjective, no longer holds water. The situations in which it should come into effect have now been defined in the laws — but the punishment is not a penalty-kick, but expulsion from the game. The ruling, in the form of an International Board decision, came into force in 1991. It reads: "If, in the opinion of the referee, a player who is moving towards his opponents' goal with the obvious opportunity to score a goal is intentionally impeded by an opponent, through unlawful means, i.e., an offence punishable by a free-kick (or a penalty-kick), thus denying the attacking player's team the aforesaid goalscoring opportunity, the offending player shall be sent off the field of play for serious foul play in accordance with Law 12(n)." Another Board decision makes handball, in similar circumstances, also a sending-off offence.

This is not the answer. It does not fit the punishment to the crime; it often punishes the offender out of all proportion to the offence, while devaluing the "ultimate" sanction; and it has not served its purpose, namely to eradicate the "professional foul".

But the definition is there — and the referee has been entrusted to use his judgement to apply it. So why can't he use his judgement in the same situation to award different punishments? If referees could award a penalty-kick for particular offences wherever they occurred — and a goal for certain offences, such as handling the ball on the line — they could administer the laws far more consistently than they do at present, and the punishment would instantly and fairly penalize the offence. A sending-off does not punish the offence, merely the offender — and this is little consolation to the side offended against.

Players, as the laws stand, will still commit the "professional foul" in extremis — to protect a lead or save a game in the dying minutes, and risk being sent off at the expense of a free-kick or even a penalty-kick. They would surely not commit the same offence if they knew they were giving away a penalty-kick or a goal, respectively. It is as plain as that. After all, how many penalty tries have to be awarded in rugby?

Mind-reading

The main reason players and coaches, among others, are reluctant to give referees too much scope to use their judgement is that they don't trust referees to do so. Admittedly, many referees who have reached high levels in football do not inspire confidence in their judgement. But football and its laws get the referees they deserve. At the risk of upsetting the profession, it has to be said that referees, like goalkeepers, must be crazy. How else can you explain their willingness to suffer abuse from players, managers and spectators, for next to no remuneration, and at the same time try to apply a set of rules that are full of contradictions, inconsistencies and inadequacies?

To understand their dilemma, you need only look at one word in the laws, the fourth word in Law 12, Fouls and Misconduct: "A player who intentionally commits any of the following nine offences ..." At the end of this law, there is some "Advice to Referees", namely that the correct application of the law "depends on the referee's ability to make up his mind whether or not a player's action is intentional".

But there is no way a referee is equipped to do this. He cannot read a player's mind. In some cases it might be obvious; but in the large majority of instances it is impossible to say whether a player went for the ball or for his opponent. And surely, if a player intentionally kicks or trips an opponent, he should be cautioned or even sent off. If all the fouls punished by free-kicks were intentional, there would be many more cautions and dismissals than there are. And this proves that referees regularly do not apply the law as it is written — that is, they give free-kicks for fouls that are not intentional.

Again, the answer is simple. Delete the word "intentional". It only confuses the issue. If a player, making a sliding tackle, say, goes for the ball but, because of his own lack of judgement or the superior skill of his opponent, makes contact with the opponent instead, the referee must give a free-kick (or a penalty). Why should the offence have to be intentional?

A beautifully executed "professional foul" — now a red-card offence in certain circumstances.

A case of obstruction

The trouble with the law-makers is that they are obsessed with the letter of the law.

The most infamous "professional foul" of all — Schumacher (West Germany) fells Battiston (France) in the 1982 World Cup semi-final.

Example: at a goal-kick, if a player touches the ball before it leaves the penalty area, the kick has to be retaken. Why can't the referee give an indirect free-kick? Answer: the ball did not leave the penalty area, so it was not in play, as defined in the Goal-Kick Law, which apparently is carved in stone.

In May 1981, the Welsh FA submitted a proposal to the International Board that the offence of obstruction should be punishable by a direct rather than an indirect free-kick. This was thrown out at a meeting of the Referees' Committee, held prior to the International Board meeting, because the committee "unanimously agreed that an obstruction in the penalty area should not be penalized by a penalty-kick". This may be a reasonable attitude to take for minor obstruction offences, but the definition of obstruction in the laws has wider implications.

According to the convoluted Law 12 on Fouls and Misconduct, obstruction is not an offence while a player is in possession of the ball and it remains "within playing distance". It is an offence when "running between an opponent and the ball, or interposing the body so as to form an obstacle to an opponent". But this covers a multitude of sins, from preventing an opponent reaching a ball before it goes out of play to a virtual body-check that deprives an opponent of an obvious goalscoring opportunity. An indirect free-kick is adequate punishment for the former, but a penalty-kick is more appropriate for the latter, which comes under the "professional foul" category. Again, it is a matter of degree, and the referee should be empowered to judge.

State of the laws

The laws of football are in a terrible state. They are divided into subsections under arbitrary headings, are full of anomalies, and some of them are open to a wide range of interpretation. They contain a hotchpotch of riders, decisions and insertions. As a result of all this, it is difficult for the International Board, when drawing up changes in the laws, to make their intentions crystal clear. Time and again, a major law change has to be rewritten the following year, perhaps more than once, because the original wording was too vague, there were loopholes in the practical interpretation, or for some other reason the change did not produce the desired effect.

There are several aspects of the laws that have not kept pace with the modern game, that were originally framed when the old traditions of sportsmanship were still alive and gamesmanship was just a twinkle in Stephen Potter's eye. Players and coaches cannot be blamed for taking full advantage of the laws as they stand. If they don't, their opponents will. The game is crying out for a proper "advantage" law, as practised in rugby. And what about rugby's 10-yard penalty for encroachment at free-kicks and contested decisions?

Nowhere in the laws does it say that the offending side are allowed time to form a defensive wall against a free-kick. Yet this is universally accepted, and referees allow it to happen. Former Football League referee Clive Thomas was vilified by managers and media for booking as many as five players or more for failing to retreat ten yards at free-kicks. But he was bravely employing the only option within this power to punish a common and deliberate attempt to gain unfair advantage. It would not be difficult, however, to frame a law that made it impossible to form an effective wall, and then perhaps defenders would be more careful about conceding free-kicks.

It has been patently obvious for years that the system of control is no longer adequate. The referee needs more help — an official at each end, perhaps, who could act as another pair of eyes — to spot the off-the-ball incidents and the "hand of God" goals, and serve as goal judge. The common excuse that lower levels of the game would not be able to afford extra officials does not hold up: they simply would not have them. But at the top level, it is farcical for millions of TV viewers to be shown quite clearly that the ball has gone over the line, and no goal is given because the officials were not in a position to judge. They rarely can be.

Following the worldwide adverse criticism of the quality of the football in the 1990 World Cup, FIFA have attempted to introduce law changes intended to improve the entertainment value of the game and stamp out some of the unfair practices. These include dismissal for the "professional foul", the "back-pass" law restricting goalkeepers' handling, and experiments to replace the throw-in with a free-kick. But until the laws are completely tidied up, with all anomalies removed, and punishments are devised to fit the crime, no amount of arbitrary tampering is going to solve the deep-rooted problems of the world's most popular game.

A "professional foul" by Gale (West Ham) on Crosby (Nottingham Forest) meant a red card in the 1991 FA Cup semi-final.

Triumph for Venables as Sugar saves Spurs

AFTER A LONG-drawn-out saga, manager Terry Venables has finally won his battle to take over ailing Spurs, teetering on the brink of oblivion with debts of some £20 million. Backed by multi-millionaire businessman Alan Sugar, chief of the Amstrad computer giant, Venables fought off a last-minute bid by Derby chairman Robert Maxwell, who would have had to sell his shares in that club had he been successful. The £7.25 million deal was formally signed on 22 June to end almost a year of uncertainty. As the football world takes in the magnitude of what Mr Venables has done — while guiding Spurs to their Cup final triumph at the same time — they learnt that he had, according to Mr Sugar, put in a "gi-normous" amount of his own money, thought to be about £3.6 million.

Mr Sugar will become non-executive chairman and Venables non-executive MD, working in tandem at the club with a first-team coach, probably his assistant Doug Livermore. The first priority of the new consortium will be to put Spurs on a more solid financial footing, and Mr Sugar warned fans not to expect the club to be involved in the transfer market for some time. The on-off move of Paul Gascoigne to Lazio will be sorted out one way or another, but it will be surprising if they can afford not to sell him. And to add a twist to a day of high financial dealing, Blackburn confirmed that they have made a bid of £2 million for Spurs and England striker Gary Lineker.

Happy days at Spurs: Sugar (left), Gascoigne and Venables.

SOCCER SOUNDBITES

"You'd have to be mad not to want to keep Gascoigne, but if there has to be life after Gazza, so be it."

TERRY VENABLES.

Souness spends £5m for starters

LIVERPOOL MANAGER Graeme Souness forked out £5.1 million on two players in mid-July in the space of two days: England centre-back Mark Wright and Wales striker Dean Saunders, both from Derby County. In doing so, the tough-talking Scot confirmed his promise, made when he took over the Anfield hot seat last April, that he was prepared to axe old favourites and introduce new faces to keep Liverpool at the top of British soccer.

Wright's fee was £2.2 million, while Saunders cost £2.9 million, a new record for a British club. Wright faces the difficult task of stepping into the shoes of Alan Hansen, who retired last season after recurring problems with knee injuries. Mr Souness, who stole Saunders — the son of a former Liverpool player — from under the noses of Everton and Forest, expects him to link up well with John Barnes and Ian Rush.

Bari bust record for £5.5m Platt

DAVID PLATT BECAME the most expensive player in British football history when Italian club Bari paid Aston Villa £5.5 million for him on 20 July. Platt, the versatile, goalscoring England midfielder, was given a free transfer by Manchester United seven years ago. And although Crewe made a tidy £200,000 profit when they sold him to Villa three years later, manager Dario Gradi ruefully points out that he accepted the deal from Graham Taylor, then Villa manager, rather than an alternative £150,000 plus a percentage of a future transfer. By joining unfashionable Bari, Platt has gambled that a bigger Italian club will later step in and acquire his services.

SOCCER SOUNDBITES

"David can go on to become a truly great player."

DARIO GRADI,
Platt's manager at Crewe.

No Turkish delight for England

ENGLAND'S unsatisfactory 1–0 victory at Wembley over Turkey — a team they twice demolished 8–0 in the 1980s — leaves them needing a draw in Poland to go through to the finals of the European Championship, when a more convincing win would have put them virtually out of reach of their rivals. As the crowd chanted "What a load of rubbish" at the end, it was Graham Taylor's first experience of this familiar Wembley anthem of disappointment. And had it not been for Alan Smith's 22nd-minute goal, and then the agility and outstretched fingertips of Chris Woods, who denied Unal the honour of scoring what would have been Turkey's first ever goal against England, the evening would have been even more embarrassing for Mr Taylor. Woods, indeed, found himself the busier of the two keepers, as Mr Taylor's pre-match instructions to shoot on sight seemed to have reached the wrong dressing-room. Now we must wait until next month, when the last matches in the group are played, to know the outcome.

Alan Smith (left) heads England's winner.

SOCCER SOUNDBITES

"... a team that could not possibly play together... a selection mistake by the manager..."

SIR ALF RAMSEY'S
unusually harsh criticism of England and Graham Taylor.

Lineker rescue act clinches England's place in Sweden

GARY LINEKER, not for the first time, came to the rescue of England in Poznan on 13 November to book them a place in Sweden for next summer's European Championship finals. With England only 13 minutes away from defeat — and elimination — he scored an equalizer that, though well deserved, had begun to look increasingly unlikely the more frustrated they became.

Panic had set in after 31 minutes, when sweeper Szewczyk gave Poland the lead with a 40-yard shot that took a deflection off Mabbutt's heel. Only five minutes earlier, Andy Gray of Crystal Palace, thrown into this crucial match for his international debut, had missed a golden opportunity. At half-time, Graham Taylor replaced Gray with Alan Smith, to give Lineker some company up front, but England made and missed several chances.

They also survived a strong penalty appeal after Woods spilled a shot and, Poland claimed, impeded Furtok as he went for the ball. Almost immediately, Lineker, England's captain, made a powerful run on the right and won the latest in a stream of corners. Mabbutt headed Rocastle's kick to the far post, where Lineker improvised an acrobatic volley to beat the stunned Polish keeper. Had he not done so, it would have meant Jack Charlton's Republic of Ireland going through, not Poland, as their 3–1 win in Turkey gave them by far the best goal difference.

Lineker celebrates the goal that puts England into the European Championship finals.

Soccer crisis: League clubs £130m in debt

ACCORDING TO AN independent survey, Football League clubs are collectively up to £130 million in debt and are "not capable of either managerially or financially facing that challenge". The report, "The Bankrupting of English Football", privately produced by sports consultant Dr Simon Pitt, also warns that more than a dozen of the 93 League clubs face extinction. Dr Pitt's findings were drawn from a voluntary and confidential response to his questionnaire, which produced replies from 61 clubs.

The report blames the crisis in football on the spiralling cost of players' wages, signing-on fees and transfers, allied to a drop in spectator interest and revenue in the last decade, which has left more than 75 per cent of the clubs in the red. Another increasingly heavy burden is the cost of policing matches, which has almost doubled to £6.1 million in the last year. The biggest problem most leading clubs face is the implementation of the Taylor Report, where the revenue needed to build all-seater stadiums by the 1994 deadline has outstripped ability to raise it.

Dr Pitt says the game is "undercapitalized and over-borrowed", and in any other business circumstances small companies such as these, with high fixed overheads and declining marginal revenues, would have gone bankrupt long ago.

United out of Cup on penalties

MANCHESTER UNITED earned the dubious distinction in the fourth round of the FA Cup of becoming the first Division One side in the history of this illustrious competition to be knocked out by the gimmicky method of a penalty shoot-out.

Following their goalless draw at the Dell, United were the firm favourites to beat lowly Southampton at Old Trafford. But after going two goals down inside 21 minutes, to goals by Stuart Gray and Alan Shearer, they were grateful to be given the opportunity of taking part in the ritual lottery. For that they have to thank their Ukrainian winger Andrei Kanchelskis, who scored just before the interval, and the ever-persistent Scot, Brian McClair, who equalized a minute into injury time.

United appeared to have won it in extra time, when Bryan Robson's header looked to have crossed the line; but the referee did not have the benefit of a television replay, which would have confirmed the score, so the penalty decider came into play. The two United players who will be haunted by their misses were England's Neil Webb and teenage Welsh international Ryan Giggs. The Saints put all four of theirs away, without recourse to their regular penalty-taker Matthew Le Tissier, and when Tim Flowers saved the last shot, United had only the dismal consolation of a place in the record books.

Robson's header: surely over the line.

Keegan returns to Newcastle: Ardiles sacked

KEVIN KEEGAN bustled back into the life of Newcastle United on 5 February as the struggling Second Division side sacked Ossie Ardiles and took the astonishing gamble of appointing the glamorous, but untried, former England star as their 15th manager since the war. Presented with the formidable challenge of saving the north-eastern giants from the indignity of relegation to the Third Division for the first time, Mr Keegan struck a positive attitude that will be familiar to those who saw him play in a career that took in successful spells at Liverpool, Hamburg, Southampton and finally Newcastle, where he enjoyed an Indian summer and a love affair with the Geordie fans. And it is because of those supporters that Keegan — who, as the first English footballing millionaire, doesn't need the money — allowed himself to be lured out of retirement. While listening to Mr Keegan's rallying cry, the media were still trying to work out exactly how it was that Mr Ardiles, in the job for only 11 months, had been sacked only three days after director Douglas Hall and his father, the chairman Sir John Hall, had taken the trouble to deny rumours of such an event. Mr Keegan, nearly 41, has not yet signed a contract, and he and his No. 2, Terry McDermott, have 16 games left to save second-from-bottom Newcastle from the drop.

Ossie Ardiles — sacked.

Kevin Keegan back at Newcastle: a tough task.

SOCCER SOUNDBITES

"Let's kill off once and for all the rumours that Ossie's job is on the line. If he leaves the club, it will be of his own volition."

SIR JOHN HALL,
Newcastle chairman, 2 February.

"I feel absolutely dreadful about what has happened... when I said those words, I meant each and every one of them."

SIR JOHN HALL,
5 February.

New Premier League confirmed

THE BREAK-UP OF the 104-year-old Football League was given official confirmation at Lancaster Gate on 20 February when the FA Council approved the formation of the new FA Premier League, to start in August. The unpaid, non-executive chairman, appointed in December, is Sir John Quinton, former chairman of Barclays Bank, and the chief executive is accountant Rick Parry. They have still to make their peace with the PFA's Gordon Taylor, who is demanding a say in the new League's decision-making process.

The Premier League will have 22 clubs, to be reduced to 20 by the end of the 1994–95 season, a compromise forced upon the FA by the clubs' chairmen despite the original idea having been to cut down on the amount of football played. It will be linked by three-up/three-down promotion and relegation to what will be the First Division of the old Football League, merely the Second Division under a new name. Referees in Premier League matches will wear a green uniform (first change, black); there will be a 15-minute half-time interval; and three substitutes (including a goalkeeper) will be permitted on the bench, any two of whom may be used.

The confirmation must have been particularly satisfying for FA chief executive Graham Kelly, after all the fuss since it was first proposed 10 months ago in the FA's "Blueprint for the Future of Football". But he must be disappointed with the rejection of the original 18-club concept, and has found it hard to explain how it will differ from the current First Division — apart, that is, from the few cosmetic changes detailed above and the higher prices that its member clubs will no doubt feel entitled to charge.

First riot for two years

IN THE FIRST SERIOUS case of hooliganism inside an English football ground for two years, rioters at St Andrews caused the Third Division match between Birmingham City and Stoke City to be held up for half an hour. It was announced that the game was abandoned but, after the ground was cleared, the managers agreed to play out the last 35 seconds, and the two sides just kicked the ball to each other until the referee blew for time.

The trouble began within seconds of Stoke's equalizer in injury time. About 400 angry Birmingham supporters swarmed on to the playing area and made towards the Stoke end. One of them, who was later identified and arrested, hit the referee, Roger Wiseman.

After being involved in several notorious crowd incidents in recent years, Birmingham have worked hard on rebuilding their image. But in the light of this latest incident, Birmingham manager Terry Cooper has said he is seriously considering leaving the club, and chairman Samesh Kumar admitted that he was in despair for the club's future.

However, Mr Kumar's remarks alleging "some scandalous decisions by the referee" are at best counter-productive. At Anfield, Liverpool manager Graeme Souness similarly described the referee after his team's match with Southampton as "a disgrace". It is comments such as these, rather than controversial decisions by match officials, that are more likely to cause crowd trouble, and it is about time that the FA took stronger measures to put a stop to irresponsible public condemnation of those officials by people within the game.

'Always look on the bright side...'

AS MANCHESTER UNITED suffered the final blow to what were only a short while ago heavily odds-on chances of winning their first Championship for 25 years — going down 2–0 to Liverpool at Anfield on 26 April — it did not help manager Alex Ferguson and his men much when the Kop choir burst out into a chorus of "Always look on the bright side of life". With Leeds being crowned champions after their same-day victory at Bramall Lane, there is only bitter disappointment for Manchester, who a week ago were two points ahead with a game in hand over their rivals. But three defeats in that time — their first home reversal of the season, by Forest, and losses to bottom club West Ham and now Liverpool — have seen them snatch failure out of the very jaws of triumph.

This should not be allowed to detract from Leeds's fine achievement, however. They have battled with Manchester for the leadership all season. They are unbeaten at home, and have lost only four League matches altogether. All credit to manager Howard Wilkinson, who in less than four years has transformed Leeds from a side fighting to stay in the Second Division into the champions of England. In doing so, he has banished from Elland Road the ghosts of the Revie era for good.

Leeds have been strong in all departments, but their midfield has been outstanding: the evergreen Gordon Strachan, Wilkinson's most inspirational signing, the combative David Batty and the elusive Gary McAllister, and Gary Speed playing wide. It is ironic that newly elected Footballer of the Year Strachan, the key man in the Leeds revival, should have been put out to grass by Alex Ferguson three years ago, with doubts surrounding his ability to keep up with the pace of top-level football. In goal, John Lukic won his second Championship medal, while other ex-Arsenal men shone in the centre: Chris Whyte in defence and Lee Chapman up front. Wilkinson added an extra touch of flair and finesse with the introduction of French international striker Eric Cantona for the last third of the season, usually as substitute, and the popular chant of "Ooh, ah, Cant-o-nah" became a familiar sound on the terraces as Leeds fought their way to the title.

Cantona, who came out of self-imposed retirement to inspire Leeds.

Leeds captain Gordon Strachan, still full of running at 35.

Strike threat averted

THE THREAT OF A strike by England's leading footballers was averted, following a meeting between the Professional Footballers' Association and the newly formed Premier League on 27 April, when PFA chief executive Gordon Taylor agreed to accept a minimum £1.5 million of television revenue next season. This represents a remarkable 50 per cent increase on the original offer. After that had been made, the PFA had circularized First Division players and received an overwhelming mandate to strike.

The deal means that, in addition to receiving 10 per cent of the first £10 million of TV income, the PFA will collect five per cent of the balance. This money is to be used for benevolent, educational and insurance purposes.

FINAL SCORE

Football League
Division 1: Leeds United
Top scorer: Ian Wright (Arsenal 24, Crystal Palace 5) 29
Division 2: Ipswich Town
Division 3: Brentford
Division 4: Burnley
Footballer of the Year: Gary Lineker (Tottenham Hotspur)

FA Cup Final

Liverpool	2	Sunderland	0

League Cup Final

Manchester United	1	Nottingham Forest	0

Scottish League
Premier Division: Rangers
Top scorer: Ally McCoist (Rangers) 34
Division 1: Dundee
Division 2: Dumbarton
Footballer of the Year: Ally McCoist (Rangers)

Scottish FA Cup Final

Rangers	2	Airdrieonians	1

Scottish League Cup Final

Hibernian	2	Dunfermline A	0

European Cup Final

Barcelona	1	Sampdoria	0
(after extra time)			

Cup-Winners' Cup Final

Werder Bremen	2	Monaco	0

UEFA Cup Final
Ajax Amsterdam beat Torino 2–2, 0–0 (on away goals)

European Footballer of the Year 1991
Jean-Pierre Papin (Marseille & France)

Leading European Scorer (Golden Boot)
Ally McCoist (Rangers) 34

World Club Championship

São Paulo (Brazil)	2	Barcelona (Spain)	1

Non-qualifiers Denmark are European champions

A POPULAR QUIZ question of the future may be: who won the European Football Championship after failing to qualify for the finals? The answer is Denmark, who came into the 1992 finals in Sweden after UEFA decided that Yugoslavia, torn by civil war, could not take part. Denmark, who had finished second to Yugoslavia in their qualifying group, were invited to step in at only 11 days' notice.

With their squad hastily assembled, Denmark kicked off with a match against England, joint favourites along with France to qualify from their group. The Danes were the tournament outsiders, and played like it in the first half. But after the interval they got on top, and in the 61st minute went closest to a goal when a shot from John Jensen hit the inside of a post. A 0–0 draw was a satisfactory start.

In their second match, in Stockholm, the Danes were the better side in the first half against Sweden, but went down to Swedish enthusiasm and industry when Brolin scored in the 58th minute. With one match to come, Denmark were bottom of the group. France had been playing well within themselves, with the "easy" match against Denmark to come, but their aristocratic air was disturbed when Henrik Larsen put the Danes ahead after eight minutes. Jean-Pierre Papin equalized on the hour, and Denmark remained as good as out until 12 minutes from time. Then Lars Elstrup, who had gone on as a substitute 11 minutes earlier, scored the winner. And Sweden's defeat of England meant that Denmark had squeezed into the semi-finals, along with the host nation.

In the semis, the Danes took on the powerful favourites Holland, who had clinched their group with a superb 3–1 defeat of Germany. Denmark shocked the confident Dutch after only five minutes, when Larsen again headed them into the lead. Holland, tackling strongly, then forced themselves back into the game and Bergkamp equalized in the 23rd minute. But Larsen struck for a second time nine minutes later to restore Denmark's lead. Holland pressed throughout the second half, and the Milan connection finally produced the equalizer five minutes from time when Gullit and Van Basten combined for Rijkaard to score brilliantly.

Now, with Brian Laudrup and Henrik Andersen off injured and defender John Sivebaek limping at centre-forward, the Danes once more had their backs to the wall. But they somehow survived extra time, and in the penalty shoot-out Peter Schmeichel saved Holland's second kick, from Van Basten. No one else failed, and Kim Christofte accepted the honour of putting Denmark into the final.

Germany had played in fits and starts during the tournament, and had edged out Sweden 3–2 in the other semi. But any relief they felt at not having to face Holland again soon vanished when Denmark went ahead after 18 minutes with a goal by Jensen, set up by Vilfort and the impressive Povlsen. The Germans came strongly, but Denmark remained cool and in control. They had chances in breakaways and, in the 78th minute, Christiansen headed the ball down for Kim Vilfort to control it and slip it in off a post. The latecomers, the rank outsiders, had beaten the world champions and won the European title.

John Jensen scores Denmark's first goal in the final.

"We still don't understand what we have done."

PETER SCHMEICHEL,
Manchester United and Denmark goalkeeper, after his team won the European Championship.

"They came at us playing direct football. They were more English than the English."

GRAHAM TAYLOR,
explaining England's defeat by Sweden.

Taylor's trusty combinations come badly unstitched

ENGLAND, WITH HIGH expectations, flopped badly in the European Championship, coming last in their group. They looked good for a while in their first match, against substitutes Denmark, whom they confidently expected to beat. But all they scored were two yellow cards, for Martin Keown and Keith Curle in the first 10 minutes, and they were lucky not to concede a goal in the second half.

The match against France was disappointing, with the French playing for a draw and getting it. Stuart Pearce, badly butted in the face by Boli in a nasty off-the-ball incident, returned straight from treatment to shiver the cross-bar with a free-kick, but the match ended goalless.

England needed to beat Sweden to be sure of a semi-final place. They made a promising start, Platt scoring in three minutes with a volley after a fine move on the right involving Batty and Lineker. But they still lacked imagination. Eriksson equalized after 51 minutes, and Brolin scored a fine winner with eight minutes left.

Graham Taylor inevitably came in for considerable criticism over his team selection. Injuries before the finals had robbed him of three right-backs, Gary Stevens, Rob Jones and Lee Dixon, and three other players occupied this spot in England's games — Keith Curle, Andy Sinton and David Batty — none of whom was a natural in the position. John Barnes and Mark Wright were also late withdrawals.

Taylor shuffled his team around trying to find a winning combination, even switching from a back four to a sweeper and back again in the three matches. Skipper Gary Lineker had three partners up front: Smith, Shearer and Platt. Taylor failed to instil any flair into the play, however, and was criticized for not including Nigel Clough, who might have brought a touch of subtlety into the build-ups.

But Taylor's main crime in the eyes of the Press and the fans was his decision, in the game against Sweden, to take off Lineker half an hour from the end of what turned out to be his last match for England, thus depriving him of the chance of overtaking Bobby Charlton's record goal total, and appearing to cast the blame on his skipper for England's failure.

Lineker is taken off, and denied the chance of a record.

Premier League reaches for Sky

WATCHING LIVE Premier League soccer on television will cost viewers a fee in its first season. The BBC and BSkyB signed a £304 million deal that gives them both Premier League action for five seasons. Sky will transmit matches live — on Sunday afternoons and Monday evenings — while the BBC will revive the Saturday evening "Match of the Day" highlights programme. But the three million owners of Sky satellite dishes will have to take out a subscription to watch their 60 live matches a season.

FOOTBALL FOCUS

- FIFA rule that all international referees must be able to speak English.
- Everton's Northern Ireland international Norman Whiteside, 26, is forced to retire in June 1991 after an unsuccessful struggle against a knee injury.
- The convictions of UEFA (ordered to compensate Heysel disaster victims and their families) and secretary-general Hans Bangerter (three-month suspended sentence for gross negligence) were confirmed in Belgium's highest court in the third and final hearing of the case in October.
- Cup-final tradition was reversed, with the losers going up first to receive their medals, but the FA boobed, Sunderland getting the winners' medals, Liverpool the losers'.
- Gary Lineker went to Sweden with 48 international goals to his name, one behind Bobby Charlton's England record, and was odds-on to equal and beat it — but he failed to score.
- The Paul Gascoigne transfer saga was finally completed at the end of the season, after the knee injuries and the operations, and he joined Lazio to a hero's welcome after a year in limbo.
- Scotland enjoyed a more successful European Championship than England, despite also failing to reach the semi-finals. They were unlucky to lose to Germany after matching them for much of the game; they held Holland for 76 minutes, and they outplayed the CIS. And their fans behaved impeccably, unlike the English with their drunken revelling and the Germans, who rioted in Gothenburg after their defeat by Holland.

Souness takes heart from final

HAVING TWICE survived elimination from the FA Cup by the width of the cross-bar against Second Division clubs — Ipswich in the fifth round and Portsmouth in the semi-finals — Liverpool faced yet another Division Two club in the final. Their opponents, Sunderland, had already put out three First Division sides in West Ham, Chelsea and Norwich.

Manager Graeme Souness, recovering from heart surgery, was on the Liverpool bench against doctor's advice, and could not bear to watch at times. In the event, Liverpool's class asserted itself, and his team won comfortably enough, thus earning themselves a place in Europe for 1992–93. Steve McManaman was the man of the match, and Michael Thomas and Ian Rush — with a record fifth goal in FA Cup finals — scored.

Sunderland's run to the final at least ensured that the job of manager went to Malcolm Crosby, who was for weeks only the caretaker as Sunderland's successes went on and on.

Little stress for Souness at the Cup final.

FINAL SCORE

EUROPEAN CHAMPIONSHIP 1992

Group 1

Sweden	1	France	1
England	0	Denmark	0
England	0	France	0
Sweden	1	Denmark	0
Sweden	2	England	1
Denmark	2	France	1

	P	W	D	L	F	A	P
Sweden	3	2	1	0	4	2	5
Denmark	3	1	1	1	2	2	3
France	3	0	2	1	2	3	2
England	3	0	2	1	1	2	2

Group 2

Holland	1	Scotland	0
CIS	1	Germany	1
Germany	2	Scotland	0
Holland	0	CIS	0
Holland	3	Germany	1
Scotland	3	CIS	0

	P	W	D	L	F	A	P
Holland	3	2	1	0	4	1	5
Germany	3	1	1	1	4	4	3
Scotland	3	1	0	2	3	3	2
CIS	3	0	2	1	1	4	2

SEMI-FINALS

Germany	3	Sweden	2
Denmark	2	Holland	2

(aet) Denmark won 5–4 on penalties

FINAL

Denmark	2	Germany	0

Gothenburg, 26 June 1992. Attendance 37,800

Denmark: Schmeichel, Sivebaek (Christiansen), Nielsen K, Olsen L, Christofte, Jensen, Povlsen, Laudrup B., Piechnik, Larsen, Vilfort (Scorers: Jensen, Vilfort)
Germany: Illgner, Reuter, Brehme, Kohler, Buchwald, Hassler, Riedle, Helmer, Sammer (Doll), Effenberg (Thon), Klinsmann

Blackburn Rovers back in top flight

BLACKBURN ROVERS chose the right season to win promotion from the Second Division. They went straight into the new Premier Division after winning a Wembley play-off final against Leicester City.

The last Premier spot was not decided until 25 May, more than two weeks after the Cup final. Rovers' David Speedie was brought down in the penalty area, and Mike Newell scored from the spot for the only goal of the game. Blackburn's appearance in the top flight will be their first since 1966.

There were two ironies in their achievement. Their late chairman, Bill Fox, as president of the Football League, had fought tooth and nail against the new Premier League, which his club were now joining. And Kenny Dalglish, their manager, who had been lured to Blackburn by retired steel magnate Jack Walker, with the help of £5.5 million to spend in the transfer market, found himself returning to the pressures of the top division, which had forced him to give up the Liverpool managership only 15 months earlier.

Dalglish: feeling the pressure at Blackburn?

Vinny pays for video nasty

THE FA CAME DOWN hard on Vinny Jones for his part in the now notorious video "Soccer's Hard Men". At a disciplinary hearing on 17 November, they handed the Wimbledon midfielder a record £20,000 fine and a six-month suspension, itself suspended for three years. The fine is the heaviest imposed on a footballer in England, dwarfing the £8,500 Aston Villa's Paul McGrath was fined for newspaper comments about his previous club, Manchester United.

Vinny Jones (left): no stranger to trouble.

Wimbledon chairman Sam Hammam, whose initial reaction when he first heard about the offending video was to describe his wayward player as a "mosquito brain", felt the punishment was unduly harsh. He accused the FA of having double standards, citing some of the recent indiscretions of Paul Gascoigne, for example, which, he suggested, had been treated as innocent pranks.

The FA, however, felt otherwise about a video that attempts to portray the unsavoury aspects of the game, and which has been described as a manual on how to commit fouls. Jones, who pleaded guilty to bringing the game into disrepute, had offered an apology as soon as the furore erupted, and announced that he would be handing his fee — said to be £1,300 — to a charity. He'll need it now, however, to help pay his fine — unless the video's producers pay it for him.

The end of Magpies' overture

NEWCASTLE'S barnstorming start to the season finally came to an end on 24 October, when it was least expected, at home to Grimsby Town. So after 11 straight wins — only two away from equalling Reading's record start — Kevin Keegan's men have at last given some hope to the chasing pack, now "only" nine points or more behind.

Without the injured Kevin Sheedy and David Kelly, the Magpies appeared subdued, and lowly Grimsby won a thoroughly well-deserved victory with a 25-yard drive from Clive Mendonca, who had twice earlier hit the woodwork. If the Mariners continue to play like this, they will have no trouble staying in the First Division, while Newcastle's momentum towards the Premier League is unlikely to be affected by this first setback.

The tremendous interest generated by this remarkable run has paid off at the gate and helped to defray Keegan's salary.

Brave new world, familiar feeling

THE ENGLISH FOOTBALL season began on 15 August to a metaphorical fanfare of trumpets ushering in the new FA Premier League. At first glance, the nine-match programme appeared to suggest that they had reverted to the original idea of an 18-club "Super League". But that was forgetting the needs of BSkyB and its satellite dishes, which look like becoming a major influence on the scheduling of fixtures, with their live telecasts of regular Sunday afternoon and Monday evening fixtures. On Sundays, they would be competing with a regional First Division (old Second Division) match on ITV and a plum from the Italian Serie A on Channel Four.

With stadiums in the process of being converted to all-seaters, building work took the gloss off the historic opening. Arsenal's bright idea of covering their North Bank eyesore with a huge mural of spectators — already criticized for being ethnically unrepresentative — backfired on their team, who could not score at their hitherto favoured end, and the Premier League favourites were beaten 4–2 by Norwich after leading 2–0 at half-time.

Anyone looking for evidence of a brave new world on this first day would have noticed a difference in the play. But this was not due to the much-heralded Premier League, but to a fundamental change in the laws that came into practice this season, known familiarly as the "back-pass law". Framed to cut down on time-wasting, this revolutionary legislation made it an offence for a goalkeeper to handle the ball, on pain of an indirect free-kick, when it was deliberately passed to him by a team-mate, unless the ball was headed or chested. Some keepers soon showed a flair for this additional "sweeper" role with hefty kicks upfield, while others demonstrated how easy it was to get in a tangle when under pressure from an onrushing striker.

A "subdued" North Bank for Arsenal's 1992–93 opener, as the mural screening development work gets its first airing.

FOOTBALL FOCUS

- Norwich, who disputed the Premier League title for most of the season and led the table on several occasions, finished third despite conceding more goals than they scored (61–65). On 16 January, having played 24 matches, they found themselves in the unusual situation of being the leaders with a negative goal difference (35–36).

- AC Milan paid Torino a world record £13m for 23-year-old Italian international winger Gianluigi Lentini in July 1992.

- Leeds United enjoyed an incredible reprieve against Stuttgart in the first round of the European Cup, after fighting back from 3–0 down in the first leg to win 4–1 at Elland Road and going out — so they thought — on goal difference. Then it was found that the German champions had played four, instead of the permitted three, foreign-born players, and Leeds won a hastily arranged decider 2–1 in Barcelona. But they went out to Glasgow Rangers in the second round after two 2–1 defeats.

- Albion Rovers, bottom of Dvision Two in Scotland, used 44 players in their 39 league games.

Fergie woos Frenchman for scoring power

ALEX FERGUSON ended his long search for a new striker when he persuaded the popular French star Eric Cantona to join Manchester United from Leeds on 26 November. This sensational coup has not pleased Elland Road fans, who took the much-travelled Cantona, 26, to their hearts last season as he helped them win the title.

Leeds manager Howard Wilkinson felt the move was in the interests of all concerned, and that Cantona would stand a better chance of a regular first-team place with Manchester. The fee, believed to be in the region of £1.5 million, takes Ferguson's spending to over £18 million. Since pulling out of a close-season duel with Blackburn for Alan Shearer, who went to Ewood Park for £3.6 million, he paid Cambridge £1 million for Dion Dublin, who promptly broke a leg, and had a £3.5 million bid for Sheffield Wednesday's David Hirst turned down.

Manchester's lack of goals lately has been worrying, and it will be interesting to see how Cantona's flair and touch combines with the more explosive skills of Mark Hughes up front. There is another intriguing aspect of the move: how will the fiery Cantona settle at such a big club?

Gascoigne's ill wind blows nobody any good

PAUL GASCOIGNE'S tendency to play the fool in front of the television cameras has landed him in more trouble. The England midfielder incurred the wrath of an Italian member of parliament, who has called for him to be fined for belching into a microphone. Gascoigne was asked to comment on his exclusion from the Lazio team on 24 January, and his undignified response was broadcast on national television. Although the enraged MP, Giulio Maceratini, has a point when he says that a top sportsman who earns millions has a duty to set a better example to young people, it is difficult to take seriously any politician who complains about wind.

Lazio's Claudio Schlosa (No. 4) finds it doesn't pay to turn your back on Gazza.

Peter Shilton sent off for first time

PETER SHILTON was sent off for the first time in his career, in his 971st League game, after conceding a penalty with a "professional foul" in Plymouth's 2–0 Second Division defeat at Hull on 28 August. The Plymouth goalkeeper-manager, who is in his 42nd year, brought down Hull's Graeme Atkinson after 26 minutes, and received his marching orders from referee Paul Harrison.

Stand-in keeper Nicky Marker, a defender, saved the penalty, but Hull scored two late goals against Plymouth's 10 men to go top of the table.

Why do FIFA need a kick-in?

A MEETING OF the International Board, the game's law-making body, in February, gave FIFA permission to experiment with substituting a "kick-in" for the throw-in. The trials will take place in UEFA and FIFA junior tournaments later in the year. The idea — the brainchild of FIFA general secretary Sepp Blatter — is so flawed that it could only come from the muddle-headed confines of Zurich.

The hitherto ultra-conservative guardians of the game's laws have panicked since the welter of adverse criticism hit them following the 1990 World Cup, and have in recent years come up with all kinds of gimmicks to "improve" the game as a spectacle.

It is one thing to cut down on unnecessary time-wasting, but speeding the game up, which is one reason given for the kick-in, will not necessarily make for more entertaining football. There are many who believe that the game has become too fast as it is. And, anyway, why they think that a kick-in will be taken any quicker than a throw-in is a mystery. Swindon player-manager Glenn Hoddle, when he heard of the experiment, described it as a farce, and said he might as well pack the game in, and leave it to the 6ft 4in strikers and long-kicking merchants. If this hare-brained idea had come from anywhere but FIFA, it would surely have been kicked into touch by the International Board. The actual experiments will be unrepresentative, scheduled as they are for youth football. And, of course, there is the usual piece of nonsense written into the experimental law — as with the throw-in, a player can not be ruled offside from a kick-in. In other words, if the ball is near the touchline, it will be cheaper to foul an opponent than kick the ball into touch. Let's see how long it takes FIFA to spot that one.

Bobby Moore dies: a true hero of football

Bobby Moore: universally mourned.

WHEN BOBBY MOORE died on 24 February, just nine days after announcing to the world that he had cancer, not only the footballing world mourned, but all those whose hearts had been filled with pride when he held the World Cup aloft at Wembley in 1966, as captain of England, felt a great sense of loss. For Bobby Moore was more than a gifted footballer and an inspirational captain. He came to represent the ideals of a long ago age, when sportsmanship still had a place in the game.

It would be naive to think that these ideals were not crumbling long before Moore finished playing. But he was the epitome of the footballing hero, blessed with a wonderful temperament and an unquenchable will to win — but not if it meant compromising his principles of fair play. Three years running, he climbed the Wembley stairs as captain to receive a valued trophy — the FA Cup and European Cup-Winners' Cup with West Ham, then followed by the crowning glory of the World Cup.

Not for Moore the crunching tackle made with no respect for life and limb. He was unsurpassed as a reader of the game, and as No.6 to a stopper centre-half, he won the ball by anticipation. His distribution, especially his long passing, was the envy even of the midfield generals. Moore won more friends and admirers in the 1970 World Cup, and his duel with Brazil's Pele was as memorable as any goal. After he retired, he was never really a success as a manager or as a businessman. But he made an indelible impression on the game, as one of its true heroes. His death, at 51, leves the world a poorer place.

City beaten by Nayim hat-trick and shamed by crowd

THE FACT THAT Manchester City's Terry Phelan scored arguably the best goal of the season, albeit in a lost cause, when he ran through the entire Tottenham team, was lost in the havoc that ensued at Maine Road in the FA Cup quarter-final on 7 March. Ostensibly to celebrate this gem of a goal, which pulled City back to 2–4 down with three minutes left, the home fans poured from the new £6 million all-seater Umbro Stand onto the pitch in the forlorn hope of having the tie abandoned. Although there was no violence, it required 13 mounted police to clear the pitch so the game could be finished.

City fans were understandably disappointed that Spurs had overwhelmed them after Sheron had given them an early lead, and, thanks largely to a Nayim hat-trick, had put the result beyond doubt before full-back Phelan's piece of bravado. But there is no possible excuse for the sort of behaviour that has almost been eradicated inside grounds over the last few years, and City might well find themselves in trouble with the authorities.

Mounted police on the Maine Road pitch.

Adams banishes those 'donkey' jibes

TONY ADAMS, 26, whose England career seemed to have taken a nose-dive since those early days of much promise and potential as a future captain of his country, established himself as a defensive rock in England's heartening triumph over Turkey on 31 March. In a sinister atmosphere of violence and intimidation from the 50,000 crowd in Izmir, he stood firm at the back while goals from Platt and Gascoigne ensured England stayed on course for World Cup 94. Then, just four days later, he led Arsenal to victory over Spurs in the second FA Cup semi-final between the North London rivals held at Wembley in three years. And it must have given him immense satisfaction to avenge that bitter defeat in 1991, by heading the only goal of the game 11 minutes from time.

Arsenal fans have never lost faith in Adams, despite his off-field transgressions, and he has repaid them by leading the club to two Championships. Those unwarranted "donkey" jibes he has stoically suffered at grounds around the country appear pretty asinine themselves now.

The life of Brian

BRIAN CLOUGH, 58, said farewell to his adoring Nottingham Forest fans at the City Ground on 1 May. It was Forest's last home match, and it mattered little that Sheffield United beat them 2–0 and consigned them to relegation, after the most unsuccessful season of Mr Clough's long, colourful and hugely controversial career. And, true to form, it ended in controversy, too, as he announced his retirement amid persistent rumours, and issued libel writs against a Sunday newspaper and a club director over allegations of excessive drinking.

Despite Forest's lack-lustre performance, their biggest crowd of the season, 26,752, preferred to remember the many major honours this gifted eccentric had brought them. He arrived 18 years ago, after triumphs at Derby and tribulations with Leeds and Brighton, and put the name of Nottingham Forest on the football map again, not only in England but all over Europe. When his teams won, they did so with style, a brand of passing, on-the-floor football that became the hallmark of the teams he built and coached along with his partner, the late Peter Taylor. A showman, a maverick and an individualist, he was always at the centre of the great debate, the rallying cry when things went wrong on the international scene — "Clough for England!". Whether he would have been a success is another matter, and it is highly unlikely that the FA would have put up with his arrogance for long.

So the fans paid a last tribute to their hero. He'd taken them from the Second Division to the First, to League Cups, to the Championship and to double glory in Europe, and now he'd taken them down again. But what a trip it had been!

Brian Clough: the one and only.

Steve Morrow: pride before the fall.

Morrow sorrow — dropped after scoring winner

STEVE MORROW scored Arsenal's winning goal in their 2–1 victory over Sheffield Wednesday in the Coca-Cola (League) Cup at Wembley and then broke an arm in a freak accident during the celebrations at the end of the game. Morrow, 22, an Irish international full-back, but unable to establish a place in the Arsenal first team, came into the midfield because of injuries, and did an excellent marking job on Sheridan in the final. The goal, his first for the club, came after 68 minutes, when Carlton Palmer failed to clear a Merson cross and Morrow appeared out of nowhere to crash the ball past Woods.

Wednesday had made an encouraging start when John Harkes, who two years ago became the first American to play at Wembley, became the first American to score there, after only nine minutes, slamming the ball home after a cross from King was not properly cleared. Waddle failed to justify the media and public protest mounted when he was excluded from the England squad during the week, and it was Arsenal's Merson who played the star role. Always a danger when he ran at the Wednesday defence, he equalized with a swerving volley from outside the box that had Woods stretching in vain.

At the final whistle, Tony Adams hoisted Morrow onto his shoulders. He fell awkwardly as his skipper let him down, and was in obvious agony. He was given oxygen and a pain-killing injection before being carried off, while his subdued team-mates collected their medals and the sorrowful Adams hoisted the Cup. Sheffield will have their chance of revenge when the two sides meet again in the FA Cup final in May, but Morrow will not be facing them.

Zambian team killed in air crash

ALL BUT FOUR members of the Zambian football squad were killed on 28 April, when the aircraft taking them to a World Cup qualifying match against Senegal crashed into the sea after taking off from Libreville, Gabon, following a refuelling stop. The 30 people on board all died. Four squad members who play for European clubs escaped — they were to join the party in Dakar. Early signs are that Zambia are determined to carry on and try to qualify for the World Cup finals for the first time.

'Excuse me, Mr Ferguson, you are champions'

ALEX FERGUSON had taken nearly seven years to put Manchester United back on top of English football, to guide them to their first League Championship since 1967. And when the great moment arrived, on 2 May, he was not in the dugout urging his men on and leaping up at the final whistle. He was on the golf course, oblivious to the progress of Aston Villa, who had fought for the title tooth and nail with United over the last few weeks and were the only side now that could prevent a Manchester triumph. He was putting on the last green when a fellow member approached, with the words: "Excuse me, Mr Ferguson, you are the champions. Oldham have won at Aston Villa."

The following evening saw the biggest party in the history of modern British soccer, as United's team captain Steve Bruce and club captain Bryan Robson collected the new Premier League trophy in front off 40,000 delirious fans at Old Trafford and then celebrated by beating Blackburn 3–1. It was a night of high emotion, and Sir Matt Busby, the last manager to taste such success, was there to share the glory. In between, five managers — Wilf McGuinness, Frank O'Farrell, Tommy Docherty, Dave Sexton and Ron Atkinson — have tried and failed to fill the shoes of Sir Matt, who built three great United sides. Mr Atkinson, now in charge of Villa, did his best to spoil Alex Ferguson's season. And at one stage, it looked as if United might repeat last year's attack of spring nerves, when they blew their chances in one fateful week, and Mr Ferguson was desolate. But he kept faith with his team — and his own belief in them — added a touch of French spice during the season to pep them up, and won the title with style and panache commensurate with the club's best traditions.

Bruce and Robson with the new Premier League trophy.

It was entirely appropriate that Bryan Robson, again plagued with injury, played enough matches to earn a Championship medal. He has been a wonderful servant to the club. For once he did not play a leading role, but this season Paul Ince has filled his shoes admirably, for England as well as United. The side, which gave a joyous demonstration of their individual and collective skills against Blackburn for their celebrating faithful fans, was: Schmeichel, Parker, Irwin, Bruce, Sharpe (Robson), Pallister, Cantona, Ince, McClair (Kanchelskis), Hughes, Giggs — the "class of 93".

United's fourth great side since the war contains names that can be mentioned in the same breath as such mighty icons of the past as Best, Charlton, Law and Edwards. Eric Cantona — Ferguson's master-stroke, when he signed him from Leeds in November — became the first player to win Championship medals with different clubs in successive seasons. And Mr Ferguson, having had considerable success with Aberdeen, became the first manager to win League titles north and south of the border. With the precocious young talents of Lee Sharpe and Welsh genius Ryan Giggs flowering into maturity, Mr Ferguson can look forward to further triumphs in seasons to come.

Champion style: Ryan Giggs scoring for United against Southampton in February.

Linighan leaves it late

Ian Wright (left) puts Arsenal ahead in the replay.

ANDY LINIGHAN, Arsenal's stopper, broke the hearts of Sheffield Wednesday fans at Wembley on Thursday, 20 May, when he headed Arsenal's winner a minute before the end of extra time in their FA Cup final replay. But he won the undying gratitude of the majority of neutral fans who detest the penalty shoot-out, which would have been the method used to decide the winners for the first time ever in an FA Cup final.

It was not a classic final, only marginally better than Saturday's grinding bore when Wednesday's Hirst equalized a first-half goal by Wright. Linighan had made that Arsenal goal, heading a Davis free-kick back across goal for Wright, nursing a broken toe, to head in. And it was the quicksilver Wright who gave Arsenal a 35th-minute lead in the replay, running on to an Alan Smith flick to beat Woods and score his 10th goal of Arsenal's Cup campaign — before having to be substituted again.

In the second half, however, as Wednesday wrested control from Arsenal, Waddle equalized in the 68th minute and Bright missed a great chance to put them in front three minutes later. He did not, however, miss Linighan's face with his elbow in what was one of many unsavoury clashes that soured the game.

Linighan, for two years a £1.3 million misfit at Highbury, jeered by the fans, had forced his way into the side earlier in the season when Bould was injured. His last-minute, point-blank header from Merson's corner not only won Arsenal a place in next season's Cup-Winners' Cup, but it put his former club Norwich in the UEFA Cup.

Historically, Arsenal, playing in their record 12th FA Cup final, recorded their sixth win and became the first club to pull off the FA Cup/League Cup double in one season. George Graham completed a unique feat of winning the three major English domestic honours as both player and manager. In seven years at Highbury, he has built a formidable, winning team. His next ambition must be to produce a team that everyone can love.

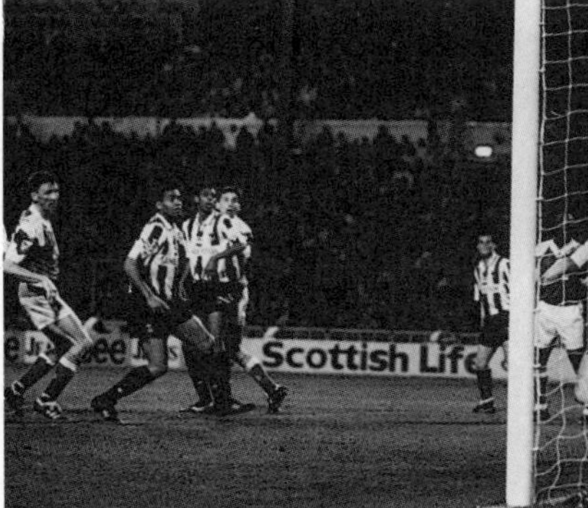

The battered Linighan (far left) becomes Arsenal's hero with a towering last-minute header.

Souness stays on at Anfield

LIVERPOOL CREATED a sensation at the end of the season by not sacking their manager, Graeme Souness. Director Tony Ensor, presumably the only member of the Anfield board not to go along with what was a startling and mysterious U-turn, resigned when the decision to keep their controversial manager was announced. The team, which was never in the running for the League title, finished sixth in the table and did not qualify for Europe — failure for a club that has dominated English football for so long. A subdued Souness put the rumours of his imminent dismissal down to Press speculation, and insisted that the team he took over was never going to win anything. He was not dissatisfied with the way rebuilding was proceeding. Of more concern to the directors, however, must be Liverpool's disciplinary record, as six players were sent off during the season. They must surely fear that Souness is hardly the man to reverse this disturbing trend.

Venables gets the sack as Sugar turns sour

WHILE ARSENAL were winning the FA Cup at Wembley, another soccer drama was unfolding on the other side of North London, at White Hart Lane, where Spurs chief Terry Venables was once more desperately trying to get backing to buy out the current major shareholder, Alan Sugar. Two years ago, it was electronics tycoon Sugar who came to Venables's aid when the club looked like going under or being taken over by Robert Maxwell. Now Sugar was himself cast in the role of villain, having sensationally, and completely out of the blue, sacked Mr Venables as chief executive of Spurs on 14 May. The following day, Mr Venables was temporarily reinstated by a High Court order, and battle commenced.

As a player, Venables helped Spurs to win the FA Cup in 1967, then completed a double by managing the club to a repeat performance in 1991. The immediate reaction of players and fans to the dismissal of such a popular figure was one of complete shock. Venables, hailed as the club's saviour, is regarded as "Mr Tottenham", and it was hard to find an ally for Mr Sugar inside the club — apart, that is, from the three directors who voted Mr Venables off the board.

Mr Sugar has been slow to assert that he had no quarrels with the chief executive's handling of the footballing side, and that the dispute was about the interference of Mr Venables and his advisers in financial matters. But the fans, the players and the club's administrative staff have made it only too clear that the removal of a man who exerts such a profound influence at every level of Tottenham's operations could well bring the whole edifice crashing down.

FINAL SCORE

Football League
Premier Division: Manchester United
Top scorer: Teddy Sheringham (Nottingham Forest 1, Tottenham Hotspur 21) 22
Division 1: Newcastle United
Division 2: Stoke City
Division 3: Cardiff City
Footballer of the Year: Chris Waddle (Sheffield Wednesday)

FA Cup Final

Arsenal	1	Sheffield Wed	1
(after extra time)			
Replay: Arsenal	2	Sheffield Wed	1
(after extra time)			

League Cup Final

Arsenal	2	Sheffield Wed	1

Scottish League
Premier Division: Rangers
Top scorer: Ally McCoist (Rangers) 34
Division 1: Raith Rovers
Division 2: Clyde
Footballer of the Year: Andy Goram (Rangers)

Scottish FA Cup Final

Rangers	2	Aberdeen	1

Scottish League Cup Final

Rangers	2	Aberdeen	1
(after extra time)			

European Cup Final

Olympique Marseille	1	AC Milan	0

Cup-Winners' Cup Final

Parma	3	Royal Antwerp	1

UEFA Cup Final
Juventus beat Borussia Dortmund 3–1, 3–0

European Footballer of the Year 1992
Marco van Basten (MAC Milan & Holland)

Leading European Scorer (Golden Boot)
Award discontinued

England humbled by USA in another Taylor shambles

IT COULDN'T HAPPEN again – but it did. The nightmare of England's humiliating World Cup defeat in Belo Horizonte in 1950 at the hands of the United States was relived in Foxboro, Massachusetts, where Graham Taylor's "team", still smarting from their disastrous display in Oslo, succumbed 2–0 to the unrated 1994 World Cup hosts in the US '93 Cup.

The beleaguered England manager, lifted earlier by the news of Norway's draw in Rotterdam, fielded a weakened side against the Americans, with Nigel Clough replacing the absent Paul Gascoigne. He saw his new central-defence partnership of Gary Pallister and Carlton Palmer embarrassed by the skill and vision of Coventry's Roy Wegerle, but it still came as a shock when England went a goal down two minutes before half-time. It was scored with a header by Thomas Dooley, the German-born Kaiserslautern striker who had not visited the USA until last year.

England's humiliation was completed midway through the second half when the gangling, red-bearded Alexi Lalas, on as substitute for the injured Dooley, headed home a corner. US keeper Tony Meola made two brilliant saves when Ian Wright broke through to deny England even a consolation goal. The defeat has left England in utter disarray, with public and press baying for Taylor's resignation.

Roy Wegerle shows a clean pair of heels to David Batty.

SOCCER SOUNDBITES

"I don't think there is a need for a new manager."

PETER SWALES,
chairman of the FA's international committee.

Sugar–Venables saga unearths sensational allegations

THE RUNNING BATTLE between Spurs chairman Alan Sugar and former chief executive Terry Venables for control of the club reached the High Court on 10 June with 2,500 pages of sworn statements. Among these were the sensational allegations by Mr Sugar of corrupt practices he found at the club and in football, including under-the-counter payments to managers of other clubs to ease through big transfer deals.

One incident, in particular, was highlighted, namely a "bung", as it is called, to Nottingham Forest manager Brian Clough when his striker Teddy Sheringham moved to Spurs for £2.1 million. This allegation – quickly denied by Mr Clough – was in the form of a sworn affidavit by Mr Sugar, and mentioned a considerable cash payment said to have been handed over at a secret meeting in a motorway service station.

Mr Sugar, who also heads the computer and electronics company Amstrad, is contesting an injunction to prevent him removing Mr Venables from the Tottenham board. He received a hostile reception from Spurs fans outside and inside the court. Mr Venables, although enjoying the support of a section of the club's fans, is opposed by the majority of directors.

Superficially, it is a case of two powerful personalities competing for control of a club. But as allegations unfold of the seamier side of football, it is the game that is really on trial.

Tottenham supporters show their support for Venables.

Double-Dutch misery for England

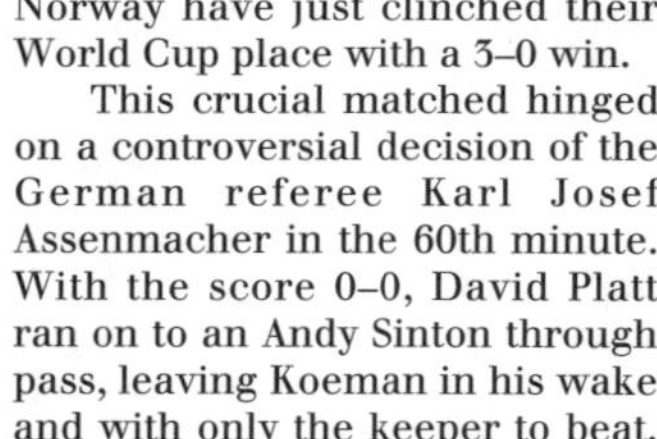

ENGLAND'S American dream was dashed at Rotterdam on 13 October when Holland beat them 2–0 and left them requiring a minor miracle next month to qualify – a seven-goal win in Bologna over San Marino plus a Dutch defeat in Poland, where Norway have just clinched their World Cup place with a 3–0 win.

This crucial matched hinged on a controversial decision of the German referee Karl Josef Assenmacher in the 60th minute. With the score 0–0, David Platt ran on to an Andy Sinton through pass, leaving Koeman in his wake and with only the keeper to beat. But Koeman desperately pulled him back on the edge of the box. It was a blatant red-card offence, as Koeman later himself admitted, but the referee gave only a free-kick. Tony Dorigo, who had hit a post with a free-kick in the first half, took it, but had his shot charged down. This was particularly galling for England and her supporters when exactly the same thing happened at the other end, but the referee ordered the kick to be retaken, booked Paul Ince for arguing and – irony of ironies – Koeman chipped the wall to beat David Seaman and put Holland ahead.

Platt is fouled by Koeman.

For all Graham Taylor's bleating afterwards, it must be said that Frank Rijkaard had a perfectly good goal for Holland disallowed in the first half for offside. Taylor, whose job was well and truly on the line, had to be cautioned by a FIFA official for encroaching too near the pitch. Dennis Bergkamp clinched it for Holland with a low shot after 70 minutes, and when Paul Merson hit a post with another free-kick, it was typical of England's luck on the night.

To add to England's woe, some 1,400 football fans were arrested before the game, most of them reported to be English, although it appeared that the Dutch police overreacted, detaining 600 of them for not having tickets.

Ooh ah, off you go – Eric Cantona sent off as United go out of Europe

GALATASARAY, thanks to their remarkable 3–3 draw at Old Trafford a fortnight ago, eliminated Manchester United from the European Cup when they held the English Champions to a goalless draw in Istanbul. And to complete United's night of misery, French star Eric Cantona was sent off in the mayhem that followed the final whistle.

It was an expensive defeat for the English champions, who looked to have booked their place in the lucrative league phase of the competition when they took that 2–0 lead against the unfancied Turks after only 13 minutes of their home leg. In a night of frustration, Cantona complained throughout about Galatasaray's time-wasting tactics, at one stage causing an ugly scene on the running track when he went to retrieve the ball from the home bench. At the final whistle, after shaking match referee Kurt Rothlisberger by the hand, he gestured and said something to the Swiss French-teacher that had him reaching for the red card.

United were lucky to go in level at half-time, and after the interval their play became more ragged as desperation set in. Cantona's reactions and his inability to control his temper incited an already hostile and hysterical crowd, and at the end both he and Bryan Robson were struck by police in the players' tunnel. The banners proclaiming "Welcome to Hell" on United's arrival were indeed prophetic.

Eric Cantona (second right) is given his marching orders.

England out – misery against San Marino

ENGLAND'S elimination from the 1994 World Cup was confirmed on a dismal night in Bologna in front of the smallest crowd ever to watch an England match – the 2,378 who turned up to see them face the part-timers of San Marino in a last, desperate attempt to score the seven goals that might have saved them. They scored the seven all right, but only after San Marino had scored what is believed to be the fastest ever goal in a competitive international.

Less than 10 seconds had elapsed when computer clerk Davide Gualtieri latched on to a pathetic Stuart Pearce back-pass to give the tournament's minnows a sensational lead. It took England 22 minutes to recover their composure and equalize through Paul Ince, and, with Ian Wright hitting four, they went on to rack up seven. It was not quite the seven-goal victory they needed if Holland were to lose by a goal in Poland. But in the event it was academic, because the Dutch side won 3–1 and took the second qualifying place in the group, Norway having already gone through.

This was only San Marino's second goal in the tournament, their other coming against Turkey last October, and in the end they conceded 46 in their 10 matches. England have reached their lowest ebb since 1977, when they last failed to qualify for the World Cup finals. The thousand England fans in Bologna were predictably chanting for Graham Taylor's head, and San Marino almost embarrassed England further before Wright scored the seventh goal, when Bacciocchi hit an upright.

SOCCER SOUNDBITES

"My foul was outside the area, but I expected to see the red card."

RONALD KOEMAN,
the Dutch captain, who scored Holland's opener a few minutes after the referee failed to send him off for bringing down David Platt in a clear goalscoring position.

Hounded Taylor steps down at last

ENGLAND MANAGER Graham Taylor finally resigned from the job a week after England's failure to qualify for the 1994 World Cup. It was perhaps one of the more predictable acts of a man who has baffled the press, the public and even his own players with his team selection and tactics.

It was evident after his handling of England in Sweden last year that Taylor was not the man for the job. But no one should have had to endure the vilification Taylor has suffered from sections of the popular press in a puerile campaign that breached all principles of reputable journalism. It was a campaign that possibly backfired, because it precluded sensible debate and made it almost impossible for the FA to remove him without seemingly capitulating to the rabble.

Like his predecessor Bobby Robson, Taylor was allowed to go on too long. Also like Robson, Taylor was an outstanding club manager who failed to reproduce his success at the highest level. This in part was due to lack of vision, but most England managers have been hamstrung by a governing body still run by club chairmen who sometimes do not appear to regard the interests of the national side as paramount, and who must take their share of the blame for England's fate.

Creator of the Busby Babes dies, aged 84

SIR MATT BUSBY, one of the outstanding figures in post-war British football, died in hospital at Cheadle on 20 January after a long illness. He was a gentle Scot who became the father figure of English football and one of the greatest managers in its history.

During an illustrious career, Sir Matt achieved success first as a player, a wing-half with Manchester City and Liverpool, winning a single cap for Scotland in 1936, and after the war as a manager, the far-seeing architect of three outstanding Manchester United sides. Under Busby, United, without a major trophy since before the First World War, soon became one of England's leading clubs.

As his ageing side broke up, he replaced them with the "Busby Babes", potentially the greatest club side of all time before they were decimated in the Munich Air Disaster of 1958. Busby was haunted regularly by memories of this tragedy, in which he came so close to death himself. But he not only recovered his health, he was able to draw on infinite resources of courage and determination to build yet another great team, one that was to become, in 1968, the first English side to win the European Cup. He was knighted shortly after this, became a director of United in 1971, and had been president of the club since 1980.

But Busby's influence in football was not just as the creator of a great club. He led English club football into Europe when the rest were prevaricating, and he captured the imagination of soccer fans all over the world with the style of his teams.

Busby was a family man, and he was a paternalist, too, in the tough world of football. He always cared, he always forgave. He earned loyalty and love from all who worked with and for him. And he won the respect and admiration from everyone he came in contact with. Above all, he was a humble man, a symbol of sport on its highest plane.

As tearful fans, some of them children, laid flowers outside Old Trafford and stood silently in the Manchester drizzle, tributes to Sir Matt poured in. Bobby Charlton, however, himself a Munich survivor and one of the most famous of the Babes, was too distraught to say anything at this time.

SOCCER SOUNDBITES

"Winning isn't the test of real achievement. There should be no conceit in victory and no despair in defeat."

SIR MATT BUSBY

Sir Matt's hearse stops outside Old Trafford for two minutes' silence.

Venables in, Souness out

Terry Venables appointed as England's new coach.

AS ENGLAND announced their new supremo, or "coach" as Terry Venables will be called, another controversial character, Graeme Souness, stepped down from what has become the hottest seat in English club football, manager of the declining Liverpool side. While Venables has been charged, at least until the 1996 European Championships, with restoring the national side to its former glory (a heady triumph some 30 years earlier), Souness departed because he failed to restore Liverpool to the high plane they occupied until relatively recently.

Venables was not only the people's choice, but the professionals' choice, and he owes his selection largely to the fact that the FA employed ex-pro Jimmy Armfield to make soundings within the game. Venables, despite his extra-curricular activities, emerged as the outstanding candidate. It was clear at the press conference on the Wembley pitch, however, that both sides have negotiated a get-out clause in the event of unforeseen circumstances.

The new coach knows that he will inherit many of the frustrations that have plagued his predecessors, not least the fact that international football too often comes second to the domestic game. It will be fascinating to see not only how he goes about rebuilding the England side, but how he faces up to the enigma of the FA, who give the impression of being 100 per cent in favour of progress yet at the same time are reluctant to change their system.

The formal announcement of Souness's departure from Anfield was made by Liverpool chairman David Moores, who last May saved him from dismissal when there was widespread expectancy that a change of management was imminent. While Souness could be forgiven his occasional lapses, in the end it was his lack of success that brought his downfall. He has reached an agreement with the club over the unexpired 27-month portion of his £1.25 million five-year contract.

Roy Evans, promoted to assistant manager at the end of last season, will take charge until a successor is appointed.

SOCCER SOUNDBITES

"I want to play good football but not fantasy football (playing well and losing). We must have a system that the players understand. It's up to me to make it as simple as possible."

TERRY VENABLES

"Liverpool Football Club is all about winning things and being a source of pride to our fans. It has no other purpose."

DAVID MOORES,
Liverpool chairman.

Villa put paid to United's dream of treble

ASTON VILLA destroyed Manchester United's dream of the domestic treble at Wembley on Sunday 27 March when they beat the League leaders and FA Cup semi-finalists 3–1 in the Coca-Cola Cup final. It was a thoroughly deserved victory in which Villa out-thought and outplayed United to clinch a place in next season's UEFA Cup. To add to United's troubles, Andrei Kanchelskis became their fourth player to be sent off in five games and will miss the FA Cup semi-final.

Steve Staunton engages in a touch-line chase with Roy Keane.

The win was particularly sweet for Villa manager Ron Atkinson, sacked by United in 1986, who enjoyed a repeat of his triumph three years ago when he led Sheffield Wednesday to victory over his former club in a League Cup final. His tactics worked to perfection. With Dean Saunders as a lone striker, his five-man midfield swamped United. The masterstroke was using striker Dalian Atkinson in an unfamiliar position on the right of midfield, and he and Tony Daley on the other side gave full-backs Earl Barrett and Steve Staunton superb protection against deadly wingers Ryan Giggs, who was substituted, and Kanchelskis.

Villa took the lead in the 25th minute through Atkinson, who beat Les Sealey, deputizing for the suspended Peter Schmeichel, from 10 yards after good work by Townsend and Saunders. The game turned on a 70th-minute tackle by man-of-the-match Kevin Richardson, Villa's captain, which robbed Lee Sharpe of an almost certain goal. Five minutes later Saunders touched in a Richardson free-kick at the near post to put Villa two up.

Mark Hughes brought United back into the match with a goal seven minutes from time. But Kanchelskis handled a goal-bound Atkinson effort on the line. The referee had no choice but to send the Russian off, and Saunders converted the penalty to clinch the trophy for Villa.

United are now only three points ahead of Blackburn in the Premiership and face Oldham in the FA Cup semi-final in a fortnight without three key players – Andrei Kanchelskis, Eric Cantona and Roy Keane.

Arsenal's triumph a boost for English pride

A FLASH OF brilliance by veteran striker Alan Smith in the 20th minute was enough to give underdogs Arsenal victory over holders Parma in the Cup-Winners' Cup final in Copenhagen on 4 May. Without four key players, including the suspended Ian Wright, they showed that the traditional virtues of the English domestic game are still good enough to beat Europe's elite. And, as well as increasing the quota for English clubs in European competition next season, their victory gives England a much needed boost after the disappointment of elimination from the World Cup.

This is not the first time they have triumphed without the inspirational Wright, their leading scorer. In the second round, back in November, they went to Belgium, albeit with a 3–0 lead, and sensationally beat Standard Liege 7–0 at a time when they had only three goals in six Premiership away games to their credit.

Without the injured John Jensen and David Hillier, George Graham had no qualms about playing the young Ian Selley and Steve Morrow in central midfield, and they were both outstanding. Morrow, the Irish international full-back who seems to have been around for ages yet is still only 23, is best remembered for breaking his arm celebrating Arsenal's Coca-Cola Cup win last year (more so than scoring the winner). In Copenhagen he played a key role in subduing the small Gianfranco Zola, a pivotal figure in Parma's success, and typified Arsenal's expertise in nullifying the opposition's strengths.

Smith, as always relentlessly competitive but scrupulously fair, led his line in his usual unselfish way, winning particular praise from his manager for his overall performance – and his goal was a bit special, too. Lorenzo Minotti, the Parma captain, attempted to bicycle-kick the ball clear, but it fell to Smith, who chested it down and, with two opponents converging on him, hit a sweet left-foot volley in-off the near post from the edge of the box.

Parma had no one to compare with Arsenal captain Tony Adams, who has matured into one of the most effective and inspirational defenders in Europe, while his partner Steve Bould was as valuable on the night. Apart from a couple of early efforts, one of which hit a post, Tomas Brolin – the Swede who made Graham Taylor a turnip in 1992 – was ineffective. And the dangerous Colombian Faustino Asprilla was given little chance to shine.

Arsenal, although having less of the play, made the more clear-cut chances. David Seaman, in Arsenal's goal, needed pain-killing injections before the start, but was never really tested – a tribute to Graham's tactics and to his team's ability to carry them out. With six major trophies in his eight seasons at Highbury, Graham has established himself as one of the finest managers in the history of English football.

SOCCER SOUNDBITES

"Arsenal were the better side. They showed how to control our system of play, and to me they are the least typical English team I have seen."

NEVIO SCALA,
Parma coach

Steve Morrow is safely at the back as Arsenal celebrate.

Manchester United secure double: Chelsea capitulate after disputed penalty

Eddie Newton brings down Dennis Irwin.

MANCHESTER UNITED, who retained their Premiership title 12 days earlier when Blackburn finally cracked, beat Chelsea 4–0 at Wembley on 14 May to win the FA Cup and become only the fourth club this century to complete the double - after Spurs (1961), Arsenal (1971) and Liverpool (1986).

It wasn't the classic Cup final everyone hoped for, nor was it by any means as one-sided as the score suggests, United's first two goals coming from penalties. Chelsea, who had inflicted United's only League defeat at Old Trafford as well as one of their three away defeats during their Premiership campaign, both by 1–0 with the goal scored each time by Gavin Peacock, were desperately unlucky to go in at the interval without at least a goal lead. They had the only real goal attempts of the half – four of them – the last of which came after 25 minutes when Peacock picked up a poor Pallister clearance and hit a dipping 20-yard volley over Schmeichel's head but on to the cross-bar and back into play.

United began to press more at the start of the second half, although still without looking dangerous. Suddenly, on the hour, it all changed, and within nine minutes they were three up and the game was over. But it was Chelsea who handed the match to the champions rather than United taking charge.

First, Eddie Newton made an unnecessary late tackle on Dennis Irwin in the box – a clear penalty, and Cantona stroked the ball low to the right, sending Kharine the wrong way.

Five minutes later came the controversial second penalty. David Elleray, whose firm refereeing – he had booked Chelsea defender Erland Johnsen in the second minute, United captain Steve Bruce in the 18th – could not be faulted up to this point, had a difficult decision to make. Sinclair misjudged a diagonal through-ball from Hughes and had to bring down Kanchelskis. Elleray was in a good position to judge that deliberate unfair contact had been made, but should have consulted his linesman, for TV replays showed it occurred outside the box. In any event, he should have sent Sinclair off, as the Russian winger was clear with only the keeper to beat. Perhaps he felt that by awarding a penalty he would get himself off this undesirable hook. Anyway, Cantona produced a carbon copy spot-kick and justice was done.

Chelsea player-manager Glenn Hoddle brought himself on to calm things down, but it was too late. His young, inexperienced side had started chasing the game after the first penalty and were playing right into United's hands. A slip by Sinclair gave Hughes the ball and the Welsh striker clinically moved into the box and placed the ball past Kharine.

The rest of the play was academic. Cantona missed a sitter immediately after the third goal, and in injury time Paul Ince took the ball round the Chelsea keeper and unselfishly put a fourth goal on a plate for substitute McClair.

Manchester United have proved themselves outstandingly the best team in the country, not only by their magnificent double, which was so nearly an unprecedented treble, but also with the heights their football has reached so many times during the season. But at Wembley Chelsea exposed tactical shortcomings that will have to be corrected if United are to conquer Europe.

Derby players attacked as fans invade pitch

DISGRACEFUL SCENES of crowd violence at the New Den, in which visiting Derby players were assaulted, may lead to Millwall having their ground closed again. The second leg of the First Division play-off was halted twice because of invading spectators, in the first half (for 19 minutes) because of an apparent problem with tickets, but in the second (13 minutes) as a result of a concerted effort to cause trouble. Millwall, who had their old ground closed four times in the past, must now fear receiving similar punishment.

Derby scored their second goal to go 4–0 up on aggregate after 22 minutes, but this prompted fighting in the east stand, and some 10 minutes later some fans moved on to the pitch as they fought with police. A few people from the west stand then ran on, and referee Brian Hill took the players off. Derby scored again on the resumption.

The crowd trouble persisted after the regular interval, and the referee had to take the players off again 15 minutes from the end. About 50 people ran on to the field and Derby keeper Martin Taylor was knocked to the ground. Their defender Paul Williams had to body-swerve attempts to obstruct him. He had received racist taunts throughout the game, and he and their other black player Gary Charles were substituted three minutes before the end for their own safety – a sad reminder of the hooliganism that once dogged English football.

FOOTBALL FOCUS

- On 16 October, in a Division Three match at Hereford, Colchester became the first League club to have both keepers sent off – John Keeley and Nathan Munson – for "professional fouls". They lost 5–0.

- In July, Rangers broke the British transfer record with £4m for Duncan Ferguson from Dundee United, and Manchester United paid Forest an English record £3.75m for Roy Keane. Blackburn Rovers signed Tim Flowers from Southampton in early November for £2m, a world record for a keeper.

- Non-League Kidderminster Harriers won 2–1 at Birmingham (Division One) in the third round of the FA Cup, then beat Preston (Division Three) 1–0 in the fourth round, before losing 1–0 to Premier side West Ham in the fifth round. They finished top of the GM Vauxhall Conference but, because they had not brought their ground up to the required standards by the deadline of 31 December, they were denied entry to the League, and Division Three bottom club Northampton were reprieved.

- Barry Town beat 22-times winners Cardiff 2–1 in the final of the Welsh Cup to qualify for the European Cup-Winners' Cup.

- Last year's European Cup winners Olympic Marseille were rocked by a bribery scandal involving an end-of-season (1992–93) league fixture with Valenciennes. Repercussions were still being felt at the end of this season, by which time Marseille had been stripped of the French title, expelled from this season's European Cup and lost the right to contest the Super Cup and Toyota Cup, relegated to the 2nd Division for 1994–95 and banned from signing new players. Their chairman Bernard Tapie, business tycoon and former government minister, was bailed on charges of corruption and interference with witnesses, and ordered to give up ownership of the club. General manager Jean-Pierre Bernes was banned from football for life, and players Eydelie (Marseille) and Robert and Burruchaga (Valenciennes) were banned until 1996.

- Tottenham Hotspur were hit by punishments unprecedented in English football for breaking League rules in the 1980s with illegal loans to players. The north London club were barred from the 1994–95 FA Cup, given a 6-point penalty in the 1994–95 Premiership and fined a record £1.5 million.

Milan masters win European Cup

AC MILAN gave notice to European Champions Cup aspirants such as Manchester United that it will take something special to prise their hands from a trophy they have won in devastating fashion with a 4–0 victory over Barcelona in Athens. Italian champions this season for the third time in succession, they were, however, underdogs as they took on Barcelona without their suspended key defenders Baresi and Costacurta.

Yet instead of sitting back and trying to catch the Spanish champions on the break, as might have been expected, Milan proceeded to take them apart with a magnificent display of positive, attacking football that was a delight to watch. And at the same time, they defended so well that their keeper was hardly tested by the much-vaunted Barcelona strikers, the Bulgarian Hristo Stoichkov and the Brazilian Romario, or anyone else for that matter.

Daniele Massaro opened the scoring midway through the first half after the elusive Dejan Savicevic had broken clear on the right and closed in on goal. The former Yugoslav star popped the ball across for the unmarked Massaro to squeeze in at the far post. The second goal, in first-half stoppage time, came as the climax to a 14-pass movement, including the throw-out by Rossi, which finished with Donadoni breaking down the left and cutting the ball back from the bye-line for Massaro to drive in from 15 yards.

If Barcelona coach Johan Cruyff harboured any thoughts of a comeback, they were killed off two minutes after the break, when Savicevic dispossessed Nadal near the touchline on the right and struck an exquisite volley with the inside of his left foot from the edge of the box, over Zubizarreta into the far corner of the net. Ten minutes later man-of-the-match Savicevic hit a post after a quickly taken free-kick, but the influential midfielder Marcel Desailly, on the winning side also last year with Marseille, then powered his way through and curled the ball past the hapless Barcelona keeper.

Milan played out the last half-hour without extending themselves, and indeed Savicevic missed a fine chance to make it 5–0 near the end after a cross from the bye-line by Donadoni.

It was Milan's third European Cup in six years, their fifth in all, and with Ruud Gullit returning next year, they will certainly take some stopping.

Marcel Desailly.

FINAL SCORE

Football League
Premier Division: Manchester United
Top scorer: Andy Cole (Newcastle United) 34
Division 1: Crystal Palace
Division 2: Reading
Division 3: Shrewsbury Town
Footballer of the Year: Alan Shearer (Blackburn Rovers)

FA Cup Final

Manchester Utd	4	Chelsea	0

League Cup Final

Aston Villa	3	Manchester Utd	1

Scottish League
Premier Division: Rangers
Top scorer: Mark Hateley (Rangers) 24
Division 1: Falkirk
Division 2: Stranraer
Footballer of the Year: Mark Hateley (Rangers)

Scottish FA Cup Final

Dundee Utd	1	Rangers	0

Scottish League Cup Final

Rangers	2	Hibernian	1

European Cup Final

AC Milan	4	Barcelona	0

Cup-Winners' Cup Final

Arsenal	1	Parma	0

UEFA Cup Final
Inter-Milan beat Salzburg 1–0, 1–0

European Footballer of the Year 1993
Roberto Baggio (Juventus & Italy)

Dundee United beat 'jinx' to win Scottish Cup

DUNDEE UNITED defied bookmakers' odds of 9–2 against them as well as their 20-year-old jinx – they had been losing finalists six times since 1974 – to beat Rangers 1–0 at Hampden and win the Scottish FA Cup for the first time in their history. The goal was scored by Craig Brewster two minutes after the interval and was the result of a terrible defensive blunder. But against a Rangers side attempting to achieve an unprecedented back-to-back domestic treble, they were worthy winners.

Great credit must go to Ivan Golac, in his first season as manager, whose bold policy of playing three in attack paid off. The endless harassing of this trio – Brewster, Christian Dailly and Andy McLaren – never allowed Rangers to settle and was, indeed, responsible for the goal. Dave McPherson fatally played the ball back to Ally Maxwell, whose attempted clearance was blocked by Dailly and cannoned back off the keeper again. Dailly then took the ball round him and, from the narrowest of angles, rolled it against the far post for the alert Brewster to tap in.

The United fans were thrilled by the pace and adventure of their side, but Rangers were always in the game. Their greatest effort came late on, when Stuart McCall made a magnificent run down the left, beating man after man with his power and skill before pulling the ball back, only for Van de Kamp to make an astonishing save from Mikhailichenko's six-yard shot on the turn. It was clear, then, that Dundee United's name was on the Cup at last.

Rangers' McPherson (left) and United's Brewster in action .

The best team won

Despite a goalless final, this was a successful World Cup, well organized by the Americans, who justified FIFA's faith in them. It was blessed with record crowds (average 68,592), impeccably behaved, and played for the most part in the best of spirits. Television schedules meant that many matches were played in conditions of intense heat and humidity, however, but FIFA's new law interpretations had the desired effect of producing open, attacking play and allowing skill to flourish.

Brazil's captain Dunga celebrates victory in time-honoured fashion.

THE FORMAT for the finals was retained with the exception that, in the first-round groups, a win would be worth three points instead of two. FIFA, still not recovered from the panic that beset them after the much-criticized 1990 finals in Italy, introduced a number of late instructions to referees for interpreting the laws. They were brought in with good intentions, to make the game more attractive and increase goal-scoring. For the most part they worked well, although there was some confusion and a few referees were over-zealous with their red and yellow cards.

The two most contentious rulings on interpretation involved making the "tackle from behind" a red-card offence and giving attacking players more advantage in offside situations. Both new interpretations needed more clarification and testing before being put into practice fairly, and Brazil's first two goals against The Netherlands in the quarter-finals should probably not have been allowed.

The mandatory stretchering-off of injured players worked very well and prevented the feigning of injury, although "diving" for free-kicks remained a problem. Using true linesmen rather than referees to run the lines was a welcome return to sanity, although FIFA's continued insistence on spreading appointments around their membership deprived the tournament of some of the world's best officials.

A capacity crowd of 94,000 packs the Rose Bowl in Pasadena, California, for the climax of World Cup USA '94.

Disappointment

Cameroon were a disappointment after their brilliant showing in 1990, but Nigeria confirmed Africa's wealth of talent by finishing top of their group with a goal difference bettered only by Brazil. Perhaps the biggest disappointment was the much-vaunted Colombian side, who came bottom of their group and were beaten 2–1 by the United States in a match that confirmed the hosts as a team to be taken seriously. The captain of the vanquished, defender Andres Escobar, who put through his own goal, was murdered in a Medellin car park on his return home to Colombia, a tragedy that puts into perspective the ups and downs of success and failure on the football field.

This followed close after the disgrace of Diego Maradona, who failed a random drugs test after Argentina's second match and was soon expelled from the tournament.

With no sides in the finals, British allegiance was switched to the Irish team, coached by Jack Charlton, and made up entirely of players from the English and Scottish leagues. They brought off the first sensation of the finals when Ray Houghton's spectacular goal gave them a 1–0 victory over Italy. All four teams in the group finished level on both points (four) and goal difference (zero), with Norway, scorers of only one goal, the team to miss out.

Among the personalities to

The World Cup was decided on penalties for the first time, and Roberto Baggio's miss that gave Brazil victory was a sad climax to what had been a thrilling tournament deservedly won by the best team.

Romario won the Golden Ball as the best player of the tournament, confirming his pre-tournament boast.

make their mark in the first round was Saudi striker Saeed Owairan, who scored the finest individual goal of the finals, against Belgium. But the individual performance of the tournament was supplied by Valencia's Russian star Oleg Salenko. Without an international goal to his name before the finals, he scored five – a World Cup record – as Russia beat Cameroon 6–1 in a vain effort to qualify for the next round of the competition.

Knock-out stages

In the last sixteen, Ireland again found themselves in the heat of Orlando, where they could not recover from defensive lapses by Phelan and keeper Bonner against Holland. An error of another kind marked Belgium's exit, when Swiss referee Kurt Rothlisberger refused them a penalty against Germany. He admitted his mistake after seeing a video, and FIFA decided not to use him again in the tournament.

Brazil, despite having Leonardo sent off for elbowing American Tab Ramos, went through, thanks to Bebeto, while Nigeria were on the verge of taking a mighty scalp, after Italy's Zola had been sent off. They led until the 88th minute, when Roberto Baggio finally came alive, equalized, and scored the winner from the spot in extra time. Argentina succumbed 3–2 to the Romanians and the genius of Hagi in one of the most memorable matches of the tournament, and Eastern Europe made it two in the last eight with Bulgaria's victory over Mexico on penalties.

In the quarter-finals Bulgaria chalked up a famous triumph over holders Germany. Romania, however, suffered the mortification of going out on penalties for the second successive World Cup, beaten by Sweden after a dramatic see-saw game. Meanwhile, Italy had beaten Spain 2–1, and Holland lost a five-goal thriller to Brazil after clawing back a two-goal deficit.

In the first semi-final, the Italians at last put on the style, with Roberto Baggio scoring two magical goals to defeat Bulgaria. But he injured a hamstring to threaten his appearance in the Rose Bowl.

Brazil made heavy weather of beating Sweden in the second semi-final despite controlling much of the game. Romario clinched a final place with an 81st minute header from Jorginho's cross.

Stalemate

In the final, the defensive qualities of both sides triumphed. Italy brought back Baresi, three weeks after keyhole surgery to his knee, for the banned Costacurta, and the AC Milan veteran was magnificent. So, too, was Paolo Maldini, who started in the middle of defence before reverting to his natural left-back position when Mussi went off in the first half. Brazil's central defensive pair, Aldair and Marcio Santos, were outstanding, but they lost their influential right-back Jorginho after 20 minutes. The latter's replacement Cafu, however, provided some of the best chances, which Romario and Bebeto uncharacteristically squandered. A cameo performance from young substitute Viola in the second period of extra time injected some spice into the game.

But the match finished goalless, and for the first, and hopefully the last, time a World Cup final had to be decided on penalties. The battling Baresi ballooned the first kick over the bar. Pagliuca saved Brazil's first, from Marcio Santos, but Taffarel saved Italy's fourth, from Massaro. Brazil's captain Dunga shot his team into the lead, before finally Roberto Baggio lifted his kick over the goal to give Brazil victory.

In the end, the best side won. Despite the 120-minute deadlock, Brazil were a joy to watch, and they thoroughly deserve to be the first country to win the World Cup for a fourth time.

FINAL SCORE

Group A

United States	1	Switzerland	1
Colombia	1	Romania	3
United States	2	Colombia	1
Romania	1	Switzerland	4
United States	0	Romania	1
Switzerland	0	Colombia	2

	P	W	D	L	F	A	P
Romania	3	2	0	1	5	5	6
Switzerland	3	1	1	1	5	4	4
US	3	1	1	1	3	3	4
Colombia	3	1	0	2	4	5	3

Group B

Cameroon	2	Sweden	2
Brazil	2	Russia	0
Brazil	3	Cameroon	0
Sweden	3	Russia	1
Russia	6	Cameroon	1
Brazil	1	Sweden	1

	P	W	D	L	F	A	P
Brazil	3	2	1	0	6	1	7
Sweden	3	1	2	0	6	4	5
Russia	3	1	0	2	7	6	3
Cameroon	3	0	1	2	3	11	1

Group C

Germany	1	Bolivia	0
Spain	2	South Korea	2
Germany	1	Spain	1
South Korea	0	Bolivia	0
Bolivia	1	Spain	3
Germany	3	South Korea	2

	P	W	D	L	F	A	P
Germany	3	2	1	0	5	3	7
Spain	3	1	2	0	6	4	5
S Korea	3	0	2	1	4	5	2
Bolivia	3	0	1	2	1	4	1

Group D

Argentina	4	Greece	0
Nigeria	3	Bulgaria	0
Argentina	2	Nigeria	1
Bulgaria	4	Greece	0
Greece	0	Nigeria	2
Argentina	0	Bulgaria	2

	P	W	D	L	F	A	P
Nigeria	3	2	0	1	6	2	6
Bulgaria	3	2	0	1	6	3	6
Argentina	3	2	0	1	6	3	6
Greece	3	0	0	3	0	10	0

Group E

Italy	0	Ireland	1
Norway	1	Mexico	0
Italy	1	Norway	0
Mexico	2	Ireland	1
Ireland	0	Norway	0
Italy	1	Mexico	1

	P	W	D	L	F	A	P
Mexico	3	1	1	1	3	3	4
Ireland	3	1	1	1	2	2	4
Italy	3	1	1	1	2	2	4
Norway	3	1	1	1	1	1	4

Group F

Belgium	1	Morocco	0
Holland	2	Saudi Arabia	1
Saudi Arabia	2	Morocco	1
Belgium	1	Holland	0
Morocco	1	Holland	2
Belgium	0	Saudi Arabia	1

	P	W	D	L	F	A	P
Holland	3	2	0	1	4	3	6
S Arabia	3	2	0	1	4	3	6
Belgium	3	2	0	1	2	1	6
Morocco	3	0	0	3	2	5	0

SECOND PHASE

Germany	3	Belgium	2
Spain	3	Switzerland	0
Saudi Arabia	1	Sweden	3
Romania	3	Argentina	2
Holland	2	Ireland	0
Brazil	1	United States	0
Nigeria	1	Italy	2
(after extra time)			
Mexico	1	Bulgaria	1

Bulgaria won 3-1 on penalties

QUARTER-FINALS

Italy	2	Spain	1
Holland	2	Brazil	3
Bulgaria	2	Germany	1
Romania	2	Sweden	2

Sweden won 5-4 on penalties

SEMI-FINALS

Bulgaria	1	Italy	2
Sweden	0	Brazil	1

THIRD-PLACE MATCH

Sweden	4	Bulgaria	0

FINAL

Brazil	0	Italy	0

Brazil won 3–2 on penalties

Pasadena Rose Bowl, Los Angeles, 17 July 1994, Attendance 94,194

Brazil: Taffarel, Jorginho (Cafu), Aldair, Marcio Santos, Branco,Mauro Silva, Dunga, Mazinho, Zinho (Viola), Babeto, Romario

Italy: Pagliuca, Mussi (Apolloni), Baresi, Maldini, Benarrivo, Berti, Albertini, D Baggio (Evani), Donadoni, R Baggio, Massaro

Leading scorers

6 Salenko (Russia), Stoichkov (Bulgaria)

5 K.Andersson (Sweden), R.Baggio (Italy), Klinsmann (Germany), Romario (Brazil)

INDEX

Page numbers in italics refer to captions to illustrations

INDEX

INDEX

INDEX

PHOTOGRAPHIC ACKNOWLEDGEMENTS

Most of the pictures used in this book were supplied by Colorsport and Syndication International, or came from the author's private collection. Thanks are also due to the following for permission to reproduce photographs: Allsport, Associated Press, Associated Sports Photography, Herald & Evening Times, Hulton Deutsch Collection, Liverpool Daily Post & Echo, Press Association and Bob Thomas Sports Photography.

It has not been possible to trace the copyright of some of the photographs, and any queries relating to pictures used should be addressed to the author through the publishers, Carlton Books. We apologize if anyone's copyright has been inadvertently infringed.